2006

The Essential Guide to Pricing a Business

16th Edition

Written and Compiled by Tom West

www.bbpinc.com

Cover design by CaseyDzn, Worcester, Massachusetts

ISBN: 0-9748518-2-5

introduction

The 2006 Business Reference Guide is the 16th Edition of the Guide Series. It also represents a big departure from previous Guides. For the first time, the book contains only rules of thumb and pricing information plus, of course, our 2006 list of Industry Experts – that's it! And, it still is about the same number of pages. Clearly, our pricing information continues to grow replacing the other portions of the Guide. Little did we know that the rules of thumb and the related pricing information would take up over 725 pages. Our very first Guide had 20 pages of rules of thumb and had a total of 340 pages.

Our current plan is to update the information that was previously in the Guide and include it in a new book primarily for the business brokerage profession. It will contain sample wording, forms, letter agreements, checklists, court cases and the like. It will be a reference book that we feel will help business brokers go that extra step.

As with every year's Guide there are people to thank. The first Guide was practically a one-person operation. This year's book requires quite a few people. Last year we thanked Barbara Bernstein for doing the indexing. This year she practically did the entire book: she did much of the research and found information that we didn't know existed; she did the proofing; she created a style chart to eliminate a lot of my mistakes; and, with all that she still did the indexing. She is a wonderfully talented lady and so easy to work with. Barbara, thank you for all of your advice and help.

Then there is the Business Brokerage Press (South) gang. DJ Phelps did some research for us this past year, but I suspect his real contribution was behind the scenes doing a lot of the work I used to do, which leaves me free to focus on getting the Guide done. Jeremy Morris continued to provide the computer programming for our Industry Expert program which has made my life a lot easier. It's amazing what BBP has accomplished thanks to Jeremy's help in making us technologically advanced. Sean Lacy was with BBP (South) for most of last year and learned enough that he now has his own business brokerage office. Thanks to my son Ron, Business Brokerage Press has stayed in the forefront of the profession. Whenever we need something – a way of making the Industry Expert program work a bit better, getting the survey launched, following through on a project, he's always there and gets the job done. Business Brokerage Press is in good hands, leaving me to write and help business brokers on a daily basis.

Then there is Elizabeth Lutyens, who has been my editor for over 20 years. Her hand is in everything I write. Thanks also to David Proctor who continues to bail me out in Maine so I can work on the Guide. Jim Casey has done the cover for the book for the second year and we think the book looks better than ever. Pamela Delaney has contributed her talents as a graphic designer for a lot of our materials.

This book could not be done without my daughter Sue who has done the layout and design for 13 years now. In fact, she has done it for so long she thinks it is just one of the chores she has to do as part of her family responsibilities. Of course, she does have husband Mark, son Isaac and daughter Lucie who should be given credit for allowing her to do the Guide every year. Sue you make the book a whole lot easier. Thanks!

For 16 years now, I have dedicated this book to my wife – and best friend Barbara. Because this is an annual book that is released in mid-January, the "crunch time" always runs into the holiday season. She has to make the last minute changes, work with the printers, make me proof-read the book, make the changes from Barbara (the other one) who really proofs it, and coordinates every detail to make it all work. The list of things she does to put this book "to bed" as they say is almost endless. But, she does it. Every year I promise myself I will get the book done earlier and I really try, but…! Barb, I know I say it every year, but I couldn't do this without you. As I said last year, this book is dedicated to you because you allow me to do what I feel I was meant to do – and love to do. Thanks Barb!

Tom West
December 2005

alphabetical listing of **businesses**

advertisers

rules of thumb

Despite all of the caveats about using rules of thumb in pricing businesses, they are commonly used to do just that. The answer is quite simple—the rules are very easy to use. But how accurate are they? A lot more than many people think. They may supply a quick fix, but if used properly, rules of thumb can come pretty close to what the business will ultimately sell for.

Most rules of thumb are market-driven; that is, they are the result of actual sales. This means that they come closer to being a sale price than an asking price. Many of the rules of thumb in this Guide come from Industry Experts. The vast majority of our Industry Experts are business intermediaries, which puts them about as close to the transaction as one can get.

Rules of thumb in the Guide usually come in two formats. The most commonly used rule of thumb is simply a percentage of the annual sales, or better yet, the last 12 months of sales. For example, if the total sales were $100,000 for last year, and the multiple for the particular business is 40 percent of annual sales, then the price based on the rule of thumb would be $40,000.

The second rule of thumb used in the Guide is a multiple of earnings. In small businesses the multiple is used against what is termed Seller's Discretionary Earnings (SDE). It is usually based on a multiple (generally between 0 and 4) and this number is then used as a multiple against the earnings of the business.

Other terms used to express earnings are as follows, along with a definition of SDE.

EBDIT (EBITDA)—Earnings before depreciation (and other noncash charges), interest, and taxes.

EBDT—Earnings before depreciation (and other noncash charges), and taxes.

EBIT—Earnings before interest and taxes.
Source: Pratt et al., *Valuing a Business*

SDE—Seller's Discretionary Earnings

Seller's Discretionary Earnings: "The earnings of a business enterprise prior to the following items:

- income taxes
- nonrecurring income and expenses
- nonoperating income and expenses
- depreciation and amortization
- interest expense or income
- owner's total compensation for one owner/operator, after adjusting the total compensation of all owners to market value."

Keep in mind that the multiples for the different earnings acronyms will be different than the multiple of SDE, which, as mentioned, generally is a number between 0 and 4. The rules contained in the Guide are very specific about what is being used. It will say 2 times SDE or 4 times EBIT, etc.

> This price, based on the rule of thumb, does not include inventory (there is some debate on whether inventory is included in the rule of thumb price—see discussion of inventory in the Retail—Quick Profile), real estate, and other balance sheet items such as cash and accounts receivable. The price derived from the rule of thumb is for the operating assets of the business plus goodwill. It also assumes that the business will be delivered free and clear of any short and long-term debt. If any debt is to be assumed by a purchaser, it is subtracted from the price based on the rule of thumb method.

The Basics

The rules are arranged alphabetically. In some cases the business may go by two name descriptions, for example: gas stations and service stations. We use the one that we feel is the most common, and we try to cross-reference them. If you can't find what you are looking for, see if it is listed under another name. If there is a particular franchise you are working on and it's not in the rules, check the type of business for more information. For example, if the franchise is an ice cream store, check the name of the franchise; and if it's not there, go to ice cream stores or other ice cream franchises. If the business is not listed, try and find as similar a business as you can, and start with that figure.

The number just below the type of business is the approximate number of businesses of that type in the U.S. In most cases we have used information from the InfoUSA catalog (www.infousa.com). We have also provided the Standard Industrial Classification Code (SIC) and American Industry Classification System (NAICS). It is labeled (the Guide. If a code isn't there, it's because either we had difficul the business with the system—or it just wasn't listed. For the best NAICS and SIC site that we have discovered, go to www.naics.com.

The Rules of Thumb

Following the type of business are the Rules of Thumb.

Pricing Tips

After the Rules of Thumb, are the Pricing Tips. These provide information from industry experts and other sources. They are intended to amplify the rules themselves. We include lots of new information every year, while keeping pertinent information from prior years. We asked our Industry Experts and others to provide us with their assessment or rankings for seven (in some cases we have used only the last three) of the more important areas in calculating a multiple of the Seller's Discretionary Earnings (SDE). In many cases we had to meld more than one opinion. You may find after reviewing the Pricing Tips that you will increase or reduce the multiplier on the business under study. Here are the ratings:

Industry Experts' Ratings

Amount of Competition (1 = Lot of: 4 = Not much) ....
Amount of Risk (1 = Very: 4 = Not much) ....
Historical Profit Trend (1 = Down: 4 = Up) ....
Location & Facilities (1 = Poor: 4 = Excellent) ....
Marketability (1 = Low: 4 = High) ....
Industry Trend (1 = Declining: 4 = Growing) ....
Ease of Replication (1 = Easy: 4 = Difficult) ....

Directly underneath the Industry Expert Ratings are comments that may explain or amplify why the rating is as listed. These comments may also lead you to raise or lower your own assessment for a particular business.

Benchmarks

This is a new area that we have included in the Rules of Thumb section. There is more on this very important subject later in this introduction. We feel it is very important in analyzing and pricing a business that you can compare it to similar businesses or benchmarks that are unique to this type of business. One common benchmark unique to each business is the expenses. We have included as many of these as we could find. They are presented as follows:

Expenses as a percentage of annual sales:	
Cost of Goods Sold	20%
Payroll/Labor Costs	40%
Occupancy Cost	20%
Profit (estimated)	20%

There are also a lot of informative benchmarks such as sales per square foot, sales per employee, etc.

Some of the Benchmark data is from www.bizstats.com. The estimated sales data, especially for restaurants, is from *Nation's Restaurant News*, an invaluable resource, and the *Franchise Times*, also an excellent resource.

General Information

We then provide General Information that provides industry information and data. The purpose of this section is to give you information that we believe will be helpful in understanding the business or industry to which it belongs. The more you know about a particular business or industry, the easier it is to put a price on it.

Advantages and Disadvantages

By reviewing the advantages and disadvantages of a particular business, you will gain a bit more insight into it.

Industry Trend

Some entries have a current trend section. However, for additional trend information, we suggest that you review the Industry Expert ratings discussed earlier.

Resources

Here we provide any resources that we have, including publications, books, etc. We also suggest that if you need additional information you e-mail or call an Industry Expert. They are listed in the Industry Expert section. A more current list may be found on our Web site www.bbpinc.com under Industry Experts.

Also included in Resources are trade associations related to this particular type of business. For most of the associations, we have included their Web site if available. Some are very informative; others are really only for members or consumers. However, many of the associations offer books or pamphlets or studies that can be informative.

Seller Financing

Following Resources is Seller Financing. This information has been supplied by industry experts and will give you an idea of what sellers have done regarding seller financing.

Benchmarking and Using the Information

We mentioned at the beginning of this section that if the rule of thumb was used properly, the price derived could be more accurate than simply multiplying the sales by the percentage rule or the SDE multiple. Reviewing market-driven data, one can reasonably assume that a five percent swing (that's our number, yours may higher or lower) on either side of the percentage multiple would allow for the additions or subtractions to arrive at a more accurate multiple of annual sales. Using our example above, the 40 percent figure, as well as available data and information, we could lower or raise that percentage by no more than five percent, and our multiple would be a lot more accurate.

Critics of rules of thumb claim that a rule is simply an average and doesn't allow for the variables of each individual business. Comparing the business under review with industry standards—benchmarks—can allow one to raise or lower the percentage accordingly. A 40 percent figure then could be as low as 35 percent, or as high as 45 percent. The review of market data has, for some businesses, percentages that range from almost zero percent to 100 percent; however, these extremes are quite rare. They are usually based on some quirk in the calculations or in the business itself—oddities such as it was closed when sold, or was so small that the selling price was not reflective of the sales.

The first step is to review any of the Pricing Tips, Benchmarks and the other information available about the business under review. Many of the Pricing Tips are contributed by our Industry Experts and can help in this process.

The Benchmark section can help you look at the vital signs of the business and compare them to similar businesses. For example, looking at the expenses as a percentage of annual sales can be a good start.

For example, if the business under review has an occupancy percentage of 12 percent against the average eight percent, then perhaps the price should be reduced to compensate for the higher rent. The rent is pretty much a fixed expense.

Certainly a new owner could lower some of the expenses, but a trained labor force, for example, is hard to replace. Obviously, reducing the percentage multiple is a judgment call, but let's face it, even business valuation is not a science, but an art—and judgment plays a large part in it.

Another important benchmark is based on employee productivity. For example, under AAMCO transmissions in the Guide, there is the following statement: "A shop should generate $3,500 to $4,000 per technical employee per week." If you are pricing a transmission business or even a similar one, the "$3,500 to $4,000 per technical employee per week" is an important benchmark. Does the business you are reviewing stack up against the benchmark?

Here are some Revenue per Employee figures from BizStats (www.bizstats.com):

Type of Business	Cost of Labor	Revenue per Employee
Ice cream & soft serve shops	23.0%	$30,539
Donut shops	25.9%	$37,926
Drinking places	21.5%	$38,269
Convenience stores	9.5%	$109,481
Beer, wine & liquor stores	7.5%	$173,645
Gasoline stations	5.8%	$214,916
Sporting goods, hobby & musical Instrument stores	11.6%	$114,100
Book stores, in general	11.8%	$103,517
Family shoe stores	11.0%	$112,517
Misc. store retailers	13.0%	$103,733
Florists	21.3%	$52,359

Note: The figures include both full-time and part-time employees and are not what they earn, but rather the sales they generate in a given year. BizStats contains many others—the above are just some examples. The revenue per employee is another benchmark that can be used to 1. see how the business under review stacks up against its peers, and 2. provide an excellent way to see how the business can be improved—a good selling point. If, for example, the business under review doesn't stack up very well with the benchmarks, then a new owner may be able to increase the sales and profits.

Another common benchmark is Sales per Gross Square Foot. Here are examples from some large restaurant franchises and chains, again from www.bizstats.com . It will give you an idea of what these popular restaurants do. You can compare them with similar businesses to see how they stack up with these successful operations.

Company	Sales Per Foot	Avg. Store Size	Avg. Sales Per Store
Cheesecake Factory	$1,020	10,730	$10,940,800
Krispy Kreme	$859	4,600	$3,952,000
Papa John's	$575	1,300	$747,000
McDonald's	$543	3,000	$1,628,000
Applebee's	$454	5,000	$2,975,000
Panera Bread	$418	4,400	$1,840,000
Denny's	$270	4,800	$1,294,765
Scholtzsky's Deli	$147	4,000	$588,000

These are just a few examples. Keep in mind that many of the businesses above are company-owned operations. They are essentially completely help operated, but can be a good gauge when compared to the businesses you are reviewing. Owner-operated businesses should be more tightly controlled than management-operated.

Benchmarking allows one to look at a business from an entirely different viewpoint. Look at the Revenues per Employee, the Sales per Square Foot and Average Sales per Store. These can play a part in the success, or lack of it, of a business. Even rough comparisons can provide sufficient data to raise or lower the percentage to arrive at a more accurate multiplier.

The data above gives you an idea of the information that is available. We have found that BizStats has a lot of valuable information. Go to www.bizstats.com. *Nation's Restaurant* has a lot of data on the restaurant and quick-service businesses. For subscription information go to www.nrn.com . *Franchise Times* is also an excellent resource for benchmarking. For a subscription go to www.franchisetimes.com.

Some Final Thoughts

A price derived from the rules of thumb, except for a multiple of EBIT, EBITDA or otherwise mentioned, is plus inventory. We have tried to put "plus inventory" on the entries, but when in doubt, multiples of annual sales and SDE are plus inventory. For more information, go to Retail in the Rules and read the Quick Profile.

We realize that many people rely on the rules of thumb and pricing information that is included in the Guide. One reason is that we continue to maintain pricing information from previous editions if we believe that it is still pertinent. The same is true for some of the data, statistics and related information. Some associations conduct their studies and surveys only every other year—or even further apart. In some cases we have done a particular section prior to the new data becoming available. However, we attempt to keep the Guide as current as possible.

We know that some of the information may be contradictory, but since we get it from those whom we believe to be experts, we still include it. The more information you have to sort through, the better your final conclusion. We think the information and data are reliable, but occasionally we find an error after the book has been printed. Also, keep in mind that rules of thumb can vary by area and even by location. For example:

The most recent editions of BizComps, the leading resource for comparable sale data (www.bizcomps.com) provides some interesting information on small business pricing based on the three major regions of the country—Eastern states, the Central states and the Western states. It covers thousands of actual business sales over a ten year period. Here is the breakdown:

	Average Sale Price
Western states	$299,500
Central states	$221,951
Eastern states	$285,941

Using the Western states as the base, since that region of the country has the highest average price business, businesses in the Central states sell for 74 percent of the average price in the Western states; and the average price in the Eastern states is 78 percent of the Western states average.

We want to thank all of those who contributed rules of thumb, industry data and information to this section. It is a tribute to them that they are willing to contribute not only a rule of thumb, but also their knowledge on pricing.

We are focusing on the Industry Experts and are offering to put them on our Web site, provide BBP Industry logos and anything else we can do to set them apart, in gratitude for their contribution to the Guide and the profession. If you're interested and feel that you are qualified, go to www.industryexpert.net or www.businessbrokeragepress.com and click on Industry Experts.

"A Rule of Thumb is a homemade recipe for making a guess. It is an easy-to-remember guide that falls somewhere between a mathematical formula and a shot in the dark … Rules of Thumb are a kind of tool."

From the Introduction to *Rules of Thumb* by Tom Parker

And When All Else Fails

Keep in mind that if it's not in the Guide, we really don't have a rule of thumb for that business. We get calls from people asking for a rule of thumb for some oddball type of business like Elephant Training Schools (not really). Honestly, if we knew of one, it would be in the Guide. We're always happy to help if we can; but unless there is sufficient sales data, there generally isn't a rule of thumb available. Here are some suggestions if you can't find what you need in the Guide

- Call a similar business in your area and see if they are aware of one.
- Check with a vendor, distributor or equipment manufacturer and see if someone there can help.
- Call a trade association for that particular industry and see if they can direct you to someone who can help. Don't do it by e-mail or fax, but call and speak to someone. Trade associations really don't want to get involved, but an individual might get you to the next step.

If none of the above helps, then we're afraid you just have to accept the fact that there isn't one for the business you are checking on.

Franchise

A&W Restaurants (A&W Root Beer)

Estimated Annual Sales per Unit (485 Units):	$365,000
Approximate Total Investment:	$75,000–$1,500,000

Rule of Thumb:

- 45 to 55 percent of annual sales

General Information

At the end of 2004, only 4 percent of the restaurants were company owned. The company is changing the name of many of its units to A&W All American Food Restaurants. A&W Restaurants is part of the Yum Brands chain of restaurants that includes: Taco Bell, Pizza Hut, KFC (Kentucky Fried Chicken) and Long John Silver. Yum Brands is "co-branding" many of its restaurants. For example, A&W may be sharing space with one of the other Yum Brands restaurants. Yum Brands is publicly held and listed on the NY Stock Exchange.

Franchise

AAMCO Transmission *(See also Auto Transmissions)*

Estimated Annual Sales per Unit (700+ Units):	$620,000
Approximate Total Investment:	$180,000–$190,000

Rule of Thumb:

- 42 percent of annual sales plus inventory
- An industry rule of thumb for AAMCO is 20 times average weekly sales for the past 16–26 weeks for a shop that has average weekly sales of less than $20,000 per week, and up to 27 times average weekly sales for shops above $20,000 per week.

Pricing Tips

"Detailed Weekly Reports provided to the franchisor are more important documents for analyzing historical performance than financial statements and tax returns, as these reports will reveal the prices charged ratio of major/minor repairs and warranty repairs."

"The following information is also appropriate for most of the other transmission franchises; e.g., Cottman, Eagle (primarily in Texas), and also for transmission shops in general.

"Established shops with a manager in the expenses:

Small Shops—Less than $20,000 per week
Sixteen to twenty (16–20) times weekly sales for the last 26 weeks—and/or one and one half (1.5) to three (3) times adjusted earnings (EBITDA). If the seller is the manager or builder—assets plus one year's SDE.

"Minimum sale price for an established, poorly performing, franchised transmission shop that is in a proven location which historically has been profitable but has recent sales which at least are "breakeven" ($8,000 to $10,000 per week) is no less than the total cost it would take to put in a new franchise and reach breakeven—typically $195,000 to $225,000."

"Large Shops—$20,000 per week and higher
Twenty to Thirty (20 - 30) times average weekly sales for the last 26 weeks—and/or two (2) to three (3) times adjusted earnings (EBITDA).

- High parts cost implies theft and/or high warranty repairs.
- Usually the buyer assumes responsibility for warranty repairs for previous work. If they are unusually high, a provision in contract price might be a consideration.
- If the owner is the manager, be careful in adding back manager's salary and replacing with "first-time" buyer unless the shop is a national franchise with a training program."

Benchmarks

Expenses as a percentage of annual sales	
Production labor costs	20%
Sales/Labor	8–10%
Occupancy	6–10%
Bottom line	10–20%

■"A shop should generate $3,500 to $4,000 per technical employee per week."

■"If parts costs are less than (15 percent), suspect that used parts are sold, which will go up if a new owner uses new parts."

■"A typical shop has four employees—1 manager, 2 mechanics (Remove & Replace), and a builder; the manager and the builder are key employees. Typical breakeven is $8,000 to $10,000/week, with the manager included in the expenses."

" Percentage of Gross Sales: (Where they should be)	
Sales	100%
Cost of Sales:	
Parts & Fluids	22%
Production Labor (All Technical Employees)	20%
Towing	1%
Misc. Production Supplies	3%
Total Cost of Sales	46%
Sales & Administration Expenses:	
Salaries (Center Mgr. & Office)	10%
Rent	8%
Insurance	3%
Utilities	1%
Advertising—Yellow Pages	8%
Telephone	1%
Legal/Accounting	1%
Bank Fees/Bad Debt	1%
Training	1%
Total Sales & Administration Expenses	34%
Net Profit	20%"

General Information

"Since 9-11-2001, the auto repair market has changed. Improved/extended warranties on new vehicles, technology which makes it difficult to separate engine from transmission problems, and pressure from auto dealers to keep their customers is resulting in transmission shops taking on general auto repairs, and vice versa. The more profitable transmission shops have added outside sales representatives, to augment or decrease the high cost of yellow page ads for reaching the traditional retail customers and increasing sales to commercial accounts, who prefer one shop to handle minor auto repairs as well. AAMCO has changed their business model and is now encouraging franchisees to add general auto repair to their services—common rules of thumb for all auto repair shops, such as 2-3 times EBITDA, are more applicable."

"Many owners of transmission shops feel that the relationship between the commercial account and shop is tied personally to the sales rep, and initially take on this function themselves. A sales oriented buyer can capitalize and transfer past skill to this industry."

Seller Financing

- "50 percent down—five (5) years"

Resources

AAMCO – www.aamco.com
Eagle Transmission – www.eagletransmission.com

Accounting Firms/CPAs *(See also Accounting Firms)*

CPAs – 97,500	SIC: 8721-01	NAIC: 541211

Rule of Thumb:

- 125 percent of annual sales plus inventory
- 1 to 1.5 times annual revenues plus inventory
- 2 to 4 times SDE plus inventory

Pricing Tips

"Generally sold based on a multiple of 1to 1.5 times gross annual revenues of the firm"

"Quality of revenues determines actual multiplier, as does the type of revenue. Quality tax planning and compliance work would be at a lower multiplier. Fewer categories of work is also a plus; in other words, a mixture of audit, write-up and tax may be less desirable than an office that has a niche in tax planning and compliance. Qualified personnel that will remain with the firm are also a plus."

Industry Experts' Ratings:

Amount of Competition (1 = Lot of: 4 = Not much)	1.5
Amount of Risk (1 = Very: 4 = Not much)	2.8
Historical Profit Trend (1 = Down: 4 = Up)	3.4
Location & Facilities (1 = Poor: 4 = Excellent)	3.0
Marketability (1 = Low: 4 = High)	3.0
Industry Trend (1 = Declining: 4 = Growing)	3.5
Ease of Replication (1 = Easy: 4 = difficult)	2.4

"Most accounting firms are labor intensive. Keeping labor cost down will produce above average net income to the owners. This can be accomplished through strong management skills and use of the latest technology."

"Most accountants do a poor job of marketing."

Benchmarks

"$100,000 billings per staff accountant"
"3:1 billing-to-salary ratio"
"Charge for client work at a rate of three times the employee cost."

Expenses as a percentage of annual sales/revenues:

Labor	30–32%
Occupancy	9–12%
Profit (estimated pre-tax)	35–45%

Advantages of this Business

- "Strong net income to the owner(s)"

Disadvantages of this Business

- "Long hours during tax season"

Industry Trend

"Upward trend with the complexity of the tax system and the need for full service tax, financial, and retirement planning under 'one roof'"

"February 18, 2005 (www.smartpros.com)—A research report released this week by Glass Lewis & Co. shows that one-fourth of more than 2,500 public companies changed outside auditing firms in 2004, a 78 percent jump from 2003, *The Wall Street Journal* reported.

"...Hiring overseas costs about 20% more, once you figure in visas, lawyers, and temporary housing. But BDO [BDO Seidman] says it couldn't find enough qualified U.S candidates to handle 40% to 60% more audit hours required by Sarbanes-Oxley."

Source: Nanette Byrnes, *Business Week*, July 4, 2005

"Glass's research shows that small companies changed auditors most. The disclosed reasons for the switch included regulatory requirements, lower fees at the new firm, and corporate mergers.

"There is no law requiring that companies switch outside auditing firms, but the high turnover tells that boards of directors are doing so anyway, which contradicts the past argument by accounting firms that switching auditors reduces audit quality, WSJ cited.

"Also, smaller accounting firms are gaining business—former Big Four clients. Second-tier firm BDO Siedman gained the most clients (109) while Big Four firm Ernst & Young lost the most (200)."

Source: *The Wall Street Journal* as it appeared in smartpros.com, February 19, 2005

U.S. Census Bureau data (2002, released 2004)

NAICS	Type of Firm	# of Firms	Receipts/ Revenues ($1,000)
541211	CPAs	56,720	$48,548,817
541213	Tax preparation svcs	19,222	$5,446,167
541214	Payroll svcs	4,064	$20,167,144
541219	Other accounting svcs	32,217	$10,442,340

Seller Financing

- "3 to 5 years"

Resources

See Accounting Firms/Practices

Accounting Firms/Practices

(See also Accounting Firms —CPAs and Bookkeeping Services)

Accountants (in general):		114,000
Accounting & Bookkeeping (General SVC):		26,000
	SIC: 8721-01	NAIC: 541219

Rule of Thumb:

- There are three rules of thumb generally cited: #1—.75 to 1.25 annual revenues, depending on characteristics of practice; #2—9 to 15 times monthly net sales, depending on characteristics of practice; and #3—2 to 5 times the seller's SDE. Rules of thumb normally include FF&E, Lease and Intangibles. Current assets, real estate, and all related liabilities must be considered separately.
- One to 1.25 times annual revenues (non-CPA)
- Generally sold for a multiple of 1 to 1.5 times gross revenues depending upon net earnings. Rarely sell below one times gross.
- One times prior year's annual gross billings (revenues) with premium for above average earnings, billings or net income; specialized work, experience-trained staff, etc. (CPA firms)
- One times gross for low-level billings, up to 1.5 times gross for high-level billings
- 100 percent to 115 percent of one-year's revenue + FF&E with one-year guarantee of gross
- 90 to 110 percent of anticipated annual revenues under new ownership, subject to seller guarantee and earnout provisions
- 100 to 115 percent of annual revenues, plus fixtures & equipment; seller keeps accounts payable & accounts receivable
- Sales price generally 100 to 125 percent of annual revenue; higher in some metropolitan areas such as New York City, Dallas, Atlanta, etc.

Pricing Tips

Questions sellers should be asked: "Break down the composition of fees on an annual basis (percent from tax, bookkeeping, payroll, accounting, auditing, technology, consulting, etc.). Also ask if fee structure is based on hourly or fixed-fee arrangements. What is the effective percent of production hours (total firm hours billed/total firm hours spent)? What are the rate realizations (total fees billed/standard rates x hours billed)? Clients making up over 10% of annual fees? Any major clients coming to end of service agreements, and details? Answers indicating poor production and rate realizations have a negative impact on pricing, while positive statistics have positive impacts on pricing."

"Client mix and buyer personality are key to a successful transition."

"The rule of thumb is from .75 to 1.5 times annual gross revenues; the higher number is usually for CPA firms or firms that have an excellent profit margin."

"In the larger deals ($350K and up), usually the furniture, fixtures and equipment are included; in the smaller deals they are sold at fair market value."

"Name recognition and reputation in the area. Fee structure, length of service of firm's clientele."

"Higher percentage of write-up work, higher multiple (versus tax work). Higher hourly rate charged to customers, higher multiple. Higher average monthly fee (write-up) or tax return, higher multiple. Prolonged cooperation, involvement of seller post-closing, higher multiple. Flexible lease terms, higher multiple."

"One-third down payment and one-year guarantee of gross"

"Location, fees, length of time in business, length of relationships with clients, quality of client base, quality of staff & profitability"

"...steady, historical growth in number of accounts and revenues. High 'averages' per monthly accounts and tax returns (corporate & individual). Reasonable, documentable relationships between dollars charged and total work completed. At least 50 percent of revenues generated from monthly write-ups to balance hectic tax season. Lengthy, committed transition phase to maximize retention. Existing trained staff willing to remain at new owner's discretion. Dollar for dollar seller guarantee (difficult/impossible to sell without). Either short term or month-to-month lease allowing new owner to eventually move clients to his/her existing location. Lack of substantial 'one-time only' work such as IRS representation or specialized consulting services. Substantially all revenues collected as earned; i.e., no material advance billings (unearned revenue). Absence of 'audit work,' which carries great liability (insurance is often cost-prohibitive)."

"Sales of accounting practices range from .5 to 1.6 times gross revenues, with a very high concentration at 1.0 times annual gross revenue. However, in the majority of cases, the price was contingent on retaining the clients for some period of time, most typically one year, with the final price reduced by the amounts for any clients not retained. The median ratio of price/SDE was 1.64."

"Metro areas on the high side (New York City maybe 200 percent of annual billings). High fee structure adds to price unless highly specialized. Compliance work (recurring type) increases price. All tax work reduces price."

"One times gross annual billings retained during first year of new ownership plus the FMV (fair market value) of equipment."

"Perhaps the most unique feature of accounting/tax practice sales is the presence of a dollar-for-dollar seller guarantee; i.e., the purchaser will ultimately pay only for the business (revenues) retained during an agreed-upon time period (typically the first year after closing). Secondly, cash flow...is not extremely important (as opposed to revenues). Obviously, without a seller guarantee, the price would be substantially less. Also of importance (all other things being equal) is the mix of monthly write-up work versus seasonal tax work. Generally, the greater the write-up percent, the more valuable. Also, any highly specialized consulting is less valuable. Finally, the higher the 'averages' the better (e.g... average monthly write-up, and average personal and corporate tax returns). The amount and length of cooperation from the seller during the transition phase also impacts value and the ease with which the practice is sold. The seller will often introduce the buyer as a new partner to allow clients to become familiar with the new practitioner (this maximizes retention). Additionally, the presence of a long-term lease actually detracts from value (most acquisitions are made by established practitioners with an existing office)."

Industry Experts' Ratings:

Amount of Competition (1 = Lot of: 4 = Not much) 1.6
Amount of Risk (1 = Very: 4 = Not much) 2.4
Historical Profit Trend (1 = Down: 4 = Up) 3.2
Location & Facilities (1 = Poor: 4 = Excellent) 2.0
Marketability (1 = Low: 4 = High) 3.4
Industry Trend (1 = Declining: 4 = Growing) 2.8
Ease of Replication (1 = Easy: 4 = Difficult) 2.0

"Generally works the same as CPA firms. Fee structure may be somewhat lower in some cases."

Benchmarks

"Fees generated per employee or staff person ($50,000 to $100,000)"

"More than half of gross income is earned, on average, from the preparation of tax returns. The typical firm charges an average of $208 to prepare an itemized Form 1040 and $102 for a non-itemized Form 1040. Fees average $92 an hour to prepare financial statements and $112 an hour for estate and financial planning services. Fees vary sharply by state and region."

Source: National Society of Accountants

Expenses as a percentage of annual sales/revenues

Labor	30–32%
Other Expenses	n/a
Occupancy	8–12%
Profit	40% (prior to owner's draw)

General Information

The National Society of Accountants (NSA) recently released its 11th Income and Fees Survey of independent practitioners. The Survey, conducted in late 2002, reflects responses from a sample of 6,000 NSA members and provides a composite picture of the typical, independent practitioner as a 58-year-old male, in practice for 23 years, in a sole proprietorship with three full-time and two part-time employees. On average nationwide, slightly less than 50% are Enrolled Agents, 21% are CPAs, and 17%

are licensed or registered in the state where they practice.

Source: National Society of Accountants

Advantages of this Business

- "Businesses always need accounting"
- "Above average income to the owner"

Disadvantages of this Business

- "Long hours at various times of the years due to deadlines"
- "High level of work necessary in 'tax season,' Work compression"

Industry Trend

"Strong growth trend with more outsourcing in the industry to keep labor costs down. Substantial amount of this work is repetitious and clerical driven."

"Consolidation and firms sending work offshore"

"Technology is changing the way accounting practices operate. The firms owned by older practitioners who do not keep up with IT updating will either die off, or will provide younger and more savvy CPAs great opportunities (at lower P/R multiples). More CPA firms are finding that it is necessary to use 'off-site' employees who have computers at home. Firms without adequate non-compete and employment contracts in place may pose greater risks to potential buyers. I think we will see many smaller firms being put on the market, because they cannot attract the talent to keep them going in this 'standards-overloaded' environment. Mid-size firms will develop more innovative ways to bring professionals into the profits of the firm, and eventually into equity positions. Group practices will grow, as there is strength in numbers and it is easier to spread fixed overhead costs over a greater number of professionals."

Seller Financing

- "Earnouts are very typically between one to two years"
- "30 percent down payment, 70 percent seller carry back, five years, eight to 10 percent"
- "20 to 40 percent down, financing three to five years for small practices; seven to10 years for larger ones"
- "Three years average"
- "Three to five years"
- "30 to 35 percent down, balance financed over three to five years with one-year client retention guaranteed by the seller to the buyer"

- "Usually seller financed—25 percent to 40 percent down. From three to 10 years, depending on size of the practice"

Resources
American Institute of Certified Public Accountants (AICPA)
www.aicpa.org

National Society of Public Accountants
www.nsacct.org

BookkeeperList.com—an interesting site with lots of resources including an excellent *glossary* of terms.
www.bookkeeperlist.com

Buying a Practice by Leon Faris & Vance Wingo. Contact: Professional Accounting Sales, 100 Galleria Parkway SE, Ste 1010, Atlanta, GA 30339-5947. (800) 729-9031. www.cpasales.com. This is a leading brokerage firm dealing exclusively in CPA and accounting firms.

"Valuing Accounting Firms," *Handbook of Business Valuation* by West & Jones, 2nd Edition, published by John Wiley & Sons. www.wiley.com

Valuing Accounting Practices by Robert Reilly & Robert Schweihs, published by John Wiley & Sons. www.wiley.com

Guide to Managing an Accounting Practice published by Publishers Publishing Company. (800) 323-8724. www.ppcnet.com

Texas Society of CPAs, Management of an Accounting Practice Survey, National Results, (published annually). (972) 687-8519. www.tscpa.org

Accounting/Tax Practices

Tax Practices 68,754	SIC: 7291-01	NAIC: 541213

Rule of Thumb:

- One times annual revenues

Benchmarks
"Generates approx. $100,000 in fees per employee. Franchise operations

compensate tax preparers based on a percentage of fees billed to client—30%."

"The average fee per office client as of Feb. 15 this year was $135, up from $131 last year and $122 in 2002."

Source: "H&R Block," *Forbes*, March 29, 2004

General Information

"Other related services can be offered such as the sale of financial products and services (retirement products, mortgages, financing, etc.)."

Industry Experts' Ratings:

Amount of Competition (1 = Lot of: 4 = Not much) 2.0
Amount of Risk (1 = Very: 4 = Not much) 3.2
Historical Profit Trend (1 = Down: 4 = Up) 2.8
Location & Facilities (1 = Poor: 4 = Excellent) 3.6
Marketability (1 = Low: 4 = High) 4.0
Industry Trend (1 = Declining: 4 = Growing) 3.6
Ease of Replication (1 = Easy: 4 = difficult) 1.2

"Easily transferable. High visibility of offices necessary to attract large number of walk-in clients. Majority of clients are seen only once a year for tax preparation and filing of tax returns. Office location is critical."

Advantages of this Business

- "Electronic filing will increase demand for these services"

Disadvantages of this Business

- "Tax system may change as Congress moves toward other types of tax revenues structures such as a flat tax or a value-added tax (VAT) similar to the one in Europe."

Industry Trend

"Upward trend with electronic filing and rapid refund popularity; IRS moving toward full compliance of electronic filing by all taxpayers"

"... The number of Americans filing returns has grown 1.3 percent a year, a pace the Internal Revenue Service expects to be fairly steady through 2006..."

Source: The New York Times, Sunday, March 11, 2001

Franchise

Ace Cash Express *(See also Check Cashing)*

1,200 + units

Approximate Total Investment: $109,200–$229,100

Rule of Thumb:

- 1.25 times annual sales plus inventory

Benchmarks

Percentage of Total Revenue	
Check Cashing & Tax Check Fees	52.4%
Loan Fees and Interest	31.2%
Bill Payment Services	6.9%
Money Transfer Services	4.5%
Money Order Fees	2.6%
Franchise Revenues	1.1%
Other Fees	1.3%

Source: 2004 Annual Report

General Information

Only about 200 of the total units are franchised; the rest are company owned and operated. In fiscal year 2004, the company opened 53 company-owned stores and 32 franchised stores.

The company offers the following franchise options:

Full-service store franchise

This is the traditional store capable of offering the complete variety of financials.

- Investment: $30,000 initial franchise fee and an initial total investment of $236,700–$279,100
- Royalty: The greater of $1,000 or 6% of monthly gross receipts
- Size: Full-service centers are typically 1,000 to 1,500 square feet

Small-market franchise

This is a small-market store located in a town with a population of 15,000 or less and not adjacent to or near a larger metropolitan area.

- Investment: $15,000 initial franchise fee and an initial total investment of$180,700–$229,100
- Royalty: The greater of $850 or 6% of monthly gross receipts
- Size: Small-market centers can be opened as full-service or kiosk stores

Kiosk franchise
This is a self-contained store that can be located within a convenience store and offer check cashing, money orders, wire transfers and other services.

- %Investment: $15,000 initial franchise fee
- %Royalty: The greater of $850 or 6% of monthly receipts
- %Size: Kiosks are typically 100 to 250 square feet

Conversion franchise
Existing check cashing operators are welcomed to join the ACE family through our program.

- Investment: $15,000 conversion fee and an initial investment of $153,200–$239,100
- Royalty: The greater of $1,000 or 6% of monthly gross receipts

Note: As with all franchises, all information is subject to change; and the company's Uniform Offering Circular (UFOC) should be checked for updates and changes.

Industry Trend
The company plans on adding 500 new stores by the end of fiscal 2008. The company's annual report for 2004 stated that it believes "our targeted markets could potentially support an additional 1,800 Ace franchise stores across the United States."

Resources
Ace Cash Express
www.acecashexpress.com
Note: The company is publicly held, and their annual report is available online and is an excellent resource.

Ace Hardware *(See also Hardware)*	
5,100 units	
Approximate Total Investment:	$750,000–$1,500,000
Startup Cash:	$250,000–$300,000
Rule of Thumb: ➢ 45 percent of annual sales plus inventory	

Pricing Tips

Sales seem to indicate that smaller sales bring a higher multiple (50% +) than stores with sales over a million, which seem to bring lower multiples. Price is plus inventory, and that may be the reason for lower multiples for larger stores.

General Information

Ace Hardware stores are not franchises. Ace is a cooperative, and the stores are the members and shareholders. It is a supplier and provides common advertising, support services, and allows use of its name. The stores are independently owned and operated.

Ace Hardware has 4,800 stores in 50 states and 70 countries and operates 15 distribution centers in the United States.

Affiliation Process	
Membership Application	$5,000
Initial Ownership Stock Investment	$5,000
Liquid Capital	$250,000
Total Investment*	$900,000

*Total investment figure is based on a 12,000 square-foot retail store. Total Investment will vary based on store size. Items included in this figure are store fixtures, inventory, office equipment, computer system, decor, signage and operating capital. These costs do not include such things as land and building costs or leasehold improvements.

Incentive Benefits

Qualified individuals will have access to an exclusive incentive package.

Initial fees

Comprehensive Training Program	$27,000 value
Complete Store Design	$6,000 value
Store Setup Services	$22,000 value
Grand Opening Event Assistance	$30,000 value
Inventory Discount	$110,000 value
Total Value of Incentives	$195,000

Resources

www.myace.com —An interesting site

Adult Club/Nightclub *(See Bars)*

Advertising Agencies

24,000	SIC: 7311-01	NAIC: 541810

Rule of Thumb:

- 70 percent of annual revenues (billings); may require earnout

Pricing Tips

"Valuation expectations have risen at high end from 5.5x to 6.5x pre-operating profits for ad agencies, and from 6x to 7x for both marketing services firms and interactive shops."

Source: Advertising/Marketing Survey 2005, www.admediapartners.com

"Although virtually all of the large, multinational agencies are members of the AAAA, more than 60 percent of our membership bills less than $10 million per year."

Source: American Association of Advertising Agencies

Resources

American Association of Advertising Agencies
www.aaaa.org

International Advertising Association
www.iaaglobal.org

Franchise

Advertising Material Distribution Services

	SIC: 7319	NAIC: 541870

Rule of Thumb:

- 3 times SDE plus inventory

General Information

This industry is represented by several large franchise companies such as Money Mailer, Supercoups and Valpak—all with about the same number of units—approximately 200.

Direct mail is a $49 billion industry

Source: Direct Marketing Association

"This is a category with a wide variety of services/products. Door-to-door distribution, direct-mail services, etc. Good opportunity for solid earnings but limited market for resale of this type of business. Low cost of entry. Highly labor intensive business which requires constant supervision of personnel."

Air Conditioning Contractor *(See also HVAC)*

55,000	SIC: 1711-17	NAIC: 235110

Rule of Thumb:

- 30 percent of annual sales plus inventory
- 1.5 times SDE plus inventory

Resources

Air Conditioning Contractors of America
www.acca.org

American Society of Heating, Refrigerating and Air-Conditioning Engineers
www.ashrae.org

Air Conditioning, Heating and Refrigeration News
www.achrnews.com

Aircraft Manufacturing—Parts, Supplies, Engines, etc. *(Kit-built & Ultralight aircraft industry)*

	SIC: 3724	NAIC: 336412

Rule of Thumb:

- 75 percent of annual sales includes value of equipment

Pricing Tips

"There is none [rule of thumb]. Each business varies so greatly from the next. It takes someone who knows the industry to know the exact business being described before a price can be established."

"What is the reputation of the aircraft or related product being sold? What is the reputation of the company? Is business up or down? What about accidents—any deaths? A company with a great reputation may be worth little because of their product—or, vice versa."

"When very specialized equipment is needed, add some if a good business. Add value of real estate."

"Where are sales today in comparison to one, two ... years ago? Why are they up or down?" [We don't know if the pun was intended or not.] "Have there been any structural failures or successful liability suits against them? Is it moveable or must buyer move?"

General Information

"Ultralights: experience on the part of the broker means more than anything. Factors that influence value are: how popular is the aircraft (this is not the same as 'what are the sales'); are sales increasing or decreasing, holding steady; what is the safety record; how advanced is the design? Then come the questions regarding financials."

Seller Financing

- "3 years max, 1 year least"
- "We've never sold a 'seller-financed' ultralight aircraft business. It is always a cash deal"

Alarm Companies *(See Security Services/Systems)*

Franchise

Allegra Printing *(See also Printing)*

400 units	
Approximate Total Investment:	Starting under $200,000

Rule of Thumb:

- 65 percent of annual sales plus inventory

General Information

The 400 units in the Allegra Network include Allegra Print and Imaging, and also American Speedy Printing Centers (118), Instant Copy, Insty Prints (144), Quik Print (7), Speedy Printing Centers (Canada) and Zippy Print (Canada).

Resources

www.allegranetwork.com

Ambulance Services

12,254	SIC: 4119-02	NAIC: 922160

Rule of Thumb:

- 40 percent of annual revenues plus inventory
- 2.3 times SDE plus inventory
- 7 to 8 times EBIT

General Information

Vital U.S Ambulance Statistics

Number of Ambulance Services	12,254
Number of Ground Ambulance Vehicles	23,575
Number of EMS Personal	840,669

Source: American Ambulance Association

"Over two-thirds of the nation's largest 200 cities are served by non-fire-based emergency ambulance services."

Source: American Ambulance Association

Resources

American Ambulance Association

www.the-aaa.org—The site is primarily for members

Franchise

American Poolplayers Association (APA)

272 units

Approximate Total Investment:	$10,632–$13,000

Rule of Thumb:

- 1.4 times annual sales
- $1,000 to $1,800 per team in sales: selling price–$2,000 to $2,500 per team

Resources

www.poolplayers.com

Amusement Routes *(See Routes and Vending Routes)*

Answering Services *(See also Call Centers & Secretarial Services)*

5,000	SIC: 7389-03	NAIC: 561410

Rule of Thumb:

- 10 to 12 times current monthly billings for larger services; may require earnout
- 5 to 7 times current monthly billings for smaller services; may require earnout plus

General Information

"It appears that the term *answering services* has been replaced with the term *call center*."

"Telemessaging clients no longer accept having the call center take messages and hold them until they pick them up later in the day. Clients want the information immediately. They also want to control how they receive the messages based on the time of day, their current location, or the type of device they may be using. In other words, clients demand intelligent messaging."

"The Future of Telemessaging," by Kevin Beale, *Connections Magazine*, January/February 2004

"And quite often we are doing more screening for the clients – between spam e-mails, telemarketing calls and the various media, information overload is rampant. This can provide us with an opportunity to be a 'screener' for some of our clients, allowing them to focus on the things that are important to them and we take care of the rest."

Source: Kelli Harrigan, *Connections Magazine*, January/February 2004

Industry Trends

"The future of telemessaging is strong. A human touch will always be required; the industry will continue to grow as long as we stay flexible."

Source: *The Future of Telemessaging* by Kevin Beale, *Connections Magazine*, January/February 2004

Resources

Association of TeleServices International (ATSI)
www.atsi.org

Online magazine for answering services
www.incoming.com

Online magazine for answering services
www.connectionsmagazine.com

Antique Malls

5,000

Rule of Thumb:

- 2 to 4 times EBITDA with a minimum of $100,000 EBITDA not including real estate

General Information

AntiqueLand USA. (www.antiquelandusa.com.) filed for Chapter 7 bankruptcy and it was granted in July, 2004. The court realized that dealers are the "lifeblood of the business" and that without them, there is no business. It appears that AntiqueLand USA was way above board in its dealings with its dealers. The company appears to have resolved the issues that placed them in bankruptcy and their business of owning and managing antique malls continues.

The National Association of Antique Malls (NAAM) estimates that there are 10,000 antique-mall owners and managers.

Antique malls may be real-estate intensive and a real estate license may be necessary to sell them.

National Association of Antique Malls (NAAM)
www.antiqueandcollectible.com/naam

Antique Shops/Dealers

41,500	SIC: 5932-02	NAIC: 453310

Rule of Thumb:

- 20 percent of annual sales plus inventory

General Information

"Handling inventory can be a real problem. Antiques by their very nature may have been acquired at one price and the value at sale may be considerably more (even possibly less). There are many pricing guides available for most antiques that should help in finding the value in the current market. The price at sale should be the original acquisition cost plus or minus the current average profit margin for the business."

One leading expert has said that there are no rules of thumb for this type of business. The legal definition of an antique is "an article of one hundred or more years of age; when this 'qualifier' is used, a much narrower meaning emerges. The recognized periods in furnishings . . . end with the introduction of mass-manufactured, machine made goods . . . " This expert told us that many antique shops are started by collectors, and the value of the business is really just what the antiques themselves are worth.

Many antique shops do not really sell antiques. Others sell what politely could be termed "used furniture." The association listed under Resources represents the elite of antique dealers, and there are only about 100 members who have qualified for membership.

Resources

Art and Antique Dealers League of America
www.artantiquedealersleague.com

Apparel *(See also Clothing Store)*

25,500	SIC: 5136	NAIC: 448190

Rule of Thumb:

.75 to 1.5 times SDE plus inventory

Pricing Tips

Women's Apparel— "try 23 percent of annual sales + inventory and/or 1.1 times SDE."

General Information

"People get into trouble because they don't know how much their rent should be in ratio to the amount of sales their store is generating," says Don Paul, an industry consultant with retail consulting firm, RSMA. "The fact is that rent should be kept between 5 and 6 percent of your total sales … you can figure you'll need $18,000 a year for rent. That means in order to keep rent at 6 percent, your store will have to generate $300,000 in sales."

Source: www.entrepreneur.com

Key considerations when pricing an apparel store:

- How is the store different from the competition?
- What quality merchandise is sold? What kind of image does the store present?
- What customer services are offered?
- Who are the customers?
- Why do the customers buy from this store?

Adapted from a report on Clothing Stores appearing in www.entrepreneur.com

Resources

American Apparel and Footwear Association
www.apparelandfootware.org

Appliance Repair

14,800	SIC: 7623	NAIC: 811412

Rule of Thumb:

- 1 to 1.5 times SDE, add inventory, fixtures & equipment

General Information

"More than 20 percent of repairers are self-employed. About 40 percent of salaried repairers worked in retail establishments such as department stores, household appliance stores, and fuel dealerships. Others worked for gas and electric utility companies, electric repair shops and wholesalers."

Source: *Occupational Outlook Handbook, 2000-03 Edition*, U.S Department of Labor

Industry Trend

"Employment of home appliance repairers is expected to increase more slowly than the average for all occupations through the year 2010. Prospects should continue to be good for well-trained repairers, particularly those with a strong background in electronics. The number of home appliances in use is expected to increase with growth in the number of households and businesses. In the past, employment growth of home appliance repairers has been limited because of the need for less frequent repairs due to solid-state circuitry, microprocessors, and sensing devices in appliances. Also, many consumers tended to purchase new appliances when existing warranties expired rather than invest in repairs on old appliances, further reducing the need for home appliance repairers. These employment limitations could be somewhat offset over the next decade as more consumers purchase higher priced appliances designed to have much longer lives, making consumers more likely to use repair service than to purchase new appliances. Moreover, as home appliance repairers retire or transfer to other occupations, additional job openings will arise."

Source: *Occupational Outlook Handbook, 2000-03 Edition*, U.S Department of Labor

Appliance Stores *(See also Furniture/Appliance)*

17,100	SIC: 5064	NAIC: 443111

Rule of Thumb:

- 2 times monthly sales plus inventory

Benchmarks

"Markup is about 27 percent with some discounters working on a 25 percent markup."

Resources

National Association of Retail Dealers of America (NARDA)
www.narda.com

National Appliance Parts Suppliers Association
www.napsaweb.org

Appliance News—Online newsletter for the appliance service industry
www.asnews.com

Association of Home Appliance Manufacturers
www.aham.org

Appraisal Services

17,800	SIC: 7389	NAIC: 562499

Pricing Tips

"For a firm with less than 10 professionals—1.25 to 1.5 times EBITDA. This would include all FF&E and related software and exclude Accounts Receivable and Accounts Payable. Most of the deals are where there is a merger of firms or a buyout by a CPA firm wanting to get into the appraisal business. They usually want the seller to manage the operation for several years."

Resources

Institute of Business Appraisers (IBA)
www.go-IBA.org

American Society of Appraisers (ASA)
www.appraisers.org

National Association of Certified Valuation Analysts (NACVA)
www.nacva.com

American Association of Independent Appraisers (AAIA)
www.aaia.com

Architectual Practices

39,300	SIC: 8712-02	NAIC: 541310

Rule of Thumb:

- 40 percent of annual revenues plus inventory

Pricing Tips

Goodwill is at a minimum due to the non-repetitiveness of the clients.

Franchise

Arctic Circle

84 units

Rule of Thumb:

- 50 percent of annual sales plus inventory

General Information

The company operates 27 company stores and has approximately 60 franchises in eight western states.

Art Galleries and Dealers

25,921	SIC: 5999-69	NAIC: 712110 (Galleries) NAIC: 453920 (Dealers)

Rule of Thumb:

- 30 percent of annual revenues plus inventory

Pricing Tips

"You'll have better luck trying to count the stars in the sky than collecting meaningful art market sales data."

Source: www.artbusiness.com

"A surprising number of people search for answers to these and similar questions in attempts to quantify the art market. The art market, however, is not quantifiable, and the answers to these questions don't exist. To begin with, art is not a commodity that can be regulated. Anyone can call him or herself an artist, anyone can call anything that they create 'art,' and anyone can be an art dealer. Anyone can sell art wherever, whenever and under whatever circumstances they please, and price or sell whatever they call "art" for whatever amounts of money they feel like selling it for, as long as that art is offered without fraud or misrepresentation."

Source: www.artbusiness.com

Resources
Art Dealers Association of America
www.artdealers.org

Art Supplies *(See also Arts & Crafts and Hobby Stores)*

9,000-	SIC: 5999-65	NAIC: 453998

Rule of Thumb:

➤ 30 percent of annual sales plus inventory

Arts & Crafts/ Retail Stores
(See also Gift, Needlepoint, and Hobby Shops)

Craft Stores 4,000 Art Supplies 7,400	SIC: 5085	NAIC: 453998

Rule of Thumb:

➤ 32 percent of annual sales plus inventory

Resources
National Craft Association—An excellent resource with an informative Web site
www.craftassoc.com

www.whereoware.com – A good site for craft and gift, retail, supplies and information

Trade Publications
The Craft Report—excellent publication and Web site
www.craftsreport.com

Arts & Crafts Industry

Pricing Tips

Those people who actually create the finished arts and crafts (craftspeople) are unique and their business would be difficult to sell because of the very nature of what they produce. Their skill is not usually transferable.

General Information

There seems to be a thin line between arts and crafts, hobby shops, and gift shops. In addition, arts and crafts can be broken down into retail stores that sell the supplies and the stores that sell the finished products.

There are 106,000 to 126,000 crafts people working in the United States today. The average gross sales/revenue per craftsperson is $76,025.

National Craft Association (the figures above are several years old)

Arts and crafts tend to differ from gift shops since the products offered are generally handmade by craftspeople. Arts and crafts may be available in gift shops. Crafts people may sell their wares outright to the gift shop or may have items placed on consignment. Consignment sales represent about 14 percent of sales, while outright sales on a wholesale basis are about 23 percent. The balance is sold directly to the consumer. In pricing both, it is important to investigate the inventory to see if it is owned or on consignment. Craftspeople may have products on consignment to gift shops in addition to having it in their own shop.

"Crafts themselves, however, are big business, in fact, a $14 billion business. "The fine crafts market is a $13.8 billion industry. As a point of comparison, the crafts industry is about half the size of the $29.9 billion toy industry. It is roughly three times the size of the $4 billion organic foods industry. And it is just slightly smaller than the $16 billion retail floral market."

Source: *Crafts Report*

Gross Sales from Various Sources by Full-Time Artists and Craftspeople

Wholesale Shows	$3.85 million
Sell Direct to Galleries	$3.07 million
Consign to Galleries	$728,000
Retail Shows	$5.35 million
Internet	$321,000
Other	$450,000

Note: the above figures do not include part-time artists and craftspeople

Source: *Crafts Report*

The Highest Average Sales per Medium (Top Five)

1. Jewelry
2. Ceramics
3. Glass
4. Metal
5. Fiber

Demographic Profile of Artist and Craftspeople

- 64% of craftspeople are female
- 41% are between the ages of 46 and 55; the median age is 49
- 79% of craftspeople work in a studio located on their residential property
- 78% are members of a craft organization
- 64% work alone in a studio, 18% work with a partner or family member, and 16% work with paid employees

Asian Restaurants *(See also Restaurants)*

Rule of Thumb:

- 30 to 32 percent of annual sales plus inventory

General Information

"Once associated primarily with Chinese and Japanese foods, today's offerings reflect a greater range of cultures from the Asian region."

Source: www.dailynews.com

Asian food includes not only Chinese and Japanese, but also Thai, Indian, Vietnamese, Hawaiian, etc. This category also includes such rapidly growing chains as Panda Express and P.F. Chang's.

Industry Trend

"Sales of Asian foods—both authentic and 'Americanized'—grew by 27 percent between 2000 and 2004, according to a report by MarketResearch, a consumer tracking firm based in Maryland."

Source: www.dailynews.com

BBP Industry Expert Program

The Business Brokerage Industry Expert Program is designed to recognize those business brokers who have expertise in a specific business or industry (or more than one). We have developed an Industry Expert logo which is awarded to all Industry Experts approved by BBP. Its purpose is to allow our Industry Experts to use this logo in their printed material and in any other way that would benefit them and their businesses. In addition , we list them in our Business Reference Guide Series, on our Web site (www.bbpinc.com) and other BBP resources. A viewer can search our database by industry and locate the appropriate Industry Expert(s).

We believe that this recognition and publicity is invaluable and will provide additional business from other professionals such as: accountants, appraisers, attorneys and other business intermediaries. Many of our Industry Experts have received excellent public relations from newspapers, magazines and other media as a result of this program. We intend to continue to expand the visibility and professionalism of the program.

We know of no other resources that list and promote Industry Experts in the business brokerage profession.

The is no charge to be approved as an Industry Expert. All we ask is that you complete a brief questionnaire providing information on the business(s). We use this information in our annual Business Reference Guide. We do not use names in publishing this information. However, being listed in the Industry Expert section may produce some telephone calls from those who have questions on your Industry.

It is only with some assistance of our Industry Experts that we can provide information on so many different businesses to our readers. Such information, as industry trends, pricing tips and rules of thumb, is invaluable to our readers and no one knows this information like our Industry Experts.

To learn more about our Industry Expert Program, or to join, please visit www.industryexpert.net or click on Industry Expert link on the Business Brokerage Press site noted above.

If you have any questions, please call Tom West at 978-692-0323.

Assisted Living Facilities

16,621	SIC: 8361-05	NAIC: 623311

Rule of Thumb:

- 75 percent of annual revenues
- $30,000–$60,000 per bed. Pricing above this range typically raises a red flag for individual buyers.
- This business is based on net operating income divided by a capitalization rate of 10 to 14 percent.

Pricing Tips

"Real-estate-intensive business. SBA pays extra attention to this industry to ensure that the buyers are not acting as 'passive real-estate investors,' but rather as small business owners."

"Capitalization of income for going concern value including real estate."

"Occupancy in market area. Going cap rates at that specific time. Whether Medicaid or private pay?"

Industry Experts' Ratings:

Marketability (1 = Low: 4 = High) 2.0
Industry Trend (1 = Declining: 4 = Growing) 2.8
Ease of Replication (1 = Easy: 4 = Difficult) 2.0

Benchmarks

"Total expenses excluding debt service should average 68 percent."
"Operating expense ratio 65 to 70 percent."

General Information

"*Levels of Assistance:*
Home Health Care – Provides assistance for those who can remain in their homes with services such as: nursing, personal care and home maintenance.

Overall, the largest 50 providers have a total resident capacity of 174,563, up eight percent from 2004.

Source: Assisted Living Federation of America

Congregate Living – Provides residence housing including meals, housekeeping and other services. Residents are assumed to be fairly self-sufficient.

Assisted Living – The same as above except that services are provided for those who are not self-sufficient, such as 24-hour nursing care, if required, and other medical programs.

Continuing Care – Provides all services for the retired including housing, meals, social programs and medical. It offers independent living all the way to 24-hour medical care. Generally, residents buy into the facility, but are guaranteed housing and medical care for life.

Nursing Home – Provides round-the-clock care for those who can no longer care for themselves."

Advantages of this Business

- "Senior population is growing at an unprecedented rate."

Disadvantages of this Business

- "High risk, 24/7 operation. Temporary market glut in some regions of country."

Industry Trend

"The annual Assisted Living Executive Largest Providers list is the definitive ranking of the largest companies in the industry," said ALFA CEO/ President Richard grimes. "Not only does the list reveal the top players, it also sheds light on the consolidation trend and growing size of the leading providers."

Source: Assisted Living Federation of America

The top five companies, ranked by total assisted living resident capacity:

1. Sunrise Senior Living
2. Emeritus Assisted Living
3. Alterra Healthcare Corp.
4. Sunwest Management Inc.
5. Extendicare Health Services Inc.

Source: Assisted Living Federation of America

According to the Assisted Living Federation of America, one factor contributing to the growth and popularity of the assisted living industry is the aging of the American population, including the dramatic increase in the number of persons aged 85 and older. According to information summarized from the U.S. Census Bureau, the population of people 85 and older is expected to increase by 33.2 percent between the years 2000 and 2010. According to census figures, about 6.5 million older people need assistance with daily living activities. As the number of older Americans continues to increase, that number is expected to double by 2020.

Seller Financing

- "5 to 10 years"

Resources

American Association of Homes and Services for the Aging
www.aahsa.org

Assisted Living Federation of America publishes *Assisted Living Today*
www.alfa.org

National Center for Assisted Living
www.ahca.org

The Directory of Retirement Facilities, published by HCIA, Inc., (800) 568-9429. www.hcia.com

Here is an anecdote that is as old as it is accurate...

A Greek restaurant owner had his own bookkeeping system. He kept his accounts payable in a cigar box on the left-hand side of his cash register, his daily cash returns in a cash drawer of the register, and his receipts for paid bills in a shoe box on the right side of the cash register. When his youngest son graduated as a CPA, he was appalled by his father's primitive bookkeeping methods. "I don't know how you can run a business that way," he said. "How do you know what your profit is?"

"Well, son," the father replied, "when I got off the boat from the old country, I had nothing but the clothes on my back. Today, your brother is a doctor. Your sister is a speech therapist, and you're a CPA. Your mother and I have a nice car, a city house, a country house, and plenty of money for retirement. We have a good business and everything is paid for. Add all that together, subtract the 'clothes on my back,' and there is your profit."

Franchise

Atlanta Bread Company

172 units	
Approximate Total Investment:	$629,700–$1,300,000
Estimated Annual Sales per Unit:	$1.4 million

Rule of Thumb:

➢ 28% of annual sales plus inventory

General Information

Bakery/Café quick-casual restaurants

Audio and Film Companies

		NAIC: 512120

Rule of Thumb:

➢ 4 to 6 times EBDITA

Pricing Tips

"Ownership of the intellectual property is key to value. Companies that provide work-for-hire services are not as valuable as those that own the final production. Since this medium ages quickly, the economic life span of the films/videos is critical."

Seller Financing

■ "3 to 7 years"

Quick *Profile* Automotive Aftermarket

"What Is the Motor Vehicle Aftermarket?

The motor vehicle aftermarket is a significant sector of the U.S. economy. This industry encompasses all products and services purchased for light- and heavy-duty vehicles after the original sale including replacement parts, accessories, lubricant appearance products, service repairs, as well as the tools and equipment necessary to make them.

Automotive Segment—companies providing replacement parts and accessories as well as maintenance and repair services for passenger cars and light trucks (pick-up trucks, minivans and sport utility vehicles/SUVs).

Heavy Duty Segment—distributors and manufacturers providing parts and service for commercial, industrial and agricultural vehicles.

Paint Body and Equipment Segment—companies providing vehicle-refinishing products and services.

Tool and Equipment Segment—firms providing the tools and equipment needed to repair and maintain motor vehicles.

Trim Segment—companies that manufacturer, distribute or install interior and exterior fabrics, associated hardware and products for the repair of cars, trucks, boats and aircraft.

Auto Electric Segment— firms providing electrical and lighting products for commercial vehicles. (Statistics for the auto electric segment are not provided. Auto electric products are included/counted in the automotive and heavy-duty segments, making it impractical to extract reliable data for the auto electric segment.)"

Source: Automotive Aftermarket Industry Association

"…Continued growth in the number of registered vehicles, licensed drivers and miles traveled are factors driving another strong year in 2005."

Source: Kathleen Schmatz, President, Automotive Aftermarket Industry Association (AAIA)

"The industry is also broken down into DIFMs (do-it-for-me) and DIYs (do-it-yourself). The motor vehicle aftermarket is also divided into the automotive portion and the heavy- duty one—heavy-duty being trucks and other delivery vehicles."

Selected Aftermarket Outlets (2005)

Outlet	Number
Auto Parts Stores	35,492
Tire Stores	17,871
New Car/Truck Dealers	21,650
Discount Stores	6,511
Warehouse Clubs	4,119
Automotive Specialty Repair	11,435
General Repair Garages	76,975
Gasoline Service Stations	107,163
Quick Lubes	7,612

Source: Automotive Aftermarket Industry Association

The Size of the Market

Motor Vehicle Aftermarket Retail Sales (in Billions) by Category:	
Motor Vehicle Aftermarket 2005 (Forecast)	$269,498
DIY (Do-It-Yourself) Products	$35,856
Tires	$19,392
Service Repair	$143,750
Labor	$64,687
Parts, chemicals	$79,063
Total Automotive Aftermarket	$198,998
Total Heavy-Duty Aftermarket	$70,500
Paint & Body Equipment Aftermarket	$3,210

Source: Automotive Aftermarket Industry Association

The above data is from the Automotive Aftermarket Industry Association (AAIA), www.aftermarket.org. This is an excellent Web site with lots of useful information. Anyone who wants more information on this subject should purchase the *AAIA 2005 Aftermarket Factbook*. www.aftermarket.org.

Auto Service and Repair Resources & Publications

Aftermarket Business .... www.aftermarketbusiness.com
Alliance of Automotive Service Providers (AASP) .... www.autoserviceproviders.com
Auto Rental Market News .... www.fleet-central.com
Autofacts .... www.autofacts.com
Automotive Aftermarket Industry Association (AAIA) .... www.aftermarket.org
Automotive Body Repair News .... www.abrn.com
Automotive Detailing .... www.automotivedetailing.com
Automotive News .... www.autonews.com
Automotive Oil Change Association .... www.aoca.org
Automotive Recyclers Association .... www.autorecyc.org
Automotive Service Association .... www.asashop.org
Body Shop Business .... www.bodyshopbusiness.com
Car Care Council .... www.carcarecouncil.org

Car Wash Forum (Self-Serve Car Wash Info) .... www.autocareforum.com
Chek Chart (Information Tools for Automotive Professionals) .... www.chekchart.com
Chilton Manuals .... www.chiltonsonline.com
Collision Repair Insight .... www.collision-insight.com
Convenient Automotive Services Institute .... www.fastoil.com
Equipment and Tool Institute (ETI) .... www.etools.org
General Car Dealer .... www.nada.com
Hand Tools Institute .... www.hti.org
Haynes Manuals .... www.haynes.com
International Automotive Technicians' Network .... www.iatn.net
International Carwash Association .... www.carwash.org
Mitchell Manuals .... www.mitchellrepair.com
Mobile Air Conditioning Society (MACS) .... www.macsw.org
Modern Car Care (Car Wash Trade Publication) .... www.moderncarcare.com
Modern Tire Dealer .... www.mtdealer.com
Motor Age Magazine .... www.motorage.com
Motor Magazine .... www.motor.com
National Auto Dealers Association .... www.nada.org
National Glass Association .... www.glass.org
National Inst. For Automotive Service Excellence (ASE) .... www.asecert.org
National Oil & Lube News /Auto Care *Industries News Magazine* .... www.noln.net
National Oil Recyclers Association (NORA) .... www.naroli.com
National Petroleum News .... www.npnweb.com
National Windshield Repair Association .... www.netrax.net
Retail Merchandiser .... www.retail-merchandiser.com
Service Technicians Society .... www.sts.sae.org
Tire Business information .... www.tirebusiness.com
Tire Industry Association .... www.tana.net
Used Car Dealer .... www.niada.com
US Glass Magazine .... www.usglassmag.com

Quick Check Pricing for Automotive
Aftermarket Related Businesses

Auto Body Repair	35% of annual sales
Auto Brake & Alignment	30% of annual sales
Auto Car Washes	1.5 to 2 times annual sales
Auto Detailing	45% of annual sales
Auto Glass Repair/Replacement	25% of annual sales
Auto Lube/Tune-Up	40% of annual sales
Auto Muffler	35% of annual sales
Auto Parts—Retail Store	45% of annual sales
Auto Parts—Accessories, Etc.	30% of annual sales
Auto Repair	40% of annual sales
Auto Service/Tire Store	40% of annual sales
Auto Towing	70% of annual sales
Auto Transmission	35% of annual sales

Rules are plus inventory

"Industry growth was led by the medium- and heavy-duty segment, which expanded 7.1 percent to $66.5 billion. The automotive light-vehicle segment increased 4.8 percent to $190.5 billion."

Source: Automotive Aftermarket Industry Association

Note: Several Industry Experts have cautioned that some of the businesses listed above that deal with auto maintenance and auto repair will have lower demand in the marketplace coupled with lower price multiples. There are more new cars on the road with longer warranties. In addition, more automakers and dealerships are providing free services such as oil changes, tune-ups, etc. for the first 30,000 miles (more or less depending on the make and dealership). Check the specific business listing for more information.

Auto Body Repair

34,681	SIC: 7532-01	NAIC: 811121

Rule of Thumb:

- 35 percent of annual sales plus inventory
- 3 times SDE plus inventory
- Top quality business— #1 or #2 in the local market; good insurance contacts; growing sales = multiple range of 3 to 3.8 x SDE

Pricing Tips

"If real estate is part of the deal, are the painting/baking facilities included as part of the real estate or part of the FF&E?"

"Out-front owner should have a can-do attitude and must be reasonably positive. Most customers coming in are in a bad mood."

Industry Experts' Ratings:

Marketability (1 = Low: 4 = High) 2.4
Industry Trend (1 = Declining: 4 = Growing) 2.4
Ease of Replication (1 = Easy: 4 = Difficult) 2.8

"Long-standing business with major agreements in place with insurance companies is very important."

Benchmarks

"The number of service bays and the size of the average facility are similar to 2003 figures of 18 bays and approximately 12,400 total square feet. Square footage averages include 1,550 of office space and 10,235 of shop space; the remaining is used for parts and storage."

Source: *Business Collision*, December 2004, Automotive Service Association, www.asashop.org

Average dollar amount of a repair order this year (2004)—$1,779
Average backlog of work this year (in days)—4

Source: Collision Repair Industry *Insight*

"Annual gross volume of approximately $150,000 per year per employee, including hands-on owner."

"What percentage of your sales is attributed to parts and labor?

Labor 56.8%
Parts 43.2%

On average, gross profit margin on parts is 26.9% and on labor is 46.8%"

Source: *Body Shop Business*, June 2003

Bay Distribution

# of Bays	% of Shops
1–4 bays	02%
5–9 bays	12%
10–14 bays	28%
15–20 bays	27%
21–25 bays	16%
25+ bays	15%

Source: *Business Collision*, December 2004,
Automotive Service Association, www.asashop.org

Gross Annual Sales

Sales	% of Shops
$250,000 or less	03%
$250,000–$500,000	09%
$500,001–$750,000	13%
$750,001–$1 million	14%
$1 million– $2 million	40%
$2 million–$4 million	18%
$4 million +	03%

Source: Source: *Business Collision*, December 2004,
Automotive Service Association, www.asashop.org (Based on 2003 figures)

Average Annual Gross Sales Volume

Non-DRP Shop Average	$293,750
DRP Shop Average	$776,734
Industry Average	$520,442

Source: *Body Shop Business*, 2004 Industry Profile

Note: See general Information on definition of Direct Repair Program (DRP)

Average # of Employees by Annual Shop Sales Volume

Annual shop sales volume	# of employees
Up to $249,999	2.8
$250K–$349,999	3.9
$350K–$749,999	5.4
$750K–$1million	9.8
More than $1 million	15.5

Source: *Body Shop Business,* 2004 Industry Profile

General Information

"DRP means Direct Repair Program. These DRP shops have an affiliation with one or more insurance carriers, and the carriers refer their business to the DRP shops. This does not mean that the DRP shops necessarily get all of the business; however they do get first crack at much of the business, since most auto owners have insurance to repair their cars."

Industry Trend

According to *Body Shop Business,* 70 % of shop owners say their shops will be more successful in the next five years than they are today, and 57% of all shop owners say their businesses are better off today than five years ago.

"From a list of 19 issues, the five issues cited by respondents as having a positive impact on their individual business were consumer awareness (71 percent); their relationship with insurance companies (64 percent); retaining technicians (59 percent); the availability of service information (52 percent); and cycle time (50 percent). Two areas cited by a majority of respondents as having a negative impact on their individual businesses are the quality of aftermarket parts (62 percent) and labor time allowances (56 percent)."

Seller Financing

- "Sellers carry for three to five years with SBA requiring the seller not to receive payments for the first two years."

Resources

Automotive Service Association, (ASA)—Great site with lots of information, www.asashop.org

Body Shop Business is an excellent publication for the industry, and also offers an excellent Web site. The site has a lot of information and offers back issues. It is a good example of what a trade publication Web site can be. www.bodyshopbusiness.com

Collision Repair Industry Insight is also an excellent publication and Web site. It's interesting that body shops with two good publications also have informative Web sites. www.collision-insight.com

Note: This industry has three of the most informative Web sites we have seen. If you're working on an auto body repair shop, you're in luck, because these sites will provide you with lots of valuable— and interesting— information.

Auto Brake Services *(See also Auto Services)*

31,500	SIC: 7539-14	NAIC: 811118

Rule of Thumb:

- 30 percent of annual sales plus inventory
- 4 times monthly sales plus inventory

Pricing Tips

"Depreciated value of fixtures and equipment plus the inventory, plus approximately one half year's net profit."

Resources

See Auto Aftermarket

Auto Car Washes *(See Car Washes)*

Auto Dealers—New Cars

21,640	SIC: 5511-02	NAIC: 441110

Rule of Thumb:

- 3 times EBIT
- Depending on the franchise, makes three to six times EBITDA plus real estate and hard assets
- Blue Sky—two to four times EBIT Earnings
- Total transaction value in the industry currently ranges from two to four times pre-tax earnings
- Blue Sky—two to three times net profit or new unit sales (most recent year) times average front-end gross profit per unit
- Hard assets at cost—new parts, FF&E– Book + 50 percent depreciation,
- Blue Sky—3 times recast earnings

Auto Dealers—New Cars *(continued)*

- The goodwill component of the sale price of an auto dealership (franchised only) normally falls within the range of two to six percent of gross revenues. Where added to the assets or book value of the business, this is a reliable method of determining price.

- Goodwill = 1–3 times pre-tax earnings (recast)
  Parts = current returnable parts
  FF&E = book value + one-half depreciation
  New Vehicles = net dealer cost
  Used Cars = as agreed

Pricing Tips

Questions to ask seller: Are there manufacturers' restrictions and/or facility requirements? What about future planning and product allocation? Would seller like to remain with new owner?

"Watch for phantom profits in both car sales and warranty sales. Some dealers miss proper submission of warranty and rebate claims. Profits can be overstated as a result."

"The current value is two to four times net profit of the most recent year. However, the new car franchises that are bringing up to five times net profit are Honda, Toyota and Mercedes Benz."

"The two most important characteristics are brands sold, and location within a market. Competing outlets also affect value. Market analysis, including measuring consumer demand in the area, is critical. Facility age is also a factor."

"Adjusted book value + blue sky is calculated as a multiple of adjusted pre-tax earnings. These multiples vary with the popularity of franchise, consolidated acquisition trends, vehicle market location, historical performance, etc."

> "Consumers are as likely to visit an auto Web site as they are to visit a dealer when shopping for a new car or used car, according to a new study by Keynote Systems."
>
> Source: www.theautochannel.com

"FF&E—Priced at book price + one-half accumulated depreciation. Parts inventory = as inventoried—current returnable parts. Used cars—take or leave. New Vehicles—dealer net less holdback."

"Other pricing methods include: (1) application of industry averages for gross profit as percentage of sales to the total revenues of the dealership being evaluated; (2) assessing financial data and applying appropriate multiples to recast net profit; (3) projection of potential based on industry average penetration statistics times appropriate multiples."

"The goodwill of an auto dealership can generally be valued at one year's pre-tax profit plus the dealer's salary and benefits, plus any adjustments from normalizing the financial statement against standard industry operating data."

"Automobile dealerships are sold for the depreciated value of fixtures and equipment, parts at wholesale cost, equity value of new cars, and used cars at low book value."

"...Market penetration. The new-car franchise held (Ford is worth more than Mazda)."

"Franchises held, demographics of area of responsibility, total registrations for area—all influence value of business."

Industry Experts' Ratings:

Amount of Competition (1 = Lot of: 4 = Not much)	1.6
Amount of Risk (1 = Very: 4 = Not much)	1.6
Historical Profit Trend (1 = Down: 4 = Up)	2.6
Location & Facilities (1 = Poor: 4 = Excellent)	3.6
Marketability (1 = Low: 4 = High)	2.2
Industry Trend (1 = Declining: 4 = Growing)	2.0
Ease of Replication (1 = Easy: 4 = Difficult)	2.2

"GM is consolidating its brands, with significant impact on its dealers. Brand risk is high."

"Each year the total number of new car dealerships is declining and fewer new points are being awarded to new or existing owners. Well-run, profitable dealerships are not being sold unless at very high pricing. The profit trend in general is up per store even with slightly fewer units being sold per dealership."

Benchmarks

"Each sales manager should be creating $55,000 to $70,000 per month in gross profit on his or her sales efforts. Everything else being at normal levels, the store will make a good profit, whether a large or small store. This is a very good benchmark."

"$1,750 GPNV"

"Cost of Goods + Payroll/Labor Costs—88 percent

Occupancy Cost—Total rent factor should not exceed 1 percent of gross sales."

"Occupancy Cost—$300 to $400 per new car sold per year."

"Profit (estimated)—3 percent of sales"

"Number of new units sold, and number of units in operation, are important metrics."

According to the 2005 National Auto Dealers Association (NADA) data, the average sales for dealerships for 2003 was $32,296,859. The average dealership had 52 employees and an average payroll of $2,312,000.

2003 vs. 2004 comparison

	2003	2004
Total Sales	$32,296,859	$33,009,335
Total Dealership Gross	$4,315,654	$4,363,870
As % of total sales	13.4%	13.2%
Total Dealership Expense	$3,751,511	$3,804,184
As % of total sales	11.6%	11.5%
Net Profit before taxes	$564,143	$559,686
As % of total sales	1.7%	1.7%

Source: 2005 National Auto Dealers Association (NADA) Data

Major expenses for the average dealership in 2004

Payroll	$2,332,000
Advertising	$384,000
Rent and equivalent	$321,000

Source: 2005 National Auto Dealers Association (NADA) Data

Share of total dealership sales dollars in 2004

New Vehicle	60.9%
Used Vehicle	27.6%
Service and Parts	11.5%

Source: 2005 National Auto Dealers Association (NADA) Data

Expenses as a percentage of annual sales:

Cost of Goods	87%
Payroll/Labor	.8–10% of gross profit
Occupancy Cost	10% of gross profit
Profit (estimated pre-tax)	1.8–2%

For additional benchmark information, for example the 2004 total sales by state, and the average sales per dealership by state, go to www.nada.org and click on NADA Data Study.

General Information

"The public will always need transportation and personal transportation will always be important for the masses. The auto dealership business is fun and very profitable when managed properly with the right people. The number-one concern for the dealer today is Employee Satisfaction; once this is achieved, the profits and Customer Satisfaction Index will increase to their highest levels."

"High profits, constant supply of new vehicles, when sales are good."

Advantages of this Business

- "The risk is low and the rewards are high. The value of the dealership will never fall to a distressed price because there are only so many points available."
- "Opportunity to grow"
- "High profits, constant supply of new vehicles, when sales are good"

Disadvantages of this Business

- This is a people business, and people can make or break the reputation, the profit and the future growth of the business. It is more difficult to find and retain good people than ever before; more young people are entering into other fields that require fewer hours and are more stable for tenure and growth.

- "Capital and labor requirements"
- " High risk, including brand and business risk. Manufacturer pressure to make expenditures, which sometimes are unnecessary."

Seller Financing

- "3 years—very small percentage of selling price is carried."
- "Seller financing occurs in less than 30 percent of our transactions and does not normally extend beyond a five-year term."
- "5 years—only goodwill is seller-financed."

Industry Trend

"A decline in the total number of points and more profit for the better run stores and less profit for the poorly run stores"

"Good"

"Consolidation; increasing ownership by dealership groups; more dealerships being owned by investors that also have interests in competing (e.g., Ford and Chevy) brands"

Note: The information in the Benchmarks and Profile and Trend sections is from the National Automobile Dealers Association industry analysis contained in their *AutoExec* magazine. They also have one of the best association Web sites we have visited. If you are selling auto dealerships or even thinking about it, visit the site at www.nada.org and subscribe to *AutoExec.*

Resources

National Automobile Dealers Association
www.nada.org

American International Automobile Dealers
www.aiada.org

"Valuing Car Dealerships," *Handbook of Business Valuation*, 2nd Edition, West & Jones, published by John Wiley & Sons.

Guide to Dealerships, published by Practitioners Publishing Company. (800) 323-8724. www.ppcnet.com

A Dealer Guide to Valuing an Automobile Dealership by David A. Duryee. National Automobile Dealers Association, 8400 West Park Drive, McLean, VA 22102-3522. (800) 252-6332.

"Valuing closely held automobile dealerships using public dealership acquisitions," *Shannon Pratt's Business Valuation Update*, November 1999.

Trade Publications
Automotive News
www.crain.com

Quick *Profile* Automobile Dealers - New Cars

"Last year ranked fourth among the six best years ever for new unit sales by franchised new-vehicle dealers. Sales in all departments increased for the year, and the U.S. economy grew by 4.4 percent in 2004, well ahead of the 3 percent in 2003. The unemployment rate started 2004 at 5.6 percent and fell slightly, to 5.4 percent, by December, falling further to 5.2 percent in March 2005. Consumer confidence measures rose through the second quarter of 2004 to peak in July, but modest employment gains, volatile energy prices, and conflict and political unrest in the Middle East were major concerns. Early 2005 shows modest improvements in consumer confidence; fortunately for consumers and dealers, the cost of borrowing stayed low last year as the Federal Reserve made measured increases in short-term interest rates. Short-term rates are expected to continue to rise moderately in 2005 with the strengthening economy.

"In 2005, vehicle sales continue to be driven by generous incentives, such as cash rebates, low-rate financing and attractive lease options. New light-duty sales exceeded 16.86 million units in 2004, 1.5 percent below 2003's 16.6 million. Analysts on Wall Street had expected a repeat of 2003 sales, but they came in slightly above NADA's 2004 estimate. In 2004, with a recovering economy and modest gains in employment nationwide, new-car dealers were able to maintain strong light-vehicle sales and profits.

The largest number of dealerships was in 1982 when there were 25,700.

"Total dealership dollar sales in 2004 exceeded $714 billion, up more than 2 percent from 2003. This allowed dealers to maintain payroll employment of 1,129,600, about equal to 2003. Total payroll

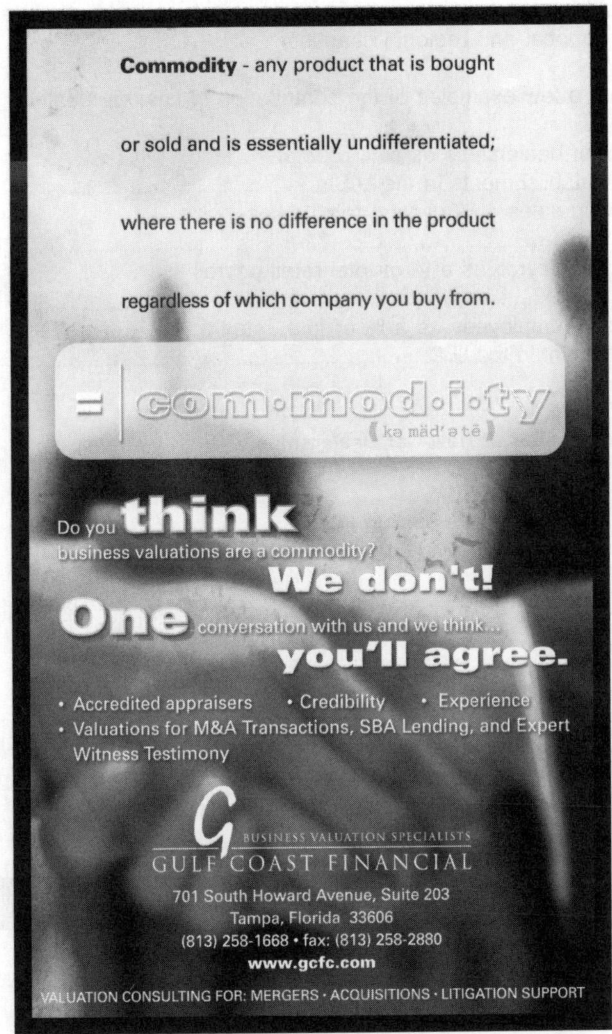

Commodity - any product that is bought
or sold and is essentially undifferentiated;
where there is no difference in the product
regardless of which company you buy from.
= com·mod·i·ty
(kə mäd'ə tē)
Do you think
business valuations are a commodity?
We don't!
One conversation with us and we think...
you'll agree.
• Accredited appraisers • Credibility • Experience
• Valuations for M&A Transactions, SBA Lending, and Expert Witness Testimony
BUSINESS VALUATION SPECIALISTS
GULF COAST FINANCIAL
701 South Howard Avenue, Suite 203
Tampa, Florida 33606
(813) 258-1668 • fax: (813) 258-2880
www.gcfc.com
VALUATION CONSULTING FOR: MERGERS · ACQUISITIONS · LITIGATION SUPPORT

in 2004 exceeded $50.5 billion, up 1 percent. Dealership expenditures, excluding cost of goods sold, reached $82 billion. With many of these expenditures made locally, dealerships provided vital support to the economic well-being of their communities. Franchised dealers were also major players and generators of federal, state, and local tax revenue, as well as major contributors of both time and money to local and regional charities."

Here are a few examples of the contribution of new car dealers:

Number of dealerships as a % of total retail establishments in the U.S.	02.1%
Dealership sales a % of total retail sales in the U.S.	18.9%
Dealership payroll as a % of total retail payroll in the U.S.	12.6%
Dealership employees as a % of total retail employment in the U.S.	07.6%

Number of New-Car Dealerships	
1998	22,600
1999	22,400
2000	22,250
2001	22,150
2002	21,800
2003	21,725
2004	21,650
2005	21,640

Note: All of the above was excerpted from information found at The National Automobile Dealers Association Web site, www.nada.org.

Auto Dealers — Used Cars

92,219	SIC: 5511-03	NAIC: 441120

Rule of Thumb:

- Wholesale book value of cars plus inventory; no goodwill; add parts, fixtures & equipment

General Information

"Franchised new-car dealers sold almost 20 million used vehicles last year Of these, 11.8 million were retailed and 7.9 million wholesaled. The average selling price of a used unit retailed in 2004 was $14,250. [$13,500 in 2003.]"

"New-car dealers acquired 55 percent of the used units they retailed from trade-ins and the remaining 45 percent from auctions, street purchases, or other sources. As a source of used vehicles, auctions have made the biggest inroads during the past decade—from less than 10 percent of the dealer's inventory in the early 1980s to a record 33 percent in 2004."

Source: National Automobile Dealers Association (NADA) www.nada.org

By the Numbers

- 230 million U.S vehicles in operation.
- 43 million U.S. sold.
- 9.5 million used vehicles.
- $9,926 Latest average used-vehicle price.

Source: From *Forbes* magazine, September 5, 2005

Industry Data

- "Sales volume by independent dealers: 13,650,000
- Number of independent dealers in the U.S.: 58,750
- Average price of used vehicles by independent dealers: $7,172
- Independent dealers hold a 24 percent share of the market in terms of used cars
- Independent dealers account for 49 percent of buyers at auctions"

Source: *Used Car Dealer* magazine

General Questions

What types of sales transactions did you have for the year under examination?

a. Any sales at auctions? If yes, which?
b. Any sales to wholesalers? If yes, which?
c. Any sales to other dealers? If yes, which?
d. Any consignment sales? If yes, describe.
e. Any scrap sales? If yes, describe.
f. Any in-house dealer financing sales?
g. Any third-party financing sales?

h. Did you have any other types of sales transactions?
i. Did you have any sales that resulted in a loss on the sale? If yes, describe the nature of these sales.
j. What sales did you have to relatives or family friends during the year? Identify.

The above is excerpted from an IRS Audit Technique Guide (Market Segment Specialization Program—MSSAP). This is an excellent source of information and is available at wwwbookstore.gpo.gov. (Search under IRS—IRS Audit Technique Guides.)

Resources

National Independent Automobile Dealers Association (ADA)
www.niada.com

See Auto Dealer—New Cars

Auto Detailing

14,857	SIC: 7542-03	NAIC: 811192

Rule of Thumb:

- 45 percent of annual sales plus inventory

Benchmarks

"Operating Costs (Approximate)

Rent	20%
Equipment/ Supplies/Maintenance	10%
Chemicals	08%
Utilities	08%
Labor	36%
Advertising	05%
Insurance	05%
Other Costs	08%"

Source: *Auto Laundry News*, 2000 Detail Survey (the latest available)

"Average Number of Cars Detailed Annually

Free-Standing Units	2,306
Car Wash Combo	2.371
Mobile Service	1,463"

Source: *Auto Laundry News*, 2000 Detail Survey (the latest available)

Resources

International Carwash Association—also has classified ads to buy and sell, www.carwash.org

Automotive Detailing—good site www.automotivedetailing.com

Modern Car Care—good site www.moderncarcare.com

Professional Carwashing & Detailing—informative site www.carwash.com

"A skilled detailer, who is working hard but not rushing, can probably complete a car in about 4 to 4.5 hours and make it look great. The average car would be only a few years old, be a mid-size, and be in average cosmetic condition with no major scratches or blemishes, and no major stains or excessive dirt on the interior."

Source: www.dealermarkclicks.com

Auto Driving School *(See Driving School Instruction)*

Auto Glass Repair/Replacement

2,382	SIC: 5231-10	NAIC: 811122

Rule of Thumb:

- 25 percent of annual sales plus inventory
- 1.6 times SDE plus inventory

General Information

"Insurance companies have dramatically affected the prices of auto-glass replacements and repairs, according to an analysis released in September 2004 by Frost & Sullivan of New York City. In the highly competitive auto-glass industry, installers, distributors and manufacturers tend to yield to the insurer's terms, placing immense pressure on their profit margins …"

Source: www.autoglassmagazine.net

"The North American automotive-glass aftermarket achieved revenue worth $1.27 billion in 2003, according to the Frost & Sullivan study. Revenues are projected to climb to $1.61 billion by 2010."

Source: www.autoglassmagazine.net

Resources

National Windshield Repair Association—good site with an excellent overview of the industry, www.netraxx.net/~nwra

National Glass Association (NGA)
www.glass.org

Auto Lube/Tune-Up

14,469	SIC: 7549-03	NAIC: 811191

Rule of Thumb:

- 40 percent of annual sales (Tune-up) plus inventory
- 3 times EBIT (Tune-up)
- 45 percent of annual sales (only Auto Lube businesses)
- 40 percent of annual sales (only Tune-Up businesses)
- 2 to 2.5 times SDE plus inventory

Auto Lube/Oil Change (no tune-ups, brakes, etc.)
Pennzoil, Jiffy Lube, Shell Rapid Lube, Quaker State, etc.

Index		Owner's (SDE)
1 .5 x	to	$50K + SDE (approx. $450K gross annual sales)
2.0 - 2.5 x	to	$100K + SDE (approx. $650K gross annual sales)
2.5 x	to	$150K+ SDE (approx. $900K gross annual sales)
3.0 x	to	$200K + SDE (approx $1.2M gross annual sales

Low-tech business operation with high cash flow generates greater multiple. Most names above are franchises deriving greater multiples.

Pricing Tips

"There are two different service and working environments applicable to this business. The first, being an oil and lube facility only, no service work is performed. The second being a tune-up business, oil and lube, in addition to service work, brakes, tune-ups, smog inspection, etc.

"The first auto lube business generally shows a greater multiple 2.5 SDE, while the auto tune-up business described above normally shows a 2.0 SDE.

"The reasoning for the difference in the multiples above is the first business described is generally in a low-tech environment, non-specialized training and employee wages are lower in comparison to specialized standards in this industry. In addition, most owners have multiple locations. The owner is absentee in this operation and a manager is trained to perform all facets of operation and office functions as required. Demand is also higher.

"The second business described above requires a higher skilled employee (usually certified) and in most states the employees need to be tested. In addition the owner needs to be involved in the everyday functions of the operation, if only as an administrator. Most have a manager in place as well.

"Critical factors affecting business value are as follows: franchise vs. independent, manager and staff, customer base and vehicle count per day, average ticket per day, lease terms, equipment leased, owner's participation and location."

Industry Experts' Ratings:

Marketability (1 = Low: 4 = High) 2.6
Industry Trend (1 = Declining: 4 = Growing) 3.2
Ease of Replication (1 = Easy: 4 = Difficult) 2.8

Benchmarks

Auto/Lube—Oil change facility (no minor repair)	
Expenses as a percentage of annual sales:	
Cost of Goods	19 to 24% (average 22%)
Payroll Costs	20 to 25% (with manager 25%)
Occupancy	10 to 16%
Royalty Fees (franchise)	5 to 8% (average 6%)
Profit (estimated)	15 to 20%

Auto/Lube—Repair Services	
Expenses as a percentage of annual sales:	
Cost of Goods	24 to 30% (average 27%)
Payroll Costs	22 to 26% (with manager 26%)
Occupancy	10 to 16%
Royalty Fees (franchise)	4 to 8%
Profit (estimated)	12 to 23%%

Tune-Up Services "Average sales volume per bay (single) $13K/mo. If you have eight bays the sales volume should be $100K per month if you have the proper equipment, mechanics and car count."

General Information

"Things to look for: franchise vs. independent, royalty fees, gross minimum 70 percent, payroll maximum 23 percent (+ payroll taxes), owner cost/price per gallon of oil, underground pits (minimum of two), supplier contacts & obligations. Things to add in the value of the business: more than one location to be purchased, minimum gross profit 72 percent, strong manager in place, multiple locations, lube & oil change only, high profile franchise, long-term leases & good rents, volume of minimum $30k per month, reputation, absentee owner. Things to subtract in this business: owner-operated, volume less than $25k per month, long-term oil supplier contract, car count low, only one bay, non-drive-thru capabilities, gross profit less than 65 percent, appearance, geographical site, most equipment on lease."

Oil Change—Market Share by Type of Chain

Automotive Chains	38%
Non-Automotive Chains	11%
Department Store Chains	03%
Discount Store Chains	48%

Seller Financing

- "4 years"

Resources

Automotive Service Industry Association
www.aftermarket.org

Independent Automotive Service Association
www.autoinc.org

Auto Mufflers

15,200	SIC: 7533-01	NAIC: 811112

Rule of Thumb:

- 35 percent of annual sales plus inventory
- 1 to 1.5 times SDE plus inventory

Resources

www.AftermarketBusiness.com

Auto Parts — Retail Store

35,500	SIC: 5531-11	NAIC: 441310

Rule of Thumb:

- 45 percent of annual sales plus inventory

Pricing Tips

"New cost of fixtures and equipment plus inventory at wholesale cost, nothing for goodwill. The inventory should turn over 4-6 times per year."

Resources

Automotive Service Industry Association—for members only
www.aftmkt.com

Automobile Parts and Accessories Association (APAA)
www.apaa.org—same as aftermarket.org

Auto Parts—Accessories, Etc. *(See also Auto Parts—Retail)*

Rule of Thumb:

- 30 percent of annual sales plus inventory

Auto Race Tracks *(See Race Tracks)*

Auto Rental

15,250	SIC: 7514-01	NAIC: 532111

Rule of Thumb:

- Number of cars times $1000

Pricing Tips

"Reservation system for franchisor is critical, as most business arrives through that system for franchised agencies."

Industry Experts' Ratings:

Amount of Competition (1 = Lot of: 4 = Not much) 1.2
Amount of Risk (1 = Very: 4 = Not much) 1.2
Historical Profit Trend (1 = Down: 4 = Up) 2.0
Location & Facilities (1 = Poor: 4 = Excellent)......................... 2.8
Marketability (1 = Low: 4 = High)... 2.0
Industry Trend (1 = Declining: 4 = Growing) 2.0
Ease of Replication (1 = Easy: 4 = Difficult) 2.8

"Franchisors are consolidating, as some (Budget, National) have gone bankrupt, and later were reorganized into consolidated entities."

Benchmarks

"Income comes from two sources: operating income from rental and add-on services and resale of vehicles. Accounting treatment (depreciation schedules for vehicles) can distort these sources."

General Information

Market Shares at U.S. Airports

Avis/Budget	30.4%
Hertz	29.6%
National/Alamo	19.8%
Dollar/Thrifty	12.2%
Enterprise	6.0%
Other	2.0%

Source: *Business Week*, July 18, 2005

Advantages of this Business

- "Increasing U.S. travel"

Disadvantages of this Business

- "Brand risk is significant; franchisor consolidation and yield management carry significant risks."

General Information

"Consider both on-airport and off-airport sites. These tend to be different business segments."

Industry Trend

"The company may be hoping to sell stock again near 16 times earnings, as in 1997. On Hertz's $390 million in profit over the 12 months ended March 31, 16 times earnings indicates an equity value of more than $6.2 billion. If instead we use multiples from 2001, when Ford was a buyer, the math implies an equity value for Hertz of much less— somewhere in a range of $4.2 billion to $5.1 billion. To get a real steal, a buyer wouldn't pay over the nine times earnings Ford initially bid in 2000. That would put the value of Hertz's equity today at $3.5 billion."

Source: *Business Week*, July 18, 2005

"Increasing transparency of pricing with Internet travel sites. Increasing use of "yield management" in pricing. Regulatory scrutiny of merged entities."

Auto Repair (Auto Service Centers)

184,000	SIC: 7514-01	NAIC: 811111

Rule of Thumb:

- 2 times SDE plus inventory
- 1.75 times SDE plus inventory

Auto Service Centers (minimum 4 bays)

Index		Owner's Cash Flow (SDE)
1.0-1.5x	to	$50K+ SDE (approx $375K gross annual sales)
2.0-2.5x	to	$100K+ SDE (approx $525K gross annual sales)
2.5-3.0 x	to	$200K+ SDE (approx $1M+ gross annual sales)

"It's important to note that there should be a manager in place for the higher multiples.

The above multiples take into account the FF&E (approx. $75K for most auto service centers). Manager in place is critical for buyers with no prior experience.

"Updates in the Auto Service Center Market—2005

"In the last year I've seen some pretty dramatic changes in the market place in regards to auto service centers. More business owners are calling to list, and hopefully exit, their current business. Some business owners have been in their business 15 to 25 years and are calling it quits.

> "Stand-alone auto shops provide roughly three-quarters of the nation's car repairs. Consumers will be the big losers if independent shops are driven out of business or forced to send work to their competitors."
>
> Source: *The Boston Globe*, April 4, 2005

"Why the sudden change? From my personal observation there has been a major influx of new vehicles on the roads. From SUVs, sedans to coupes, all makes and models. In addition the dealerships and auto makers are providing free services on oil changes, tune-ups, etc. for the first 30,000 miles. On my 2004 model, they'll even do a free alignment for the first year.

"What does this all mean for the average auto center? Fewer older models on the road and less opportunity to service late-model vehicles. Most of my core auto center business owners are down from 5% to 18% in sales over the last couple of years.

"I would say this is evolving in a major way on the West Coast, and in other areas of the country you should also be feeling the effects within the next 12 to 18 months.

"My final observation will show that for at least 3 to 5 more years and/or until the market place has a slowdown on new-vehicle sales, the demand and multiples will be down for this type of business.

"How does this affect the multiples? With less demand for this type of business and more auto centers on the market the multiples will normally go down from their past levels.

"I've reduced the rule of thumb above from 2.3 x SDE to 2.0x SDE."

"Eighty-eight percent of my automotive purchasers are buyers with no prior experience. The multiple on this type of business has dropped from previous years. Why? Lack of skilled technicians, overabundance of service centers, low unemployment. Most buyers in today's market are not looking for a business that falls under the heading of a low- paying job. Rule of thumb is applicable for Franchise or Non-Franchise Centers."

Pricing Tips

"Sometimes I will use 2.5 times SDE. This depends on if the business is located on a prime corner, how much equipment the business has, and how new the equipment is. A shop that has a very low SDE, or possibly is losing money, is able to sell for between $100K to $135K just for its location, built out, and equipment."

"1.5 to 2 times net annual tax income. These businesses are the most difficult to sell and market due to the very personal nature of the business. It is very helpful if the owner stays for 1–2 months to ease the buyer into the business especially creating a comfort level with the customers."

"Most auto repair businesses carry very little inventory, so it's included in the selling price; however, if the business does carry a large inventory it is very often in addition to the selling price."

"1. Owner's participation (tech or administrative). 2. Family members. 3. Equipment age. 4. Client core base. 5. Computer & software in place."

Industry Experts' Ratings:

Amount of Competition (1 = Lot of: 4 = Not much)	2.0
Amount of Risk (1 = Very: 4 = Not much)	1.6
Historical Profit Trend (1 = Down: 4 = Up)	2.5
Location & Facilities (1 = Poor: 4 = Excellent)	2.8
Marketability (1 = Low: 4 = High)	1.5
Industry Trend (1 = Declining: 4 = Growing)	1.6
Ease of Replication (1 = Easy: 4 = Difficult)	1.8

"It is a labor-intensive business, the labor being specialized mechanics who have to be managed well, as mechanics can be lured away by car dealerships for a better wage."

"A very good automotive repair business is difficult to replicate because of the time necessary to build a customer base. Today's automotive technicians are very skilled people and very difficult to replace."

"There are thousands of vehicles on the road. The industry is becoming more complex, slowly eliminating the backyard mechanic and limiting the large chain stores on what they do (brakes, basic services). This allows the good independents to work on high margins due to limited quality competition if you have a qualified staff. Location is key to continued success in this industry. Buyers do not have to be mechanics to operate these businesses, which allows brokers to sell at higher multiples."

Benchmarks

"$98,000 annual sales per employee (technician). Typical garage has two employees + the owner-operator, who may or may not work the bays."

"If each tech produces at least $35K per month, it is a productive shop."

"The average [auto repair] business has seven bays and is nearly 6,323 square feet in size."

Source: Auto Services Association, 2004 Survey

"By breaking the number of bays into categories, we see movement within the industry from one to three bays to 10 or more bays. It is too early to tell if this is an industry trend. As for bay categories, 15 percent have one to three bays and 36 percent have four to six bays. Twenty-three percent have seven to nine bays and 17 percent have 10 to 12 bays. Nine percent have 13 or more bays."

Source: Auto Services Association, 2004 Survey

"Two percent of businesses reported having an average ticket up to $100. Twenty-seven percent recorded an average ticket from $101–$200. The largest percentage (33 percent) reported an average ticket from $201–$300. Although $302 is the average, 21 percent had repair orders from $301–$400. Ten percent cited a repair order average from 401– $500. One percent acknowledged an average ticket from $501–$600, and two percent averaged $601–$700. The remaining four percent have repair orders averaging $700 or more.

Source: Auto Services Association, 2004 Survey

"The average repair order is broken down into 49 percent parts and 51 percent labor. Overall, a business uses 32 percent OEM parts and 62 percent aftermarket parts. Recycled OEM parts make up four percent of the parts breakdown. Recycled, non-OEM parts come in at two percent."

Source: Auto Services Association, 2004 Survey

"... the average of repair orders per month was determined to be 194. Twenty-four percent of businesses had between one and 100 repairs monthly; 37 percent had from 101–200 repairs monthly; 21 percent had 201–300; eight percent had 301–400 repair orders; five percent had 401–500 repair orders; and two percent had 501–1,000 repair orders. The remaining three percent accounted for the largest and smallest repair orders, which were removed from the calculations."

Source: Auto Services Association, 2004 Survey

Expenses as a percentage of annual sales:

Cost of goods sold	20%
Payroll/Labor Costs	20%
Occupancy Cost	10%
Profit (estimated)	20%

General Information

"Demand for this service business has gradually decreased over the last four years. The smaller (Mom & Pop operations of $25,000 gross/month or less) are becoming non-existent in many larger cities."

"Factors to look for: the gross profit of the business pre-wages, equipment leased vs. free and clear, management & certification of techs, percentage of wages, the length of lease and terms. The business should do a minimum of $30K per month in sales revenue (excluding smog Certs). Any special licenses required? Does the owner work as a mechanic? Things to add to value: volume exceeds $50K per month, the owner works only in administrative capacity, number of bays (minimum 6 bays), all equipment is free and clear, all mechanics have at least two years' experience, rent is eight percent of sales or less, strong manager in place, gross profit exceeds 60 percent. Things to subtract from value: owner is active as mechanic, monthly sales under $25K per month, appearance, location, most equipment on lease, the age of the equipment, lack of professional management, inexperience of mechanics, unable to expand in capacity or sales, rent high, short term lease."

Advantages of this Business

- "This is not a luxury industry. Consumers will always need a repair shop and the number of cars on the road is increasing."
- "High profit and normal day hours"

Disadvantages of this Business

- Annual investment in diagnostic equipment; and in some areas, it may be difficult to get qualified technicians.
- "Difficult employees and risk of liability for shoddy workmanship"

Industry Trend

"Specializing in the type of service and types of cars, vans, etc."

"There are many automotive consulting firms that do a great job for minimal investment in teaching new owners how to run an automotive business profitably and productively."

"According to survey results, the average owner is 49 … 22 percent are 55 to 64 … The largest percentage of owners are between 45 and 54."

Source: Auto Services Association, 2004 Survey

"The smaller shops are having a very difficult time keeping mechanics and often are a training program for dealers. Dealerships are trying every way they can to keep the service business, and technology is getting more complex. Specialty shops seem to be doing well. Drugs and alcohol are a very serious problem. There are a lot of old cars, and the need will always be there. I think the trend is for shops to become larger; smaller ones, especially where the owner is a mechanic, are fading fast, and difficult to sell to a non-experienced buyer. Mechanics in general do not have money to buy, and many [of these smaller shops] will end up as asset sales or for FF&E value."

Seller Financing

- "3 to 5 years, average 8 percent interest per annum"

Resources

Automotive Service Industry Association—excellent and informative Web site www.aftmkt.com/asia

Auto Services Association—an excellent site. If you are working in the auto repair/collision field, this is the site to visit.
www.asashop.org

Auto Service Stations *(See Gas Stations)*

Auto Tire Stores

42,000	SIC: 5531-23	NAIC: 441320

Rule of Thumb:

- 2 to 3 times SDE plus inventory

"Domestic replacement tire sales totaled a record $24.3 billion in 2004, a 7.8% increase over the previous year. Passenger tires accounted for $14.7 billion, light-truck tires—$4.0 billion, and truck tires—19.4%"

Source: *Modern Tire Dealer*, January, 2005

Auto Tire Centers (minimum 5 bays)
Franchise; e.g., Big O Tire, Goodyear, Firestone, etc.

Index		Owner's Cash Flow (SDE)
1.5 x	to	$50K+
2.0 x	to	$75K+
2. 5 x	to	$100K+ (sales normally exceed $700K)

Above are plus inventory. Rule of thumb for independent tire center: deduct 20 percent from above figure.

"The first business generally shows a greater multiple 2. 5 x the SDE. If the business does not have a name identity; e.g., Goodyear, Big O Tire, Bridgestone—you need to deduct from the above multiples, normally 20 percent of the SDE."

"The second performs tire mounting and balancing in addition to service work; e.g., brakes, tune-ups, smog certifications, alignment, front-end service, etc."

Benchmarks

Expenses as a percentage of annual sales:

Cost of goods sold	35 to 40%
Payroll/labor costs	24 to 26%
Occupancy costs	10 to 14%
Profit (estimated)	16 to 23%

Profit varies on total revenues and royalty fees

Summary of the Average Independent Tire Dealer's Automotive Service Operations

Service as a percentage of total sales	44%
Service as a percentage of total earnings	47%
Bays per outlet	5.5
Technicians per outlet	3.8
Percentage of technicians certified	49%
Domestic vehicles serviced	68.8%
Imported vehicles serviced	31.2%
Age of vehicles serviced (in years)	6.7
Annual wages per technician	$31,180

Source: *Modern Tire Dealer*, January 2005

Tire dealer profile

"Close to 67% of the 26,000 independent retail, wholesale and commercial tire dealers in the United States are single-store owners. The average independent dealer sells 10 different tire brands. While some 95% of all dealers have Internet access, only 8% offer nitrogen tire-filling service, although that percentage is higher than it has been in the recent past. The average annual compensation for an automotive service technician working in an independent tire dealership is $30,180. The average number of technicians employed per outlet is 3.8."

Source: *Modern Tire Magazine*, January, 2005

Dealer Sales Volume

Sales	% of Independent Dealers
$0–$499,999	33%
$500,000–$999,999	26%
$1million–$2,999,999	25%
$3 million–$4,999,999	06%
$5 million–$9,999,999	05%
$10 million and over	05%

Source: *Modern Tire Magazine*, January 2005

General Information

Financial Analysis of Automotive Services Offered

Service	% offering service	Average ticket/job	# of jobs per mo	Profit margin
Air conditioning	51%	$262	17	52%
Alignment	80%	$69	70	63%
Battery/electrical	91%	$88	20	35%
Bearings/seals	74%	$127	11	52%
Brakes	94%	$160	35	51%
Chassis/suspension	80%	$191	23	51%
Cooling system	60%	$99	18	54%
Eng.diag./tune-up	55%	$157	28	53%
Exhaust system	53%	$138	17	50%
Mounting/balancing	95%	$59	173	63%
Oil/lubrication	84%	$26	148	42%
Shocks & struts	85%	$207	13	49%

Source: *Modern Tire Dealer*, January, 2005

"Critical factors that make an overall difference in the business value are as follows: key employees including manager, lease terms, equipment owned and leased, geographical location, years established and customer base, family members involved, owner participation."

"The average independent tire dealer employs 3.8 technicians per outlet.

Source: *Modern Tire Dealer*

Industry Trend

"So for the full year [2005], I'm looking for about a 2% increase in replacement passenger tire shipments, a 3% increase in light truck tire shipments and a 4% increase in medium truck tire shipments."

Source: Saul Ludwig, industry analyst, *Modern Tire Dealer*, January 2005

Seller Financing

- "5 Years"

Resources

Automotive Service Industry Association
www.aftmkt.com

Trade Publications
Tire Business, published by Crain Communications www.crain.com

Modern Tire Dealer—a great Web site—one of the best we have seen in our research. If you are working in a tire store, this site and the publication are a must. www.mtdealer.com

Auto Towing *(See Towing Companies)*

Auto Transmission Centers

(See also AAMCO Transmission Centers)

17,056	SIC: 7537-01	NAIC: 811113

Rule of Thumb:

- 35 percent annual sales plus inventory
- 1.7 times SDE and includes inventory
- Also, 16 to 20 times average weekly sales for a shop doing less than $20,000 a week plus inventory

Auto Transmission Centers;
e.g., Franchise, Cottman, Sparky's, AAMCO

Index		Owner's Cash Flow (SDE)
1.0 x	to	$50K+ SDC
1.5 – 2.0 x	to	$100K+ SDC
2.0 – 2.25 x	to	$150K+ SDC (sales normally exceed $800K)

Rule of thumb—deduct 20 percent for independent centers.

Pricing Tips

Industry Experts' Ratings:

Marketability (1 = Low: 4 = High) 2.0
Industry Trend (1 = Declining: 4 = Growing) 2.0
Ease of Replication (1 = Easy: 4 = Difficult) 2.0

"Competition from Auto Repair Shops. Zero-interest dealer incentives to trade cars rather than repair, technology and improvement in manufacturer's warranties, and the dealers trying to keep their new-car customers. Small independent shops are giving a hard time competing."

"Updates in the Market Place for Transmission Centers — 2005

This service business has really taken a hit on the West Coast. Sales are down on average 22% from previous years and continue to slide. Look for similar trends in your geographical areas as well.

"Demand is off dramatically for this type of business and who can blame the buyers. Why the sudden drop in sales and demand? New car makers have increased their warrantees on drive trains to 6 years and 70,000 to 100,000 miles. A greater abundance of new vehicles each year has significantly affected the transmission replacement and or repair business.

"Lastly, vertical market businesses such as auto service centers can now replace transmissions on almost any vehicle in about three hours or less. They take out the old existing transmission and it's replaced with a GM, Ford or Chrysler manufactured transmission that includes a full warrantee from the factory.

"I've reduced the average rule of thumb on this business from 2.0x to 1.7x SDE."

Benchmarks

"$3,500 to $4,000 per shop employee. Parts cost lower than 15% indicates used parts being used. High parts cost indicates high warranty costs, and/or skimming. High ratio of commercial sales to retail sales indicates a personal relationship that may not be transferable. Average invoice less than $1,000 on transmission repairs is an indication of a poor manager. Ratio of major to minor repairs should be high."

Expenses as a percentage of annual sales:	
Cost of goods sold	28%
Payroll/labor costs	25% to 30%
Occupancy costs	8% to12%
Profit (estimated)	12% to 18%

General Information

Questions to ask seller: "What does the owner do? Analyze weekly sales reports, if available; they provide a real insight as to what is going on. How many techs on payroll? A typical shop has three—a builder and two mechanics. What are they paid, and how is the manager compensated? Ratio of major repairs to minor, ratio retail to commercial accounts, look at 'comebacks.'"

"If one is buying a franchise, talk to all the other locations and determine that they are working together and cooperating with regard to advertising expense, and whether or not they feel that the franchisor is assisting them."

"1. Franchise versus independent. 2. Owner's duties. 3. Inventory in stock. 4. Manager in place. 5. Geographical location."

Industry Trend

"New-car extended warranties have impacted the business—hopefully short term. Unprofitable shops are being weeded out, and are difficult to sell. Good shops, especially the large independent and franchises, are doing well. Trend is changing to average."

Seller Financing

- "3 to 6.5 years"

Resources

Independent Automatic Transmission Rebuilders Association (ATRA)
www.atra-gears.com

Auto/Wrecking/Recyclers/Dismantlers/Scrap/ Salvage Yards (Auto parts—used & rebuilt)

14,581	SIC: 501502	NAIC: 333923

General Information

"A common problem has always been inventory valuation of salvage cars on the property with no particular value as collision parts. Generally some nominal value, like $50, had been used. With the changes in the manner of construction of newer cars to more plastics (which is a disposal expense) and more galvanized metals (a lower-value scrap), this number is $0; or perhaps a negative number if they have been only selectively picked for the removal of high value parts.

"Automotive recycling currently ranks among the largest industries in the U.S., with more than $3.7 billion in annual sales.

"The automotive recycling industry recycles more than 11 million motor vehicles annually nationwide."

Source: Automotive Recyclers Association of New York

Seller Financing

- "Seller financing, if more than a nominal sale price if desired, is very long term: 15–40 years, with a very minimal down payment, which may not be even enough to cover the commission, and a sharing/offset of future liabilities for past activities."

Resources

Automotive Recyclers Association of New York
www.arany.com

Benchmark Data for Selected Auto Aftermarket Franchises

The data below is provided for benchmarking purposes only and is not current information. However, we believe the data still provides important benchmark data. The companies below are successful; and by comparing gross sales and percentages for the various expenses with a similar business (independent or franchised), and adjusting for inflation, one may get a ballpark idea of how it's doing.

Jiffy Lube (for year of 2002)

Range of Gross Sales			
Expense Category	$280,802– $493,641	$495,221– $703,175	$704,074– $1,432,535
Median:	$426,511	$585,005	$861,644
Cost of Goods	27.74%	26.19%	24.87%
Oper-Salaries/Wages	22.84%	20.55%	18.98%
Mgr-Salaries/Wages	7.42%	5.48%	4.00%
Bonus Wages	1.70%	1.65%	1.95%
Vacation/Holiday Pay	0.82%	0.67%	0.60%
Employee Benefits	8.58%	7.43%	6.67%
Payroll Burden	0.00%	0.00%	0.00%
Employee Expenses	0.14%	0.11%	0.09%
Employment Costs	0.05%	0.05%	0.04%

Valvoline Instant Oil Change
(Year ending September 30, 2002

Average Oil Changes per Day	40.32
#of Service Centers (All Company Owned)	337
Net Sales	$168,363,076
Cost of Goods Sold	$38,131,536
% of Net Sales	22.6%
Total Labor	$52,256,794
% of Net Sales	31.0%
Total Other Expenses	$14,716,150
% of Net Sales	8.7%

Above information does not include footnotes.

Car X Centers (2002)

More than two years in business—169 centers, 139 franchised

Average Annual Sales—$690,000

Lee Myles Transmissions (2001)

Average sales of 70 centers open one year—$534,389

Merlin Muffler & Brake

Fifty of these shops have been open two years or longer as of December 31, 2002. The average sales of these shops for the period was $619,659. For the period, the sales of 20 of these shops exceeded this average, and the sales of the other shops were less than the average.

Cottman Transmissions (Year ending April 30, 2000)

Total Sales	$553,741
Total Cost of Sales	44%
Gross Profit on Sales	56%
Total Selling Expense	13.5%
Total Overhead Expenses	22.3%
Net Income before Taxes	20.2%

Bagel Shops

6,955	SIC: 546101	NAIC: 722110

Rule of Thumb:

- 30 percent of annual sales plus inventory
- 2.5 SDE plus inventory

Pricing Tips

"Generally worth 1/3 of gross sales volume, with a decent rent. Higher rent or upcoming increase will lower price."

"Rent a large factor; hand-rolled or frozen product?"

Industry Experts' Ratings:

Marketability (1 = Low: 4 = High)	2.0
Industry Trend (1 = Declining: 4 = Growing)	1.6
Ease of Replication (1 = Easy: 4 = Difficult)	1.6

"Easy to duplicate. Setup cost expensive. Most shopping centers already have a bagel shop."

Benchmarks

Expenses as a percentage of annual sales:

Cost of Goods Sold	10%
Payroll/Labor Costs	25%
Occupancy Cost	20%
Profit (estimated)	20%

"Rent and payroll the most important factors."

General Information

"Bagel-baking machines, a fairly recent innovation, were developed to enhance production…. This primed the market for the bonanza during the 1990s, when Americans turned to bagels as a low-fat alternative to doughnuts and croissants…. In their purest form, bagels are 90 percent flour and water, and contain no sugar…. Bagels quickly became as mainstream as tacos and pizza, and soon chains like Einstein's/Noah's and Bruegger's were in a fast-growth mode, opening hundreds of shops nationwide…. American bagel consumption doubled between 1995 and 1999, according to Business Trend Analysts, a marketing research company…. And while some of the chains are struggling, the overall sale of bagels—whether fresh-baked, frozen, refrigerated or off the shelf—is still purring along, with an estimated $4.7 billion in sales this year…. What has hurt the chains and their fast-casual restaurant concept is simply the tremendous availability of bagels—including supermarkets, java joints, and Dunkin' Donuts, which added bagels to its sweeter menu. Now Dunkin' Donuts is the nation's largest bagel chain, even while riding the crest of a doughnut revival."

Source: Article by Rose Atkin, www.csmonitor.com (2001)

"Most people think of bagels as a New York food. In fact, they were first made in the late 17th century by a Jewish baker in Austria and became popular in Eastern Europe. Bagels came to America with Jewish immigrants 200 years later. Since many Jewish newcomers settled in New York, the bagel became associated with the city. And the large, dense, chewy bagels with a hard crust, the ones made by the immigrants, became the most widely known."

Source: The *Boston Globe*, Wednesday, March 16, 2005

Advantages of this Business

- "Cash business, high gross profit."

Disadvantages of this Business

- "Long hours, at the mercy of employees."

Industry Trend

Many bagel shops, especially the franchised outlets, are adding extensive lunch items including soups, salads, and sandwiches, in addition to the usual bagel items. Some of the bagel shops are changing their name and dropping the word bagel from it.

Resources

(See Restaurants)

American Bakers Association (ABA)
www.americanbakers.org

Bait and Tackle Shops

Bait and Tackle:	10,000		
Fishing Supply Stores (Bait):	4,000	SIC: 5941-33	NAIC: 451110
Fishing and Tackle:	6,000	SIC: 5941-31	NAIC:339920

Rule of Thumb:

- 25 percent of annual sales plus inventory

Resources

www.baitnet.com—this site contains listings of many fishing-related businesses including bait and tackle shops.

Bakeries

28,618	SIC: 5461-02	NAIC: 311812

Rule of Thumb:

- 45–50 percent of annual sales plus inventory
- 2 times SDE plus inventory

Pricing Tips

"Receivables; years in business; scope of market; new 'state of art' equipment vs. old"

Industry Experts' Ratings:

Marketability (1 = Low: 4 = High) 3.6
Industry Trend (1 = Declining: 4 = Growing) 2.0
Ease of Replication (1 = Easy: 4 = Difficult) 2.0

"The product line (especially bread) is a highly marketable item."

Benchmarks

Expenses as a percentage of annual sales:

Cost of goods sold	Food—10–5%
Payroll/Labor Costs	30–35%
Occupancy Cost	6–8%
Other Overhead	10–15%
Profit (estimated)	20+%

General Information

"The U.S. baker industry has about 2,600 commercial bakeries, with a combined annual revenue of $25 billion, and 7,000 small retail bakeries, with $2 billion total revenue. Large companies include Interstate Bakeries (filed for Chapter 11) and Flowers Foods, plus divisions of companies such as Sara Lee, Nabisco, and Best Foods. The industry is highly concentrated: three companies produce almost 45 percent of industry sales. Over 75 percent of baked goods come from 380 large facilities, each having over $45 million in revenue and over 100 employees. Although big companies may operate dozens of bakeries, the typical baker operates just one facility.

Competitive Landscape

"Demand comes from commercial entities, such as restaurants and specialty food and grocery stores that don't have their own bakeries. Profitability for individual companies is determined by efficiency of operations and favorable materials prices. Large companies have scale advantages in procurement, production, and distribution. Large commercial bakeries' sales-per-employee average $150,000. Small companies can compete by offering specialty goods or superior distribution services.

Products, Operations & Technology

"Baking is a low-technology business that produces low-priced products from commodity ingredients. Fifty percent of industry volume is from baked breads, mainly white, wheat and rye; 20 percent from rolls, buns, muffins, bagels and croissants; 11 percent from soft cakes; and the rest from pies, pastries, doughnuts and a variety of sweet goods. Annual U.S. per capita consumption of bread is close to 60 pounds,..."

Source: Bakeries—Industry Profile, www.researchandmarkets.com/reports

"What is a full-line bakery? A small family-run operation that produces a variety of cakes, cookies, breads and donuts for retail sale? Sometimes, but quite often not…. Entrepreneurs continue to enter the retail bakery business. Busy discussions on bakery associations' e-groups offer proof positive that a new generation of full-line retail bakery operators is alive and well…. Now they are better connected to the resources of seasoned bakery operators through the Internet. The new retailers offer a full line of products, but they likely fill niches untapped by traditional 'American' retail bakeries. Gourmet tortes, cakes, artisan breads and rustic pastries are among the new generation's specialties."

Source: *Modern Baking and Baking Management* at www.bakery.net

"Percentage of full-line retail bakery operators offering the following items:

1. Sodas, juices, teas 61%
2. Conventional coffee service 56%
3. Sandwiches 45%
4. On-site dining 31%
5. Espresso, other gourmet coffee 30%

Other deli (salads, cheeses, etc.) .... 30%"

Trend

"The Top 50 largest in-store bakery operators find themselves at a crossroads. Amid intense competition from mass merchandisers, convenience stores, drug stores and other non-traditional food retailers, supermarket companies are debating how best to compete: on price or quality. Some are choosing price, such as Giant Eagle's recent announcement to go EDLP in all its 221 stores by cutting prices seven percent, and Albertson's new Super Saver limited-assortment, discount grocery stores. For others among the Top 50, such as Whole Foods Market and Wegman's Foods Market, price is not a primary focus.

"For bakery, the Top 50 operators have proven time and again that taking the high road with quality and price is the most direct route to achieving profitable in-store bakeries. The most important consideration for in-store bakery customers is product quality, but bakery's track record for customer satisfaction has been mixed through the years. Customer loyalty as a regular shopper has fallen 16 percent during the last seven years, according to FMI's Consumer Attitudes and the Supermarket report"

Source: *Modern Baking*, December 2004

Resources

Modern Baking magazine

www.bakery-net.com—an excellent site. It offers downloadable surveys that are not inexpensive, but if you want to sell bakeries, they would be well worthwhile.

Independent Bakers Association
www.bakingnetwork.com

National Confectioners Association of the U.S.
www.candyusa.org

Bakery & Restaurant *(See also Bakeries & Restaurants)*

Rule of Thumb:

- 35 to 40 percent of annual sales plus inventory

Bakeries—Commercial *(See also Bakeries)*

6,044	SIC: 5149-02	NAIC: 422420

Rule of Thumb:

- 65 percent of annual sales plus inventory
- 2.5 times SDE plus inventory

Pricing Tips

"Be careful to check if one or two customers comprise a high percentage of the bakery's revenues."

"Don't be fooled by the owner's overstatement of the value of the equipment. Most bakery equipment is valued at between 10%–25% of replacement cost new. The larger equipment requires riggers to move it. The dismantling and re-installation of ovens requires specialized skill and knowledge."

Industry Experts' Ratings:

Amount of Competition (1 = Lot of: 4 = Not much) 1.0
Amount of Risk (1 = Very: 4 = Not much) 2.0
Historical Profit Trend (1 = Down: 4 = Up) 1.6
Location & Facilities (1 = Poor: 4 = Excellent) 1.6
Marketability (1 = Low: 4 = High) 2.4
Industry Trend (1 = Declining: 4 = Growing) 1.6
Ease of Replication (1 = Easy: 4 = Difficult) 3.2

"This is an old industry. Many of these businesses are passed from one generation to the next. This does not create an environment for growth or innovation. Ease of replication is influenced by high asset cost to enter this industry."

"Industry is declining due to eating habits of population. Cost of entry is very high due to equipment cost, unless used equipment is purchased. Marketability is limited by the size of the marketplace of professional bakers. In some parts of the U.S., facilities tend to be old. Competition is growing a bit due to the business education of young professional bakers."

Price dependent on the scope of distribution; whether they sell retail as well; their receivables, plus value of depreciated equipment (which in most cases is not worth much) and any product inventory kept in-house (flour and sugar are not cheap).

Receivables are very important since they determine the amount of start-up capital needed. It was the cause of the demise of many a big wholesaler in New York.

"Price will vary greatly depending on the volume and types of labor-saving equipment. This is an industry where payroll can be significantly reduced by machinery. Commercial contracts with restaurants, hotels, etc. are also a source of value."

Benchmarks

"Difficult to measure since many of these businesses operate from facilities that are old and much larger than required with new highly automated equipment."

Expenses as a percentage of annual sales:	
Cost of Goods Sold	20%
Payroll/Labor Costs	35%
Occupancy Cost	07%
Profit (estimated)	15%

"Commercial bakeries vary from those generating $500K–$1 million in sales to factory- style operations. I have not developed or seen any 'Benchmarks' that apply across all sizes and styles of commercial bakeries. Those that I've included above apply to businesses baking bread products—not pastry or novelty products. Each of those businesses is unique."

Advantages of this Business

- "It is seen as an art form by those who take baking seriously. There is a great deal of pride in a baker's creations."
- "It is not subject to the supermarket bakeries' impact on the retail bakery business. Most large accounts will sign contracts for the provision of products."

Disadvantages of this Business

- "Tough work. Plenty of competition. Equipment is expensive. Need to train personnel. Oftentimes unusual hours (2a.m.–10 p.m.)"

- "It is a seven-day-per-week operation that requires expertise in baking, business, food chemistry and awareness of trends in eating habits."

Industry Trend

"Flat. Carbs-R-Out."

Seller Financing

- "5 years"

Banks

92,395	SIC: 6021-01	NAIC: 522110

Pricing Tips

"Rules of Thumb Don't Always Nail It—Financial institutions have specific interest-rate, credit, technology and liquidity risks that an experienced firm is best able to assess and benchmark. The rule of thumb for community banks and thrifts is that valuations average between 1 and 2 times the price-to-book ratio. But overrelying on rules of thumb can be dangerous. Take two recent thrift acquisitions by the same company in a 10-month period that perfectly highlight the danger in depending on averages. The first deal was priced at 1.7 times the price-to-book ratio and the second at 3.0 times—a 76 percent difference."

BVS Valuation Quarterly published by Business Valuation Services

Resources

Moody's Bank and Finance Manual, published by Mergent Fis Inc.
www.fisonline.com

American Bankers Association
www.aba.com

Barbecue Restaurants *(See Restaurants)*

6,427		

Rule of Thumb:

- 30 percent of annual sales plus inventory

Barber Shops

51,669	SIC: 7241-01	NAIC: 812111

Rule of Thumb:

- 10 to 25 percent of SDE plus inventory; add $1500 per chair

General Information

"Barbers, cosmetologists, and other personal appearance workers held about 790,000 jobs in 2000. Nine out of ten jobs were for barbers, hairdressers, hairstylists, and cosmetologists. Of the remaining jobs, manicurists and pedicurists held about 40,000; skin care specialists about 21,000; and shampooers about 20,000.

"Most of these workers are employed in beauty salons or barber shops, but they are also found in department stores, nursing and other residential care homes, and drug and cosmetics stores. Nearly every town has a barbershop or beauty salon, but employment in this occupation is concentrated in the most populous cities and states.

"Approximately half of barbers, cosmetologists, and other personal appearance workers are self-employed. Many own their own salon, but a growing number lease booth space or a chair from the salon's owner."

Source: *Occupational Outlook Handbook, 2002-2003 Edition*, published by the U.S. Department of Labor

Industry Trend

"Overall employment of barbers, cosmetologists, and other personal appearance workers is projected to grow as fast as the average for all occupations through 2010, because of increasing population, incomes, and demand for cosmetology services."

Source: *Occupational Outlook Handbook, 2002-2003 Edition*, published by the U.S. Department of Labor

Bars (See Cocktail Bars, Brewpubs & Breweries)		
53,544	SIC: 5813-01	NAIC: 722410

Rule of Thumb:

- 40 to 50 percent times annual sales— business only plus inventory
- 2.5–3 times SDE plus inventory
- 2 times EBIT
- 3–3.5 times EBITDA
- 4 times monthly sales + game revenue (net) plus inventory
- 4 times monthly gross sales + liquor license and inventory
- Dollar for dollar on gross sales if property is included plus inventory

Pricing Tips

Questions to ask seller: "Is the seller reporting all income? What is seller's pour cost? Is seller hands-on owner?

"Location is key to success....as is longevity for resale unless major renovations will occur. Location needs to have sufficient parking."

Types of Bars

Neighborhood bar
Sports bar
Brewpub
Beer bar
Cocktail lounge
Nightclub
Adult club/Nightclub

"It is easier to go thru the receipts of the business than go thru returns."

"Long lease a must"

"Lease terms a huge factor; ratio of food to liquor drinks; current market wants light food, less than 25%"

"Multiples of earnings are similar to full-service restaurants. However, income statements for bars show a loss, even after non-operating expenses."

"Value and type of liquor license is always a key consideration. Ownership of real estate is always a big plus. Many buyers are looking for real estate as part of the purchase."

"Location, value of lease, liquor license value, willingness of seller to hold note, cooperation of seller to supply necessary financial information, beware of 'red' flags."

"+/- value of the liquor license
+/- lease value
+/- location
+/- seller financing"

Industry Experts' Ratings:

Amount of Competition (1 = Lot of: 4 = Not much) 1.0
Amount of Risk (1 = Very: 4 = Not much) 1.2
Historical Profit Trend (1 = Down: 4 = Up) 2.0
Location & Facilities (1 = Poor: 4 = Excellent) 2.8
Marketability (1 = Low: 4 = High) 2.4
Industry Trend (1 = Declining: 4 = Growing) 2.5
Ease of Replication (1 = Easy: 4 = Difficult) 3.0

"I think the competition is intense for the local neighborhood places, brought on by the chain-type concepts opening up in suburban markets. Some of the rent factors make it cost-prohibitive for the local venue to compete. Neighborhood bars are always a popular pick since it is a recession-proof business."

"Lots of taverns, one on each corner. Liquor license may be the majority of the value."

"Must buy an existing liquor license in New Jersey, no new licenses available."

"Location is key to success....as is longevity for resale, unless major renovations will occur. Location needs to have sufficient parking."

Benchmarks
"Lite food is a plus"

"$327 sales per sq. ft. in a bar generating $850,000 in sales with a 5% net profit."

"Food costs in the 40s %—too high. Beer costs in the mid-20s % and under 30%—good."

Expenses as a percentage of annual sales:	
Cost of goods sold	Food—28–35% Bar—25–30%
Payroll/Labor Costs	25%
Occupancy Cost	5–10%
Profit (estimated)	10–20%

"Twenty-eight percent COGS is at the high end; some operators can be in the low 20s depending on the price points. Labor can be significantly lower or higher depending if the state has a tip credit for minimum wage. Ten percent to the bottom line is only a rule of thumb."

General Information

"High degree of owner involvement on a day-to-day basis. Ability to contain costs and prevent 'shrinkage.' Creating a customer-friendly environment which provides good value. Owner usually must have excellent people skills, not a business for introverts."

"Never trust the books. Check sales tax returns, bank statements, etc. Also, check the price points and compare to the actual COGS. Are the comps legitimate on the P&L? Are COGS high due to the owner skimming, or are they giving the house away? We never address a value to skimming and never represent it to buyers. Experienced buyers will recast the financials using their own labor percentage, etc."

"Food costs must be controlled. Lots of businesses fail due to ineffective food and liquor cost controls."

Advantages of this Business

- "Cash business with high profit margin, low cost of help due to tips and limited product line."
- "Great cash flow"
- "Perceived to be 'fun' and having 'status'—Cash business with good profit margins."

Disadvantages of this Business

- "Major chains and large players taking the market share from the smaller bars."
- "Long hours, at mercy of employees"
- "Long hours!!! Hard work!!! Difficult customers. Employee theft."

- "Employee turnover"
- "It is a very complex type of business to sell with all of the licensing, taxes, being a cash business. Banks don't like to get involved in these transactions. It can be difficult to get a complete picture of the business."
- "Maintaining food and liquor costs to manageable levels"

Industry Trend

"Diminished demand for bars due to influence of major chains with large bar followings and promotions"

"People are always going to frequent bars to socialize. The bar business will grow as the population increases."

"Bars are easy to sell"

Seller Financing

- "3 to 5 years"

Resources

Bar Confidential;Running a Successful Bar by Bob Johnson—to order, go to www.barproducts.com. This is an interesting site.

Bars - Adult Only | Adult Clubs/Nightclubs

Rule of Thumb:

➢ 1.5 times SDE plus inventory

Pricing Tips

"Adult clubs are zoning sensitive. The municipality, the state, political environment, and competition all factor in also, of course."

Advantages of this Business

- "Cash flow can be quite high. Profitably can be much better than 25% if properly managed."

Disadvantages of this Business

- "This industry is not for the faint of heart. It is highly policed/overseen. It is a much more demanding operation than a mainstream bar or club due to the operational requirement."

Industry Experts' Ratings:

Amount of Competition (1 = Lot of: 4 = Not much) 2.4
Amount of Risk (1 = Very: 4 = Not much) 0.0
Historical Profit Trend (1 = Down: 4 = Up) 1.6
Location & Facilities (1 = Poor: 4 = Excellent) 2.8
Marketability (1 = Low: 4 = High) 1.2
Industry Trend (1 = Declining: 4 = Growing) 1.6
Ease of Replication (1 = Easy: 4 = Difficult) 4.0

"Adult Clubs are a distinctive subset of alcoholic establishments."

Benchmarks
"No more than 8% of gross income for rent"

Expenses as a percentage of annual sales:

Cost of goods sold .... 15 %
Payroll/Labor Costs 08%
Occupancy Cost 08%
Profit (estimated) 25%

Industry Trend
"Trended down about 7–9% in Gross Sales for 2004, first half of '05"

Bars — Nightclubs

9,451

Rule of Thumb:

➢ 2 times SDE plus inventory

Pricing Tips

Industry Experts' Ratings:

Amount of Competition (1 = Lot of: 4 = Not much)	0
Amount of Risk (1 = Very: 4 = Not much)	0
Historical Profit Trend (1 = Down: 4 = Up)	3.2
Location & Facilities (1 = Poor: 4 = Excellent)	3.2
Marketability (1 = Low: 4 = High)	4.0
Industry Trend (1 = Declining: 4 = Growing)	2.4
Ease of Replication (1 = Easy: 4 = Difficult)	2.0

"Hot nightclubs generally have a two to three year lifespan. Fortunately, this is generally more a function of promoters than the physical location. Unfortunately, this takes the critical success factors somewhat out of owner's hands, as it is often difficult for management teams doing 'In-House' promotion to adjust to ever-changing trends."

Benchmarks

"While such benchmarks work with typical bars, these vary widely with nightclubs."

Expenses as a percentage of annual sales:

Cost of goods sold.	25%
Payroll/Labor Costs	30%
Occupancy Cost	20%
Profit (estimated)	15%

Advantages of this Business

- "These businesses are considered highly 'sexy,' however, many owners in large markets operate marquee venues as 'vanity' businesses rather than the profitable enterprises they can be. These are high cash businesses, with all too willing investors that do not seek economic returns."

Disadvantages of this Business

- "Conditional use permits and city/county regulators may wreak havoc on a successful enterprise. Definitely a lifestyle business; owners need to work long hours and maintain strong audit measures to prevent theft."

General Information

"Top-end venues in major cities attract buyers with deep pockets. We saw a $20 million cash offer on a hot venue doing $3 million in profit—it was turned down. From a brokerage standpoint, beware that every promoter in the state that has ever dreamt of ownership will seek to ascertain the venue name/location to protect their promotion night; others will tout that they are backed by teams of investors. Much time is saved by only working with the investors directly."

Quick *Profile* **Bars**

Bar Confidential: Working with Sellers

By Terri Sokoloff, CBI, CRB, GRI/Broker/Realtor

I have had many brokers over the years confuse the openings we attend to with the so-called glamour of the business The smarter ones have always known that oftentimes these buyers and sellers lead to many dead ends. It's not challenging finding a bar owner who wants to sell, but finding one that is motivated and cooperative is strategic. The economy has had its fluctuations resulting in consumers tightening their pocket book for white tablecloth dining. The Russian Tea Room didn't even survive. Consumers perceive the bar differently. It is a place to go to relax with friends, meet new people, and have some fun with hopefully decent food. Everyone has a "Cheers" of his or her own to patronize. I have talked with hundreds of bar owners this year and yes business was off a little but they didn't suffer like their fellow restaurateurs we spoke to. People drink in good times and in bad times. My father-in-law, who owned 30 bars in his day, said it was a recession-proof business and he was right. The dollar has shrunk in value but the attraction to the bar business hasn't. People from all walks of life contact us to turn their dream of owning into reality.

I have found after eighteen years of dealing with bar owners that they are a tough breed. It is about survival for them. Most sellers we have met have a story—some are poignant and oftentimes heartbreaking situations. This business destroys lives and habitually drains the seller emotionally and occasionally financially. Sellers never seem to inquire when they should be putting their business for sale except when they are forced to. I have observed numerous sellers are past help because they have buried themselves in a situation often associated with professionals more interested in lining their pockets than helping. If you still say, "I'm going to sell bars," then keep reading. I have attempted to share a few topics in considering the listing and the red flags associated with bars that are fundamental for you to detect.

Do Your Homework

The first step when someone calls to sell is doing your homework on him or her and the establishment. We check into court records. I scour the legal journal daily to find out who is litigious, who doesn't appear to pay their purveyors and so forth. If they have more secured creditors than the establishment is worth, then how do I get compensated? We aren't in the business as nonprofit business. If they sue everyone, or everyone is after them, what are the odds even with an ironclad contract that I will have to fight to get paid? Is this worth it? I don't think so, even if starting out you will be spinning your wheels. The sellers that called—are they truly the sellers? Check the corporate bureau to see who the officers are. Who has the stock? We have seen many sons and daughters attempting to sell "Dad's" business without his authorization. Have they had any reviews? Anything controversial? I just got a call from an owner who was under investigation for underage drinking and shut down two weeks later. I knew his attorney and picked up the case in the legal journal. It saved us a long dead end. With the Internet, another approach is to "Google" someone. On the buyer side—we had a potential buyer from outside our county that attempted to purchase a two million dollar facility from us. The buyer and his mother were in litigation in the other county on a similar size transaction for bad checks and deceptive business practices, and his mother was charged with embezzlement from her former job. Who would have ever thought after meeting these buyers? The article appeared online and we were fortunate to have known.

Motivation

What is truly going on? We always hear about wanting to spend more time with the family and about health problems, and for most they are legitimate. Are these sellers one breath away from filing bankruptcy? When you ask them who their attorney is and they name the top bankruptcy lawyer in your town, walk the other way. Or they are not really sure but want to have you test the market and put some feelers out? Run. Are they on COD with their purveyors? Do the employees seem pleasant? What is really going on is your job to find out.

Cooperation

I always request a minimum of three years tax returns and financials. I have experienced the mainstream is to file extensions. Some of them fall in arrears not paying their accountant, so their work is a last priority. A requisite in selling is information. If you can't get the records upfront, be prepared to walk. Don't play the game. If you bring a buyer and get me an offer, I will show you everything. The seller can only meet you at 7 a.m. on Sunday. I don't know about you, but I'm either going to sleep in or play golf. If you're meeting me with a cash offer, sure, but time is our commodity. The seller tells you he wants to give you an open listing or one for three months. I always recommend a year exclusive on an operating business. Another situation we have seen is that the lease is almost expired and the seller is telling you no problem, his landlord will give you a new lease. The seller doesn't want you to contact the landlord and he can't show you anything in writing confirming his conversation. These places are very intricate to sell, and not being able to control your listings is a recipe for failure.

Up Front Fees

We incorporated project fees into our listings a few years ago. It really separates sellers that appear to not value your services from those that are motivated and respect you as a professional. If you think about it, the seller wouldn't expect to meet with his attorney and have agreements drawn up and not expect to have a bill associated with their time and costs. We have incorporated project fees from $750–$5000 on listings. Our time is a commodity, and it certainly costs money to run an office.

Cash Business

He put all of his kids through school and didn't borrow a dime. He has Fort Knox on his hand; lives in the yuppie neighborhood, but his sales reported are minimal. He brags about his machine revenue that doesn't materialize on the records. We can work with this so far, but then the seller desires twice as much as the business is grossing. Can you achieve this? Probably not without landing in jail with the seller. The additional challenge you encompass is this: who is going to want to finance this loss? If you don't have any alternative lenders and the seller won't hold a note...you need to refocus. I haven't met too many poor bar owners. Sometimes they were poor cash managers, but most need to be educated on the reality of selling. If you can't find financing in your area for bar deals, you are better off to shift to an alternative type of business sales. Also, the IRS Criminal Investigation Unit can show up at YOUR door. Be prepared to substantiate anything that has been given to you from the seller and always document all conversations.

Licensing

Our state is regulated. If yours is, it's essential to form a relationship with a consultant or lawyer specialized in this area and also to educate yourself in the process. You need to locate in advance if there are any citations issued on the current owner. This will delay your sale. Does the buyer qualify for a liquor license in your state? Not knowing the time cycle and progression can sabotage a good deal with misinformed parties and ineffectual contingencies. If the place was unsaleable or the buyer not qualified, you want to know this before proceeding."

Terri Sokoloff, CBI, CRB, GRI/BROKER, President of Specialty Bar & Restaurant Brokers and VP of Specialty Group

Resources for Businesses with Alcoholic Beverage Licenses

Distilled Spirits Council of the United States .... www.discus.org

National Alcoholic Beverage Control Association .... www.nabca.org

National Association of Beverage Retailers .... www.nabronline.org

National Restaurant Association .... www.restaurant.org

Wine and Spirit Wholesalers of America .... www.wswa.org

Trade Publications

The Beverage Media .... www.bevaccess.com

Beverage Alcohol Market Report
160 E. 48th St.
New York, NY 10017
(212) 371-5237

Modern Brewery Age .... www.breweryage.com

Nation's Restaurant News .... www.nrn.com

Bars with Slot Machines

Rule of Thumb:

- 3 times SDE plus inventory

Pricing Tips

"Drinks are free to slot players. Pay close attention to only the net, providing other operating costs are in line."

Benchmarks

Expenses as a percentage of annual sales:	
Cost of goods sold	32%
Payroll/labor costs	30%
Occupancy costs	10%
Profit (estimated)	17%

Seller Financing

- "Where the debt service does not exceed 35 percent of the SDE."

Baseball Teams (professional)

Pricing Tips

"Triple-A teams are selling for around $10 million, Double-A for an average of $7.4 million and Single-A for $5 million, according to Baltimore advisory firm Moag & Co. Even independent-league, unaffiliated clubs can be hot properties."

Source: *Smart Money*, April 2004

According to *Forbes* magazine, the average value of a big league baseball team is $332 million (up $295 million from last year). The NY Yankees led the way with a valuation of $950 million, with the Tampa Bay Devil Rays at the bottom at $176 million. A footnote adds that the value is "based on the current stadium deal (unless new stadium is pending), without deduction for debt (other than stadium debt."

Source: *Forbes,* 2005

"In an interview with the Globe (*Boston Globe*, September 11, 2001)

Salomon Smith Barney officials said that the last 10 major-league franchises sold have fetched an average of three times the team's gross annual revenue...."

The Sports Industry's Resistance to Bear Markets

In response to the recent decline in the U.S. economy, Moag and Company has examined the impact of declining economies on the sports industry in the United States. Our analysis focuses on the U.S. economy from 1970 through November 2001, when the S&P 500 grew at a compound annual growth rate ("CAGR") of 8.4%. During this 30-year period, however, five bear markets have occurred, as shown in Exhibit 1. Based on our analysis, we conclude that the sports industry has performed better during the broader effects of a declining economy and, is therefore an attractive investment during both robust and declining economies.

Source: Moag & Company
www.moagandcompany.com

Basketball Teams (professional)

Pricing Tips:

The National Basketball Association (NBA) average value for all teams is approximately $301 million up from $265 million last year.

Source: *Forbes*, 2005

Franchise

Baskin-Robbins Ice Cream *(See also Ice Cream)*

4700 + units

Estimated Annual Sales per Unit: $200,000

Approximate Total Investment: For a single store, the minimum initial cash required is $750,000 with a net worth at least $1,500,000.

-cont'd-

Franchise

Baskin-Robbins Ice Cream *(Continued)*

Rule of Thumb:

- 46 to 56 percent of annual sales plus inventory

General Information

There has been a recent trend for placing two or more franchises under one roof. Baskin-Robbins has been doing this with Dunkin' Donuts. Baskin-Robbins, along with Dunkin' Donuts and Togo Great Sandwiches, is owned by Allied Domecq PLS, based in the U.K. The company has recently been acquired and as of this writing, Dunkin' Donuts and the other food operations are rumored to be on the market."

Resources

www.baskinrobbins.com—Specific information

www.dunkin-baskin-togos.com—Franchise information

Beauty Salons *(See information under Barber Shops)*

245,727	SIC: 7231-06	NAIC: 812112

Rule of Thumb:

- 30 percent of annual revenues; add fixtures, equipment & inventory
- 1.0 to1.5 times SDE plus inventory
- 4 times monthly sales plus inventory
- 3 times EBIT
- 2 times EBITDA

Pricing Tips

"Check reason(s) for empty stations—turnover? Are stations rented?"

"1. Check on chair rental versus commissioned stylist. 2. Check on staff turnover. It can be very high. 3. Reputation and location very important."

"...installation of beauty shops in today's market costs from $2,000 to $2,200 per station (verify), but selling price is usually about $1,500 to $2,000 per station. The ultra modern shops usually have a considerable amount of tenant's improvements which should be taken into consideration...Rents are from $50 to $75 per station or the operators rent a station and retain a portion or all of the commissions earned...with resulting loss of goodwill value. Other approaches: (1) is to price the salon at 20 percent of gross sales, (2) 1–1.5 times recasted cash flow, or (3) 35 percent of gross sales plus equipment & inventory."

Industry Experts' Ratings:

Amount of Competition (1 = Lot of: 4 = Not much) 3.0
Amount of Risk (1 = Very: 4 = Not much) 2.0
Historical Profit Trend (1 = Down: 4 = Up) 2.5
Location & Facilities (1 = Poor: 4 = Excellent)........................ 2.7
Marketability (1 = Low: 4 = High).. 2.0
Industry Trend (1 = Declining: 4 = Growing) 3.0
Ease of Replication (1 = Easy: 4 = Difficult) 2.3

"Levels of competition are high due to market saturation. The beauty industry needs education and direction to avoid the pitfalls of market saturation."

"Market saturation has occurred likely due to the creative nature of the salon professional wanting to expand yet not completing the necessary business market research. The risks are considered low because of the small monetary initial investment. The beauty industry trends will always grow due to vanity and fashion."

"Fair amount of turnover, but fair amount of buyers."

Benchmarks

"Full time operators should produce a minimum of $50,000 annual gross revenue."

Expenses as a percentage of annual sales:	
Cost of goods sold	14–20%
Payroll/labor costs	50–60%
Occupancy costs	08–0%
Profit (estimated)	10%

- "Full-time operators should produce an average minimum of $50,000 gross sales annually."

General Information

"Beauty salons have multiple profit centers; when all available services and products are provided, the profit margins can be very rewarding."

"This industry needs organizations to support as one voice for upcoming situations such as independent contractors verses employee status, reporting of tip income, and licensure regulations."

"There is a trend toward full-service salons with spas."

"Adds to value—owner who does not work directly with customers; staff longevity; automated; and systems in place. Subtracts from value—part-time or unproductive staff; owner who does it all: manages, 'chair work' and cleans up; and short lease remaining. The industry has become, in some cases, very profitable and sophisticated. Individual salons vary greatly."

Advantages of this Business

- "The industry has thrived through even the worst of economic times because of one strong human trait—vanity."
- "Beauty!"
- "Repeat customers"
- "Owner-operators usually do better than manage-owners."

Disadvantages of this Business

- "The prime locations are commonly the high-end rent districts."
- "Market saturation"
- "Stylist turnover"
- "Very competitive, stylists are somewhat fickle & move around easily if able to maintain some customer base. Must remain informed with new trends & styles."

Industry Trend

"Mainstream beauty services will continue. Natural processes for beauty treatments. Minor cosmetic surgery/treatments will interchange with spa and salon services. Male client services are increasing."

Seller Financing

- "4 to 5 years"

Resources

The Salon Association (TSA)
www.salons.org

Building A Business Building A Buyer: How To Aggressively Manage And Eventually Sell Your Salon by Aaron Shiley. For a copy, mail $50.00 + $3.00 shipping and handling to Aaron Shiley, 512 N. President Ave., Lancaster PA 17603.

Trade Publications

Modern Salon
www.modernsalon.com

Bed & Breakfasts *(See also Inns)*

14,323	SIC: 7011-07	NAIC: 721191

Rule of Thumb:

- 4.2 times gross room sales for small B&Bs (less than eight rooms); a little higher for dinner-service inns, 4.5; these are for businesses as opposed to real estate driven small properties
- 8 times SDE
- Priced 4 to 4.5 annual gross sales
- $50,000 to $100,000 per guest room
- In the Midwest, the year-round larger inns are selling from $80,000 to $100,000 per guestroom.
- 3 times net operating income + $20,000 to $40,000 for the aesthetics & tax benefits + value of real estate & furnishings.

Pricing Tips

"Midwest value is usually $80K to $100K/guestroom; 8 to 10 times operating income prior to debt based on the degree of seller financing. Smaller (less than seven rooms), non-urban B&Bs may not have any net cash flow and are typically sold for slightly above real estate value."

"Yovino-Young tracked three indexes typically used to appraise bed and breakfasts for 103 properties which changed hands between 1994 and 2000. These are the same indexes we use at Yellow Brick Road to report recent inn sales. They include Price Per Room, which is the total sales price divided by the number of legal rooms. The Gross Income Multiplier is the sales price divided by the gross annual income; this typically ranges between 3.5 and 5 with the lower number being more desirable. The Capitalization Rate, or overall rate of return on investment, is calculated by dividing the net operating income by the price; it typically ranges between 9 and 14 percent."

From: *Yellow Brick Road*, an industry newsletter

Industry Experts' Ratings:

Marketability (1 = low; 4 = high) 3.2
Industry Trend (1 = declining; 4 = growing) 2.0
Ease of Replication (1 = easy; 4 = difficult) 2.8

"For the past five years, many smaller B&Bs sold/converted back to homes than we've had homes being converted to inns! Start-ups are more difficult to accomplish today versus the mid-1980s primarily due to rising real estate values, high conversion cost, zoning restrictions, tougher lending practices, and a lack of market demand for innkeeping (during a strong economy.) Some of the smaller inns in less popular areas were converted to alternative uses, and a minority of inns closed for avoidance of taxes from capital gains and depreciation recapture."

Benchmarks

"The smaller the inn and lower the business income, the more the real value factor weighs heavy in the formula. The larger the inn and the

> Running a bed-and-breakfast sounds like a dream job for many folks, and plenty are willing to give it a shot. Today there are more than 20,000 licensed bed-and-breakfasts in the U.S. according to the Professional Association of Innkeepers International, up from a mere 1,000 in 1980. With guests spending a collective 55 million nights at B&Bs last year, according to PAII estimates, many innkeepers often find themselves struggling to manage even the basics, which can turn your dream getaway into a weekend of hassles.
>
> Source: "10 Things Your Bed & Breakfast Won't Tell You" by Sarah Robertson, *Smart Money*, July 2004

higher the business income, the less this factor affects total value. Many of the larger inns have been selling in the 8 to 10 capitalization rate of net income, less any needed repairs, and up to a 20% discount if seller financing is not involved."

- "Average number of rooms: 8.5; 95% have private baths
- Overall occupancy for B&Bs: 38%
- Overall Average Daily Rate: $136.70
- 39.1% of B&Bs added sleeping rooms; average cost $49,362/unit
- 95% of properties have their own domain name
- 8% of B&Bs were sold: average purchase price of $653,981
- 6% of country inns were sold; average purchase price of $1.1 million"

Source: 2002 PAII Industry Study

Expenses as a percentage of annual sales:

Cost of goods sold	15%
Payroll/labor costs	10%
Occupancy costs	10%
Profit (estimated)	10%

"Payroll/Labor Costs	12–15% with working owner
Profit (estimated)	40–45% of sales"

General Information

"Many resort inns within three hours of a metro area can produce occupancy in the 40%– 50% range. Urban inns can produce 50%–80% occupancy. Most non-urban inns below seven guestrooms provide only supplemental income. It's kind of like owning a duplex; you can live in a better location & house than you could otherwise afford, but you don't give up your day job. About 50% of the U.S. B&Bs are this size."

Breakdown of B&B's

The following definitions attempt to codify what is presently being used in the field. They are only approximations and will vary by region or individual innkeeper.

"Bed and Breakfast Inn (B&B)

Both a home for its owners and a lodging establishment usually operated at a higher level of professionalism than a home-stay. Some B&Bs have the word "inn" as part of their name. A professional B&B meets all the appropriate tax, fire, building, zoning, and health requirements. Many B&Bs have been inspected by a state association or an inspection rating service such as AAA or the Mobil guides. The owners advertise and may legally post a sign. Breakfast is served to overnight guests and may be quite lavish. Many smaller B&Bs provide a part-time or seasonal occupation for their owners, who do most of the work, often with some help for housekeeping and other chores. Most larger B&Bs (eight rooms or more) require the full-time year-round attention of one or more owners. There is always a high degree of personal service to guests. Reservations may be made directly with the property or through a service. The inn may host events such as weddings or family reunions. Increasing numbers of inns also cater to the business traveler and have facilities to host small business meetings.

"While buying a B&B is a lot like buying a house, there are some differences. If you're more than six months from making your move, you should be reading the B&B books and magazines, attending a B&B seminar, visiting B&Bs as a guest, vacationing in your area of interest, and volunteering your time at a local B&B to experience the "feel" of innkeeping. Once you're within six months of moving, you should put your house up for sale and begin looking at B&Bs for sale. If you slightly over-list your house, the worst that can happen to you is that someone may pay you more than you thought it was worth and you may move twice. We've had a number of B&B dreams crushed when the buyers couldn't sell their house during the time they needed to. Why let the past control your future? If you're thinking about relocating to an unfamiliar area, you should consider renting in that area for a year or so, so that you experience a full cycle of your dream spot—not just a one-week vacation."

"Country Inn

This kind of lodging property has all the characteristics of a B&B inn, but serves an evening meal in addition to breakfast. Some country inns serve dinner to overnight guests only, and the cost of dinner and breakfast is generally included in the room rate (called the Modified American Plan). A country inn with a "full-service restaurant" serves meals to the general public. Generally, the owner or owners are actively involved in daily operations of the inn, and often live on site. To be a country inn, a property does not have to be located in a rural area, though historically, restaurants were added so travelers in remote locations could enjoy a good evening meal. Most country inns have 10 or more rooms.

"Bed and Breakfast Hotel

These are properties in which the historic structure, unique decorating components, guest amenities, and breakfast offering provide the atmosphere of a B&B. Many of these properties formerly were standard hotels, apartment buildings, or other commercial structures in urban or rural areas; some have been built specifically as bed and breakfast hotels. Most of these B&B hotels have fewer than 40 rooms.

"No matter the type of property, innkeepers seek to provide the following to B&B travelers:

- A high level of service with a personal touch from the owner or owners
- Generous hospitality and good value
- Unique ambiance and surroundings
- Architecturally interesting or historic structure
- Individually decorated rooms that are clean and comfortable."

Professional Association of Innkeepers International (PAII)

"Smaller B&Bs (less than 8 rooms) are usually real-estate driven."

"69 percent of all inns have employees. 50 percent of the owners are dependent on an income outside the inn."

Source: PAII

Advantages of this Business

- "B&Bs primarily cater to affluent, Baby Boomer travelers. That market appears to be growing. This is also the market that the next generation of innkeepers is coming from.
- "What other occupation affords you a nicer house than you otherwise could afford, a desirable location and hosting the cream of the crop for travelers? None!"

- "Affords an excellent opportunity for a couple to live in a vacation location, in a beautiful property with quality guests. A perfect bridge between career and retirement for baby boomer empty nesters. There's nothing like it."

Disadvantages of this Business

- "Lack of privacy and time away from home occupation. It's kind of like having a sick child. Innkeeping doesn't work well for folks who like to travel every weekend. It works best for homebodies who enjoy hospitality. In innkeeping, the world comes to you!"

Industry Trend

"B&Bs primarily cater to affluent, Baby Boomer travelers. That market appears to be growing. This is also the market that the next generation of innkeepers are coming from."

Seller Financing

- "7 years"
- "Seller is often 2nd 10 percent of sales price, 20-year term, 7-year balloon."
- "5 to 8 years; partial financing."

Annual Revenues, Expenses & Income

	1–4 Rms	5–8 Rms	9–12 Rms	13–20 Rms	21+ Rms
Total Revenues	$46,706	$128,027	$283,830	$515,398	$897,585

Note: Includes Salary & Wages, Benefits, Commissions, Housekeeping, etc. The big jump from 5–8 Rooms to 1—20 Rooms is the increase in Salaries & Wages.

	1–4 Rms	5–8 Rms	9–12 Rms	13–20 Rms	21+ Rms
Total Operating Expenses	71%	67%	63%	55%	61%
Net Operating Profit/Loss	29%	33%	37%	45%	39%

Source: A 2000 Survey conducted by the Professional Association of Innkeepers International (PAII). The complete study is available through the PAII—see Resources.

The PAII has a 2002 study that is available. Their site has price information and ordering instructions. The above data is for informational purposes.

Resources

Yellow Brick Road—an industry newsletter that also has an excellent Web site. www.yellowbrickroadnl.com

American Bed and Breakfast Association (ABBA)—provides a list of inns only. (800) 769-2468

National Bed-and-Breakfast Association (NB&BA)
www.nbba.com

Professional Association of Innkeepers International—This is an excellent site with lots of information. They also have an "Inns For Sale" section and conduct important studies of the industry.
www.paii.org

Inns for Sale—This site has Inns and B&Bs for sale and also offers educational programs.
www.innsforsale.com

www.bedandbreakfast.com

www.bbonline.com—information for B&B owners.

An IRS Audit Technique Guide (Market Segment Specialization Program—MSSAP) is available for this type of business. It is an excellent source of information and is available at www.bookstore.gpo.gov (search under IRS-IRS Audit Technique Guides).

Beer & Wine Stores—Retail

Rule of Thumb:

- 4 times monthly sales plus inventory

> "Beer-related businesses, including brewers, wholesalers, retailers and brewery suppliers, contribute more than $162 billion annually to the U.S. economy."
>
> Source: The Beer Institute and the National Beer Wholesalers Association, February 16, 2005

Beer Distributorships/ Wholesalers

Wholesale 3,700	SIC: 5181-01	NAIC: 422810

Rule of Thumb:

- $5.00 to $15 per case sold over the last 12 months; add hard assets & inventory. Multiple per case is dependent on brands sold—the popular ones command the higher multiples.
- "These types of distributing businesses are usually sold for the price of inventory at cost, plus the rolling stock, plus the land and improvements, if these are part of the sale, plus $1.00 for each case delivered per year, plus $1.50 for each keg delivered per year."

Pricing Tips

"The two most important characteristics are: (1) the brands carried, and (2) the territory.

Brands vary considerably in market sales, and also vary regionally. Territories that are densely populated tend to be serviced more efficiently."

Industry Experts' Ratings:

Amount of Competition (1 = Lot of: 4 = Not much)	3.2
Amount of Risk (1 = Very: 4 = Not much)	2.4
Historical Profit Trend (1 = Down: 4 = Up)	2.8
Location & Facilities (1 = Poor: 4 = Excellent)	2.0
Marketability (1 = Low: 4 = High)	1.6
Industry Trend (1 = Declining: 4 = Growing)	2.0
Ease of Replication (1 = Easy: 4 = Difficult)	2.0

"Franchise restrictions are important constraints on resale."

Benchmarks

"Market values for beer distributors tend to be discussed as a multiple of cases sold in the past 12 months. These often vary from $5 to $15 per case sold, for well-established brands and successful operations. Struggling brands and operations can be priced less. There is no comparable metric for wine or spirits."

General Information

"The beer industry is comprised of brewers, wholesalers [distributorships] and retailers. ... On the average, a beer wholesaler [distributor] has annual sales of $11.8 million and employs 36 workers. Nearly all wholesaler distributorships are family-owned and-operated, often by descendants of their original post-Prohibition founders. The typical wholesaler maintains a temperature-controlled warehouse and operates a fleet averaging 12 delivery trucks."

Source: The National Beer Wholesalers Association (NBWA)

Advantages of this Business

- "Risks of brand decline; flat overall consumption; possible implied liability for underage drinking or over consumption, although this normally rests with the retailer."
- "Low risk, consistent profitability for good operations with good brands"

Disadvantages of this Business

- "Many distributorships are captive of the brands they offer, and the market areas they have. Without good brands—which are largely outside the control of the distributors—the wholesalers are in a weak position. Also, the wholesalers must deal with the risk of termination of the brand and of their franchise rights."

Industry Trend

"Consolidation among beer wholesalers is continuing. Overall alcoholic beverage consumption is flat in the U.S. The ongoing battle over interstate commerce in wine will affect supplier and wholesaler valuation in the future."

"Changes in state laws and judicial interpretation of the XXI amendment should be considered"

"The industry will continue to face many of the same market challenges in 2005 as it did in 2004. Overall industry performance is not expected to be different in 2005 compared to 2004. Competition from the hard-liquor industry encouraging new and existing beer drinkers to try hard liquors will continue in 2005 with increased advertising and new product rollouts. An aging baby boom generation will also continue their move towards the wine category encouraged in part by increased supply from domestic and foreign sources and an overall flat-pricing movement."

Source: *Beer Institute Bulletin*, March 2005

"The 'three-tier' system set up in most states after Prohibition is being challenged, at least on the edges, by interstate shipping of wine. Legal developments in this area will affect the value of wine distributors, although not beer distributors, over the next few years. Once you have a good operation in a decent area, this business will keep producing cash. Remember, the beer and wine business is over 2,000 years old."

1 U.S. BBL (beer barrel) = 31 U.S. gallons = 13.778 = 24/12oz cases

Resources

The National Beer Wholesalers Association (NBWA)—an informative Web site, www.nbwa.org

Beer Taverns—Beer & Wine *(See Bars, Brew Pubs)*

Rule of Thumb:

- 6 times monthly sales plus inventory
- 1 to 1.5 times annual EBIT
- 55 percent of annual sales plus inventory

Pricing Tips

"There are 1,980 ounces in a keg, less 10 percent waste, about 1,700 net ounces per keg. If there are 12 ounces (net) in a glass of beer, divide 12 ounces into 1,700 net ounces per keg to determine cost and number of glasses that should be poured from that keg. Determine what a 12-ounce glass of beer is selling for, then multiply that times the number of glasses that is poured from the keg. This will give you the total gross per keg."

General Information

"Beer taverns should not be confused with brew pubs. Some states such as California have distinct taverns that only offer beer (and in some cases wine). California also has cocktail bars that offer spirits, beer and wine. They each require different licenses. Brew pubs tend to be more upscale and offer food in addition to their own brewed beer.

"... Consumer interest continues to grow in a wide range of beers, ales, and other malt beverage products. Approximately 2,800 malt beverage brands are now produced in the U.S., three times the number of brands produced a decade ago. U.S. and international brewers continue to produce a tremendous array of beer styles with solid niche markets continuing to develop for industry members of every size.

"Consumer demand has sharply increased the number of U.S. brewers during the past 15 years. The number of domestic brewers in the U.S. has surpassed 1,800, seven times the number in business in 1990.

"Microbreweries and brewpubs account for this increase, and their presence has helped bolster the industry's long tradition as a dynamic part of the American economy. Smaller brewers have helped sustain the brewing industry's 'on-premise' business, particularly in urban centers and tourist destinations."

Source: Beer Institute, www.beerinstitute.org

Resources

Beer Institute—has an excellent site
www.beerinstitute.org

Anheuser-Busch—has an interesting site
www.beerprofitguide.com

Franchise

Ben & Jerry's

500 + units	
Estimated Annual Sales per Unit:	$360,000
Approximate Total Investment:	$129,500 to $316,000

General Information

Ben & Jerry's Franchising, Inc. is part of Unilever.
www.benjerry.com

Franchise

Between Rounds Bagels

7 Units

Approximate Total Investment: $80,000 to $210,000

Rule of Thumb:

- 48 percent of annual sales plus inventory

Resources
Between Rounds
www.betweenroundsbagels.com

Bicycle Shops

6,843	SIC: 5941-41	NAIC: 451110

Rule of Thumb:

- 20 percent of annual sales plus inventory
- 1.5 times SDE plus inventory

Pricing Tips
"If shops don't repair as well as sell, they could lose most of their income. Need to have mechanic in store!"

Benchmarks
"According to the most recent research from the National Bicycle Dealers Association's (NBDA) Cost of Doing Business Study 2004, the average specialty bicycle dealer has gross sales of $550,000 per year; 91% of them had one location; and average store size was 4,822 square feet.

"The profile of the average member of the National Bicycle Dealers Association certainly reflects that. The average NBDA member reports gross revenue of $622,917 per year—22% higher than non-member stores. While the average NBDA member's store is slightly larger than the average, they are also much more productive in generating $128 in revenue per square foot—20% higher than the industry average."

Source: National Bicycle Dealers Association

"5,000 — Cycling specialty stores, down from 6,260 in 2001."

Source: *Forbes*, July 25,2005

Note: The difference between the two stores used in the above two comments is that the first one is specialty bike dealers, in general, while the one directly above is for NBDA members.

"According to the NBDA's Cost of Doing Business Study 2004, the average bicycle dealer's revenue is 47% bicycles, 35.1% parts and accessories, 11.4% bicycle repair, 1.6% bicycle rental, and 4.9% 'other' that includes fitness equipment. The average store sells approximately 650 bicycles per year, carries five bicycle brands, and numerous accessories brands. Gross margins on bicycles average about 37%, though the break-even point has been shown to be 42.5% for the average store (the average 'cost of doing business'). Margins on hard goods are generally higher than those for bicycles (48% gross margin)."

Source: National Bicycle Dealers Association

Here are the average expenses for specialty bicycle retailers from the National Bicycle Dealers Association (NBDA) article "Want to Start a Bike Shop."

Expenses as a percentage of annual sales:	
Payroll Expenses	20.5%
Occupancy	7.7%
Advertising/Promotion	3%
Auto/Delivery	0.5%
Depreciation	0.9%
Insurance	0.8%
Licenses/Other Taxes	0.5%
Professional Services	0.5%
Office Supplies/Postage	1.2%
Telephone	0.6%
Travel/Entertainment	0.4%
Other	1.3%
Total Operating Expenses	37.7%
Net Income Before Tax	4.2%
Gross Margin on Bicycle Sales	36%
Gross Margin on Clothing Sales	43%
Gross Margin on Other Equipment	48.1%

Bicycle Retailer Profile

Annual Gross Sales	
More than $2 million	5%
$1.5 to $1.99 million	3%
$1 to $1.499 million	7%
$500,000 to $999,000	20%
Less than $500,000	65%

How many people do you employ?

Average number of full-time employees	3.6
Average number of part-time employees	3.0

"Add all that to the overall slim profitability in the bicycle industry, and you can really get depressed. NBDA studies show the typical bicycle dealer needs about a 36% profit margin to cover the costs of doing business and break even financially. Studies also show the average realized profit margin on bicycles to be around 36%, which is a break-even proposition devoid of profit. Fortunately accessories products generally carry a higher profit margin than bicycles. Still, the average bike dealer's profit is less than 5% at year's end—about $25,000 for an average size store of $500,000 in annual sales."

Source: "Want to Start a Bike Shop." Published by the National Bicycle Dealers Association

General Information

"Bicycle sales are accomplished in this country through four primary and distinct channels of distribution—the specialty bicycle retailer, the mass merchant, full-line sporting goods stores, and 'other,' which is comprised of a mixture of retailers, including multi-sport stores such as REI, outdoor retailers and mail order.

"Department, discount and toy stores sell mostly price-oriented products. Approximately 74% of bicycle units were sold through the mass merchant channel in 2004, but this represented 37% of the dollars due to the declining average selling price of $69.

"The approximately 5,000 specialty bicycle retailers feature higher quality merchandise, and also rely on adding value through added customer service such as bike fitting, expert assembly and repair. This channel commanded approximately 16% of the market in terms of unit sales in 2004, but 47.5% of the dollars, a dominant dollar share. Dealer price points generally start at around $200, with the average at approximately $400, though prices can range into the thousands. While the number of specialty bicycle stores has declined in recent years due to consolidation, this is the only distribution channel that maintained or increased average retail bicycle selling price. The recent trend has been for mass merchant gains in unit sales market share, but stability in dollar market share due to declining prices in the mass segment.

"Chain sporting goods stores sold approximately 5% of the bicycles in

2004, and 9.7% of the dollars, at an average price of $270. These are merchants that fall somewhere between mass merchant and bicycle dealers on the spectrum, and include merchants such as The Sports Authority, Champs Sports, JumboSports, Sportmart and Big 5.

"The 'other' category sold 4% of the units, representing 5.7% of the dollars, with an average price of $199.

"Specialty bike dealers commanded the vast majority of parts and accessories sales, and virtually 100% of the service market. They dominate the market in bicycles selling for $250 and up."

Source: *Industry Overview 2005* published by the National Bicycle Dealers Association

Industry Trend

"Nationally, bicycle sales have leveled off at around $5.3 billion, or 12.9 million adult bikes sold in 2003, the latest figures available from the National Bicycle Dealers Association. That's a slight dip from 2002 when 13.6 million bikes were sold. Bike sales peaked in 1973 with 15.2 million bikes when high oil prices helped boost sales.

"The latest trend is a shift back to road bikes, away from mountain bikes that dominated in the 1990s, especially for models costing more than $600. Just as with sport utility vehicles, a lot of riders discovered they rarely ventured off-pavement, especially as they got older."

Source: *The Boston Globe*, Sunday, March 6, 2005

Resources

National Bicycle Dealers Association (NBDA)
www.nbda.com
This is a wonderful (one of the best) site, offering lots of information and data. It contains an informative article titled "So, You Want to Start a Bike Shop..." The NBDA offers a 56-page *Cost of Doing Business Study*, 2000 edition, for $150 for non-members. They also publish the *Bicycle Retailer & Industry News.*

Outspoken
Published by the NBDA
(See above)

Bicycle Product Suppliers Association (BPSA)
www.bpsa.org—an informative site, especially relating to the various segments of the industry

Bicycle Retailer & Industry News—an informative site
www.bikeretailer.com

Franchise

Big Apple Bagels

175 + units

Approximate Total Investment: $175,000 to $350,000

Rule of Thumb:

- 42 percent of annual sales plus inventory

Resources
www.babcorp.com

Billboard Advertising Companies *(Outdoor Advertising)*

2,582	SIC: 7312-01	NAIC: 541850

Rule of Thumb:

- 11 times EBITDA
- 500 percent of annual sales

Pricing Tips
"Prices are based on annual multiples of revenue or cash flow."

"Values of billboard companies tend to be higher in large metropolitan areas, and lower in rural areas. Prices tend to be between 3 x and 6 x annual revenue."

"OAAA's nearly 1,100 members represent more than 90% of industry income..."

Source: Outdoor Advertising Association of America

"EBITDA is normally 45% to 50%. Cap rates tend to be very low, usually more like real estate than an operating business. Acquirers prefer long-term leases at low rates for existing billboard locations."

"Billboard companies are usually worth surprisingly high prices in the market. Buyers and sellers rely almost exclusively on market multiples that are widely recognized as the best measures of fair market value. Discount rates and capitalization rates in this industry are more closely aligned with real estate yields than returns on operating businesses."

Source: "Appraising Billboard Companies" by Jeffrey P. Wright, ASA, CFA, *Business Valuation Review*, September 2003

Industry Experts' Ratings:

Amount of Competition (1 = Lot of: 4 = Not much) 1.2
Amount of Risk (1 = Very: 4 = Not much)................................ 3.2
Historical Profit Trend (1 = Down: 4 = Up) 2.8
Location & Facilities (1 = Poor: 4 = Excellent)........................ 1.0
Marketability (1 = Low: 4 = High).. 3.2
Industry Trend (1 = Declining: 4 = Growing) 3.2
Ease of Replication (1 = Easy: 4 = Difficult) 3.6

Benchmarks

"Occupancy Cost = 20%
Profit (estimated pre-tax) = 20%"

"EBITDA margins are very high in this industry, usually around 45% to 50%. Fixed expenses normally represent a rather high percentage of fixed expenses, with 75% to 85% typical for larger companies. This includes site leases, taxes & licensing, lighting, vehicles, and to some degree labor. Workers must be employees to change advertising even if ad revenue is not strong. Variable expenses include a small number of items like printing and sales commissions."

Source: "Appraising Billboard Companies" by Jeffrey P. Wright, ASA, CFA, *Business Valuation Review*, September 2003

General Information

"There are hundreds of small companies with 5 to 50 signs, but the market is dominated by three large corporations. Viacom and Clear Channel are large international companies with other media holdings such as TV and radio, while Lamar Advertising is the largest pure play in the U.S billboard industry."

Source: "Appraising Billboard Companies" by Jeffrey P. Wright, ASA, CFA, *Business Valuation Review*, September 2003

Advantages of this Business

- "Low risk, revenue growth opportunities"
- "Market monopolies exist because restrictions on new permits have created a huge barrier to entering the market."

Disadvantages of this Business

- "Difficulties getting permits"
- "Since citizen groups frequently want to remove billboards, legal efforts are often required to entering the market."

Industry Trend

"Digital boards"

Seller Financing

- "5 years"

Resources

Outdoor Advertising Association of America (OAAA)
www.oaaa.org

BPS Outdoor—a monthly publication
www.bpsoutdoor.com

Billiards

3,256	SIC: 7999-12	NAIC: 339920

Rule of Thumb:

- 45 percent of annual sales plus inventory

Industry Trend

"Billiards is in a growth cycle that we expect to continue in 2005. After 2004 participation and wholesale shipments figures are published, we expect the recent growth trend to continue. In 2003, nearly 41 million people over the age of six picked up a cue at least once, and nearly 10 million people played twice a month or more. Wholesale shipments of billiard equipment and accessories were last reported at $255 million, with single-digit increases expected in the next report.

"Key sports business issues and stories: Women's and junior billiards are emerging segments, with more opportunities to play at both the amateur and professional levels. Over 37% of billiard players are women, up from previous years. Expect businesses to continue to focus on this segment, with talc and cue designs to focus on fashion as well as functionality.

"Over four million youths, age 7-17, played two or more times in 2003, with increases expected in the 2004 figures. Various leagues systems offer junior leagues, programs, tournaments and scholarship opportunities, as the industry comes to ensure the next generation of players and consumers."

Source: The Billiard Congress of America (BCA)

Resources

Billiard Congress of America
www.bca-pool.com

Billiard and Bowling Institute of America (BBIA)
(561) 840-1120

Trade Publications

BBIA Newsline
published by BBIA
(See above)

Franchise

Blackjack Pizza

45 units

Rule of Thumb:

- 40 percent of annual sales plus inventory
- 3 to 4 times SDE (15% discount for cash) plus inventory

Franchise

Blimpie Subs and Salads

1,500 units

Approximate Total Cost:	$60,000 to $200,000
Estimated Annual Sales per Unit:	$160,000

Rule of Thumb:

48 percent of annual sales plus inventory

Resources

www.blimpie.com

Boat Dealers		
9,759	SIC: 5551-04	NAIC: 441222

Rule of Thumb:

- 1 times annual adjusted earnings; add fixtures, equipment & inventory
- 2 to 3 times SDE includes used boat inventory, parts and FF&E
- "Most dealerships finance their new boat inventory with flooring companies which are now requiring some type of industry background and/or experience. In most cases the new owner will take over the financing arrangements with the flooring companies for all current and future new boat inventory. The multiple can vary depending."

Pricing Tips

"Boat dealerships in the Pacific Northwest typically sell for 2–3 times SDE which includes used boat inventory, parts and FF&E."

Benchmarks

- "Approximately 870,000 new boats were sold in 2004, up 4 percent over 2003.
- New boat and motor sales reached $13.6 billion in 2004, an 8 percent increase from $12.6 billion in sales in 2003.
- Average price of a new boat in 2004 was $7,850.
- Average price of a pre-owned boat in 2004 was $7,850.
- Average price of a new outboard engine was $9,131.
- Average price of a pre-owned outboard engine was $3,287.
- Average price of a new outboard boat, motor, trailer package was $24,079, a four percent increase from 2003.
- Demonstrating seasonality, 43 percent of new boat sales took place in the second quarter of 2004, followed by 31 percent in the third quarter of 2004.
- Florida ranks number one in total expenditures for new powerboats, motors, trailers and accessories followed by California, Texas, New York and Minnesota respectively. The top five states account for almost 35 percent of total expenditures."

Source: National Marine Manufacturers Association

General Information

- "Recreational boating contributed approximately $33 billion to the nation's economy, up more than 8 percent from 2003.
- 32,200 more boats were sold in 2004 than in 2003—a four percent increase in unit sales.
- Sales growth of recreational boats continued to outpace U.S. economic growth in 2004, increasing an average of eight percent annually since 1997, when compared to the Gross Domestic Product, which averaged 3.4 percent annual growth during the same period.
- Most segments enjoyed unit and dollar sales increases highlighted by the growth in outboard boat unit sales, which increased by 9,500 boats.
- Seven out of ten boat segments showed positive growth in unit sales.
- In 2004, aftermarket accessory sales increased an estimated 14 percent to $2.4 billion vs. 2003. Over the past seven years, aftermarket accessories sales have doubled from $1.2 billion in 1997 to $2.4 billion in 2004.
- Based on revised 2003 estimates, recreational boating participation increased an estimated 300,000 in 2004 to 69 million from 68.7 million in 2003."

Source: National Marine Manufacturers Association

"The number of boats in use grew to 17.6 million in 2004, an increase of 210,000 from 2003."

Source: National Marine Manufacturers Association

Book & Stationery Stores

Pricing Tips

"Fixtures and equipment value plus inventory at wholesale cost, plus one-half year's net profit"

Book Stores—Christian *(See also Book Stores—New)*

3,570

Pricing Tips

These specialized book stores would probably sell for a bit higher than other book stores would sell for. Christian bookstores seem to do a bit better business than regular book stores. However, these bookstores also sell many other non-book Christian items. The Christian Booksellers Association has approximately 2,400 retailing members and also reports that their sales in 2002 were $4.2 billion—that works out to approximately $1,750,000 per store.

Book Stores—New

18,524	SIC: 5942-01	NAIC: 451211

Rule of Thumb:

- 15 percent of annual sales plus inventory
- 1.6 SDE plus inventory

Benchmarks

"The average of all reporting companies [book stores] with sales below $500,000 is negative. Although small stores can be and are profitable, size makes the task much easier."

Source: American Booksellers Association

Approximate Allocation of Net Sales for Independent Booksellers:

Cost of Goods Sold	60–61%
Gross Profit Percentage	39–40%
Payroll	21–22%
Occupancy	8–9%
Advertising	2%
Total Operating Expenses	41–42%
Net Income before Tax	-1–2%

Average Sales per Selling Square Foot

Annual Sales	Sales per Sq. Ft.
Under $250,000	$122
$250,000–$500,000	$209
$500,000–$1 Million	$337
$1 Million–$2.5 Million	$370
$2.5 Million–$5 Million	$456
Average	$302
General	$302
Specialty	$298

Average Sales per Selling Square Foot - (cont'd)

Annual Sales	Sales per Sq. Ft.
Single Location	$293
Multiple Location	$349
Lower Profit	$251
Higher Profit	$405

Source: American Booksellers Association

The average annual inventory turns is 3.22

Source: American Booksellers Association

General Information

"Of course, independents can't match either the discounts or the selection at superstores or Internet outlets. Competition from non-bookstore outlets, such as kitchen and hardware stores, doesn't help. If independent store owners sound frustrated when they talk about the bottom line, it's because, for all of them, the wolf is at the door.

"If it's so hard to scrape by owning a small bookstore, why does anyone bother? For all of the booksellers profiled here, the answer is passion. Instead of markdowns and huge inventories, these booksellers offer up a part of themselves; their stores reflect their personalities. They love books and their communities, and they'll often go to bat for lesser-known writers they admire."

Source: "Read All About It" by Betsy Block, *The Boston Globe*, July 31, 2003

"The typical Barnes & Noble or Borders superstore carries about 100,000 titles, while large independent bookstores stock about 40,000."

Source: *The New York Times*, April 22, 2004

Industry Trend

"The number of new titles published last year, 195,000, increased by 14 percent over 2003, according to a new report from R.R. Bowker, the publisher of *Books in Print* and other references. The biggest chunk of the increase was in adult fiction—the number of novels published in 2004 was 25,184—43 percent higher than 2003.

"What's driving the big increase isn't obvious, since sales are not expanding at the same rate. It is clear, however, that small publishers—and self-publishers—account for a big part of it.

"Even so, the flood of books may be daunting for the book-buyer—the industry has shown only minor sales increases in recent years, according to the authoritative Book Industry Study Group. While the total number of titles published increased 14 percent, total sales jumped only three percent over 2003, and are projected to grow only five percent this year. Price competition is one of the reasons. The average retail price for adult hardcovers, Bowker found, fell 10 cents in 2004, to $27.52."

Source: *The Boston Globe*, June 4, 2005

"For the author, the thousands of new titles and billions of actual books—2.2 billion in 2004—aren't necessarily cheery news, either. Many more books are chasing not-so-many-more readers."

Source: *The Boston Globe*, June 4, 2005

"Supermarkets, long the domain of paperback romances, pulp thrillers and astrology guides, are the new frontier of book selling. Chains like Wegmans, Kroger and Albertsons have greatly expanded their book sections, adapting the techniques that move large amounts of Velveeta and Count Chocula and applying them to Nora Roberts and John Grisham."

Source: *The New York Times*, April 28, 2005

Resources

American Booksellers Association
www.bookweb.org
This informative site is what a trade association should have—lots of information.

Book Hunter Press
www.bookhunterpress.com—a great site with lots of valuable and interesting information, especially in the used-book area.

Christian Booksellers Association
www.cbaonline.org

Trade Publications

Independent Bookselling Today
Paz & Associates
www.pazbookbiz.com
This site offers good information on opening a bookstore.

Publishers Weekly
www.publishersweekly.com

Book Stores—Rare and Used *(See also Book Stores)*

5,445	SIC: 5932-01	NAIC: 453310

Pricing Tips

"In response to your question about a pricing rule of thumb [We had emailed our request for this to Susan Spiegel of Book Hunter Press, and perhaps the leading authority on used bookstores in the U.S.], I'm not aware of any, but I doubt that even if one existed it would be helpful. But then, I must confess that I haven't been involved in buying or selling a business.

"The reason for my skepticism: even among just-open shops, there is such a wide, wide range of inventory, that the same pricing mechanism could not automatically be used for all shops. Two shops may each have 10,000 books—but very, very different books in terms of wholesale or retail value.

"The inventory in new bookstores is pretty homogeneous; this is not the case in a used bookstore. Even within a given store, there could be a range of value in the inventory with mass market paperbacks selling at one price point and hard-to-find hardcovers selling for $25-50+.

"Stores with vastly different size inventories can have the same gross sales, depending on what types of books they are selling. In my humble judgment, one would have to arrive at a selling price based on the value of the inventory for that particular store, as well as that store's sales records.

"One problem is that most dealers have only a small portion of their inventory computerized. And I have no idea of what type of pencil and paper records they keep for tax purposes on the cost of what they've bought.

"Open shops that have gone out of business have disposed of their inventory in several different ways. Assuming that they can't sell the business to someone else who will continue it as a used bookstore (usually the first choice), some sell off their inventory to another, larger dealer. This may or may not involve donating the undesirable volumes to a library.

"Some dealers close their shops, sell off a portion of their inventory, and continue selling online with a smaller inventory, often, but not always, in a specialty area/s."

Source: Susan Spiegel, Book Hunter Press

Benchmarks

"Three quarters of the dealers [open shops] sold an average of more than 200 books per month with 23% selling 200–499 books, followed closely by 21% selling 500–999 books a month. Sixteen percent of the open shops sold 2,000 or more books per month.

> Bookstore: Cost of Goods Sold – 60.2%;
> Gross Margin – 39.8%
>
> Source: American Booksellers Association

"For shops in the most frequent open-shop size category (25,000–44,999 volumes), 31% of the dealers sold an average of 500–999 volumes per month, followed by 28% selling 200–499 volumes. Only 8% of the dealers within this size category sold fewer than 200 books per month and, at the other extreme, 16% sold 2,000 books or more."

A Portrait of the U.S. Used Book Market, published by Book Hunter Press.

General Information

"Most popular places to buy used books	
Online	54.4%
Bookstores	29.5%
Book fairs	14.2%
Print catalog	03.7%
By appointment	02.7%"

Source: Book Hunter Press

A new report by Book Hunter Press, A *Portrait of the U.S. Used Book Market*, states there are 4,079 used "open" book shops. Open means a "brick and mortar" store. In addition there are hundreds of used paperback exchanges. And, according to the study, there are about 8,000 to 10,000 online dealers in used books.

Resources

Book Hunter Press

www.bookhunterpress.com—a great site with lots of valuable and interesting information on the used book market. If this subject interests you, you have to get a copy of A *Portrait of the U.S. Used Book Market* and their guide to used book stores—we did and they're great.

Bookkeeping Services *(See also Accounting)*

25,743	SIC: 8721-02	NAIC: 541219

Rule of Thumb:

- 50 percent of annual revenues
- 2 times monthly revenues

Bottled Gas *(See Liquefied Petroleum Gas)*

Bottled Water

Rule of Thumb:

- 90–100 percent of sales

Industry Trend

"Bottled water emerged as the second largest commercial beverage category by volume in the United States in 2003, and, despite its significant stature, it continued to grow at a rapid pace in 2004. In recent years, U.S. volume has been increasing more rapidly than dollar sales, but on both fronts, the industry's performance is unparalleled.

"In 2004, total U.S. category volume surpassed 6.8 billion gallons, an 8.6% advance over 2003's volume level. The category includes sparkling and non-sparkling water, domestic and imported water, water in single-serve bottles (the PET segment, named for the plastic used for packaging) and larger packages, as well as vended and direct-delivered waters. U.S. residents now drink more bottled water annually (23.8 gallons per person in 2004) than any other beverage other than carbonated soft drinks (CSDs)."

Source: Beverage Marketing Corporation, April 2005

"Before taxes, the company (Niagara Bottling) makes 7.5 cents on the dollar—$10.5 million on $140 million in revenues last year. The firm is tiny alongside Poland Spring (Nestlé), Dasani (Coca-Cola) and Aquafina (PepsiCo). What Niagara offers is low prices:..."

Source: *Forbes*, June 2005

Resources

International Bottled Water Association (IBWA)—informative site on bottled water itself, www.bottledwater.org

www.bottledwaterweb.com—same as above site

Bowling Centers

5,985	SIC: 7933-01	NAIC: 713950

Rule of Thumb:

- 5 to 6 times SDE plus inventory
- 5.5–7 times EBITDA—if real estate is included
- 3–5 times EBITDA—if real estate is leased
- 1.5 to 2.0 times annual sales plus inventory

Pricing Tips

"Necessary capital expenditures are deducted. Location/market are critical factors."

"Important: updated appearance and new amenities"

"Revenues over $30,000/lane a plus. Location, physical condition and appearance are big factors."

"Bowling is a social equalizer. How fabulous can any one person be when everyone's wearing the same shoes?"

Source: Patrick Lyons bowling center owner, in *The Boston Globe*

Industry Experts' Ratings:

Amount of Competition (1 = Lot of: 4 = Not much) 1.0
Amount of Risk (1 = Very: 4 = Not much) 2.4
Historical Profit Trend (1 = Down: 4 = Up) 3.3
Location & Facilities (1 = Poor: 4 = Excellent) 3.6
Marketability (1 = Low: 4 = High) 2.9
Industry Trend (1 = Declining: 4 = Growing) 2.6
Ease of Replication (1 = Easy: 4 = Difficult) 1.5

"Location and quality of facility are critical. Revenue trends are also important."

Benchmarks

"Revenues of $35,000 per lane"

"2004 Revenue Rankings

The following evaluations are based on our ongoing studies of both individually owned and chain-owned centers in all parts of the country. Revenue figures are for bowling, bar, food, vending, video games and billiards. Pro shop revenues are excluded because this activity normally produces only modest profits at best. This also assumes a normal 'bowlers' bar' without entertainment, a disco, etc.

Expenses as a percentage of annual sales:	
Cost of goods sold	10%–20%
Payroll/Labor Costs	25%–30%
Occupancy Cost	15%
Profit (estimated)	25%

Gross Revenues per Lane per Year

Excellent	$37,000 or more
Good	$32,000 to $37,000
Average	$27,000 to 32,000
Inadequate	$27,000 or less"

Courtesy: Sandy Hansell & Associates, Inc.

Target Costs vs. Cost of Goods

Target Costs	Cost of Goods
Bar	28%–30 % of total bar revenues
	22%–25% of liquor revenues
	28%–30% of draft beer revenues
	30%–33% of cans, bottles revenues
Supplies	2%
Food/Beverages	30% of total food/beverage revenues
Supplies	3%
Pro Shop	60%–65% of total pro shop revenues
Vending, Other	60% of total vending revenues

Target Costs vs. Cost of Goods (cont'd)

Target Costs	Cost of Goods
Controllable Expenses	
Payroll—Bowling	30% of lineage revenues
Payroll—Bar	20% of bar revenues
Payroll—Food	25%–30% of snack bar revenues
Total Payroll	25%–28% of total revenues
Payroll Taxes	13% of total payroll
Employee Benefits	5%–7% of total payroll
Total Employee Costs	28%–33% of total revenues
Advertising & Promotion	3% of total revenues
Repair, Maintenance & Supplies	5%–6% of total revenues*
Utilities	5%–7% of total revenues

**Varies with age and condition of center, building and equipment*

Operating Income as % of Total Revenues**

Above Average	Average	Below Average
33%–35%	25%–28%	20%–24%

***Operating Income is defined as the funds generated by an operation before interest, real estate rent, non-recurring expenses, principal payments, capital improvements, depreciation and owner's salaries (above normal limits) and fringe benefits.*

Courtesy: Sandy Hansell & Associates, Bowling's Only Full-Service Brokers, Appraisers & Financial Advisors. (800) 222-9131. 2005

General Information

Questions to ask seller: "1. League bowler count; 2. Recent facility/equipment upgrades; 3. Demographics within five miles."

Advantages of this Business

- "Cash business, family-oriented, stable, long-term popularity"
- "Cash business providing fun"

Disadvantages of this Business

- "Management intensive, busiest nights and weekends"

- "Management and capital intensive"

Industry Trend

"More entertainment and recreation oriented; more diversified profit venues inside the buildings"

"Good centers will demand strong prices."

"Surveys also show that about 25 percent of all league bowlers are not sanctioned, and that upward of 50 million report bowling at least once a year."

Source: www.bowlercentral.com

Seller Financing

- "15 years with 5–10 year call; not done very often, mostly all-cash sales"
- "Usually bank financed"

Resources

Bowling Proprietors Association of America
www.bpaa.com

"Valuing Bowling Centers," *Handbook of Business Valuation*, West & Jones, 1st Edition, published by John Wiley & Sons

Franchise

Bread Franchises

Atlanta Bread Company–165 units, Estimated Annual Sales per Unit: $1.4 million

Au Bon Pain–230 units, Estimated Annual Sales per Unit: 41.5 million

Great Harvest Bread Company–167 units, Estimated Annual Sales per Unit: N/A

Panera Bread –701 units, Estimated Annual Sales per Unit: $1.87 million

Franchise

Bresler's Ice Cream

Rule of Thumb:

- 35 to 40 percent plus inventory

Brew Pubs *(See Bars, Beer Taverns & Breweries)*

Rule of Thumb:

- 40 percent of annual sales plus inventory

Breweries *(See also Beer Distributorships/ Wholesalers)*

1,430		

General Information

Craft beer industry definitions

"Microbrewery: A brewery that produces less than 15,000 barrels (17,600 hectoliters) of beer per year. Microbreweries sell to the public by one or more of the following methods: the traditional three-tier system (brewer to wholesaler to retailer to consumer); the two-tier system (brewer acting as wholesaler to retailer to consumer); and, directly to the consumer through carryouts and/or on-site tap-room or restaurant sales.

"Brewpub: A restaurant-brewery that sells 25% or more of its beer on-site. The beer is brewed primarily for sale in the restaurant and bar. The beer is often dispensed directly from the brewery's storage tanks. Where allowed by law, brewpubs often sell beer "to go" and/or distribute to off-site accounts. Note: BA re-categorizes a company as a microbrewery if its off-site (distributed) beer sales exceed 75 percent.

"Contract Brewing Company: A business that hires another brewery to produce its beer. It can also be a brewery that hires another brewery to produce additional beer. The contract brewing company handles marketing, sales, and distribution of its beer, while generally leaving the brewing and packaging to its producer-brewery (which, confusingly, is also sometimes referred to as a contract brewer).

"Regional Brewery: A brewery with the capacity to brew between 15,000 and 2,000,000 barrels.

"Regional Specialty Brewery: A regional brewery whose flagship brand is an all-malt or specialty beer or whose production is 50% or greater of craft

beer. For example, Sierra Nevada, New Belgium Brewing Co. and Magic Hat are regional specialty breweries.

"Craft Beers: Generally, "all-malt," domestic beers produced using 100 percent malted barley. Craft beers that are not all-malt sometimes substitute a percentage of malted wheat (for wheat beers) or malted rye (for rye beers). Their inspiration can be traced to British, German or Belgian traditions or is often uniquely American. Craft beers range from pale to dark in color and from mild to strong in alcohol content. Sometimes they include unusual ingredients such as fruit, herbs or spices. Compared with other beers, their emphasis is more on flavor, and less on appealing to a mass market. (The best-selling American beers are brewed using 30 to 40 percent rice or corn "adjunct," resulting in a paler, lighter-bodied and lighter-flavored beer).

"Craft Brewer: A brewpub, microbrewery, regional specialty brewery or contract brewing company whose majority of sales is considered craft beer."

Source: Brewers Association. www.beertown.org

Industry Trend

"2004 was a difficult year for the beer industry, but it was a huge year for craft breweries. Overall consumption was up 0.5 percent, and import's growth rate of 1.4 percent was the lowest figure for import growth in 13 years. What this means is that craft beers are increasingly making headway in the areas of market share and consumer enjoyment."

Source: Paul Gatza, Director of the Brewers Association

2004 Overall U.S. Brewing Industry Dollar Volume: $77 billion

Source: Brewers Association. www.beertown.org

U.S. Market Shares by Segment

	2004	2003
Domestic Large Brewers + Traditional Regional Brewers	85.17%	85.42%
Imports	11.64%	11.58%
Domestic Specialty or "Craft" Beers	3.19%	3.0%

Source: Source: Brewers Association. www.beertown.org

U.S Breweries Operating in 2004:

57 Regional Specialty Breweries
351 Microbreweries
988 Brewpubs
21 Large Breweries
13 Regional Breweries

1,430 Total U.S. Breweries

2004 U.S. Openings:

46 Brewpubs
26 Microbreweries

2004 U.S. Closings YTD:

77 Brewpubs
12 Microbreweries

Source: Source: Brewers Association. www.beertown.org

Resources

Beer Institute
www.beertown.org

Brewers' Association of America
www.brewersadvocate.org

www.BeerServesAmerica.org
A very interesting site

Bridal Shops

7,731	SIC: 5621-04	NAIC: 448190

Rule of Thumb:

- 10 to 15 percent of annual sales plus inventory

General Information

"Some 2.3 million couples marry each year in the United States, and weddings are a $43 billion business, says the Fairchild Bridal Group, publisher of *Bride's* magazine. Bridal dresses account for $1.4 billion of the total. Although a national chain that relies heavily on off-the-rack sales has grown rapidly in the last decade or so, about two-thirds of bridal gown sales are still handled by boutiques and independent retailers—a fiercely competitive market in which brides often find the sales pitches sweet but the business practices sometimes veering toward the gray area of the law."

Source: *The New York Times Sunday*, June 27, 2004

"Whether you view this process with that much cynicism or not, most brides come face to face with the ugly reality of bridal retail shops at some point in their wedding planning. A recent survey by a bridal magazine revealed that about two-thirds of all brides buy their dress at a full-service bridal shop.

"(For the curious, another 12 percent found their dress at a department store; 11 percent had a gown sewn by a friend or professional; 3 percent of brides purchased a dress from a mail-order discounter, 2 percent wear a family heirloom and another 2 percent of brides borrowed or rented a wedding dress.)

"The first thing most folks realize after getting over the shock of having to plan a wedding is that the bridal business is, well, a business. And a big business. Engaged couples spend $10 billion a year on weddings and receptions. Dresses are a $1.2 billion chunk of that market ($800 million is spent on wedding gowns, $400 million for bridesmaids' dresses).

"So, you thought the tough part about getting married was finding the right guy?

"Wait until you start shopping for THE DRESS. For some reason, the bridal dress industry has decided to turn the process of obtaining a bridal gown into some sort of merciless test of wills between the Bride (wearing white, weighting 120 pounds, in one corner) and the Evil Apparel Industry (wearing black, weighing 320 pounds, in the other corner). BridalGown.com is here to even the odds."

Source: www.bridalgown.com

"Let's take a look at the numbers. The average wedding dress sells for $800. What does the shop pay for that? About $400, leaving a $400 gross profit. Not bad, eh? Well, hold it. The shop has to pay all their overhead, advertising, rent, salaries and other expenses from that amount. What's left over is a pittance, on average about 5 percent to 10 percent (or $40 to $80).

"The truth is: bridal retailers are just middlemen. When the dress manufacturer screws up, they are left holding the bag. Of course, some bridal shops are to blame as well—far too many mismanage their business, falling behind in their bills. They 'forget' to pay a manufacturer, who then puts them on a credit hold. As a result, your dress is held hostage in the cross-fire."

Source: BridalGown.com

"Special-order gowns require deposits—many bridal stores don't put the deposits aside but co-mingle funds during the normal course of operations (a liability issue that could be deadly for a new buyer unless appropriate safeguards are in place). A bridal store's inventory is made of samples and the samples should be considered 'amortized over the ordering life of the gown style.'"

"Bridal is not retail—to be successful in bridal, an owner has to treat it as a sales company and recruit and train salespeople. Traditional bridal is special-order and requires an excellent control system to monitor the progress of the customer's gown. Most bridal stores have 40 percent to 60 percent of their gown inventory tied up in 'one- of-a-kind' gowns. These are styles that are discontinued by the manufacturer and no additional orders can be placed. This severely curtails potential for a store. Some manufacturers are notorious for discontinuing their styles quickly. The bridal business is extremely sensitive to word-of-mouth; one horrendous experience and that bridal transaction will cost the company about $50,000 in sales over a period of 18 months, according to my estimations. Liquidation of our bridal inventory was 23 cents on the dollar—guaranteed."

Franchise

Budget Blinds

200 + units	
Estimated Annual sales Per Unit:	$780,000
Approximate Total Investment:	$50,000 to $90,000

Rule of Thumb:

- 2 times annual EBIT plus inventory & equipment

Resources

www.budgetblinds.com

Franchise

Buffet Nest

Rule of Thumb:

- 40 percent of annual sales plus inventory

Building Materials/Home Centers *(See also Lumber Yards)*

Rule of Thumb:

- 4 times EBIT
- 25 percent of SDE; add fixtures/equipment & inventory

Pricing Tips

"As to a rule of thumb estimate of value, we see that most reasonably profitable businesses (5 percent EBT [earnings before taxes] on sales) in this industry sell for Fair Market Value on all the assets, including real estate, inventory and equipment, plus up to a year's EBT in the form of a goodwill non-compete agreement. Marginally profitable businesses sell for Fair Market Value of Assets only, and extremely profitable businesses, those with 5 percent to 10 percent EBT on sales, bring premium prices, FMV of assets plus up to 2 times EBT in goodwill/non-compete, etc. Key factors are earnings, inventory and accounts receivable turnover. Competition, profits and niche determine salability."

"Many are sold on net asset value."

"If sales $1.5 million to $20 million, and if operating net profit 0 to 5 percent, on sales, before tax, likely sell for fair market value; if 5 to10 percent, on sales, before tax will likely sell for 1.5 to 2 times annual net before tax + fair market value of assets."

Benchmarks

Expenses as a percentage of annual sales:

Cost of Goods	75%
Payroll/Labor Costs	14%
Occupancy Cost	2%
Profit	5% (industry average)

2005 Market Measure

Income Statement Data	Home Centers	Lumber/Bldg Materials
Net Sales Volume	$4,251,403	$4,440,931
Cost of Goods Sold	70.9%	76.3%
Total Expenses	28.3%	22.5%
Net Profit (Before Income Taxes)	2.1%	1.9%

	Home Centers	Lumber Yards
Average Size of Selling Area (sq. ft.)	14,300	7,485
Sales per sq. ft. of Selling Area	$297	$593
Inventory per sq. ft. of Selling Area	$65	$97
Total Sales per Employee	$218,021	$269,147"

Source: *2005 Market Measure*, National Retail Hardware Association (NRHA). Figures are for 2003.

Note: This is an annual report titled "Where Are We Headed? By Shelly Bucksot, Chris Jensen and Dan Tratensek and is from "Do-It-Yourself Retailing." The NRHA site www.nhra.org is a wonderfully informative site. (See also Hardware Stores.)

Seller Financing

- "Buyers are sophisticated and well financed. It is rare to have seller financing of any kind."

Resources

National Lumber and Building Material Dealers Association
www.dealer.org

"Valuing Home Centers & Lumber Yards," *Handbook of Business Valuation*, 2nd Edition, West & Jones published by John Wiley & Sons.

Franchise

Burger King

11,220	
Estimated Annual Sales per Unit:	$1,045,000
Approximate Total Investment:	$294,000 to $825,000

Rule of Thumb:

- 40 percent of annual sales plus inventory

General Information

"Ninety-one percent of Burger King restaurants are owned and operated by independent franchisees, many of them family-owned operations that have been in business for decades."

Source: Burger King Corporate Facts Sheet. www.bk.com

Approximately 58.8% of Burger King business is drive-thru and 19.6% is take-out.

Source: Burger King Corporate Facts Sheet. www.bk.com

Industry Trend

"Burger King Corporation (BKC) today announced that its April 2005 results show U.S. system-wide same store sales up 6.7%, with sales at company-owned restaurants up 6.6 percent, and sales of U.S. franchised restaurants up 6.7 percent year-over-year. April marks the 15th consecutive month of positive U.S. same-store sales."

Source: Burger King Corporate Facts Sheet. www.bk.com

Resources

www.burgerking.com

Bus Companies (Bus Lines, Charter & Rental)

10,097		

Rule of Thumb:

- 35 percent of revenues plus asset value of busses plus inventory

Benchmarks

"What is your annual revenue per coach?

For companies with...

Fewer than 10 coaches	$130,284
10 to 19 coaches	$112,513
20 to 29 coaches	$125,761
30 to 39 coaches	$28,126
40 or more coaches	$201,044

How many coaches are in your fleet?

Fewer than 10	44%
10 to 19	30%
20 to 29	10%
30 to 39	06%
40 to 49	02%
50 or more	08%"

Source: 2001 "Industry Survey," Destinations magazine, August 2001
(the latest we could find)

General Information

"The motorcoach industry comprises thousands of mostly small businesses. Sixty-five percent of known carriers operate fewer than 10 buses, but those smallest of companies carry an estimated 97 million passengers... Only about 50 companies own more than 100 coaches, and these account for 56 percent of passengers."

Source: American Bus Association. July 10, 2005 – www.buses.org

"The average cost of a new 45-foot motorcoach is more than $350,000."

Source: American Bus Association. July 10, 2005 – www.buses.org

"The [motorcoach] industry is composed largely of small entrepreneurial businesses. There are over 4,000 companies, 90 percent of which have fewer than 25 buses. These entrepreneurial companies, with about 19,000 motorcoaches, account for almost 40 percent of the total industry mileage, and carry one in five passengers.... In a recent survey, almost all carriers (96 percent) reported providing charter services. Nearly one-third provide tour services, one-quarter provide sightseeing services, one-fifth provide airport service, and one-fifth provide commuter service. Twelve percent provide scheduled service."

Source: Overview of the Motorcoach Industry, American Bus Association, June 24, 2004

Resources

American Bus Association

www.buses.org—a very informative site and their magazine, *Destinations*, is also very informative

United Motorcoach Association

www.uma.org—also an informative site

Bus Ride magazine

www.busride.com—and another interesting site

Seller Financing

- "3 years"

Business Brokerage Offices

3,543	SIC: 7389-22	

Pricing Tips

"An earn-out based on existing listings"

General Information

"Is it an agency or a one-man show? Is it low-end, mid-market or M&A?"

Resources

International Business Brokers Association

www.ibba.org

Call Centers *(See also Answering Services)*

SIC: 7389-12		

Rule of Thumb:

- 10 to 12 times current monthly billings for larger services; may require earnout
- 5 to 7 times current monthly billings for smaller services; may require earnout

Benchmarks

■"Call center staffing averages 202 full-time agents and 92 part-time agents average call center budget is $11,800,417. Inbound call volume averages 14,427,106 calls annually. Outbound call volume averages 1,097,237 calls annually."

Source: BenchmarkPortal, Inc

Industry Trend

"There are currently 50,600 call centers in the U.S., containing 2.86 million agent positions. However, the U.S. market is actually shrinking; by 2008 there will be 47,500 call centers and 2.7 million agent positions. This reduction in market size is due to a combination of self-service technologies, offshore outsourcing, and the effects of the federal do-not-call list."

Source: McDaniel Executive Recruiters' 2004 North American Call Center Report, 9-23-2004. www.incoming.com.

" Indian revenues from call centers have grown an estimated 107% over the past year. Indian call centers employ over 120,000 people today."

Source: Research and Markets, 10-4-04. www.incoming.com.

"There are currently 4,500 call centers in Canada, and 212,000 agent positions. By 2008, there will be 5,300 call centers, and 305,500 agent positions."

Source: McDaniel Executive Recruiters' 2004 North American Call Center Report, 9-23-2004. www.incoming.com.

"The worldwide market for customer service outsourcing is set to grow from $8.4 billion (in 2004) to $12.2 billion in 2007, but the offshore component will remain small, according to Gartner Inc. Despite the hype surrounding offshore call centers, offshore customer service outsourcing only represents a tiny fraction of the market—less than 2 percent in 2005, increasing to less than 5 percent in 2007. Gartner also reports that, through 2007, 80 percent of organizations that outsource customer service and support contact centers with the primary goal of reducing cost will fail."

Source: Gartner Inc. 3-13-05. www.incoming.com.

"The average agent [call center] base wage in the U.S. is $14.16 per hour."

Source: 2004 Call Center Best Practices Report. – www.incoming.com

"Spending on recruiting and staffing services will increase to $94 billion worldwide by 2008, with a compound five-year annual growth rate (CAGR) of 8.7%. The U.S. market will continue to lead in this area, and will increase to $40 billion in 2008."

Source: IDC, 11-24-04. www.incoming.com.

"According to Datamonitor, speech-enabled self-service technology will compete with offshore call center agents as it provides a more cost-effective approach to service low-level transactions. When compared to a call center in the domestic market, a center in an offshore location like India saves a U.S. company approximately 25% to 35% per transaction—significant savings. However, a call serviced through speech automation costs approximately 15% to 25% of the cost of a call handled by an agent in India."

Source: Datamonitor, 11-28-04. www.incoming.com.

Resources

Incoming Calls Management Institute
www.incoming.com—a great site full of interesting and valuable information—one of the best.

Camera Shops *(See also One-Hour Photo Labs)*

3,199	SIC: 5946-01	NAIC: 443131

Rule of Thumb:

- 10 to 15 percent of annual revenues plus fixtures, equipment & inventory

Benchmarks

Camera Shops

	# of Retail Outlets	Sales per Outlet
Camera stores w/o minilabs	302	$959,375
Camera stores w minilabs	2,939	$580,242
Minilabs	3,855	—
All specialty retail outlets	7,096	$384,928
Mass retail outlets w/minilabs	23,464	—
Speciality outlets+ Mass retail outlets w/minilabs	30,560	—
All mass retail outlets	79,578	—
One-hour minilab	—	$294,558
Digital imaging firm	—	$770,833

Source: PMA 2003–2004 Industry Trends Report, Photo Marketing Association International (PMA)

General Information

Major retail photo channels—The traditional channels for photo-products and services are:

Independent & chain minilabs
Camera stores
Mail-order
Retail portrait studios
Mass retailers (supermarkets, drugstores, discount stores & warehouse clubs)
Department stores
Electronics/video stores
Office-supply stores
Internet firms
Source: PMA 2003-2004 Industry Trends Report, Photo Marketing Association International (PMA)

Industry Trend

"Camera stores without minilabs, while offering overnight processing, focus more on equipment sales and have been less affected by these trends. A typical camera store experienced at least a 35 percent increase in the number of digital cameras sold in 2003 compared to 2002. Of course, camera stores face severe competition from electronics/video chains, discount stores, and Internet retailers. They have to carefully balance their merchandise across unique selections, support, and value. Sales of digital cameras are also expected to peak in the next couple of years."

Source: PMA 2003-2004 Industry Trends Report, Photo Marketing Association International (PMA)

"Last year, Kodak said 1.9 billion digital images were printed by all methods, with 57 percent done at home, 33 percent at retail locations and 10 percent through online services. The company predicts that by 2007 the number of printed images will rise to 10.7 billion a year and that the share printed at kiosks will grow to 37 percent."

Source: The New York Times, March 17, 2005

"According to the 2003-2004 PMA U.S. Industry Trends Survey: Retail Markets, specialty retailers received an average of 2,194 digital orders per location in 2003, and the average value of each digital order was $20.94 ("specialty retailers" includes camera stores with minilabs, camera stores without minilabs, and retail minilabs). Growth in the number of orders was modest in the first half of 2004. Prints from digital files are increasing, but the overall volume of digital prints is expected to be flat in 2005 compared to 2004. Retailers looking for growth in photo services will have to shift their attention away from the number of prints and towards customer and order value by utilizing marketing schemes such as memberships, bundles, and personalized products."

Source: PMA 2003-2004 Industry Trends Report, Photo Marketing Association International (PMA)

Resources

Photo Marketing Association (PMAI)
www.pmai.org—good site

Campgrounds *(See also RV Parks)*

14,910	SIC: 7033-01	NAIC: 721211

Rule of Thumb:

- 8.5 times EBITDA
- 3.5 times SDE (after cost of mdse. for store)
- 7 to 7.5 times SDE; add store inventory.
- "The above always includes real estate and, 90 percent of the time, owner financing. Real estate value may be much higher than the value as a campground. Rules of Thumb generally do not apply to the 'low end' or to large RV resorts."

Pricing Tips

Industry Experts' Ratings:

Marketability (1 = low; 4 = high) 3.6
Industry Trend (1 = declining; 4 = growing) 3.6
Ease of Replication (1 = easy; 4 = difficult) 3.6

Benchmarks

"When we look at rules of thumb, the following would apply to the 'typical campground' with a camp store and average amenities:

"Registration income (site rental only) x 4.5

"Gross profit (after cost of goods for the store) x 3.5

"Adjusted net income (SDE) x 7.5

"Multiply each one out and see if they come out reasonably close. If they are within $50,000 or so, they really mean something. If they are way off, it can mean some of the following: If the GP multiple is much higher than the RI, it is positive because they have strong store sales. If the GP multiple is lower, they are probably doing a bad job in the store or they are eating too much inventory (literally).

"Obviously the net is very important, but I would tend to place a great deal of importance on the GP. This gives credit to strong store sales, good registration fees and the overall ability of the park to produce revenue. It also shows a picture before bad management. We know that a properly run park should net 40 percent to the bottom line, or they are not good managers. (Could be a good opportunity for the new owner.)

"The net income multiple will float with interest rates. Since most are sold on a contract, the multiple goes up when interest rates are down. As in any business, you really need to understand how the adjustments were made. It is very normal for some owners to work very long hours with not enough employees. This is a pace that wore them out, and that is why they are selling.

"When we look at the above multiples, I would qualify it with the following:

"This is assuming that the park has modern utilities (some 50 amp service, most 30 amp), a good source of water and sewer (city services best). The sites need to be large enough for newer modern RVs with wide roads and level sites, and many pull-thru sites. The buildings need to be in good repair and include a game room, laundry and convenience store."

Expenses as a percentage of annual sales:	
Cost of Goods Sold	10%
Payroll/Labor Costs	10%
Occupancy Cost	40%
Profit (estimated)	40%

General Information

"First, campgrounds and RV parks are the same business. Some just prefer to call themselves RV parks if they are looking for the higher end of the business, and they might exclude tent campers from the park. A much more important aspect for valuation purposes would be if they are open all year or seasonal, if they rent sites on an overnight basis or weekly, monthly or for the whole season.

"Campgrounds that have a high percentage of seasonal sites have sometimes become more like a trailer park with lots of junk stored outside and they sometimes do not keep up with modern electrical etc. for the newer RVs. Campers do not want to stay in parks like this.

> "The estimated percentage of summer camps that ban cell phones—90%"
>
> Source: American Camp Association

"The most value tends to be in overnight parks near destination areas like National Parks. They can charge a much higher rate for the site, the people tend to buy more items from the camp store, and there are usually extra people in the family who pay another $2 to $5 per night to stay on the site, and all want to go home with T-shirts and souvenirs from the gift shop. Some also do very well with breakfasts, etc. This type does not need to have much of an advertising budget either because they feed from the other activities in the area.

"One perception that is often wrong is that the highest registration fees come from the huge motor homes on a 50-amp site with sewer hookups. They would have two people who brought all of their groceries with them, and they sit inside with the air conditioner running, using up electricity for $30 per night. On the other hand, you have a family of five who stays in a pop-up trailer on a water and electric site. They paid $25 for the site, $3 each for the extra three people and didn't have room to bring groceries. The kids spent $15 in the game room, Mom spent $5 in the laundry, they each bought a $12 T-shirt and bought $16 worth of soda pop and groceries. And....the owners are only open for six months out of the year and spend their winters in Florida.

"Another type with a high value is the resort park. They need to be looked at very differently because they are much more like a hotel. The income, amenities, land values, etc. are much more and they require more employees. Also, the type of buyer is not the same. The owner is not behind the counter checking in the campers, and their kids are not cleaning the restrooms.

"Another thing that has changed the business is camping cabins. KOA did a great job of developing this into a substantial source of income for many campgrounds. The whole industry copied the concept too. They rent for much more than a campsite and are very popular with people who used to camp in a tent, the baby boomers. I could go on and on about cabins, but that should probably be another discussion.

"You also need to be very careful about zoning and how well accepted the park is with neighbors. If they are operating on agricultural land with a special use permit and the area is surrounded by residences...look out! If they are on leased land, the value would be half of normal. Some who are operating under special permits are prevented from making improvements to the park (can't get a building permit) and are eventually forced out of business.

"Some buyers are looking for a year-round facility so they can make more money. Actually, the value is set by the income produced over a year. I would rather work for six months for the same price! This is another lengthy subject.

"Many campgrounds are sitting on land that is worth much more than the business and it is very difficult to obtain permits to build a new park. These two things will make it more attractive to purchase an outdated park with the right zoning and make it more modern."

Advantages of this Business
- "Family owned and operated"

Disadvantages of this Business
- "Long hours when you are open"

Resources
National Association of RV Parks and Campgrounds
www.gocampingamerica.com

Camps

8,864	SIC: 7032-03
Camps (except day, instructional) Camps (except instructional) day Camps, sports instruction	NAIC: 721214 NAIC: 713990 NAIC: 611620

Rule of Thumb:

- 2 times annual sales or 5 to 8 times SDE plus inventory

Pricing Tips

"Expect to pay $3 million to $5 million for a 200-bed camp in good condition and operating at capacity, and $1 million to $2 million for one needing renovations and operating at half-capacity."

Source: "Bunk and Breakfast," Forbes, December 8, 2003

"Only a dozen of the 2,000 or so private sleep-away camps in the U.S. are openly listed for sale right now. That's because most camps are handed down within a family or sold through word of mouth to, say, the assistant director who has worked there for 20 years."

Source: "Bunk and Breakfast," *Forbes*, December 8, 2003

Benchmarks

Expenses as a percentage of annual sales:	
Cost of Goods	5 to 10%
Payroll/Labor	25%
Occupancy	10 to 20%

General Information

"According to the association [American Camp Association], there are about 12,000 summer camps in the United States, 8,000 of them residential, meaning that children spend their days and nights there…"

Source: *The New York Times*, Sunday, March 6, 2005

"Fantasy camps are hardly new. The model for many of them—'Field of Dreams' gatherings of baseball fans and their aging idols—goes back more than two decades. But the camps have grown into a $1 billion industry that goes far beyond sports. The boom has been fueled by the spread of reality television, on which almost anyone can become a star, and by the interest of more celebrities in taking part."

Source: *The New York Times*, Sunday, June 12, 2005

"Over the last decade, however, camp has grown into a $19.8 billion industry serving nearly 12 million kids and is more than ever focused on specialties—from the popular (soccer, computers) to the obscure (fencing, yoga)—that bolster college applications or win sports scholarships."

Source: *Business Week*, June 13, 2005

"About 23 percent of the 2,400 accredited camps across the nation now offer family programs. That percentage has more than doubled in the last 15 years, according to the American Camp Association, which accredits summer camps."

Source: *The New York Times*, Sunday, May 8 2005

Resources
American Camping Association
www.acacamps.org

Candy Stores		
7,643	SIC: 5441-01	NAIC: 445292

Rule of Thumb:

- 30 to 35 percent of annual sales + inventory
- 1.7 times SDE plus inventory

Resources
National Confectioners Association of the United States
www.candyusa.org

Candy Industry magazine
www.candyindustry.com—an excellent and informative site

Car Washes—Full Service/Exterior		
18,000	SIC: 7542-01	NAIC: 811192

Rule of Thumb:

- 6 times EBITDA
- 1.5 to 2 times annual sales plus inventory
- A car wash should be worth double its yearly gross, no more

Pricing Tips
"Tax returns are not easily available and estimating is generally the rule; therefore using water bills,etc. to figure out the sales is one common method."

"95 percent of car washes sold with real estate, equipment and assets. Very seldom sold with business only."

"Car washing is a total cash business—strongest figure to be used is Gross Annual Sales in determining strength of business."

"Key factors include current market conditions, owner salary, benefits, condition of equipment… these are just some of the typical costs and items buyers and sellers negotiate over."

"4 times SDE without land"

"2 times SDE + land & equipment"

"Research shows that 52% of Americans wash their cars less than once a month—and 15% never wash their cars. An estimated 37 million cars even smell because of interior garbage, according to a consumer survey conducted by the International Carwash Association (ICA)."

Industry Experts' Ratings:

Amount of Competition (1 = Lot of: 4 = Not much)	1.2
Amount of Risk (1 = Very: 4 = Not much)	1.6
Historical Profit Trend (1 = Down: 4 = Up)	2.0
Location & Facilities (1 = Poor: 4 = Excellent)	2.0
Marketability (1 = Low: 4 = High)	1.2
Industry Trend (1 = Declining: 4 = Growing)	2.0
Ease of Replication (1 = Easy: 4 = Difficult)	2.0

"Car washes take time to be approved through a town/city due to the traffic restrictions and noise factors, also including water recycling."

Benchmarks

"Car washes usually run at 1/3 profit from gross. Example: $90,000 gross = $30,000 net."

Benchmark Data

Payroll/Labor Costs	$20,000 to $30,000
Occupancy	$3,000 to $8,500 approx (depending on location)

Benchmark Data (Continued)

Carwash Type	Cost (in millions)	Labor	Facilities	Expenses
Full-Service	$1.8 mil.	35%	10,000	$17,300
Exterior-Only	$1.2 mil.	21%	5,000	$7,900
Self-Service	$0.8 mil.	8%	30,000	$761
IBA @ Gas C-store	$0.5 mil.	0%	30,000	n/a

Cost—includes land, site improvements, construction and equipment

Labor—labor-to-revenue ratio

Facilities—ICA estimate of the number of carwash facilities

Expenses—annual advertising expenditures (industry averages)

Source: *Professional Carwashing & Detailing* magazine, April, 2003

Expenses as a percentage of annual sales:

Cost of goods sold	20%
Payroll/Labor Costs	25%
Occupancy Cost	25%
Profit (estimated)	25%

Good locations can be very successful. Get an expert to figure one out, as it is very difficult to understand a business by just counting cars only.

Advantages of this Business

- "It's a high-margin business with good returns."

Disadvantages of this Business

- "It requires constant marketing, and equipment breakdown and cost can be high."

The car wash industry has traditionally been segmented into three categories of operations:

"**Self-Service**—Commonly referred to as wand-style, quarter, do-it-yourself, etc. Here the owner washes his own vehicle. You provide only the space and equipment; he handles the labor. The wash quality is variable as it depends totally on the vehicle owner. This type of facility is generally not attended; however, it does require regular maintenance and housekeeping.

"**Conveyor**—Commonly referred to as full-serve, exterior or flex-serve. In this case, the vehicle is placed on a conveyor that moves it through a series of applicators, washers, rinses and dryers. Whether the owner exits the vehicle depends on the type of service selected. In a full-serve, he leaves the vehicle, and you provide the labor to clean the interior and detail the exterior. The customer enters the building to complete the sale and waits for the wash to be completed. In an exterior wash, the facility cleans only the outside of the car. In flex-serve, you offer the option of interior or exterior only. A conveyor facility is always attended; the number of staff depends on the services offered.

"**In-Bay Automatic**—Commonly referred to as a rollover, in-bay or automatic. Here the vehicle passes by an automatic teller. The owner selects the method of payment and type of wash and enters the facility. At a petroleum site, the transaction occurs at the pump. The equipment may be touch-free (relying on wash solutions and high-pressure water to clean), or it may be a friction-style unit that relies on soft foam or fiber to make contact with and clean the vehicle."

Industry Trend

"The number of car washes being built are growing slowly."

Seller Financing

- "20 percent down, 80 percent financing, 20 year amortization"

Resources

International Carwash Association
www.carwash.org

Other sites of interest:
www.carlove.org
www.carcarecentral.com
autocareforum.com

Professional Carwashing & Detailing magazine
www.carwash.com—an excellent site

See IRS Audit Technique Guide (Market Segment Specialization Program—MSSAP) on the Car Wash Industry. It is an excellent source of information and is available at bookstore.gpo.gov; (search under IRS—IRS Audit Technique Guides).

Car Washes—Coin Operated/Self-Service

32,000	SIC: 7542-05	NAIC: 811192

Rule of Thumb:

- Operations less than five years old generally sell for cost of original real estate, equipment, and improvement cost, plus negotiated figure 2 to 3 times EBIT.
- 4 times annual gross sales—"A good place to start"

Pricing Tips
"Total cash business. Passive investment, almost labor free."

"90 percent of self-service car washes will have combination of self-service and automatic bays."

"98 percent of self-service/automatic car washes are sold with real estate, equipment and assets."

"Nearly impossible to sell business only."

"Takes 5 years to build new operation—gross annual sales volume to maturity."

Benchmarks
"Income & Expenses:
The estimated monthly income for a self-serve facility in an average location is $1200– $14,000 per bay.

Your average operating expenses are 17%–20% per month (not including debt service.) The estimated income for an automatic unit is approximately $4800 per month.

The average monthly operating expenses for automatic units is approximately 21%."

Source: Magic Wand Car Wash Systems, www.magicwandcarwash.com

"The typical self-service facility:

- Has five wand-bays and five vacuums;
- Serves an estimated market population of 30,000 to 40,000 people;
- Has an estimated 10-mile market radius;
- Competes against two other self-service carwashes; and
- Is open 7 days per week and 24 hours per day.
- Produces average monthly revenue of $1,330 per wand-bay ($1,500 to $2,500 for new facilities), $176 per vacuum, and $395 for all merchandise vending.
- Has average operating expenses between 25 percent and 40 percent of gross sales.
- Pays an average debt service (principal and interest) of 26 percent of gross sales."

"ProForma—Annual

	Good Site	Better Site
Revenue		
Wand-Bays	$90,000	$150,000
Vacuums	$12,000	$20,000
Vending	$5,400	$9,480
Gross Revenue	$107,400	$179,480

	Low Side	High Side	Low Side	High Side
Operating Exp.	$26,850	$42,960	$44,870	$71,792
Gross Margin	$80,550	$64,440	$134,610	$107,688
Debt Service	$27,924	$27,924	$46,665	$46,665
Profit*	$52,626	$36,516	$87,945	$61,023
*before depreciation and tax	49%	34%	49%	34%"

General Information

"Prime commercial property may cost as much as $8 to $15 per square foot, and each wand bay will require a minimum of 3,000 square feet of land. Actual development costs can be as much as $20,000 to $30,000 per bay for buildings; $15,000 to $20,000 per bay for equipment; and $100,000 to $200,000 or more or more for site improvements such as excavating, grading and paving, tap and impact fees, permits, professional fees, and landscaping. The information table that follows provides a model for a five-bay self-service carwash to illustrate how these factors can impact a projected budget.

"As you can see, building a new self-service carwash is an expensive proposition. With estimated budgets of between $470,000 and $740,000, an investor would need cash injections of between $141,000 and $222,000 to adequately fund these projects. Adding an in-bay automatic will increase the initial capital investment and operating expenses.

"Takes up to 3 years to plan, permit and zone a new car wash. Existing operations will generally sell in range of $400,000 to $1,750,000."

Income

"What Level of Gross Income Can Be Expected?

This is a very difficult question to answer because income per bay can vary, depending on many factors. Income per bay will usually range from a low of $250 per week to a high of $450 per week. Many operators indicate that they have kept their prices constant while they have cut washing time from 5 minutes to 3 1/2 minutes. Others have increased charges from $1.00 to $2.00 for 4 minutes.

"How Much Business is Needed to Support the Bays?

We generally use the principle of 1 bay per 1,000 area residents, but in some instances that general yardstick can be unreliable. As self-serve car washes can be located in a variety of areas, a good location is secondary to great service and an excellent price. We find that self-service car washing customers will travel to a good self-serve car wash, and customer loyalty tends to be high.

"Tunnel Car Wash

According to industry trade magazines, the national average for traffic entering a tunnel car wash is .76%. Based on this figure, an area traffic count of 30,000 vehicles per day would result in approximately 228 cars entering your business. While regional differences may affect your average revenue per wash, the national average wash generates $9.75 per car.

"Based on the above figures:

228 vehicles per day x $9.75 per vehicle = $2,223.00 per day for the projected average income. If your facility is open 320 days per year, then your gross revenue from a single site will be approximately $711,360.00 per annum. The following guidelines are listed for the additional costs.

Additional Cost Guidelines	
Supplies	6.0%
Utilities	7.5%
Variable Expenses	5.5%
Fixed Expenses	29.8%
Labor	32.0%
Subtotal	80.8%

Therefore, you could assume that the gross profit generated from one typical self-serve site would be $711,360.00–$574,778.00 + $136,582.00"

Resources

An IRS Audit Technique Guide (Market Segment Specialization Program—MSSAP) is available for this industry. It is an excellent source of information and is available at bookstore.gpo.gov: (search under IRS—IRS Audit Technique Guides).

Franchise

Car X Muffler & Brake Shop

170 units	
Approximate Total Investment	$214,000–$326,000

Benchmarks

In 2002, according to their franchise disclosure documents, a Car X center that was in business two years or more averaged $690,000 for the year.

Resources

www.carx.com

Card Shops *(See also Gift Shops)*

6,544	SIC: 5947-10	NAIC: 453220

[Note: We debated whether to leave card shops as a stand-alone business, but there are few, if any, pure card shops. However, card shops still have a SIC and a NAICS number, so someone feels that they are still a stand-alone business. On the other hand, we have seen few gift shops that didn't have cards. In either event, we suspect that the rule of thumb would be about the same.]

Card Shops (Hallmark) *(See Hallmark Gift Shops)*

Carpet Cleaning

37,722	SIC: 7217-04	NAIC: 561740

Rule of Thumb:

- 45 to 50 percent of annual revenue plus inventory
- 1.8 times SDE plus inventory

Benchmarks

Following are some averages based on the 10 largest and most successful carpet cleaning companies in the United States. The information is from data collected by the Carpet Cleaning Industry Leaders Review (Cleanfax). (www.cleanfax.com) Geographically, the range is from California to New Jersey. Interestingly, the make-up of each category is not necessarily the same companies. We did the math for averaging the responses to the questions—only the data is from Cleanfax.

"How many carpet cleaning trucks does your company operate?" The average is 21.4 cleaning trucks. The numbers range from 45 trucks to 10.

"How many miles (estimate for past 12 months) did you put on your most-used trucks?" The average is 83,364

"How many people does your company employ full-time?" The average is 113. The numbers range from 20 to 186 employees.

"How much revenue did your company generate from carpet cleaning and closely related services?" The average is $3,991,500. The figures range from $9,850,000 to $1,300,000.

"What is the total square footage of your company's carpet cleaning accounts?" The average is 9,881,000 square feet. It ranges from 35,000,000 to 2,175,000 square feet.

General Information

"There are approximately 40,000 carpet cleaning companies in the U.S.; about 8,000 are run by eight franchisors. Start-up costs for franchises range from $43,000 to $104,000…. Most carpet cleaning companies are very small, and nearly one-quarter of them are part-time operations. To progress beyond $100,000/year in receipts requires a significant investment in either 'truck-mounts' or the purchase of a franchise."

Source: Professional Carpet and Upholstery Cleaners Association (PCUCA)

Resources

International Society of Cleaning Technicians (SCT)
www.isct.com

Carpet and Rug Institute
www.carpet-rug.com

Association of Specialists in Cleaning & Restoration
www.ascr.org

Professional Carpet and Upholstery Cleaners Association—This is a regional association, but has some good information.
www.pcuca.org

Carpet/Floor Coverings

Rule of Thumb:

- 20 percent of annual sales plus inventory

Resources

Flooring Magazine
www.flooringmagazine.com

Floor Covering Weekly
www.floorcoveringweekly.com

Franchise

Carvel Ice Cream *(See also Ice Cream)*

490 units

Approximate Total Investment:	$250,000

-cont'd-

Franchise

Carvel Ice Cream *(See also Ice Cream) (cont'd)*

Rule of Thumb:

- 60 percent of annual sales or $20 to 25 times the number of gallons of liquid ice cream mix purchased plus inventory
- 2 times SDE plus inventory

Pricing Tips

"Some franchised ice cream businesses with a positive history, updated facilities and verifiable sales numbers will move to 2.5 SDE. Conversely, a short lease and less than five years on franchise agreement will result in less than 2 times SDE."

"Location drives price higher and typically has higher returns on product usage, therefore more profit. Free standing buildings with volume in excess of 10,000 gallons, rule of thumb would be 60 percent of annual sales, with average lease of 7 years remaining."

Benchmarks

"Food cost percentage typically is equal to SDE unless rent is above $25 per sq. ft."

Expenses as a percentage of annual sales:

Cost of Goods Sold:	26%
Payroll/Labor Costs	21%
Occupancy Cost:	11%
Profit (estimated)	25%

Advantages of this Business

- "Not affected by downturns in the economy"

Disadvantages of this Business

- "Health concerns in America/seasonality"

Seller Financing:

- "3 to 5 years"

Casinos/ Casino Hotels

Rule of Thumb:

- Las Vegas Strip average: 8.1 times EBITDA
- Indian Gaming management contracts: 30 to 40 percent net (this is pulled from the top in "Operating Income" and should be calculated before debt service). 5 to 7 percent of gross used to be standard for Indian Gaming contracts. The NIGC must approve all contracts and agreements between management and tribal nations. The NIGC (National Indian Gaming Commission) is an independent federal regulatory agency of the United States. Management cannot own any part of the Indian casino. Contracts are typically five years with options to renew. The tribe will be responsible for paying down the debt service.

Pricing Tips

Industry Experts' Ratings:

Marketability (1 = low; 4 = high) 3.2
Industry Trend (1 = declining; 4 = growing) 2.8
Ease of Replication (1 = easy; 4 = difficult) 3.6

Benchmarks

Hotel Casino Revenue Contributions:
(Industry Average)

"Casino (slots, tables, etc.):	52%
Hotel Rooms:	18%
Food & Beverages:	15%
Retail Stores & other Entertainment:	15%"

"Take slot machines. These workhorses produce about 70 percent of a typical casino's gambling revenue."

Source: *U.S. News & World Report,* May 23, 2005

Expenses as a percentage of annual sales:	
Payroll/Labor Costs	21%
Profit (estimated)	08%

General Information

"Wells Fargo & Bank of America are the leading financial service providers to Native Americans and to the tribal gaming industry. Wells Fargo provides capital and financial services to more than 150 Tribal Nations."

The gaming industry is divided into two sectors: commercial gaming and Native American or tribal gaming. Commercial gaming exists in 11 states and includes casinos and casino/hotels in places like Las Vegas and Atlantic City, and riverboat and dockside gaming in Indiana, Mississippi, Louisiana, and other states. Tribal gaming can be found in 28 states and includes casinos and other gaming on Native American reservations and tribal lands. In 2001, commercial and tribal gaming generated an estimated $38.3 billion in total revenues. Of this total, commercial gaming generated 67 percent ($25.6 billion) and tribal gaming generated 33 percent (an estimated $12.7 billion).

Advantages of this Business

- "Gallup data (released in March 2004) revealed that 66% of American adults say they have gambled in some form in the past 12 months."

Disadvantages of this Business

- "Impact of State Taxes:
  Casinos can be taxed at higher rates than other businesses. Gaming offers states an alternative to raising taxes. When states need more money, casinos and race tracks are natural targets.

- "Capital Intensity:
  Most gaming companies in the industry have a high debt-to-equity ratio which exposes them to interest rate risk.

- "Gaming Sensitivity in Economic Cycles:
  In a slower economy, consumers cut leisure spending."

Industry Trend

"Indian casino revenues continued to grow rapidly last year, reaching $19 billion, a sum that makes the casinos two-thirds as big as all the commercial casinos, according to a report released yesterday by the Analysis Group, a consulting firm.

"With revenues generated by Indian casinos climbing 12 percent last year, compared with 6.7 percent for commercial casinos, the gap between the categories continues to shrink and is quite likely to become smaller, the report said. As recently as 2001, the revenues of Indian casinos were half those of commercial casinos, the report found.

"The report said 228 tribes operated 405 casinos in 30 states compared with 443 commercial casinos. The Indian casinos supported 539,000 jobs and paid $19.4 billion in wages last year, the report said."

Source: *The New York Times National*, Thursday, June 16, 2005

"Revenue at the Mohegan Sun has jumped an average 14% a year since 2000 to $14 billion last year, when the business pulled in $344 million in operating income (earnings before interest, taxes, depreciation and amortization)—making it one of the most profitable casinos in the U.S.

"Native American gambling is quite some business. Last year, reports the National Indian Gaming Association, 411 operations grossed $18.5 billion (that's the excess of bets over payouts), accounting for 37% of the U.S. casino industry total."

Source: *Forbes*, June 20, 2005

"Last year [2004], the 445 commercial casinos in 11 states generated nearly $29 billion in gross gaming revenue, surpassing 2003 gross gaming revenues by more than 7 percent."

Source: American Gaming Association, as written in www.prnewswire.com

"It's a story being repeated millions of times across the country. A record 73 million Americans, up nearly 20 million from just five years ago, will patronize one of the nation's more than 1,200 casinos, card rooms, or bingo parlors this year. The average gambler visits a casino nearly six times a year—almost twice as often as he did a decade ago. At least 6 million Americans will click a bet on one of the 2,300 online gaming sites. Altogether, gamblers will lose more than $80 billion on everything from the Triple Crown to the flop of a card this year. There seems to be no stopping America's gambling mania."

Source: *U.S. News & World Report*, May 23, 2005

Casino Market 2004 Annual Revenues

1.	Las Vegas Strip	$5.333 billion
2.	Atlantic City, NJ	$4.806 Billion
3.	Chicagoland, Ind.,/IL.	$2.346 billion
4.	Connecticut (Indian)	$1.646 billion
5.	Tunica/Lula, Miss.	$1.199 billion
6.	Detroit	$1.189 billion
7.	Biloxi/Gulfport, Miss.	$911.45 million
8.	Reno/Sparks, Nev.	$903.54 million
9.	Lawrenceburg/Rising Sun/Elizabeth/Vevay, Ind.	$885.90 million
10.	St. Louis, Mo./Ill.	$848.41 million

Source: American Gaming Association

Resources

American Gaming Association
www.americangaming.org

North American Association of State & Provincial Lotteries
www.naspl.org

Interactive Gaming Council
www.igcouncil.org

National Indian Gaming Association
www.indiangaming.org

Gaming Magazine
www.gamingmagazine.com

Caterers/Catering

44,388	SIC: 5812-12	NAIC: 722320

Rule of Thumb:

- 30 percent of annual sales plus inventory

Resources

The National Association of Catering Executives (NASE)
www.nace.net

International Caterers Association (ICA)
www.ncacater.org

CaterSource Journal
www.catersource.com

Catering Trucks *(See Routes)*

Rule of Thumb:

- 40 percent of annual sales plus inventory

Cellular Telephone Stores

Rule of Thumb:

- 50 + percent of annual revenues plus inventory
- "Most cell-phone stores receive a small percentage of the usage fees based on the sale of the plan purchased by the customer with the telephone."

Resources

Cellular Telecommunications & Internet Association (CTIA)
www.wow-com.com

Cemeteries

6,825	SIC: 6553-02	NAIC: 812220

Rule of Thumb:

- 6 times SDE
- 8 times EBIT
- 6 times EBITDA

Pricing Tips

"This is a very difficult business to value without industry experience. The value is directly proportionate to the success of the sales program (pre-need)."

"Valuations will vary depending on the strategic fit of the buyer. A local funeral home is generally the best strategic fit and should, therefore, be willing to pay the most."

Benchmarks

Profit (estimated pre-tax) = 15%

General Information

Questions to ask seller: Trust fund information is critical. What are the liabilities? Are they properly funded? Is there a successful sales organization/program in place?

"The cemetery analysis is much more difficult for several reasons. The number of acres, whether it is a memorial park or whether they allow upright markers, the type of ground and terrain and more, all have an effect on maintenance & labor costs. Each state has different requirements for handling endowment care; merchandise and the permitted use will affect the bottom line. I would suggest that anyone that has an opportunity to sell a cemetery should involve an industry expert immediately. They are tricky but very lucrative businesses."

Check Cashing Services

20,000	SIC: 6099.03	NAIC: 522390

Rule of Thumb:

- 75 percent of annual revenues
- 2 times SDE

"Collectively, Check Cashers process over 180 million checks annually, worth over $60 billion, which generates almost $1.5 billion in revenues. Roughly 80% to 90% of these checks are payroll checks with an average size of between $500 and $600."

Source: Financial Service Centers of America (FISCA)

Pricing Tips

"The check cashing business is growing; every state has its own rules and regulations. Lease terms and whether a franchise or independent will affect pricing."

Industry Experts' Ratings:

Amount of Competition (1 = Lot of: 4 = Not much)	2.0
Amount of Risk (1 = Very: 4 = Not much)	3.2
Historical Profit Trend (1 = Down: 4 = Up)	2.4
Location & Facilities (1 = Poor: 4 = Excellent)	2.4
Marketability (1 = Low: 4 = High)	3.2
Industry Trend (1 = Declining: 4 = Growing)	3.2
Ease of Replication (1 = Easy: 4 = Difficult)	1.2

"This is a growing industry, inventory is cash,more people using these types of services."

Benchmarks

"Check cashing should provide the owner with 1% of total gross sales as owner's discretionary income."

Expenses as a percentage of annual sales:

Cost of goods sold..	99%
Payroll/Labor Costs	01%
Occupancy Cost	01%
Profit (estimated)	01%

General Information

"Location is important—doesn't work well in high income areas."

"Although there are a few large chain operations, most FISCA [Financial Service Centers of America] are local neighborhood organizations, that on average, operate one and three stores."

Source: Financial Service Centers of America (FISCA)

"Consumers who use financial service centers are:

- slightly younger than the general population
- employed full-time (80%)
- primarily lower to middle class in income
- maintaining at least one traditional bank account (58%)"

Source: Financial Service Centers of America (FISCA)

"Scope of Their Activities:
Here is a checklist that includes those activities and many other items commonly found among their product and service offerings: [Other than routine check cashing]

- Cash payroll or government checks for a fee. About 1/3 of all AFDC checks are cashed at check cashing businesses.
- Offer "payday loans" or advances for a personal post-dated check.
- Sell money orders, used to pay bills, etc., and receive a fee.
- Distribute welfare payments and food stamps, as a paid agent for the government.
- Make utility payments, charging a fee for each payment.
- Wire transfers, such as through Western Union.
- Sell lottery tickets.
- Sell phone cards, normally buying at around 70% of the card's face value.
- Sell prepaid cell phones on a buy and resale basis.
- Sell beepers on a buy and resale basis.
- Sell public transportation tickets and passes at no profit, basically to bring in customers.
- Sell cigarettes and sundry items.
- Buy and sell gold jewelry.
- Offer tax preparation services, including serving as an IRS authorized e-file provider."

"Stephens Inc., an investment bank that tracks the payday industry, estimated that at least nine million households had used payday loans in 2002. Gregory Elliehausen, senior research scholar at the Credit research Center at Georgetown University, said that a survey he did found that about 2 percent of payday loan customers were in the military.

"It would be reasonable to conclude, he said, that 2 percent, or 180,000 of those nine million households are military families. That would be just under 26 percent of all military households, based on Pentagon personnel figures."

Source: *The New York Times*, December 7, 2004

"Risks they Take:

There are two primary risks that check cashing businesses accept as part of their business:

- Check cashing businesses accept the risk that a check they accept for deposit will be no good. This is one reason they charge a fee. A bank generally will not accept this risk without the customer having funds on deposit to cover the check.
- Security and robbery are significant threats since check cashing businesses hold large amounts of cash during the day (most make one or more daily deposits) and are perceived as being less secure than a bank."

The above is from an article by Don Coker on www.website.lawinfo.net

Advantages of this Business

- "Inventory never spoils, services always needed"

Disadvantages of this Business

- "Might be security issues"

Industry Trend

"Growing due to the increased costs of doing business with the banks"

Resources

Financial Service Centers of America

www.fisca.org—an excellent site with lots of information

Chemical Product and Preparations Manufacturing (Miscellaneous Chemical)

Pricing Tips

"Pricing would roughly be between 4–9 trailing EBITDA—there is a wide variety of businesses in the industry, therefore rules of thumb on pricing and ratios are not really applicable."

Resources

Chemical Week, Chemical Marketing Reporter, and Chemical & Engineering News

Franchise

Chester's International (Fried Chicken)

9 units

Approximate Total Investment:	$60,000 to $400,400

Rule of Thumb:

- 45 percent of annual sales plus inventory

Resources

www.chesterfried.com

Franchise

Chicago Style Pizza

200 + units

Rule of Thumb:

- 26 percent of annual sales plus inventory

Chicken Restaurants—Food-To-Go *(See Restaurants)*

Rule of Thumb:

- 30 to 35 percent of annual sales plus inventory

Chinese Restaurants *(See Asian Restaurants & Restaurants)*

413,000		

Rule of Thumb:

- 30 percent of annual sales plus inventory

Chiropractic Practices

62,321	SIC: 8041-01	NAIC: 621310

Rule of Thumb:

- 30 percent of annual fees; may require earnout

Pricing Tips

"Pricing varies widely by location and type of practice, cash or insurance-dominated. Insurance reimbursement is still trending downward; Medicare is planning further reductions which other insurance companies will follow. Statistics are similar to medical family practice."

"Are you and the doctor a compatible personality match? Is the personality of the selling doctor vivacious and outgoing, while the 'new' doctor is a little reserved? Is your chiropractic technique compatible with the seller's? Every instance of non-compatibility may mean one fewer patient will remain with you.

"In my experience, I have found that patients do not mind the doctor leaving the practice as long as they can continue a similar experience with another doctor. If the change is too noticeable, patients are going to face change anyway, but history doesn't lie.

"With compatibility being addressed, I value the practice and goodwill to be equal to one-year net income. This figure will be corrected based upon a few factors:

- Blend of patient financial classes
- Insurance dependency/non-dependency
- Selling doctor's philosophy (pain practice/wellness practice)
- Percentage of actual overhead (high overhead lowers value)

"Purchasing a practice is a very smart thing to do. I would always look for a practice to buy rather than start fresh."

Source: From an article by Bruce A. Parker, D.C. in *Today's Chiropractic*.
For more information, go to www.bruceparkerconsulting.com.

Benchmarks

"The 'Typical' Chiropractor

According to the survey data, the typical full-time chiropractor is a Caucasian male who is in professional practice from 30 to 40 hours per week. Most chiropractors (61.8%) practice in a single-practitioner office. Typically, doctors of chiropractic also have a baccalaureate degree and participate in continuing education exceeding 21 hours per year; however, about two-thirds have not worked toward certification in a specialty area. Similar to the 1998 survey data, which showed 46.6% of chiropractors had practiced 5 to 15 years, 42.3% of those in the current survey have been in practice for 5 to 15 years; a weighted average of responses reveals that the average chiropractor was in practice for 13.2 years in 1998 and 15.6 years in 2003."

Source: National Board of Chiropractic Examiners

Components of Chiropractic Practice

Direct patient care	52.9%
Documentation	18.9%
Patient education	15.1%
Business management	13.2%

Source: National Board of Chiropractic Examiners

Reimbursement Categories, Managed Care, and Referral

Private Insurance	21.5%
Private pay/cash	21.2%
Managed care	19.4%
Personal injury	13.6%
Medicare	10.8%
Workers' Comp.	07.8%
Pro Bono	03.9%
Medicaid	01.8%

Source: National Board of Chiropractic Examiners

Expenses as a percentage of annual sales:

Cost of goods sold	07%
Payroll/Labor costs	24%
Occupancy cost	05%
Profit (estimated)	35%

Resources
National Board of Chiropractic Examiners
www.nbce.org—an excellent site

Today's Chiropractic
www.todayschiropractic.com

Cigar/Tobacco Stores

2,500	SIC: 5993-01	NAIC: 453991

Pricing Tips
"Usually carry $2,000–$3,000 inventory. Purchaser will pay as much as $10,000 to $20,000 for the opportunity of owning his own business. Definitely just a livelihood proposition."

Resources
Tobacco Merchants Association (TMA)
www.tma.org

Franchise

Closets by Design

27 units	
Approximate Total Investment:	$88,000–$220,000

Rule of Thumb:

- 50 percent of annual sales plus inventory

Resources
www.closets-by-design.com

Clothing Stores (Retail) *(See also Apparel)*

	SIC: 5699-77	NAIC: 448140

Rule of Thumb:

- 40 to 50 percent of annual sales plus inventory

Clothing Store (Retail) *(See also Apparel) (cont'd)*

- 2.4 to 2.8 times SDE plus inventory

Note: In both rules of thumb above, price includes inventory.

General Information

"Key factors are the rent costs and payroll expenses. Good businesses: big sizes, custom- made shops, children's, bridals, upscale resort-wear do well. Very important—age of the inventory or/and excessive inventory. Inventory one year or older should be sold by the owner buyer's take-over."

Benchmarks

Expenses as a percentage of annual sales:	
Cost of goods sold	46–52%
Payroll/Labor costs	14–18%
Occupancy cost	6–10%
Profit (estimated)	12–15%

Seller Financing

- "5 - 10 years"

Coatings, Adhesives & Specialty Chemical

Pricing Tips

"Environmental considerations are important."

Cocktail Lounges *(See also Bars)*

11,139	SIC: 5813-03	NAIC: 722410

Rule of Thumb:

- 40 percent of annual sales plus inventory
- 3 to 4 times monthly sales; add license (where applicable) and plus inventory

Cocktail Lounges *(cont'd)*

- 1.5 to 2 times SDE; add fixtures, equipment and inventory
- $ for $ of Gross sales if property is included, 40 percent of annual sales for business only plus inventory

Benchmarks

"Sales price 2 ½ to 3 times the annual liquor sales. Rent should never exceed 6 percent of the gross sales."

"When buying liquor, only purchase what you can sell. Ignoring this simple rule has put many bars out of business...The only way to maintain a profitable operation is to establish a firm system of liquor control, and usage, that lets you know, to the penny, exactly how much each drink costs, and how much liquor is poured...Each dollar tied up in inventory is a dollar not working for you. And cashflow is the name of the game. So keep your inventory lean.... If you sell one-ounce drinks for $2 each, a quart bottle can generate 32 drinks, and $64 in revenues. If the quart bottle costs you $12, your gross profit will be $52. Subtract about $15 to cover labor and overhead, and you should clear $37.... However, if your bartender 'free pours' liquor, and his shots average 11/2 ounces, the number of drinks you get from a quart will be cut from 32 to 21. This will cut your revenue from $64 to $42. And your gross profit will fall from $52 to $30. And, if your bartender also gives away 4 free drinks out of the same bottle, your gross profit will drop to $22, minus your $15 in labor and overhead, which will leave you with just $7. That's why your liquor should be guarded like cash."

from "Eleven Tips to Owning a Profitable Bar," Specialty Group, Pittsburgh, PA

Expenses as a percentage of annual sales:

Cost of goods sold	Food—30–40%; Beverages—18–22%
Payroll/labor costs	25%
Occupancy costs	8%
Profit (estimated)	10%

Industry Trend

"Demand for this type of business seems to be declining."

Resources

See List of Businesses with Alcoholic Beverage Licenses page 104

Coffee Shops *(See also Restaurants)*

18,522	SIC: 5812-28	NAIC: 722213

Rule of Thumb:

- 4 times monthly sales plus inventory
- 40 to 45 percent of annual sales plus inventory
- 2 to 2.2 times SDE plus inventory

General Information

Note: Some years ago, coffee shop was another name for a restaurant that did not serve liquor and usually specialized in breakfast, lunch and other short-order items. A place like Denny's still is considered a coffee shop by many, but it really is a restaurant, in our opinion. Now, a coffee shop is just that—Starbucks, Peets, and similar establishments.

"Is all cash going in the cash register? Based on gross sales, every other number is predictable."

Benchmarks

Expenses as a percentage of annual sales:	
Cost of goods sold	28–32%
Payroll/Labor costs	20–25%
Occupancy cost	8–12%
Profit (estimated)	16–20%

Resources

Specialty Coffee Association of America
www.scaa.org

National Coffee Association of USA
www.ncausa.org

Web sites:
www.coffeeuniverse.com
www.virtualcoffee.com

Coffee Shops (Gourmet)

Rule of Thumb:

- 45 percent of annual sales plus inventory

Benchmarks

Benchmarking the Big 3

	Sales Per Foot	Avg. Store Size	Avg. Sales Per Store	# of Stores
Starbucks Coffee	$521	1,500	$731,000	3,880
Peets Coffee	$696	1,800	$1,252,206	65
Tully's Coffee	$317	1,200	$380,000	104

Source: BizStats.com & Nation's Restaurant

Resources

See Coffee Shops

Coin Laundries

13,479	SIC: 7215-01	NAIC: 812310

Rule of Thumb:

- 3.5 to 5 times SDE plus inventory (Higher multiple for newer equipment and long lease)
- to 100 percent of annual revenues plus inventory
- 1 to 1 ½ times gross annual sales plus inventory
- "Generally 2.5 to 5.0 times annual SDE; depends on various parts of the U.S.— California, for example, sells between 4 to 5 times SDE, whereas in Nebraska it's 1.5 to 2.5 times SDE.

"Comparable Sales Report

Price/Sales multiple .... .88 [88% of annual sales]
Price/SDE multiple 2.31

Down payment: Typically between 50% and 75% of the purchase, though many will sell for all cash

Financing: Seller note over 2 to 4 years at 8% to 10% interest (personally guaranteed)

Training: One week

Other: non-compete agreement"

Source: Arrow Business Appraisers—an interesting and informative site, with sample appraisal reports www.arrowappraisers.com

Pricing Tips

"Coin operated laundries typical based on a 20% return on capital."

"Try and achieve a 25% return on capital; not including owner's salary."

"Utility costs are the single largest operating expense in a coin laundry."

Source: Coin Laundry Association

"Higher multiplier for businesses with newer equipment (3–4 years) and long-term lease (10+ years) increase business value."

"Here are the steps used to calculate how many times the washers would have to be used to use all the water reflected in the water bill: (1) Get the water bills for the last year, (2) Since water bills are usually in cu. ft., you will have to figure out how many gallons of water were used (there are approximately 7.5 gallons per cu. ft.), (3) Find out how many gallons of water the particular washer type uses, (4) Calculate how many times the washers have to be used to use all the water based on the bill. That should give you the number of washes. Multiply that by the cost per wash. The national average for 'turns' is 5—the number of times the washer is used. Dryer income is generally half that used of washer income, and vending income can produce 10 percent of total.

"Historically, laundries have been priced to sell at some multiple of their annual gross. Primarily because of tradition, this multiple varies from one section of the country to another, but normally it's within the 90 percent to 150 percent range.... Variations on the annual gross formula include such rules of thumb as 12 to 18 times monthly gross, or three to five times annual net income (before taxes)."

Ben Russell

Benchmarks

Expenses as a percentage of annual sales:

Utilities	25 % (can be higher depending on area)
Payroll/Labor	8–10%
Occupancy Cost	25%
Profit (estimated)	35%

"Coin laundries need a gross profit margin of 50 percent."

General Information

Questions to ask seller: "Age & condition of equipment. Is equipment mix suitable for market area? Are they taking in wash & fold or dry cleaning? Is store attended? Easy loading and parking? Environmental compliance and local government fees and restrictions? Length of increase value of business. Typically, the lease should be at least 10 years or more."

"Location, location, location"

Advantages of this Business

- "Less than full-time at site, limited or no payroll"
- "Cash flow"

Disadvantages of this Business

- "Security in low income neighborhoods"
- "Competition"

Industry Trend

"Changing from cash operations to debit card operations"

"Great potential for growing areas, especially in dense population areas with large numbers of renters"

There is a trend to adding ancillary businesses to coin laundries. Owners have added mini-marts to their laundry. This allows a full-time person to tend the laundry and to work the mini-mart. In one 4,900 square foot laundry, the owner carved out 300 square feet for the mini-mart, that sells not only laundry supplies, but snacks and cold drinks. In another store, the owner has added a fast-food operation; another an espresso bar, and still another a tanning salon. It seems the additional businesses are limited only by the owner's imagination.

"If you've got a lease and you can't assign it to somebody else when you sell it, then it's going to cost you a lot of money."

"When the stock market is down, more buyers look to cash flow businesses and the demand exceeds supply of available businesses. This has caused selling prices of coin laundries to exceed the price determined by rule of thumb."

"A lot of saturation in major urban markets, with stores opening in both urban and country markets which will impact smaller, less profitable competition"

Seller Financing

- "7 to 10 years"

Resources

Coin Laundry Association—They have an excellent Web site.
www.coinlaundry.org

Note: The above association publishes an excellent book: *Today's Coin Laundry: A Comprehensive Guide to Entering the Self-Service Laundry Industry.* Part II of this book is titled: Purchasing an Existing Coin Laundry. For more information, contact the Coin Laundry Association. They also have a monthly publication The Journal. You can look at lead articles

Financing of new stores according to a survey conducted by the Coin Laundry Association:

27%	Local Bank
17%	Equipment Manufacturer
05%	Independent Financing
12%	SBA
41%	Family & Friends

by going to the Association's site. They have a feature, Store Profile, which contains an equipment list and price structure—very interesting and informative.

American Coin-Op
(312) 337-7700

See Web sites mentioned in the Coin Laundry Quick Profile that follows

The [Coin Laundry] Lease

We have bracketed Coin Laundry because the following is taken from an article on coin laundry leases, but the information applies to almost all businesses and directly impacts— positively or negatively—the price of the business under review.

"The main thing to focus on when negotiating your lease is the time factor. You've got to give yourself enough time on the lease to make it worth your while. If you're going in with a new store [coin laundry], it's highly recommend that you get 15 to 20 years as an absolute bare minimum—with 25 years being the ideal situation.

"One of the things you need to negotiate is an 'exclusive' in that [shopping] center to do your type of business, as well as the ability to offer the ancillary services you'd like to provide.

"You should protect yourself in the event that your [shopping] center becomes more than a certain percentage vacant and/or if the major tenant, such as a supermarket, should leave. In such cases, you should have the right to get out of the lease or at least be entitled to some sort of rent abatement or credit."

Source: "The Coin Laundry Lease" by Bob Nieman, The Journal, March 2003

The above are just brief excerpts from an article that is probably the best one we have ever read on the business lease. Down-to-earth, practical advice, this should be read by anyone involved in business transactions, including buyers and sellers. To read it in its entirety, go to www.coinlaundry.org and click on the Journal; then go to past articles and March 2003—hopefully it will still be there.

Quick *Profile* Coin Laundry

"The term coin laundry is defined as 'commercial grade, self-service laundry equipment placed into service in a retail space.' Coin laundries generally occupy the retail space on long-term leases (10–25 years), and generate steady cash flow over the life of the lease. Coin laundries are unique small businesses in that they have no inventory or receivables, and no traditional employees. A minority of coin laundries employ attendants.

"Coin laundries range in market value from $50,000 to $1,000,000, and can generate cash flow between $15,000 and $200,000 per year. Business hours typically run from 6:00 a.m. to 10:00 p.m. The stores usually occupy 1,000 to 4,000 square feet of retail space, with the 2002 average being 2,260 square feet. New coin laundries are valued based on actual construction and equipment costs; while existing ones are valued based primarily on revenues. Coin laundries are perfect examples of passive-income generators. Coin laundries are also referred to as 'coin-op laundries,' 'coin-operated laundries,' or 'laundromats.'"

Source: Coin Laundry Association

"The three crucial items of a location are:

- The total number of renters
- The total number of households
- The number of families in a lower-income range. Of course, the dollar amount that defines "lower income" is different in different parts of the country. For instance, while $25,000 per year and lower is a good barometer, keep in mind that in some areas $25,000 may be considered middle class.... No. 1 is renters ... Renters, by and large, make up the bulk of coin laundry users."

Source: "By the Numbers" by Bob Nieman, The Journal, September 2002

What Does it Cost to Buy a Coin Laundry?

"Coin laundries usually sell for between 1 and 1.5 times their annual gross sales. For example, a laundry with gross sales of $50,000 will probably sell for $50,000 to $75,000 depending on the profit, lease, location, equipment and other factors.

"Most sellers require a down payment of 1/3 to ½ of the asking price, and most provide seller-financing for the remaining balance. This eliminates the need for bank or outside financing."

Source: Coin Laundry Sales.com

Equipment Necessary

According to a survey conducted by the Coin Laundry Association, the average number of washers contained in the stores that responded was 37.7. The mix of equipment breaks down to 18.6 top loaders; 8.6 18-lb. front loaders; 4.5 25-lb. front loaders; five 35-lb. front loaders; and one 50-lb. front loader. Most dryers are 30 lb. And the rule seems to be that there should be one dryer for every two to three single-load washers. A washer may only get used four or five times a day, but the dryers may get used 15 to 20 times a day. There appears to be a trend among the manufacturers of dryers to make single-load machines. In this case, the store would probably need one dryer for every washer.

"The accepted standard of 'useful life' for commercial coin laundry equipment is as follows:

- Top-load Washers—(12 lbs. to 14 lbs.) 5 to 8 years
- Front-load Washers—(18 lbs. to 50 lbs.) 10 to 15 years
- Dryers—(30 lbs.–60 lbs.) 15 to 20 years
- Heating systems 10 to 15 years
- Coin Changers 10 to 15 years

"This schedule will vary upon usage, sales volume, and maintenance. 'Useful life' may differ for accounting or tax purposes."

Source: Coin Laundry Association

"Economic Analysis of a Store

In any laundromat operation, there are both fixed and variable costs. Fixed costs continue at a set rate each month, no matter what volume of business is conducted. Fixed Cost items are:

- Rent
- Payroll & Cleaning Costs
- Trash Collection
- Insurance
- Repairs
- Note Payments

"Variable costs are a direct function of the volume of business and consist of those utilities consumed such as water, sewer, gas or oil, and electricity. These utilities will generally run approximately 16 to 25 percent of the total volume of business, or gross. (The following example is figured at a conservative 20 percent.)

"A formula which has proved to be accurate in determining the weekly breakeven point (and thus provide a basis for calculation of profitability at various levels) is as follows:

"Multiply the sum of the monthly fixed costs by 0.28. This equals the weekly breakeven point. (This factor of .28 figures in the variable costs of utilities at 20 percent of gross and that there are 4.3 weeks per month.)

"An example of a 20-washer store would be as follows:

- Rent $1800 per month
- Cleaning $450
- Trash $100
- Insurance $200
- Repairs $100
- Fixed Costs (less note) = $2650

"To this figure, add the monthly payment for notes. Assuming that the total cost of the store was $180,000 and that $60,000 was the down payment and the balance was financed at 10.5 percent interest, the monthly note payment (covering interest and amortization) would be $2254 per month for 72 months.

"Therefore your total Fixed Monthly Cost would be:

- Rent, Cleaning, etc. $2650
- Note Payment $2254
- Total Fixed Costs = $4904
- Conversion Factor x .28
- Weekly Breakeven Point = $1373

"Almost without exception, the coin-op laundries which we have constructed during the last five years show a weekly gross of between $1800 to $4500. Assuming the lower end of this range as a conservative estimate we have:

- $2600 Weekly Gross Business
- Less—$1373 Breakeven Point
- $1227 Difference

"But because a portion of this difference must be allocated to pay the increased utility costs (above the breakeven point), only 80 percent of this difference is profit. In this example the profit is $982 per week or over $51,000 per year. This is a ROI of 85 percent—not too bad! In this, the store owner is making a handsome profit while building equity in the store at a rate of almost $27,000 per year.

"If you increase your business by an additional $200 a week, your profit is now almost $60,000 per year. For every dollar above the breakeven point, 80 percent is profit. This is a tremendous multiplier. Just a little more business can make a big difference!"

From: "Things You Should Know Before Investing in a Coin Laundry" prepared by Sunburst Sales.

Note:This is an excellent site prepared by a firm that sells coin-laundry equipment. It's well worth a visit to read the entire article. We like companies that provide valuable information and don't just try to sell their stuff. Sunburst Sales is one of them.

Store Inspection Checklist

Following are some suggestions about visiting a coin laundry and the things to look for on your visit. They are designed for those considering buying a specific store, but are also most appropriate for those considering brokering or valuing a laundry. These suggestions are excerpts from a Coin laundry Association publication, *Today's Coin Laundry*. The association has an excellent Web site and offers informative publications on the coin laundry business.

"The Visit

It's recommended to visit the store during one of the busier days of the week (Friday, Saturday, or Sunday), in order to get a feel for how the business operates during a high-volume period.

"Store Inspection Checklist

General Store Appearance: Take a good look at the store from the outside. Does this store give the appearance of being a properly managed, attractive, safe, and inviting coin laundry store?

"Above all, try to capture the "first impression" of the store. Would you consider doing your laundry there? Don't be disappointed by a few negative answers to your initial questions…many of these characteristics can be improved through remodeling.

"The floor: The appearance and condition of the floor is important to examine. Floors are expensive to replace, but having the right floor has everything to do with a bright appearance and customer safety.

"The Washers: Inspect the condition of the washers in the store. Do they look like they've been abused or neglected? How many have "out of order" signs?—one or two are acceptable, more than 10 percent out of commission indicates either poor management or a number of machines that are beyond repair. Also check for signs of vandalism, such as "pry" marks on coin vaults of the washers.

"Check the floor around the washer for signs of water puddles that may indicate equipment leaks. Water stains could indicate something minor like a loose hose connection, or a major maintenance problem—investigate further!

"The Dryers: You'll want to inspect the dryers as closely as you did the washing machines. Begin by making certain that the dryers look reasonably well-maintained from the outside...do they look run down?

"Some Points For the Cautious Buyer

You must understand what you are buying and you must be careful what you pay—very careful. Key to price is gross sales. In fact, it is fair to say that a 10 percent difference in gross sales can impact the overall value of a coin-laundry business by some 20 percent, and maybe considerably more; therefore, you must ask the right questions, and be able to assess the veracity of the answers. For just one example:

"Find out exactly what portion of gross sales comes from coin and what portion comes from service. Is the attendant inserting coins into machines in order to do service work? If so, you must make an adjustment in order to arrive at the correct gross. For example: if, on average, a $12.00 sale of service work takes $4.00 in coins to launder, the net sale for service is $8.00; therefore, if service work is $900 per week and total coin receipts are $3000, the gross is correctly calculated by subtracting $300 from $3900 = $3600 (i.e.; by the above example, 1/3 of drop-off sales is actually coin sales, so take 1/3 off total drop-off sales to avoid counting it twice.) Is all of the service work drop-off or is some of it being picked-up somewhere? Are there any institutional customers? If so, who are they and how secure are the accounts?

"Do your homework. Do not rely on 'trial' periods. Devise your own rough estimate of gross sales before entering contractual agreements and/or commencing a 'trial' period (which is customary in a Laundromat sale):

- Count each washing machine in the store and note the price per wash (e.g.,. three Wascomat W-244 (75 pounder) at $7.50 per wash; three Wascomat W-184 (50 pounder) at $5.00 per wash; 16 Wascomat W-124 (30 pounder) at $3.00 per wash; 14 Wascomate W-74 (18 pounder) at $1.75 per wash.

  Note: Price per wash is, of course, directly tied to overhead. As rent, utility and labor costs vary greatly across the U.S. and

Canada, prices in your area may differ significantly.

- Find the rough average price per wash and divide by the total number of washers. The result is the rough average price per wash.

- Find out approximately how much water per wash each type of machine in the store uses (ask to see the machine manual, or call the distributor.)

- Find the rough average water use per wash by taking the calculations used to find the average price per wash and substituting gallons of water per wash for the various prices.

- Calculate the estimated revenue per gallon of water used

- Review the water bills and calculate the number of gallons per month the operation uses (one cubic foot of water = 7.48 gallons.)

- Multiply the monthly water usage in gallons by the revenue per gallon. Unless service is being done in non-coin machines, the resulting rough estimate of washing machine sales should be about two-thirds of total coin sales per month.

- Multiply the washing machine revenue by 150 percent to get the estimated total coin sales per month.

- Divide the estimated total coin sales per month by 4.3 to get a rough estimate of total coin sales per week.

"I refer to 'rough' average because the use pattern of laundry machines is not necessarily consistent with the store layout. If, upon your visits to the store you identify equipment that is rarely (or very frequently) used, it is recommended that you adjust your calculations accordingly. In fact, all of the above calculations should be adjusted to tailor them to the operation you are analyzing. For example: my calculation assumes a ratio of washer revenue to dryer revenue of 2:1. My experience has proved that to be a fair approximation, but the ratio can vary. Ask questions and figure things out. There is no substitute for diligent analysis."

From: An excellent article by Gary Ruff, an industry consultant who is also an attorney

Gary Ruff can be reached via his informative Web site: www.laundromatadvisor.com or at (212) 696-8502 or (631) 389-2800. He maintains two offices; if you need advice or legal services in the coin laundry business—he knows his stuff.

Following is some basic pricing information from BIZCOMPS. For a study based on your area of the country, contact BIZCOMPS at: www.bizcomps.com.

BIZCOMPS data ranges from 90 percent, on average, of annual sales, and 2.8 SDE in the western states, to 87 percent, on average, of annual sales, and 2.1 SDE in the eastern states, to 72 percent in the central states and 2.1 SDE

Editors Note: We should mention again that the Web site for the Coin Laundry Association is full of useful information. It offers lots of publications and studies on the industry, including a manual for those considering going into the business. It would also be a very useful tool for the business broker professional who wants to handle this type of business. The Web site is: www.coinlaundry.org

Collection Agencies

7,326	SIC: 7322-01	NAIC: 561440

Rule of Thumb:

- For agencies with revenues of $1 million +: 75 percent to 125 percent of annual revenues
- 6 times recasted EBIDTA
- 100 percent of annual revenues

Pricing Tips

"Collection agencies are being valued on a multiple of adjusted EBITDA, with the multiples ranging typically between four and eight times, depending on the amount of current annual revenues, historical and future growth, client diversification, strength of management team and company's area of specialization."

"Collection agencies typically sell based on four to six times EBITDA. The size of the company is the greatest determinant of how large the multiple is."

"Debt collection agencies have contracts with clients that are usually only for 30 days or less. In addition, client concentration is a major force as well."

"Collection Agencies are typically priced on a recast EBITDA income stream which includes earnings before interest, taxes, depreciation and amortization and should add shareholders' salaries, perks and non-recurring expenses and then subtract a replacement salary for the shareholders. The valuation multiple typically ranges between 4 and 6 times EBITDA. The primary determinant of the multiple is the size of the company."

Industry Experts' Ratings:

Amount of Competition (1 = Lot of: 4 = Not much) 1.6
Amount of Risk (1 = Very: 4 = Not much) 1.2
Historical Profit Trend (1 = Down: 4 = Up) 2.6
Location & Facilities (1 = Poor: 4 = Excellent) 2.2
Marketability (1 = Low: 4 = High) 2.0
Industry Trend (1 = Declining: 4 = Growing) 2.6
Ease of Replication (1 = Easy: 4 = Difficult) 2.4

Benchmarks

"Sales per collector in successful collection agencies typically exceed 3–4X the collector's compensation on a monthly basis."

"50% of revenues are employee cost."

"The average collection agency employed 19 collectors and 10 other full-time staff members in 2003."

Source: ACA International's 2004 Benchmarking/Cost of Operations Survey

"The average number of phone calls a typical collector attempts per hour is 20. A typical collector will reach six debtors in an hour with at least two promises."

Source: ACA International's 2004 Benchmarking/Cost of Operations Survey

"Employee compensation accounts for nearly half (46.68 percent) of the total expenses at the average collection agency."

Source: ACA International's 2004 Benchmarking/Cost of Operations Survey

"The average annual base salary for a collector is $22,487, with an average commission rate of 12 percent—totaling $31,812."

Source: ACA International's 2002 Compensation & Collection Agency Operations Study

Expenses as a percentage of annual sales:	
Payroll/Labor	50–60 %
Occupancy Cost	05–10% (Varies by area)
Profit (estimated pre-tax)	20%

General Information

"The median profit margin for commercial collection agencies in the year 2000 from collection operation was about 9 percent. Looking back to 1995 it was 12 percent, a decline of about 25 percent from 1995 to 2000 … For example, in 1998, accounts placed with members of Commercial Collection Agency Association (CCAA) totaled approximately $5.5 billion. In 2000, accounts totaled about $8.6 billion. This year they are on a pace to perhaps exceed $10 billion."

From: An article by Emil Hartleb, Commercial Collection Agency Association

"What is a professional debt collection service? Third-party collection services collect on past-due accounts referred to them by various credit grantor-credit issuers, banks, care dealers, retail stores, healthcare facilities, funeral homes – any business that extends or offers payment installment plans. Since third-party collection services use specialized phone systems and computers and software specifically for the collection industry, they are effective…."

"Most accounts are referred for collection because they have gone unpaid for an average of eight months and the creditor has not received communication from the consumer …the amount of new business placed for collection in 1999 was $59,766,196 and the average collection rate was 10.8 percent."

Source: The American Collectors Association

Advantages of this Business

- "There will always be a need for companies that can help other businesses to collect their delinquent debts. This industry is highly fragmented, so there are substantial opportunities to grow both organically and inorganically."
- "Cashflow business and trends are positive."
- "Growing, highly profitable, consistent profit margins, low capital intensive as compared to other businesses."

Disadvantages of this Business

- "There are stringent legal requirements set forth by the Federal Trade Commission, as well as various state governments. You need to understand these requirements and make sure that you comply with all of them to the best of your ability, or you will be penalized severely."
- "High employee turnover"
- "Legal and compliance requirements, high rates of collector turnover and non-recurring client contracts."

Industry Trend

"More and more collection agencies are continuing to specialize in either one or multiple industries, or in collecting a specific stage of delinquent paper."

"The Bureau of Labor Statistics estimates employment in the collection industry will increase 21 to 35 percent between 2002 and 2012."

"Consumers have borrowed a bundle in recent years—to the tune of over $2 trillion in credit card and auto debt, according to the Federal Reserve. Add mortgages, and the figure jumps to nearly $10 trillion. All in all, the average U.S. household is deeper in the hole than it was four years ago, carrying debt of about $9,200, up from $7,200.

"Credit card charge-offs, or the bad debt that banks and others write off the books, were expected to hit a record $65 billion in 2004, up from $57.3 billion in 2003, according to the Nilson Report, a consumer credit newsletter, Nilson forecasts the market for such debts will increase to $2.8 trillion by 2010."

Source: *Business Week*, January 10, 2005

A Basic Limitation of Rules of Thumb

"In general, rules of thumb should not be used as the only valuation method. However, they are useful in evaluating the reasonableness of the values indicated by other methods. Limitations on rule of thumb methods include inability to identify enough comparable sales and specific factors (such as the fact that a sale was a distress sale) affecting sales of comparable businesses. In other words, the basic limitation of rules of thumb is that they are intended to apply to 'typical' businesses. However, in actual transactions, there is no such thing as a 'typical' business as far as the buyer and seller are concerned."

From: *Guide to Buying and Selling Small Businesses* published by Practitioners Publishing Company

Resources
American Collectors Association
www.collector.com

The Kaulkin Report—It provides a detailed review of the industry as well as market trends.
www.kaulkin.com

International Association of Commercial Collectors
www.commercialcollector.com

Association of Credit and Collection Professionals
www.ccascollect.com

www.collectionindustry.com—A site prepared by a major collection agency brokerage firm, containing a lot of valuable information.

Comic Book Stores

2,170	SIC: 5942-05	

Rule of Thumb:

- 12 percent of annual sales plus inventory

General Information
"According to Diamond Comic Distributors, Marvel's market share was 35.54 percent in 2004, while DC's was 30.63. The rest of the market was split among more than 15 other publishers.

"The comic book industry generates $400 million to $500 million in book sales each year, down from nearly a billion dollars at its peak in the early 1990s."

Source: *The New York Times*, Monday, May 9, 2005

Community Newspapers *(See Newspapers)*

Computer Consulting

Resources
Independent Computer Consultants Association
www.icca.org

Franchise

Computer Pro

Rule of Thumb:

- 33 percent of annual sales plus inventory

Computer Programming Services (custom)

Pricing Tips
"Traditional methods use some multiple of revenues for valuation; however, this is fraught with problems. Growth in revenues is a key aspect, prized in establishing higher value. Earnings are not unimportant, although high-growth companies may be more attractive even without earnings. Look for stability or managed growth in operations.

"Because software companies must be nimble to respond to market actions, and are vulnerable to loss of key persons, control premiums (and lack of control discounts) and discounts for illiquidity are typically enhanced in this industry."

Industry Experts' Ratings:

Marketability (1 = low; 4 = high) 3.2
Industry Trend (1 = declining; 4 = growing) 2.8
Ease of Replication (1 = easy; 4 = difficult) 1.6

Computer Sales

Rule of Thumb:

- 30 percent of annual sales plus inventory

Computer Services

Rule of Thumb:

- 55 percent of annual sales, plus fixtures, equipment & inventory

Concrete Bulk Plants

Rule of Thumb:

- 33 1/3 percent of SDE; plus fixtures, equipment & inventory

Franchise

Conroy's Flowers

71 units

Rule of Thumb:

- 55 to 60 percent of annual sales plus inventory

Construction (In General)

Rule of Thumb:

- 2.2 times SDE
- 1.8 times EBIT
- 2 times EBITDA

-cont'd-

Construction (In General) *(cont'd)*

- 25 percent of annual sales

Note: "Some construction firms own significant equipment and some are run from storefronts, so rules of thumb are misleading. The business history is very important, as is the value of signed contracts to be completed, and understanding how a company bills its work in progress. Accounts receivable can average over 45 days, increasing the working capital required and decreasing the business value. Once again rules of thumb are not very useful."

Pricing Tips

"Good supply of buyers doing over a million in EBIT with 20 percent or better profit margins. Smaller ones fairly difficult and best practice is to merge with larger company that doesn't have a presence in that area. Important for owner to stay after transaction. Individual to individual transactions are the most difficult."

"Stock vs. assets, employment agreements."

"Construction companies are relatively hard to sell, with the exception of ones that have been established many years and enjoy an established name and reputation. These should be [priced at] depreciated value of fixtures and equipment and rolling stock, plus 10 percent of the sale price for goodwill, plus 25 percent of the part of the business period which has already been contracted for."

Industry Experts' Ratings:

Amount of Competition (1 = Lot of: 4 = Not much)	2.0
Amount of Risk (1 = Very: 4 = Not much)	2.0
Historical Profit Trend (1 = Down: 4 = Up)	2.0
Location & Facilities (1 = Poor: 4 = Excellent)	2.0
Marketability (1 = Low: 4 = High)	1.2
Industry Trend (1 = Declining: 4 = Growing)	2.0
Ease of Replication (1 = Easy: 4 = Difficult)	2.8

"Because of the many categories in construction, I generally applied the average value. Construction companies are difficult to sell and relatively difficult to replicate because of capital requirements."

Benchmarks

Expenses as a percentage of annual sales:	
Cost of goods sold..	70%
Payroll/Labor Costs	15%
Occupancy Cost	5 %
Profit (estimated)	10 %

Advantages of this Business

- "Construction companies can be very profitable and have made a lot of money for a lot of people."

Disadvantages of this Business

- "High risk and high working-capital requirements. Many construction companies fail from lack of capital even though they are profitable."

Seller Financing

- "5 to7 years, however SBA loans up to 10 years can be obtained"

Construction—Heating & AC *(See also Heating Contractors)*

Rule of Thumb:

- 20 to 25 percent of annual revenues

Consumer Products & Services

Rule of Thumb:

- 4 to 6 times EBIT
- 50 to 100 percent of sales plus inventory

Contract Manufacturing *(See also Machine Shop)*

2,700	SIC: 3999-06	

Rule of Thumb:

- 3 to 4 times EBITD plus, and reasonable owner's compensation
- 2 to 4 times SDE plus inventory

General Information

Questions to ask seller: "Customer concentration and who has technical skill to operate."

"High client concentration = lower multiple. Prototype production more profitable than short/medium run work = higher multiple."

"Be careful of client concentration, especially if capital equipment is custom tailored to 'special' clients."

"Look for rate of growth over last several years, not just one year. Look for consistency or improvement. What is outlook for industry—for the company? Why does seller want to sell and will seller be willing to keep a piece of the business?"

Benchmarks

Expenses as a Percentage of Annual Sales:	
Cost of Goods Sold	45%
Payroll/Labor Costs	20%
Occupancy Cost	15%
Profit (estimated) EBITDA	20%

Industry Trend

"Industry trend has been downward as ripple effect of OEM manufacturers continues. Short-term future flat."

"It could not get any worse."

An introduction to Convenience Stores

There are different types of convenience stores. A mini-mart may be priced differently than a convenience store with gas. Obviously, the more profit centers there are, the higher the price. However, some buyers may be more interested in a plain convenience store than one with gas and/or alcohol. Keep in mind, also, a store may have higher sales and profits because it is open 24 hours, but in the eyes of a buyer it may lose value due to the long hours. Here is a brief description of the different types:

- Convenience store without gas or beer
- Convenience store with just beer (possibly wine also)
- Convenience store with full liquor license
- Convenience store with gas—These operations are more convenience stores than gas stations such as a 7-Eleven or Circle K.
- Gas station with convenience store (mini-marts)—These operations are more of a gas station than convenience store such as Mobil, Shell and Exxon gas stations that have a convenience store. In many cases the garages and station itself have been retrofitted to be a convenience store. These operations may include a car wash.
- Convenience stores with food franchises—Fairly new concept, integrating a fast food franchise within a convenience store. Dunkin' Donuts and Taco Bell are good examples of this concept.

Note: We realize that the different "types" of convenience stores can cause confusion. Is it a convenience store with gas or a gas station with a convenience store? We hope that the information in this section will help; but, when in doubt, we think the overall appearance of the business will really define what type it is. In pricing the convenience store, it helps to make the determination whether it is a gas station that has added a few convenience items. If so, refer to Service Stations.

It is also difficult today to distinguish between convenience stores with gas and gas stations with mini-marts or convenience stores. Since the sale of gasoline is so important to the profitability, and therefore the price of the business, we strongly suggest that you review the section on Gas Stations to learn more about this multi-product business.

Convenience Stores—In General

(See also Convenience Stores with Gas, Gas Stations/Mini-Marts & Grocery Stores)

105,476	SIC: 5411-03	NAIC: 445120

Rule of Thumb:

- 5 times EBITDA less cosmetic renovation to receive a national brand of fuel; inventory is separate and above
- 2 to 3 times EBITDA plus inventory—C-store only
- 6 to 8 times EBITDA plus inventory—real estate + business
- 15 to 30% of annual sales plus inventory
- 2 to 2.5 times SDE plus inventory

Pricing Tips

One industry expert reported: "Should strive for an overall 'weighted' inside gross profit margin of 30 percent. Included in this margin, you should attempt to get a margin between 50 percent and 60 percent for deli sales. Outside gasoline/fuel sales margins will vary all over the place depending on competition. You're in the ballpark, generally, if you get a bottom line profit of between 6.5 percent and 7.0 percent of total sales after taxes, depreciation and amortization."

"Interstate location more desirable"

"(1) Gas included, (2) Location, (3) Owner works, (4) Beer and wine license, (5) Franchise or independent"

"Location and brand of gasoline very important"

"(1) Age and condition of petroleum equipment is important, (2) Environmental issues must be dealt with prior to closing. Phase I and II reports required."

"58% of C-stores are under single-store ownership while 13% are operated by chains with more than 50 units."

Source: C Store News

"An up-to-date current property appraisal is helpful. Also, there is software available for measuring the potential value and potential revenue/gallonages of a new-build location, or for measuring the

Top 10 C-Store Companies arranged by # of Franchised/ Licensed Units

Name of Company	Total Stores	# Franchised/ Licensed	Store Names
Shell Oil	5,937	5,559	Shell, Texaco
7-Eleven	5,717	2,048	7-Eleven
BP North America	4,904	3,621	BP Express, Connect, Amoco Food Shop, am/pm
Exxon Mobil Corp.	4,313	3,412	Mobil Mart, On the Run, Tiger Mart,Tigermarket
ChevronTexaco	2,693	2,171	Chevron, Texaco Extra Mile
ConocoPhillips	1,350	968	Kicks 66, 76, Coastal, Conoco, Breakplace Speedway
SuperAmerica	2,541	830	SuperAmerica, Marathon, Bonded, United, Gastown
CHS	810	810	CENEX, Ampride
Sunoco	1,484	807	APlus

investment value of an existing location based on the gallonage, inside sales, quick food sales, and car wash sales."

"Usually valued at 3 to 4 times the monthly gross depending upon age of the structure, a new versus mature business, location, etc. This price would not include the real estate or inventory, but would include the fixtures and equipment at market value. The value of the food inventory for a super market is about $12 per sq. ft."

"The buyers/jobbers and lenders all accept the 5 times EBITDA."

"Beer and wine license a plus; good deli counter a plus; 3,000+ sq. ft; ample parking; easy in-out; extra storage; good corner location, ample inventory."

"High sales volume with profit important; need loss leaders especially milk and bread, good personnel, customer service important; open early morning; clean facility."

Industry Experts' Ratings:

Amount of Competition (1 = Lot of: 4 = Not much) 1.0
Amount of Risk (1 = Very: 4 = Not much) 1.0
Historical Profit Trend (1 = Down: 4 = Up) 2.0
Location & Facilities (1 = Poor: 4 = Excellent)......................... 3.2
Marketability (1 = Low: 4 = High).. 2.0
Industry Trend (1 = Declining: 4 = Growing) 3.3
Ease of Replication (1 = Easy: 4 = Difficult) 2.0

"C-Stores depend more on inside sales now because of high gas prices."

Benchmarks

"Should strive for average 30 per cent 'weighted' inside margin on merchandise sales."

Expenses expressed as a percentage of annual sales:

Cost of Goods .... 70% or less—Good Store
Payroll/Labor Costs.......... 20 –% +/- (Owner operator will lower)
Occupancy Cost .... 7%–10% +/- (Rent or Mortgage Payment)
Profit (estimated) 3%–5%
(Gasoline Profit Should Cover Rent/Mortgage +)

"Selected Expense Profile (as a percent of gross profit)

	2001	2002	2003
Labor*	38.6%	42.1%	38.5%
Depreciation/Amortization	9.8%	9.1%	9.9%
Utilities	5.2%	5.3%	5.7%
Credit/Debit Fees	5.0%	4.8%	5.8%
Insurance	0.4%	0.9%	——
Occupancy	6.8%	7.1%	9.1%
Interest	2.85%	3.0%	——
General & Administration	14.3%	12.5%	——
Repairs/Maintenance	4.0%	4.4%	4.3%

*Labor includes wages, payroll taxes, workers' compensation, health insurance and other benefits. A line item followed by —— signifies that it was not supplied for 2003."

Source: National Association of Convenience Stores (NACS)

"Top Ten In-Store Product Categories (As a percentage of in-store sales)

	2004
Cigarettes	34.7%
Packaged Beverages (non-alcohol)	12.2%
Foodservice	11.9%
Beer (1)	11.9%
Other Tobacco	3.5%
Candy	3.4%
Salty Snacks	3.3%
Fluid Milk	2.5%
General Merchandise	2.0%
Edible Grocery	1.9%

Source: news@nacsonline.com, April 12, 2005

"C-stores annual sales $767,000; food service annual sales $115,000"

"High volume, easier to sell. Small stores under $25,000 month, very hard to sell."

"Secondary Income (About 1.7% of Total Sales; $250,000 = $4,250 and at

$150,000=$2,550)

- Rebates & Allowances
- Product Placement Fees
- Special Promotions
- Pay Phones
- Car Vacuums/Air/Water
- ATMs
- Money Orders
- Lottery
- Prepaid Cards"

Source: "How to Evaluate a Listing or Sale in the C-Store Industry," a Presentation by Jim Town, Business Evaluation & Appraisals, Inc.

"Average store size (new construction—2002): 3,291 Sq. Ft. (1.2 acres) Average 'existing' older store: 2,490 Sq Ft."

Source: National Association of Convenience Stores (NACS)

General Information

<u>Questions to ask seller</u>: "Location, location, location; traffic count and number of rooftops dictate the best locations, along with traffic patterns, red lights, curb cut access, etc. Age and condition of petroleum and other equipment are important; environmental issues must be dealt with prior to closing. Phase I and II reports are almost always required for financing and property transfer. What is the mixture of sales? How do your sales break down concerning gas, merchandise/cigarettes, beer, grill, deli? Have all of your EPA requirements been completed? How many robberies have you had since you bought the store? Do you have key people? Who supplies your gasoline? Who owns the gasoline equipment? Who is your wholesaler that supplies the majority of your groceries? Are there any convenience stores being built within two miles of the store?"

"Indian-American C-Store Owners

It made sense, he said. U.S. census numbers quoted on Shaw's Web site say that there are 132,000 convenience stores in the country. Of those, Shaw said, roughly 80,000 are owned by Indian immigrants. And about 60,000 of those Indian-American store owners, he said, come from the same state in India: Gujarat."

Source: Convenience Store News, July 16, 2005

"Looking at a C-Store:

- Look at the four (4) primary profit centers in a convenience store, including typical sales, cost, margins, and cash flows;
- Consider the impact of real-estate ownership versus leasehold;
- Review the various petroleum products supply agreements to determine normal parameters for valuation;
- Calculate with accurate books and records a possible market value that can be financed; and
- Review crucial 'reality checks' that may help you determine whether or not to list a particular store for sale."

Source: "How to Evaluate a Listing or Sale in the C-Store Industry," a presentation by Jim Town

"Petroleum Supply Agreement:

- How long does it have remaining?
- Are there any financial strings such as loans, unamortized rebranding costs, volume rebates, buyout penalties?
- Is the brand competitive in the trade area, or should rebranding be considered?
- Are the financial terms competitive, can they be renegotiated to take advance of current market practices? Sometimes sales volumes have increased that would qualify for better competitive allowances, prepayments, etc. not being offered by the supplier to the current operator.
- For sites with petroleum sales greater than 1,000,000 gallons per year, or about 83,000GPM, there are some lucrative arrangements if a supplier is 'buying' market share ... timing is important.
- Don't take the supply agreement as an administrative function ... it's a very important part of the sale."

Source: "How to Evaluate a Listing or Sale in the C-Store Industry," a presentation by Jim Town, Business Evaluation & Appraisals, Inc

"Check store on their gross/traffic count; compare to average hours that generate profit, not 1 a.m. to 5 a.m., most stores do not generate enough business at this time."

"Demand for this type of business has in general declined in the last two years, mainly due to the hours of operation the owner needs to put in for an average salary of $50K to $60K annually."

"Small volume, marginal stores are nearly impossible to sell in this bad-margin market. "

"With all due respect, rule of thumb pricing for a gas/convenience store can be extremely misleading. Need to know gasoline supply agreements & margin that the operator is working on.... High volume, good margins.... The most important factor to determine justification of the seller's asking price is the profitability of the business. A convenience store working on a high margin on inside sales and having high monthly sales will sell for a higher price than a high-volume store working on a low margin. A convenience store operating at 30 percent + gross profit & monthly sales over $50K is very attractive to a buyer & should sell for a higher price."

"Korean Approach: Annual Gross Profit divided by 12 months x 4 plus inventory."

Advantages of this Business

- "Cash business, high gross profit"
- "High traffic and cash sales"
- "Easy operation, customer demand if good location"
- "This primarily is a cash business, which means you turn your inventory costs into cash very rapidly with minimum accounts receivable collection problems and bad debt."

Disadvantages of this Business

- "High employee turnover. High investment versus return on investment."
- "Hard to find good employees—and safety"
- "Long, long hours, some 24-hour locations. Employee theft can be a problem without good inventory controls in place."
- "Health issues, high rent costs, inventory control"

Industry Trend

"Convenience Stores Ripe for Mergers

The North American convenience-store industry, dominated by mom-and-pop operators, is ripe for consolidation, a trend that would favor the large publicly traded store operators, analysts at Merrill Lynch say.

"More fast food franchising in stores

'With significant scale advantages, economics favor large chain operators in the c-store industry,' the analysts said in a report released Tuesday. 'With a still high degree of fragmentation, the publicly traded c-stores stand to be beneficiaries of the inevitable consolidation we foresee.'"

Source: Convenience Store News, July 16, 2005

"Cigarette sales, which are by far the largest in-store sales category (34.5 percent of all in-store sales), increased 1.8 percent to $400 billion ... to $304,250 per store."

Source: National Association of Convenience Stores (NACS)

"I believe that there will be an increase in all sales, especially gasoline. I expect an increase in merchandise sales of 3 to 6% and gasoline products 5 to 8%. I feel the gas price to the consumer is so unstable that everyone down the profit line will take advantage and increase their profit margins. The general public that shops convenience stores are only gasoline-price sensitive and will pay the higher price for convenience. Stores must focus on fast foods to increase sales in this area to increase overall gross profit. The average gross profit is 28% to 32%. The focus should be 33% to 38%. With average gasoline profit only 5% to 10%, the focus must be on inside sales."

"Trend is towards the hypermarkets in the more populated areas, while the smaller stores can do well in less populated niche markets where the big boys do not have much interest. The big box stores and supermarkets are also entering the industry as a one stop location, and often use fuel as a loss leader."

"Trend is up"

Seller Financing

- "5 years all due and payable with 15 year amortization"
- "5 to 7 years"

"A convenience store in Japan gets global, local and personal

"The convenience store is a model of Japan in miniature: the triumph of function over fuss and of ease over embarrassment. Just as you can buy whiskey, eggs, pornography and even (it is said) women's underwear in vending machines, so you can all but live in convenience stores. I pay my phone bills and send my packages through the local branch of the national Lawson chain (named after the defunct American Lawson); I buy my bus cards there and tickets for Neil Young concerts. I make the convenience store my de facto office, lingering by the photocopier for hours on end and then faxing an article, say, to New York. Yet the first law of Japan, even in Lawson, is that nothing is what it seems, and that you can find all the cultures of the world here, made Japanese and strange. Here, in the four thin aisles of my local store, are the McVitie's digestives of my youth—turned into bite-size afterthoughts. Here are Milky Bar chocolates, converted into bullet-size pellets. Here are Mentos in shades of lime and grape, cans of "Strawberry Milk Tea" and the Smarties I used to collect as a boy, refashioned as "Marble Chocolate." Were Marcel Proust to come to Lawson, he would find his madeleines daily but made smaller, sweeter and mnemonically new."

Source: "Our Lady of Lawson" by Pico Iyer, *The Sunday New York Times*, 2005

Resources

National Association of Convenience Stores
www.cstorecentral.com

www.nacsonline.com
This is an excellent site—lots of valuable information.

Convenience Industry News—online magazine
www.convenienceindustrynews.com

CS News Online
www.csnews.com

Association of Convenience Store Managers
www.c-storemanagers.com

Convenience Stores—No Beer/Gas

(See Convenience Stores)

Rule of Thumb:

- 10 percent of annual sales plus inventory
- 4 to 6 times SDE

Convenience Stores with Gas

(See also Convenience Stores & Gas Stations w/C-Stores/Mini-Marts)

Rule of Thumb:

- 22 percent of annual sales plus inventory
- 2.5 to 3.5 times SDE plus inventory
- "3.0 to 3.5 times EBITDA—including the real estate is a good rule of thumb for convenience stores with gas. 2.0 to 3.5 times EBITDA for leased sites. Age and condition of the petroleum equipment and environmental issues are important considerations in selling these businesses. A Phase I & II are required."

Convenience Store with Gas, e.g., Circle K, Citgo

Index (multiple)		SDE	Gals/Mo
1.0x	to	$50K+	50K
2.25x	to	$90K+	75K+
2.75x	to	$150K+	100K+

The above value multiples do not include inventory (at cost).

Influence Factors

"Factors that have a direct bearing of value in today are market. Store sales should be greater than $30K per month (do not include lottery sales) to be considered above average. What percentage is gross profit on average? The rent is a straight fee or a percentage of sales. Things to add into the value of this business: volume is greater than $40K per month; gross profit should be a minimum of 30 percent; appearance; part of a large gas station and/or car wash; long-term lease. Things to subtract in this business: volume is below $25K per month; gross profit is below 27 percent; major competition in the neighborhood; virtual free standing without a gas station or car wash.

"7-Eleven convenience stores without gas are primarily controlled by the parent company (51%), thus your profit picture is relatively lower than the businesses shown above and therefore your multiples will be lower as well."

Pricing Tips

Industry Experts' Ratings:

Amount of Competition (1 = Lot of: 4 = Not much) 1.0
Amount of Risk (1 = Very: 4 = Not much) 1.2
Historical Profit Trend (1 = Down: 4 = Up) 2.2
Location & Facilities (1 = Poor: 4 = Excellent) 2.5
Marketability (1 = Low: 4 = High) 2.6
Industry Trend (1 = Declining: 4 = Growing) 2.4
Ease of Replication (1 = Easy: 4 = Difficult) 2.2

"Very competitive industry today with the hyper markets, grocery stores and big box retailers all getting into the convenience store industry. Location is everything with traffic count, population, and highway access critical to success."

-cont'd-

Industry Experts' Ratings: ***(continued)***

"A larger location is better. A full liquor license is harder to obtain. Tobacco products have a high cost and low profit. Higher rent costs."

"A convenience store is not too difficult to open by itself, especially if it's without gasoline. Convenience stores come in all kinds of formats: corner stores, main street, highway exits, inside malls, inside airports, inside college campuses, etc. Location is very important to get the walk-in traffic."

"High profit margin with varied merchandise and lots of smaller profit centers: cell phones, phone cards, money orders, lottery, Western Union, bill payment centers, deli, ATM, copy center, etc."

Benchmarks

"A good store should do a minimum of $750,000 to $1,000,000 in yearly sales plus lottery, and be at least 3,000 sq. ft. It should have a good deli counter and liquor, and a large parking lot with easy in and out. A free-standing building is better with extra storage."

"$480 per sq. ft. approx."

Expenses expressed as a percentage of annual sales:

Cost of Goods	70% or less—Good Store
Payroll/Labor Costs	20-% +/- (Owner Operator will lower)
Occupancy Cost	7–10% +/- (Rent or Mortgage Payment)
Profit (estimated)	3–5%

"Factors that influence price and things to look for: Store sales should be greater than 30K per month to be considered a good business. When addressing the sales, do not add in the lottery sales. What percentage is the gross profit on average? The rent is a straight fee or a percentage of sales. Things to add into the value of this business: volume is greater than $40K per month, gross profit should be a minimum of 30 percent, appearance, part of a large gas station and/or car wash. Things to subtract in this business: volume is below $25K per month, gross profit is below 27 percent, competition in the neighborhood, part of a small gas station; e.g., Circle K or 7-Eleven, location, appearance."

Industry Trend
"Labor intensive, long hours, and there is competition"

General Information
"Location, Location, Location—very important."

Advantages of this Business
- "Mostly a cash business. Low-tech business with large labor pool to draw from. Convenience shopping will continue to be favored by the public."
- "Convenience shopping, many profit centers, repeat customers, credit card sales"
- "Easy Access"

Disadvantages of this Business
- "Competition—your store can be wiped out by a major player buying the better corner and putting up a superior store. Long hours, employee turnover, employee and customer theft, and insurance costs are disadvantages."
- "Relatively high real-estate investment for high-volume sites. Average to above average competition, especially in gasoline/fuel sales."
- "More competition, especially from large chains"
- "Competition from larger stores, long hours, high employee turnover"

Industry Trend
"Higher cost of doing business"

"Greater investment will be required. Lower volume convenience stores will continue to decline. Overall investment will increase. Average store size will increase."

Quick *Profile* — Convenience Stores

"It's all in the Numbers
"Total convenience store sales rose to $396.2 billion, an 18.2 percent

rise. However, that top-line growth is somewhat deceiving. Much of this gain came from increasing motor fuel pricing, and the number doesn't take into consideration the higher cost of goods and runaway operating expenses (particularly escalating credit-card fees.)

"Gasoline continues to be a challenging category for the industry, making up 70 percent of sales and only 35 percent of gross profit dollars. Inside the store is where retailers' opportunity lies—and, indeed, operators are making a greater effort. Savvy retailers are embracing new product introductions and changing pianograms more frequently to create customer awareness and interest, and working at the store level to address local market needs. They are renewing interest in foodservice programs, perhaps the biggest point of differentiation inside the store.

"A convenience store, on average, posted $3.0 million in sales in 2003, which includes $2.1 million in motor fuels sales."

Source: National Association of Convenience Stores (NACS)

"In-store sales per store increased by 6.6 percent and operators posted a hard-won 10.8 percent increase in gross profit dollars. The flip side to that good news is that pre-tax profit per store declined 3 percent despite sales and gross profit gains. Although the overall in-store gross margin percent still fell below the magic 30 percent mark, it did improve slightly in the past year."

Source: csnews.com, July 16, 2005

The National Association of Convenience Stores (NACS) rated the factors important in the decision customers make on whether to shop at a particular store. The top five were:

Convenient location	70.0%
Can also buy gasoline	42.1%
Easy in and out of lot	31.8%
Fast in and out of store	23.9%
Reasonable merchandise price for the convenience	14.2%

What is a Convenience Store?

"NACS defines convenience store as: '... a retail business with primary emphasis placed on providing the public a convenient location to quickly purchase from a wide array of consumable products (predominantly food or food and gasoline) and services.'

"There are six convenience store formats, as identified by a National Association Convenience Store (NACS) research report, as prepared by Gene Gerkle of Gerkle & Associates, Inc.

"Kiosk—This format is less than 800 square feet and is intended to provide some additional revenue beyond gasoline sales... This store sells only the fast-moving items found in traditional convenience stores (tobacco, beverages, snacks, and confectioneries)...Store sales may be only about ten percent of revenues in such locations...

"C-stores sold more than $4.8 billion in coffee in 2003. That works out to, on average, coffee sales of about $36,276 per store."

Source: NACS 2004 State of the Industry

"Mini Convenience Store—This store format, usually 800 to 1,200 square feet in size, is extremely popular with the oil companies, and the emphasis is on gasoline sales. However, in such locations, the owners view store sales as an important part of the revenue and margin picture....

"Limited Selection Convenience Store—These stores, which range from 1,500 to 2,200 square feet, are becoming more numerous. They are often affiliated with oil companies and are in the size range of a converted two-bay service station...They differ from the 'mini convenience store' in a broader product mix and grocery offering.... Also, simple foodservice...may be offered.

"Traditional Convenience Store—Most of the original convenience stores fall into this category. They are about 2,400 to 2,500 square feet in size and offer a product mix which includes dairy, bakery, snack foods, beverages, tobacco, grocery, health and beauty aids, confectionery, and perhaps prepared foods to go, fresh or frozen meats, gasoline, various services, and limited produce items.... Such operations are normally owned by convenience store chains, but oil companies have also built or acquired stores of this size.

"Expanded Convenience Store —Growth is occurring in the number of stores in the 2,800 to 3,600 square feet range. Such stores can accommodate ... additional grocery products or room for significant fast food operations and seating ... taking advantage of the niche which has developed as supermarkets increasingly move above the 40,000 square foot range.... A greater percentage are using the space to take advantage of the high profit margins in fast food....

"Hyper Convenience Store— These are very large stores (4,000 to 5,000 square feet) that usually offer an array of products and services arranged in departments. For example, such stores may offer variations such as a bakery, a sit-down restaurant area, or a pharmacy. Many of these locations do sell gasoline...In some locations, such stores are mini-truck stops, which obviously affects product mix and the customer base."

Advantages of this Business

- It is mostly cash sales, a relatively low-tech business and easy to operate. Repeat customers with high inventory turns and good margins. Many different profit centers such as gasoline, lottery, convenience items, tobacco and alcohol products (in many stores), etc.

Disadvantages of this Business

- Long hours, sales of tobacco and alcohol to minors, and employee turnover. Employee and customer theft can also be a problem. Environmental issues with gasoline sales. Business is susceptible to robberies. Due to alcohol and tobacco sales, coupled with the resulting liability, insurance can be costly. Also, there seems to be no letup in the building of new stores—very competitive business.

Additional Pricing Data

Following is some basic pricing information from BIZCOMPS. For a study based on your area of the country, contact BIZCOMPS at: www.bizcomps.com. (702) 454-0072.

Pricing ranged from 26 percent of annual sales and 2.2 SDE in the western edition, to 26 percent of annual sales and 1.7 SDE in the eastern states, to 23% of annual sales and 1.5 SDE in the central states.

Franchise

Cost Cutters Family Hair Care

676 + units	
Approximate Total Investment:	$100,000 to $300,000
Rule of Thumb:	
➢ 57 percent of annual sales plus inventory	

Resources

www.costcutters.com

Franchise

Cottman Transmission Systems

(See also Auto Transmissions)

415 units

Approximate Total Investment: $150,000 to $200,000

Rule of Thumb:

- 56 percent of annual sales plus inventory

Pricing Tips

See Pricing Tips under Aamco Transmissions/Auto Transmissions

Benchmarks

For the year ending September 30, 2003, Cottman reported in their franchise disclosure the following figures:

Average sales for the year were: ($489,050)	(100%)
Total Cost of Sales	43.2%
Gross Profit on Sales	56.8%
Total Selling Expenses	12.4%
Net Profit on Sales	44.4%
Total Overhead Expenses	24.3%
Net Profit	20.1%

Resources

www.cottman.com

Country/General Stores

Rule of Thumb:

- 20 percent of annual sales plus inventory

General Information

"'Village stores are very challenged and very fragile these days,' said Paul Bruhn, the executive director of the Preservation Trust of Vermont, who estimated that about a dozen country stores have gone out of business in the past three years. ... Bruhn said keeping country stores open is a quality-of-life issue. 'If you go to a place that has lost its village store, it's not much more than a suburban subdivision,' he said."

Source: "Bill Would Aid Country Stores," Boston Sunday Globe, May 15, 2005

Resources

"Valuing Country Businesses," Handbook of Business Valuation, West & Jones, 2nd Edition, published by John Wiley and Sons.

Coupon Books

Rule of Thumb:

- 2 to 4 times EBITDA

General Information

"Coupon books can be defined as direct mail coupon magazines and envelopes."

"Check finance regulations carefully for no-sell clauses or corporate office transfer change."

Seller Financing

- "Not usually seller financed. If financed, 2 to 3 years."

Courier Services

2,346	SIC: 4215-01	NAIC: 492110

Rule of Thumb:

- 70 percent of annual sales

Resources

Courier Service—magazine of the messenger, courier & expedited delivery industry
www.couriermagazine.com

Franchise

Coverall Cleaning Concepts (Commercial Cleaning)

8,000 + units	
Approximate Total Investment:	$6,000 to $32,200

Rule of Thumb:

- 2 to 3 times monthly volume
- Master/Area developer—sell for 3 to 5 times earnings plus some blue sky for size and potential of market (some cases).
- 4 times EBITDA

Pricing Tips

"Quinn (an Ohio franchisee) said he'd like to have between 60 and 80 local franchisees in a year. Local franchise costs range from $1,000 to $20,000, depending on how much business they can handle. Quinn would not specify how much his "master franchise" fees were to acquire the rights to the Dayton market. However, the company Web site said it costs between $100,000 and $185,000."

Source: *Dayton Business Journal*, April 9, 2005. www.bizjournals.com

"The four basic components of determining the value and price of a Master Franchise of Coverall include the collective principal amount of Franchisee Notes outstanding, the value of the exclusive rights to the population territory inclusive of the number of businesses with 5 or more employees, the value of the business structure (number of commercial accounts serviced and the number of franchisees) and the cash flow of the territory."

Industry Experts' Ratings:

Marketability (1 = low; 4 = high) 3.2
Industry Trend (1 = declining; 4 = growing) 3.2
Ease of Replication (1 = easy; 4 = difficult) 3.2

Benchmarks

"Pricing of its commercial cleaning contract @ $0.10–$0.14 per sq. ft. or $16–$17 per hour for services provided. Average size of Cleaning Package sold to franchisee is $3,000 per month for services to be provided.

"Account loss ratio of less than 2% is ideal as larger loss ratios contribute to the revolving back door effect. Each field service representative should procure an average of $3,000 per month in new accounts for the franchisor."

Expenses as a percentage of annual sales:	
Cost of Goods Sold	80%
Payroll/Labor Costs	04%
Occupancy Cost	01%
Profit (estimated)	10%

General Information

"A well-managed master franchisor can be a very solid and respected competitor in its marketplace. Compared to the predominant workforce employed by the independents, which consists of low-wage, less motivated employees who are paid a few dollars over minimum hourly wage, a franchisee invests a significant portion of his or her net worth in buying the right from the franchisor to provide cleaning services to a commercial customer."

Disadvantages of this Business

■"As in any business which ultimately depends upon the end service provider, a franchisor must depend on its franchisees to provide good service to the local accounts. Having to manage directly or indirectly many different franchisees who may have intelligence, language, focus and discipline challenges, does come at a mental stress price which requires both a dispassionate and understanding as well as an astute task master."

Resources

www.coverall.com

Franchise

Culligan International – Franchise/Dealership

700 + units

Approximate Total Investment: $104,500 to $695,000

Rule of Thumb:

- 80 to 120 percent of gross annual sales—dependent on several things: market size, current penetration rental base, water quality, etc.

General Information

Cost of goods, payroll/labor costs, occupancy costs and profit vary by profit center: residential, commercial, medical, bottled water—sales/rental.

Seller Financing

- "Frequently 7 to 10 years."

Resources

www.culligan.com

"What's around the curves

"'Ever since 8,000 Curves of Waco, Texas, became the fastest-growing franchise in the world, at least 20 other franchises have jumped into the 30-minute fitness circle,' wrote Julie Bennett in Franchise Times for August 2005. Such franchises are Slender Lady, 21-Minute Convenience Fitness, and Butterfly Life. However, it's difficult to compete with the front runner. In interviewing franchisees of the Curves 'wanna-bes' she received such comments as: 'she, too, closed down, after months of effort yielded only 35 members and she needed 300 to break even,' 'who's been open since February 2004, has 80 members, and needs 226 to make it go,' 'signed on 127 members in her first year and is breaking even,' and 'so far, they have 85 members and need 120 just to pay their monthly bills' The lady who signed on 127 members in her first year said, 'but you can't expect to unlock the store and watch it fill with women. You have to know your market and be active in your community.'"

Source: *Franchise Times*, August 2005.

If you do any work involving franchises you need to subscribe to Franchise Times. For information, visit www.franchisetimes.com

Franchise

Curves for Women (See also Fitness Centers)

8,750 units

Approximate Total Investment: $36,425 to $42,850

Rule of Thumb:

- 60 percent of annual sales
- 2 times SDE

Pricing Tips

Note that last year the percentage of annual sales was 35%; it has increased dramatically because of the popularity of the stores. Curves is growing rapidly and must be able to sustain its growth or sales volumes. When in doubt, use the multiple of SDE.

"1.5 to 2 times SDE. The number of monthly check drafts and club size and location are important value factors along with membership trends."

Industry Experts' Ratings:

Amount of Competition (1 = Lot of: 4 = Not much)	2.0
Amount of Risk (1 = Very: 4 = Not much)	3.2
Historical Profit Trend (1 = Down: 4 = Up)	2.4
Location & Facilities (1 = Poor: 4 = Excellent)	3.2
Marketability (1 = Low: 4 = High)	2.0
Industry Trend (1 = Declining: 4 = Growing)	2.8
Ease of Replication (1 = Easy: 4 = Difficult)	2.0

"Popularity has hit a new low in 2005. Curves franchises hit the 'wall.' Statewide town overlap has hurt many individual franchisees. Many locations were up for resale."

Benchmarks

"1.5 employees per $100K sales"

Expenses as a percentage of annual sales:	
Cost of goods sold	0%
Payroll/Labor Costs	15%
Occupancy Cost	8%
Profit (estimated)	30%

General Information

"Curves franchises are 100-percent independently owned and operated. With more than 8,500 locations and 4 million members worldwide, Curves is the world's largest fitness center franchise."

Advantages of this Business

- "Low overhead, good franchise training and equipment. Circuit training is still popular. Concept has been successful."

Disadvantages of this Business

- "Membership is dropping in 2005. Many franchises compete with nearby Curves in towns next door. Will they return to popularity in 2002-2004?"

Industry Trend

"Curves needs an injection of energy to rival the success of prior years. Lawsuit against company founder could bring Curves down like exercise fads before them."

Seller Financing

- "3 years"

Resources

www.curvesforwomen.com

Dairy Drive-Through

Rule of Thumb:

- 3 times monthly sales plus inventory

Franchise

Dairy Queen

5000 + units

Estimated Annual Sales per Unit: $446,000

Approximate Total Investment: $171,000 to $514,000

Rule of Thumb:

- Price = 1.1 to 1.2 times annual sales for stores w/real estate
- Price = .45 times sales for leased facility. Rent = variable item
- "Walk-up"— two windows with real estate—1.24 (+/-) times annual sales
- Without real estate —.5 (+/-) times annual sales
- Full Brazier— with real estate—1.15 (+/-) times annual sales
- Without real estate—.5 (+/-) annual sales."

Pricing Tips

"Dairy Queens: With Real Estate = 1.1X sales. IDQ leaning toward "Corporate" type ownership, moving away from "Ma & Pa" owners."

"Capitalization Requirements: Net worth (exclusive of home and personal property) of 50% of purchase price; liquid assets of 20% of sale price; additional liquid assets 33% of annual operating costs (90 days.)"

Industry Experts' Ratings:

Amount of Competition (1 = Lot of: 4 = Not much)	1.0
Amount of Risk (1 = Very: 4 = Not much)	2.0
Historical Profit Trend (1 = Down: 4 = Up)	3.2
Location & Facilities (1 = Poor: 4 = Excellent)	3.2
Marketability (1 = Low: 4 = High)	3.3
Industry Trend (1 = Declining: 4 = Growing)	3.2
Ease of Replication (1 = Easy: 4 = Difficult)	2.0

"Many players in this market"

Benchmarks

"Dairy Queen 'Grill & Chills' are doing pretty well. Very high 'entry' cost of 1.5 million +/-, which requires $2 million sales to be profitable."

Expenses as a percentage of annual sales:	
Cost of Goods Sold	31%
Payroll/Labor Costs	25%
Occupancy Cost	08%
Profit (estimated)	15%

General Information

<u>Questions to ask seller</u>: "Leased facility—rent important
Owned facility—loan & taxes important"

"Franchise fees— 4 percent of sales; Advertising fees—5 percent. Franchise cost— $35,000. Age of major pieces of equipment is important to value (soft-serve machines, grills, freezers, etc.). Employee training/supervision important and directly related to cost of goods in terms of portioning, waste, etc."

Dairy Queen is a Berkshire Hathaway Company. Dairy Queen also owns Orange Julius and Karmelkorn brand popcorn.

"The initial franchise fee for a DQ Grill & Chill restaurant is $35,000."

"Site Improvement: .... $190,000–$350,000
Construction: .... $400,000–$525,000
Equipment: .... $340,000–$450,000
Non-Recurring Costs: .... $100,000–$150,000"

"You are required to demonstrate a minimum net worth of $750,000. In addition, you must have liquid assets of $400,000, of which a minimum of $300,000 will be used in the project as equity. The minimum required liquid assets must be verified prior to completing the approval process."

"The initial franchise fee for a Dairy Queen/Orange Julius Treat Center store is $25,000."

"Leasehold improvements: .... $90,000–$175,000

Equipment: .... $115,000–$160,000
Non-Recurring Costs: .... $45,000–$65,000"

"You are required to demonstrate a minimum net worth of $200,000. In addition, you need liquid assets of $175,000, of which a minimum of $125,000 will be used in the project as equity. The minimum required liquid assets must be verified prior to completing the approval process."

Advantages of this Business

- "Clean business"

Disadvantages of this Business

- "Hours, problems with employees"

Industry Trend

"Sales & profits increasing 5–10%/year."

"Even as the chain, which has 3,400 DQ/Brazier units in North America and 5,700 worldwide, moves ahead with plans to grow its fast-casual DQ Grill & Chill concept, it wants consumers to know that its more traditional brazier outlets also boast a broad array of items.

"Dairy Queen has been steadily trying to reposition itself since 2001, when it launched DQ Grill & Chill, its fast-casual concept with a more upscale design and a larger kitchen than traditional Dairy queen units."

Source: *Nation's Restaurant*, January 17, 2005

Seller Financing

- "Rarely seller financed."
- "5 years with balloon payment."
- "SBA financing—17 to 18 years with real estate; 7 to 10 years without real estate."

Resources

www.dairyqueen.com

"DQ still has full Braziers, limited Braziers, and now the Grill & Chill. They are trying to make any new franchises into Grill & Chills, but existing stores have the option of becoming a Grill & Chill or remaining a full Brazier. The limited Braziers do not serve any cooked/fried food, only hot dogs, chips, DQ, etc."

Day Care Centers/Adult *(See Assisted Living, Nursing Home)*

3,300	SIC: 8322-10	NAIC: 624120

Day Care Centers/Children

76,716	SIC: 8351-01	NAIC: 624410

Rule of Thumb:

- 3 times SDE
- 2.5–3 times EBIT
- 2 times EBITDA
- 45 percent of gross sales
- Depending on the size of the facility (licensed capacity), location, and demographics of the area, the rule of thumb is:

Center Size	
<40	1 to times SDE
40 to 85	2 to 3 times (depending on expansion possibilities) SDE
100+	3 to 4 times SDE

- "Pricing ranges from 1.5 to 4 times EBITDA depending upon the size (licensed) of the facility. The larger the facility, generally the higher the multiple."
- Two times cash flow for smaller centers (licensed for under 75) Up to four times cash flow for larger centers (licensed for 100 +)

Pricing Tips

"Multiples of EBITDA vary depending upon the sixe of the operation and depth of management. The larger the operation, the higher the multiple. Smaller operations will sell for over 2 times EBITDA, while larger operations with competent management will sell for in the 3 to 4 times EBITDA range. Reconstructed EBITDA should include adjustments to FMV for arms length transactions (salaries, rent, etc.)."

Industry Experts' Ratings:

Amount of Competition (1 = Lot of: 4 = Not much) 1.5
Amount of Risk (1 = Very: 4 = Not much) 2.6
Historical Profit Trend (1 = Down: 4 = Up) 2.4
Location & Facilities (1 = Poor: 4 = Excellent)......................... 2.8
Marketability (1 = Low: 4 = High)... 3.0
Industry Trend (1 = Declining: 4 = Growing) 3.2
Ease of Replication (1 = Easy: 4 = Difficult)............................ 2.0

"Business very popular at this time; full centers generate lots of profit."

"Size and demographics will have a positive impact on the ratings."

"Other than 'occupancy costs' all other expenses are pretty proportional to enrollment or gross revenues and are easily managed as such. If rent can be tied to enrollment, then risk is greatly reduced (example: 10% of gross receipts for rent)."

"$1,000 to $2,500 per licensed child capacity depending on the success of current business"

"Attractors are: good location, appealing type of building, low or fixed rent , high current enrollment, high historic enrollment, low staff turnover rate, very good reputation, many years in service, several program types. Detractors are pretty much the opposite."

"If no one is watching the children, it doesn't matter how many different jobs are created because people will not be able to work."

Source:Jen Wohl , National Economic Development and Law Center

"Number of children, location and competition. Track record helpful"

"Real estate can be the largest value in a day-care transaction. Rent should be adjusted to reflect Fair Market Value (FMV) rent based on a) comparable information available or, b) a percentage of the real estate appraisal value and, c) cross-checked by making sure, if financed, that the rent will cover the debt services (and a return on the down payment)."

"Are children state-subsidized?"

"Popping up all over the state. New locations opening rapidly on excellent and visible locations."

"Industry is very competitive and regulated in California. Almost impossible to move existing business to alternate location if facility lease is not renewable. License to operate not transferable to buyers."

Benchmarks

"EBITDA should range from $1,000 to $2,000 per licensed child, providing owner operates a compliant business. Salaries below 40 percent of sales should be investigated to ascertain the operation is [being] legally operated. Salaries above 45 percent of sales could indicate (a) inefficiency in the physical facility layout, (b) too many employees, or (c) lots of long-term employees (some turnover of staff is expected in the industry, and can actually help the earnings of the business)."

"Enrollment or licensing per square foot is regulated by each state's Department of Welfare or Child/Family Services. Check with the state for regulations in your state."

"Food Costs	2.2% of Gross
Supplies & Materials	6.5% of Gross
Insurance	1.5% of Gross"

"Owner/Operators should expect to net approximately $1,000 per licensed child capacity per year if operating at 90 percent capacity."

"Number of children key to sucess."

Expenses as a percentage of annual sales:	
Cost of Goods Sold	20%
Payroll/Labor Costs	40–45%
Occupancy Cost	20%
Profit (estimated)	20%
"Sales per employee	$23,988"

"Number of children and their ages. Ratio of students to teachers."

Selected Day Care Franchises (1)

School & # Units	Approximate Total Investment (2)	Estimated Annual Sales
Computer Tots (95)	$42,000–$48,000	$91,000 (3)
Goddard School (159)	$425,000	$877,610 (4)
Huntington Learning Center (263)	$180,250–$298,300	$405,713 (5)
Kiddie Academy (57)	$218,300–$719,100	$665,455
Primrose (148)	$2–$2.4 million	$1,060,522 (6)
Sylvan Learning (742)	$153,465–$227,915	$508,382 (7)
Kuman Math & Reading Centers (1,197)	$9,250–$28,265	n/a

(1) Information is from Child Development & Educational Services Survey 2004 (based on data from company's FTC/UFOC disclosures, the SEC and misc. company data), published by Franchise Help (www.franchisehelp.com, a great site. Sales data is from 2002. Information is also from the Spring Summer 2005 Franchise Opportunities Guide published by the International Franchise Association (IFA), www.franchise.org, an invaluable franchise resource.

(2) See above.

(3) Top 50 percent of the schools averaged $136,486.

(4) The results shown above were for schools opened for 18 months; those that had been open for only 12 months averaged $729,048. Operating expenses based on $877,610 were as follows:

Payroll	41%
Rent	14%
Misc. expense	30%
Total expense	85%
Operating Income	15%

(5) 43% of the schools did better than the figure shown.

(6) The figure above is for large facilities; the figure for smaller facilities was $806,462.

(7) The figure above was for an A territory; the figure for a B territory was $341,905.

General Information

Questions to ask seller: "Make sure the labor cost is in line with industry standards, and inquire as to deviations to make sure the facility is staffed properly (legally). Child care is a state-regulated business which mandates child-to-staff ratios. Look at the demographics in the area, as birth rates have an impact on future business. Location of the facility near affordable housing (which turns over) is a benefit. Rules of thumb based on gross sales can be misleading, as they do not incorporate operating-cost efficiencies."

"There is need for both 'mom & pop' operations as well as larger 'institutionalize' type businesses. Each can serve their own niche and be literally right next door to one another. A good, clean, quality service provider can be profitable in almost any competative environment."

"Striking the right balance between quality and profit is critical to long-term success. Many parents will place cost as a secondary consideration to quality and reputation."

"Average daily attendance"

"Check out licensing authority for complaints against the business. Understand frequency of rate increases. (Rate increases should be annual if only a couple of dollars.) Look at staff longevity to understand the caring nature of the business, which is critical to the reputation of the business."

"Check to see if state-subsidized."

"People look for unique program structure and location which they deem desirable (which vary by buyer)." As birth rates stabilize and decline, program will be what keeps the progressive centers open and thriving in the future."

"Salaries as a percentage of revenues should be between 40 to 45 percent of gross revenue. If they are less than 40 percent, it could indicate the facility is exceeding staff-to-child ratios as established by the state. 45 to 48 percent indicates the current owner is not effectively managing staff, or has too many part-timers, (or the facility is older and does not optimize child-to-staff ratios) which a new owner may be able to improve, and therefore, add a little to the price…buyers don't care as much what type of community it is in, as long as the center has a good reputation and earnings."

"Expected profit should be $1,000 per licensed child per year, or 20 percent return on investment. Monthly rental and length of lease or value of real property if included in sale are important factors."

"If the facility was built for day care— rather than converted from another use—it will bring a higher price. As always (+ -) depending on profitability."

Advantages of this Business

- "Fairly stable industry which is desireable to a cetain segment of the buyers. It can be a 'feel good' industry."
- "Advantages include stability, steady profits (if operated correctly), and good opportunity to build a solid professional reputation. Easy for high quality independent centers to compete with local or national chains."
- "Big profit, five days per week, short hours"
- "Stability. The birth rate continues at a good pace. This, combined with dual-income families being the norm today, means parents need child care."
- "Most families have working parents today. High gross profit in this business. No inventory, no theft and no spoilage; very popular with business buyers today."

Disadvantages of this Business

- "Staffing can be a difficult job. And occupancy costs (as real estate prices generally continue to escalate) is a concern. Be carful not to pay too much in occupancy costs as clients will only pay so much for the service."
- "This is a highly regulated industry. There are not many other businesses where government (usually state) mandates the amount of space you're required to operate in, the staff required to operate, the methods of operation, etc."
- "Heavy competition, lots of employees"
- "In certain 'desirable' markets competition can be fierce. Service rates charged to parents can only go so high before alternative care will be found; e.g., spouse stays at home with 2+ children of similar age. Adding a second or third location may increase earnings in a linear fashion versus exponentially."
- "Employees can make or break you. Risk of new competition. State regulations constantly changing."
- "No guarantees that parents will like a new operator or that the state will not impose unreasonable regulations or go into competition through public school programs. Staffing and facility-size regulations make it difficult to increase gross revenues beyond market rates."

Industry Trend

"According to census statistics, grandchildren of 'baby boomers' are going to present the largest population of school-age children in our history. The opportunity is being born every day."

"Industry growing by leaps and bounds"

"The industry trend is good and positive, however check the immediate area demographics which are a better gauge of future growth or decline."

Seller Financing

- "Business only—7 to 10 years"
- "Most are 90 percent SBA financed."

Resources

National Association for Family Child Care (NAFCC)
www.nafcc.org

National Child Care Association
www.nccanet.org

State regulations for day care centers

Quick *Profile* Day Care

"Nationwide, the industry employs 900,000 workers as licensed providers and teachers, according to the National Child Care Association. Another 2 million are family, friends, or neighbors who serve as child-care providers. National revenues for direct child care were an estimated $43 billion in 2002, the MIT-legal Momentum report said.

"The Bureau of Labor Statistics reported that they earned, on average, $9.50 per hour in 2002, less than the $14.95 average paid other workers at private firms."

Source: *The Boston Globe*, Tuesday, April 19, 2005

"The $40 billion child-care industry includes everything from large national day-care chains, to local mom and pop centers, to private homes that care for just a few children. Into those hands every day parents send more than 13 million infants and toddlers, according to the Children's Defense Fund."

Source: *The Dallas Morning News*, Sunday, February 3, 2002

"Signs of a bad day care center:

"A so-so reputation—If other parents aren't thrilled with the center, it's best to keep looking.

"Loose rules—If a home daycare doesn't have rules and organization, it's not likely to be right for you. Keep looking.

"A curriculum in hiding—Your child need age-appropriate activities to encourage his development. If the center doesn't offer them, move on.

"An unqualified staff—If a center is understaffed, it's not for you. The National Association for the Education of Children (NAEYC) has set these guidelines:

- 'For babies, the ratio is one caregiver for every three children if a group has six infants, one for every four if a group has eight babies.
- 'For toddlers (12 to 24 months), the ratio is 1:3 for six children, 1:4 for eight children or kids, and 1:4 for children.
- 'For children between 24 and 36 months, the ratio should be 1:4 for a group of eight, 1.5 for a group of ten, and 1:6 for a group of 12.'

"When you tour the facility, watch carefully to see whether babies are tended to quickly or if the staff, overworked and overwhelmed, lets them wail.

"An under-compensated staff—If the staff's training isn't up to snuff, they seem overworked, or they don't stick around very long, the center isn't for you.

"Dirty, unsafe facilities—If the center seems dingy, cramped, or dangerous, move on.

"An expired license—A license isn't everything, but if a center doesn't have one, it's not for you."

Source: www.family.msn.com

Comments from *Retail Insights:*

"As a marketing perspective for day care centers, what were the average child care expenses, including education, during the past year in three different household income groups?

"Annual research conducted by the U.S. Department of Agriculture found that husband- wife families earning less than $39,100 a year paid an average of $840 in 2001 in child care/education expenses for a child 0–2 years, and $950 for a 3–5 year old child; husband-wife families earning between $39,100 and $65,800 a year paid an average of $1,380 during 2001 in child care/education expenses for a child 0–2 years, and $1,530 for a 3–5 year-old child; husband-wife families earning more than $65,800 a year paid an average of $2,090 during 2001 in child care/education expenses for a child 0–2 years, and $2,270 for a 3–5 year-old child. U.S. Dept. of Agriculture, 2003.

"As a marketing perspective for the growth of day-care-center based programs, what percent of 3–5 year old preschool children were enrolled in some form of day care program during the past two years?

"A total of 59.6% of 3–5-year-old preschool children were enrolled in some type of center-based program, such as day centers, nursery schools, prekindergarten, preschools and Head Start programs. This group included 46.1% of 3-year-old youngsters, 70.1% of 4-year olds and 76.3% of 5-year olds. National Center for Education Statistics, 2003.

"Various categories of child care during the past two years?

"Relative care: 23.3%; non-relative care: 15.9%; center-based program (includes day care centers, nursery school, prekindergarten, preschools and Head Start): 59.3%."

Source: *Retail Insights*, www.retailinsights.com

"Research by Runzheimer International determined that U.S. families spend an average of 9.6% of their income for child care."

Source: *The Wall Street Journal*, 2003

Early Childhood Education for All

"And, early education is itself a significant industry, providing millions of jobs nationwide, paying billions of dollars in wages, purchasing billions in goods and services, and generating billions in gross receipts. In many states, it is often one of the largest employers and producers of revenues.

- In Massachusetts, it employs more people than telecommunications, computer manufacturing, or pharmaceuticals;
- In New York, more than hotels and lodging, air transportation, and public transportation;
- In Washington state, more than in agriculture, and
- In North Carolina, it produces more gross receipts than wholesale leaf tobacco.

"Yet while virtually every state has maintained economic development funding at high levels in order to aid job growth, state after state has made cutbacks in child care and early education."

Source: "Early Childhood for All," www.familyinitiative.org

Pricing tips

Following is some basic pricing information from Bizcomps. For a study based on your area of the country, contact Bizcomps at www.bizcomps.com.

The price based on a percentage of annual sales ranges from 46 percent in the western edition to 52 percent in the eastern edition and 40 percent in the central states edition.

The multiple of SDC is from 2.3 in the West to 1.9 in the East and 1.7 in the central states.

Franchise

Deck the Walls

120 units	
Approximate Total Investment:	$ $180,900 to $245,200

Rule of Thumb:

- 34 percent of annual sales plus inventory

General Information

Deck the Walls retails art, custom framing and wall décor.

Source:www.dtwfraninfo.com

Resources

www.franinfo.com

Delicatessens *(See also Restaurants)*

40,656	SIC: 5812-09	NAIC: 722211

Rule of Thumb:

- 2.5 times SDE plus inventory

"It the deli is open five days a week, it's 50 percent of annual sales; if it's open six days a week, it's 40 percent of annual sales; and, if it's open seven days a week it's 30 percent of annual sales."

Retail	40 percent of annual sales plus inventory
Industrial	50 percent of annual sales plus inventory
Office Buildings ...	50 percent of annual sales plus inventory

General Information

"Shopping Frequencies

Ninety-four percent (94%) shop in supermarkets that have a service deli. Eighty-five percent (84%) say their supermarket has a self-service deli. Consumers shop their service delis on average once a week, while they shop both the self-service deli and the wall deli slightly less often (an average of 0.8 times a week). They shop for deli foods outside of their supermarkets an average 0.2 times a week. Three in ten (31%) consumers are shopping more frequently at their supermarket delis than they did five years ago, 45% are shopping the same amount, and 23% are shopping less frequently."

Source: International Dairy-Deli-Bakery Association (IDDBA) February 21, 2005

"Opinions about Supermarket Deli Characteristics & Services

Delis in 2004 are offering consumers more services than they did in 1999. Eighty-five percent (85%) have a self-service deli—up dramatically from 34% in 1999 and 27% in 1994. Forty-five percent (45%) offer recipe and serving suggestions for the items they sell—up from 40% in 1999. Forty-three percent (43%) provide information about how long food can be stored—up from 40% in 1999. Ninety-three percent (93%) agree that deli foods tend to be fresher than packaged foods."

Source: International Dairy-Deli-Bakery Association (IDDBA) February 21, 2005

Resources

International Dairy-Deli-Bakery Association

www.iddba.org

Delivery Services *(See also Courier Services)*

11,243	SIC: 4212-05	NAIC: 492210

Rule of Thumb:

- 2 times EBITDA for businesses under $1 million
- 3 times EBITDA for businesses from $1 to 5 million
- 4 times EBITDA for businesses over $5 million

General Delivery

"The express delivery and logistics industry, which XLA represents, specializes in fast, reliable transportation services for documents, packages and freight. XLA members include large firms with global delivery networks, such as DHL Express, FedEx, Purolator, TNT Express and UPS, as well as smaller businesses with strong regional delivery networks. Together, XLA members employ more than 510,000 American workers. Worldwide, XLA members have operations in over 200 countries, move more than 20 million packages each day, employ more than 800,000 people, operate 1,200 aircraft and earn revenues of approximately $60 billion annually."

Source: Express Delivery & Logistics Association

Resources

Express Delivery & Logistics Association
www.wxpressassociation.org

Franchise

Del Taco

475 units

Estimated Annual Sales per Unit:	$940,000
Approximate Total Investment:	$910,000 to $1,750,000

Rule of Thumb:

- 90% of annual sales plus inventory

Resources

www.deltaco.com

Dental Laboratories

11,835	SIC: 8072-01	NAIC: 339116

Rule of Thumb:

- 1 times SDE plus equipment and inventory
- 2 times SDE including equipment & inventory

Dental Practices

208,426	SIC: 8021-01	NAIC: 621210

Rule of Thumb:

- 60 to70 percent of gross annual sales
- 70 percent of collections, not including accounts receivable, but including equipment
- 50 to 70 percent of annual collections subject to how weighted practice is towards managed care versus private fee for service (cash pay) and condition of equipment
- 1.5-2 times SDE; add fixtures, equipment & inventory; may require earnout

Pricing Tips

"It varies by specialty, with prosthodontia being lowest, followed by perio and pedo. Endo is highest."

"It depends upon the dental specialty, practice style, patient mix, clinical staff, payer mix, location, referral patterns, and many other factors specific to the practice."

"Mathematical approach—Simple math can be used to check the alleged number of active patients for reasonableness. Divide the yearly collections (as verified by tax returns) by the number given for patient files. This will give you the average income per patient for the year. In many regions, you can expect this number to be between $285 and $385. If your answer to this math problem is less than that, there may be more patient files than reported. A higher answer indicates fewer patient files. The seller should explain any deviations from the average yearly collections per patient. The fee schedule may be high, driving the average up. A high average also might indicate that patients want quality dentistry that simply costs more. Either of these explanations means good news. But, a lower average may indicate the patient base does not desire good dentistry or that the patients just cannot afford it. Although there may be more patients in terms of actual numbers in the latter situation, you'll have to work harder to get the gross collections desired. Until the law changes, use any method available to find out all you can about the patient base. The exact restrictions of the Patient Privacy Act and its impact on information available to

a practice buyer are yet to be determined. We recommend that you watch for updated information from the ADA as further developments on this legislation unfold."

Source: *Practice Transitions* by Dr. Gene McCormick and Bob Fitzgerald, CPA, www.dentalsales.com

"How much managed care or third-party pay versus fee for service; number of actual patients; quality of staff; condition of equipment; any expansion possible"

"A lot depends on the number of patients that are in a practice, the location of the practice, the type of medicine/dentistry that is being done, the overhead, the lease, etc."

"Specialty practices are somewhat more risky and for the same numbers will generally sell for a little less. For a partnership, the price may be skewed depending on how income is split."

"Managed care brings down value, while private fee practices have highest value."

Benchmarks

Expenses as a percentage of annual revenues:	
Cost of Goods Sold	10–15%
Payroll/Labor Costs	22%
Occupancy Cost	5–7%
Profit (estimated pre-tax)	40%

Gross over $500,000 is a successful practice

General Information

Questions to ask seller: "What type of procedures performed on patients? Type of insurance accepted?"

"Why shouldn't I open my own dental office, and just start from scratch? Some dentists will do this, and most will suffer financially for that decision. Research has proven that if one compares a new practice start-up with the purchase of a good quality existing practice, over a five-year period of time, the purchaser of the existing practice will have earned

Why Dentists are Earning More

"On average, general dentists in 2000, the most recent year for which comparative data are available, earned $166,460—compared with $164,100 for general internal-medicine doctors, $145,700 for psychiatrists, $144,700 for family-practice physicians, and $137,800 for pediatricians. All indications are that dentists have at least kept pace with physicians since then."

."So why are dentists so handily outpacing doctors? In part, it's because dentists have avoided being flattened by the managed-care steamroller, and instead many have turned into upscale marketers. Dental care makes up less than 5% of the overall U.S. health bill, and hasn't been a major focus of cost-cutting."

Source: *The Wall Street Journal*, January 10, 2005

approximately $500,000 more than the start-up dentist, in the same time frame. Need I say more?"

Source: Professional Practice Associates; www.ppa-brokers.com

"Equipment, location, socio-economic conditions, fee schedule and transfer terms"

Advantages of this Business

- "More stable than medical specialties, with higher value. Easier to set up and sell businesses than medical specialties. Passive income through use of hygeinists. Cosmetic income opportunities."
- "High incomes for dentists in today's market relative to other professions"

Disadvantages of this Business

- "Higher competition than medical in most markets."
- "Education, training and licensure requirements limit qualified purchasers."

Industry Trend

"Many dentists will be wanting to transition their practices."

"Strong for adult specialties as baby boomers age. Much dentistry is elective, and a general economic slowdown could quickly affect dentistry."

"Dental expenditures will increase from $70.9 billion in 2002 to a projected

$84.1 billion this year, the report said. Government actuaries predict annual increases of 6.3 to 6.9 percent in dental service expenditures to $146.9 billion in 2014. National health expenditures overall are projected to rise within an annual range of 7.1 to 7.9 percent during the same period, although that rate declines throughout the next decade."

Source: American Dental Association, www.ADA.org February 23, 2005

"Washington—Dental spending will exceed $84 billion this year, according to the government's latest national health spending estimates."

Source: American Dental Association, www.ADA.org February 23, 2005

"Dental services spending for selected calendar years from National Health Expenditures report:

1993	$38.9 billion
1998	$53.2 billion
2002	$70.9 billion
2003	$74.3 billion

Projected expenditures:

2004	$79.1 billion
2005	$84.1 billion
2006	$90.0 billion
2014	$146.9 billion"

Source: American Dental Association, www.ADA.org February 23, 2005

Seller Financing

- "Very good 3rd party financing available—sometimes even 100 percent."
- "3 to 7 years."
- "5 to 7 years; most are bank financed."

Resources

American Dental Association
www.ada.org

Diners *(See also Restaurants)*

Rule of Thumb:

- 30 percent of annual sales plus inventory

Direct Mail—Advertising

4,500	SIC: 7331-05	NAIC: 541860

Rule of Thumb:

- 40 percent of annual revenues plus inventory

Resources

Direct Marketing Association
www.the-dma.org

Direct Selling Businesses

Rule of Thumb:

- 5 times EBITDA

Pricing Tips

Industry Experts' Ratings:

Amount of Competition (1 = Lot of: 4 = Not much) 1.2
Amount of Risk (1 = Very: 4 = Not much) 2.0
Historical Profit Trend (1 = Down: 4 = Up) 2.8
Location & Facilities (1 = Poor: 4 = Excellent) 2.0
Marketability (1 = Low: 4 = High) 2.8
Industry Trend (1 = Declining: 4 = Growing) 2.0
Ease of Replication (1 = Easy: 4 = Difficult) 1.0

Benchmarks

$1,100,000 revenue per sales department

Expenses as a percentage of annual sales:

Cost of Goods Sold 60%
Payroll/Labor Costs 01%
Occupancy Cost 01%
Profit (estimated) 10%

Disadvantages of this Business

- "Postal regulations and costs rising. competition, difficulty of obtaining capital and operational financing through typical commercial lenders, reliance on UPS/FEDEX labor negotiations."

Display Advertising *(See Billboards)*

Distributors—Electrical Products

Rule of Thumb:

- 35 percent annual revenues plus inventory

Resources

National Association of Electrical Distributors, Inc
www.naed.org—a good site with sales information & data

Distributors—Food Products

Rule of Thumb:

- 50 percent of annual sales plus inventory

Distributors—Industrial Supplies

Rule of Thumb:

- 50 percent of annual revenues plus inventory

Distributors—In General *(See Wholesale/Distribution)*

Rule of Thumb:

- 1.5 to 2 times SDE plus inventory
- 50 percent of annual sales plus inventory

Distributors—Janitorial

Rule of Thumb:

- 40 percent of annual revenues plus inventory

Distributors—Medical Equipment & Supplies

Rule of Thumb:

- 50 percent of annual revenues plus inventory

Dog Grooming

23,218	SIC: 0752-04	NAIC: 812910

Rule of Thumb:

- 50 percent of annual revenues plus inventory
- 1.5 times SDE plus inventory

Benchmarks

Following are a few results of the 2004 survey conducted by Pet Groomer. It answers almost any question one would have about the subject of the dog-grooming business. This site, www.petgroomer.com, is one of the best we have seen. If you are researching this industry, this site is all you will need.

What is the average gross revenue your business earns from pet-grooming services only in one year (before taxes or expenses)? Do not include retail sales amount.

A. Under $10,000 .... 02%
B. $10,001 to $20,000 .... 06%
C. $20,001 to $30,000 .... 04%
D. $30,001 to $50,000 .... 31%
E. $50,001 to $75,000 .... 40%
F. $75,001 to $100,000 .... 05%

G $100,001 to $150,000 .... 04%
H. $150,001 to $250,000 .... 05%
I. Over $250,000 .... 03%

What is your present, or most recent, annual wage net earnings from your business employment (prior taxes)? Your answer should reflect your personal net income before taxes that you earned from the business, not the gross revenue of sales or services earned by the business.

A. Under $10,000 .... 09%
B. $10,001 to $20,000 .... 20%
C. $20,001 to $30,000 .... 33%
D. $30,001 to $40,000 .... 27%
E. $40,001 to $50,000 .... 07%
F. $50,001 to $75,000 .... 02%
G Over $75,000 .... 02%

If you pay rent for your commercial salon or shop, or you rent a grooming department, how much rent do you pay per month?

A. Under $500 a month. 22%
B. $501 to $1,000 a month 56%
C. $1,001 to $1,500 a month 18%
D. $1,501 to $$2,000 a month 03%
E. $2,001 to $3,000 a month 01%
F. $3,001 to $4,000 a month 0%
G. Over $4,000 a month 0%

Which description below best describes your operation?

a. Home-based business 20%
b. Mobile grooming business 28%
c. Commercial location shop or salon 41%
d. Leased operation from a retailer or veterinarian or similar 11%

Source: www.PetGroomer.com

Resources

PetGroomer.com Career Center
www.petgroomer.com
This site sets a standard for what can be accomplished with Web sites. These are some of the most informative sites we have visited. PetGroomer.com may be the best site we have visited for providing infor-

mation about a particular business or profession. If you are considering this profession or need information on it, you will find what you're looking for on this site.

89 percent of the respondents "plan to sell [their] business someday, for either a career change or to retire." The previous survey reported that 78 percent planned to sell. And this year's survey did not ask the question.

Source: www.PetGroomer.com

National Dog Groomers Association of America (NDGAA)
www.nauticom.net/www/ndga

www.dogwise.com—This site contains several books that are of interest to anyone entering the dog grooming or dog kennel business—or brokering them.

Dog Kennels

2,016	SIC: 0752-05	NAIC: 812910

Rule of Thumb:

- "One way of calculating the market value of a boarding kennel would be to figure the present market value of just the real estate and add to that 1 or 1½ times the annual gross. Now, the difference between 1 and 1½ times would be determined by the area. For example, if the kennel is in a growing area, you would be more inclined to go 1½ times. If the kennel is in an area that is static, and there is reason to feel that the kennel will continue to do more business, then you could use 1 times the annual gross."

Benchmarks

"Another set of numbers you might find useful is this: the average kennel occupancy nationwide is 55.9 percent; the average income per run is $2.902 annually. Now these numbers can have some significance in helping people figure out how much a kennel should be making. For example, if you have 100 runs that are occupied 55.9 percent of the time, you can figure that the kennel would be doing average business. Multiply that by the daily charge for customers. The numbers should come out somewhere near what the present owners say they are grossing for the year on boarding. If they say they are making a lot more than that, it means that they are claiming that they have more than 55.9 percent occupancy. And that would merit some further investigation."

Source: www.kennelsource.com March 22, 2005

Estimated Sales of Boarding Facilities in U.S.

Size of kennels (dog runs)	Average Gross Income
Small (under 50; average— 27)	$134,000
Large (100+; average—137)	$654,500
Avg. Daily Charge per Dog Run	$16.65
Avg. Annual Income per Dog Run	$2,902
Avg. Dog Occupancy	55.9%
Avg. Days' Stay per Dog	6.5

Dog Kennel Expenses

Expenses (As a % of gross sales)	Size of Kennels (See above for size) Small	Medium	Large
Payroll	30.63%	49.95%	26.37%
Employee Benefits	1.33	1.22	1.56
Auto/Truck	1.93	0.94	1.38
Travel & Entertainment	0.31	0.36	0.33
Kennel Insurance	2.02	1.26	1.08
Repairs & Maintenance	4.01	2.5	1.93
Office Supplies	1.18	0.89	1.29
Utilities	2.61	2.34	2.81
Telephone	1.48	0.89	0.54
Yellow Page Ads	1.69	1.29	1.60
Other Advertising	2.15	0.95	1.11
Office & Administration	0.75	0.67	1.68
Professional Services	0.82	0.61	0.77
Veterinary Expense	1.44	0.43	0.43
Licenses	0.39	0.31	0.10
Other	3.97	3.91	4.0

The above are recent estimates. Not all kennels have all of the services above. The information was furnished by the American Boarding Kennel Association (ABKA).

General Information

"A recent survey of our membership revealed that 83% of our members board cats as well as dogs, 57% sell retail supplies, and 78% offer professional grooming services."

Source: www.kennelsource.com March 22, 2005

Industry Trend

"Recently, the American Pet Products Manufacturers Association (APPMA) released new figures proving that the pet care industry has experienced an explosive growth over the last 10 years. In 1994, the total industry expenditures were $17 billion, nearly doubling in 2003 to $32.4 billion. It's estimated that the number rose nearly $2 billion more for 2004."

Source: www.kennelsource.com March 22, 2005

Add-on Services

A trend that has been observed in the boarding kennel industry over the past several years is that kennels are offering more add-on services such as playtime and doggy day care. In addition, these add-on services are contributing a much larger percentage to the kennel's income. The industry statistics reflect this change in a number of ways. There are very few direct costs (such as supplies) associated with many of these services, but they do require additional personnel costs.

"In the United States, there are more pets than people, 377.8 million pets versus 290 million people. 64.2 million U.S. households own a pet.

Source: www.kennelsource.com March 22, 2005

ABKA Predictions

"ABKA expects that add-on services will continue to grow in popularity and will make up a larger and larger portion of the kennel's income. In particular, we will see more kennels offering doggy day care, playtime and luxury accommodations.

"As the cost of doing business increases, kennels will be forced to raise their boarding prices. Look for the cost of boarding to increase 15%–20% over the next two years. This increased cost will come partly from an increase in base boarding prices and partly from an increase in add-on services."

Source: American Boarding Kennels Association (ABKA)

Resources

The American Boarding Kennel Association (ABKA)
www.abka.com

Note: The above Web site offers several books on the subject including *Building, Buying and Operating A Boarding Kennel.* It also contains a Web site that lists kennels for sale. The ABKA also publishes an annual survey—a portion is reprinted above. If you are considering handling the sale of animal boarding kennels, you should join this association — they do an excellent job and they are very cooperative.

Note: Dog kennels can be real-estate intensive. If real estate is involved, a real-estate license may be necessary.

Franchise

Dollar Discount Stores

165 franchised units

Approximate Total Investment: $99,000 to $195,000

Rule of Thumb:

- 11 percent of annual sales plus inventory

General Information

Mostly rented in strip malls in high foot-trafffic areas. Seems to do well in all kind of demographics.

Dollar Stores

Rule of Thumb:

- 10 to 12 percent of annual sales plus inventory
- 2 times EBITDA

Pricing Tips

"Dollar Stores are the fastest growing channel in the country today with torrid growth. Typically between 2 to 2.5 times annual net income."

Industry Experts' Ratings:

Amount of Competition (1 = Lot of: 4 = Not much) 1.6
Amount of Risk (1 = Very: 4 = Not much) 2.0
Historical Profit Trend (1 = Down: 4 = Up) 2.4
Location & Facilities (1 = Poor: 4 = Excellent) 2.0
Marketability (1 = Low: 4 = High) 2.4
Industry Trend (1 = Declining: 4 = Growing) 2.4
Ease of Replication (1 = Easy: 4 = Difficult) 1.2

"Not too difficult to repicate; needs a large amount of inventory; the larger the store, the better the variety and the sales."

Benchmarks

"Good ones do over $600 per sq.ft."

Expenses as a percentage of annual sales:	
Cost of Goods Sold	70%
Payroll/Labor Costs	15%
Occupancy Cost	10%
Profit (estimated)	30%

General Information

"The stores offer a variety of hardlines and softlines merchandise. Hardlines merchandise includes primarily household chemical and paper products; candy, snack and other food; health and beauty aids; electronics; housewares and giftware; pet food and supplies; toys; stationery and school supplies; seasonal goods; hardware and automotive supplies. Softlines merchandise includes men's, women's, boys', girls' and infants' clothing; shoes; and domestic items, such as blankets, sheets and towels. During the fiscal year ended August 30, 2003, hardlines accounted for approximately 76.7% of the Company's sales. Softlines accounted for approximately 23.3% of sales (with hanging apparel and shoes representing 12.4%, basic apparel 4.4%, and domestics 6.5%.)"

Source: Family Dollar Tree Annual Report 2003

The following table shows the percentage of purchases of each major product group for the year ended January 31, 2004 and December 31, 2002

	January 31, 2004	January 31, 2002
Variety categories	49.5%	50.6%
Consumable	41.2%	40.5%
Seasonal	09.3%	08.9%

Source: Dollar Tree Stores Annual Report, January 31, 2004

Advantages of this Business

- "Very easy to operate; mom & pop operaters are moving in at great speed; mostly all cash business"

Disadvantages of this Business

- "Easy replication. Possible squeeze in margins down the road"

Trend

"Keep growing and possible margin shrinkage; bigger chains will have more buying clout."

Franchise

Domino's Pizza

7,757 units

Estimated Annual Sales per Unit:	$640,000
Approximate Total Investment:	$98,850 to $346,350

Rule of Thumb:

- 45 percent of the first $400K in annual sales, 50 percent of the next $100K ($400 to $500K) in annual sales, then 55 percent of the next $250K of annual sales (from $500 to $750K)

Resources

www.dominos.com

> "It [Domino's Pizza] sells one million pizzas a day … and franchises in more than 50 countries. The company plans to add as many as 250 stores a year and increase sales by as much as 6 percent a year…"
>
> Source: FranchiseHelpOnline, www.franchisehelp.com

Donut Shops *(See also Dunkin' Donuts)*

10,668	SIC: 5461-05	NAIC: 722213

Rule of Thumb:

- 50 percent of annual sales plus inventory (and can go to 100 percent of sales for a great store)
- 2 to 2.5 times SDE plus inventory

Pricing Tips

"Higher coffee sales (60 percent of sales) produce higher value. Very low coffee sales produce lower values."

"Length & cost of lease? Retail vs. wholesale business? Percentage of business that is coffee (the higher the percentage of coffee sales, the higher the price)"

Benchmarks

Expenses as a percentage of annual sales:

Cost of Goods	21% food (+ 4.2% paper goods)
Payroll	20 to 23%
Occupancy Cost	10%

"The store needs to be located on the morning side of traffic flow in order to do a high volume and to minimize … risk of failure. The donut business is not an absentee business."

Source: The Donut Factory

General Information

Cambodian Americans own some 90 percent of California's donut shops "Winchell's Donut's VP of Brand Management, Lou Franson reckoned that the donut market in the United States is worth a whopping $3 billion dollars. Though good statistics are hard to find, Franson said that there are 1,800 independently Cambodian or Korean-owned donut shops in Los Angeles alone. And the *San Jose Mercury* reported that California has approximately 5,000 independent donut shops and that Cambodians own as many as 90 percent of those independent franchises.

"Nonetheless, the hard work and pooling of family resources pays off and many donut stores are very successful. Franson says that because donut stores run by close-knit family members—who usually put in long hours without wages—have low labor costs, the small donut businesses usually gross about $100,000, bringing in roughly $40,000–$50,000 profit a year. Depending on the size and location, rewards reaped can be even greater. Lee said that while profits fluctuate, his upscale Powell Street Donut Cafe can bring in up to $80,000 in profit a year."

Source: www.Asianweek.com, June 22 – June 28, 2000

"The prices paid for some of the company's acquisitions have also raised eyebrows. Krispy Kreme shelled out $67 million in cash for the Dallas and Shreveport franchises, a total of six stores. That's more than $11 million a store. Just months before, Krispy Kreme was paying an average of $6.5 million a store."

Source: *Business Week*, August 16, 2004

Note: We realize the above article is several years old, but is still current and, we think, of interest.

Industry Trend

"The closing later this month of one of Rochester's most popular donut shops begs the question, can small 'mom and pop' stores survive in this era of the national chain stores? It's not just Main Street, USA that's hurting. Even in a big metro area like Rochester, it seems that only the strong survive.

"The point was driven home this week when Donuts Delite announced it was closing after nearly 50 years. It has been a fixture at Culver Road and Empire Boulevard. Bob Malley is the owner of Donuts Delite and he said that the times are changing. "We just could not compete with the multi-million dollar advertising budgets that these national companies had. And by sheer force of numbers, people were patronizing the new places, and passing us by."

Source: www.whee.com

Resources

Independent Bakers Association
www.bakingnetwork.com

Franchise

Dr. Vinyl

282 units	
Approximate Total Investment:	$44,000 to $69,500
Rule of Thumb:	
➢ 75 percent of annual sales plus inventory	

General Information

"...takes care of cracked dashboards, torn vinyl and leather seats, windshield dings, faded colors, dents, paint touch-up, auto graphics and pin-striping, etc."

Resources

www.drvinyl.com

Dress Shops *(See also Apparel)*

36,535	SIC: 5621-01	NAIC: 448190

Rule of Thumb:

- 20 percent of annual sales plus inventory
- 2 times monthly sales plus inventory

General Information

"Should turn its inventory 4 times per year. The better dress shops should sell for fixtures and equipment, plus depreciated tenant's improvements, plus inventory at cost, plus one-half year's net profit before taxes. Rent can run as high as 8 percent of gross sales."

Drive-in Restaurants *(See also Restaurants)*

Rule of Thumb:

- 6 times monthly sales plus inventory
- 35 to 45 percent of annual sales plus inventory

Drive-In Theaters

General Information

"A group of Vineland [NJ] businessmen bought the 17-acre property for $1.8 million. The property already had a screen that 'was still in good shape. . . .There is capacity for 700 cars, which will be reduced by half next when the skate park opens. . . . Instead of paying by the carload as in the old days of drive-ins, the Delsea will charge $6 for adults and $3 for children for the double feature.'"

Source: *The New York Times*, Friday, July 23, 2004

For more on drive-in theaters go to www.driveintheatre-ownersassociation.org—It is a wonderful site whether for information or just nostalgia. The site says that there are now 405 drive-ins as of November 2004, a new one has been built [we suspect the one mentioned above] and seven closed.

"Of the 405 drive-ins:

- 278 (69%) are single-screen theatres
- 75 (19%) are two-screen
- 23 (6%) are three-screen
- 16 (4%) are four-screen
- 5 (1%) are five-screen
- 6 (1%) are six-screen
- 1 (<1%) is nine-screen
- 1 (<1%) is thirteen-screen"

Source: United Drive-in Theatre Owners Association

Industry Trend

"More than 25 drive-ins have been built since the 1990s, over 50 have reopened since 1990s. Though drive-in numbers will never be as high as they were in the 1950s, the industry seems to be on an upswing."

Source: United Drive-in Theatre Owners Association

Resources

United Drive-in Theatre Owners Association
www.driveintheatre-ownersassociation.org

Driving Schools (Instruction)

6,589	SIC: 8299-02	NAIC: 611692

Rule of Thumb:

- 1 times SDE + fair market value of fixed assets

General Information

"High barrier to entry due to increasingly higher and stricter state regulations and standards."

The rule of thumb above applies to "learn-to-drive schools" that primarily teach teenagers to drive and pass a state driving test. It is mandatory in many states. However, there are many other types of driving schools such as: winter driving, commercial driving (trucks, etc.), race driving, etc. For information on these schools, see Schools—Vocational

Drug Stores *(See Pharmacies)*

Dry Cleaning

48,226	SIC: 7212-01	NAIC: 812320

Rule of Thumb:

- 75 to 100 percent of sales. Plants with on-site laundry equipment will get a higher multiple. Plants with over-the-counter sales of $35,000 will receive higher multiples.
- 5.5 times SDE plus inventory
- 2.5 times EBIT
- 2.5 times EBITDA
- "80% of annual gross sales if equipment is under five years old. If equipment is between six and 10 years old, it will be 60% of annual gross sales. If equipment is over 11 years old, it will be between 40% and 50% of the annual gross sales."
- "Purchase price ranges from 70 % of annual sales to 100%. Single stores with full garment pricing (no discounts, no coupons) & having monthly retail sales over $35,000 will achieve the higher multiple. Retail pick-up stores (no equipment) 25% to 50% of annual sales."
- "One can get 3 times cash flow (SDE) if the owner is a manager and does not perform a specific job such as counter, dry cleaner or presser. If the owner does perform a specific job, such as dry cleaner, etc., the cash flow should include the owner's salary and the business would be valued at 2.5 times that cash flow."
- "Dollar for dollar (100 percent of sales) on a plant that has dry cleaning equipment and a single buck or double buck shirt unit, assuming all sales are over-the-counter, not from pick-up stores or hotels or other cleaners. 75 percent of sales for plant w/o shirt unit, & 50 percent of sales on pick-up stores, assuming sales are $125,000 or more."
- "75 to 100 percent of annual gross sales for complete retail plants, must be able to verify. Pick-ups (drop stores) go for 30 to 50 percent of annual gross sales. Routes vary greatly, but can sell for 25 to 50 percent of actual paid gross sales."

Pricing Tips

"Make sure you know where sales are coming from—over-the-counter or wholesale, etc."

"If equipment is under 5 years old, the price can be 80 to 90 percent of gross sales; if equipment is 6 to 10 years old, the price can be between 70 and 80 percent of gross sales; and if the equipment is 11 to 20 years old, the price can be 50 to 70 percent of gross sales."

"The most common rule of thumb for determining the marketing price used by sellers and buyers (and brokers!) is still one times the annual gross sales for a full plant, and 50 percent of annual gross sales for a pickup store. The actual selling price is then a percentage up or down from that starting point (usually down), depending on specific features of the business. The more important features are the type and length of the lease; type, age and condition of equipment; ability to verify actual annual gross sales; and the location. Due to environmental issues, the most important feature is a lease that allows for dry cleaning with perc or petroleum on the premises and at least 10 years of term (five years with five-year option to renew). Most sellers today want to be 'cashed out' and outside financing is available. Many buyers feel that if they are paying cash with outside financing (usually with higher interest rates), then the seller should discount his selling price. Often when outside financing is available, the seller will still be required to provide a small promissory note to make up the difference between the agreed selling price, down payment, and funds provided by the lender."

The traditional buyers' method:

The long-held mind set is that buyers will generally pay for a "perfect" dry cleaning business dollar for dollar on retail over the counter sales; $.75 on a dollar for sales from a pickup outlet or a route under the same ownership as the plant; and $.50 on a dollar for wholesale work performed for outside businesses.

The immigrant buyers' method:

Immigrant buyers often look at prices as multiples of weekly gross sales. Typically: 50 times weekly sales for retail, approx. 30 times weekly sales for pickup stores and routes (owned and operated by the seller). Immigrant buyers often have little interest in wholesale businesses and may not be willing to pay for this type of sales.

"'A business is worth what a buyer is willing to pay for it and what the seller is willing to sell it for.' We hear this a lot and cannot argue with this wisdom. The majority of dry cleaners are small cash businesses and family owned and operated. Many cannot provide substantial financial information with accurate cash flow/net profit figures. Consequently, buying decisions are based more on the buyer's approval of the location and equipment. If the contingencies for sales verification and satisfactory lease are met, then buyers can feel comfortable with the simple multiple of gross sales method. Depending on the variables present with each business, most desirable plants are selling for 75–99 percent of verifiable gross sales. Pickup stores are selling for 20–50 percent of sales, and routes can go for 15–40 percent."

"Dry cleaners and laundry nation-wide sold for 60 to 80 percent of gross sales; the variation in percent is based on the age of the equipment."

"Dry cleaning plants without laundry equipment have been selling for 75 to 85 percent of annual net total sales. Dry cleaning plants with laundry equipment have been selling for 85 to 100 percent of annual net sales. Also, selling price ranges from 2.65 to 3.5 x discretionary cash flow earnings before owner's compensation and debt service."

"In pricing a dry cleaning plant today, the single most important consideration is the premises' lease. How long is it, and does it allow dry cleaning on the premises? Many new shopping centers will not allow dry cleaning with 'perc'; if this is the case, then processing must be done elsewhere, involving more expense. Not having the ability to dryclean does affect the value of a location. The ideal dry cleaning situation which would demand the highest value on the market would be as follows: (1) A strong retail location with a drive-thru. (2) No previous contamination problems. (3) Permission to use dry cleaning machine and chemicals on the premises. (4) At least 5 years' lease, with a 5-year option to renew. (5) New EPA approved dry cleaning machine with proper installation and spill containment tray. (6) Good shirt pressing equipment. (7) Good gas- fired boiler. Anything less than the above would reduce the price accordingly from the one times annual gross sales rule of thumb."

"Value added: Retail over-the-counter vs. wholesale & drop store income. Shirt equipment in-house. Shirt volume & pricing to equal general dry cleaning margin. All equipment to meet environmental regulations. Seller financing vs. all cash & SBA financing. Is payroll under 30 percent of gross sales? Is shirt volume no more than 20 percent of gross volume?"

"If equipment is under 5 years old and store is all retail, 70–80 percent of annual gross. Decreases to 50 percent if equipment is over 5 years old. "

Industry Experts' Ratings:

Amount of Competition (1 = Lot of: 4 = Not much)	1.0
Amount of Risk (1 = Very: 4 = Not much)	2.0
Historical Profit Trend (1 = Down: 4 = Up)	1.8
Location & Facilities (1 = Poor: 4 = Excellent)	2.6
Marketability (1 = Low: 4 = High)	2.6
Industry Trend (1 = Declining: 4 = Growing)	1.6
Ease of Replication (1 = Easy: 4 = Difficult)	1.6

"The discount cleaners and laundries are not money-makers with very poor quality control. When they come into a market, they hurt the professional cleaners and laundries."

"Historic Profit Trend: Profit is down due to fixed expenses going up, such as rent, employment. Also, competition from discount cleaners."

"Dry cleaning is a long-term business with not a lot of drastic ups and downs."

Benchmarks

"Supply costs (hangers, bags, cleaning solvent, etc.): approx 6% to 8% of gross sales. Payroll costs for an owner-operated store: 25% to 28% of gross sales. SDE profit: approx 25% to 32%."

"Valuation can be as high as 100% of gross sales if it is a full operating plant (with a shirt unit). Valuation can be 75% of gross sales if only does dry cleaning and sends shirts out to be cleaned. Valuation can be based on 3 times SDE if owner manages only and 2.5 times SDE if the owner helps in production (such as dry cleaner or presser)."

"A plant should generate at least $300K per year to be successful."

Expenses as a percentage of annual sales:

Cost of Goods	10%
Payroll/Labor Costs	30–35%
	(lower figure with owner working full-time)
Occupancy Costs	15–20% + R.E.Taxes&C.A.M.
	(top locations may be higher)
Utility Costs	5–9%
Profit (estimated pre-tax)	20–25%:

General Information

Questions to ask a seller: "How can you verify your actual sales? What is your lease, concerning assignments? Has the property been tested for environmental problems? How old is your equipment? Are you willing to do all or part of financing? Is it possible for the buyer to observe the business during business hours? Are sales: retail, from owned pickup, commercial accounts, wholesale to other cleaners, delivery routes, or other? Check lease, equipment, prices and environmental compliance. Dry cleaning machines type: perc or hydrocarbon? Garment pricing. Advertising/ coupon programs if any. Environmental problems? Landlord lease transferability issues? Will the landlord allow an on-site operating plant to continue within its premises? Does owner have environmental insurance? Does landlord require environmental insurance? Age, condition & capacity of equipment?"

"With approximately 30,000 dry cleaners in the United States, dry cleaning is one of the largest industry sectors that is still recognized as a 'Mom and Pop' small business. Although the size of dry cleaners varies, most commercial dry cleaners are single-facility, family-owned operations. An average number of five employees work at a plant. Commercial dry cleaning is not a high-profit business, with the median annual revenues below $250,000."

Source: International Fabricare Institute (IFI)

"Stores with up-to-date 5th generation dry cleaning machines, no coupon retail garment pricing in growth upper income trade areas will bring top dollar. Must pay attention to any environmental insurance. Be familiar with the different dry cleaning solvents (perc, Exxon DF 2000, etc.). Stores in changing trade areas, where the household incomes may be declining, will bring a lower value. However, these stores may have low rent rates. Absentee owners are attractive for buyers. Buyers may pay a higher value."

Advantages of this Business

- "The amount of investment to start up a dry cleaning business is very high, which makes it very difficult for someone to start new. This is a service business and is most successful if owned and operated by the owner and/or the owner's family, which makes this industry difficult for absentee owners to operate successfully."
- "Flexibility of hours that owner wants to work. Also, half day on Saturdays, closed on Sundays. Not a difficult business to learn."
- "Cash, production business easy to expand and diversify."
- "A service business which is very appealing to the owner-operator. It is very expensive to build new because of the high cost of installation and equipment."
- "If a store generates over $400,000 in gross sales, owner's hours are short with no weekends (not including discount cleaners)."
- "5 ½ to 6-day-week business. Sunday closed. Good cash flow business. Little to no receivables. Everyone will always need dry cleaning services. Owner can control the quality of his products & services. Always seems to be an active buyer market so you can sell the business in the future."

Disadvantages of this Business

- "Competition, lack of employees available and working conditions (heat in summer, etc.), environmental problems and regulation."
- "In order to be successful, the owner needs to be on site full time."
- "There is quite a bit of competition."
- "Growing competition from discount cleaners."
- "Increased competition from one-price cleaners. Cost of equipment & installation has increased dramatically. Dry cleaning is a task master business requiring hands-on oversight. Requires semi-skilled labor force."

Industry Trend

"Will continue to be a basic service, but discounters and immigrant population sweat shops affect profit picture of industry."

"The sales and profits should continue to grow, but not at a fast rate."

"In metropolitan cities, competition from discount cleaners"

"Industry sales trend will be flat. Because of new regulations on perc solvent, the cost of doing business will increase. Competition from new locations is creating a flat sales trend. Business will improve as the general economy improves. Still a basic business. Will not become obsolete. People still need to get their clothes cleaned. State of Texas has assessed a perc surcharge/tax of $15/gallon and an annual fee of $2,500/year/plant location."

"Saturated in major urban cities with low-price immigrant operations and large discounters."

Seller Financing

- "Seller, 2 to 5 years and 8 to 12 percent interest; banks/lenders, 3 to 7 years and 2 to 5 points over prime with sufficient collateral, often a second position lien on a home if real estate is not included with the business."
- "5 to 10 years"
- "Sellers have not been keen to offer seller financing. Typical transaction is bank financed for all cash to the seller. Sometimes we can get sellers to carry back 10 to 15 percent of the purchase, subordinate to the bank."
- "Sellers on the East Coast have to hold paper 99 percent of the time—usually 50 to 80 percent financed for 5 to 10 years."

Resources

International Fabricare Institute (IFI)
www.ifi.org

Dry Cleaning Pickup Outlets/Stores *(See dry cleaning)*

Rule of Thumb:

- 25 to 50 percent of annual sales
- 30 times weekly sales

Dry Cleaning Routes

Rule of Thumb:

- 15 to 40 percent of annual revenues

Quick *Profile* Dry Cleaning

State of the Dry Cleaning Industry
By Richard Ehrenreich, CBI, CED, SBA

A dry cleaner is a service business that functions in the capacity of a personal valet to its retail customers through the dry cleaning and pressing of suits, dresses, slacks and jackets (approximately 60 percent of volume); laundering and pressing of shirts, wearing apparel and personal laundry (approximately 20 percent of volume); repairing the customer's shoes and clothing (approximately 10 percent of volume).

Other miscellaneous services make up the remaining income, including fur, suede and leather cleaning, formal wear rental, reweaving and sales of miscellaneous retail items. Some dry cleaners do commercial account services for hotels, restaurants, theaters and other cleaners. Others may possibly offer wedding gown cleaning/restoration, on-site household goods cleaning or fire and flood damage restoration work.

The full-service plant is the most common and the most profitable form of dry cleaning business. In these operations all or most of the processing is performed on the premises. They often include additional pickup and drop-off points that feed the main plant. The grand majority of the plants do dry cleaning, laundry and alterations on the premises while sending out specialized items such as reweaving, shoe repair, as well as fur, suede and leather cleaning.

A dry cleaning business may also exist as a pickup store or a valet unit. In these businesses, all of the dry cleaning and laundry production is performed at a remote location, while tailoring or shoe repair may be done on site. They are the least profitable because the owner must pay from $.40 to $.60 on the dollar to the business providing the dry cleaning and laundry. Beyond a doubt, owners of dry cleaning plants run the most profitable pickup and/or valet shops.

In general, the most profitable and desirable dry cleaners are the ones with retail, walk-in or truck route sales that do the processing of the work in-house where the owner has control of costs, schedule and quality.

Background

In the past thirty-five years the industry has gone through two cycles of "Feast and Famine." The early 1970s brought about a devastating period to the industry due to tough economic times, wash-and-wear polyester, the growth of the big-box discount cleaners, the oil crisis, the casual clothes/"hippie" movement and a saturation of the cleaning industry, resulting in a loss of approximately 40 percent in the industry, nationally.

In the late 1970s and 1980s, the economy improved, and natural fabrics requiring dry cleaning returned to fashion. Today, more households have two working adults with higher incomes and less time or interest to do the family cleaning. Cleaners that survived the early 1970s re-established their revenues, and their values soared. Everyone wanted to become the "Drycleaning Millionaires" written about in the *New York Times*! The industry became a particular target of Asian and Middle Eastern immigrants who arrived on the U.S. shores with cash, a willingness to work hard, a family labor force and high hopes for new opportunities in this country.

Currently in most major cities with a large immigrant population, the industry has again become saturated, with retail prices either fixed or dropping. Thus, profits and values have dropped in many areas of the country. Heavy discounting of prices has become an increasingly popular trend in many large urban markets where the saturation is already particularly heavy.

While this period does not have the polyester kicker of the early 1970s, the many current environmental issues, in addition to the growing discount trend of the 1990s, have given the industry new areas of concern.

Is there anything unique about the business?

Successful dry cleaners are business owners who should have an industrial mentality rather than the "buy-and-sell" merchant manner of thinking. Dry cleaning and its allied products consist of labor-intensive services in which the customer sends in a (dirty) raw product and the cleaner must turn around a (cleaned and pressed) finished item at a competitive price. All the elements of a small factory are present; e.g., production, machinery, labor, supplies, accounts receivable, customer relations and promotion. It is not the trade for an owner who is unable to handle the multi-dimensional demands of this business: labor, technology and customer relations.

What type of location is best?

Outstanding locations can be found both in town and in suburban areas. They should be crime free and with sufficient population density of a socioeconomic level appropriate to the targeted group desired by the store. Urban locations should be convenient to large masses of white-collar office workers. Suburban locations can be free-standing with easy access to morning drop-off on main arteries or in shopping centers, hopefully with popular food, drug, and other neighborhood convenience shopping.

Important factors include visibility, accessibility, ease of parking, plus various environmental and utility considerations; let us not forget to mention competition and market area demographics.

In recent years there has been a growing concern among landlords for the environmental impact of a dry cleaning business on their property. The contamination of a property by hazardous materials, such as perchloroethylene or "Perc," the most common dry cleaning solvent, can create serious problems for a shopping center owner and the cost of cleanup can be staggering. This concern has caused some landlords to not renew leases of dry cleaning businesses with plants, especially those using Perc, on the premises, in their shopping centers.

What kind of major equipment is necessary to operate this kind of business?

A complete, newly installed dry cleaning plant (without laundry, shoe repair, etc.) can cost from $100,000 to $150,000 or more, depending on the projected volume and wall office decorations, etc. The breakdown of costs shows 70 percent for machinery with the rest going for installation and fixtures. The major equipment purchases are the dry cleaning machine, which costs approximately $1,000 for each pound of capacity (usually 35 to 70 pound loads), finishing equipment, as well as the boiler and other power plant items.

Financial information

Income: Extremely important is annual gross sales income and base price of key products. With the proper sales income, a successful owner/operator will be able to maintain higher margins after advancing through the various levels of fixed, variable and fixed expenses for the business operation. A smart, hard-working owner/operator in an above average location can produce an SDE of 20% to 25%.

Expenses: There are various business finance items to be concerned with when listing a dry cleaner for sale, but three or possibly four items make up the majority of expenses and should be scrutinized most carefully. First and foremost, is payroll and related costs, which accounts for 30 to 40 percent of the total annual expenses.

As mentioned earlier, dry cleaning is a labor-intensive business in which the company hires staff to perform tasks. Thus, our first consideration is the total labor rate, which is roughly equal to the cost of goods in a retail buy/sell type of business, and the value of this item can make the difference between success and failure of the enterprise.

The next important item, number two, is the real-estate-related costs. Whether purchased or leased, the premises are a major investment. Rental rates are a particularly strong concern of many immigrant buyers. Some long established businesses may find themselves in shopping center locations with long-term leases that have escalated over the years. Often these rents are not in line with today's rates and should be re-negotiated if at all possible.

Number three is the cost of supplies, including: solvent, hangers, bags and tickets that may account for another 10 to 12 percent. These three expense categories—payroll, premises, and supplies—easily account for 50 percent of the expenses, 50 cents on every dollar that enters the cash register.

The fourth item is subcontracted services for outside laundry, shoe repair, fur-suede-leather cleaning, and other miscellaneous services which each individual operator may or may not offer and may perhaps, do themselves.

The pluses of this type of business

Some of the strong points of owning a dry cleaning business are: diversity in operations and in vertical or horizontal expansion. Basic operations can be adjusted to expand production by adding payroll-hours and/or equipment; strong customer contact opportunity; labor intensive allowing an owner to earn by his or her own efforts. Additionally, the dry cleaning industry is considered to be relatively recession resistant.

The minuses of this business

Some of the negative aspects of this industry are: long owner hours and the need to cope with many personalities of employees and customers, etc.; labor intensive from shrinking labor pool that requires technical training, especially for production and customer-service functions; strong competition from Asian and East Indian immigrants and nationally franchised discount chains that are holding down prices and trimming profits; enforcement of various labor and environmental laws governing air, ground water, toxic waste, as well as Perc surcharges and fees in some jurisdictions.

A recent trend towards heavy discounting to counter serious problems from over- saturation has created unstable market conditions in many of the larger urban areas. The appearance of large discounting chains, as well as the cutting of prices by established cleaners, has caused a change in the habits of many customers who traditionally have chosen quality and service over lower prices. This has created a very tight market for many of the smaller "middle of the road" drycleaners that are neither discounters nor high-end.

Evaluation & Pricing Techniques

As is true in many small businesses, much of the dry cleaning business owner's benefits are buried in the expenses of the business. We recast the financial statements and use various Multiples of the Discretionary Earnings, usually between 2 and 3 times Seller's Discretionary Earnings (SDE).

Our evaluation process uses a multi-level approach to arrive at a realistic *Fair Market Value* range. The first step is to work with the owner to review all relevant financial material, building leases, promotional aspects, current prices, competition and sales, in-addition to the labor and equipment elements of the business.

The most desirable sales from the typical buyer's perspective are in the plant's retail over-the-counter "cash & carry" sales. This type of income is considered to be the most reliable and profitable. Sales from pickup stores or valet units owned by the same business, or other types of income are rated less than the plant's retail sales. The more removed from the control of the owner the income becomes, the lower its value. Wholesale cleaning processed for other businesses, as well as many commercial accounts, has little appeal to most buyers and is given little or no value.

Mid-Atlantic Asian Market

The following appears to be true in the Maryland, Washington, DC and Northern VA down to around Spotsylvania, but not PA or WVA or NC. Richmond is still in the stone ages.

No one likes to use cash flow as a measure. The common measure is a multiple of weekly gross sales.

Good drycleaning plants (as previously discussed in this article) are selling for up to 65 to 70x weekly gross. Lately there has been an increase in the number of Landlords forcing cleaner tenants to yank out Perc machines at lease renewal and sometimes even at lease assignments (at sale). Whether the latter is legal or not may be debatable depending on the text of the lease. Whereas there are alternative dry cleaning technology, HC (DF-2000, Greenearth, Purdry), CO_2, most LLs are not even considering plants in new retail centers, period!

Even arguments for the latest emergent technology, wet or water based "dry" cleaning, gets the boot. Therefore, in many cases, the price of dry cleaning plants with solid leases and the ability to do DC have gone up due to lack of supply.

The good news is that many landlords are beginning to understand HC technology, and many are welcoming it as a replacement to Perc. Furthermore, the price of HC based dry cleaning machines have gone down at least 20-30% over the past 5 years as more manufacturers of DC equipment have entered the field. So this alternative technology is much more affordable and getting more reliable.

Pick-up stores doing over 5K per week are selling for up to 40x gross weekly. In some extraordinary cases where the sales are $8K+ the ask has been 50x (our old plant pricing) gross weekly sales. Under 3K hardly sells and sells for around 30X. Crazy, but how long will this last? I don't know. I remember in the late 80's we were seeing 60x multiples until the market crashed and we were back to 50x i.e. 1 year gross.

<u>The West Coast</u>
On the West Coast there are only two differences: first, the market for good stores (over $30,000 retail sales per month) is very good; the market for smaller stores doing under $15,000 gross sales is poor and the pricing of these stores reflects the market conditions. A store doing $30,000 retail will go for 13 to 14 times monthly sales but a store doing $10,000 will go for only 6 to 7 monthly sales. Stores doing over $60,000 Per month retail are getting 17 times gross all cash via bank financing.

As far as the second difference, we do not continue to have the discounters coming into our market that we saw a few years ago. At this point, they are slowly moving their prices up.

Levels of Expertise
The various levels of expertise, and profitability, of dry cleaners can be thought of like one would view a multi-level apartment building.

The cleaners dwelling in the basement are mostly first generation immigrants with limited English language skills, who run the 20 percent off "retail prices," offer a $.99 shirts and function in a "work harder – NOT smarter" environment. Their sweatshops provide the owners' "jobs" rather that giving their businesses true "value." This segment of the industry is extremely saturated in the cities hosting a large immigrant population. These basement dwellers are having an increasing difficult time standing up to both the well-run higher priced competition, as well as to the big-box deep discounters.

The first floor is the home of the professional cleaners who have learned to build a profitable business based upon quality and service at a realistic price. They have worked to develop a strong retail following from the mile or so radius of the prime trade area out of their front doors. They have learned to "work smarter rather than harder!" They are increasing the "value" of their businesses, rather than just creating "jobs" for themselves.

The upper levels of our building contain the niche marketers. These distinguished dry cleaning professionals are the masters of dry cleaning and have developed specialized niches in various products areas (commercial accounts, "carriage trade clientele," restoration work, hotel accounts, route delivery, pick-up stores, etc.) and through the use of their trucks parked behind their plants, are able to service larger geographic areas. Capitalizing on their skills and knowledge, they are developing their operations into unique and increasing profitable businesses through diversification, growth and specialization.

The penthouse is reserved for the empire builders, who have been fortunate enough to have the time, money, education, ability, dedication, and yes, luck to build chains of stores. This group may include mature local and regional firms, as well as national franchises, so of which may be the well run deep discounters.

Industry Sales Trends

Industry sales trend should remain flat, due to the competition from new locations, except in the lucrative niche markets. The industry is saturated in major urban cities with low-price immigrant operations and large discounters. The dry cleaning industry is currently depressed with many locations, suffering as a result of new or/or discount competition could be down 15% to 30% when compared to recent prior years. Because of new regulations on Perc solvent, the cost of doing business should increase. The fabricare business should improve as the general economy, as well as the workplace dress standards improve.

There are not as many qualified buyers as in the past. The ones who are looking are only interested in the very best volume stores, especially those who have concentrated on the various niche markets. Average or worst stores are not selling for premium amounts. Also landlords are becoming more difficult to work with for new lease or assignment of current leases.

Dry cleaning will always be a basic business and will not become obsolete. People will always need to get their clothing cleaned and restored.

About the Author

The above has been excerpted from an article contributed by Richard Ehrenreich, CBI, CED, SBA. Ehrenreich is a former principal in an organization that developed and sold over 90 dry cleaners and laundries. He was the vice president of the International Fabricare Institute, and has held many positions in local and regional dry cleaning associations.

Ehrenreich has owned and operated a chain of dry cleaning stores employing 40 people. Some of the 10-year accounts included The White House, The Mayflower Hotel, The Army and Navy Club, as well as the Russian Embassy. Ehrenreich & Associates, LLC. is a consulting and brokerage firm that specializes in the evaluation and brokerage of dry cleaning and laundry businesses. They are willing to assist other brokers as consultants or joint venture partners.

Drycleaner brokers, Robin Rix of Rix Business Sales, Long Beach, California (rix@ctecomputer.com) and Kwang Chul "KC" Whang, W Group Commercial Real Estate, Laurel, Maryland (kcwwgroup@netzero.net) collaborated with Richard Ehrenreich on this article.

More Pricing Information

Following is some basic pricing information from Bizcomps . For a study based on your area of the country, contact Bizcomps at: www.bizcomps.com

The price based on a percentage of annual sales ranges from 75 percent in the western edition to 74 percent in the eastern edition to 56 percent in the central states edition.

The multiple of SDE is from 2.5 in the West to 2.3 in the East to 2.3 in the central states.

Franchise

Dunkin' Donuts

4,736 units	
Estimated Annual Sales per Unit:	$750,000
Approximate Total Investment:	For a single store the minimum initial cash required is $750,000 with a net worth at least $1,500,000. Minimum five-store development required.

Rule of Thumb:

- 70–110 percent of annual sales plus inventory
- " ... Dunkin Donuts shops now sell for 75%–125% of annual sales, depending mainly on geography. It's about 125% in New England, 100% of sales in the Mid-Atlantic, and lower in the South and Midwest. There really is not a Dunkin market in the West."

Benchmarks

"The average check at Dunkin' is about $2.50 to $3.50."

Source: *The Boston Globe*, April 13, 2004

Expenses as a percentage of annual sales:

Cost of Goods	23–24% +4% supplies (paper)
Payroll/Labor Cost	22%
Occupancy Cost	8–10%
Profit (estimated)	15–23%

General Information

"Price adjusted down if a remodel is imminent."

"The knowledgeable buyer of a Dunkin' Donuts shop will pay a base price based on the annual volume of the business. The multiplier will change somewhat from market area to market area. In the extreme case of much of New England, and some parts of the Mid-west, where Dunkin' Donuts franchises are very successful, the multiplier is now between 50 and 70 percent. The most important factor is the basic law of supply and demand. In New England, essentially all the areas have been assigned to franchisees for further development. Stores are rarely available for resale. Hence the higher multipliers. The next important factor is the business mix. In New England, units can have coffee sales over 60 percent of sales. Coffee sales have both lower food cost, and lower labor costs...volume itself somewhat changes the multiplier. In parts of the South, certain parts of the Midwest, and the Far West, where Dunkin' Donuts shops do not operate at the higher volumes of the 'better markets,' multipliers fall lower. Another way to state this is that lower volumes attract less potential buyers and investors, and supply and demand result in lower valuations per unit of sales."

"Average annual sales of a Dunkin' Donuts store in New England are just over $1 million...."

Source: Jon L. Luther, CEO, Dunkin' Donuts, in the *Boston Globe*, April 29, 2003

Industry Trend

"...Krispy Kreme isn't viewed as a direct competitor for the same reason Dunkin' Donuts hasn't experienced the same financial hit from low-carb diets. We're not a doughnut shop ... we're a coffee shop." Coffee is big business and in many stores represents 70 percent of the business. Dunkin' Donuts is teaming with a sister company, Baskin-Robbins, with combined stores. The company hopes to open approximately 800 stores in 2004.

Seller Financing

- "7 years—usually are bank/SBA financed."

Resources

www.dunkindonuts.com

E-Commerce (Electronic Shopping)

Rule of Thumb:

- 3 times SDE
- 4 times EBIT

Pricing Tips

"Length in business, barriers to entry such as keyword/search engine results, partners, vendors, etc. can all add to the valuation. Also additional hard asssets such as servers, as well as the website technology."

"Natural search results and third-party rankings (e.g., Google) can play a significant role as an asset."

Industry Experts' Ratings:

Marketability (1 = Low: 4 = High)	2.8
Industry Trend (1 = Declining: 4 = Growing)	3.6
Ease of Replication (1 = Easy: 4 = Difficult)	1.6

Benchmarks

"Revenue per unique visitor should be around \$.30 to \$.50. Also the conversion rate should be .5% to 2% (that is orders per visits)."

Expenses as a percentage of annual sales:

Cost of Goods Sold	50%
Payroll/Labor Costs	10%
Occupancy Cost	05%
Profit (estimated)	30%

Advantages of this Business

- "Work at home, work anywhere, few employees"
- "Location—live anywhere you want (as an owner). Another might be flexibility to add/change product, and customer acquistion is quite low."

Disadvantages of this Business

- "Compeition, rise in advertising rates in the past year—and that will continue for a while (i.e. Google's ppc costs)."

Industry Trend

"Every year the overall percentage of online retail site sales as compared to traditional retail is growing and will continue to do so for the forseeable future."

Employee Service—Leasing (PEO)

(See also Employment Agencies & Temporary Services)

2,300	SIC: 7363-03	NAIC: 561330

Rule of Thumb:

- 6 to12 times EBITA

Employment Agencies

28,364	SIC: 7361-03	NAIC: 561310

Rule of Thumb:

- 50 percent of annual revenues; may require earnout
- 1 to 1.5 times SDE; add fixtures equipment & inventory; may require earnout

Engineering/Architectural Practices

Rule of Thumb:

- 40 percent of annual fee revenues; add fixtures & equipment; may require earnout

Franchise

Environment Control (Commercial Cleaning Services)

60 units

Rule of Thumb:

- 42 percent of sales plus inventory

Resources

www.environmentcontrol.com

Equipment & Party Rental (General Rental)

(See Rental, Equipment & Party)

Event Companies

2,977		

Rule of Thumb:

- 3 times EBITDA plus asset value.

Pricing Tips

"Are there events on the books going forward? How many repeat clients?"

General Information

"The event planning business is very dependent on networking..."

Source: Danielle Nunez, Owner, Grand Events of Florida, *Tampa Bay Business Journal*, January 31, 2005

Seller Financing

- 2 ½ years

Fabric Stores

7,146	SIC: 5949-02	NAIC: 451130

Rule of Thumb:

- 3 times monthly sales plus inventory

Resources

The Fabric Shop Network—an online resource
www.fabshopnet.com

Facilities Support Services

Rule of Thumb:

- 50 percent of annual sales

Pricing Tips

Industry Experts' Ratings:

Marketability (1 = Low: 4 = High) 2.4
Industry Trend (1 = Declining: 4 = Growing) 2.4
Ease of Replication (1 = Easy: 4 = Difficult) 2.4

Benchmarks

Expenses as a percentage of annual sales:

Profit (estimated) 18%

Advantages of this Business

- "More large corporations are outsourcing this traditional in-house organization."

Disadvantages of this Business

- "Clients are always looking at this service to cut overhead costs."

Family Entertainment Centers

Rule of Thumb:

- 3 times EBITDA

General Information

"FEC's that are generally 50,000 to 80,000 sq. ft. in size with several profit centers. Many include bowling, laser tag, arcade, redemption, fast food, party areas, billiards, etc."

Franchise

Fantastic Sam's

1,364 units

Approximate Total Investment: $138,000–$188,000

Rule of Thumb:

- 25 percent of annual sales plus inventory

Resources
www.fantasticsams.com

Fast Food—also called Quick-Service

(See also Restaurants and Franchised Food Businesses)

Rule of Thumb:

- 1 to 1.5 times SDE; plus fixtures, equipment & inventory
- 35 to 45 percent of annual sales plus inventory

Resources
National Restaurant Association
www.restaurant.org

Nation's Restaurant
www.nrn.com

Franchise

Fast Signs

450 units

Approximate Total Investment: $152,360–$225,000

Rule of Thumb:

- 42 to 46 percent of annual sales plus inventory

Resources
www.fastsigns.com

FedEx (Ground)

Rule of Thumb:

- 60 percent of annual sales

General Information

FedEx ground is a fairly new program for FedEx and uses independent contractors who actually operate their own business under the FedEx name. There are several pending lawsuits in which FedEx Ground contractors claim that they are forced to operate as employees. FedEx Ground claims that their independent contractor's agreement is legal and that these operators are free to sell their businesses and are indeed independent contractors.

Feed and Seed Stores

General Information

"Should have a relatively high gross profit in order to make it profitable to a purchaser. Price is fixtures and equipment at depreciated value plus inventory at cost. Absolutely nothing for goodwill. Caution: Rent should never exceed two percent of gross sales."

Film Companies *(See Audio & Film Companies)*

Fine Dining *(See also Restaurants)*

Rule of Thumb:

- 30 percent of annual sales plus inventory

Fitness Centers *(See also Racquet Sports Clubs)*

26,830	SIC: 7991-01	NAIC: 713940

Rule of Thumb:

- "One year's annual revenues; usually reduced (or pro-rated) by memberships already contracted and paid for"
- "The clubs today have the electronic transfer money systems.... One rule of thumb would be ten times the monthly amount...so if the club has $10,000 a month going through the electronic transfer, then the price would be $100,000 plus the value of the equipment...taking into consideration that the lease has sufficient time on it...most clubs today have $30,000 and up on the electronic transfer money. If there is 10 years on the lease, added value can be given for that."

Pricing Tips

"The total purchase should be pro-rated for memberships that have been 'paid in full' and up-front. The owner has likely already spent this money, so if the new owner fails to pro-rate these specific memberships, they must honor the 'paid in full' memberships without receiving any financial benefit."

"Fitness and/or health centers historically have been priced at 10 times the Electronic Transfer Money. Example: If the club has $15,000 a month on the electronic transfer money, times 10 equals $150,000 plus value of equipment. Equipment can be about $100,000 (depreciated), plus a ten-year lease is added value... so market price would be on or about $300,000.00 to $350,000.00 depending on condition of the facility...naturally all of this would be assuming the $15,000 cash flow covers the net, plus...."

"...there are about 10,000 express workout facilities in the United States, about 37 percent of the total health club market."

Source: International Health, Racquet & Sportsclub Association (IHRSA)

The major franchise companies in the fitness business:

Name	# of Units	Approximate Investment
Bally Fitness	420	$100,000–$1.5 million
Contours Express	315	$34,000–$49,000
Curves	8,750	$36,425–$42,850
Gold's Gym	658	$500,000–$2.2 million

Industry Experts' Ratings:

Marketability (1 = Low: 4 = High) 3.2
Industry Trend (1 = Declining: 4 = Growing) 2.4
Ease of Replication (1 = Easy: 4 = Difficult) 2.0

"Profitability is concurrent with owner experience in the field. Employee sales and management training programs are important to the success of this business. It is an entity of its own that cannot be learned in MBA programs."

Benchmarks

"Estimated median of $655,000 in revenue per club"

"Estimated median of 9 full-time and 34 part-time employees per club"

"Based on a median payroll cost of 41% of total revenue"

Source: International Health, Racquet & Sportsclub Association (IHRSA)

"The average fitness company has annual revenues of $500,000 or less with about 15 employees."

"Revenues are generated from two major sources:
1) Memberships account for 75%–80% of a club's revenues. Personal training fees, clothes & food account for the other 20%–25%."

"Theodore J. Forstmann, the financier who said he planned to wind down his firm next year, made what was likely to be his last big bet yesterday by acquiring a private fitness company for $1.6 billion.

"Mr. Forstmann's firm, Forstmann Little & Company, has agreed to buy 24 Hour Fitness Worldwide, the world's largest privately owned chain of fitness centers, executives with both companies said. The deal is expected to be announced today. The chain, based in San Ramon, California, has 345 clubs in 15 states with 2.8 million members, mostly on the West Coast, and another 15 clubs in Asia. Last year, the company had more than $1 billion in revenue."

Source: *The New York Times*, May 3, 2005

Club Operating Benchmarks: sample averages

	2003
Total Revenue (thousands $)	2,099
EBITDA % of total revenues	14.6%
EBIT of total revenues	6.0%

Source: International Health, Racquet & Sportsclub Association (IHRSA)

	Key Ratios
Revenue Growth	5.0%
Total Payroll as a % of Revenue	43.8%
Rate of Member Retention	65.5%
Net Membership Growth	3.9%
Revenue/Member	$653
Indoor Sq. Ft./ Member	13.5
Revenue/Indoor Sq. Ft.	$47
Non-Dues Revenues as a % of Revenue	28.3%

Note: Figures are for 2003.

Source: International Health, Racquet & Sportsclub Association (IHRSA)

Expenses as a percentage of annual sales:

Payroll/Labor Costs	33%
Occupancy Cost	10%
Profit (estimated)	35%

General Information

"The Scope of the U.S. Health Club Industry (industry estimates)

Number of U.S. Clubs:	26,830 (2005)
Number of Health Club Members:	39.4 million (2004)
2003 Total Industry revenues:	14.1 billion"

Source: International Health, Racquet & Sportsclub Association (IHRSA)

Clubs' Most Profitable Programs and Services

"The following figures indicate what percentage of clubs cited a given program or service as being among their five most profitable.

1. Personal Training	50.5%
2. Massage Therapy	28.2%

3. Pro Shop 26.2%
4. Aquatics Programs 24.3%
5. Tennis Programs 20.5%
6. Food & Beverage sales 11.7%
7. Tanning 9.7%
8. Physical Therapy 7.8%
   Summer Camps 7.8%
9. Kids Programs 6.8%
   Martial Arts .... 6.8%"

Source: International Health, Racquet & Sportsclub Association (IHRSA)

Questions to Ask: "Does the company buy or lease its exercise and weight equipment? Leasing is very common. How many members are there on average? It should be about 3,000. What is the referral rate for new members? It should be about 75–80%. What is the member attrition rate? It is usually about 30–37%."

"About fifty companies control a third of the U.S. market (e.g., Bally's, Gold's Gym, etc.)."

Advantages of this Business

- "Upward Trend in Memberships:
  (1) Health club memberships increased about 9% in 2003 (accounting for approximately 40 million). Health club membership numbers have steadily increased for the past 5 years—growing 32% from 1998 to 2003." (2) 2003 Industry Revenues increased to $14 billion."
- "National Health Concerns:
  About 60% of adults in the U.S. are either overweight or obese. As the number of overweight Americans continues to grow, national campaigns increase on all government levels to encourage both exercise and diet. Naturally, fitness centers will benefit from the growing obesity concern in the U.S."
- "It can be a good cash flow. It caters to the professional! Creates an ambiance of health and fitness."

Disadvantages of this Business

- "Poor management will put you out of business. You must be on top of service, cleanness, upgrading equipment often."
- "Attrition Rates:
  About 34% of fitness club members do not renew their membership at the end of their contract. This increases marketing costs for attracting

new members, while contributing to the unpredictability of revenues."

- "Market Saturation:
  In some markets, consumers can choose from up to a dozen fitness centers within a 10- mile radius. The density of competition will limit a center's ability to raise prices and reduce profit margins."
- "Economic Cycles:
  People are not as willing to pay membership costs during hard economic times."
- "Legal Liabilities:
  If a member is injured while training, liability might fall on both the personal trainer and the club. Most states will allow 'exculpatory clauses' in membership contracts (which release clubs from liability); however, some states find that fitness is 'essential to human life' and void the 'exculpatory clauses.'"

Industry Trend

"Employment in the fitness sector is expected to grow, as indicated by the U.S. Bureau of Labor Statistics. According to a 2005 U.S. Department of Labor report, fitness trainers and group exercise instructors are among the fastest growing occupations in the United States, with faster than average growth expected through 2012. IDEA continues to take a leadership role in collecting important salary and compensation data to assist both employers and fitness professionals in making informed decisions."

Source: IDEA Health & Fitness Association. www.ideafit.com

Resources

International Health, Racquet and Sportsclub Association (IHRSA)
www.ihrsa.org —This is a superb site and should be visited by anyone interested in this industry.

www.americansportsdata.com

Fitness, Racquet Sports, and Spa Projects: A Guide to Appraisal, Market Analysis, Development, and Financing by Arthur E. Gimmy, MAI, and Brian B Woodworth, published by the Appraisal Institute, 875 N. Michigan Ave., Chicago, IL 60611-1980. (312) 335-4100

Flower Shops (Florists)

48,670	SIC: 5992-01	NAIC: 453110

Rule of Thumb:

- 30 percent of annual sales plus inventory
- 2 times SDE plus inventory (after adjustment for fair market value for ownership based on their labor contribution)

Pricing Tips

"Review the Profit and Loss Statement to determine if wire service revenues and expenses (FTD, Teleflora, etc.) are tracked on separate line items to ensure that the sales are not overstated and cost of goods is not understated."

"A premium should be given for stores with a significant number of commercial accounts (especially if there is a credit card on file for ease of billing) which helps protect revenues from big box stores that also sell flowers and plants."

"Florists with a significant number of weekly or house accounts are very attractive in the marketplace and can command slightly higher multiples. Below market rent can also justify higher multiples. Conversely, shops located near grocery stores with large floral departments or near big box discounters should expect lower multiples."

"The value of a florist shop is typically 2 to 4 times the adjusted cash flow, after a fair market rate for the owner's labor contribution is deducted from the adjusted cashflow [EBIT]."

Industry Experts' Ratings:

Amount of Competition (1 = Lot of: 4 = Not much) 1.0
Amount of Risk (1 = Very: 4 = Not much) 1.2
Historical Profit Trend (1 = Down: 4 = Up) 1.2
Location & Facilities (1 = Poor: 4 = Excellent) 2.4
Marketability (1 = Low: 4 = High) 2.4
Industry Trend (1 = Declining: 4 = Growing) 1.2
Ease of Replication (1 = Easy: 4 = Difficult) 2.0

Industry Experts' Ratings: (continued)

"Owning a flower shop continues to be a desireable lifestyle business for creative entrepreneurs who wish to provide an artistic and meaningful contribution to their community."

"The floral industry has been deeply affected by the economy and online 'orders.' Grocery stores and discount warehouses have also taken market share from retail florists."

Benchmarks

"The average florist generates $250,000 per year in sales."

Flower Shops

"Retail florist shops: (2004)	22,753
(Average annual florist sales: $290,000)	
Supermarkets selling flowers:	23,000
Plant nurseries and garden centers:	16,432
Floral wholesalers (estimate)	1,000
Domestic floriculture growers:	11,193"

Source: Society of American Florists. www.aboutflowers.com

"For a florist to be profitable, the rent should not exceed 15% of gross sales."

"Local business is generally more profitable than wire-service-generated income."

Expenses as a percentage of annual sales:

Cost of Goods Sold	33%
Payroll/Labor Costs	20%
Occupancy Cost	10%
Profit (estimated)	20%

General Information

"Floral shops are among the few types of retail businesses that conduct significant sales over the phone, without ever seeing or meeting consum-

ers, and, often, without the customers ever seeing the purchased products. In fact, some florists strive for strong phone sales, aspiring to achieve 80 percent, even 90 percent, of revenues from telephone orders, perhaps because these types of transactions can be quicker, easier and more cost-effective than in-store transactions. They can also allow for greater labor efficiency, since designers can focus on designing rather than talking to walk-in shoppers, some of whom might be browsing with no intention of purchasing."

Source: www.floristsreview.com

Questions to ask a seller: "Percentage local business versus wire service?"

There are an estimated 30,000 U.S. florists, many of them mom-and-pop operations, and the highly fragmented, $18.5 billion floral industry has generally resisted national chains.

Source: *The Boston Globe*

"How important is Valentine's Day?
Valentine's Day is 10 times busier than our average day, our highest volume day by far. We'll do about $700,000 of business that day. Mother's Day is next; it's six times busier than a normal day. December is our best month, but with the holidays, business is spread out. With Valentine's Day, it's got to get done on that day or you're in trouble.

"How has the flower business changed?
We've definitely become more of a gifts and special events business. There are so many more outlets where you can buy flowers. Twenty-five years ago, you had to go to a florist if you wanted flowers. Now you can go to supermarkets or big-box stores. A lot of big chains use flowers as loss leaders. So we've evolved into more of a service-oriented business that's about quality, design, and same-day delivery."

Source: From an interview with David Winston, of Winston's Flowers, *The Boston Globe*, February 13, 2005

Advantages of this Business

- "Being a florist can be a very rewarding and profitable business if operated by adhering to industry operating standards and not as a hobby."
- "This is one of the few industries that allow a business owner to marry an artistic aptitude with income generation via entrepreneurship."
- "Owning a flower shop is a 'lifestyle' business that if run professionally, can be very profitable. Florists also enjoy a favorable position within their communities as they are often an integral part of many

local activities and celebrations. Also with many florists located in a concentrated area, successful florists have the opportunity to acquire additional stores to increase profits and lower expenses all within close geographic proximity."

Disadvantages of this Business

- "Success is often contingent on finding and retaining quality design staff."
- "Increasing loss of marketshare to Internet 'order gatherers' or florists."
- "There is increasing competition with many online order gatherers spending significant advertising dollars to reach consumers directly."

Industry Trend

"Survey results reveal that U.S. florist shop owners, on average, are currently older than those in 'Old Europe.' Results suggest that a substantial turnover in florist shop ownership may be expected in the U.S. over the next ten years."

Source: Survey conducted by Prince & Prince P-and-P@worldnet.att.net
for the September 27th, 2004 edition of *Flower News*

Age Profile of the U.S. Retail Florist Industry, 2003

Age of Florist Shop Owner	% of Florists
Under 35	06%
35–44	20%
45–54	37%
55–64	26%
65 or Older	11%

Source: Survey conducted by Prince & Prince P-and-P@worldnet.att.net
for the September 27th, 2004 edition of *Flower News*

Seller Financing

- "3 to 7 years"

Resources

Society of American Florists—for members only
www.safnow.org

www.aboutflowers.com—information on retail florists

Wholesale Florist & Florist Supplier Association
www.wffsa.org

www.floralmarketresearch.com—some free information, but lots of data available for a fee

Florists' Review
www.floristsreview.com

Definitions

Distribution—In commerce, the process of moving merchandise from the producers to the consumer or retail or wholesale point of sale.... The term *distribution* also refers to the channels through which goods move from the producer to the market.

Wholesaling—The act of purchasing products and materials from the producer and selling them to retailers and other businesses, which in turn sell them to consumers. The function of the wholesaler, also referred to as a middleman or jobber, is to evaluate much broader regional, seasonal, and consumer needs than those merchants at the retail level are able to do, and to anticipate supplies and demands. Among the functions that come under the responsibility of the typical wholesaler are advertising and sales promotion, warehousing, allocating inventories to locations convenient to retailers, transporting merchandise on request, servicing products and merchandise after they are purchased, extensive bookkeeping, and in many cases providing their retailer customers with financial assistance.

Dictionary of Business Terms by Wilbur Cross,
published by Prentice Hall Press, www.phdirect.com

Food Processing & Distribution

Rule of Thumb:

- Processing
  Branded—5 to 7 times EBIT
  Non-Branded—4.5 to 6 times EBIT

- Distribution
  Branded and Non-Branded—4 to 5 times EBIT

Pricing Tips

Rate of growth; gross margins—higher is better; customer concentration—high is a threat; management continuity, high synergies

Food Service Distribution

Pricing Tips

"Rule of thumb difficult to apply due to variance in asset base between companies, as well as diversity in product and customer mix. Key factors for consideration include gross profit percentage, average order size, and customer concentration percentages. Industry consolidation driven by larger companies subtract value for low GP, small average order size, and excessive customer concentrations that will make profitability difficult."

Seller Financing

- "5 year seller carryback is average."

Food Stores *(See Grocery Stores— Small to Medium Size)*

Football Teams (professional)

Rule of Thumb:

- According to *Forbes* Magazine of September 19, 2005, "The average value of a National Football League franchise was $733 million in 2004. *Forbes* estimates that the Minnesota Vikings is the least valuable team in the NFL at $658 million.. The Washington Redskins had the highest valuation at $1,264 million. According to *Forbes*, "Football team values rose an average of 12% during the past year to $819 million."

- The price of an Arena Football team is about $18 million (based on a pending sale of the Kansas City team). Then there is the Arena Football's minor league teams—one team sold for $1million.

Source: *Forbes* ,June 6, 2005

Arena Football—2004

Revenue—$1.2 million	Expenses—$910,558
Ticket sales 47%	Payroll 42%
Corporate sponsorship 33%	Rent 15%
Merchandise & Concessions 10%	Travel 05%
Radio & TV 09%	Liab. & Work. Comp. 10%
Other 01%	Other 42%

Source: *Forbes,* June 6, 2005

Note: We have found that *Forbes* Magazine tackles (no pun intended) some pretty interesting valuation issues. It's worth it to subscribe.

Franchises

320,000 +

What is Franchising

Webster's Dictionary defines *franchise* as: "1. A privilege or right granted a person or a group by a government, state, or sovereign. 2. Authorization granted by a manufacturer to a distributor or dealer to sell his products." The word comes from Old French *franchise,* from *franc*, meaning "free."

"There are an estimated 1,500 different franchisors (franchise companies) operating in the U.S."

Source: www.azfranchises.com/franchisefacts

In a more contemporary business context, the terms *franchising* and *franchise* are often used interchangeably to mean a business, a type of business, or an industry. Strictly speaking, the "franchise" is the agreement or license between two parties which gives a person or group of people (the franchisee) the rights to market a product or service using the trademark of another business (the franchisor.) The franchisee has the rights to market the product or service using the operating methods of the franchisor. The franchisee has the obligation to pay the franchisor certain fees and royalties in exchange for these rights. The franchisor has the obligation to provide these rights and generally support the franchisee. In this sense, franchising is not a business or an industry, but it is a method used by businesses for the marketing and distribution of their products or services.

Responsibilities of Franchisee and Franchisor

"Franchisor:	Franchisee:
Owns trademark	Licenses trademark
Provides Support:	Runs business with franchisor's support, training, advertising, marketing, financing (sometimes)
Receives fees	Pays fees

Different types of Franchises

"There are many businesses, organizations, and even some government agencies that grant franchises. In sports, teams are referred to as a *franchise*.

"The franchise industry accounts for 40% of all retail sales in the U.S."

Source: www.azfranchises.com/franchisefacts

"In telecommunications, government agencies grant licenses to radio, TV, and cable operators that are referred to as *franchises*. This research study is focused on two other types of franchises—product distribution franchises and business format franchises.

Product distribution franchises sell the franchisor's products and are supplier-dealer relationships. In general, the franchisor licenses the use of its trademark to the franchisee but may not in all cases provide the franchisee with a system for running its business. Examples of product distribution franchises are soft drink distributors (Pepsi), automobile dealerships (Ford), and gas stations (ExxonMobil.)

"A new franchise business opens every 8 minutes of every business day."

Source: www.azfranchises.com/franchisefacts

"Business format franchises not only sell the franchisor's product or service, with the franchisor's trademark, but operate the business according to a system provided by the franchisor. The franchisor provides training, marketing materials, and an operations manual to the franchisee. There are many examples of business format franchises, including quick-service restaurants (McDonald's), automotive services (Meineke Car Care Centers), lodging (Marriott), real estate agents (RE/MAX), convenience stores (7-Eleven), and tax preparation services (H&R Block).

"There are other methods of business expansion, including wholly company-owned chains. As an economic model, however, franchising has been so widely embraced because it provides the franchisor:

- a method of expansion using the franchisee's capital, which allows for a faster rate of system expansion as well as a source of capital;
- the motivation of franchisees that comes from owning their own business rather than being employees.

Who Does What?

	"Franchisor:	Franchisee:
Site selection:	Probably oversees, may choose	Chooses with approval
Design:	Provides prototype design	Implements design; pays
Employees:	Generalized recommendations	Actually hires, supervises and fires
Menu:	Set by franchisor	Changed only by approval
Prices:	Recommendations, possible caps	Decides actual prices
Supplies:	May offer bulk purchasing program or lists approved suppliers orlists quality requirements or requires supplies from franchisor	Complies with program
Advertising:	Designs national program Requires or suggests local amounts	Pays into advertising fund Gets franchisor approval
Quality control:	Sets standards; trains franchisees; inspects	Trains employees, carries out systems"

Source: "Economic Impact of Franchised Businesses," prepared by PricewaterhouseCoopers for the International Franchise AssociationEducational Foundation, 2004. For the full study go to www.franchise.org

Franchise Resales

Shown below is our current list of rules of thumb for the resale of various franchises. We have received many of these rules from the business brokerage community who have been kind enough to supply them.

> "The average initial franchise investment is $250,000—excluding real estate."
>
> Source: www.azfranchises.com/franchisefacts

Keep in mind that the following rules of thumb are simply rough guidelines. In some cases, the sampling was limited, but we included a rule of thumb to provide at least a starting point. The bigger the franchise, the more likely it is that we have a fairly representative number of sales. In other cases, where we received a lot of "rules" for the same franchise, we had to average them out, so to speak. Whenever there was a fairly large gap in the information we received, we created a range. Where there is a number in parentheses, we have supplied a footnote that may contain important pricing or additional information. Some of the rules may pertain to franchises that are just regional; and in others, the rule of thumb may just represent a unit (or units) that pertains to just one particular area. For example, by reading the comments that follow, one would see that Dunkin'Donuts has a much higher multiple in the Northeast than it does in the West.

> "Most franchise companies have fewer than 100 units."
>
> Source: www.azfranchises.com/franchisefacts

If you don't find a franchise that you are working on listed below, use a rule of thumb for a similar franchise. And, again, remember these are guidelines only. The information we have received reveals a wide disparity within the same franchise family. Also, the rules don't account for cash sales or attractive terms. If you use them carefully, they will, hopefully, provide a starting point for your work. They should be used for ballpark pricing and not valuation work.

[And, when your sale is completed, how about going to our Web site www.bbpinc.com, clicking on Franchise Resales on our Home page, and completing a very brief questionnaire.]

For up-to-date information on franchise fees, total investment required or the number of existing units, check the individual franchise in this Guide and then visit their web site. We have provided a web site for most of the franchises listed in the Guide

What types of franchises are in the top 25 percent?

"The top 25% were defined as those with the highest profit from franchising as a percentage of total franchise revenues.

Personal Services	29%
Retail	29%
Business Services	14%
Food	14%
Maintenance	14%"

Source: 2004 IFA Educational Foundation and Business Resource Services

Franchises

Name of Franchise	Selling Price as a % of Sales
AAMCO Transmission	42%
A & W Restaurants	45%–55%
Ace Cash Express	1.25%
Ace Hardware stores (1)	45%
Allegra Printing	65%
American Poolplayers Association (APA) (2)	1.4%
Arctic Circle	50%
Atlanta Bread Company	28%
Baskin-Robbins Ice Cream	46%–56%
Between Rounds(3)	
Big Apple Bagel	42%
Black Jack Pizza	55%–60%
Blimpies	48%
Bresler's Ice Cream	35%–40%
Budget Blinds (4)	
Buffet Nest	40%
Burger King	40%
Carvel Ice Cream/Restaurants	60%
Chester International	45%
Chicago Pizza	26%
Closets by Design	50%
Computer Pro	33%
Conroy's Flowers	55%–60%
Cost Cutters	57%
Cottman Transmission	50%–55%
Coverall North America (5)	2–3 times monthly sales
Culligan Dealerships	80%–120%
Curves for Women (6)	35%

Name of Franchise	Selling Price as a % of Sales
Dairy Queen	50%
Deck the Walls	35%–40%
Del Taco	90%
Dollar Discount stores	11%
Dr. Vinyl	75%
Dunkin Donuts (7)	75%–80%
Environment Control	42%
Fantastic Sams (8)	25%–30%
Fast Signs	42%–46%
Franklin's Printing	52%
Godfather's Pizza	28%
Goodyear Store	35%
Grease Monkey	58%
Great Harvest Bread Co. (9)	
Great Steak & Potato	55%–60%
Grout Doctor	89%
Hallmark Cards	40%
Harley-Davidson Motors (10)	87%
Heavenly Hams	48%
Home Pros Home Improvement	56%
House Doctor	24%
Hungry Howie's Pizza & Subs	30%
Iceberg Drive Inn	40%–45%
Jani-King	26%
Jersey Mike's	50%
Kentucky Fried Chicken (KFC)	30%–35%
Kwik Kopy (printing)	40%
Kuman Math & Reading Centers	40%–45%
Liberty Tax Service	32%
Lil' Dinos Subs (11)	64%
Little Caesar's Pizza	55%
Logan Farms (honey-glazed hams)	30%
Lube-Pro	38%
MAACO Auto Paint	40%
MaggieMoo's Ice Cream (12)	32%
Maid Brigade	50%
Mail Boxes, Etc.	39%
Marble Slab Creamery	44%
Mountain Mike's Pizza	27%
Moto Photo	72%
Mr. Jim's Pizza	35%
Mr. Payroll	1.3%
Mr. Rooter Plumbing (13)	
Mrs. Fields Cookies	68%
Oil X Change	30%
Once Upon A Child	25%
One Hour Martinizing	60%

Name of Franchise	Selling Price as a % of Sales
Orange Julius	32%
Pak Mail	50%
Pasquales Pizza	35%–40%
Petland	57%
Pizza by George	50%
Pizza Inn	47%
Play It Again Sports	45%
Precision Tune Auto Care	36%
Purrfect Auto	75%
Quick Stop Oil Change	30%
Quizno's Classic Subs (14)	50%–60%
Red Robin Gourmet Burgers	32%
Rita's—Ices, Cones, Shakes	.80%–1.3%
Roly Poly Sandwiches	34%
Sears Carpet & Upholstery Care	30%
Service Master	45%
Shell Rapid Lube	51%
Signarama	55%–60%
Sir Speedy (printing)(15)	25%
Subway (16)	50%–60%%
Superior Inspection	1.3%
Swisher (restroom hygiene service)	75%
Taco Johns	31%
TCBY	50%
Texaco Express Lube	30%–40%
Two Men and a Truck	43%
Your Office USA	60%
U Save (auto rental) (17)	10%–15%
We the People	86%
Wingstop Restaurants	33%
Ziebart International (auto services)	42%

Note: All rules are plus inventory

(1) Sales seem to indicate that smaller sales bring a higher multiple (50% +) than stores with sales over a million, which seem to bring lower multiples. Price is plus inventory which may be the cause of lower multiples for larger stores.

(2) $1,000 to $1,800 per team in sales; selling price: $2,000 to $2,500 per team

(3) 3 to 4 times earnings

(4) 2 times annual EBIT, plus inventory & equipment

(5) Master/Area developer—Sell for 3 to 5 times earnings plus some blue sky for size and potential of market (some cases).

(6) Prices for Curves for Woman seem to be all over the

place. Some sales have been reported at 75% + of sales. One sale reported was 1.31 times sales for four units.

(7) In ... Dunkin' Donuts shops now sell for 75 to 125% of annual sales, depending mainly on geography. It's about 125% in New England, 100% of sales in the Mid-Atlantic States, and lower in the South and Midwest. There really is not a Dunkin' Donuts market in the West. A sale in Colorado was reported that sold for 22% of sales.

(8) These stores sell for maximum 2 times SDE versus $120,000 to $125,000 for new. 10 to 12 sales have been reported at 2 times SDE for absentee owner stores (most are) and 2 times SDE + manager's salary of owner operated.

(9) 3.3 to 3.4 times SDC

(10) Netted $2,100,000 and seller retained 20% of ownership

(11) One sold for 80% of sales, but it was located in an office building with vending rights

(12) One MaggieMoo's Ice Cream & Treatery sale was reported at 92%, three years old, great location, growth at approx 15% a year; but only 15% down payment

(13) 1 to 4 times SDC plus hard assets. The number between 1 and 4 depends on several factors, such as the owner operating a truck, etc.

(14) Two sales in the western states were reported at 99% of sales and another at 65% of sales. However, two sales in the lower Midwest were reported at 38% and 40%.

(15) One sale was reported at 70% of sales.

(16) On stores with gross sales of $300,000 to $500,000, multiple of 40% of annual sales. On stores with sales of $500,000+, multiple of 50% of annual sales. Franchisor would like 30% as a down payment on resales. "I would suggest for Subway, in New England and maybe all of New England, due to the high number of pizza restaurants, Subways tend to sell for a much lower of percentage of sales than 47%—sometimes as low as 20 to 25%."

(17) Price does not include cost of vehicles, and revenues do not include auto sales.

Resources

Nation's Restaurant—If you're involved in anything to do with food franchises or the restaurant/food industry itself, you have to subscribe to this publication. It is a weekly and has all sorts of necessary information about the food industry. For subscription information, go to www.nrn.com or call (800) 944-4676. You can't be involved in this field in any capacity without reading *Nation's Restaurant*.

International Franchise Association—This trade association publishes many different kinds of material, all relating to franchising. Their semi-annual *Franchise Opportunities Guide* is a wealth of information on all the various franchisors. In order to be included, the franchisor must be a member; however, many are members, including the major ones.

The Business Brokerage community—We want to thanks all those business intermediaries who contributed to our list of rules of thumb for the resale of various franchises.

***Entrepreneurs* 26th Annual Franchise 500**

1. Subway
2. Curves
3. Quizno's
4. Jackson Hewitt Tax Service
5. UPS Stores
6. Sonic Drive-In Restaurants
7. Jani-King
8. 7-Eleven
9. Dunkin' Donuts
10. Re/Max Int'l

Source: *Entrepreneur Magazine*

Franchise Food Businesses

Rule of Thumb:

(This category is dominated by McDonald's, Burger King, Wendy's, KFC, Dominos, Pizza Hut, Arby's, Dairy Queen, Taco Bell & Denny's—others are Subway, Blimpie's, Baskin Robbins & Schlotsky's)

- 50 percent of annual sales plus inventory
- 1.7 to 2.3 SDE plus inventory
- 4 to 6 times monthly sales plus inventory
- Asset value plus 1 year's SDE plus inventory

Pricing Tips

"The multiples are a bit above the level for the industry in which the franchisee participates."

"Stability of income, down payment & quality of franchisor"

"Labor costs typically represent 15 to 20 percent of gross food sales. Food costs generally run from 28 percent to a high 40 percent for red meat on the menu. Pizza shops run about 28 to 30 percent. Rent should not exceed 10 percent."

"Check the franchise agreement. Who pays transfer and training fees? Does the franchisor have the first right to purchase the business? Will the transition require the facilities to be upgraded to franchisor's current standards? If yes, the upgrade cost can be substantial."

Seller Financing

- "5 to7 years; however, SBA loans up to 10 years can be obtained."

Pricing Existing Franchised Businesses

Pricing the franchise resale obviously depends on the franchise. Is the franchise value added or—as in some cases—value subtracted? Does franchising add value to the business or would the same business—independent of a franchise label—bring as high a price in the marketplace? When calculating a multiple of annual sales, is it before subtracting the royalty fees, or are they included in the annual sales? After all, 6 percent of just $500,000 in annual revenues is $30,000, but just $12,000 at 40 percent of annual sales. The $12,000 probably doesn't have much of an impact on pricing unless the sales are really astronomical.

McDonald's has always been the franchise that everyone compares others to, but that has changed recently. However, it probably hasn't hurt the price of a McDonald's—it is still a very strong brand. One disadvantage of franchising is that, like Burger King, the company gets sold several times, and the direction of the new owners can play havoc with operational support, advertising and growth of the company. In most cases, franchisees have no control over this. The strength of a franchise is the success of the brand name and the reputation created in the marketplace. Many franchises have been able to create that brand-identity and awareness to add a lot of value

"It should be confirmed with the franchisor that the existing royalty and co-op fees are going to remain the same for a new buyer. It has been my experience that the existing franchise agreement is not transferable to a new buyer, who has to sign a new agreement that is in effect at the time of closing, which normally will have a higher franchise royalty and co-op advertising fee than the existing franchisee's, since the existing franchisee has been around for some time. For example, some of the old Kwik Kopy franchises have royalties as low as 3%, but the current royalty is 10%. A 7% differential on a typical Kwik Kopy gross yearly revenue of $300K is $21,000, which would equate to an approximate reduction of $50,000 in the selling price of the business."

Source: An email from Dick Flamos, Certified Business Brokers, on franchising, August 8, 2004

to the price of one of the units. And, if you want to buy a very popular franchise in a particular geographical marketplace, you have to pay the going rate.

Some prospective business buyers like the security and the support of a franchise. Still others want the independence of owning and controlling their own business. Buying an independent business provides just that. No answering to the franchisor, no royalties and no heavy advertising fees, no forced purchasing from certain suppliers—and no politics. Owning your own independent business also allows you to expand, change, add or delete products and/or services. Independent businesses can be very quick to adjust to changes. Franchises, especially large ones, are very cumbersome and slow to adapt to new trends and ideas.

The choice is personal one. Some very strong independent operators have chosen, after years of independence, to buy a franchise, while some franchisees felt stifled and changed to an independent business.

As for pricing a franchise, we don't see much of a difference between an independent business and the franchised one, except for the very big players, where the franchise label probably adds a lot of value, maybe 10 to 20 percent, based on the same gross. On the other hand, the fledging franchise with just a few units has some real problems on the resale side. If it's fairly new, there are plenty of new units available, the name doesn't really mean anything yet, and the age old question is asked—why is the business for sale? In cases like this, the percentage multiples might be reduced by the same figure as is added for the well-known brand name—most likely lower.

Despite what the franchise industry would like us to believe, not all franchises are successful. What has always struck us as strange is the buyer who is very number- oriented and turns down a very good business due to some slight anomaly in the financial statement from two years ago, and who will be the same buyer who purchased a franchise (a new one) where he has seen no books and records and has no idea whether the location will work out or not.
Source: *The Business Broker*

Key Considerations When Pricing a Franchise

"Lease Terms—If the lease doesn't contain a provision for at least 10 years remaining, the price can be affected accordingly.

"Franchise Rights—If there aren't at least 10 years left in the franchise agreement, a price adjustment downward should be made. This may not be applicable in those states where the franchisor may not terminate the agreement unless there is a default.

"Territorial Rights—If the franchise agreement does not provide for territorial rights, this could be a minus. In other words, if the franchisor can open additional units in the immediate area, the value of the existing franchise could be diminished. However, if the franchisee has additional territorial rights then the value may be increased.

"Business Mix—If the bulk of the sales is in low profit items, value may be diminished; whereas if high profit items make up a substantial part of the business, value may be increased. Is there wholesale business? Do one or two customers make up a majority of the business? Business mix should be considered.

"Remodel Requirements—Does the franchise agreement state that the business has to be remodeled periodically? How often and how much remodeling? The value of the business may be reduced by the cost of the remodeling, depending on when it has to be done.

"Hours of Operation—Does the franchisor require specific hours and days open? Some franchisors, especially food related, donuts/ convenience stores, may state that the business has to be open 24 hours a day, seven days a week. The shorter the hours, the better the price.

"Location—Obviously, the better and more desirable the location, the better the price.

"Cash Flow—The price of a small business may be based on its sales history rather than on reported profitability. Some businesses are just not operated efficiently from a cash management point of view. Certainly, strong cash flow benefits the price asked, but a poor cash flow coupled with strong historical sales does not necessarily detract from the price."

Excerpted from a presentation to the American Institute of Certified Public Accountants by Bernard Siegel, Siegel Business Services, Philadelphia, PA.

Franchise

Franklin's Printing

50+ units

Approximate Total Investment:	$305,000 to $395,000

Rule of Thumb:

- 52 percent of annual sales plus inventory

Resources

www.franklins-printing.com

Fruits and Vegetables (Wholesaler)

Rule of Thumb:

- 1 times SDE plus inventory

Pricing Tips

"Actual gross sales achieved is not an important analysis tool ... since there is usually an inverse relationship between sales volume & amount of profit that may be achieved (for instance, the more a box of tomatoes costs, the less profit may be added on). Better to determine how many packages/boxes of product are handled weekly & what 'profit per unit' is achieved."

Industry Experts' Ratings:

Marketability (1 = Low: 4 = High) 1.0
Industry Trend (1 = Declining: 4 = Growing) 2.0
Ease of Replication (1 = Easy: 4 = Difficult) 1.0

Benchmarks

$ profit per package (see Pricing Tips)

Expenses as a percentage of annual sales:

Cost of Goods Sold 25%
Payroll/Labor Costs 45%
Occupancy Cost 15%
Profit (estimated) 20%

Fuel Dealers (Wholesale)

Rule of Thumb:

- 1.5 times SDE plus inventory
- 1.5 EBITDA

Pricing Tips

"Wholesalers/distributors are large-volume, low-margin operators; therefore the price is 1–2 times EBITDA."

Industry Experts' Ratings:

Marketability (1 = Low: 4 = High) 1.2
Industry Trend (1 = Declining: 4 = Growing) 1.6
Ease of Replication (1 = Easy: 4 = Difficult) 2.8

"Requires a huge amount of capital, and the further risk is that money is lent out on credit to retail gasoline operators at least a few days at a time"

Benchmarks

"Typical wholesaler does $30 million in annual sales."

General Information

"Big advantage if you own your own gas stations along with this business, otherwise is risky"

Advantages of this Business

- "Moderate competition, steady and stable business"

Disadvantages of this Business

- "High risk since fuel is supplied on credit often, low margin business"

Resources

National Liquid Gas Association
www.npga.org

Butane Propane News
www.bpnews.com

Funeral Homes/Services

9,208	SIC: 7261-02	NAIC: 812210

Rule of Thumb:

- Under 75 funerals per year, 3 to 4.5 times EBITDA; 75 to 150 funerals, 4 to 5 times EBITDA; and 150 + funerals, 4.5 to 6 times EBITDA
- 5 to 6 times EBITDA if real estate is included. If real estate is not included, long-term triple net lease is a must (8 to 10 percent of sales); purchase price would be 4 times EBITDA or approx. 1 times trailing 12 months sales.
- 1.5 to 2.0 times revenue plus inventory
- 5 times EBITDA
- 6 times EBIT
- 175 percent of annual sales plus inventory

Pricing Tips

"Valuation can vary greatly depending on profitability of business and stategic fit for buyer."

"Amount of pre-need & how it is funded, volume trends; e.g., market share, change in business mix (at need versus pre-need & burial versus cremation. Is the owner staying in community or are there other plans?"

"The U.S. cremation rate is 27.81% and it is expected to reach 35.07% by 2010 and 42.96% by 2010."

Source: Cremation Association of North America

"Funeral home values are driven by the projected cash flow of the business. Funeral homes that perform a large percentage of cremations are typically less profitable and therefore less valuable than businesses that perform more traditional funerals."

"You need to understand the value or non-value of pre-needs."

"Reduce purchase price by the amount of underfunded/unfunded trust funds. Size of market? Is real estate included? Number of services performed per year?"

Industry Experts' Ratings:

Amount of Competition (1 = Lot of: 4 = Not much)	2.4
Amount of Risk (1 = Very: 4 = Not much)	2.8
Historical Profit Trend (1 = Down: 4 = Up)	2.8
Location & Facilities (1 = Poor: 4 = Excellent)	2.0
Marketability (1 = Low: 4 = High)	2.2
Industry Trend (1 = Declining: 4 = Growing)	2.0
Ease of Replication (1 = Easy: 4 = Difficult)	3.0

"Local heritage is important to communities, so it's difficult for a new funeral home to open and compete successfully."

Benchmarks

"50–100 funerals per full-time Funeral Director"

"The average cost of a funeral in the United States is nearly $6,500. This cost includes:

- Casket
- Embalming
- Visitation/Viewing
- Cosmetology
- Professional charges
- Transportation"

Source: www.funeralandcemeteryinfo.org

Expenses as a percentage of annual sales:	
Cost of Goods	20%
Payroll/Labor Cost	25–28%
Occupancy Cost	10–12%
Profit (estimated)	35%

General Information

"The primary reasons people select a particular funeral home are because:

- It previously served their family
- It is close to their residence
- It has a good reputation
- They previously visited their facilities
- They felt the cost was competitive."

Source: www.funeralandcemeteryinfo.org

Questions to ask seller: "Service mix varies considerably from region to region, has major impact on value of the business." "Check volume trends and average sales trends for at least 5 years." "Businesses can fluctuate dramatically with the death rate. However, it is not uncommon for market share to change as competitors open. A buyer should be very comfortable with the trends in the number of annual services."

The average member funeral home conducts 160 services per year. Approximately 85 percent of NFDA member funeral homes are family-owned and operated and average 57 years in business.

Advantages of this Business

- "Very fulfilling work for those drawn to the industry"
- "Very low failure rate"
- "Fairly easy to accurately project future earnings"

Disadvantages of this Business

- "As an operator, it's a 24/7 business. Government regulation may be increasing."
- "Owners can work 24 hours a day. Vacations are difficult to plan."

Industry Trend

"There will be a shortage of qualified young funeral directors to hire as employees. Younger mortuary school graduates want to either own their own business or work 40 hours per week."

"Old notions die hard for funeral professionals in changing times
Funerals will increasingly be colored green—not as in money, but as in the environment. The percentage of people who select cremation, which saves precious land, is already around 30 percent nationally. That figure is expected to rise above 50 percent within a generation or two.

"The national average cost for a traditional funeral is around $7,000. For a cremation, it's about $1,500. You do the math.

"In an apparent contradiction of the back-to-nature trend, funerals will often be, simultaneously, more high-tech. People want what amounts to a cinematic short of their life. The eight-minute-or-so digital presentation, typically built around family photos and any old footage, is to be played at a service, even broadcast live over the Web for those who can't make it. Later, the short, perhaps the entire service, will be archived on the Internet, where it will achieve its own kind of immortality."

Source: www.lubbockonline.com

Seller Financing

- "10–15 years"
- "15–20 percent of purchase price for 10 years"
- "7–10 years"

Resources

National Funeral Directors Association
www.nfda.org

Furniture/Appliance Stores *(See Appliance Stores)*

Furniture Stores: 43,626	SIC: 5712-16	NAIC: 442110
Appliance Stores: 17,188	SIC: 5722-02	NAIC: 443111

Rule of Thumb:

- 2 times monthly sales plus inventory

Pricing Tips

Large privately held profitable furniture stores may bring as much as one times annual sales.

Benchmarks

"Industry average is about $325 in sales per sq. ft."

General Information

"…Are usually not salable unless they are high-credit-account stores, bringing in foot traffic. Usually they are then sold for inventory only, and furniture stores usually can spend up to 10 percent of the gross sales for rent."

Resources

National Home Furnishings Association
www.nhfa.com

Furniture Refinishing

7,827	SIC: 7641-05	NAIC: 811420

Rule of Thumb:

- 50 percent of total annual revenues

Garage Door Sales & Service (Garage Door Operating Devices)

4,264	SIC: 5211-02	

Rule of Thumb:

- 25 percent of annual sales plus inventory

Garbage/Trash Collection

12,780	SIC: 4953-02	NAIC: 562111

Rule of Thumb:

- 1.5 to 2.5 times annual sales

Pricing Tips

"In the larger cities, garbage routes are selling from $30 to $34 for each dollar taken in per month. Perimeter routes around the larger cities sell for $18 to $22 for each dollar taken in per month, with the smaller communities selling from $14 to $18 for each dollar taken in during the month. If the dump is owned by the garbage collector, you should also add the amount of the land and permit value."

Garden Centers/Nurseries *(See also Lawn Care)*

8,000	SIC: 5261-04	NAIC: 444220

Rule of Thumb:

- 4 times monthly sales plus inventory

General Information

"While the number of U.S. farms of all types has declined over the last two decades, the number of nursery and greenhouse farms has increased.... In terms of economic output, nursery and greenhouse crops represent the third most important sector in U.S. crop agriculture, ranking seventh among all commodities in cash receipts, and among the highest in net farm income.

"Nursery and greenhouse crops are the top five commodities in 27 states and the top 10 commodities in 42 states.

"The nursery and landscape industry is made up of thousands of small family businesses that grow, install, and care for plants and landscapes."

Source: American Nursery & Landscape Association (ANLA)

"Seven states account for almost two-thirds of all nursery-crop output: California (24%), Texas (11%), Florida (09%), North Carolina (09%), Oregon (07%), Ohio (4%), Maryland (3%)."

Source: American Nursery & Landscape Association (ANLA)

Here are some key questions to get answered in analyzing garden centers:

- How many months are you open for business (determine season)? If not open all year, which months are you open?
- What method do you use to value your ending inventory (e.g., cost)?
- What makes up your inventory in the winter months?
- How are obsolete/damaged goods accounted for?
- What is your policy regarding returns and allowances for plants?
- Do you have a slow season? Which months? What other sources of income do you have during the slow season?
- Who are your major suppliers (any related parties)?
- What services do you provide? (Landscaping, lawn service, delivery, plant rental, etc.?)

The above is excerpted from an IRS Audit Technique Guide *(Market Segment_Specialization Program—MSSAP).* These guides are an excellent source of information and are available at www.bookstore.gpo.gov: (search under IRS— IRS Audit Technique Guides).

Resources
American Association of Nurserymen
www.anla.org
This is a good site.

Trade Publications
American Nurseryman
www.amerinursery.com

Gas Stations—Full and/or Self-Serve

84148	SIC: 5541-01	NAIC: 447110

Rule of Thumb:

- 2 to 2.5 times SDE plus inventory
- 1 to 2.0 SDE (with service bays, business only) plus inventory
- 3 to 4 times EBITDA—business only
- 4 to 6 times EBITDA—business and real estate

Gas Stations—Full and/or Self-Serve *(cont'd)*

- "3 to 5 times EBITDA including the real estate is a good rule of thumb for convenience stores with gas. 2 to 3.5 times EBITDA for leased sites. Age and condition of the petroleum equipment and environmental issues are important considerations in selling these businesses. A phase I & II report are required for both purchased and leased sites."

Pricing Tips

"Dealer stations in our market sell for 2.2 to 2.5 post due diligence SDE for the business only. I value gas stations with the land by starting with SDE and deducting the buyer's required income for managing the station and any necessary reserves, and then I capitalize that amount by what I feel is the market cap rate. This is basically a real estate approach to the value."

"Fewer and fewer stations surviving in today's competitive market."

"2 or 3 times net SDE)—most stores have horrible records.. proof of numbers is thru gas reciepts and store invoices. Gallons per month, pool margin, inside sales, other income and do the tanks meet 2009 standards..."

"3 to 4 times EBITDA including real estate is a general rule. Location, traffic count, brand and population are important considerations."

"Factors that most influence value are: volume of gasoline sales, location, length, C-store versus service bays, traffic count and major brand identity."

"Age of tanks; does station have canopy (is it cantilever or mech. attached); is it clean (environment); location, location, location."

Gas only	2 to 2.5 times SDE plus inventory
Gas with Food Market	2.5 to 3 times SDE plus inventory
Gas with Car Wash/Food Mart	2.5 to 4 times SDE plus inventory
Gas with Garage/Repair ...	1.5 to 2 times SDE plus inventory

"The geographical site/location is key to a buyer in many offers and subsequent sells. Near freeways or interstates, high visibility corner locations or locations near major malls all come with a premium price tag to the buyer."

"How Much Can I Make?

What are the expenses of a gas station?

For an average station open 18 hours a day, pumping up to 150,000 gallons per month, and store sales between $20,000 and $40,000 monthly, you should expect to have the following monthly expenses:

- Payroll: There are 540 man-hours in a month times $7 per hour—$3,780. Add payroll taxes and workman's compensation and it brings the payroll expense to $4,200.
- Utilities: Electric, water, sewer, garbage collection, phone—approximately $1,400.
- Credit card fees: Range depending on the oil company and the gas volume. A fair amount is between $600 and $1,000.
- Insurance: Liability insurance ranges between $1,400 and $2,200. In some cases full coverage is expected by the oil company or landlord. In this case the cost will vary depending on the structure.
- Accounting: Most accountants charge $150.00.
- Maintenance: $250.00.

If the station has fast food or deli, add payroll and increase utilities by 25%.

Car washes increase electric and water by 25 to 30%.

Add to these expenses the rent or the mortgage.

You have to keep in mind that a small operation may require the owner to work more hours. We recommend that for the first year the new owner should work at least 50 hours per week and cut expenses as much as possible.

To calculate the gross income, multiply the gallons by the profit per gallon. Take 30% of the store sales. Lottery income is 5% of Lotto [Florida] sales. Car wash income is about 80% profit. Fast food profit is between 60 and 70% of sales. Auto repair shops make 44% profit of all sales (this includes mechanics and parts)."

Source: Mike Amendolagine, www.gasstationsusa.com

Gas Stations USA is a gas station business broker. This was on Mike's site and we think it provides a lot of information.

"Other Considerations:

- Multiples vary with:
- Marketing demographics
- Facility image
- Business trend over past 3 years
- Business tenure
- Owner tenure
- Exclusivity"

"Pool margin is what is referred to as the gross profit on all grades of gasoline."

(Regular gas gross profit x gal. sold) + (medium-grade gas GP x gal. sold)
+(premium gas GP x gal. sold)
Total Gallons Sold"

Benchmarks

"Gas stations' earnings come from a number of profit centers. These are gas sales, c-store sales, misc. sales such as lotto, ATM, phone, money orders, car wash, etc. My benchmarks are gas sales above 100,000 gals a month, C-store margins above 30% and rent less than $12,000 a month."

"Inside sales (for C-stores); gross profit should be 25–30 percent of sales (including rebates, buy-downs, etc)."

"High net profit C-Store/Gas Businesses make 4 to 6 percent of sales. Median net profit C-Stores/Gas Businesses make 3 to 4 percent of sales."

"Most stations now include other services such as car wash or convenience stores to be sucessful."

Expenses as a percentage of annual sales:

Cost of Goods Sold	80%
Payroll/Labor Costs	11%
Occupancy Cost	8.5%
Profit (estimated)	5–8.0%
Food (C-Store)	60 to 70%
Repairs	20 to 30%

Industry Experts' Ratings:

Amount of Competition (1 = Lot of: 4 = Not much) 1.6
Amount of Risk (1 = Very: 4 = Not much) 2.4
Historical Profit Trend (1 = Down: 4 = Up) 1.8
Location & Facilities (1 = Poor: 4 = Excellent) 2.4
Marketability (1 = Low: 4 = High) 2.4
Industry Trend (1 = Declining: 4 = Growing) 2.0
Ease of Replication (1 = Easy: 4 = Difficult) 2.0

"Very competitive industry today with the hyper markets, grocery stores, and big box retailers all getting into the convenience store industry. Location is everything with traffic count, population, and highway access critical to success."

"Stand-alone gas stations are dwindling in number. The trend is towards convenience stores. Some gas stations with service bays can do OK in the right market."

"Gas stations should not be risky if managed properly. They are a cash business requiring good management."

"Hard to replicate due to site work needed and tank cost"

"In South Florida, staions with land will not cover the note payment."

General Information

"C-store is only way to make a profit; the gas sales cover the rent at best. ONLY MAKE MONEY when gas prices move down."

"It is important to understand the different options in getting into the business. There is also an amazing amount of misinformation in the marketplace. Also many gas station listings in our market do not accurately present the earnings, so due diligence is critical."

"Very few good mechanics in this sector, most have been moved to the large auto dealers."

"This industry has gone through some major changes within the core structure from 5 or 10 years ago. Mergers and buy-outs have affected the competition in the market place. With only 4 majors now in the network we have seen a steady rise in consumer retail prices at the pumps. Along with the mergers and billion dollar buy-outs we have also noticed within the industry substantial increases in the franchisee rents as well as diminished profits. The major oil companies are the ones who have greatly enhanced their pockets over the last 2 to 3 years. If the trend continues, I foresee Federal controls of some magnitude, price caps versus the price per barrel of crude oil. Owner pool margins have increased to, on average, $0.15 per gallon."

"Average gallons pumped on a monthly basis (minimum 100K) is normally a good station. Another factor is the pool margin (minimum 12 per gallon is good). Things that can subtract from value are gas with mechanical bays or gas only, short-term lease, oil company does not own property, history of soil contamination, low volume in sales, appearance, poor geographical location."

"Some factors that detract are small lot size and access issues."

Advantages of this Business

- "Convenience shopping, many profit centers, repeat customers, credit card sales"
- "The business is not cyclical and is scalable. If you like the business, you can open multiple stations."
- "Easy to run, minimum wage employees & a comodity necessity."
- "Convenience; local service garage"
- "Only if you have large size multiple locations and own the real estate. Large gas marts with food service and car washes preferred."

Disadvantages of this Business

- "Competition—your store can be wiped out by a major player buying the better corner and putting up a superior store. Long hours, employee turnover, employee and customer theft, and insurance costs are disadvantages."
- "There is a high cash cost to purchase a station because financing is virtually non-existent in our market. It is a cash business so you have to manage the business carefully."
- "Employees"
- "Potential for ground contamination"
- "Gas margins are shrinking, street corners have competitive uses."
- "Tough business today, with trend towards hypermarket C-stores, big box & supermarket gasoline"

- "Higher rent expense from major oil companies. Lower profit margins. More competition from large mass merchandisers. More taxes and E.P.A."

Industry Trend

"In South Florida trend is to LARGER stores, 2000sq feet or more. More food service inside the larger C-store; repair bays are history."

"Growing business until electric cars become more widely accepted."

Seller Financing

- "3 years, on average 8 percent interest per annum."
- "As much as 50 percent of sales price could be financed—3 to 5 years typical."
- "Franchise—2 to 3 years (5 to 10 percent)"
- "Property—10 to 15 years (8 to 11 percent)"

I would suggest you visit the website www.abbunitedstates.com. On this site you will find a complete glossary for the convenience store industry and some useful data that will help you understand the industry. As with every business, there are different terms and slang that are used, and the site has tried to answer some of the common questions.

Gas Stations w/Convenience Stores/MiniMarts

(See also Gas Stations above and also Convenience Store w/gas & beer)

Rule of Thumb:

Note: The information that follows is also in C-Stores with Gas. It is a confusing issue, and perhaps there is no difference between a C-store with gas and a gas station with a C-store, but many experts still feel that there is. So here goes, again: Convenience stores with gas—these operations are more convenience stores than gas stations such as a 7-Eleven or Circle K. Gas stations with convenience stores (mini-marts)— these operations are more gas stations than convenience stores, such as Mobil, Shell and Exxon gas stations that have convenience stores. In many cases, the garages and stations themselves have been retrofitted to be convenience stores. These operations may include a car wash.

- 2.75 to 3 SDE with mini-mart (minimum 800 sq. ft.), 200K gals/ mo., with the mini-mart $35K+/mo

- 2.75 to 3 times EBITDA

Pricing Tips

"The rule of thumb when valuing a convenience store with real estate is 5–6 x EBITDA; without real estate, it is 2–3 x EBITDA plus inventory. Questions to ask from the seller are: Is the store branded (Mobil, BP, Shell etc.) and if so how long is the contract to the brand? You need to know this, because the buyer may want to change the brand, and there will be a financial obligation to the brand to get out of the commitment."

"3 to 5 times EBITDA including real estate; 2.0 to 3.5 times EBITDA for leased sites. Age and condition of petroleum equipment, and environmental issues are important considerations in selling these businesses. A phase I & II are required."

"A business including real estate could command a 5 multiple of EBITDA. Multiples can be shaded by exclusivity, barriers to new competition, quality of the improvements, etc."

"One times annual gross profit plus inventory for business only. 2.5 to 3.5 times annual gross profit plus inventory for business & real estate. 50% to 60% annual gross sales plus inventory for business & real estate."

"Self-serve car washes add little or nothing to the above multiples. Most customers are charged a minimum of $2.99 for these washes, the equipment is generally inferior, prone to breaking down and increases the rent factor approx. $1,500 per month with escalation of leases. Beware of rent increases for most major oil companies. Mergers have caused a great deal of disturbances within the ranks of many dealers/owners. Most major oil companies have pushed the dealers out and now have a good number of company owned stations."

"In the gas station industry, the 2 to 3 times net income rule does change when it comes to stations (assuming owner does repair work) with repair. The price has to be reduced by a factor of 1 at least, since the minute the seller leaves, he takes most but not all of his customers away with him which negatively affects the business. How steady is the business? Can it run with simple training? Is there owner financing? Is it a low or high crime area?"

Industry Experts' Ratings:

Amount of Competition (1 = Lot of: 4 = Not much) 1.0
Amount of Risk (1 = Very: 4 = Not much) 2.0
Historical Profit Trend (1 = Down: 4 = Up) 2.2
Location & Facilities (1 = Poor: 4 = Excellent) 2.4
Marketability (1 = Low: 4 = High) 2.6
Industry Trend (1 = Declining: 4 = Growing) 2.2
Ease of Replication (1 = Easy: 4 = Difficult) 2.6

"More competition and larger facilities. More local land restrictions. Higher land and building costs."

"The convenience store industry is in turmoil due to entry of the big box retailers and the reduced profit margins on fuel sales. As with many other industries, people continue to build the newer, brighter, bigger, shiny stores and cannibalize the older ones. The big get bigger, and the weak get shoved out."

"Consolidation! But, newer and better sites are being built. Small operators are constantly buying and selling sites discarded by the majors and many are doing better than previously (when being run by larger corporations). Replication is easy, but the cost is prohibitive. Average build-up cost is $1.8 million to construct a new gas/C-store."

"Tough industry today; location, traffic count, highway access, and rooftops are all critical to success in the C-Store industry."

Benchmarks

"A good gas station should pump at least 1.2 million gas gallons yearly, and take in $540,000 yearly in the Mart plus any lotto sales. Most higher sales gas stations will have a car wash and some type of food service."

"The basic things to look for in a convenience store with fuel are the monthly gallons and then the inside sales. Gasoline has generally stopped being a profit generator due to the big box retailers getting into the business (Wal-Mart, Sam's, K-Mart etc.) so there isn't much profit in the fuel; however the more gallons a store does, generally the better the inside sales are. The gas has become the hook to get the people into the store."

"Approx $400 [in sales] per sq.ft"

Expenses as a percentage of annual sales:	
Cost of Goods Sold	70 to 75%
Payroll/Labor Costs	2 to 5%
Occupancy Cost	7 to 9%
Profit (estimated)	3 to 5%

"High volume a must in today's stations; lower volume stations difficult to sell; repairs not as desirable."

"$0.10 to $0.15 profit per gas gallon, 25% to 30% gross profit margin C-store; pump 120,000 to 150,000 gas gallons monthly minimum; $45,000 to $60,000 C-store + Lotto monthly minimum; $6,000 car wash monthly minimum; open 24/7; 1,200 sq. ft. C-store with food service."

"Gas stations go upscale to lure customers, boost profits
"The change comes at a crucial time for the nation's 138,000 convenience stores. At the same time profit margins are shrinking, the $395 billion industry is facing tough new competition from grocers adding fuel pumps and drug stores that offer more food than pharmaceuticals.

"The economics of the transformation make sense. A good price on fuel might get people in the door once or twice a week. Great coffee, brick-oven pizza, and gelato could pull them in daily.

"Since many customers are more loyal to good coffee than to gasoline brands, that's money well spent, said Russ Ritenour, Exxon Mobil's hot beverages manager. The company even has added a new position at its stores—brew master."

Source: *The Boston Globe*, Thursday, April 28, 2005

Advantages of this Business

- "Everyone needs gas. If the product changes it will be still sold through a 'gas' station. It's a steady, neccessary commodity. It's still cheaper than most of the world. The household driving has still not decreased even with gas being over $2. The income from a gas station is approximately $75K a year, which is a pretty good income to support a middle-income life style. Most are family-owned businesses."

- "The convenience store business is still a profitable business if you have a good location, keep your overhead low and give your customers good service. Convenience stores are just what their name implies. They were built for convenience for customers to run in and run out and will continue to have a long life if managed properly and control their costs."
- "Relatively easy to get into; good family enterprise"
- "High sales and profits of the larger locations"
- "Convenience shopping, many different profit centers, repeat customers, cash or credit sales"
- "Not a luxury item. Everyone has to purchase gas."
- "Very stable because without gas, the country stops; recession proof; ease of operation; easily saleable/marketable"

Disadvantages of this Business

- "The main disadvantage is that, as with any retail business, once you have your store you are stuck in that location and cannot relocate without incurring major expenses. Try to look ahead and see where the customers are coming from and going to."
- "Long hours; high employee turnove; mostly upfront cash required if buying only the business."
- Much competition in the industry."
- "Auto repair gas stations in less demand and other facilities being closed; more competition from mass merchandisers and drug store chains for corner locations"
- "Long hours, high employee turnover, cash business, security, customer theft, insurance costs"
- "Most good locations are controlled by major oil companies."

Industry Trend

"We see the industry to continue in turmoil especially with the announcement by Wal-Mart in early 2005 that all new Wal-Marts would have fuel sales, and any existing Wal-Marts that were not slated for remodeling in the next five years would have fuel sales also."

"Larger facilities with larger marts"

"The creative entrepreneurs, people with deeper pockets, unique locations, newer fancier locations, stations catering to ethnic groups, stations with varied amenities[one-stop shop]will have better chances of surviving."

"Trend is towards the hypermarkets in more populated areas, while smaller stores can do well in rural areas. The big box stores and supermarkets are putting in gasoline islands as a one-stop location, and often use fuel as a loss leader."

"Doing this since 1986 and things are still going strong and with steady growth in the marketability of gas stations"

Resources
Gasoline and Automotive Services Dealers Association
www.ssda-at.org

Gas Stations with C-Stores (business only)	2.5 to 3 times SDE
Gas Stations with Garages (business only)	1 to 2 times SDE
Gas Stations with C-Store (with property)	7 to 10 times SDE
Truck stops (with property)	7 to 10 times SDE

Updates in the Market Place, Gas Stations
By Hal Janke, haljanke@adelphia.net

What's happening with gasoline prices? Blink once, you're now at $2.50 a gallon, blink twice and you'll soon be at $3.00 [or more] a gallon, ouch. Yes, it does hurt and ultimately the price of gas will start affecting not only driving habits and pocketbooks but the proliferation of many other vertical markets and non-related retail businesses as well.

The oil companies are making billions of dollars in profits annually, and who is paying the ultimate price? You and I, along with millions of others, are feeling the effects of a doubling of gasoline prices in the last 12 months. On the West Coast we are now at $2.55 per gallon for regular and it's still climbing. Is this ever going to stop? I believe when it hits close to $3.00 a gallon, we'll finally see a slow down.

What does this mean for gas stations and their overall value? In our area of California, I've seen major oil companies buying many gas stations that are on the market. Do realize that all franchisee gas station owners sign a contract that gives the oil companies the first right of refusal to purchase their branded gas station that is on the market for sale.

Oil companies continue to merge with each other, and now at last count we have only four major brands within the network. This cause and effect minimizes the competition, thus less price gouging and more stability for the oil companies. It's time to start selling the gas guzzling SUVs and buy that Honda or Nissan, unless of course you never drive anywhere, and who does that?

Now there are ethanol (made from corn), hydrogen and battery-driven vehicles, known as hybrids. Environmentally sensitive vehicles proclaimed to deliver 40 to 50 miles per gallon. This is one way to stop OPEC from twisting us in the wind.

I see values on gas stations dropping as mpg increases, but not for a while. There is still demand for this business sector. On the norm, there are fewer and fewer service stations (with service bays) and a conversion to gas stations with markets and car washes.

My final analysis on this business is that for now it's a hold, with multiples still in the 2.5 x to 3.0x multiple range, some areas slightly higher. Hazardous issues, EPA and the federal government are demanding this industry tighten its standards, and as this fallout continues you'll see the prices continue to go up at the pump. Is it time to write your congressman? Yes—Help!

Quick *Profile* — Gas Stations

"There are (3) types of gas station ownership: company, dealer or independently owned and operated. These business sites are either oil-company-owned property or leased land. Gas stations with mini-marts are the most popular and always in high demand. The newest innovation in this industry is the addition of fast food franchises.

"The gas station owner/operator is in most cases a separate owner, not the franchisee of the fast food business. The oil companies prefer separate ownership for maximum efficiency and optimum sales in each respective business. Major oil companies can now collect a double rent and/or a percentage of the sales from both operations.

"Usually there will be anywhere from 12 to 28 nozzles (self-serve) and the mini-marts will carry food, drinks, dairy products and sundry items [see Convenience Stores]. If the site has a car wash, it will be in most cases a self-serve car wash. Lastly, you have the service bay station mostly in the two or three bay set up (usually full and self-serve). This type of facility is a dying operation with most oil companies going to the more updated version of gas and mini-marts, car washes being optimal.

“Many gas station sites are now franchised through the oil company. This seems to give a buyer a greater sense of security knowing they are buying a franchise and that there will be training and support from the parent company. The oil companies prefer the franchise concept as well for they now have more operational control over the owner/franchisee. Additionally the oil companies feel more justified when it comes to increasing fees, rents, royalties, etc., because of the franchise agreement. Most all gas station leases run for a period of three years and are automatically renewed, but rents are usually increased with the oil companies reserving the rights to also increase other fee items.

“When a station is sold, the oil company has first right of refusal (unless so specified to the contrary in the lease agreement), such as an independent station. If the oil company does exercise this option, it usually will not occur until after the new buyer has been approved and has gone to the training school. The buyer signs an agreement with the oil company and is aware this may happen. If the seller of the business takes back a note on the sale of his business and the buyer goes into default, the seller may have great difficulty in taking back the business. The oil company can take back possession of the entire gas station. This is a major reason why a seller of a gas station needs all cash or a large down payment. At the very least, collateral if there is a note. Additionally, most oil companies may demand a fair share of the sale price. This goes under the heading of a franchise transfer fee.

“What type of location is best? Freeway and/or interstate off and on ramp sites provide the easiest accessibility and greatest visibility. Most consumers will take advantage of these locations either going to or coming from work and once their habits are formed, the volume and sales will normally be reflected in these prime locations. Pros and cons exist as to whether a station is better suited to the side of the street that most commuters travel on their way to work. The neighborhood station is usually surrounded by residential housing with very little retail or commercial businesses in the area. Stations that are situated in or near large shopping malls seem to do very well in overall sales.

“Some Key Questions

A buyer would want to ask the current owner if the oil company owns the property or if the land is leased to the oil company. The value of the business will be less if the land is leased from another entity. The reason is that when the lease expires, even if there are options, the oil company may decide not to renew. Make sure the oil company owns the property; worst case make sure the lease for the station runs at least for another 10 years (when the oil company does not own the land). Buyers should also be concerned about the types of tanks that are underground—are they steel or fiberglass? If the owner has steel tanks, find out why the tanks have not been replaced with fiberglass. Ask the current owner if there have been any leaks or contamination. If the answer is yes, find out when and to what extent. Has the problem been corrected?

"One should also find out who is responsible for any and all contamination that lies above or below the surface of the site. Always require, in an offer to purchase agreement, a clause that states that the buyer will perform as part of the due diligence a Phase I report by an accredited environmental or chemical engineer who has a license to do so, with the results approved to the buyer's satisfaction. If a Phase II or III report is required, it is strongly suggested that it be done as well.

"Financial Information

Most P&L statements will show the gallons pumped per month as well as the pooled margin (profit margin per gallon). The key is the pooled margin or profit per gallon. Most owners work on margins of 12 to 22 cents per gallon. There are exceptions where the margin will be greater or less than shown above. (Pooled margin is defined as the difference between the owner's costs per gallon plus all taxes versus the price indicated at the pump which the consumer pays.)

"The owner who keeps the costs of goods in the service bay at 30 percent to 35 percent before wages will have a good profitable business. A station that has gas and service bays needs to stay within 25 percent to 32 percent salary/wages to sales, per sales tax. The turnkey financial elements for a successful operation are spelled out above: pool margin vs. gallons per month, cost of goods, and your wages and salaries. A gas station with a mini-mart has a difference in one category: the mini-mart should operate on a gross profit of 32 percent minimum with the pool margin 14 cents per gallon minimum.

"Pricing Information

Seller's Discretionary Cash Flow (SDE) is a method most commonly utilized for this type of business. Some of the variables that will affect this multiple are:

a. Whether the station has service bays or gas with mini-mart, fast food or car wash
b. Average monthly gallons pumped and the pool margin
c. Who the owner of the property is and what, if any, contamination has occurred within the site
d. Franchise vs. independent
e. Brand name of the oil company
f. All cash price vs. down payment and note
g. Geographical location

"The pricing factor and multiple used does not include the land value (priced separately). I've utilized multiples from 1x to 4.5x SDE, with the core variables depending on the above a. through g. The average multiple is normally 2.75x plus inventory including equipment. The gas station with mini-mart and full-service car wash will generally bring the higher multiple from 3x to 4.5x SDE. The station with a minimum monthly gallonage of 125,000 plus and a margin of .12 cents or greater, without service bays, is very high on the demand scale."

Pricing Tips

Gas Stations: Following is some basic pricing information from Bizcomps. For a study based on your area of the country, contact Bizcomps www.bizcomps.com.

Gas stations ranged in price from 21 percent of annual sales in the Western states to 12 percent of annual sales in the Eastern states. The SDE in the West was 2.3 SDE to 1.5 SDE in the Eastern states.

Gas Stations w/Mini-Marts: The price ranged from 21 percent of annual sales in the Western states to 18 percent of annual sales to 16 percent of annual sales in the Eastern states.

The multiple of SDE in the Western states was 2.3, 1.8 in the Central states, and 1.5 SDE in the Eastern states.

About the author

The above information, except for the information from Bizcomps, was taken from an article, with permission, written by Hal Janke. To meet space considerations, we have abbreviated it. He is President of Hal Janke & Associates, Inc. and has been in the automotive industry for the past 23 years as a business consultant and advisor. He has been actively involved in sales transactions of gas stations, tire & service centers, car washes, quick lubes, etc. Hal Janke, CBI, IBBA, CBC, SBA, haljanke@adelphia.net

Gift Shops *(See also Card Shops & Hallmark Gift Shop)*		
67,496	SIC: 5947-12	NAIC: 453220

Rule of Thumb:

- Inventory @ cost + FF&E + 1 to 2 times SDE
- 2.5 times SDE including inventory
- 1.5 times SDE plus inventory
- 35 percent of annual sales plus inventory
- 3 to 4 times EBITDA

Pricing Tips

"Inventory should be valued separately and include any costs associated with shipping inventory to the point of sale and preparing it for sale. Example: beads are bought in bulk. They are heavy and require extra costs to ship and require time and cost to re-package and weigh into smaller sellable units."

"1. Location weighs heavily. 2. Products are very important in relation to value. Is the store a card + gift shop? Does it carry high-end American crafts and upscale gifts, gifts + toys? The mix is important along with profit margins."

Benchmarks

"Rent at 10% of GAS (Gross Annual Sales); Sales Per Square Foot at $150–$175; Sales Per Employee at $75,000–$125,000; Advertising at 3%– 4% of GAS."

"Small store sales are usually $200–$300 per sq. ft.; Larger stores $300–$500 per sq. ft. Small stores should average $125,000 per employee."

Expenses as a percentage of annual sales:

Cost of Goods	50%–55%
Payroll/Labor	10%–15% (larger stores)
Occupancy Costs:	6%–8% /mall stores 8%–15%
Profit (estimated)	20%–25% for sole proprietor;
	5%–10% for larger stores

Industry Experts' Ratings:

Amount of Competition (1 = Lot of: 4 = Not much)	1.0
Amount of Risk (1 = Very: 4 = Not much)	1.2
Historical Profit Trend (1 = Down: 4 = Up)	1.6
Location & Facilities (1 = Poor: 4 = Excellent)	2.4
Marketability (1 = Low: 4 = High)	2.0
Industry Trend (1 = Declining: 4 = Growing)	1.8
Ease of Replication (1 = Easy: 4 = Difficult)	1.4

"For smaller stores, unreported cash sales may exist. For larger stores, management, location and experienced buyers are key. Volume/type of products sold is very important. Merchandise buyers can make or break profitability, image, etc."

"Relatively easy to get into a craft business but difficult to obtain and maintain profitability. Smaller independently owned stores tend to be operated by owners with a passion for the craft rather than a passion for business."

General Information

"Companies with multiple store locations have a much higher survival rate. Buyers will not pay for obsolete inventory."

"You need to understand which segment of this industry you are working with (craft type). Also, are you working with the retailer, the distributor, or the manufacturer?"

Advantages of this Business

- "Great advantage if you are a lover of crafts. Different segments of the industry gain in popularity for a few years at a time. Interaction with customers that are excited about being in your store. Constant learning process for new products and techniques."
- "An enjoyable type of work for many folks. Successful owners have an opportunity for significant financial rewards. Exciting new products are fun to sell. Riding a 'hot trend' for a new product can be lucrative. Opportunities for travel."

Disadvantages of this Business

- "Profitability is difficult to achieve for smaller stores. Long retail hours.

Reasonable leases and terms are difficult to negotiate. Small retail gift stores are difficult to sell. Good employees are often difficult to find. Theft and inventory shrinkage must be controlled. Increase competition from big box stores who are increasing their gift offerings."

- "Managing employees, managing profitability, being open for retail hours, increased 'spot' competition that comes and goes."

Industry Trend

"According to CHA this is a $29 billion a year industry with a small but steady growth rate of 1%–2% per year."

"Large stores have survived recession, etc. Small stores are becoming extinct due to rising costs, difficulty in obtaining knowledgeable/motivated employees, the inability to buy with volume discount, difficulty moving old inventory, poor buying decisions."

Seller Financing

- "3 to 4 years"

Resources

Craft & Hobby Association
www.craftandhobby.org—a good site. For the best information, click on Press Room and review executive summaries.

Golf Carts—Sales & Service

1,500	SIC: 5571-02	NAIC: 441229

Rule of Thumb:

- 25 to 30 percent of annual sales plus inventory

Trade Publications

Golf Shop Operations
www.progolfed.com

Golf Courses

Private—4,005 Public—12,566	SIC: 7997-06 SIC: 7992-01	NAIC: 713910

Rule of Thumb (Private):

- 2.5 to 5 times SDE plus inventory

Rule of Thumb (Public):

- Net income multipliers—8 to 11, typically 9 to 10
- 4 times golf related income ("green fees, golf carts, driving range—does not include pro shop or food & beverage")

Pricing Tips

We asked one industry expert why the price had dropped this year versus last year and his response was, "Yes they have dropped but more importantly, as I mentioned, cap rates are being used more as a pricing guideline. The trick in using cap rates is to get to an NOI or EBIDTA that is accurate. This is true for real estate and golf courses which have a strong real estate orientation."

"Nearly 3 million golfers give up the game each year"

Source: *Business Week*, December 13, 2004

"Real estate value big determinant in price of a golf course"

"Golf courses are priced like real estate, with current values being at a 10% cap rate."

"Personal property + equipment (FF&E) usually accounts for 3 to 10 percent of the purchase price depending on the amount of equipment leased and type of operation (daily fee vs. private). From 4 to 7 percent of price is typical."

"Profit estimated—40 percent."

""Due to weather-related conditions, a 5-year average for cash flow should be used— capital reserves of 5 percent should always be accounted for."

"Add to price for additional assets such as development land. Also check rounds of golf, P&L and type of facilities."

"Be careful to look at non-golf income for 'normal' distribution."

Industry Experts' Ratings:

Amount of Competition (1 = Lot of: 4 = Not much)	1.0
Amount of Risk (1 = Very: 4 = Not much)	1.5
Historical Profit Trend (1 = Down: 4 = Up)	2.4
Location & Facilities (1 = Poor: 4 = Excellent)	3.0
Marketability (1 = Low: 4 = High)	2.6
Industry Trend (1 = Declining: 4 = Growing)	2.4
Ease of Replication (1 = Easy: 4 = Difficult)	2.8

Benchmarks

Expenses as a percentage of annual sales:

Cost of Goods	20%
Payroll/Labor	45%
Occupancy Costs:	15%
Profit (estimated)	20%

General Information

Questions to ask seller: "Is there adjoining acreage that could be used for golf community homes? This can greatly increase value of the golf course."

"Need deep pockets and need reserves to get through the bad years due to bad weather conditions."

Advantages of this Business

- "Real estate values"
- "Pleasant environment, upscale clientele, limited seasonality, income"

Disadvantages of this Business

- "At the will of the weather"

Industry Trend

"Stagnant"

"Look beyond the pro circuit, however, and the grass isn't so green. According to the National Golf Foundation, the number of rounds played by all golfers has declined over the past three full years and was up just 1.3% through the first nine months of 2004. Equipment makers are struggling, with sales of clubs and balls largely flat since the late 1990s.

"These statistics suggest that many of the newcomers lured into the game by Woods [Tiger] have concluded that golf is an expensive, time-consuming, and frustrating endeavor. While industry officials boast of the 26 million people who now play golf, the dirty secret is that nearly 3 million quit the game each year—leaving the industry hunting for new players just to stay even."

Source: *Business Week*, December 13, 2004

Seller Financing

- "5 to 7 years"
- "20 years"

Resources

National Golf Course Owners Association
www.ngcoa.org

Golf Courses and Country Clubs: A Guide to Appraisal, Market Analysis, Development, and Financing by Arthur E. Gimmy, MAI, and Martin E. Benson, MAI, published by The Appraisal Institute. www.appraisalinstitute.org

www.golfcoursestoplay.com—an interesting and fun site for golfers

Golf Shops

Rule of Thumb:

- 30 percent of annual sales plus inventory

Resources

Golf Shop Operations
www.progolfed.com

Franchise

Goodyear Tire Stores *(See Auto Tire Stores)*

Rule of Thumb:

- 35 percent of annual sales plus inventory

Gourmet Shops *(See also Restaurants)*

3,000	SIC: 5499-20	NAIC: 445299

Rule of Thumb:

- 20 percent of annual sales plus inventory

Franchise

Grease Monkey *(See Auto Lube/Tune-up & Other Lube Franchises)*

240 units

Approximate Total Investment:	$200,000 to $250,000

Rule of Thumb:

- 58 percent of annual sales plus inventory

Resources

www.greasemonkeyintl.com

Franchise

Great Harvest Bread Company

167 Units

Approximate Total Investment:	$210,000 +

Rule of Thumb:

- 3.2 to 3.4 SDE plus inventory

Resources
www.greatharvest.com

Franchise

Great Steak & Potato

220 Units	
Approximate Total Investment:	$150,000 to $260,000

Rule of Thumb:

- 55 to 60 percent of annual sales plus inventory

Resources:
www.thegreatsteak.com

"Green" Businesses

The Evergreen Group (Sustainable Business Brokerage) is the only business brokerage firm in the country (that we know of) that specializes in helping people buy and sell "green" businesses. Since 2001, the company has handled business valuations and sales of such businesses as: organic food products, natural and organic body-care products, natural and organic clothing, renewable energy, recycled furniture, handmade wooden toys, locally owned organic/natural retail stores, and eco-friendly cleaning services. For more information contact the Evergreen Group (Sustainable Business Brokerage) at 415-750-1120. www.theevergreengroup.com

Grocery Stores *(See also Convenience Stores)*

101,403	SIC: 5411-05	NAIC: 445110

Rule of Thumb:

- 2 times monthly sales plus inventory
- 11 percent of annual sales plus inventory
- 1/2 of SDE; add fixtures, equipment plus inventory
- 16 to 18 percent of annual sales; includes equipment

Grocery Stores

Stores	# of Stores	$ Sales Billions
Supermarket ($2 million +)	34,252	$457.4
Chain Supermarkets	22,453	$386.4
Independent Supermarkets	11,799	$71.1
Grocery (under $2 million)	13,182	$17.4
Wholesale Club Stores*	1,034	$32.6
Convenience**	138,205	$114.0
Convenience/Gas Kiosk**	25,205	$13.2

* *Supermarket items only*
** *Excluding gas*

Source: "Facts & Figures," Food Marketing Institute, April 2005

Benchmarks

Sales and Expenses

	2004
Supermarket Sales ($2 million +)	$457.4 billion
Net profit after taxes	0.88%
Median average store size in sq. ft.	45,561
Weekly sales per supermarket	$348,130
Weekly sales per sq. ft.	$24.64
Sale per labor hour	$79.77

Source: "Facts & Figures," Food Marketing Institute, April 2005

Payroll Expense	12.2%
Total Employment Cost	15.7%
Supplies	1.2%
Utilities	1.2%

Source: Food Marketing Institute, April 2005

General Information

"Supermarket $2 million + —A full-line, self-service grocery store with sales volume of $2 million or more. This definition applies to individual stores regardless of total company sales or size, and therefore includes both chain and independent locations.

"Supercenter—A retail unit with a full-line discount merchandiser under one roof. May have separate or combined checkouts.

"Limited Assortment/Gourmet—A store that has a limited selection of items in a reduced number of categories. The focus of the selection limitation may be natural products, gourmet quality, or special pricing. Principal differentiation from a conventional supermarket is often in the reduced size and completeness of nonfoods categories such as Health and Beauty Care (HBC), cleaning supplies, and paper products.

"Superette/Small Grocery <$2 Million—A grocery store with a sales volume ranging from $1 million to $2 million annually. Typically superettes are independent, but many are affiliated with groups like IGA, Inc. Small grocery is defined as a grocery store with sales below $1 million annually.

Convenience Store Trade Class—This class includes small-format stores (between 200 and 3,000 square feet and 500 and 1,500 SKUs) selling beverages, snacks, and tobacco plus limited grocery items including milk and bread. These stores may also sell gasoline and offer fast food services.

"Conventional C-Stores—By far the majority of stores making up this trade class, these include any stores with selling space dedicated primarily to consumables. Examples: 7-Eleven, On the Run, Texaco Star Marts, Circle K.

"Gas Service—These units are first and foremost gas stations, many with service bays, that also sell small amounts of beverages, snacks, and tobacco. Items are sold via vending machines or office merchandisers, not from dedicated selling spaces.

Source: Trade Dimensions as used in *Progressive Grocer*

Industry Trend

"New Formats Edging Out Traditional Supermarket

The popularity of the conventional grocery store, a mainstay of food retailing for half a century is on the wane. In 1988, traditional grocery formats accounted for nearly 90% of grocery and consumables sales. By 2003, these retailers, which can be found under a variety of banners, accounted for only a 56% share. By 2008, that share is expected to drop to just 49% according to data released at The Outlook for Food Retailing Through 2008, a Webinar featuring Willard Bishop Consulting (WBC), and The Food Institute, an Elmwood Park, NJ-based food industry information association.

Traditional grocery store formats will account for less than 50% of the grocery and consumables market by 2008, losing share to non-traditional formats," Bill Bishop, president of WBC told Webinar attendees. At the presentation, Mr. Bishop discussed the popularity of alternative formats, from dollar stores to supercenters, and offered predictions about their respective futures.

The future success of supermarkets hinges on whether or not they want to re-invent the center of the store. In a survey of participants in the Webinar, an astounding 94% said it was very, or somewhat, important for these retailers to do so in order to succeed in the future. However, when asked, "What do you think will stop the growth of supercenters?" 44% replied, "Nothing."

Source: www.foodinstitute.com/wbcwebinar.cfm

Resources

National Grocers Association (NGA)
www.nationalgrocers.org

Progressive Grocer
www.progressivegrocer.com

Food Marketing Institute (FMI)
www.fmi.org

Grocery Manufacturers of America (GMA)
www.gmabrands.com

The Food Industry Center
www.foodindustrycenter.umn.edu

Grocery Stores—Markets (Small to Medium Size)

(See also Convenience Stores)

Rule of Thumb:

- 2.5 to 3 times SDE plus inventory
- 10 to 15% of annual sales plus inventory
- "Real estate, business, inventory (total package)—4 times recasted cash flow not including owner's salary." [EBIT]

Pricing Tips

"…Up to $2,000,000 gross sales…these stores are usually sold for fair market value of fixtures and equipment plus the inventory at retail cost less 27–36 percent. Rent should never exceed 2.5 percent of the gross sales. Markup of these small stores usually runs between 17 percent and 20 percent of wholesale cost. Or, value of business is 3 to 5 times weekly gross (per United Grocers), plus fixtures and equipment, plus inventory."

"Breakeven sales approximately $ 160,000 year."

Industry Experts' Ratings:

Amount of Competition (1 = Lot of: 4 = Not much)	1.0
Amount of Risk (1 = Very: 4 = Not much)	1.6
Historical Profit Trend (1 = Down: 4 = Up)	2.0
Location & Facilities (1 = Poor: 4 = Excellent)	2.4
Marketability (1 = Low: 4 = High)	2.4
Industry Trend (1 = Declining: 4 = Growing)	2.0
Ease of Replication (1 = Easy: 4 = Difficult)	1.2

"Larger gross sales easier to market"

Benchmarks

"Must have turnover, long lease, and good employees."

Expenses as a percentage of annual sales:	
Cost of Goods Sold	60%
Payroll/Labor Costs	15%
Occupancy Cost	15%
Profit (estimated)	10%

General Information

"Good operators very sucessful"

"Recasted cash flow is a recast statement net of all owner benefits including salary or draw, no interest, depreciation, amortization or other non-cash expenses, also no debt service—recasted cash flow is the cash flow available to the owner and the bank (debt service)."

"After 13 years of selling stores, and resisting 'rules of thumb' I have researched my sales and found that the only meaningful ratio has been that stores have sold for a price that is roughly four times the net cash flow before debt service and with no owner's wages and no non-cash expenses such as depreciation and interest."

Advantages of this Business

- "High volume possible, cash business"

Disadvantages of this Business

- "Spoilage, employees, health costs"

Industry Trend

"Business growing"

Resources

National Grocers Association
www.nationalgrocers.org

"Valuing Grocery Stores," *Handbook of Business Valuation*, 1st Edition, West & Jones, published by John Wiley & Sons.

Ground Transportation Companies

(See also Bus Companies & Transportation)

Rule of Thumb:

- 3 times EBITDA plus vehicle value for small to midsize operations; 4 times EBITDA + for over 15 vehicles

Pricing Tips

"Who controls the groups? The quality of the drivers and how long have they been with the company? Are the groups preformed or do they sell into them? Condition of equipment counts."

Franchise

Grout Doctor

43 units

Approximate Total Investment:	$15,660 to $28,850

Rule of Thumb:

- 89 percent of annual sales plus inventory

Resources

www.groutdoctor.com

Guard Services *(See also Security Services/Systems)*

9,233	SIC: 7381-02	NAIC: 561612

Rule of Thumb:

- 25 percent of annual sales plus inventory

Hallmark Gift Shops

Approximate Total Investment:	$115,000 to $220,000

Rule of Thumb:

- 40 percent of annual sales plus inventory

> "There's little room for expansion [greeting card business] because American already has 40% of the market (and privately held Hallmark Cards has 50%)."
>
> Source: *Business Week*, May 16, 2005

Pricing Tips

"Inventory valuation is crucial; inventory should be no more than one third of annual volume. If it is more, then it is probably old and over-valued. Many stores have collectibles that are very slow moving, and very high in value. Unless inventory over-valuation is anticipated, deal can fall through because of this very contentious issue."

Benchmarks

Expenses as a percentage of annual sales:	
Cost of Goods	50%
Payroll/Labor	12%
Occupancy Costs:	max 14%
Profit (estimated)	18%–20%

General Information

Initial Investment

	Low	High
Fixtures	$55,000	$85,000
Inventory	$90,000	$170,000
Leasehold Improvements	$20,000	$110,000
Retail Equipment	$20,000	$35,000
Misc. Expenses	$15,000	$20,000
Working Capital	$50,000	$80,000
	$250,000	$500,000

Source: www.newbiz.hallmark.com

Hallmark Gold Crown Stores

"About 4,200 Hallmark Gold Crown stores can be found nationwide, most of which are independently owned and operated."

"Gold Crown stores are between 4,000 and 6,000 square feet; stores are in regional shopping malls and strip centers. They offer more than 18,000 different products, of which approximately 60 percent are Hallmark brand products.

"'Hallmark Gold Crown' store is a distinct specialty retail network, a store that should be referred to as 'Hallmark Gold Crown store' (not 'Hallmark store') in print and electronic coverage."

Hardware Stores

23,249	SIC: 5251-04	NAIC: 444130

Rule of Thumb:

- 30 percent of annual sales plus inventory
- 3 times monthly sales plus inventory
- 1.2 SDE plus inventory
- Note: One industry expert had a bit higher multiple of SDE and for the percentage of annual sales multiple

Pricing Tips

Industry Experts' Ratings:

Amount of Competition (1 = Lot of: 4 = Not much) 1.0
Amount of Risk (1 = Very: 4 = Not much) 1.0
Historical Profit Trend (1 = Down: 4 = Up) 2.4
Location & Facilities (1 = Poor: 4 = Excellent) 3.0
Marketability (1 = Low: 4 = High) 2.8
Industry Trend (1 = Declining: 4 = Growing) 2.0
Ease of Replication (1 = Easy: 4 = Difficult) 2.4

"Heavy industry consolidation by the big boxes means that small operators must be aligned with a major franchisor. Local dealer advertising groups are also a must. Plenty of help on the store floor, convenient parking, knowledgeable staff, and quick service are far more important to today's hardware shoppers than price. Therefore, small neighborhood stores that possess those characteristics will survive the big boxes quite well."

Benchmarks

"Should turn their inventory 2.5 to 3 times per year. Fixtures and equipment should not exceed 16 percent of the average stock carried per year. These stores are sold for fixtures and equipment at depreciated value plus the inventory at wholesale cost. Markup runs from 35 to 40 percent."

Financial Profile of Hardware Stores

Operating Profile	
Average Size of Selling Area (sq. ft.)	8,025
Total Sales	$1,169,035
Total Asset Investment	$555,281
Total Inventory	$369,817
Income Statement	
Net Sales	100%
Cost of Goods Sold	60.6%
Gross Margin	39.4%
Patronage Dividend/Purchase Rebate	0.7%
Total Gross Margin	40.1%
Total Expenses	38.6%
Gross Operating Profit	1.5%
Other Income	1.0%
Net Profit (before taxes)	2.5%

Source: *Market Measure 2005* issued by the National Retail Hardware Association

Sales per Sq. Ft. of Selling Area:	$146
Total Sales per Employee:	$129,893
Inventory per Sq. Ft. of Selling Area:	$46
Net Sales to Total Inventory:	3.2 times
Average size of Transaction:	$17

Source: *Market Measure 2005* issued by the National Retail Hardware Association

General Information

"Retail Store Performance

Average hardware stores reported a sales gain of 2.1 percent, almost double the previous year's 1.1 percent increase. However, bottom line net profits continued to hover at 2.5 percent. Two key profitability measurements—return on assets and return on net worth— were stable at 5.2 percent and 8.6 percent, respectively.

"Customer count declined again, continuing a four-year trend, but the average transaction size increased. Average inventory turnover dropped below two turns with a corresponding drop in the sales-to-inventory ratio. Hardware stores maintained the number of employees, but payroll and productivity ratios slid slightly.

"High-profit stores generated an average net operating profit of 7.7 percent, more than three times that of typical stores. That performance traces directly to higher margins and lower expenses. Gross margin for the high-profit stores was 1.7 points higher than typical stores while payroll was two points lower and other operating expenses were 1.3 points lower.

"The high-profit stores turned inventory faster than the typical store and produced higher sales and gross margins per square foot—10 and 15 percent, respectively. Because they do this with the same number of employees, their employee productivity ratios are higher as well. They produce these sales on less inventory, reporting inventory per square foot 17 percent lower than typical stores.

"Hardware stores are primarily independent, family-owned operations. Most are affiliated with dealer-owned or co-op wholesalers or wholesaler merchandising groups that offer marketing programs.

"Hardware stores can range in size up to 20,000 or 30,000 square feet or larger. Sales volumes can exceed one million dollars per unit. They tend to serve neighborhood markets, tailor their mix of products and services to their individual markets, and position themselves as offering personal service and well-informed salespeople. They advertise aggressively and are open during evening and weekend hours. Primary customers are homeowners.

"Aggressive hardware stores can compete well with chains because they

Number of Outlets—2005

Hardware Stores	20,100
Home Centers	10,000
Lumberyards	11,300

Source: *Do-It-Yourself Retailing*, www.nrha.org

can distinguish themselves from big-box retailers. Most consumers know what a hardware store is.

"Many hardware stores identify with their primary wholesaler's stores program. True Value, Ace, Do it Best, Trustworthy, Sentry and PRO are among the most widely known marketing identities."

Source: *The Market Measure: The Industry's Annual Report.* National Retail Hardware Association's (NRHA)

"Independent family-owned stores tend to belong to marketing and buying programs offered by wholesale organizations. In addition to purchasing merchandise from wholesalers, retailers receive marketing and advertising support. As a general practice, they buy at least 60% of their merchandise from a primary wholesale source and use secondary or specialty distributors for most of the rest. A small portion is purchased directly from manufacturers.

"Because independent retailers frequently use the store identity program offered by their primary wholesaler, they appear to the consuming public to be a chain. They are not corporate chains, nor are they franchises in the sense that McDonald's is a franchise. Stores are individually owned and the retailers maintain a strong independence about what they buy. There are very few true corporate chains in the hardware segment and virtually all are privately owned. Sears Hardware is a notable exception."

Source: "The Retail hardware/Home Improvement Market," National Retail Hardware Association/ Home Center Institute

Advantages of this Business

- "Stores often exist for two or three generations. Very family oriented. Hardware ownership still carries a fantasy image in most peoples' minds."

Disadvantages of this Business

- "Long hours"

Industry Trend

"Computerization, renovation, innovation. Do or die."

"Looking into the future, NRHA estimates that industry sales will grow at an average annual rate of 5.2 percent between 2002 and 2007. During this time, [do-it-yourself] sales are expected to grow more than twice as fast as professional/remodeler sales."

Source: *Market Measure 2004* issued by the National Retail Hardware Association

Resources

National Retail Hardware Association

www.nrha.org

This is an excellent site with lots of valuabl e information and statistics on the entire home improvement/hardware industries. It is a very good trade association site and represents what they all should be like.

Harley-Davidson Motorcycle Agencies

(See Motorcycle Dealerships)

Rule of Thumb:

- "87% of annual sales. In this case the agency netted $2,100,000 and seller retained 20 percent of ownership."
- 3.5 SDE plus net assets plus inventory

Resources

www.harley-davidson.com

Health Care Companies

Rule of Thumb:

- 3.5 to 5 times EBITDA excluding rental equipment depreciation

General Information

"Less value in retail; more value in service related"

"Large number of contracts, the higher the multiple. Effect of Medicare cuts can be plus or probably a minus."

"Varies with product mix."

Expenses as a percentage of annual sales:	
Cost of Goods	45%
Payroll/Labor Costs	20%
Occupancy Cost	8%

More Rules of Thumb

Following are some percentages that may help you "ballpark" a price for certain businesses. They are actual sales prices, as gathered by BIZCOMPS, shown as a percentage of gross. The study has detailed information on 1,125 transactions from January 1993 through March 2004. The businesses sold, on average, for $1,026,566. These figures are from the 2004 Annual National Industrial Edition. For more information on current studies and other publications contact: Jack Sanders, Bizcomps www.bizcomps.com

Manufacturing .... 71% of annual gross sale
Wholesale/Distributor .... 54% of annual gross sales
Service Businesses .... 68% of annual gross sales

Others:

Printing .... 61% of annual gross sales
Electronics (Mfg.) .... 62% of annual gross sales
Machine Shops (Mfg.) .... 92% of annual gross sales
Plastic Products (Mfg.) .... 70% of annual gross sales
Tool & Die (Mfg.) .... 88% of annual gross sales
Automotive (Whsle) .... 46% of annual gross sales
Medical Supplies (Whsle) .... 66% of annual gross sales
Electronic Products (Distr) .... 46% of annual gross sales
Industrial Products (Distr) .... 49% of annual gross sales
Janitorial Supplies (Distr) .... 53% of annual gross sales
Food Products (Distr) .... 41% of annual gross sales
Equipment Rental .... 1.02% of annual gross sales
Janitorial Services .... 49% of annual gross sales
Accounting Practices .... 97% of annual gross revenues
Temporary Manpower .... 57% of annual gross revenues
Trucking/Courier .... 67% of annual gross sales

The above figures are asset transactions and do not include cash, accounts receivable or payables, but they do include inventory.

Note: Many of the above percentages are lower than the previous year. Since the percentages are cumulative, it can be assumed that the figures for last year were significantly lower than the prior year. It is also interesting to note that the overall asking price versus actual selling price is 91 percent.

Seller Financing

- "3 to 5 years"

Resources

T*he Analysis and Valuation of Health Care Enterprises* by Arthur E. Gimmy, MAI, and Charles R. Baumbach, published by the Appraisal Institute, 875 N. Michigan Ave., Ste. 2400, Chicago, IL 60611-1980. (312) 335-4100.

Health Clubs *(See Fitness Centers & Racquet Sports Clubs)*

	SIC: 7991-01	NAIC: 713940

Health Food Stores

16,651	SIC: 5499-01	NAIC: 422480

Rule of Thumb:

➢ 1 to 1.5 times SDE plus inventory

General Information

"The $20.5 billion in the naturals channel market... and includes eight store categories plus the biggest chains—Whole Foods Market and Wild Oats Markets (together $4.3 billion in 2003 sales), GNC (approximately $1.7 billion), Vitamin World (owned by NBTY and recording $212 million in 2003 sales)—and the natural-product sales of other specialty retailers (co-ops, gourmet shops, personal care stores, health clubs, mall stands, herb shops, etc., totaling $920 million.)

- Natural Foods Stores were defined as stores with less than 40 percent of sales from supplements. In our sample, 28.5 percent of respondents were in this group.
- Health Food Stores were defined as having more than 40 percent but less than 80 percent of sales from supplements. In our sample, this group consisted of 35.9 percent of the total.
- Vitamins/Minerals/Supplements Stores were defined as having 80 percent or more of sales from supplements. In our sample, 28.4 percent of respondents had VMS stores.
- Note that 2.8 percent of the sample respondents classified themselves

as 'other,' including co-ops, pharmacies and personal care outlets. Conventional grocery stores made up 4.4 percent of the sample."

Source: *Natural Foods Merchandiser*, www.naturalfoodsmerchandiser.com

Industry Trend

"The U.S. nutrition industry reached sales of $68.6 billion in 2004."

Breakdown of Products

	Sales in billions	Growth in 2003	Growth in 2004	Growth in 2005-2008
Functional Foods	$24.5	6.9%	7.6%	6–8%
Supplements	$20.3	5.7%	2.6%	3–5%
Natural/Organic Foods	$18.4	13.1%	13.2%	8–10%
Natural Personal Care	$5.5	8.7%	11.3%	10–12%"

Source: *Nutrition Business Journal*

Health & Safety Industries

Rule of Thumb:

- 3 to 5.5 times EBIT (Distribution)
- 3 to 7 times EBIT (Manufacturing)

Hearing Aid Sales

11,612	SIC: 5999-79	NAIC: 446199

Rule of Thumb:

- 50 to 55 percent of annual revenues plus inventory

General Information

"Hearing aids are better today and most people do benefit from them. The combination of technology, programming software and ongoing follow-up enables hearing aids to be optimized to meet individual needs like never before.

"Still, there is no single 'best' hearing aid for everyone. The most critical factor is matching technology to individual communication needs and expectations. This can only be achieved through teamwork between you and your hearing healthcare professional, who retains the crucial role of providing the appropriate selection, fitting and follow-up tools to ensure the best possible outcome."

Source: "Hearing Aids: Is High Tech Really Better?" *Hearing Health,* a publication of Deafness Research Foundation, www.hearinghealthmag.com

Industry Trend

"On the Horizon - A perplexing issue confronting the hearing aid industry is the fact that only 20 to 25 percent of people with measurable hearing loss routinely obtain hearing aids. Needless to say, this limits greatly the number of people who experience benefits of amplification. Baby boomers comprise a significant portion of the many millions who are not addressing their hearing loss. Members of this storied generation are often characterized as insistent on personal attention and quality outcomes, data-driven, convenience-oriented and creative rather than conforming. This list certainly describes a challenging consumer group. Add to that what may be the most significant obstacles for the hearing aid market: they tend to think of themselves as 10 to 15 years younger than their chronological age. This does not mesh well with the stigma that hearing loss is an 'older person's' problem.

"Of necessity, new products will be created to meet the demands of baby boomers. They will likely include both small size and better performance in addition to convenience and improved functionality."

Source: "Hearing Aids: Is High Tech Really Better?" *Hearing Health,* a publication of Deafness research Foundation. www.hearinghealthmag.com

Heavy Equipment Sales & Service

Rule of Thumb:

- 50 percent of SDE plus fixtures, equipment and inventory

Heating Contractors *(See also HVAC)*

46,800	SIC: 1711-02	NAIC: 235110

Rule of Thumb:

- 24 percent of annual sales plus inventory

Heating, Ventilating & Air Conditioning (HVAC)

(See also Air Conditioning)

Rule of Thumb:

- 30 percent of annual sales plus inventory
- 2.5 times SDE plus inventory
- 3 times EBIT
- 2.75 times EBITDA

Pricing Tips

"Mix drives value. There is an enormous range of pricing based on the mix of business. Prices for these businesses range from under 10% of revenue to over 100% of revenue. This is an enormously fragmented industry and therefore every company mix, set of controls, recurring nature, and margins will drive value."

"Biz mix is a critical value driver. Must evaluate the mix in order to price."

Industry Experts' Ratings:

Amount of Competition (1 = Lot of: 4 = Not much) 3.2
Amount of Risk (1 = Very: 4 = Not much) 1.2
Historical Profit Trend (1 = Down: 4 = Up) 2.0
Location & Facilities (1 = Poor: 4 = Excellent) 2.0
Marketability (1 = Low: 4 = High) 1.2
Industry Trend (1 = Declining: 4 = Growing) 2.4

"Competition: highly fragmented, over 50,000 contractors. Risk: a required recurring market. Historic profit trend: as varied as there are contractors. Location: proximity to market important, but not a driving factor as services provided off-site. Marketability: tough to carry sustainability based on typical owner influence. Growth: somewhat mature slow growth industry. Ease of replication: these businesses are easily replicated."

Benchmarks

"$100,000 per employee is typical."

Expenses as a percentage of annual sales:	
Cost of Goods Sold	65%
Payroll/Labor Costs	22%
Occupancy Cost	3%
Profit (estimated)	5%

General Information

Questions to ask seller: "Pricing is dependent on business mix. Service vs. contracting and commercial vs. residential—all play a part."

"Too many owners focus on the required technical abilities rather than the service they are providing."

Advantages of this Business

- "The industry offers significant margins and competitive advantages that can be obtained through certain controls and differentiation. This is an enormous industry offering significant opportunity (on the order of $100 billion)."

Disadvantages of this Business

- "Often smaller companies have too much owner influence."

Trend

Rising Insurance Costs - "PHCC members recently ranked rising insurance costs as the biggest issue they face. We've heard horror stories such as liability insurance premiums increasing up to 600%, health insurance premiums soaring to all-time highs, and contractors being told they don't qualify for insurance at all.

"Finding affordable health insurance is also disturbing, especially when you consider that small businesses pay nearly 30% to 50% more than large businesses to cover the insurance costs of employees.

Indoor Air Quality - "Mold and related indoor air quality (IAQ) issues are also of concern. In fact, sometimes the risks associated with these are convincing some contractors not to pursue work on some projects. Mem-

bers who do HVAC work are becoming educated on the subject of mold, and are considering, or have implemented, protective measures for their companies.

Business Expansion - "PHCC members are often extremely flexible when needed—readily adapting their business to changing times or market demands. In these situations, they typically seize an opportunity to improve profits by diversifying or adding to their business mix.

"Here's what's happening:

- Plumbing companies moving into the HVAC business
- HVAC companies adding plumbing to their service offerings
- Contractors adding specialty services to their businesses. Some examples include irrigation, lawn fertilization, water softeners, bottled water, geothermal market, water-well drilling
- Business scope changes—large, residential new-construction contractors change to primarily commercial
- Single-family home contractors beginning to do multi-family condos
- Service and repair contractors entering the single-family market
- Single-family specialists moving into multi-family construction
- Radiant work is becoming more marketable in upscale homes, particularly in the Northeast. It's used in just under 25% of homes in Canada, and the trend is moving south."

Source: "An Industry Forever Changing" by Eddie Hollub. *Contracting Business;* www.contractingbusiness.com

Resources
Air Conditioning Contractors of America
www.acca.org

Heating Oil Dealers

Rule of Thumb:

- 1 to 1.25 times gross profit + inventory and accounts receivable, but can vary significantly depending on location. Companies are often sold on a per-gallon basis.
- 4 times EBITDA (normalized earnings) is also used in some areas.

Pricing Tips

"Generally 4–5 times adjusted EBITDA plus inventory and accounts receivables. Gross profit per gallon is a major consideration for strategic buyers, and a typical heating oil business may sell for between 1.0 and 1.25 times total gross profit depending on the location and customer mix."

"6 to 7 cents/gallon on annual basis; add fixtures, equipment & inventory"

"Gross profit per gallon drives the value of a heating oil business. Our data base indicates most of these businesses are sold in a range of 1 to 1.5 times gross profit. High margin & full HVAC service firms bring top dollar. Petroleum bulk plants are hard or impossible to sell."

"Usually are sold for 6 to 6.5 cents per gallon the company pumped per year, plus the rolling stock, plus the inventory at cost, plus the cost of the real property in the event it is included in the sale. Usually a high volume low net profit type of business."

"It depends on the amount of hard assets. Gross profits generally drive the value of these businesses. The higher the gross profit, the higher the value. Gross profit per gallon is a key ratio. Some things that detract from value are high real estate values (land & bldgs.), and other outdated petroleum bulk plants, & petroleum equipment. Any environmental problems are a concern."

"Three-year history of dollar sales, gallonage + gross profits. financials, # of customers by product, & type of dispatch (automatic vs. will call). Age and condition of equipment."

Industry Experts' Ratings:

Amount of Competition (1 = Lot of: 4 = Not much)	1.0
Amount of Risk (1 = Very: 4 = Not much)	1.0
Historical Profit Trend (1 = Down: 4 = Up)	2.0
Location & Facilities (1 = Poor: 4 = Excellent)	1.6
Marketability (1 = Low: 4 = High)	2.4
Industry Trend (1 = Declining: 4 = Growing)	1.6
Ease of Replication (1 = Easy: 4 = Difficult)	2.5

"The heating oil industry is a mature industry with significant environmental regulations. The major growth opportunity is through acquisitions, as the older generation exits the business. Discounters can adversely affect margins near supply point terminals."

Benchmarks

"Gross profit per gallon should be in the $0.35 to $0.60 gallon range, and even higher in the major metro areas. Full-service companies, including HVAC service, are in higher demand in the market today."

General Information

<u>Questions to ask seller</u>: 1. A full-service, high-margin, residential customer base is desirable and will bring the best value. 2. Environmental concerns are an issue, w/property transfers requiring Phase I and Phase II reports and usually remediation for the seller. 3. Older bulk plants and petroleum equipment are difficult to sell.

"Full service companies w/ HVAC service and a high margin residential customer base are preferable with strategic buyers."

"Oil-related businesses usually buy other oil-related companies; not much diversification, and people outside oil industry seldom buy into it."

Advantages of this Business

- "Still a viable, cost-effective heating fuel in many areas, particularly in the Northeast and Midwest. New highly efficient furnaces and boilers help conversion efforts. Provides a warm comfortable heat versus electric pumps."

Disadvantages of this Business

- "Environmental concerns, discounters, price spikes during peak heating season; older bulk plants are difficult to sell and/or dismantle."

Industry Trend

"Flat to slow decline as people move towards gas and electric heating systems"

Seller Financing

- "We typically get cash at closing for fixed assets, and finance the intangibles over 2 to 5 years."
- "3 years."
- "5 to 7 years"

Resources

Petroleum Marketers Association of America (PMAA)
<u>www.pmaa.org</u>

American Petroleum Institute (API)
<u>www.api.org</u>

Franchise

Heavenly Hams

160 + units

Rule of Thumb:

- 48 percent of annual sales plus inventory

Resources

www.heavenlyham.com

High Tech and Electronics

Pricing Tips

"Pricing varies very widely from parts, components, sub-assembly, products, combined products, systems and software with or without systems."

"Too many variables—does not lend itself to a rule of thumb. Rough valuing based on EBIT, but multiples based on technology, market and competition...Position of technology in market can add or subtract. Extensive technology, financial and finance- related knowledge essential."

Seller Financing

- "3 to 5 years"

Hobby Shops *(See also Arts & Crafts)*

7,318	SIC: 5945-08	NAIC: 451120

Rule of Thumb:

- 20 percent of annual sales plus inventory
- 1.5 times SDE + inventory plus inventory

Benchmarks

The gross profit margin for the average hobby shop is around 35 percent, before expenses and taxes. Net profit margins are usually less than 10 percent.

Source: National Retail Hobby Stores Association

Average shop sales—This was the first time the question was asked, so no trend could be determined, but average hobby-shop sales are about $390,000, translating into about a $1.5 billion market … The figures show the largest group—31 percent—sells between $100,000 and $249,000 annually, while another 18 percent sell up to $499,000 a year. About 10 percent, or more than 400 shops, report sales that topped $1 million.

Source: *Model Retailer* Magazine, October 2001(the latest we could find.)

Sporting Goods, Books, Music & Hobby Shops

Operating Ratios	All Sole Propretorships	Profitable Only
Sales	100%	100%
Cost of Goods Sold	64.5%	63.6%
Gross Profit	35.5%	36.4%
Operating Expenses	31.3%	24.6%
Net Income*	04.2%	11.8%

* Before Compensation to Owner

Source: Bizstats.com

Resources

National Retail Hobby Stores Association—www.nrhsa.org

Model Retailer magazine
www.modelretailer.com

National Hobby Association
www.hobby.org

Home Centers *(See Building Materials/Lumber Yards)*

Home Health Care *(See also Assisted Living)*

21,000	SIC: 8082-01	NAIC: 621610

Rule of Thumb:

- 3.5 to 5 times EBITDA
- 5 times EBIT
- 70 percent of annual sales

Pricing Tips

"Depends on type of contracts (Medicare-Medicaid, private pay, nursing home, etc.) and length of contracts."

"The age of the equipment may make it subject to obsolescence. A careful inventory of equipment located in patient homes must be made and evaluated by an expert."

"Multiples of EBITDA range from 3–5. Much of the pricing depends on product mix, e.g., respiratory, DME, infusion, sleep apnea, etc."

"In 17 years we have sold hundreds of home health care businesses. We have learned that it takes over 53 determinants of value among risk multiples that are weighed against the relationships among risk multiples and required rates of return. There are too many factors that impact pricing. We advocate that, because of the myriad considerations that are common in the home health care industry, there are no common rules of thumb. To use one would be misleading."

Industry Experts' Ratings:

Marketability (1 = Low: 4 = High)	4.0
Industry Trend (1 = Declining: 4 = Growing)	3.2
Ease of Replication (1 = Easy: 4 = Difficult)	3.2

"Competition is high because the market is huge and growing. Risk is low because established businesses have patient referral sources. Profits are slightly down due to more third-party 'paperwork' requirements. Marketability is high, since many large companies are growing by acquisition. Industry is growing due to an aging population."

Benchmarks

Expenses as a percentage of annual sales:

Cost of Goods Sold	30%
Payroll/Labor Costs	20%
Occupancy Cost	06%
Profit (estimated)	15%

General Information

"Ongoing consolidation provides privately held businesses to sell at high multiples. Also, new services can be added to business 'service and product inventory' using their in-place referral and distribution."

Advantages of this Business

- "Rewarding to help people stay healthy. Much dealing with non-profit hospitals which can be 'refreshing' from a business point of view. Recession proof business."

Disadvantages of this Business

- "Requires some professional expertise. Must be diligent in collecting receivables. Must be prepared to complete all forms, etc. correctly."

Seller Financing

- "Very seldom—no hard assets to secure."

Resources

National Association for Home Care
www.nahc.org

"Valuing Home Health Care Businesses," *Handbook of Business Valuation*, 1st & 2nd Editions, West & Jones, published by John Wiley & Sons

Home Heating Oil *(See also Heating Oil Dealers)*

Home Nursing Agencies

Rule of Thumb:

- 4 times EBITDA

Pricing Tips

"Multiples of EBITDA commonly used for home nursing agencies run from as low as 1 to 5 times 12 month trailing EBITDA."

Industry Experts' Ratings:

Marketability (1 = Low: 4 = High)	2.4
Industry Trend (1 = Declining: 4 = Growing)	3.2
Ease of Replication (1 = Easy: 4 = Difficult)	2.0

Benchmarks

"With the aging of America, and the growing need for health care services, this is a growth industry. Low cost of entry equals a competitive environment."

Expenses as a percentage of annual sales:

Payroll/Labor Costs	30%
Profit (estimated)	15%

Advantages of this Business

- "Growth only depends upon management capability and access to capital."

Disadvantages of this Business

- "Competitive. Nursing shortage."

Resources

National Association of Health Care
www.nahc.org

Homes—Retirement *(See Assisted Living/Nursing Homes)*

25,300	SIC: 8059-04	NAIC: 623311

Pricing Tips

"Selling price is quite varied, from $2,000 to $3,000 per bed, depending upon the number of beds. There is no hard and fast rule of thumb which will apply because of the condition of the real estate and whether or not there are quarters for the owner/operator and the size of the home."

Hospital Laundry

Pricing Tips

An industry expert states that for laundry with hospital contracts a rule of thumb is 50 percent of gross annual sales. This is because that market is a very competitive one.

General Information

The Textile Rental Services Association (TRSA) estimates the following costs that hospitals spend for on-premise laundry services:

- fringe benefits, taxes, insurance—12%
- fuel oil, natural gas—7%
- depreciation—2%
- maintenance—2%
- water and sewer—1%
- electricity—1%
- interest on investment, administration, and support—5%

Source: www.trsa.org

Resources

Textile Rental Services Association (TRSA)
www.trsa.org

Hotels & Motels *(See also Motels)*

47,584*	SIC: 7011-01	NAIC: 7211

*Based on properties with 15 or more rooms.

Source: American Hotel & Lodging Association

Rule of Thumb:

- 8 times SDE
- 10 to 14 times EBITDA
- 3 times annual room revenues
- 3.2 percent of annual sales
- 7 to 9 times cash flow
- 2.0 to 3.5 times annual room revenues—average 2.5
- Outside corridors—2.0 to 2.5 times annual room revenues
- Inside corridors—2.5 to 3.0 times annual room revenues
- Seldom seen—3.5 times annual room revenues

Pricing Tips

"Buyer pricing should always be done AFTER provision form FF&E Reserve of approximately 4%. Repairs & Maintenance and FF&E Reserve TOGETHER should total approxmiately 8–9% of total sales. Forget exterior corridor properties."

"Usually use a rule of thumb from 2.0 to 3.0 of gross sales. In extreme cases, up to 3.5 for excellent franchised property. Age and condition of property as well as FF&E makes a difference. We use several approaches to actual valuation of a property. Adequate (approx 5%) for reserves. RevPAR (Revenue per Available Room) seems to be the thing today, not gross sales."

"Hotels are based on many things, since you just don't buy a hotel business. You have real estate attached 100% of the time. Revenue per available room, occupancies, average daily rates play important parts. In general, a hotel would sell according to the amount of rooms built. In general, you could take revenue per available room per year and multiply that by number of rooms then multiply that number by anywhere from 3 to 10 to get a price; of course this would depend upon what type of flag the hotel was flying. Food and beverage operations both in hotels and free standing are similar. Basically a good rule of thumb is to take the replacement cost of the FF&E plus leasehold improvements, then add this amount to 50% of revenue or 3x seller's discretionary cash or bottom line after seller ad-backs."

Note: What is the difference between a hotel and motel? "There really is none. The term 'motel' is derived from the term 'motor hotel,' which originally meant that the hotel provided parking (circa 1950s). The term motel today generally is used for a 'limited service' property (i.e., a hotel that provides a limited number of amenities and does not provide food service."

Source: American Hotel & Lodging Association

"Hotels should be priced only after taking into consideration an ample FF&E Reserve of 4 to 5 percent of revenues (in addition to repairs and maintenance expense). Anticipate third-party financing of 60 to 70 percent of purchase price only if ample debt service coverage (1.25 to 1.5) can be proven from historical financials. Buyer's track record operating similar facilities will be paramount with lenders. Franchise affiliation an obvious advantage. Interior corridors only."

"Most appraisers use only the land plus building, plus FF&E for total valuation. We prefer to consider all of these, but add a value for the going business based on the gross and net income."

"Required equity return: Equity investor return requirements will continue to be low by historic standards due to pressure from competing buyers with an abundant supply of capital. Unleveraged equity yields from 10 percent to 12 percent are common with cash-on-cash returns dropping to 6 percent to 8 percent for highly desirable assets. Leveraged equity investor return requirements in the mid-to-high teens will remain commonplace for institutional assets with proven cash flow."

Source: Hotel & Motel Management, www.hotelmotel.com

"Beach properties: 3 ½ to 5 times sales. Ocean front: 4 to 5 times gross sales."

"Some buyers and sellers prefer to use a cap rate to determine value while others prefer a dollar amount per room."

"Whether or not the property is franchised, business hotel or resort can influence value."

Industry Experts' Ratings:

Marketability (1 = Low: 4 = High) 1.6
Industry Trend (1 = Declining: 4 = Growing) 2.2
Ease of Replication (1 = Easy: 4 = Difficult) 1.8

"Large capital investment on front-end makes the property susceptible to new, better-located competition. Need ongoing reserve for replacement of FF&E."

"Location and franchise make a great difference. Also, we must consider extended-stay motels."

Benchmarks

"Measured by stock-market value divided by number of rooms, La Quinta seems cheap at roughly $50,000 a room, according to JMP Securities analyst William Marks. Extended Stay America, one of La Quinta's rivals, was bought out earlier in 2004 for $63,000 a room."

Source: "Smart Money" column by Russell Pearlman, *Bangor Daily News*, August 14–15, 2004

"The buying binge did not translate into a corresponding increase in prices. The median price per room rose just 2.8% in southern California to $52,778; in northern California, the per-room price plunged 28%, to $43,919, according to Atlas." [Atlas Hospitality Group]

"The largest hotel sale in the state last year at $553,000 per room was the $383-million purchase of the historic Hotel del Coronado in San Diego County.

"Other large transactions in 2003 were Merv Griffin's sale of the Beverly Hilton in Beverly Hills for $135 million, or $232,000 a room. The Warner Center Marriott in Woodland Hills sold for $85.3 million, or $184,000 a room; the Sheraton Universal Hotel in Universal City went for $49 million, or $112,000 a room; and the Pan Pacific Hotel in San Francisco sold for $47 million, or $143,000 a room."

Source: *Los Angles Times*, Monday, May 3, 2004

"In the United States, tourism is currently the third largest retail industry, behind automotive and food stores."

Source: *2004 Lodging Industry Profile*, American Hotel & Lodging Association

General Information

Questions to ask seller: Are there capital expense items that need attention? How much contracted room business do they have? How much room business do they have on the books and for how long a period of time? What was their last QA score if it is a franchise hotel? Do they know of any new highways being constructed in the future that may divert traffic to or away from the hotel? Any new competition coming up in the area?

"Astute operators seek tour bus travelers and other group business. Many customers prefer a continental breakfast. Others prefer late check-out. Parking close to entrance and sufficient handicapped parking is essential. 'Across the street' parking will reduce the value. Easy and safe entrance and exit to the property is valuable. No shrubs near doors or entrances to avoid insects, etc. Use of Key Cards a plus."

2004 At-a-Glance Statistical Figures

47,040 (15 or more rooms)	properties
4,415,696	guestrooms
$105.3	billion in sales
61.1%	average occupancy rate
$50.42	revenue per available room

Source: *2004 Lodging Industry Profile*, American Hotel & Lodging Association

Advantages of this Business

- "Equity build-up and cash flow. Many motels have living quarters as a benefit. Special 'expense' items which inure to the benefit of the owner/operator."
- "Significant profit potential once operating costs are covered"
- "Ability to collateralize existing properties to finance new"

Disadvantages of this Business

- "High fixed cost and debt-service levels. Very heavy labor costs."
- "Large equity commitment required (approx 40% of initial project cost). Industry is very labor intensive. Need major 'flag' affiliation and previous background in order to qualify for most lenders."
- "Competition moving in. Aging property. Management. Franchise not paying for itself. Bad location—neighborhood changes downward/ road changes."

Industry Trend

"Effect of 9/11 was to deter new hotel development and drive up ADR and occupancy in existing properties as the economy recovered. Sales prices of existing properties have increased along with recent development surge."

Portsmouth, NH—"Lodging Econometrics (LE), the Industry Authority for Hotel Real Estate, has released, for the first time, its supply growth forecast for 2007 in its mid-year report to the lodging industry. Additionally, LE revised its forecast for supply growth in both '05 and '06 after reviewing over 3,000 project records in the Development Pipeline with individual Developers and re-verifying anticipated start and completion dates with various Brand Managers.

"Patrick Ford, President, said, 'LE forecasts that 917 hotels with 100,559 guestrooms will open in '07. That's the highest total for new openings since '01, but far removed from the peak set in 1998 when 1,532 hotels with 156,471 rooms opened. Because the supply increase forecasted for '07 is modest—just 16,101 more rooms than '06—and because the industry has already seen 26 consecutive months of improved demand, which is expected to continue well into the expansionary phase of the present cycle, 2007 is on track to become the second record-breaking profit year in a row. It's expected to exceed the record $26 billion anticipated for '06.'"

Source: www.hotelmotel.com

"The supply of long-stay lodging has surged over the last seven years, increasing 2.4 percent last year to 245,357 rooms and more than doubling from 107,000 rooms in 1997, according to the Highland Group, a hospitality consulting firm in Atlanta. And demand has been picking up even more lately, according to Smith Travel Research, growing by 4.9 percent in 2004, the fastest rate since 2000, and surpassing the 4.6 percent jump reported for the overall hotel industry.

"What is driving the trend? Tight corporate budgets, for one thing."
Source: *The New York Times*, Tuesday March 29, 2005

"Hotel property prices: Almost all Lodging Industry Investment Council (LIIC) members predicted that hotel values will continue their upward growth over the next 12 months. This is being facilitated by improving hotel operating performance, an abundance and diversity of aggressive buyers and a cooperative lending climate.

"Where are we in the cycle? From the hotel operations cycle perspective, top-line revenue growth should fuel strong bottom-line growth for the next several years. In terms of the real-estate pricing cycle, the results ranged from 'we are peaking now' to 2009. A significant number believe we are nearing the cycle peak in terms of asset pricing."
Source: Hotel & Motel Management, www.hotelmotel.com

Seller Financing
- "Not usually seller financed currently"
- "20 years"
- "5 to 10 years"

Resources
American Hotel & Lodging Association
www.ahma.com
This is an excellent and very informative site

Hotels and Motels: Valuations and Market Studies, published by the Appraisal Institute, www.appraisalinstitute.org

"Valuation of Hotels and Motels," *Handbook of Business Valuation*, 1st and 2nd Edition, West & Jones, published by John Wiley & Sons.

Hotel & Motel Management
www.hotelmotel.com

Hotel Business
www.hotelbusiness.com

Lodging Magazine
www.lodgingmagazine.com

Lodging Hospitality
www.lhonline.com—a good site with an in-depth archive of excellent articles.

Hotels
www.hotelsmag.com

Franchise

House Doctors Handyman Service

235 units

Approximate Total Investment:	$25,450–$53,550

House Doctor is a handyman service specializing in minor home repairs

Rule of Thumb:

- 24 percent of annual sales

Resources
www.housedoctors.com

Franchise

Hungry Howie's Pizza & Subs

500 units

Approximate Total Investment:	$100,000–$150,000
Estimated Annual Sales per Unit:	$500,000

Rule of Thumb:

- 30 percent of annual sales

Resources
www.hungryhowies.com

Ice Cream Trucks

General Information

"The Philadelphia-based International Association of Ice Cream Vendors doesn't keep statistics, but says the industry is doing as well as ever, and its membership is expected to grow.

"Today, ice cream trucks are owned by small regional companies that rent to independent drivers, or individuals who go it alone.

"Some, including Tanner, buy a fleet and rent to drivers such as Phillips, who take home 35 percent of their daily sales—minus the $12 daily truck rental fee and gas costs. Tanner gets the other 65 percent to cover operational and stocking costs: He supplies 64 varieties of ice cream from various suppliers to every truck.

"Phillips said that, so far, her best day netted more than $400 in sales. She's been working six days a week, now aiming for $500."

Source: *The Boston Globe*, Thursday August 18, 2005

Resources

International Association of Ice Cream Vendors
www.iaicv.org

Ice Cream Truck Superstore—a company that sells ice cream and food trucks and vans; offers a manual on how to operate an ice cream truck business, www.icecreamtrucksuperstore.com

National Ice Cream and Yogurt Retailers Association
wwwnicyra.org

International Ice Cream Association
www.idfa.org—an interesting and informative site

Ice Cream/Yogurt Shops *(See also Carvel)*

18,472	SIC: 5812-03	NAIC: 722213

Rule of Thumb:

- 45 to 50 percent of annual sales plus inventory
- 1 to 1.5 times SDE; plus fixtures, equipment & inventory

Pricing Tips

"These stores are usually sold for a little less than one half year's gross sales. If it is a franchise store, such as Dairy Queen, Arctic Circle, or A&W, 15 percent can be added to the asking price. Net profit usually runs from 18 percent to 22 percent. Lease on the property should not exceed 6 percent (upper limit) of gross profit."

General Information

Labeling Definitions

- Ice cream is a frozen food made from a mixture of dairy products, containing at least 10% milkfat.
- "Reduced fat" ice cream contains at least 25% less total fat than the referenced product (either an average of leading brands, or the company's own brand).
- "Light" ice cream contains at least 50% less total fat or 33% fewer calories than the referenced product (the average of leading regional or national brands).
- "Low-fat" ice cream contains a maximum of 3 grams of total fat per serving (1/2 cup).
- "Nonfat" ice cream contains less than 0.5 grams of total fat per serving.

Quality Segments

- "Superpremium" ice cream tends to have very low overrun and high fat content, and the manufacturer uses the best quality ingredients.
- "Premium" ice cream tends to have low overrun and higher fat content than regular ice cream, and the manufacturer uses higher quality ingredients.
- "Regular" ice cream meets the overrun required for the federal ice cream standard.
- "Economy" ice cream meets required overrun and generally sells for a lower price than regular ice cream."

Source: International Ice Cream Association

Ice Hockey Teams (Professional)

Rule of Thumb:

- The average value of a National Hockey league team is $163 million.

Source: *Forbes*, November 29, 2004

General Information

"Lockout ends with owners' approval

"New York—In a span of 90 minutes, the NHL showed off its new labor agreement and its new rules, and even had time to find a home for the league's newest phenom.

"No team's payroll will exceed $39 million or go under $21.5 million next season— including salaries, signing bonuses and performance bonuses. The six-year deal also stipulates that total player costs will not exceed 54 percent of league revenues.

"Under the new deal, players are guaranteed to receive 54 percent of league-wide revenues—projected to be between $1.7 billion and $1.8 billion next season. A portion of every player's salary will be held in escrow if it is determined that revenues are smaller, resulting in players receiving more than 54 percent."

Source: Associated Press, www.sports.espn.com

Franchise

Iceberg Drive Inn

11 units

Approximate Total Investment: $131,500–$546,000

Rule of Thumb:

- 40 to 45% of annual sales plus inventory

"Ice cream and related frozen desserts are consumed by more than 90% of households in the United States."

Source: Mintel

Incentive Travel Companies

Rule of Thumb:

- 5 times EBITDA for larger incentive houses, 4 times for mid-size, and 3 times EBITDA for smaller shops

Pricing Tips

"How many programs are on the books for the next 12 months? Are they serving various industries or concentrating on one sector? Diversity is better. Three types—travel, merchandise, debit card. Points tracking & redemption, etc. = big online registration."

Industrial Safety and Health

Rule of Thumb:

- Manufacturing—5 to 7 times recasted EBIT less debt
- Distribution—4 to 6 times recasted EBIT less debt

Information and Document Management Service Industries

Rule of Thumb:

- 4 to 6 times normalized EBITDA

Information Technology Companies

Rule of Thumb:

- 3 times SDE
- 4 to 6 times EBITDA

Pricing Tips

"Is there an SLA (Software License Agreement) for each type/copy of software being used? Are the SLAs assignable? Has the vendor given written permission to assign them and under what conditions? Has the company been reported to the Software Consortium as a company using unlicensed software? Is the technology based on open standards and/or proprietary? Is there a complete inventory list of all software and hardware being used in the business? What 3rd parties are hosting applications and providing IT Services?"

"Off-balance sheet items such as: customer/client lists, developed technology, R&D yet to be commercialized, patents, proprietary products, future potential to grow the business"

"Ask questions about client relationships that will remain, about product & market development, about other competitive advantages."

Trend

"It will be up because companies are less inclined than ever before to develop technology capabilities. They want IT products and services to be served up like a utility and priced accordingly. IT products and services that clearly distinguish between commodity services and strategic services will be very helpful to many industries."

Seller Financing

- "3 years"

Injection Molding (Privately held)

Rule of Thumb:

- 4.5 to 6 times EBITDA

Inns *(See also Bed & Breakfast—B&Bs)*

590+	SIC: 7011-02	

Rule of Thumb:

- 3 to 5 times annual income plus inventory
- $50,000 to $100,000 per guest room plus inventory

Pricing Tips

"On smaller B&Bs, take the asset value of the underlying real estate & furnishings, add to it 3 times the net operating income and add $20K to $40K for the aesthetics & tax benefits. Work backward to see if the Net Operating Income can support debt service and reduce accordingly. Most larger inns are selling from 6 to 8 times NOI based on degree of seller financing."

"Inns & B&Bs (businesses as opposed to real-estate driven small properties—small is 3 rooms or less): 4.2 times gross room sales, a little higher for dinner service; 4.51 times room sales. Factors affecting price are area, size, style & owner's quarters. Dinner food service makes a property more difficult to sell. Everyone wants a B&B."

"For motels & lodging, a commonly used rule of thumb is the GIM (Price/Gross Annual Income) which varies from 3.5 to 5.0. For these kinds of properties, a CAP rate of 10 percent is typical. More important is the cash flow for an inn to be economically feasible; the inn must have enough income to pay the expenses, debt service, and enough left over for the owners to live on."

"On larger inns, use 8 (bank-financed) to 10 (seller-financed) cap rate on Net Operating Income (NOI) before debt & depreciation. For smaller inns, take the asset value of the underlying real estate & furnishings, add it to 3 times the net operating income and add $20K to $40K for the aesthetics & tax benefits. Work backward to see if NOI can support debt service and reduce accordingly."

"Must have private baths now. Operating expense can range from $3K to $10K per room depending on occupancy and size of building. Income is usually $5K to $20K per guest room depending on location (occupancy & room rate) and amenities."

"Leased [inn] properties priced at 30–60 percent of gross sales. Owned properties priced at 50 percent plus of gross sales."

"Buyer should have a sense of good taste, common sense & hospitality ... cash flow is not great, it will mostly cover living expenses (mostly tax deductible) and there is real estate appreciation potential which you can retain tax free to the degree it is your primary residence. Future of business is excellent—has a great appeal to over-50, early-out, college-educated baby boomers; a lot of teachers. Buyer profile doesn't generalize to other typical businesses."

"...In business w/leased property, monthly rent & terms of lease are a major factor. Food cost should be plus or minus 30 percent. Labor cost should be plus or minus 25 percent. Also, how much debt does the business have? How much do the owners pay themselves? How many hours do they work?"

Benchmarks
"Operating Expenses 40 to 50 percent"

Expenses as a percentage of annual sales:
Cost of Goods .... 15% (food, cleaning supplies & linens)
Payroll/Labor .... 10% not including owner
Occupancy Costs: 7%–10%

Seller Financing
- "Most large inns are seller financed. Typically with 20 percent down and terms @ 9 percent, 30-year amortization with a 7-year balloon."
- "5 to 10 years."
- "Some owner financing, full owner financing—20 year amortization, 5–10 year balloons, 7 years normal"

Resources
Professional Association of Innkeepers International
www.paii.org

www.bb-4-sale.com
This is a Web site offering inns for sale.

Instant Print *(See Print Shops)*

Insurance Agencies

234,667	SIC: 6411-12	NAIC: 524210

Rule of Thumb:

➢ "A. Standard Multi-Lines Independent Insurance Agency
  a) under $1 million commission, Multiple of Gross Commission Income—1.25 to .85, depending on carriers represented.
  b) over $1 million commission and fee income, EBITDA, 3 to 9 times.
B. Non-Standard Auto Insurance Agency. Insurance Commis-

Insurance Agencies *(cont'd)*

sion Income, excluding add-on coverages, times last year's retention, .2 to 1.0 times commission income.

C. Surplus Lines Agency; .80 to 1.0 times commission."

- 2.5 times SDE
- 1.25–1.50 times annual gross sales
- 100% of annual commissions; applies to multi-line agencies doing $100,000– $200,000 in gross commissions
- 1.0 to 1.5 times annual renewal commissions
- 1.5 times annual commissions (property & casualty)
- 2 times annual revenues (standard agency)
- 1.0 times annual revenues (sub-standard agency)
- "Agencies with more revenue ($1.5M + in commissions) are typically valued at 5–8 times EBITDA. This roughly translates into 1.5–2.0 + times commission revenues. Hard markets yield more contingent income and increased pricing on carrier premiums. EBITDA margins after recasting should come in between 15%–40% depending on size; any brokers above $2 million in commissions due to economies of scale issues."

Pricing Tips

"The insurance products and companies represented by the agency are an important component of value. Commissions generated from the sale of securities sell at much lower multiples. An analysis of the client mix is necessary to determine the nuances of valuation."

"Persistency of policy renewals. Employee length of employment. Number of insurance companies represented."

"Agencies sell for a multiple of annual commissions received by the agency. That number can run from 1 to 4, with 2 being the most likely. Determining factors are lines of business sold (e.g., casualty, life, health), carriers appointed by size of agency, loss ratios of lines of business, persistency of book of business, diversity of clients, etc."

"Direct-bill policies have a value of 30% greater than agency-bill policies, due to retention. Personal lines have greater value than commercial line p/c due to the relationship with clients and commission of the producer. Agencies with state-of-the-art Internet-based management systems and transactional filing seem to generate greater revenue per employee."

"Contract persistency is critical to the continuation of fees. The demographics of the clientele base should be carefully analyzed. The range of valuation multiples is very wide and varies by the type of revenue stream and how it's paid. Regulation violations by the owner can severely reduce the price."

"Renewal (persistency) rate. Amount of assigned risk business. Any client that accounts for 5% of the gross revenue. Length of employment—present employees. Agency contracts with insurance companies. Lost ratio of book of business over past five years.

"The U.S. insurance industry, which is made up of property/casualty and life/health companies and agents, brokers and service personnel for all sectors, employed 2.3 million people in 2004."

Source: Insurance Information Institute. www.iii.org

"Ask if the property and casualty has standard and sub-standard, and if the percentage of each standard is 1.5 times annual commissions, but sub-standard is 1.0 times annual commissions."

"Renegotiations of agency contracts by companies as a condition of approving the new agent destroy value and kill deals. The time is perhaps right, though, because the industry is at the point in its cycle when they want all the business they can get on almost any terms. Companies often have a 'pocket' buyer, who is the only buyer they will agree to. Approval often means acceptance of a reduced commission rate. Traditional agencies aren't worth the time and effort."

"One interesting exception has come to my attention, and that is brokerage-based agencies that deal extensively in employee benefits, particularly employee group health insurance. The business tends to be high volume, stable, and consistently profitable. The contractual relationships that have been set up by many of the major HMOs etc. with brokers have volume and quality factors such that two agencies, each receiving $3 in revenue, if combined, may receive $12–$15. Beyond that, various sources have identified this as a fertile field for cross-selling opportunities and other incremental revenue.

"In one extreme case, I understand that the final deal amounted to paying approximately 8 times gross annual revenue; yep, 8 x annual gross! Payment was made in listed stock of the acquiring company, not cash though. Not sure where this will all shake out. Some of the earliest and most aggressive acquirers are now having financial indigestion as a result of their purchases, and one, last I knew, was near bankruptcy. However, there are still active acquirers, and price seems to be a minor consideration. Acquirers seem to be acquiring potential markets rather than current businesses."

"They mostly run at 1 to 2 times annual commission, taking into consideration the quality and risk level of the premiums. Does customer maintenance require a lot of work and handholding? Personal versus commercial lines, level of risk of the insured and Standard versus Non-standard."

"What kind of companies do they represent?"

"Kinds of insurance, location, number of customers? How long has the agency been established? Does any one customer represent over 20 percent of the business? What would happen to the customers if the owner left?"

"Buyers must be approved by major insurance companies."

Industry Experts' Ratings:

Amount of Competition (1 = Lot of: 4 = Not much) 2.0
Amount of Risk (1 = Very: 4 = Not much) 2.6
Historical Profit Trend (1 = Down: 4 = Up) 2.8
Location & Facilities (1 = Poor: 4 = Excellent) 3.0
Marketability (1 = Low: 4 = High) 3.2
Industry Trend (1 = Declining: 4 = Growing) 3.2
Ease of Replication (1 = Easy: 4 = Difficult) 3.0

"Insurance is usually required by state(s) and/or lending institutions."

Benchmarks

"Each agent should generate $300,000 to $1,000,000 in commissions to the agency."

"Revenue per client—$3,000
Revenue per employee—$100,000
Profit for agency under $25,000 is 18%
Profit for agency between $250,000 and $500,000 should be 30%
Profit for agency between $1 and $2 million should be 40%
Profit for agency between $2 and 5 million should be 50%"

"275 sq. ft. per employee, $100,000 in commissions per full-time equivalent employee or above is good; producers with large books of business would be in the $400,000–$1 million + range in terms of commissions to the agency."

"Percentages of Gross sales	
Payroll, Service Employees	35%
Sales	25 to 40%

"Revenue per Employee	
Paperless Agency	$75,000 to $115,000
Manual Files	$39,000 to $50,000"

Expenses as a percentage of annual sales:	
Cost of Goods Sold	32%
Payroll/Labor Costs	35%
Occupancy Cost	8–10%
Profit (estimated)	25%

General Information

"There are usually many insurance agencies in each town, city, state. You need to be very customer-oriented."

"Agencies are most often sold by word-of-mouth to local competitors. Help is available from carriers with valuation of their businesses. They also offer succession planning. A more than cursory knowledge of the industry is necessary to represent an agency in a professional manner."

"Agency commissions are under greater pressure from the carriers to be reduced, but due to the consolidation over the past 20 years, the agencies are larger; same staff, but more profitable if the agency has installed state-of-the-art management systems and is using transactional filing. Where agencies have more than one location, centralization of back- office services is most beneficial."

"It is a seller's market."

"Great time to be an independent agent, as the captive carriers, such State Farm, Allstate and Nationwide have limited their agents in getting new business."

"Industry consolidation and company efficiencies are promoting the move away from a commissioned sales force."

"Like many other service businesses, the insurance business recognizes the benefit of growing by acquisition."

Advantages of this Business

- "So long as you provide prompt courteous service, customers stay with you for many years."

Disadvantages of this Business

- Possibility of insurance companies discontinuing to provide insurance products if state regulators are difficult to deal with or risks become too great, such as hurricanes at seashore locations or other catastrophic exposures.
- "High income. Support from carriers. Community involvement. Equity building. Renewable income stream (annuity)."
- Highly competitive.
- "The insurance agency business is highly regulated, and the licensed agents are usually very professional and respected by the community."
- "Good margins, high valuations, no inventory, repeat business"
- "So long as customer service is good and pricing is reasonably competitive, customers tend to stay with the agent they are with."
- "Control of your personal daily schedule and personal income substantially above average are the top two."
- "Profit can be very difficult, if the owner does not implement state-of-the-art systems and contract with insurance carriers interested in underwriting business in the agent's marketplace."
- "Startup can cost $150K, and yet not have carriers or qualified staff to sell and service prospects and clients."
- "Difficult to manage and motivate producers, difficult to find good talent"

- "Dependent upon desire of insurance companies to do business with the agent, for the kind of coverage required, and the regulatory additive of the insurance department of the state"
- "The difficulty in developing a successful marketing plan and building equitable relationships with vendors are the top two."

Trend

"Insurance agencies are selling many more products and services and should continue to grow."

"Continued need and growth. Consolidation of smaller agencies."

Seller Financing

- "Down Payment—25 to 50 percent
  Balance—24 to 60 months, plus interest @ 2 percent over prime."
- "50% of gross commissions for 3 years"
- "3 to 5 years"
- "Sometimes owner financing on renewals. For instance, 1.50 times renewals. This can be tricky because buyer may take the cream of the crop and seller is left holding the bag."

Resources

Independent Insurance Agents of America
www.independentagent.com

Insurance Information Institute
www.iii.org,—lots of information and data

Insurance Companies (in general)

(See Insurance Agencies)

Rule of Thumb:

➢ 1 to 2 times capital and surplus

Pricing Tips

"A ton of information is required, beyond the company's financial statements and tax returns, such as reports submitted to the insurance department of the states the company does business in; actuarial reports on the adequacy of amounts in reserve to pay claims; rating of company by one or more insurers-rating organizations; status of any significant lawsuits pending against the company; its reputation in the industry; and its relationship with its sales force. Just getting an opinion as to value involves hundreds of hours of document review and analysis."

Insurance Companies (Life) *(See also Insurance Agencies)*

Rule of Thumb:

- 1 to 2½ times capital & surplus

Insurance Companies (Property & Casualty)

(See also Insurance Agencies)

Rule of Thumb:

- ½ to 3 times capital & surplus

Pricing Tips

"I have a Property & Casualty company for sale with stockholders' equity of $145 million; the asking price is 1.6 to 1.7 times stockholder's equity. Price dropped due to an adjustment in some bad risks that were eliminated."

General Information

"All of these must relate to past profitability & future prospects."

"What is their stockholders' equity? What management do they have? What is their marketing ability?"

Internet Publishing *(See Publishing—Internet)*

Investment Advice

Rule of Thumb:

- 1.5 times SDE
- 1 times annual sales

Pricing Tips

"Contract persistency is critical to the continuation of fees. The demographics of the clientele base should be carefully analyzed. The range of valuation multiples is very wide and varies by the type of revenue stream and how it's paid. The numbers above are considered to be averages. Regulation violations by the owner can severely reduce the sales price."

Industry Experts' Ratings:

Marketability (1 = Low: 4 = High) 1.0
Industry Trend (1 = Declining: 4 = Growing) 2.0
Ease of Replication (1 = Easy: 4 = Difficult) 1.0

"Industry consolidation and company marketing efficiencies are promoting the move away from commissioned sales force."

Advantages of this Business

- "Control of your personal daily schedule and personal income substantially above average are the top two."

Franchise

Jani-King *(See Coverall Cleaning Concepts)*

11,000 units

Approximate Total Investment:	$8,170 to $74,000

Rule of Thumb:

- 26 percent of annual revenues plus inventory

General Information

"Through a network of more than 100 Regional Offices, Jani-King contracts commercial cleaning services, while the work is performed by Franchisees who own and operate their own business."

Source: www.janiking.com

Resources

www.janiking.com

Janitorial Services *(See Coverall & Jani-King)*

40,376	SIC: 7439-02	NAIC: 561720

Rule of Thumb:

- 45 percent of annual sales plus inventory
- 1.5 times SDE plus inventory
- 1 times one month's billings; plus fixtures, equipment and inventory
- 4 times monthly billings; plus fixtures, equipment and inventory

Pricing Tips

"Janitorial (Contract Cleaners)—1.5 times net, depending upon the amount of hired help. An industry evaluation is 3 to 5 times the monthly gross depending upon the equipment and the type of accounts; e.g., government vs. private… a very conservative approach which could vary widely on a monthly basis. Government contracts could offer more start-up security for a prospective purchaser."

Benchmarks

"For contract janitorial services, average estimated gross sales skyrocketed to $4,153,450 [2004] from $1,418,527 in 2003. The median estimated 2004 gross sales was $550,000. Respondents who perform janitorial services reported charging an average of $0.31 per square foot."

Company is part of a franchise 12.0%

Company is not part of a franchise 77.8%

Source: *2005 Proctor & Gamble Contract Cleaning Benchmarking Survey Report*. See Notes below

"Residential maid services estimated 2004 gross sales were $111,250, and the median estimated annual gross sales for 2004 were $85,000. Residential maid services cost customers an average minimum of $80 per cleaning."

Source: *2005 Proctor & Gamble Contract Cleaning*

Benchmarking Survey Report

This survey was conducted and produced by the research department at the CM B2B Trade Group, the parent of *CM/Cleaning & Maintenance* magazine. It is being sponsored as a service by P&G ProLine ™, Proctor & Gamble's complete line of floor care, carpet care, daily cleaner, and specialty cleaner products.

Note: The above survey items are from one of the most informative and valuable surveys we have seen. It is only eight pages but crammed full of survey results. If you are doing anything in the janitorial/maid industries, you need this survey. Go to www.cminstitute.net and order a copy (we did); it's only $25 a copy.

The 2004 Pioneer Eclipse In-House Cleaning Operations Benchmarking Survey Report is featured in this month's CM *Cleaning & Maintenance Management* magazine.

"The survey found the following averages of interior building area cleaned in square feet per FTE (full-time equivalent employee) per hour, with no obstructions:

- 2–4 year college/university: 12,466
- Schools/districts (K–12): 11,388
- Private office building: 10,853
- Government facility: 7,835
- Medical facilities: 5,931

"Median square footage per FTE per hour was as follows:

- 2–4 year college/university: 5,000
- Schools/districts (K–12): 4,000
- Private office building: 4,500
- Government facility: 4,000
- Medical facilities: 2,050"

Source: "Benchmarking Survey: Which facility has best cleaning production?" by Nicole Lemperle, Associate Editor, *CM Cleaning & Maintenance Management*

General Information

"The business of cleaning and maintaining America's office buildings, retail, commercial, industrial, educational, and healthcare facilities is huge—an estimated $49 billion. The industry is not quite 'recession proof,' but is recession resistant in that demand is growing. No companies really dominate the industry. Rather, it is populated by more than 56,000 cleaning contractors, mostly small 'mom and pop' operations. This figure includes roughly 16,800 commercial cleaning franchises and 2,100 residential cleaning franchises.

Source: Building Services Contractors Association International.

Industry Trend

"Companies providing services to buildings will experience a 58 percent growth during the period 1994-2005."

Source: Building Services Contractors Association International

Resources

Building Service Contractors Association International
www.bscai.org

www.janitorusa.com—This site has instructions on how to start your own janitorial business and related information.

www.JanitorBooks.com—This site contains a list of books, software and training materials related to the janitorial business.

CM Cleaning & Maintenance Management—www.cmmonline.com—an informative site based on the magazine

Franchise

Jersey Mike's Submarines & Salads

200 + units	
Approximate Total Investment:	$94,000 to $203,000

Rule of Thumb:

- 50 percent of annual sales plus inventory

Resources

www.jerseymikes.com

Jewelry Stores

45,552	SIC: 5944-09	NAIC: 448310

Rule of Thumb:

- 4 to 6 times EBIT if inventory included
- None—too inventory intensive

Pricing Tips

Questions to ask seller: What return on assets would be expected if current owner left city?

"A destination upscale jeweler has a much better 'chance' of being sold as a going business."

"Highly capital intensive—inventory on hand most critical in pricing"

"Price is based on amount of inventory, current value, years in business, and profit of operations now and after sale is completed."

"No magic formula—jewelry is a high-capital requirement for inventory and hiring personnel; trust & confidence of owners not readily transferable. Will seller sell without inventory—or one year's supply based on sales volume that is high enough to be attractive—example: annual sales of $500,000 with inventory at cost of $200,000 is attractive if business has growth and is currently profitable."

Benchmarks

Expenses as a percentage of annual sales:	
Cost of Goods	55%–58%
Payroll/Labor Costs	22%
Occupancy Cost	8%–10%
Profit (estimated)	06%

Industry Trend

"… There was a downtrend in total sales in '00 and '01. Despite this trend, '02 industry sales were projected up to $42.3 billion with the industry projected to break the $50 billion barrier by 2005 and the $60 billion barrier by 2008."

Source: www.NationalJeweler.com

Seller Financing

- Not seller financed—inventory too portable—high risk
- 3 years

Resources

Jewelers of America (JA)
www.jewelers.org

PricePoint

Everyone has a different opinion of what a business is worth...PricePoint gets everyone on the same page.

Based on the Multiple of Discretionary Earnings Method to pricing a business, PricePoint incorporates business and industry characteristics as perceived by buyers and sellers of small to midsize businesses to arrive at a suggested selling price. PricePoint assists in structuring the deal so that the down payment and the terms of the loan can be justified to potential buyers while showing the business owner their potential gain from the deal. Throughout the program, industry rules of thumb are used as general guides and sanity checks to give a larger perspective on the detailed analysis of the business financials and industry position. PricePoint is a realistic approach to pricing that gets everyone on the same page.

PricePoint Features:

- **Three Year Annualized Analysis and Weighted Pricing**
- **Price Variances Based on Down Payment Percentage**
- **Built-in Amortization Calculator**
- **Justification for Purchase**
- **Calculation of Seller's Discretionary Earnings**
- **Multi-Year Income Statement Analysis**
- **Full-Color Graphing**
- **Printable Multi-Page Price Report**

Download a free fifteen-day demonstration from our website

PricePoint *$329*

System Requirements

- **Processor:** 486/66-MHz processor or higher (Pentium processor recommended)
- **Operating System:** Windows98 Second Edition, WindowsME, WindowsNT 4.0 (SP6a) and higher, Windows2000, or WindowsXP
- **Memory:** 16MB of RAM minimum 50MB of Hard Disk Space
- **Drive:** CD-ROM Drive
- **Display:** Super VGA (800X600) or higher-

For more information please call 800-239-5085.

www.bbpinc.com

National Jeweler
www.nationaljeweler.com

Modern Jeweler
www.modernjeweler.com

Instore magazine
www.instoremag.com

Job Shop/Contract Manufacturing *(See Machine Shop)*

Franchise

KFC (Kentucky Fried Chicken)

5,000 + units

Estimated Annual Sales per Unit:	$900,000
*Approximate Total Investment:	$950,000–$1,100,000

*Note: These figures do not include land or lease costs.

Rule of Thumb:

- 30 to 35 percent of annual sales plus inventory
- KFC is part of the YUM Brands, Inc., which includes: A&W, Long John Silver's, Pizza Hut and Taco Bell.

Franchise

Kumon Math & Reading Centers *(See Day Care Centers)*

1,197 units

Approximate Total Investment:	$9,250–$28,265

Rule of Thumb:

- 40 to 45 percent of annual sales

Resources

www.kumon.com

Franchise

Kwik Kopy Business Center (printing)

(See also Quick Printing)

17 units	
Approximate Total Investment:	$216,735–$320,600

Rule of Thumb:

- 40 percent of annual sales plus inventory

Resources

www.kkbconline.com

Land Surveying Practices

15,870	SIC: 8713-01	NAIC: 541370

Rule of Thumb:

- 40 to 80 percent of annual fee revenues; plus fixtures, equipment and inventory; may require earnout

Resources

American Congress on Surveying and Mapping
www.acsm.net

Professional Surveyor magazine
www.profsurv.com

Landscape Contractors

61,739	SIC: 0782-04	NAIC: 501730

Rule of Thumb:

- 1.5 times SDE; plus fixtures and equipment (except vehicles)
- 45 to 50 percent of annual revenues plus inventory

Pricing Tips
"Try 1.5 SDE"

Resources
Professional Landcare Network (Planet)
www.landcarenetwork.org

Association of Professional Landscape Designers
www.apld.org

Law Practices

Lawyers—496,310	SIC: 8111-03	NAIC: 541110

Rule of Thumb:

- 40 to 100 percent of annual fee revenue; firms specializing in estate work would approach 100 percent; may require earnout

General Information
Can You Sell Your Law Practice?
"An increasing number of attorneys consider getting out of the practice of law and doing something else. Whether changing careers or retiring, many attorneys leave the law by just closing their office doors one day and never returning. However, by abruptly leaving, the attorney forsakes 'cashing in' on a valuable asset that has taken many years to build.

"And, what about the situation where the attorney dies suddenly and leaves a spouse to 'mop up?' Is there anything of value that can be sold?

"Depending on where you practice, the answer to both questions is *yes.*

"In 1989, California became the first state to adopt a rule of professional conduct (Rule 2-300) that specifically permits the sale of a law practice. The American Bar Association, through the efforts of the General Practice Section, then adopted a similar rule, Model Rule 1.17. Two years ago, through the efforts of the ABA's Standing Committee on Sole & Small Firm Practitioners, the ABA adopted a modification that permits lawyers to sell part (not all) of their practices. Several states have since adopted the ABA's new version, and more than 40 states now have some version of the ABA rule and permit the sale of a law practice. The remaining states are in various phases of rethinking this issue.

"While the practice of law is personal, there is also a business component to it that enables the owner to sell the practice to another attorney, who would then step into the first attorney's shoes and provide a continuity of service to the existing clients.

"It is time that attorneys realize that their practice is something of value, and that value (not the practice) can be passed on to the heirs of the attorney at time of death or otherwise become part of the attorney's estate if the practice is sold before death.

"Is every practice saleable? Maybe not. Some practices are so small and so personal that without continuing involvement of the first attorney, a second attorney would not succeed in keeping the clients. However, most law practices—including small and personal ones —are saleable for the right price and under the right terms."

Source: Edward Poll, J.D., M.B.A., CMC, February 2005, *Law Practice Today*, www.aba.net

Sale of a Law Practice

Following are excerpts from Rule 1.17 covering the sale of a law practice promulgated by the American Bar Association. For the complete text, refer to Rule 1.17.

<u>The Model Rules - Rule 1.17: Sale of Law Practice</u>

A lawyer or a law firm may sell or purchase a law practice, including good will, if the following conditions are satisfied:

a. The seller ceases to engage in the private practice of law [in the geographical area] [in the jurisdiction] (a jurisdiction may elect either version) in which the practice has been conducted;
b. The practice is sold as an entirety to another lawyer or law firm;
c. Actual written notice is given to each of the seller's clients regarding:
    1. the proposed sale;
    2. the terms of any proposed change in the fee arrangement authorized in paragraph (d);
    3. the client's right to retain other counsel or to take possession of the file;
    4. the fact that the client's consent to the sale will be presumed if the client does not take any action or does not otherwise object within ninety (90) days of receipt of the notice.

Resources

The Tool Kit for Buying or Selling a Law Practice, published by LawBiz Publishing Co.

The Impact of Seller Financing on Full Price

Comparison of Financed and All-Cash Transactions

Average SP/SDE for financed transactions 2.15
Median SP/SDE for financed transactions 1.84

Average SP/SDE for all-cash transactions 1.84
Median SP/SDE for all-cash transactions 1.60

SP = Selling Price

The average down payment for the deals financed in the above chart was, 37 percent.

This difference is even more pronounced if we compare the all-cash transactions to those [selling] with seller financing of 70 percent or more. Here is this data:

Comparison of Financed and All Cash Transactions

Average SP/SDE for financed transactions 2.31
Median SP/SDE for financed transactions 2.03

Average SP/SDE for all-cash transactions 1.84
Median SP/SDE for all-cash transactions 1.60

SP = Selling Price

In these sales with 30 percent or less as a down payment and financed by the seller, the SP/SDE is 25 percent higher. The median is 27 percent higher. These figures are all the more meaningful since, as we mentioned, there is a very large sampling—more than sufficient, in our opinion, to make the conclusions significant.

What the data reflects is that if a seller is willing to accept a down payment of 30 percent or less, the full price will increase, on average, by 25 percent, or more. This presents a seller with a very interesting dilemma.

The figures are from a book by Toby Tatum, *Transaction Patterns.*

This firm provides consulting, management and brokerage services for law practices. They have an excellent site with articles on the sale of law practices. www.lawbiz.com.

ABA Journal
www.abanet.org—This site has an article titled "Law Firms for Sale."

The Missouri Bar Association
www.mobar.org—This site has an excellent article on selling law practices.

Lawn Maintenance & Service *(See Landscape Contractors)*

38,819	SIC: 0782-06	NAIC: 561730

Rule of Thumb:

- 50 to 60 percent of annual sales plus inventory
- 1.5 times SDE plus inventory

Benchmarks

"Hourly Service Rates - What is your average hourly rate for each of the following services in 2003?

Service	Average Hourly Rate
Residential Mowing Per Hour	$38.30
Commercial Mowing Per Hour	$45.37
Chemical Lawn Care Per 1,000 Sq. Ft.	$10.37

Source: *Lawn & Landscape*

"Approximately what was your pre-tax profit margin in 2003?

Less than 5%	10.7%
5% to 10%	28.6%
11% to 15%	20.5%
16% to 20%	15.2%
21% to 25%	9.8%
Over 25%	15.2%

Source: *Lawn & Landscape*

"Overall, 66.9 percent of contractors' clients renewed their maintenance contracts in 2003."

Source: *Lawn & Landscape*

Industry Trend

"The U.S. lawn and garden market reached a record $24 billion in sales in 2004, up a healthy 5 percent over 2003 sales, according to 'The U.S. Lawn and Garden Market,' a new report from market research publisher Packaged Facts.

"The overall lawn and garden market is being driven fundamentally by the 'Two Booms': the housing boom and aging baby boomers. 'These two macro factors have been and will continue to be overwhelmingly positive, creating strong underlying demand for lawn and garden products and services for years to come,' according to Don Montouri, acquisitions editor for Packaged Facts. 'Whether or not this strong demand is expressed or is somehow bottled up depends on the vagaries of two other macro factors—the economy and the weather.'"

The nursery and landscape industry is made up of thousands of small family businesses that grow, retail, install, and care for plants and landscapes.

Source: American Nursery & Landscape Association

"In terms of retailers, 'The U.S. Lawn and Garden Market' reports that home centers control the major retail share of lawn and garden equipment with an estimated 65 percent of sales, mostly at the expense of garden centers and nurseries. Home centers are formidable in terms of price, selection and convenience, causing the garden center and nursery sector to suffer."

Source: Primedia Business Magazines & Media Inc.

Resources

American Nursery & Landscape Association
www.anla.org

Professional Landcare Network (Planet)
www.landcarenetwork.org

Lawn & Landscape
www.lawnandlandscape.com
Note: *Lawn & Landscape* used to be one of the best sites for industry information. They have recently restricted the information to members only. In fact, one can't even enter the site unless they are a subscriber to the publication. Unfortunately, many sites are doing the same thing. It's a shame, as it make less information available to the general public and, in our opinion, does a disservice to the industry.

Quick *Profile* Lawn Care

Note: The information below is a bit dated, but is the latest we could find. It is current enough to serve the purpose, in our opinion. The figures may be a bit higher now, so you might want to take that into account.

There are well over 100,000 businesses that provide landscaping and lawn services. This figure does not include nurseries, garden equipment and supply firms, and all of the various industry support businesses. These businesses have annual sales of more than $50 billion. The overall landscaping and lawn care businesses collectively are termed the "green industry." They include companies that actually build and construct, others that provide maintenance, still others that provide chemical applications to lawns and gardens, including some well-established franchise firms, while many small businesses do primarily lawn care and mowing on a monthly basis. Following is a breakdown by revenues of the green industry.

Annual Revenues

	% of Firms
Less than $50,000	18.7%
$50,000 to $99,999	18.5%
$100,000 to $199,999	20.2%
$200,000 to $499,999	19.4%
$500,000 to $999,000	09.9%
$1 million or more	13.3%

Source: *Lawn & Landscape*, 2003 figures

Their sales are broken down as follows:

Average Sales From:	
Lawn Maintenance	36.8%
Lawn Care	12.2%
Design/Build	25.8%
Irrigation	06.2%
Tree & Ornamental Care	07.1%
Snow & Ice Removal	04.9%

Source: *Lawn & Landscape*, 2003 figures

The business is broken down as follows:

Revenue from Single-Family Homes	63.3%
Revenue from Multi-Family Residential Clients	07.5%
Revenue from Commercial/Industrial Facilities	23.7%
Revenue from Government/Institutional Facilities	03.9%

Source: *Lawn & Landscape*, 2003 figures

Geographic Region by percentage of Firms

Northeast	26.5%
Midwest	31.6%
South	29.0%
West	12.6%

Source: *Lawn & Landscape*, 2003 figures

Number of Employees

	% of Firms
1–2	19.3%
3– 4	21.7%
5– 9	28.2%
10–24	18.4%
25 +	12.4%

Source: *Lawn & Landscape*, 2003 figures

"Which services represent the largest sales volume of business for your company:

Top 10 Services	% of Contractors
1. Turf mowing	54%
2. Landscape construction/installation	39.4%
3 Turf fertilization	22.6%
4. Hardscapes	18.2%
5. Snow removal	13.5%
6. Tree & ornamental pruning	12.8%
7. Landscape construction design	11.4%
8. Fall cleanup	09.3%
9. Turf edging/trimming	09.1%
10. Irrigation installation	08.2%

"It's clear from the data provided that residential lawn care is the biggest segment of the green industry.

"Unlike most other service businesses, those in the green industries must have a variety of skills and knowledge. Many tradespeople such as plumbers need only have knowledge of their specialty. Lawn care providers must know about the different grasses, their diseases, what fertilizers to use, etc. In addition, they are expected to know about trees, bushes, irrigation systems, flowers—and where they grow best, plus soil and fertilizer requirements, diseases, pests—you name it. However, maintenance continues to be the mainstay of the industry.

"It is an industry in which 37.2 percent of the businesses do less than $100,000 and 76.8 percent have annual sales of less than $500,000. However, franchisors like TruGreen-ChemLawn have revenues in the multi-millions. It is clear, however, that the industry is dominated by small business.

Pluses

"Despite the knowledge required, the green industry is an easy one to enter. One could say that having a lawn mower and a pickup truck is a good beginning. Since the bulk of the business is residential lawn care, it may be a good start. Customer service and satisfaction are critical elements of success. However, it can also be said that one person mowing lawns is not really a business, but more like being self-employed. To build a business takes all of the attributes necessary to build any business.

Minuses

"Finding good workers is difficult and labor costs continue to increase. Add in the increasing cost of fuel and the constant problems with accounts payable—and it doesn't sound as easy as one would think. Customers continue to demand more and more—and want to pay less and less.

Pricing

Because the green industry is broken down into many segments, it is difficult to place a price on the industry as a whole. However, the lawn care segment is by far the largest within the category, and by researching the various sources, we feel that an approximate price based on a percentage of annual sales is 60 percent. The multiple of SDE is 1.5. We suggest that you refer to the rules of thumb in the Guide for some of the other types of businesses within the industry.

Franchise

Li'l Dinos Subs

30+ units

Rule of Thumb:

- 64 percent of annual sales plus inventory

Pricing Tips

"One sold for 80 percent of sales, but it was located in an office building with vending rights."

Resources

www.lildino.com

Limousine Service

15,161	SIC: 4119-03	NAIC: 485320

Rule of Thumb:

- 60 to 70 percent of annual revenues
- 2 to 2.5 times SDE

Benchmarks

"Sources of Gross Revenue

Source	% of Business by # of Vehicles Operated			
	1–3	4–10	11–20	20+
Business Travel	41%	46%	52%	67%
Weddings/Proms	28%	27%	22%	10%
Nights on the Town	22%	17%	15%	10%
Hotel/Resort Contracts	05%	06%	07%	08%
Tours	04%	04%	04%	05%

Source: National Limousine Association

Operator Revenues

Gross revenues for calendar year 2003
(the latest we could find)

Less than $100,000	33%
$100,000–$249,000	20%
$250,000–$499,000	14%
$500,000–$999,000	14%
$!,000,000–$2,900,000	12%
$3,000,000–$6,900,000	04%
$7,000,000 +	03%

Source: *Limousine & Chauffeured Transportation*

General Information

"Business travel accounts for half of operator's revenue; weddings and proms bring in an additional 22%

"The smaller the operator, the greater percentage of revenue from weddings and proms

"Sedans comprise 40% or $1.4 billion of industry income

"Smaller operators' income more likely to come from limos."

Source: National Limousine Association

"Usually the limousines bring no value to the deal—unless they are owned."

"Every month in this country, a minimum of 100 entrepreneurs open a limousine company."

Source: *A Step-By-Step Guide to Starting a Limousine Company in a Down Economy* by Tom Mazza

"Sedans make up nearly half of the industry's fleet. Sedans are also the most purchased or leased vehicles in 2004."

Source: *Limousine & Chauffeured Transportation*, October 2004

"The use of independent contractors has fallen in the past five years. They represented 51% of all chauffeurs in 1998, compared to 36% today."

Source: National Limousine Association

Resources

National Limousine Association
www.limo.org
The association has a study on this industry, but it is for members only. However, the site itself has a lot of excellent information and is well worth a visit.

Limousine & Chauffeured Transportation
www.lctmag.com

Linen Service (Supply)

1,700	SIC: 7213-02	NAIC: 812331

Rule of Thumb:

- 25 times weekly sales plus inventory

General Information

"Textile rental industry consists primarily of SIC numbers 7213 and 7218. Linen Supply, SIC #7213 and 7218, is defined as 'establishments or household users, on a rental basis, such laundered items as uniforms, gowns, and coats of the type used by doctors, nurses, barbers, beauticians, and waitresses; and table linens, bed linens, towels and toweling and similar items.' Industrial Launderers, SIC #7218, are defined as 'establishments primarily engaged in supplying laundered or dry-cleaned industrial work uniforms and related work clothing, such as protective apparel (flame and heat resistant) and clean-room apparel; laundered mats and rugs; dust control items, such as treated mops, rugs, mats, dust tool covers, and cloths; laundered wiping towels; and other selected items to industrial , commercial, and government users.' The textile rental industry has been described as a 'derived demand, business-to-business service industry.'

"Market Share

"Market share calculations are difficult for an industry that serves a wide variety of customer groups. What is clear is that textile rental has tremendous potential for expanding market share in every one of the markets. For example, less than 10 percent of the American work force wears a rental uniform on the job, less than 25 percent of the restaurants in the United States use rental cloth napkins for dinners service, and less than 25 percent of the hospital beds in the United States use rental bed linen.

"Competition

"Although industry price increases have lagged behind the CPI in this decade, textile rental companies have maintained profit margins by lowering their cost of operations. The principal area of improved efficiency has been in plant operations.

"An unusual characteristic of the industry is its performance in economic downturns. In difficult economic conditions, many potential customers find rental more attractive because it doesn't require a substantial initial capital outlay. In part due to this characteristic, bankruptcies are extremely rare in the textile rental industry."

Source: Textile Rental Services Association of America (TRSA)

Resources

Textile Rental Services Association of America (TRSA)
www.trsa.org—This site offers publications for sale that would be of interest to anyone interested in this industry.

Uniform & Textile Service Association
www.utsa.com

Western Textile Services Association
www.wtsa.org

Liquefied Petroleum Products

1,700	SIC: 5984-01	NAIC: 422710

Rule of Thumb:

- 130 percent of annual sales plus inventory
- 3 times SDE plus inventory
- 4 times EBIT
- 5 times EBITDA (Good double-check is 2.5 to 3.5 gross profit)
- 4 to 5 times EBITDA (Normalized Earnings). Some very attractive and growing markets will demand 6 times EBITDA—depends on the business and location.
- Under 1 mm annual gallons—4.5 to 6.5 times EBITDA. Over 1 mm annual gallons—5.5 to 7.5 times EBITDA. Some use a multiple of annual gallons; some use a multiple of gross margin.

Pricing Tips

"Company ownership of the tanks and cylinders at the customer's location is an important consideration. The higher percentage of company ownership the better."

"Major considerations are customer base, percentage of lease tanks, gross margin history, age of equipment and employee tenure."

"Add value—high number of company-owned lease tanks, relatively new trucks (less than 5 years), high percentage of residential accounts' back-up management and infra-structure, current safety equipment/storage controls."

"Where the company owns most all of the customer equipment, and there are good gross profits, a much better value can be obtained."

"EBITDA and gross profit per gallon are the driving forces supporting value—the higher the better. Company ownership of propane field equipment (at customer location) is important. Image & safety are also important considerations. One-million-gallon-and-up companies attract the larger & better buyers."

"...Customer mix, market position, age & condition & efficiency of equipment. The bulk of the asset value is usually in field tanks at customer locations... A large number of residential customers is generally a plus."

Industry Experts' Ratings:

Amount of Competition (1 = Lot of: 4 = Not much) 1.2
Amount of Risk (1 = Very: 4 = Not much) 1.0
Historical Profit Trend (1 = Down: 4 = Up) 2.4
Location & Facilities (1 = Poor: 4 = Excellent) 2.8
Marketability (1 = Low: 4 = High) 3.2
Industry Trend (1 = Declining: 4 = Growing) 2.8
Ease of Replication (1 = Easy: 4 = Difficult) 3.2

"The propane business is typically very capital intensive, in that most companies want to own and control the tanks at the customer locations. For this reason, it is difficult to enter, and the industry is subject to price spikes and supply displacements during the peak winter heating season."

"Extremely mature industry with little innovation"

Benchmarks

"EBITDA per gallon greater than $0.15"

"Can vary considerably by company, depending on customer mix between residential, commercial, farm & industrial type customer"

Expenses as a percentage of annual sales:	
Cost of Goods Sold	45%
Payroll/Labor Costs	13%
Occupancy Cost	03%
Profit (estimated)	12%

General Information

Questions to ask a seller: "Company ownership of customer tanks & cylinders is an important consideration. Where the company owns most of the customer field equipment, and there are good gross profits, a much better value can be obtained." "Lease tank coverage, age of equipment, age and volume of bulk storage, type of customer base."

Advantages of this Business

- "Viable, clean-burning, alternative fuel that is typically cheaper than electricity. Propane is a versitile fuel and is used for many applications in homes, farms, and industry, including cooking, water heating, central heating, space heating, motor fuel, fireplaces, dryers, fuel cells, generators, and many other farm and industrial uses."
- "Residential gas business provides service that is more necessity than luxury. Most are in rural areas where only alternative competition for space/water heat is electric, which is more expensive and provides less comfort.

Disadvantages of this Business

- "Product cost is tied to both crude oil and natural gas, and as such can be very volatile. Competition may not allow pass through. Regulation is increasing and insurance is becoming more difficult to obtain. Currently very difficult for someone without industry experience to get insurance, which is key to being licensed in most areas."
- "Capital intensive, price spikes, supply displacement during peak winter heating season, and somewhat labor intensive"

Industry Trend

"Slow growth, around 4 to 5% outside of the metro areas and beyond the natural gas lines"

Seller Financing

- "Typically cash at closing for fixed assets; intangibles are sometimes financed over five years."
- "Five years"

Resources

National Propane Gas Association
www.npga.org

Propane Education & Research Council
www.propanecouncil.org

Liquor Stores/Package Stores (Beer, Wine & Liquor Stores)

53,544	SIC: 5921-02	NAIC: 445310

Rule of Thumb:

- 40 percent of annual sales plus inventory
- 5.5 to 3 times SDE + inventory
- 3 to 3.5 times EBITDA
- 28%–32% of annual revenues or one times gross profit. "These rules tend to apply to stores with a volume of $800,000 to $1.5 million."

Note: Since many states limit the number of off-sale licenses, the price of the license can vary based on area. Therefore, in many areas, the price of the license may have to be added to the price.

Pricing Tips

"Buyers will generally pay 5 to 7 times the monthly gross sales of the store, plus inventory. Rent is the deciding factor in determining where this multiple lies. Rents closer to $1 / sf should value a store closer to 7 to 8 times monthly gross, while rents over $2 / sf will value a store between 5 to

Liquor Licenses

Note: In many states, liquor licenses have a value, a significant one in some cases. The value exists because liquor licenses are limited, generally by population; so in order to acquire a license, an existing one must be purchased. In many states, the price of a license floats in a free market—supply and demand. The transfer process can be a complicated and lengthy one. There are firms that broker liquor licenses.

These are two that we are aware of. Michael Brewer, Alcoholic Beverage Consulting, 951-753-1400, mbrewer@abcconsulting.com. This firm deals primarily in California but does have contacts in other states. James R. Stariha, 231-670-0878, jimstariha@hotmail.com. He is an attorney who handles liquor licenses and handles matters concerning the Michigan Liquor Control Commission.

6 times the monthly gross."

"3 times SDE and/or 33 percent of annual sales work for businesses with revenues from $800,000 to $1,500,000 and selling a good mix of beer, wine and liquor."

"Liquor stores: one times gross profit"

"In northeartern U.S., prices are dramatically escalating due to buyer pressure of 'New Americans'. Family ownership by this buyer group places less discount for burden of management and thus SDC/EBIT is perceived as being greater. Many times the groups of buyers will actually bid against each other. Accordingly, prices are higher than even a year ago."

"The range of SDE is up to 3 times depending upon location, GPM, years in business, condition of equipment, occupancy cost and payroll as compared to sales."

"Competition, length of lease, location, location, location, wine sales a plus, lottery sales help generate traffic."

"Product mix is extremely important as it relates directly to gross profit."

"One times annual gross profit plus inventory for business only"

"Percent of revenues in beer/wine/liquor"

"3–4 times monthly gross, add inventory, has been used in the Denver metro area. This rule of thumb is most commonly used within the Asian community. It is a wide range and is dependent upon normal fixed cost, especially rent. We have a tight retail real estate market and rental rates are high in newer retail developments. Many stores remain on the market because the occupancy cost (as a percentage of sales) is too high."

" Competition in area; length; number of liquor licenses in town—small mom-and-pop stores hard to sell"

"Wine-oriented stores (more than 40 percent of sales in wines) may sell for more but require previous wine experience on the part of a buyer."

"Heavy cigarette sales at low margins pull down price."

"Lottery commissions, if substantial over typical amount of $8,000, would add dollar to dollar to price—the excess over $8,000."

"Rent over 5 percent has negative impact on price. City stores generally sell for less than suburban stores. Big lotto/lottery commissions (over $15,000/yr) help price."

Industry Experts' Ratings:

Amount of Competition (1 = Lot of: 4 = Not much) 1.6
Amount of Risk (1 = Very: 4 = Not much) 2.8
Historical Profit Trend (1 = Down: 4 = Up) 2.0
Location & Facilities (1 = Poor: 4 = Excellent) 2.6
Marketability (1 = Low: 4 = High) 3.2
Industry Trend (1 = Declining: 4 = Growing) 2.4
Ease of Replication (1 = Easy: 4 = Difficult) 3.0

"The liquor, beer, and wine industry continues to prove itself as one of the most profitable small businesses to own, primarily due to the markup available to these products. These are generally low-risk, stable, and consistent businesses to operate, as sales are not sensitive to seasonality, and are easily managed by friends and family members of the owners."

-cont'd-

Industry Experts' Ratings: (*-cont'd-*)

"Liquor licenses are state regulated and can be a relatively high barrier to entry."

"In high income areas, competition is based on discounts and specials."

"Only products that are showing any significant market share gains are wines and white liquors, like high-end vodkas. Beer sales are flat. Sales of brown whiskies have declined."

"Must buy an existing liquor license in NJ; can't apply and obtain a new one; lottery traffic a plus"

"Very popular with buyers. Simple inventory control systems available today."

"Industry has been flat with exception of wine and high-end vodka. Most jurisdictions control the industry, making barrier to entry higher."

"Low profit margin, competition, pricing, liquor license laws, insurance cost and public liability."

Benchmarks

"Sales per sf should be at least $25 per sf per month. Occupancy costs higher than 8% will decrease the value of the business, as this is one of the main cost components analyzed when valuing a liquor store."

"Gross margins should be between 20% and 25%."

"Rental must be below 7% of Gross."

"Stores that sell more 6-packs, singles, pints, wine in 750s etc. will exhibit higher gross margins than high-volume stores selling 30-packs, wine in 1.5s or boxes."

"Gross Profit should be no less than 20% and 23% median."

"Too many variables. Example: beer store; fine wine store, etc."

"Know your market place—selling higher margin product like wine and beer area will tie up too much cash and not help the profits of the business."

"Normal product mix in sales is 60% liquor and 40% wine."

"Watch the gross profit levels. Must keep the rental figures below 7% of gross at all times."

"Gross profit percentage is a huge factor. Is the store full markup or discount?"

"Turn inventory 9 to 10 times a year."

"Typically a store with normal margins needs to do $1 million + to sustain 6-figure earnings. Smaller stores need to do more business in higher margin goods like 6-packs, singles, nips, wine and high-end liquor to sustain a livable wage."

"3,500 sq. ft., ample parking, easy in and out, free-standing building, prefer basement and/or extra storage, some food items, buying co-op with regular ads, pricing"

"The typical store grosses about $350,000/year. Overall gross profit margins in liquor stores generally are between 21 to 24 percent, the exceptions being very large (over $1,000,000/year) discount stores that operate on lower margins—and wine specialty stores."

Expenses as a percentage of annual sales:

Cost of Goods Sold	75%
Payroll/Labor Costs	10%–12%
Occupancy Cost	7%–8%
Profit (estimated)	10%

General Information

Questions to ask seller: "Length of lease, percentage of sales in each category: wine, beer and liquor." "Does the store cash checks? Does the store have lottery? Does the store sell fine wines? If so, it has higher margins. Is it a discount store? Does it sell lots of half- pints?"

"Owning the real estate can be a huge advantage in controlling occupancy cost."

"Small profitable stores are very desirable in our market. It is very common for older, established stores to be put out of business by new developments in the immediate trade area. Site selection is crucial."

IRS Audit Techniques on Inventory

The following are some questions regarding inventory from the Guide mentioned below. (This is an excellent IRS publication on liquor stores.)

- Verify that the method of inventory valuation conforms to a prescribed method.
- Compare inventory balances with prior and subsequent year returns and the taxpayer's books.
- Check for unauthorized changes from cost to cost or market.
- Check for gross percentage variations.
- Check notes to financial statements of independent auditors.
- Insure year-end purchases are included in ending inventory.
- Determine if there have been any inventory write-downs to below cost.

The above is excerpted from an IRS Audit Technique Guide (*Market Segment Specialization Program—MSSAP*). They are an excellent source of information and are available at www.bookstore.gpo.gov: (search under IRS—IRS Audit Technique Guides).

Advantages of this Business

- "Advantages of this business are that people will continue to drink in good times and bad times, times of peace and times of war. Liquor stores tend to increase revenues during poor economic times, as consumers look to save money by visiting these businesses, versus restaurants and night clubs."
- "High barrier to entry; limited number of licenses; relatively easy to operate"
- "There are very few changes—very solid industry, stores are protected by state law."
- "Ease of operation, recession proof"

- "Hedge against inflation and downturn of the economy"
- "Cash, easy to control inventory, very little spoilage."
- "Limited licenses, price controls, people tend to drink in good times and bad"
- "Recession proof, hard to enter the market because of government restrictions"
- "Cash business; easy to maintain inventory control systems and re-ordering items."
- "High barrier to entry; perception that people tend to drink during good times and bad."
- "Liquor is in demand; limited number of liquor licenses"

Disadvantages of this Business

- "Disadvantage to the business is the high cash factor. The high cash factor exposes the business to potential employee theft if not properly managed."
- "Very little real growth"
- "Competition; long hours; theft can be a problem; relatively flat sales"
- "Big box competition in beer & wine"
- "Hours, high cost of inventory"
- "Low margins"
- "Competition, diminishing margins, licensing authorities/changing laws"
- "In most areas, very tightly regulated and controlled"
- "Usually 7 days and long hours; some areas require delivery."
- "Cash business; theft a problem for absentee owners"
- "Liquor license transfer takes 2 to 4 months in many areas—so plan ahead if you want to sell by a certain date."
- "Notoriously known for high levels of shrinkage & pilferage; long hours"
- "Insurance costs, liability, local license restrictions, low profit margins especially on beer, robbery, under-age customers"

Industry Trend

"The trend for this industry should continue to grow, as these businesses are in high demand, primarily due to ease of operating and the high cash factor."

"Very little changes"

"Sales have been generally flat in the liquor and wine industry except for wine sales. Trend will probably continue in 2006."

"Growing; hard times make people drink booze."

"Demand to remain high"

"Trends are expected to be steady as long as specialty licenses to sell the product remain limited."

"Flat"

"Stores seem to be getting more valuable."

Seller Financing

- "5 years on business, 30 to 120 days on inventory."

Resources

(See Resources for Alcoholic Beverage Licenses page 104)

Franchise

Little Caesar's Pizza

1,720 +	
Estimated Annual Sales per Unit:	$390,000
Approximate Total Investment:	$106,000 to $260,000

Rule of Thumb:

- 55 percent of annual sales

Resources

www.littlecaesars.com

Lock & Key Shops

26,604	SIC: 7699-62	NAIC: 561622

Rule of Thumb:

- 4 times monthly sales; add inventory

Resources
Associated Locksmiths of America
www.aloa.org

Institutional Locksmiths' Association
www.ilanational.org

Franchise

Logan Farms (Honey-glazed Hams)

25 units

Approximate Total Investment:	$100,000 cash assets required

Rule of Thumb:

- 30 percent of annual sales plus inventory

Franchise

LubePro

30 + units

Approximate Total Investment:	$170,000 to $200,000

Rule of Thumb:

- 38 percent of annual sales plus inventory

Resources
www.lubepro.com

Home Centers or Lumber Yards or Hardware Stores?

"Home centers typically have 2/3 sales in hardware and 1/3 sales in lumber and building materials. If lumber percentage is much higher, it is a lumber yard; much lower, it is a hardware store. 1.8 to 2.2 times SDE plus inventory. Home centers with SDE/Sales of 13 percent or more will be in the top range of multiplier. Those with less than 10 percent will be in low range.

"Sales per sq. ft. for successful home centers would be >$300 for stores with retail space of 10,000 sq. ft. or more. Lumber is a low-margin (20%–25%), high-turnover (2.5 to 3.5 turns per year) product line. Therefore the more lumber the store does, the lower its overall gross profit margin, but the greater its total sales."

Lumber Yards *(See Building Materials)*

16,212	SIC: 5211-42	NAIC: 444190

Rule of Thumb:

- 25 percent of annual sales plus inventory
- 1.6 to 2 times SDE plus inventory
- "Sell for Adjusted Book Value if making 2.5% EBT (Earnings before Taxes); if making 5% EBT, add 1 to 2 years EBT as Goodwill."
- For a lumberyard selling to builders and DIYers with sales in the \$2–\$10 million range, the EBT should be 5% to make it attractive to buyers; some run 5%–10%. Those get a premium of 1 to 2 years EBT in addition to the 3 major assets in an asset sale (to include inventory at cost, FMV on real estate, and FMV on equipment).

Pricing Tips

"Average EBT is 2.5%; should do this or more; ideal is 5% EBT."

Industry Experts' Ratings:

Amount of Competition (1 = Lot of: 4 = Not much) 1.0
Amount of Risk (1 = Very: 4 = Not much) 1.4
Historical Profit Trend (1 = Down: 4 = Up) 2.0
Location & Facilities (1 = Poor: 4 = Excellent)......................... 2.2
Marketability (1 = Low: 4 = High).. 1.8
Industry Trend (1 = Declining: 4 = Growing) 1.8
Ease of Replication (1 = Easy: 4 = Difficult) 3.6

The competition from the "big boxes," Home Depot and Lowes, has hurt the retail lumberyards' DIYer business; the lumberdealer focused on the contractor/builder has done quite well in the last 10 years; this could change with a decline in housing starts.

"High capital requirement is a major deterent to entering into a market. Once a lumberyard is established in an area, few new competitors move in, unless of course it is a big box."

Benchmarks

"Sales typically are over $500 per square foot for lumberyards with retail space of more than 8,000 sq. ft."

"$250,000 to $300,000 per employee"

Expenses as a percentage of annual sales:	
Cost of Goods	70%–75 %
Payroll/Labor Costs	10%–12%
Occupancy Cost	2%
Profit (estimated)	3%

Advantages of this Business

- "Great business with good customers, good products that help people improve their homes"
- "A well-run lumber and bulding-material store can produce long-term rates of returns in the 14%–20% per year range and can provide a very good salary to its owner. The business owner must also own the real estate to get those kinds of returns, though, and the return usually is in the form of appreciated assets and retained earnings. Potentially a very satisfying business. Most of your customers will really appreciate what you do for them."

Disadvantages of this Business

- "Besides the 'big box' competition, very capital intensive; some credit risk; subject to swings in housing starts and interest rates (not so in last decade, but normally so)."
- "Long hours, very very fast pace. Your brain is on 24/7."

Industry Trend

"In a market that is an hour away from the 'big box,' some small dealers are doing OK; their business is generally 75 % to contractors and builders; those in competition with the big boxes are in trouble."

"If housing slows, could be tough"

Seller Financing

- "Very few sell on owner financing; the sales are generally to existing lumber dealers."

Resources
National Lumber & Building Material Dealers Association
www.dealer.org

Franchise

MAACO Auto Painting and Bodyworks

483 units	
Approximate Total Investment:	$299,000

Rule of Thumb:

- 40 percent of annual sales plus inventory

General Information
"MAACO commands a 47% share of the $1 billion production auto painting after- market."

Source: www.automotivefrnchises.net

Resources
www.franchise.maaco.com

Machine Shops

35,907	SIC: 3599-03	NAIC: 332710

Rule of Thumb:

- 65 to 70 percent of annual revenues plus inventory
- 2 times EBIT
- 1.5 times EBITDA

Pricing Tips
"Short-run shops having design capabilities and doing prototyping may demand a premium. Different geographical areas will have varying availability of qualified machinists. Look for stable work force that is not near retirement. Be sensitive to difference between a machinist and a 'CNC machine operator.' Backlog, client concentration and industry(s) served can also have large effects on valuation."

"Strategic buyers tend to look for excess capacity."

"Short-run prototyping shops concentrating in the medical industry tend to sell for higher multiples."

"Look for customer concentration. Determine sales mix between commercial and military/defense contractors. Age and type of equipment will affect valuation. Production capacity is important."

"Customer concentration and level of owner skill required affect valuation."

"Condition of equipment; value equipment separately. Type of equipment very important. Any agreements or contracts?"

Industry Experts' Ratings:

Marketability (1 = Low: 4 = High)	1.6
Industry Trend (1 = Declining: 4 = Growing)	2.0
Ease of Replication (1 = Easy: 4 = Difficult)	1.6

"Revenues and profitabilty are trending upwards in NE U.S. Barrier to entry high with well -quipped shops, low with antiquated equipment like retrofit CNC Bridgeports, etc. Abundance of bankers searching for businesses has grown demand as their background of lending to mfg. makes this industry 'seem' a fit. Risk of high client concentration always a concern with contract manufacturing."

"Need to be $10 million shop to get good buyers"

"Contract machining, while recovering slowly, continues to feel the ripple effect of the OEM's slowdown"

Benchmarks

Expenses as a percentage of annual sales:

Cost of Goods Sold	45%
Payroll/Labor Costs	24%
Occupancy Cost	8%
Profit (estimated)	11%

General Information

"Need to understand equipment value and replacement schedules"

"Be wary of client concentration. OEMs have a tendency to try to get all your attention; and if they slow down, the job shop follows quickly."

"There are no major players in this industry."

Geographic Spread, by % of Machine Shops

Rocky Mountains	03%
Plains	06.4%
New England	07%
Southwest	11%
Mideast	12.5%
Southeast	17.5%
Far West	18%
Great Lakes	24%

Source: Valuation Resources.com

Advantages of this Business

- "Higher margins if careful to service growth industries with demand for quick turns"
- "Diversity of customers; not subject to foreign competition (smaller shops)"
- "You make big bucks when the economy is good."
- "Competitive advantages can be developed by means of industry or production concentration."

Disadvantages of this Business

- "Short-run and prototyping shops lack residual revenues of mid to long-term runs."
- "There exists a direct correlation with OEMs, and the contract manufacturer has little control."
- "Capital intensive; dependent on few, large customers"
- "A downturn in the economy affects these types of businesses hard."

Industry Trend

"Should trend upwards with GDP going in like direction."

Franchise

MaggieMoo's Ice Cream and Treatery

140 + Units	
Approximate Total Investment:	$215,100 to $312,180

Rule of Thumb:

- 32 percent of annual sales plus inventory

Resources
www.maggiemoos.com

Maid Services *(See also Janitorial Services)*

Rule of Thumb:

- 40 percent of annual sales plus inventory
- 1.5 times SDE plus inventory

General Information
According to the U.S. Bureau of labor Statistics: "Cleaning services are expected to be the second biggest generator of new jobs for the period 1994–2005."

Mail and Parcel Centers (Also called Mail Receiving and Mailing & Shipping Services) *(See also UPS Stores)*

12,309	Mail Receiving SIC: 7299-18 Mailing & Shipping SIC: 7331-01	NAIC: 56143

Rule of Thumb:

- 40 to 45 percent of annual sales less direct cost of goods sold (pass-throughs); e.g., stamps, money orders, UPS charges
- 3 times SDE for national franchises plus inventory

Pricing Tips
"Rent is a very important factor, as it is a fixed cost. Stores below a certain

minimum of sales diminish in value exponentially as they find it more and more difficult to cover the fized costs."

Industry Experts' Ratings:

Amount of Competition (1 = Lot of: 4 = Not much) 1.0
Amount of Risk (1 = Very: 4 = Not much) 1.6
Historical Profit Trend (1 = Down: 4 = Up) 1.6
Location & Facilities (1 = Poor: 4 = Excellent) 2.4
Marketability (1 = Low: 4 = High) 2.4
Industry Trend (1 = Declining: 4 = Growing) 1.6
Ease of Replication (1 = Easy: 4 = Difficult) 1.6

"Competition is high—even from the suppliers (UPS, FEDEX) providing individual accounts to your customers."

"Barriers to entry are not strong. A new store does not cost much to open. Establishing the business is the tough part. Competition is everywhere. Your suppliers (e.g., FedEx, UPS, and DHL) are also your competition. All office supply houses are your competition."

"Buying a proven store with a steady track record may be a much better way to get into this business than opening a new one. It takes a long time to ramp up sales."

"I feel that these private mail centers are good businesses with many profit centers. They also have good hours, which is appealing to many buyers."

Benchmarks

"Must be earning at least 50% gross profit or better. The sales must exceed a certain level (usually 10 times rent) before a profit can really be seen. A good store has a decent budget for advertising."

"Most stores must be doing at least $150,000 in annual sales before they start showing any real profit. Advertising is very important; stores should not skimp on advertising. The client base is primarily within a radius of a few miles."

"Depending on fixed cost factors, there is a certain amount of minimum sales necessary to make money. If rent is less than 10 percent and advertising is about 8 percent, the breakeven should be around $125,000 in sales. No real advantage in a franchise versus an independent, as the public does not differentiate."

Expenses as a percentage of annual sales:	
Cost of Goods Sold	50%
Payroll/Labor Costs	15%
Occupancy Cost	10%
Profit (estimated)	20%

General Information

"This is a proven business concept."

Following are selected survey results conducted by the Associated Mail & Parcel Centers (AMPC), a leading trade association for the mail and parcel center industry. We have used those responses we feel will be most helpful to those who are pricing or marketing this type of business. We are indebted to AMPC for permission to use the results of the survey. The responses are done by the number of responses per item listed under the question and are based on the latest survey made available to us. See Resources below for their contact information. We tried to contact the AMPC to see if they have done a new survey; we never heard back.

Although this survey is several years old, we feel it is still representative of the industry.

Is your business:

Independently owned	540
Part of a franchise	20
Member of a group or chain	7

Indicate the number of stores in which you have an interest.

1	440
2–3	85
4–5	4
More than 5	1

How many square feet is your facility?

More than 2,000 130
1,500–1,999 163
1,000–1,499 423
Less than 1,000 151

What is your annual rental cost on a square foot basis?

$25.00 or more 122
$20.00–$24.99 127
$15.00–$19.99 151
$10–$14.99 300
Less than $10.00 160

What is the approximate population within a 3-mile radius of your facility?

500,000 or more 107
100,000–499,000 142

50,000–99,000 155
25,000–49,999 183
Less than 25,000 176

Describe the area surrounding your facility.

Primarily commercial 43
Primarily residential 180
50%/50% each 434

Within a 3-mile radius of your facility, how many other businesses are there that you consider competitive to one or more aspects of your business?

20 or more 18
15–19 19
10–14 113
5–9 148
1–4 471
None 118

If you were to advise someone else on starting a new, well-equipped mail/parcel center, what investment (including working capital) would you recommend?

$100,000 or more 190
$60,000–$99,000 307
$30,000–$59,000 164
Less than $30,000 16

If we define "profits" as all the benefits of business ownership, what percentage of total gross sales do you enjoy as "profit?" In estimating this profit percentage, include salary, owner's draw, bonuses, insurance benefits, company paid vacation, auto, etc., as well as remaining "bottom line" profit.

More than 40% 112
20%–39% 314
10%–19% 186
1%–9% 132
Less than 1% or no profit 22

If you are a full-time owner, using the same compensation criteria described in question 23, would you describe your own total compensation as:

Below $10,000 132
$10,000–$25,000 156
$25,000–$40,000 194
$45,000–$75,000 150
Above $75,000 123

In 2000, what were your total gross sales? Do not answer this question if you started up after January 1, 2001. Do not include in your sales figures such items as Western Union or MoneyGram amounts (other than your actual commission), money order total (other than your actual commission), lottery tickets, utility bill payments, bus tickets, etc. (other than your commission). Also, do not include postage stamp sales (other than your surcharge, if any).

$1 million or more 2
$750,000–$999,000 19
$500,000–$749,000 72
$250,000–$499,000 276
$100,000–$249,000 223
Less than $100,000 104

Approximately what percentage of your total gross sales comes from mailbox rentals and mail forwarding?

75%–100% 12
50%–74% 12
25%–49% 16
10%–24% 154
Less than 10% 392

Approximately what percentage of your total gross sales comes from

parcel shipping? Do not include revenues from wrapping or packing.
75%–100% 124
50%–74% 332
25%–49% 197
Less than 10% 113

Approximately what percentage of your total gross sales comes from package wrapping or packing? Include crating and gift wrapping services in these totals.
75%–100% 0
50%–74% 110
25%–49% 158
10%–24% 343
Less than 10% 153

Approximately what percentage of your total gross sales is from copying?
75%–100% 12
More than 50% 16
25%–49% 19
10%–24% 152
Less than 10% 288

What is your current opinion about the future of your business?
Will continue to grow at a satisfactory rate assuming no
  change in current services: 184
Will stagnate or decline in the next few years: 115
Needs new, more profitable services to continue to grow:.. 308
Has a very bright future and should produce excellent profits: 161

"Ratio of gross sales that are subject to pass-throughs versus more productive direct sales of services such as mail box rentals, packaging, and inventory such as boxes, cards, etc.; check on length of equipment leases or which will be paid off, and if up-to-date on the technology of the equipment."

"Breakdown of profit centers; what has worked and what hasn't; any significant changes in demographics of area served; will seller be willing to pay off any equipment leases at closing; and is training available if not a franchise."

Advantages of this Business

- "The hours are generally nice for a smaller 'mom-and-pop' business. It is not that difficult work."

- "Hours are good—closed most holidays and most of weekend. Work is not hard."
- "Good hours. Easy business to run. Many profit centers."

Disadvantages of this Business

- "If your sales cannot get past a certain volume, you are done!"
- "Competition is everywhere. You do not make a strong profit until your sales level reaches a certain point, which is not necessarily easily attainable."
- "Easy to duplicate."

Industry Trend

"No growth; steady sales; falling out of stores that are too small."

Resources

Associated Mail & Parcel Centers (AMPC)
www.ampc.org

Note: This is an excellent organization, and any serious owner of a mail and parcel center should be a member. AMPC publishes a monthly magazine that does accept listings of stores for sale.

Mail Boxes Etc. *(See UPS Store)*

Mail Order

Mailorder & Catalog Shopping 4,642	SIC: 5961-02	Mailorder Houses NAIC: 454110

Rule of Thumb:

- 6 times EBIT
- 5 times EBITDA
- 50 percent of annual sales

Pricing Tips

"Valuation of firm typically based on house account quality (house database of customers) and EBITDA sustainability and growth"

Industry Experts' Ratings:

Marketability (1 = Low: 4 = High) 2.8
Industry Trend (1 = Declining: 4 = Growing) 2.4
Ease of Replication (1 = Easy: 4 = Difficult) 1.0

Benchmarks

"Sales personnel should generate revenue of about $1.3 million per employee."

Advantages of this Business

- "Economic trends; Internet growth; ease of business"

Disadvantages of this Business

- "Ease of replication; postal regulations; governmental regulation; availability of trained work force"

Resources

National Mail Order Association www.nmoa.org—an excellent site, loaded with information

Malls—Shopping *(See Shopping Centers)*

4,762		

Management Consulting

Rule of Thumb:

- 2.5 times SDE

Manufacturing Rules of Thumb—Quick Check
(See individual business for additional information)

Manufacturing—General	3.5 times SDE 3.4 times EBIT 4-4.5 times EBITDA
Manufacturing—Small	5 times SDE
Chemical	6 times EBIT
Electrical	5 times EBITDA
Machinery	5 times EBITDA
Metal Fabrication	3 times EBITDA
Miscellaneous	3.25 times EBITDA
Furniture	4–7 times EBITDA
General Purpose Machinery	4.5 times EBITDA
Metal Valve & Pipe Fitting	7 times EBIT
Pharmacy & Medicine	6 times EBITDA
Plastic	4.5 times EBITDA
Plastic & Rubber Machinery	9 times EBITDA
Powder Metallurgy	4.5 times EBITDA
Scientific Instruments	3–6 times EBITDA
Showcase, Partition, Shelving	3 times SDE
Sign	2.5 times SDE
Valves	5 times EBITDA
Wood Kitchen Cabinets, etc.	2.5 times SDE

Manufacturing—General

11,524	SIC: 3999-03	

Rule of Thumb:

- 60 to 70 percent of annual sales
- 3 to 4 times SDE (depending on size & quality)
- 3.5 times SDE; must manufacture product; not be a job shop
- 3 to 4 times EBIT
- Hard Assets + 1.5 to 2 times EBIT
- 4 to 4.5 times EBITDA

Pricing Tips

"Multiple of EBITDA will range from 3 to 5 depending upon EBITDA. Multiple of 3 to 4 for EBITDA under $1 million, and 4 to 5 for EBITDA over $1 million."

"The industry position and growth potential and exclusivity are other crucial factors. Age of equipment , trade name/branding, and intellectual properties also have a weight in determining value. Further considerations are leases or age of facilities, location, growth potential, backlog, contracts, relationships with suppliers, availability of credit lines. etc."

"We look at the calculation for owner benefit/cash flow and apply a 2 to 3 times multiple plus the current market value of furniture, fixtures and equipment and inventory at cost. Since manufacturing is very equipment intensive, using a pure EBITDA or cash flow multiplier does not adequately give a fair evaluation, in our opinion."

"Transferablity of the customer base and maintenance capital expenditures are the two biggest issues to close a deal."

Industry Experts' Ratings:

Amount of Competition (1 = Lot of: 4 = Not much) 1.2
Amount of Risk (1 = Very: 4 = Not much) 1.6
Historical Profit Trend (1 = Down: 4 = Up) 2.8
Location & Facilities (1 = Poor: 4 = Excellent) 3.2
Marketability (1 = Low: 4 = High) 3.4
Industry Trend (1 = Declining: 4 = Growing) 2.8
Ease of Replication (1 = Easy: 4 = Difficult) 2.6

"Manufacturing is typically a complex and expensive process, creating barriers to entry."

"I find that manufacturing facilities and more technological systems are much improved over the last 20 years. Cadcam systems and computerized equipment have greatly improved productivity in the industry. When I first started selling mfg, low-tech processes and poor working facilities were the rule."

"Every business is uniqu,e but China is a big factor in California deals."

"High labor costs in U.S., relative to foreign labor, have affected manufacturing sector."

Benchmarks

"Sales per employee: $100,000

"Proprietary products are most important."

"No customer bigger than 20%"

"Gross margin >45%; Inventory turns >4"

Expenses as a percentage of annual sales:	
Cost of Goods Sold	45%–50%
Payroll/Labor Costs	25%
Occupancy Cost	8%–10%
Profit (estimated)	10%–15%

General Information

Questions to ask seller: "Inventory breakdown (WIP, raw FG), customer deposits, machinery & fixtures, number of customers, key employees, receivables (amount & days) and method of sales & distribution—all affect whether the multiple is high or low. Stock or asset sale is a function as to whether or not it is a C corporation. Most manufacturers selling are 20-plus years old and therefore are C corporations, which means a stock sale."

"Insurance considerations—is the business properly insured?" "Value and margin of backlog; asset value and basis for value;. product line breakdown & mix; 3 to 5 years P&L and balance sheets." "What are the capital expenditures required to maintain and grow the business?"

"Manufacturing will not totally disappear in the U.S. Yes, our industrial base has been decimated and is being farmed offshore where cheap labor can be found, but there are thriving industries in medical, computer-related, bio-chemical, bio-medical, pharmaceutical, leisure and many other segments."

"The ability to grew the company is a big factor."

Advantages of this Business

- "A well-run company can be very profitable—10%–25% EBITDA."
- "Close to total control over your production. The only outside influences that can affect your process are outside suppliers and competition. All other factors are within. Great liquidity of the business because of market demand."
- "Skilled labor force"
- "Lots of assets and consolidation savings"
- "One of few actual wealth-creating activities"

Disadvantages of this Business

- "Trend for overseas manufacturing is growing for certain products."
- "Labor-market changes and interest-rate fluctuations can veritably choke the financial lifeblood out of any industry. Proper projections and calculations are critical."
- "Employee turnover in the lower paid jobs. At times, more employee oversight is needed due to interaction with equipment."
- "Outsourcing, higher labor costs, insurance, competition"
- "China again is the main problem for West Coast deals."
- "Strong competition in all segments"

Industry Trend

"Niche businesses can grow rapidly. Some will be converted to distribution companies as the manufacturing process is moved overseas."

"Certain niche manufacturers where expertise cannot be taken offshore will survive.
Reasonable labor availability will be critical."

"Continued slow decline"

"As the economy picks up, manufacturers will start being profitable again."

"About the same; some sectors (labor-cost sensitive) will go down; other sectors (technology, medical equipment., etc.) will go up." "Volume will be the same, with profit margins declining, due to an increase in labor and other operational costs."

"Many manufacturing companies have gone offshore, and we are left with the smaller and more closely held companies. On a resale basis, mfg. is much in demand and supply is low."

"Outsourcing is putting a strain on manufacturing, as well as high labor and insurance costs."

"China will continue to pose big, long-term pressures."

Seller Financing
- "3 to 6 years"

Manufacturing—Chemical

Rule of Thumb:

➢ 6 times EBIT

Pricing Tips
"There is a wide variation in multiples."

Benchmarks

Expenses as a percentage of annual sales:	
Cost of Goods Sold	60%
Payroll/Labor Costs	10%
Occupancy Cost	5%
Profit (estimated)	15%

Seller Financing
- 5 years

Manufacturing—Contract *(See Machine Shop)*

Manufacturing—Electrical

Rule of Thumb:

➢ 5 times EBITDA

Pricing Tips

"Client relationships and strength of long term contracts is a major factor. Patents and proprietary processes must be evaluated. Work force productivity factor min. of $250K per man-year is essential."

Industry Experts' Ratings:

Amount of Competition (1 = Lot of: 4 = Not much)	2.4
Amount of Risk (1 = Very: 4 = Not much)	3.2
Historical Profit Trend (1 = Down: 4 = Up)	2.4
Location & Facilities (1 = Poor: 4 = Excellent)	2.8
Marketability (1 = Low: 4 = High)	2.4
Industry Trend (1 = Declining: 4 = Growing)	2.4
Ease of Replication (1 = Easy: 4 = Difficult)	2.4

"Use of third-party contract manufacturers continues to grow as more and more traditional manufacturers outsource."

Benchmarks

"Sales per employee—$250K = world class; <$100K = trouble! Inventory turns—20 = world class; <= 7 = trouble. Employee turnover: > 10% = trouble."

Expenses as a percentage of annual sales:

Cost of Goods Sold	64%
Payroll/Labor Costs	7%–8%
Occupancy Cost	4%
Profit (estimated)	12%

General Information

"Front-office productivity is the key to success; low overheads and effective use of technologies, including Internet, are essential."

Advantages of this Business

- "Relatively low risk"

Disadvantages of this Business

- "Hard to forecast short-term results. Longer term beyond one year, usually predictable; near term can be a problem."

Industry Trend

"Top-line growth, bottom-line pressure from offshore (non-U.S.) companies. Small to medium specialist will prosper with strong customer-service commitments."

Seller Financing

- "5 years"

Manufacturing—Machinery

Rule of Thumb:

- 100 percent of annual gross sales
- 5 times EBITDA

Pricing Tips

"A manufacturer of industry-specific machinery generally employs 50 to 500 people. A high price is 1x sales figure (valid if market dominant worldwide). A good price is equal to total assets. A frequently observed price is twice net assets (Stockholder's Equity) or 5 times EBITDA for a firm in good standing. Multiple of net earning is meaningless since most owners minimize net earnings through various perks."

Industry Experts' Ratings:

Amount of Competition (1 = Lot of: 4 = Not much)	3.0
Amount of Risk (1 = Very: 4 = Not much)	3.0
Historical Profit Trend (1 = Down: 4 = Up)	2.0
Location & Facilities (1 = Poor: 4 = Excellent)	1.6
Marketability (1 = Low: 4 = High)	1.8
Industry Trend (1 = Declining: 4 = Growing)	2.2
Ease of Replication (1 = Easy: 4 = Difficult)	2.8

Benchmarks

"Sales per employee: $120,000 to 250,000; varies a lot as function of manufacturing integration. Our experience (300 clients during last 10 years) is that 80% of the world machinery industry is mismanaged because of lack of market focus and deficient customer service. The remaining can be highly profitable, and utilize market downturns to acquire competitors (most of our own business)."

Expenses as a percentage of annual sales:	
Cost of Goods Sold	60%
Payroll/Labor Costs	30%
Occupancy Cost	5%
Profit (estimated)	8%

General Information

"The stock market as a rule doesn't like the machinery industry: perceived as low-tech, high-risk, slow growth..."

Advantages of this Business

- "When well managed, high profitability, high goodwill due to references and recognition, notably for spare parts and customer service business."

Disadvantages of this Business

- "The main assets are the engineers and technicians who have learned the skills. Skills are very slow to learn both from technology and market point of view. Your best assets walk out of the door when business is bad, if they do not trust the strategy."

Industry Trend

"It is moving to fast-growing economies where the biggest market is: China, India, other NICs."

Manufacturing—Metal Fabrication

Rule of Thumb:

- 6 times EBITDA

Pricing Tips

"EBITDA must be adjusted to show owner's discretionary cash flow. The multiple that is used varies by industry, geographic location, and specific business, and must be determined in a subjective manner by one knowledgeable of current market conditions."

Industry Experts' Ratings:

Amount of Competition (1 = Lot of: 4 = Not much)	2.0
Amount of Risk (1 = Very: 4 = Not much)	2.0
Historical Profit Trend (1 = Down: 4 = Up)	3.2
Location & Facilities (1 = Poor: 4 = Excellent)	3.2
Marketability (1 = Low: 4 = High)	3.2
Industry Trend (1 = Declining: 4 = Growing)	3.2
Ease of Replication (1 = Easy: 4 = Difficult)	2.0

"Proprietary products and processes can protect a company from competition, both domestic and overseas."

Benchmarks

Expenses as a percentage of annual sales:

Cost of Goods Sold	60%
Payroll/Labor Costs	20 %
Occupancy Cost	10%
Profit (estimated)	10%

Advantages of this Business

- "Control of products and proprietary processes"

Disadvantages of this Business

- "Labor costs increasing"

Industry Trend

"Increased overseas competition"

Seller Financing

- "5 years"

Manufacturing—Miscellaneous

Rule of Thumb:

- 2.75 times SDE
- 3.25 times EBITDA

Pricing Tips

"Most accurate method is to deduct cost of professional employees to replace current ownership, and then use a multiple of 4 to 6 times net earnings (EBIT) depending on industry, security of earnings, assets, growth potential, etc."

Benchmarks

Expenses as a percentage of annual sales:	
Cost of Goods Sold	50%
Payroll/Labor Costs	25%
Occupancy Cost	08%
Profit (estimated)	15%

"Successful manufacturing businesses often have sales of over $100,000 per employee. Gross margins should never be below 34 percent (unless central office is tiny compared to the whole operation."

Manufacturing—Furniture

4,148	SIC: 2599-01	NAIC: 337215

Rule of Thumb:

- 4 to 7 times EDITDA

Pricing Tips

Size, growth, condition of plant, how profitable it is, place in the market, and management can play a part.

Benchmarks

Following is a sampling of the benchmark data that is available for this industry. This is from BDO Seidman's "Furniture Executive Outlook for 2005 & 2006," from *Furniture World* magazine.

" Shipments per factory employee in upholstery also increased with current year shipments per employee at $152,000 versus $143,000 last year. Overall shipments per factory employee improved to $147,000 from $131,000 last year. Most of these increases likely relate to more imported products as well as better business conditions, allowing more products to be made and shipped without adding employees.

"Operating profits per factory employee improved in 2004 from $6,921 last year to $7,751 in 2004.

"In case goods, operating profit per factory employee increased from $6,191 in 2003 to $7,632. In upholstery, operating profits fell to $6,386 from $7,375 in 2003.

"As would be expected with lower profits overall, the return on equity fell again this year. Returns on equity were 5.64 percent in 2004 versus 8.86 percent last year and 12.08 percent in 2002."

Source: (See above) www.furnonfo.com

General Information

According to an article in *M&A Today,* the top manufacturers comprise 50 percent of the industry. Number 25 has annual sales of only $150 million, and the next 40 companies have only 16 percent of the market, with 2,600 other firms fighting for the 34 percent balance of the market.

Resources

The Business and Institutional Furniture Manufacturer's Association
www.bifma.com—a worthwhile site

Manufacturing—General Purpose Machinery

Rule of Thumb:

- 4.5 times EBITDA

Manufacturing—Metal Valve and Pipe Fitting

Rule of Thumb:

- 7 times EBIT
- 100 percent of annual sales
- Assets + 1 to 2 times EBITDA

Pricing Tips

Industry Experts' Ratings:

Marketability (1 = Low: 4 = High)	2.4
Industry Trend (1 = Declining: 4 = Growing)	1.2
Ease of Replication (1 = Easy: 4 = Difficult)	3.2

"High capital investment"

Benchmarks

"Four inventory turns, 50 percent gross margin"

Expenses as a percentage of annual sales:

Cost of Goods Sold	50%
Payroll/Labor Costs	20%
Occupancy Cost	30%
Profit (estimated)	15%

Advantages of this Business

- "Niche products can command a high margin."

Disadvantages of this Business

- "Labor content and capital investment are high."

Manufacturing—Miscellaneous Electrical and Components

Rule of Thumb:

- 8 times SDE

Pricing Tips

"Customer concentration and special skills required by owner drive the price model."

Industry Experts' Ratings:

Marketability (1 = Low: 4 = High)	2.0
Industry Trend (1 = Declining: 4 = Growing)	2.0
Ease of Replication (1 = Easy: 4 = Difficult)	2.8

Benchmarks

Expenses as a percentage of annual sales:

Cost of Goods Sold	50%
Payroll/Labor Costs	25%
Occupancy Cost	15%
Profit (estimated)	10%

Manufacturing—Pharmaceutical Preparation & Medicine

Rule of Thumb:

- 75 percent of annual sales
- 5 times SDE
- 4 to 5 times EBIT
- 6 times EBITDA

Pricing Tips

"Depends on the market size and developmental maturity of products in the pipeline"

"Because of products manufactured, it is important that the products are not on the FDA hit list."

"Much of what the company is valued at will depend on how many products they manufacture, the concentration of clients to the gross revenues, the cost margin for each product, the number of short runs versus the number of long runs, and the opportunity for expansion through existing clients."

Industry Experts' Ratings:

Amount of Competition (1 = Lot of: 4 = Not much)	1.8
Amount of Risk (1 = Very: 4 = Not much)	1.6
Historical Profit Trend (1 = Down: 4 = Up)	3.4
Location & Facilities (1 = Poor: 4 = Excellent)	3.6
Marketability (1 = Low: 4 = High)	3.8
Industry Trend (1 = Declining: 4 = Growing)	3.6
Ease of Replication (1 = Easy: 4 = Difficult)	3.6

"High risk of product failure and high barriers to entry are hallmarks of the pharmaceutical and biotechnology industries. Profits for companies that manage to bring a drug to market are high."

Benchmarks

"Development stage: number of drugs in pipeline, and the stage of development"

"Pharma businesses are premium now that many trademarked items are available and companies are getting top dollar. FDA requirements are hard, and it can take months to get a company approved for manufacturing."

Expenses as a percentage of annual sales:

Cost of Goods Sold	30%–35%
Payroll/Labor Costs	30%–32%
Occupancy Cost	15%–20%
Profit (estimated)	20%–30%

Advantages of this Business

- "Products coming off the trademark market are now available for reproduction."
- "High profit potential"
- "Tremendous growth opportunities"

Disadvantages of this Business

- "High risk of failure, high up-front capital costs, high burn rate"
- "FDA recalls"
- "FDA regulations with constant monitoring"

Industry Trend

"Huge"

"Consolidation of existing companies and emergence of many new entrants"

Seller Financing

- "5 years"

Manufacturing—Plastic

Rule of Thumb:

- 4.5 times EBITDA

Pricing Tips

"4 to 5.5 times EBITDA less maintenance cap ex."

Industry Experts' Ratings:

Amount of Competition (1 = Lot of: 4 = Not much) 1.0
Amount of Risk (1 = Very: 4 = Not much) 2.4
Historical Profit Trend (1 = Down: 4 = Up) 2.4
Location & Facilities (1 = Poor: 4 = Excellent) 3.2
Marketability (1 = Low: 4 = High) 3.6
Industry Trend (1 = Declining: 4 = Growing) 4.0
Ease of Replication (1 = Easy: 4 = Difficult) 2.0

"This is a hot industry and businesses in this industry are always in demand."

Benchmarks

"$125,000 sales per employee to be profitable"

Expenses as a percentage of annual sales:	
Cost of Goods Sold	75%
Payroll/Labor Costs	5%
Occupancy Cost	2%
Profit (estimated)	8%

Advantages of this Business

- "No obsolesence; room to compete with overseas, since labor is a small component"

Disadvantages of this Business

- "High cap ex costs. Most are custom shops dependent on OEMs."

Industry Trend

"More and more interest in plastic-products manufaturers as OEMs look to replace steel & metal with plastic"

Manufacturing—Plastic and Rubber Machinery

Rule of Thumb:

- 9 times EBITDA

Pricing Tips

"Look at customer concentration; determine age and condition of equipment; look at industry diversification."

Industry Experts' Ratings:	
Marketability (1 = Low: 4 = High)	2.8
Industry Trend (1 = Declining: 4 = Growing)	1.6
Ease of Replication (1 = Easy: 4 = Difficult)	2.8

Benchmarks

Expenses as a percentage of annual sales:	
Cost of Goods Sold	50%
Payroll/Labor Costs	12%
Occupancy Cost	08%
Profit (estimated)	15%

Advantages of this Business

- "Large market for plastic manufacturing"

Disadvantages of this Business

- "Strong foreign competition"

Manufacturing—Powder Metallurgy Processing

Rule of Thumb:

- 4.5 times EBIT

Pricing Tips

"None have any merit due to profitability variations; sanity check at 80 percent of revenue."

"Gross margins consistency and diversification of the customer base add value to PM business."
"Value is and should be a function of projected future cash flow."

"Investment value drives this and other manufacturing markets. 5 to 6 times EBITDA (adjusted for synergy) is typical, but never a firm rule."

"Transactions are driven by technology fit, growth prospects, profitability and other attributes of the selling company. Other key factors are: management, technology & systems, markets, and equipment age & mix. Markets served may have an influence and older smelting furnaces may detract slightly."

Industry Experts' Ratings:

Marketability (1 = Low: 4 = High)	1.6
Industry Trend (1 = Declining: 4 = Growing)	1.6
Ease of Replication (1 = Easy: 4 = Difficult)	2.4

"The current trend to move manufacturing to China and India is affecting the key customer groups of many PM companies."

Benchmarks

Expenses as a percentage of annual sales:

Cost of Goods	65%
Payroll/Labor Costs	15%
Occupancy Cost	10%
Profit (estimated)	10%

Advantages of this Business

- "Powder improvement opens new application which increases the effective market size."

Disadvantages of this Business

- "70% of the custom PM manufacturers are in the auto or auto-related markets. Both this segment and the remaining non-automotive markets are extremely competitive."

Manufacturing—Scientific Instruments

Rule of Thumb:

- "Company value is 3 to 6 times EBITDA."

Pricing Tips

"Where are the products in the life cycle? What new products are about to be introduced? Do they have strong patents? What is the competitive situation?"

General Information

Expenses as a percentage of annual sales:

Cost of goods sold	50%
Payroll/Labor costs	25%
Occupancy cost	15%
Profit (estimated)	10%

Manufacturing—Showcase, Partition, Shelving, and Lockers

Rule of Thumb:

- 3 times SDE

Pricing Tips

"Customer concentration and any special skills required to operate can make for a big difference in pricing."

Industry Experts' Ratings:

Marketability (1 = Low: 4 = High)	2.8
Industry Trend (1 = Declining: 4 = Growing)	1.2
Ease of Replication (1 = Easy: 4 = Difficult)	1.2

"Economy changes the profitability very quickly here."

Benchmarks

Expenses as a percentage of annual sales:

Cost of Goods Sold	35%
Payroll/Labor Costs	40%
Occupancy Cost	15%
Profit (estimated)	10%

Manufacturing—Sign

29,000	SIC 7389-38	NAIC: 339950

Rule of Thumb:

- 50 percent of annual sales
- 2.5 times SDE

Pricing Tips

Industry Experts' Ratings:

Marketability (1 = Low: 4 = High) 3.6
Industry Trend (1 = Declining: 4 = Growing) 1.6
Ease of Replication (1 = Easy: 4 = Difficult) 1.0

Resources

International Sign Association (ISA)
www.signs.org

Manufacturing—Small *(See Manufacturing above)*

Rule of Thumb:

- 5 times SDE

Pricing Tips

"For manufacturing companies with sales of $1 to 5 million, a crude rule of thumb is 3 to 4 times SDE, assuming the company is reasonably well established and viable. As company size goes up, the multiple will go up."

Factors to look for: "Sales/profitability trends; SDE (and trends); industry trends; years in operation; fixed asset value, seller financing. Risk factors: technology, competition, industry trends."

Resources

"Valuing Manufacturing Businesses," *Handbook of Business Valuation*, 2nd Edition, West & Jones, published by John Wiley & Sons.

Manufacturing—Valves

Rule of Thumb:

- 5 times EBITDA

Pricing Tips

"Special consideration given for special products, market share, industry recognition."

Industry Experts' Ratings:

Amount of Competition (1 = Lot of: 4 = Not much)	1.2
Amount of Risk (1 = Very: 4 = Not much)	2.0
Historical Profit Trend (1 = Down: 4 = Up)	2.0
Location & Facilities (1 = Poor: 4 = Excellent)	1.2
Marketability (1 = Low: 4 = High)	3.2
Industry Trend (1 = Declining: 4 = Growing)	2.8
Ease of Replication (1 = Easy: 4 = Difficult)	2.0

"A lot of competition with 'commodity' type valves; the more specialized, the less competition"

Benchmarks

"Market share, innovative products"

Expenses as a percentage of annual sales:

Cost of Goods Sold	60%
Payroll/Labor Costs	20%
Occupancy Cost	20%
Profit (estimated)	15%

General Information

"All valve company buyers are valve companies. We have over 800 valve companies in our data base which can be contacted overnight."

Advantages of this Business
- "All industries use the product."

Disadvantages of this Business
- "The margins on commodity items"

Industry Trend
"Trends toward specialization"

Seller Financing
- "5 years"

Manufacturing—Wood Kitchen Cabinets and Countertops

Rule of Thumb:

- 2.5 times SDE

Pricing Tips
"Some wood cabinet manufacturers have state-of-the-art equipment that increases the efficiency of the business. Analyzing and adding the value of the equipment is a component of the above valuation."

Industry Experts' Ratings:

Marketability (1 = Low: 4 = High) 3.6
Industry Trend (1 = Declining: 4 = Growing) 2.8
Ease of Replication (1 = Easy: 4 = Difficult) 1.2

"The sales trends are determined on the general economy of the geographic area. When housing starts are booming, demand is high."

Advantages of this Business
- "Manufacturing companies are always in demand on a resale basis."

Disadvantages of this Business
- "Qualified employees are in short supply in some markets."

Franchise

Marble Slab Creamery

450 units	
Approximate Total Investment:	$178,675 to $238,275

Rule of Thumb:

- 44 percent of annual sales plus inventory

Resources
www.marbleslab.com

Marinas *(See Boat Dealers)*

5,900	SIC: 4493-06	NAIC: 713930

Rule of Thumb:

- 12 times SDE plus inventory
- 10 times EBIT
- 11 times EBITDA

Pricing Tips

"Price of waterfront land greatly distorts the value, and multipliers are only wild guesses. A good rule of thumb is to have the slip rental/storage income be enough to cover debt service, and buyer can make his living from the other services provided at the marina."

"Rules of thumb are complicated because a marina is a combination of many businesses—berth rentals, service, perhaps new or used boat sales, and sometimes even a restaurant."

"As far as the marina part is concerned, I have a comfort level if the income from the slip rentals is enough to service the debt. The buyer's profit will then come from the ancillary businesses mentioned above. Fuel sales can also be a factor, as the markup is quite high."

Industry Experts' Ratings:

Amount of Competition (1 = Lot of: 4 = Not much) 2.0
Amount of Risk (1 = Very: 4 = Not much) 1.0
Historical Profit Trend (1 = Down: 4 = Up) 2.0
Location & Facilities (1 = Poor: 4 = Excellent)........................ 2.0
Marketability (1 = Low: 4 = High)... 1.0
Industry Trend (1 = Declining: 4 = Growing) 2.0
Ease of Replication (1 = Easy: 4 = Difficult) 4.0

"It's a reasonably risky business, because in hard times the boat is one of the first things to go. It is amazing how boats 'disappear' during a recession. They end up at a friend's dock, in the back yard or whatever. They are hard to market because profits are low, but because of waterfront, the real estate is valuable. They are very hard to replicate as sites are tougher to find, and permitting is very difficult."

Benchmarks

"The best rule of thumb is to make sure your income from slip rental/ storage is enough to cover your debt service. That is your 'nut' that must be covered come what may."

"Each business in the marina will have its own benchmark, corresponding to the activity."

Expenses as a percentage of annual sales:

Cost of Goods Sold 65%
Payroll/Labor Costs.. 20 %
Occupancy Cost 5%
Profit (estimated) 10%

General Information

"You must have a passion for boats and people. You also must be financially strong."

"Some sold as leased property; i.e., business/marina operation only. Unless good cash flow, value is in the location and real estate. Be careful of the cost of 'floor planning' each model year."

"Beware of a marina selling new boats with a large floor plan. This is a very tough business, and the only ones making money are the people flooring the inventory."

"Be careful if a restaurant is involved. This is an entirely different and sometimes dangerous business. It is always better to lease out a restaurant to a professional restaurateur. Environmental issues are at the top of the list in questioning the seller."

Advantages of this Business

- "Lifestyle, lifestyle, lifestyle"

Disadvantages of this Business

- "Very hard work for little reward"
- "Extremely low profits after debt service"

Industry Trend

"Reasonably stable—barring a bad economic downturn."

Seller Financing

- "15 years."

Resources

International Marina Institute (INI)
www.imimarina.com

Financial & Operational Benchmark Study For Marina Operators, available through the International Marina Institute (see above)

Valuation of Marinas, published by The Appraisal Institute, www.appraisalinstitute.org

Markets *(See grocery stores—markets (small to medium size)*

Franchise

Martinizing Dry Cleaning *(See Dry Cleaning)*

642 units

Approximate Total Investment:	$250,000 to $396,000

Note: Also known as One Hour Martinizing

Rule of Thumb:

- 60 percent of annual sales

Resources
www.martinizing.com

Meat Markets

9,850	SIC: 5421-07	NAIC: 445210

Rule of Thumb:

- 5 times monthly sales plus inventory

Resources
American Meat Institute
www.meatami.org

National Cattlemen's Beef Association
www.beef.org

Medical and Diagnostic Laboratories

Rule of Thumb:

- 3 times SDE plus inventory

Pricing Tips
"Multiple of SDE increases with profit levels."

Industry Experts' Ratings:

Amount of Competition (1 = Lot of: 4 = Not much)	1.2
Amount of Risk (1 = Very: 4 = Not much)	2.0
Historical Profit Trend (1 = Down: 4 = Up)	3.2
Location & Facilities (1 = Poor: 4 = Excellent)	3.2
Marketability (1 = Low: 4 = High)	3.2
Industry Trend (1 = Declining: 4 = Growing)	3.2
Ease of Replication (1 = Easy: 4 = Difficult)	2.0

"This is a marketing business. Location, ease of service, and networking with doctors and attorneys is a must."

Benchmarks

"Sales are measured on a per-technician basis. Each MRI tech should produce a certain level of revenue."

Expenses as a percentage of annual sales:

Cost of Goods Sold	3%
Payroll/Labor Costs	25 %
Occupancy Cost	7%
Profit (estimated)	25%

Advantages of this Business

- "Easy to run. You do not have to be an M.D. High Profit level."

Disadvantages of this Business

- "Relatively large overhead in equipment, and maintenance."

Industry Trend

"More personal injury MRI's"

Medical Practices

Rule of Thumb:

- "35 to 50 percent of annual fee revenue; applies to small practices; may require earnout"
- "20 to 60 percent of annual fee revenue; applies to practices with fee revenues of $125,000 +; may require earnout"
- "Worth 45 to 55 percent of one year's gross collections, based on location, age and contracts"
- "30 to 50 percent of collections not including accounts receivable, but including equity"
- 1.5 to 3 times SDE
- 2 times EBITDA

Pricing Tips

"Medical practices are small businesses and differ greatly depending on the specific owner, specialty, location, and clinicians involved in the practice. Regulation and reimbursement policy changes from day to day. In order to value a medical practice, a site visit and extensive review of financial, operational, community, and industry information is essential. Rules of thumb are not meaningful."

"Value varies widely by specialty and geographic location. The Goodwill Registry and Institute of Business Appraisers have databases on many sales, but beware of using historical data without considering current and upcoming issues, like Medicare's proposed reduction in reimbursement. Since other insurance companies base reimbursement on Medicare, this can significantly affect future profits in many specialties."

"The healthcare industry has been experiencing margin compression over the past 5 to 7 years. Third-party payers/managed care companies (insurance companies, Medicare, Medicaid) have been reducing reimbursements, while office overhead has been growing. This has created stagnation in business valuations due to smaller buyer pool."

"Depends on reason for selling— value is related to continuity of practice:

Retiring but stays on .... value up
Death .... value down
Loss of lease .... value down
Divorce .... value down"

"Pricing of health care professional practices is highly variable depending upon the specific type of health care service, geographical location (state), highly third party pay dependent versus fee for service or cash pay."

"Multiple of SDE increases with profit levels."

"Number of doctor referral relationships and strength of same"

"Specialists have more value. Multi-physician practices have more value. Sales of past physician practices to large HMOs and hospitals are not viable comps, as none have done what they anticipated."

"Located near a hospital or with other medical professionals. Positive reputation in the community. Established referral network. Type of medical specialty is a valuation factor."

"Call around for waiting times to see a new patient. If local wait times are two weeks or more, opening from scratch may be an economically viable alternative to purchasing a practice, or setting a valuation comparable. Also, will the local hospital offer income guarantees via forgivable loans to a competitor to start from scratch (decreases demand and value, but alternatively may be a source of buyer-recruitment and support)?"

"There are 23 specialties. Generally patient allegiances are salable, but doctor referrals are not. For example, a general surgery practice (based on referrals) would be worth quite a bit less than an ophthalmology practice (patients are transferable)."

"Urban practices more popular than rural"

"...Between 33 1/3 percent of gross to 55 percent depending on many things—or one times readjusted net—adding back discretionary items. Age of practice—how many provider contracts? Location—good or bad? Must show a net before doctor salary of over $100K."

"45 percent to 68 percent of gross collected revenue. Type of patients? Collection history? Location? Age of equipment, staff?"

Industry Experts' Ratings:

Amount of Competition (1 = Lot of: 4 = Not much)	1.4
Amount of Risk (1 = Very: 4 = Not much)	2.5
Historical Profit Trend (1 = Down: 4 = Up)	2.4
Location & Facilities (1 = Poor: 4 = Excellent)	2.2
Marketability (1 = Low: 4 = High)	2.6
Industry Trend (1 = Declining: 4 = Growing)	2.4
Ease of Replication (1 = Easy: 4 = Difficult)	2.6

"Due to high competition, an excellent reputation and marketability are big pluses."

"Three important overall industry factors: demographics (quite positive), government regulations (negative), and health organization (negative)"

"Competition mostly low, risk high, profit trend down, marketability low, ease of replication high."

"2004 individual income before taxes (in thousands of dollars) of family physicians, May 2005.

Median	$135.0
Mean	$143.6"

Source: American Academy of Family Physicians, www.aafp.org

Benchmarks

"All payroll and overhead together run between 40 to 60 percent, depending on specialty of doctor."

"It depends upon the specialty, physicians, location, service mix, payer mix, regulations and reimbursement policy."

"Payroll/Labor Costs: 32.23% (from MGMA cost survey 2003)
Occupancy Cost: 6.70% (from MGMA cost survey 2003)"

"High profit margin"

Expenses as a percentage of annual sales:	
Payroll/Labor Costs	25%–30%
Occupancy Cost	6%–8%
Profit (estimated)	35%–50%

"Benchmarks vary widely for 20+ specialties from pediatricians to neurosurgeons. Two good data sources by specialty are the national Association of Healthcare Consultants Statistics Reports (for practices with 10 or fewer doctors) at www.HealthCon.org, and the Medical Group Management Association at www.MGMA.com for larger groups."

Note: www.healthcon.org is an excellent site and has a lot of data; however, one must purchase it, and non-members pay a lot more than members.

General Information

Questions to ask seller: "One should look at whether the business is primary care or surgery/specialty, and what portion of the business is professional (fees) vs. technical (diagnostic or pharmaceutical/medical goods). Specific reimbursement trends are based upon specialty, provider supply (i.e., the supply of physicians to the population) and other indicators of demand for services, such as utilization demand for services in the market service area of the practice." "Things that make business sense are often illegal in medical practice, so services, leases, referral sources, etc. need to be scrutinized for Stark II and Medicare compliance. CPT coding errors can greatly affect value."

"Beware of using common sense in brokerage. Research the law, which varies state by state. There are many laws that apply only to medicine, like bans on fee splitting and licensure of buyers, that don't apply to other businesses."

"In such a turbulent health care transactional environment, information utilized in market-based methods and in market-derived rates of return of multiples for income approach methods must be carefully analyzed and evaluated in relation to the competitive strategies, trends, and forces acting within the health care marketplace."

"1) Major regulations and rulings affecting the universe of potential purchasers of medical practices. 2) Regulatory edicts affecting the cost and delivery of medical services and thus the potential profitability of the practice. 3) Issues dealing with the legality of the sale of or valuing of intangibles, particularly goodwill. Goodwill is hard to justify when buying a practice; do patients come for the particular doctor's name or the practice trade name?"

Advantages of this Business

- "Usually high income for the physician relative to other professions"
- "It is a 'needs' business."
- "Prestige"
- "Moderate to low risk; needed services (non-discretionary)"
- "Providing care for people in need, and good financial compensation"
- "The inherent high regard that society places on these highly skilled health professionals; the ability to earn substantially higher than average compensation."
- "Still good income. Licensure is a barrier to competition. Baby boom is getting older and sicker, more customers."
- "For physicians, ownership of the practice allows for more individual freedom to practice medicine, control of the schedule, more control over income, expenses, and the management of the practice."

Disadvantages of this Business

- "Competitive educational and training process, many years of education and training required, many licensure and regulatory requirements, and much of revenue stream is dependent on government policy and funding, which varies from year to year."
- "Lots of competition, high potential of being sued"
- "Stress and government control"
- "Administrative challenges"
- "Stress in dealing with people in a very personal manner, and long hours"
- "Disadvantages include the growing governmental, insurance & health organization regulations."
- "Profits trending down"
- "Malpractice liability issues, complex billing and regulatory risks; much of the revenue is controlled by third parties."

Industry Trend

"We see a trend away from managed care contracts and/or improved reimbursements. The longer term trend shows better profit margins which will generate more buyers."

"Downward profitability for insurance-dependent specialties"

"Many practitioners will be wanting to transition their practices."

"A rising trend due to the aging of America"

"Increasing due to the aging population and lower number of health care graduates at all levels"

"The market is extremely localized by specialty. One specialty may have depressed value and another inflated value in the same building."

"There is a growing shortage of physicians in many specialties, increasing paid jobs and reducing the need of new doctors to buy practices. The market is very localized."

"The health care service sector will be about the same. Demand will either remain steady or increase due to the aging of the population, but continued pressure on reimbursement and increasing amounts of uninsured patients will counterbalance demand, leading to the continued profitability at current rates."

Seller Financing

- "If Medicare patients are seen, limit payout terms to one year to comply with laws."
- "Seller financing is generally limited to one year by the Medicare 'anti-kickback' laws. Most states require that buyer be a physician."
- "3 to 5 years—more deals with seller financing happening."

Resources

American Medical Association
www.ama-assn.org

Buying, Selling, and Owning the Medical Practice published by the American Medical Association

"Valuing Medical Practices," *Handbook of Business Valuation*, West & Jones, 1st & 2nd Edition, published by John Wiley & Sons

Medical Practice Valuation Guidebook by Mark O. Dietrich, Windsor Professional Information Services

Microbreweries *(See Breweries & Brew Pubs)*

Mini-Storage *(See Self-Storage)*

Mobile Home Parks

12,500	SIC: 6515-01	NAIC: 531190

Rule of Thumb:

- 3 to 8 times monthly income

Pricing Tips

"Eight times gross or $8,000 per space (pad), depending upon the amenities, e.g., carports, recreation center, landscaping, paving, size of pad (space), closeness to city, etc."

Note*:* Mobile Home Parks are generally real-estate intensive—a real estate license is probably necessary to handle the sale.

Industry Trend

"The mobile home park, an American icon since the 1950s, is a dying institution. Parks that opened decades ago on the outer edges of cities and towns are now valuable real estate. Park after park is being snapped up by developers for condos, shopping centers or single-family homes. Sometimes, local governments themselves purchase such land to create urban parks or smart shopping promenades.

"'It's an epidemic here in Florida,' says Don Hazelton, president of the Federation of Manufactured Home Owners of Florida. 'We're seeing parks vanish every week.'

"There are those who turn around and buy another mobile home. Mobile home parks may be disappearing, but manufactured housing is not. Despite a few tough years recently, caused in part by low-interest mortgage rates that made conventional homes more affordable, the industry provides one out of every 7.5 new houses. An average singlewide home costs $32,000, a doublewide $60,000."

Source: "There Goes the Neighborhood, Mobile Home Parks, once Retirees' Oases, are Disappearing Fast" by Barbara Basler, *AARP Bulletin*

"From 1998 to 2003, shipments of mobile homes from manufacturers to dealers around the country plummeted 65 percent, to 130,000 homes."

Source: "Mobile Home Industry Experiences Downward Slide in North Carolina" by Charles Lunan, *Charlotte Observer*

Modeling Agencies

1,500	SIC: 7363-01	NAIC: 711410

General Information

"As far as selling them, haven't sold any lately, haven't seen any salable lately. It is definitely a lifestyle business whose economics defy analysis by anyone thinking in traditional financial analysis terms."

Motels *(See Hotels)*

Rule of Thumb:

- 2.25 to 3 times annual revenues; up to 5 times for resort properties
- 7 to 9 times cash flow (SDE)
- $20,000 per room
- 2.5 to 3 times room revenues
- 7.5 times SDE
- 10 to 12 percent cap rate

Pricing Tips

"We use several approaches to establish value. One is the Performance Index Method— developing a valuation table showing (a) cap rate (b) economic value (c) value per room (d) multiple of room revenue and (e) multiple of total revenue. One can then determine economic value by using either desired cap rate (best method), per room rates, X gross or Y total revenue. We also use discounted future earnings, discretionary cash flow, book value, market value and rule of thumb. We usually provide a range of values based on profitability, income risk, desirability, business type, business trend in location, competition, industry, terms of sale, along with a few other factors."

"Most ask 3 times, but sales result usually under 2.5 times—for larger and older properties, usually around 2 times gross. We usually use several approaches to establish value. We use the Performing Indexing Method showing: (1) cap rate percent (2) economic value (3) value per room (4) multiple of room revenue (5) multiple of total revenue. One can determine the economic value by selecting either the desired cap rate (best method) or the per-room rate, or the times room gross or times total revenue.

"Our general analysis using a high and low range utilizes several approaches to value (1) the income approach (2) excess earnings (3) discounted future earnings (4) discretionary cash (5) book value (6) market value (7) rule of thumb—then we have value comparisons and then a correlation and final opinion of value range and finally an opinion of value. We base the above on: profitability, income risk, desirability, business type, leasehold, and product exclusivity. A factor is assigned to each of the above for both high and low range."

"Limited-service operating expenses—50 to 65 percent; full-service operating expenses—75 to 80 percent (age influences pricing heavily). Current franchise status or possible entry? New competition coming into market?"

"Room revenue multiplier (2x to 6x), net operating income multiplier (6x to 12x). The multiplier you choose determines the capitalization rate."

"2.3 to 3 x annual gross sales. We try to avoid 'times gross' pricing. We prefer to price based on cap rate. The 'x' net room sales of 2.5 to 3 is better than using total sales. Location, age, structure, franchised or not, all make a difference in value. Some people (buyers and sellers) price based on $ per room."

"Location—highway changes—age—obsolescence—market conditions—affiliation."

Seller Financing

- "10 to 20 years—depends on age and size of property. One assumption—seller financing seldom exceeds time of original note. Last five sales have all been different with different interest rates."

Resources

American Hotel & Motel Association
www.ahma.com

The Computerized Income Approach to Hotel-Motel Market Studies and Valuations published by The Appraisal Institute, 875 N. Michigan Ave., Ste 2400, Chicago, IL 60611-1980 (312) 335-4100.

Hotel Investments: A Guide for Lenders and Owners by Stephen Rushmore, published by Warren, Gorham & Lamont

Franchise

Moto Photo

215 units

Approximate Total Investment:	$225,000 to $275,000

Rule of Thumb:

- 73 percent of annual sales plus inventory

Resources
www.motophoto.com

Motor Carriers (Freight Carriers)

(See Moving and Storage, and Transportation & Trucking)

Rule of Thumb:

- 5 times EBIT

Pricing Tips
"After December 1995 'operating rights' generally have no value. Acquisitions are almost always based on operating synergy, and pricing reflects this. Financial information generally reflects 'Operating Ratio' or 'OR' rather than more conventional accounting. 80 to 90 generally reflects a profitable company that is not in a sufficiently lucrative niche so as to attract a large number of new competitors, and would be expected to command the highest price."

"Losses, low or negative net worth is a negative—management in place is a positive."

Motorcycle Dealerships *(See Harley-Davidson dealerships)*

9,328	SIC: 5571-06	NAIC: 441221

Rule of Thumb:

- 10 to 12 percent of annual sales plus inventory
- 1.5 times SDE plus inventory
- 4 times EBIT

Pricing Tips

"The EBIT multiple above assumes that all new vehicle inventory is subject to floor plan financing that will be assumed by the buyer. Normal working capital acquired."

"The actual value of the franchise type of cycle business is fixtures and equipment plus the price of used cycles that have been taken in (prior to shop work being done) at the used motorcycle book price, plus the new cycles, plus 5 years' to ¾ year's net profit. One note of caution: contact franchisor to determine what is exactly required to satisfy their requirements for opening or buying a dealership; e.g., flooring requirements and financial strength."

Industry Experts' Ratings:

Amount of Competition (1 = Lot of: 4 = Not much) 1.2
Amount of Risk (1 = Very: 4 = Not much) 2.0
Historical Profit Trend (1 = Down: 4 = Up) 2.4
Location & Facilities (1 = Poor: 4 = Excellent)......................... 1.6
Marketability (1 = Low: 4 = High).. 1.2
Industry Trend (1 = Declining: 4 = Growing) 2.8
Ease of Replication (1 = Easy: 4 = Difficult) 3.2

"The original equipment manufacturers (Honda, Harley-Davidson, Yamaha, Suzuki, Kawasaki, etc.) control the numer of dealers permited in a marketplace. An existing dealership can block the establishment of a competing dealership of the same brand within a geographical proximity to the existing dealership."

Benchmarks

"GP% on New Unit Sales 18%
GP% on Used Unit Sales 20%
F&I Income per Major Unit Sold $500
GP% on Parts & Accessories 36%–40%"

Expenses as a percentage of annual sales:	
Cost of Goods Sold	76%
Payroll/Labor Costs	8 %
Occupancy Cost	2%
Profit (estimated)	7%

Advantages of this Business

- "Strong consumer brand identification"

Disadvantages of this Business

- "Original equipment manufacturers influence on operating procedures and floor plan debt guaranteed by principal owners."

Industry Trend

"Industry growth trends should remain remain positive with 5%–7% annual growth due to lifestyle changes and population demographics in the United States."

Resources

Motorcycle Industry Council
www.motorcycles.org

Franchise

Mountain Mike's Pizza

100 units

Rule of Thumb:

- 27% of annual sales plus inventory

Resources

www.mountainmikes.com

Movie Theaters

7,286	SIC: 7832-01	NAIC: 512131

Rule of Thumb:

- 4 times SDE
- 6 times annual adjusted earnings, 1000 plus seating
- 4 to 6 percent annual sales; add fixtures & equipment

Pricing Tips

Concession sales usually make up 24 percent of movie-theater sales. It has been said that, without concession sales, the movie theater business would not be viable.

General Information

Number of U.S. Movie Screens (Indoor) in 2003: 34,490
.... (2002, 35,170)
Number of U.S. Cinema Sites (Indoor) in 2004: 5,629
.... (2003, 5,700)
Total U.S. Box Office Gross in 2004: .... $9.53 billion
.... (2003, $9.49 billion)
Total U.S Admissions in 2004: .... $1.53 billion
.... (2003, $1.57 billion)
Average U.S Ticket Price in 2004: $6.21
.... (2003, $6.03)

Source: National Association of Theater Owners

Top 10 Circuits [Movie Theatre Companies]
(as of June 1, 2004)

Circuit	Screens	Sites
1. Regal Entertainment Group	6,076	547
2. AMC Entertainment, Inc.	3,316	218
3. Cinemark USA, Inc.	2,329	201
4. Carmike Cinemas, Inc	.2,221	291
5. Loews Cineplex Ent. Corp.	1,463	140
6. National Amusement, Inc.	1,101	94
7. Century Theatres	919	79
8. Famous Players, Inc.	800	80
9. Kerasotes Theatres	532	77
10. Marcus Theatres Corp.	488	46

Source: National Association of Theater Owners
Note: The top 10 were the same as last year, although the number of screens and sites may have changed.

Resources
National Association of Theater Owners
www.natoonline.org

Business of Show Business: The Valuation of Movie Theaters, published by the Appraisal Institute. www.appraisalinstitute.org

Moving and Storage

18,307	SIC: 4214-01	

Benchmarks
The following summary of revenues and expenses are available from the American Moving and Storage Association, www.promover.org—an informative site. Below are the averages of the Class I and Class II movers—the difference being their size and scope. For example, Class I is made up of 30 companies including such household names as United Van Lines, Mayflower, Allied and Bekins. The average below is the average for all 30 companies in Class I and for 10 companies in Class II. Class II would be more representative of smaller moving companies. For current information, go to the site above.

Carrier Class	Operating Revenue	Total Expenses	Profit Before Tax	Operating Ratio	Net Income
I	$146,113,957	$144,452,391	$1,001,600	98.86%	$855,689
I	$7,090,707	$8,349,290	($21,178)	117.75%%	$72,170

Resources
American Moving and Storage Association
www.promover.org—an informative site

National Moving and Storage Association
www.moving.org

Franchise

Mr. Jim's Pizza

75 units

Approximate Total Investment: $70,000 to $100,000

Rule of Thumb:

- 35% of annual sales plus inventory

Resources

www.mrjimspizza.com

Franchise

Mr. Payroll

140 units

Rule of Thumb:

- 130 percent of annual sales

General Information

The company is a leader in non-bank check cashing services (money orders, bill pay, wire transfer, etc.) Most of the franchises are located inside convenience and grocery stores.

Resources

Mr. Payroll is owned by Cash America International
www.cashamericaonline.com

Franchise

Mr. Rooter Plumbing

300 units

Approximate Total Investment: $25,000 to $200,000

Rule of Thumb:

- 1 to 4 times SDE plus hard assets; the number between 1 and 4 depends on several factors such as the owner operating a truck, etc.

Resources
www.mrrooter.com

Franchise

Mrs. Fields Original Cookies

400 + units	
Approximate Total Investment:	$162,400 to $247,100

Rule of Thumb:

- 68 percent of annual sales plus inventory

Resources
www.mrsfieldsfranchise.com

Music Stores

Rule of Thumb:

- 4 to 7 times SDE plus fixtures, equipment and inventory

Pricing Tips
"Usually in a store of this kind inventory turns about twice a year. The store should be located in an area where rent will not exceed 4 percent of the gross sales. National average shows a gross profit of approximately 54 percent before expenses of wages, repairs, maintenance, advertising, bad debts, utilities, insurance, taxes, etc. National average net profit is approximately 10 to18 percent."

General Information
"In the past decade, Wal-Mart has quietly emerged as the nation's biggest record store....But as Wal-Mart and other national discount operations such as Target and Best Buy have grown—approximately half of all major-label music is sold through these three —an estimated 1,200 record stores have closed in the past two years … In the same way that Wal-Mart made it difficult for local mom-and-pop retailers to compete with its low prices, it has hurt smaller music stores."

Source: www.rollingstone.com "The Killers: Wal-Mart Wants $10 CDs" October 12, 2004

"Price War: Does a CD have to cost $15.99?

The breakdown of the cost of a typical major-label release by the independent market-research firm Almighty Institute of Music Retail shows where the money goes for a new album with a list price of $15.99

$0.17	Musicians' unions
$0.80	Packaging/manufacturing
$0.82	Publishing royalties
$$0.80	Retail profit
$0.90	Distribution
$1.60	Artists' royalties
$1.70	Label profit
$2.40	Marketing promotion
$2.91	Label overhead
$3.89	Retail overhead"

Source: www.rollingstone.com

Industry Trend

"The sales of compact discs, best marked by the number of 'units' shipped, has steadily decreased since 2000. Many contribute downloading, file sharing and 'unbundling' as the reason for this decline."

Source: Recording Industry Association of America

Resources

International Music Products Association
www.namm.com

Mystery Shopping Companies

700		

General Information

"Although mystery shoppers—also called secret shoppers—have been around for decades, the business has grown rapidly in recent years… Jeff Hall, president of the mystery shopper's association and owner of Second to None, a business in Ann Arbor, Michigan that provides mystery shoppers and survey analysis, estimated that mystery shopping has grown 40 percent in 40 years with significant growth in the last five years."

Source: *The New York Times*, Sunday, March 13, 2005

"'Mystery shopping, in and of itself, is a unique type of research,' says Jeff Hall, president of the Mystery Shopping Providers Association, or

MSPA, a 150-member trade group based in Dallas. 'The type of information collected through a mystery-shop program could not be gathered through any other means.' He adds that anonymous visits provide 'insight on the customer experience' and give quick-service operators measurements on speed of service, temperature, and weight measurements of different products, and the cleanliness of the facility, including the drive-thru.

"A mystery shopper serves as the eyes and ears of the retail and restaurant industry, providing actionable feedback to field operations management concerning the quality and overall value of the customer experience."

Source: Mystery Shopping Providers Association

"He [Jeff Hall] estimates that between 70 percent and 80 percent of quick-service (restaurant) operators are using some type of mystery-shopper program. Although costs vary widely, Hall believes that a 25-unit chain would spend in the range of $15,000 to $25,000 annually on a program involving one shop per store each month."

Source: *Nation's Restaurant News*, December 13, 2004

Resources

Mystery Shopping Providers Association (MSPA)
www.mysteryshop.org

www.idealady.com—offers a book on mystery shopping and has a free e-mail course

Nail Salons

54,120		

Rule of Thumb:

- 25 percent of annual sales plus inventory

General Information

Following is some current information from surveys conducted by *Nails Magazine*—www.nailsmag.com:

Nail Salons

"Weekly earnings for salon owner (doing nails): $731.74
What commission % do you receive? .... 56.5%(average)
Average weekly income: $541.05

Ethnicity of licensed technicians:

Caucasian 43%
Vietnamese 39%
African American/Black 08%
Hispanic 07%
Korean 02%
Asian/other .... 01%"

Resources
Nails Magazine
www.nailsmag.com—an interesting and useful site, has an interesting survey of the nail salon business

Here are two sites that list salons for sale:

www.nailsalonbroker.com—a brokerage site for a firm that handles only nail salons. It is a Division of Manheim Realty.

www.salonsforsale.com—advertises all types of salons: hair, nail, tanning, spa & barber shops

Needlepoint Shops *(See Fabric Stores)*

	SIC: 5949-04	NAIC: 451130

Newsstands (News Dealers)

	SIC: 5994-01	NAIC: 451212

Rule of Thumb:

➢ 45 percent of annual sales plus inventory

General Information
"Many newspapers place their copy on the Internet, thus decreasing, or even eliminating, newsstand sales."

Nurseries *(See Garden Centers)*

Nursing Homes *(See Assisted Living)*

Rule of Thumb:

- 8 times SDE

Pricing Tips
"Return on investment—cash on hand is the guiding rule. Cost per bed varies from $20,000 to $60,000. Cost of upgrading facility a strong factor."

"Again, there is a substantial variance, depending upon the type of home and the type of patients, from $3,000 to $6,000 per bed. In addition to the amount of the rent, quality of the construction, condition and overall general appearance, and the number of beds are important whether or not the facility is licensed for Medicare."

"Growing Industry."

Industry Experts' Ratings:

Amount of Competition (1 = Lot of: 4 = Not much)	2.8
Amount of Risk (1 = Very: 4 = Not much)	2.8
Historical Profit Trend (1 = Down: 4 = Up)	3.2
Location & Facilities (1 = Poor: 4 = Excellent)	3.6
Marketability (1 = Low: 4 = High)	3.6
Industry Trend (1 = Declining: 4 = Growing)	3.6
Ease of Replication (1 = Easy: 4 = Difficult)	2.4

Benchmarks
"Most available are new facilities, fast growing business."

THE BUSINESS BROKER Newsletter

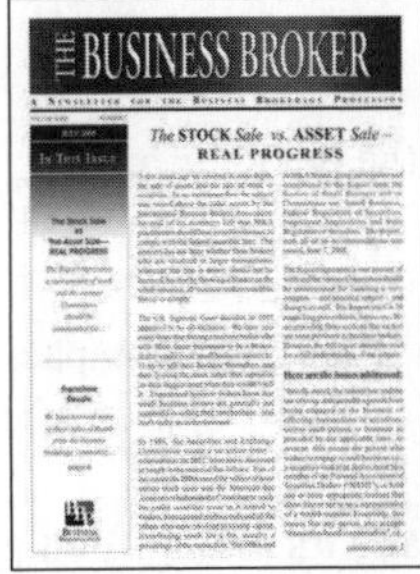
THE BUSINESS BROKER

The STOCK *Sale vs.* ASSET *Sale* — REAL PROGRESS

For over 20 years, The Business Broker has informed and educated readers about industry developments and ideas. It has provided new forms and checklists, important legislative and legal issues, and much more. Some of the latest articles include:

- ***Business Brokers: Success and Failure***
- ***Top 10 Reasons Why the Seller Should Pay a Retainer***
- ***Offer to Purchase Is Binding - Legal Update***
- ***How Far Have We Come - A Twenty Year Comparison***
- ***Top 10 Tips for Superior Listing Service***
- ***Series On Successful Offices***
- ***The Full-Price Offer***

Regular features include: Legal Update, Legislative Update, Business Brokerage Update, New Products and Services, Upcoming Events, and the annual Brokerage Industry Survey. This publication is the voice of the business brokerage industry and is advantageous reading for anyone involved in the business.

The Business Broker......... *$95.00/year*

For more information please call 800-239-5085.

www.bbpinc.com

Expenses as a percentage of annual sales:	
Cost of Goods Sold	15%
Payroll/Labor Costs	40%
Occupancy Cost	20%
Profit (estimated)	15%

General Information

"Growing industry – will see more units in the next 5 years."

Advantages of this Business

- "Most units being built are immediately filled to near capacity."

Disadvantages of this Business

- "Rules and regulations, large on-site staff, including food prep, doctors, nurses."

Industry Trend

"Growing as the health industry increases life expectancy."

Seller Financing

- "10 years."

Office Products

Rule of Thumb:

- 5 to 8 times EBIT
- 1 times sales plus inventory

Pricing Tips

"Key to higher valuation is the company's customer base. Does it include either:

(a) One or more office superstore? (Staples, OfficeMax or Office Depot)
(b) One or more national wholesaler? (United Stationers, etc.)
(c) One or more contract stationers?"

"Customer concentration—many office-product manufacturers have one major customer —a Staples, for example. This may impact valuation if too dependent. Manufactured vs. imported product—companies whose manufacturing base is not vulnerable to imports (from China or Taiwan) are more valuable than those who are."

"There is no rule of thumb for the office products industry, but in general, pricing is affected by the size of the company. The larger the EBIT, i.e., over $5 million, then the higher the multiple. If a manufacturer of office products sells half to Staples et al and half to Wal-Mart et al, it is not a pure play in the office products business, so the price would be discounted accordingly. A better, more valuable, company would sell 100 percent to office product dealers, not 50 percent to mass merchants, 50 percent to office products. Other factors: breadth of product line, channels of distribution—how broad and complete is that industry, customer and supplier mix (80/20?)? Dependency on family members means lower value; union is negative. Is M&E up to date? Growth rate correlation. Is company financeable, or only soft assets?"

"1. Customer profile—are the products well-entrenched in the office superstore channel? 2. Uniqueness of product—are items basic commodities or are they unique or distinctive? If the latter, valuation may go up."

Seller Financing

- "Not very often. If it is a good company, it is a cash deal."
- "3 years."

Resources

School and Home Office Products Association (SHOPA)
www.shopa.org

Business Products Industry Association
www.bpia.org

Office Supplies and Stationery Stores		
11,500	SIC: 5943-01	NAIC: 453210

Rule of Thumb:

- 25 percent of annual sales plus inventory
- 1.5 times SDE plus inventory
- 12 percent of EBIT
- 4 times monthly sales plus inventory

Pricing Tips
"Check inventory levels and FF&E carefully. Owners of these types of businesses tend to hide cash flow in excessive inventory and FF&E."

Benchmarks
"Historical sales against same store performance would be a good measurement. Adequate advertising budget (5% of gross is desirable.) Gross sales per square foot of $200/year would be good, $250/year would be very good, $300/year or more would be excellent."

Franchise

Oil X Change

Rule of Thumb:

- 30 percent of annual sales plus inventory

Resources
(847) 526-4041

Franchise

Once Upon A Child

215 units

Approximate Total Investment:	$119,543 to $194,389

Rule of Thumb:

- 21 percent of annual sales plus paid for inventory

Benchmarks
We found some numbers for 2002 which might help in benchmarking current operations. For stores open 12 months or more, they averaged $294,591 in sales (the range in sales was $110,867 to $524,462), and average gross profit was $179,426. The average gross profit as a percentage of gross sales was 60.91%. These figures appeared in franchise disclosure documents.

General Information
"Once Upon a Child is the largest chain of children's resale stores."
Source: *Franchise Opportunities Guide*, Spring/Summer 2005

Resources
www.ouac.com

Optical Practices

18,620	SIC: 5995-02	NAIC: 446130

Rule of Thumb:

- 68 percent of annual sales plus inventory

General Information

Product Breakdown

Lenses/Lens Treatments	53.0%
Rx Frames	31.5%
Contact Lenses	11.8%
Sunglasses/Clips	03.7%

Source: Jobson Research, 2003

Optometry Practices

39,010	SIC: 5999-04	NAIC: 421460

Rule of Thumb:

- 65 to 70 percent of annual revenues plus inventory
- 2 times SDE plus inventory
- 2.5 times EBIT
- 2 to 3 times EBITDA

Pricing Tips

"Optometry offices will typically sell for a multiple based on the SDE. This ranges from 1.5 to 2.25 times the SDE. This range is determined by the percentage of professional fees vs. dispensary (retail) revenue. If the practice grosses less than $300,000, then the cash flow method is not appropriate and may be valued based on assets."

"Wide range of values relative to gross sales and/or SDE"

Industry Experts' Ratings:

Amount of Competition (1 = Lot of: 4 = Not much)	2.4
Amount of Risk (1 = Very: 4 = Not much)	2.0
Historical Profit Trend (1 = Down: 4 = Up)	2.2
Location & Facilities (1 = Poor: 4 = Excellent)	3.0
Marketability (1 = Low: 4 = High)	2.6
Industry Trend (1 = Declining: 4 = Growing)	2.4
Ease of Replication (1 = Easy: 4 = Difficult)	1.8

Benchmarks

"Average doctors may see a $250/per patient fee. Offices with premium eyewear selections will see a significantly higher per-patient revenue."

Expenses as a percentage of annual sales:

Cost of Goods Sold	30%
Payroll/Labor Costs	20 %
Occupancy Cost	10%–15%
Profit (estimated)	30%–35%

General Information

"Generally, you should expect to receive a return in gross dollars of 10 times what you spend on marketing. For example, if you want to increase the practice by $100,000, expect to spend $10,000."

Source: "Promote Your Practice More Effectively" Review of Optometry

"Clearly this is not a general-interest business; only doctors of optometry (or, occasionally, an ophthalmologist) would be interested and allowed to own such a business/practice."

Advantages of this Business

- "Health service provided to predominantly healthy patients. Small business, often sole professional, so much independence."
- "Build equity, independence"

Disadvantages of this Business

- "Graduates leaving school with higher student loans create a demand for higher immediate starting salaries. This may create difficult situations for buyers seeking smaller practices that offer less immediate cash flow."

- "Must hold appropriate degree and be licensed by state regulatory board"

Industry Trend

"Added revenue services (scope of licensing) will continue to provide doctors with increased revenue sources."

Seller Financing

- "10 years"

Packaging (Industrial)

Rule of Thumb:

- 6 times EBIT;
- 60 to 70 percent of annual sales

Benchmarks

Expenses as a percentage of annual sales:

Cost of Good Sold: 60%–65%
Payroll/Labor Costs: 8%–10%
Profit: .... 10%–15% (before taxes)

General Information

Questions to ask seller: "How stable is your customer base—what is your customer retention record? What % of total sales do your top 10 accounts represent? Is there really any real 'free cash flow' in the business?"

Industry Trend

"Consolidation will rule the packaging industry. Cheaper to buy than to grow market share in a mundane, non-innovative business, lacking pricing power and vulnerable to relocation of key accounts to offshore facilities."

Franchise

Orange Julius

384 units	
Approximate Total Investment:	$142,100 to $349,800

Rule of Thumb:

- 32 percent of annual sales plus inventory

General Information

Orange Julius is a subsidiary of Dairy Queen International, which in turn is owned by Berkshire Hathaway.

Resources

www.orangejulius.com

Packaging and Shipping Services

(See Mail & Parcel Centers)

Paint & Decorating (Wallpaper) Retailers

15,797	SIC: 5231-07	NAIC: 444120

Rule of Thumb:

- 20 percent of annual sales plus inventory

Pricing Tips

"They should be doing a minimum of $50,000 gross and up. Also, should have nationally known brand name plus 2 competitive paint lines. A wide variety of wallpaper from lesser priced to higher priced lines should be offered. National averages tell us these stores make from 16 to 17 percent plus reasonable wages for the owner/operators. The average markup is 40 percent. These stores are sold for fixtures, equipment plus inventory at cost."

Resources

The Paint & Decorating Retailers Association (PDRA)
www.pdra.org

Starting Out: A Practical Guide to Opening or Buying a Decorating Products Business, published by PDRA (see above)

Franchise

Pak Mail

430 units

Approximate Total Investment:	$114,300 to $147,500

Rule of Thumb:

- 50 percent of annual sales plus inventory

Resources
www.pakmail.com

Franchise

Panera Bread

701 units

Benchmarks
A store's average sales for 2004 was $1.88 million

Parking Lots

Approx 5,000

Pricing Tips
"[In some cities] they have been selling for 1.5 times their annual net before taxes, plus the value of fixtures, equipment and inventory at cost—plus real estate."

Resources
National Parking Association
www.npapark.org

Parking Lot Sweeping

12,000	SIC: 1611-04	NAIC: 561790

Rule of Thumb:

- 55 to 60 percent of annual revenues
- 1.6 times SDE

Benchmarks

"Very generally speaking, using 2005 prices, it is not uncommon for a contractor with a smaller parking area sweeper, such as a three-yard-capacity sweeper on a 1-ton chassis, to be able to charge between $55 and $65 per hour, for a gross earnings of between $9,000 and $11,000 per month.

"For a larger sweeper, one which is suitable for performing a variety of duties other than parking lot cleanup, the same rule of thumb is a charge of between $65 and $75 per hour; this should net you a gross of between $11,000 and $14,000 per month. Street sweeping pricing should be about $90, since it is harder on your equipment, and the sweepers cost substantially more.

"Again, these are simply generalizations, and actual earnings are quite dependent upon work performed, charges in your area, etc. They are definitely, however, numbers which have been attained by many in the industry who have worked hard at developing their businesses."
Source: Schwarze Industries, Inc, 2003, www.american sweeper.com

Resources

American Sweeper magazine
www.americansweeper.com

Franchise

Pasquales Pizza

Rule of Thumb:

- 35 to 40 percent of annual sales plus inventory

Pawn Shops

11,371	SIC: 5932-29	NAIC: 522298

Rule of Thumb:

- 40 to 70 percent of annual sales

Benchmarks

"A typical loan is small, averaging $75 to $100. The interest rate charged by a pawnbroker is controlled by the state and varies widely across the nation. The pawnbroker is also required to hold the merchandise for a specific period of time, giving the borrower time to repay the loan. This hold period also varies widely but is typically in the 60 to 90 day time frame.

"On average, about 80 percent of all loans are repaid. Repeat customers make up most of the business, similar to any other lending or retail establishment.

"Less than half of one percent of all loans are identified as stolen goods. Thieves and robbers are a pawnbroker's worst enemy.

"What is the difference between buying at a pawnshop and buying at a retail store? Mainly price. If you go to a pawnbroker, gold can be found for about 40 percent less than at retail outlets and other products are usually 30 to 50 percent less.

"Since 15 to 20 percent of a pawnbroker's customers elect not to repay their loans, they are forced to turn 'bad debt' into a retail center to recover their costs."

Source: National Pawnbrokers Association, www.nationalpawnbrokers.org

General Information

"According to the police, the 14 licensed pawnbrokers in Boston averaged an 85 percent gross return on investment last year. Roughly 50 percent from interest on loans and 35 percent on resale of foreclosed items. Net profit runs 12 to 15 percent."

Source: "Pawnshops, in Check," by Sam Allis, *The Boston Globe*, March 9, 2003

Industry Trend

"'Payday' loans even pinch pawn shops

You would expect that here in Las Vegas, payday loan outfits would flourish ("Mass. Cracks Down on 'Payday' Loans," Feb. 9). And they do. But I live in a suburb and the usurers are rampant here, too. I counted nine 'loan centers' along a three-mile stretch of Sunset Boulevard—14 miles from the 'Strip' It's obvious that these outfits are bottom-fishing for the unfortunate and distressed, and not just in low-income areas. Curiously, one major component of the quick-loan business here is suffering as a result of the proliferation of payday loans—pawn shops."

Source: Robert Duggan, Henderson, Nevada, letter to the editor, *The Boston Sunday Globe,* February 13, 2005

Resources

National Pawnshop Association
www.nationalpawnbrokers.org

Personnel Staffing Agencies *(See Employment Agencies)*

Rule of Thumb:

- .75 to 1 times annual revenues; includes equipment

General Information

"Personnel Staffing Agencies - In the U.S., over 40,000 personnel staffing offices generate total annual revenue of more than $130 billion. Large firms include Adecco, Manpower, Vedior, and Kelly Services, with hundreds of offices. The average agency, however, has one office, $2 million in annual sales, and 15 employees. Despite strong consolidation in recent years, the industry remains moderately fragmented: the 50 largest firms hold about 40 percent of the market. Agencies with multiple offices may have agency-owned branches, independently owned franchise offices, or licensed area-representative offices."

Source: wwwfirstresearch.com. 5/16/2005

Resources

American Staffing Association
www.staffingtoday.net

Pest Control

24,500	SIC: 7342:01	NAIC: 561710

Rule of Thumb:

- 1.5 times SDE
- 5 times EBITDA
- 80 percent of annual sales

Pricing Tips

"One-person pest control companies normally sell for approximately 1.25 times cash flow (SDE). One-man operations usually sell for 75% of annual sales. A good one-man route sells for close to one year's annual sales. Larger businesses normally sell for 2 to 3 times SDE as in most service businesses."

"Normally no more than 1 year's gross sales for a good business. However, Terminix is paying in excess of 1.5 times gross on a pest control business (w/no termites). 1.5 times cash flow is another figure often used, based on monthly accounts with charges of $25 to $32 for average residential. Annual contracts might go for as high as 2 times cash flow."

"Profit is the main determining factor. Size of business is a determining factor. Potential for expansion is a determining factor. Time in business is a determining factor; the transfer of the seller's profit to the buyer's profit is a determining factor."

"The value of an exterminating and pest control business is not determined by any one single factor. The SDE is certainly a key factor in pricing this type of business, but gross sales, number of employees, value of equipment, and the general organization of the business must also be considered. As in most businesses, all aspects of the business must be taken into account when deciding the value of the business."

"Pest control with contracts—most valuable; Termite renewals—2nd; Lawn & ornamentals with contracts—3rd; Fumigation value = equipment value only"

"Earnings over 30 percent increase value as volume increases."

"In Arizona it's what the market will allow. With Terminix, Orkin and other large companies aggressively pursuing the industry, prices presently are high."

"Price depends on profit, efficiency, category, location—volume is a big factor. Most buyers prefer to buy pest control as opposed to termite. Some companies in the South do exclusively lawn & ornamental."

"Annual profit should be substantial for a greater sales price. Large companies bring a good price and are in demand."

Industry Experts' Ratings:

Marketability 2.8
(1 = low marketability; 4 = high marketability)
Industry Trend 3.2
(1 = declining trend; 4 = growing trend)
Ease of Replication 3.0
(1 = easily replicated; 4 = difficult to replicate)

"Capital is a factor when growing the business."

Benchmarks

"Companies over $1 million profit should be 18 to 24 percent of annual volume."

"Sales or production per employee = $100,000 to $150,000 per year."

"Under $500K .... 20% to 35% profit
Over $500K .... 18% to 22% profit"

Expenses as a percentage of annual sales:

Cost of Goods Sold	10%
Payroll/Labor Costs	30%
Occupancy Cost	02%
Profit (estimated)	20%

Here are a few interesting statistics from a survey conducted by *Pest Control* magazine. They also have a very informative web site: www.pestcontrolmag.com.

The national average pay per hour for technicians was "more than $11 per hour to their new technicians. This falls in line with the U.S. Bureau of Labor Statistics' contention that the national average for technicians is $12.03 (median figure is $11.13)."

2004 Annual Revenue	
Less than $50,000	11%
$50,001–$100,000	16%
$100,001–$250,000	23%
$250,001–$500,000	14%
$500,001–$1 million	13%
$1 million–$5 million	13%
$5 million–$10 million	03%
$10 million +	07%

Source: *Pest Control* magazine survey

Operating Budgets in Action	
Technician salary	29.33%
Pesticides & equipment	18.37%
Overhead	16.93%
Vehicles	14.25%
Other expenses	14.20%
Nontechnician salary	06.92%

Source: *Pest Control Magazine*, September 2004

General Information

Questions to ask seller: "Like most businesses, a quality company sells for more. New equipment, good books and records, and a high profit margin make a business worth more. Repeat commercial accounts also affect the bottom line positively when pricing a business."

"The Business of Pest Control

Year after year, small service-business owners have always had the same issues to combat, including employee turnover, customer retention, overhead costs and government regulations. And it's no secret that pest management professionals have to work hard to dispel the pop cultural stereotype of the unkempt, uneducated 'bug man' particularly when it comes to public sentiment over pesticide use, for example.

"This year, our state of the industry respondents indicate that the professional image seems to be getting on the right track, but other issues are becoming compounded by several factors, including:

- skyrocketing health care costs
- liability insurance premiums also on the rise
- high fuel costs
- uncertain economy."

Source: "2004 State of the Industry," *Pest Control Magazine*, September 2004

Advantages of this Business

- "Good profit, and business is not going away; bugs are always with us."

Disadvantages of this Business

- "Constant demand of customers can cause burnout if not handled properly."
- "Pest control companies are dealing with poisonous chemicals on a daily basis. In most states, pest control companies are licensed by the state. The owner must either employ an individual capable of being the qualified party or he must have years of training in the industry before being eligible to qualify for this license."

Seller Financing

- 5 years
- 3 to 5 years

Resources

National Pest Control Association
www.pestworld.org

Pest Control magazine
www.pestcontrolmag.com
This is an excellent site with lots of informative articles.

The Web site below is that of Al Woodward, a specialist in the pest control brokerage business. The site is informative and interesting.
www.pestcontrolbiz.com

Franchise

Petland

Rule of Thumb:

- 57 percent of annual sales plus inventory

Pet Shops

7,737	SIC: 5999-30	NAIC: 453910

Rule of Thumb:

- 35 percent of annual sales plus inventory

Pricing Tips

"Retail—treat like any other retail business."

General Information

Breakdown of pet ownership in the U.S.

Number of U.S. Households that Own a Pet (millions)	
Bird	6.4
Cat	37.7
Dog	43.5
Equine	4.2
Freshwater Fish	13.9
Saltwater Fish	.8
Reptile	4.4
Small Animal	5.7

Total U.S. Pet Industry Expenditures

Year	Billion
2005	$35.9 Est.
2004	$34.4
2003	$32.4
2002	$29.5
2001	$28.5

Estimated 2005 Sales within the U.S. Market
For 2005, it is estimated that $35.9 billion will be spent on our pets in the U.S.

Breakdown:

Food	$14.5 billion
Vet Care	$8.6 billion
Supplies/Medicine	$8.8 billion
Live animal purchases	$1.6 billion
Pet Services: Grooming & Boarding	$2.4 billion

According to the 2005/2006 APPMA National Pet Owners Survey, basic annual expenses for dog and cat owners in dollars include:

	Dogs	Cats
Surgical vet Visits	574	337
Food	241	185
Kennel Boarding	202	119
Routine Vet	211	179
Groomer/Grooming Aids	107	24
Vitamins	123	3
Treats	66	43
Toys	45	29

Source: American Pet Products Manufacturers Association, Inc. (APPMA)

Resources

American Pet Products Manufacturers Association, Inc. (APPMA)
www.appma.org

Pet Industry Joint Advisory Council
www.pijac.org

World Wide Pet Supply
www.wwpsa.com

"63% of U.S. households own a pet, which equates to 69.1 million homes."

Source: American Pet Products Manufacturers Association, Inc. (APPMA)

Pet Supply (Wholesale)

1,300	SIC: 5199-32	NAIC: 422990

Pricing Tips

"Treat like any other distribution company."

Pet Livestock (Wholesale)

Pricing Tips

"Be very careful here; you could wind up 'with a nest of rattlesnakes.'"

Pharmacies

55,013	SIC: 5912-05	NAIC: 446110

Rule of Thumb:

- 18 to 42 percent of annual sales—depending on profits and includes inventory
- 70 times average daily sales (Range 60 to 80 times) plus inventory
- 25 percent of annual sales (Range 20% to 30%) plus inventory
- 6.5 times annual net income after owner's salary & depreciation & taxes (Range 5 to 8 times) plus inventory
- 5 times annual net income after owner's salary & depreciation before taxes (Range 3 to 7 times) plus inventory

Pricing Tips

"Average total Rx filled daily, % new, % ref, & total Rx average price for year, % Rx third-party insurance & Medicaid & % cash sales, % charge sales. Inventory value in date & salable. Inventory turns per year; total cost of goods sold + inventory on hand (8 times); age analysis of all accounts receivable including welfare, Worker's Comp; hours open per day, per week, per month, # days per year open; lease."

"Good front business, e.g., gifts and greeting cards that improve profits.

Look for niche business & profits."

"Number of prescriptions filled daily, monthly, annually; divide by number of days open to arrive at number of prescriptions filled per day. Retail & cost of ingredients. In medical professional building—number of physicians in building. Does pharmacy do its own prescription compounding, & what percentage of business is third party; i.e., Medicare (welfare) & insurance company paid?"

"Try 22% of [annual] sales. Net income, i.e. return on investment. Future income of business at least 5 years down the line. Demographics and customer review."

Benchmarks

"Average number of prescriptions per pharmacy: 54,427 annually, 174 per day.

Average independent pharmacy sales: $2.855 million.

Average prescription sales: $2.55 million.

Average independent pharmacy employs 2.6 pharmacists (including owner) and 3.3 technicians."

Source: National Community Pharmacists Association (NCPA)

"Preliminary *Digest* data indicate that the average independent community pharmacy exceeded $3.46 million in total sales in 2004. That represents growth of 6 percent over 2003 figures. Net pre-tax profit held steady at 4 percent, while gross margins dropped to 22.2 percent compared to 24 percent in 2003.

"Prescription sales revenue also grew, accounting for 92 percent ($3.18 million) of total average sales — a 9 percent increase from the previous year.

"'It's going to kill the little guys,' one pharmacy owner said of mail-order drugs."

Source: *The New York Times*, January 1, 2005

"Prescription volume rose with the average independent pharmacy dispensing 59,316 prescriptions in 2004, according to preliminary *Digest* figures. That translates into an average of 190 prescriptions per day.

"In 2004, the number of independent pharmacies — including single-store independent pharmacies, independent chains, independent franchises,

independent franchises, independent long-term care and I.V. pharmacies, and independent pharmacist-owned supermarket pharmacies - increased slightly to 24,345 pharmacies. Independents make up 42 percent of the nation's total retail marketplace of 58,109 pharmacies, based on NCPDP and NCPA data.

"Independent pharmacies comprise the largest segment of the retail pharmacy market. Chains follow comprising 31 percent of the market with 18,279 drugstores. Supermarket pharmacies make up 15 percent with 8,790 pharmacies, and mass merchandisers comprise 11 percent with 6,695 pharmacies.

"Among multi-store owners, the average number of pharmacies owned is 2.8. For the independent sector as a whole, the average is 1.2 pharmacies.

"Independent pharmacies offer a wide range of patient services. The top services offered in 2004 were: delivery (85 percent), nutrition (84 percent), patient charge accounts (83 percent), compounding (73 percent), herbal medicine (70 percent), and durable medical equipment (60 percent). Blood pressure monitoring and diabetes training continue to be the top disease management services offered."

Source: 2005 NCPA-Pfizer Digest, "Total, Prescription Sales Increase at Nation's Independent Pharmacies

Expenses as a percentage of annual sales:

Cost of Goods	75%
Payroll/Labor Costs	09%
(employees + owner 5% of annual sales = 15%. Range 12 to 18%)	
Occupancy Cost	2 to 3%
(Range—1% rural, 4% metro)	
Profit (estimated)	3– 4%

General Information

"There are 23,552 single-store independent pharmacies, independent chains, independent franchises, and independent pharmacist-owned supermarket pharmacies. [They represent] 43 percent of the nation's 55,200 drugstores."

Source: National Community Pharmacists Association (NCPA)

Industry Trend

"Drugstores Fret as Insurers Demand Pills by Mail

"Mail-order drug sales rose to $32.5 billion in the 12 months ending in September, a 16 percent increase compared with the same period in 2003, according to IMS Health, a pharmaceutical consulting company.

."At least 30 pharmacies in the state were closed or sold to chains last year, according to the Michigan Pharmacists Association, a professional group that is lobbying the state legislature for a prohibition on making mail-order prescriptions mandatory.

"Medco said its mail sales rose to $3.4 billion in the third quarter, up 21 percent from the same period in 2003. Express Scripts' mail-order sales increased 41.7 percent, to $1.4 billion, in the three months ending Sept. 30. Caremark, which in March bought AdvancePCS, a big pharmacy benefits manager, doubled its mail revenues to $2.19 billion in the third quarter, a prime reason, it said, for a 41 percent increase in quarterly profits.

"These results from mail orders, not surprisingly, are considered a serious threat by drugstore chains, which are fighting back. 'Mom-and-pop stores are going out of business,' said Meredith Adler, a retail drugstore analyst at Lehman Brothers. 'But the chains would like to play in the mail-order game.'"

Source: *The New York Times,* January 1, 2005

Seller Financing

- Mostly all cash sales. Owner finance 3 to 7 years with interest at prime +/- 1% or 2 %
- 10 years

Resources

National Community Pharmacists Association
www.ncpanet.org—interesting and informative site

American Pharmacy

American Pharmaceutical Assoc.
www.aphanet.org

NCPA (National Community Pharmacy Association—*Searle Digest*, published annually

Photographic Studio *(See Camera Shop)*

Rule of Thumb:

- 50 percent of SDE; add fixtures, equipment & inventory
- 3 times monthly sales; add inventory

Pricing Tips

"They are usually sold for the new cost of fixtures and equipment, plus inventory, plus 30 percent of one year's net profit. National average states the gross profit usually runs about 62 percent, leaving a net profit of about 24 percent after expenses."

Resources

Photo Marketing Association International
www.pmai.org—This site contains valuable information on the photography business including the school market, the portrait business, etc.

Physical Therapy

Rule of Thumb:

- 75 percent of annual sales
- 2.5 times SDE
- 2 times EBIT
- 2 times EBITDA

Pricing Tips

"Private Practice Physical Therapy Clinics. We have valued over 300 in the last 20 years. My valuation rules of thumb are based on this experience. Value is typically 60% to 100% of annual collected fees, 3-4 times amount available to owner (SDCF) and 2-3 times (SDCF less reasonable replacement salary for owner.)."

Industry Experts' Ratings:

Amount of Competition (1 = Lot of: 4 = Not much)	1.6
Amount of Risk (1 = Very: 4 = Not much)	1.8
Historical Profit Trend (1 = Down: 4 = Up)	2.4
Location & Facilities (1 = Poor: 4 = Excellent)	2.2
Marketability (1 = Low: 4 = High)	2.0
Industry Trend (1 = Declining: 4 = Growing)	2.1
Ease of Replication (1 = Easy: 4 = Difficult)	1.0

"Competition is the biggie, particularly if a large healthcare provider decides to enter the market. Relationships with physicians are key."

Benchmarks

"Collected fees per full-time employed physical therapist should be $200,000 to $300,000 per year. Net profit after reasonable salary to owner should be 25%-35%. Collected fee per visit should be close to $100 and patient visits per PT should be 3000-3500."

Expenses as a percentage of annual sales:

Cost of Goods Sold	27%
Payroll/Labor Costs	21%
Occupancy Cost	07%
Profit (estimated)	12%

General Information

There was significant consolidation in this industry ten years ago, with lots of public companies competing in as feeding frenzy. Things have settled down and many of these companies are out of business.

Advantages of thes Business

- "Attractive net profit, even for single owner practice. Quite marketable."

Disadvantages of this Business

- "Price pressure. Increasing costs of therapists."

Industry Trend

"There will be continued price pressure but with the aging of the baby boomers there will be plenty of growth. Cost of therapists and supply will be problems."

Seller Financing

- "5 years"

Picture Framing

16,750	SIC: 5999-27	NAIC: 442299

Rule of Thumb:

- 40 percent of annual sales plus inventory

Resources

Professional Picture Framers Association (PPFA)
www.ppfa.com

Picture Framing magazine
www.pictureframingmagazine.com

Franchise

Pizza by George

Rule of Thumb:

- 50 percent of annual sales plus inventory

Franchise

Pizza Inn

413 units	
Estimated Annual Sales per Unit:	$435,000
Approximate Total Investment:	$49,000 to $285,000

Rule of Thumb:

- 47 percent of annual sales plus inventory

Resources
www.pizzainn.com

Pizza Shops

68,694	SIC: 5812-22	NAIC: 722110

Rule of Thumb:

- 35 to 40 percent of annual sales plus inventory
- 1.5 to 2 times SDE; plus fixtures, equipment and inventory
- 4 times monthly sales plus inventory

Pricing Tips
"Typical pricing is 20 to 24 times weekly gross sales. Industry insiders and purchasers use this barometer consistently."

"Sole ownership in this type of business results in numbers that are hard to decipher their basis in reality. Be cautious and spend a great deal of time with the owner to truly understand the earnings of the business."

Domino's Formula — 45 percent of the first $400K in annual sales, 50 percent of the next $100K ($400 to $500K) in annual sales, then 55 percent of the next $250K of annual sales (from $500–$750k)

Industry Experts' Ratings:

Amount of Competition (1 = Lot of: 4 = Not much) 1.6
Amount of Risk (1 = Very: 4 = Not much) 1.8
Historical Profit Trend (1 = Down: 4 = Up) 2.4
Location & Facilities (1 = Poor: 4 = Excellent)......................... 2.2
Marketability (1 = Low: 4 = High).. 2.0
Industry Trend (1 = Declining: 4 = Growing) 2.1
Ease of Replication (1 = Easy: 4 = Difficult) 1.0

Benchmarks
"Keep food costs below 30 percent and labor, not counting manager's salary, below 20 percent."

"Luke Bailey, owner of the two-unit Pizza Company in Davison, MI, keeps 10 to 14 days' worth of inventory on hand and schedules a running inventory only sporadically. 'If I can keep 61 percent on food and payroll, I'm OK,' he said."

"Average Sales per Unit (Forecast 2005) $528,667"

Source: National Association of Restaurants (NRA)

Avarage Pizza Sales

	2004	2003
Average Sales for the Top 25 Pizza Chains	$629,334	$607,364
Average Sales for Independents (All pizzerias not in the Top 25)	$338,745	$341,534

Source: "Pizza Power 2005," PMQ's Annual Pizza Industry Analysis, Pizza Marketing Quarterly

Expenses as a percentage of annual sales:

Cost of Goods Sold	28%
Payroll/Labor Costs	25%
Occupancy Cost	08%
Profit (estimated)	12%

General Information

"The Industry as a Whole—2005 - "There are three bits of good news when looking at the industry as a whole. First, there are 1.7 percent more pizzerias in America. Second, sales rose 2 percent, indicating more growth than the previous year. A third sign of positive change is that only 388 pizzerias went out of business according to statistics from InfoUSA, which is down from 1,139 that closed the previous year. The total number of pizzerias in the U.S. reached 69,844 as of July 2005 compared to 68,694 at the time of the 2004 Pizza Power report.

"Average per-unit sales for pizzerias in the U.S. for the period between July 2004 and July 2005 is $442,492 per location, which is up 0.3 percent from the previous year. The reason the per-unit percentage change is lower than the overall growth rate is a result of the growth rate of total pizzerias being higher than the overall sales growth.

"Independents own 64.30% of the pizzerias and control 49.22% of the sales."

Source: "Pizza Power 2005," PMQ's Annual Pizza Industry Analysis, Pizza Marketing Quarterly

"The National Restaurant Association's (NRA) Restaurant Industry Forecast for 2005 predicts a total of 900,000 restaurants and total sales of $475.8 billion by the end of 2005. This will average $528,667 per unit, leaving the pizza industry falling short of the national per-unit average for all restaurants. The NRA's per-unit sales prediction for 2004, was $501,253 per unit. The NRA's numbers show a change in average sales per unit for all restaurants between 2004 and 2005 of 5.5 percent. While the pizza industry is gaining sales and locations, it is still behind the national per-unit average for all restaurants in the U.S."

Source: "Pizza Power 2005," PMQ's Annual Pizza Industry Analysis, Pizza Marketing Quarterly

Note: If you have anything do with the pizza business, it is almost mandatory that you subscribe to the *Pizza marketing Quarterly*. Go to www.pmq.com.

Advantages of this Business

- "Low priced food with appeal to all ages, genders, etc. Widening variety of product offerings to entice a larger segment of the population."

Who Owns America's Pizza Industry?

As part of the 2005 Pizza Power Annual Pizza Industry Analysis in *Pizza Marketing Quarterly,* the question of who owns the pizza business in the U.S. was addressed. As you might guess, the states with the lowest population not only had the lowest number of pizza businesses, but the number of stores per owner was the highest, led by the state of Mississippi, where the number of stores per owner was 4.23, to Vermont at the other end, with each owner owning only 1.3 stores.

What this would seem to indicate is that there are a lot of owners with only one store. The most populated states in the East and Midwest, and include California in the list, had the most stores and the fewest stores per owner. California, New York, Pennsylvania and Ohio have a lot of pizza stores, almost 30 percent of the total number of stores, yet these four states have less than 2 stores per owner.

The pizza business is comprised of a lot of small business people operating only one store.

- "Ease of operation and ease of entry"

Disadvantages of this Business

- "High-fat food content. Increasing number of franchised and independent pizzerias limit the growth potential."
- "Hard work, long hours"

Industry Trend

"As seen by comparing the pizza industry to the entire restaurant industry, pizza is failing to pull customers away from the hamburger, taco, sandwich and chicken guys. It appears that, rather than fighting to expand pizza's customer base, the deep discounting by the major chains is simply a war of attrition that is pulling pizza customers from one pizza place to another. Perhaps there needs to be a shift and an effort with marketing towards expanding your customer base, introducing new products or a healthy angle to keep this industry 'fresh' and 'exciting.' The Big Four's move in early 2004 to offer new items was a step in the right direction, but the '555 Deal,' '$5 National Pizza Sale' and numerous low-priced pizza offers and coupons are simply going to make customers 'bargain hunt' for the cheapest pizza they can find. Americans' love for pizza won't go away, but there needs to be a movement to educate customers on the quality, uniqueness and value of pizza."

Source: "Pizza Power 2005," PMQ's Annual Pizza Industry Analysis, Pizza Marketing Quarterly

Resources

(See Restaurants)

Pizza Marketing Quarterly
www.pmq.com—This is a wonderful site. If you are serious about selling pizza businesses, you have to visit it.

Nation's Restaurant—This is one publication you must have if you're marketing any type of food operation, including pizza stores.

(See Restaurant Resources)

Franchise Times
www.franchisetimes.com

Guide to a Successful Pizza Business & *Pizza Business Manual* by Paul Shakarian. www.pizzabusiness.com

Quick *Profile* Pizza

SIC Code 5812-22
NAICS: Pizza Delivery Shops 722211
Pizza Parlors, Pizzerias—Full Serve 722110
Pizza Parlors, Pizzerias—Limited Service/Take Out 722211

U.S. Pizza Sales	% of Total Sales	% of Total Stores	Est. Annual Sales/per Unit
Pizza Hut	17.02%	10.74%	$692,300
Domino's	10.27%	07.17%	$640,000
Papa John's	5.55%	03.67%	$670,000
Little Caesar's	3.92%	03.96%	$403,600
All Other Top 25	14.02	10.16%	n/a

Here are some franchised pizza operations and their estimated annual sales per unit:

Bertucci's Brick Oven Pizza	$2,214,000
California Pizza Kitchen	$2,500,000
Chuck E. Cheese's Pizza	$1,107,000
CiCi's Pizza	$885,000
Domino's	$640,000
Donato's Pizza	$958,000
Godfather's Pizza	$523,000
Hungry Howie's Pizza	$504,000
Little Caesar's	$403.600
Mazzio's Pizza	$790,000
Papa John's Pizza	$670,000
Papa Murphy's	$475,000
Pizza Hut	$692,300
Pizza Inn	$435,000
Round Table Pizza	$792,000
Sbarro	$620,000
Shakey's Pizza	$450,000
Uno's Chicago Grill/Pizzeria Uno	$2,216,000

Source: *Franchise Times, Nation's Restaurant*, *Pizza Marketing Quarterly* and various other publications

The Independents

"For this report, independents are classified as all pizzerias not in the Top 25. Once again the independents gained market share of the total number of pizzerias in the U.S. and now comprise 64.3 percent of all the pizzerias in the U.S., which is up from 64.2 percent the previous year, but lost market share of total sales. Between July 2004 and July 2005, independents earned 49.22 percent of the industry's total sales compared to earning 50.7 percent of the total industry sales the previous year. For 2004, independents earned an average of $338,745 per unit compared to $341,534 per unit the previous year. This marks a decrease of 0.8 percent. What does this mean? Independents are opening more locations than the Top 25, but the Top 25 are outpacing independents in sales. While this may be true, it does not necessarily mean the Top 25 are doing the best job of expanding our industry as a whole."

Source: "Pizza Power 2005," PMQ's Annual Pizza Industry Analysis, Pizza Marketing Quarterly

Pluses of the Business

"Pizza restaurants are one quick-service food business where the independent can successfully compete with the chains and franchised businesses. The top independents, according to our informal survey, compare very favorably with the top franchised pizza restaurants, with volume over $1 million per year. Although pizza represents more than 50 percent of sales, most pizza restaurants sell sandwiches, Italian food, and other items. Pizza is one of the few quick-service items that are deliverable. In fact, delivery represents 99 percent of Domino's business, and this company is number 2 in the rankings of pizza chains and franchises. Delivery now represents 49 percent of sales of the number 1 company—Pizza Hut. Pizza sales are increasing every year, it is not the only food item sold, and it is deliverable—all pluses!

Minuses of the Business

"The pluses, to some extent, create the minuses. Delivery is labor intensive. Some chains and franchises specialize in delivery, while others lean towards the eat-in and take-out customer. Although very competitive, it is an easy business to enter. Customers tend to be loyal to their favorite pizza place. Because of the low per-check price, it takes a lot of customers to make the business successful. Some high-volume restaurants make well over 200 pizzas per hour in busy times. It takes a lot of dough to make a lot of dough! It can be difficult when buying an existing pizza restaurant to figure out how much business it is really doing."

Financial Information

It is also very difficult to piece together the financial information of an independent pizza restaurant if the owners have not properly maintained their records. Franchised restaurants are much easier, due to the financial reporting required by the franchisor. The Internal The

# of Pizza Stores per 10,000 People

If you like pizza, here is where you want to live:

Maine	4.13 pizza stores
New Hampshire	3.95 stores
Pennsylvania	3.93 stores
Iowa	3.84 stores
Massachusetts	3.75

And if you don't like pizza:

Mississippi	1.21 pizza stores
Louisiana	1.28 pizza stores
Hawaii	1.41 pizza stores
Alabama	1.49 pizza stores
Texas	1.54 pizza stores

Source: "Pizza Power 2005," PMQ's Annual Pizza Industry Analysis, Pizza Marketing Quarterly

Rules of Thumb for Pizza Franchises

Between Rounds	3–4 times SDE
Black Jack's Pizza	55%–60 % of annual sales
Chicago Pizza	26% of annual sales
Godfather's Pizza	28% of annual sales
Hungry Howie's Pizza	30% of annual sales
Little Caesar's Pizza	55% of annual sales
Mountain Mike's Pizza	27% of annual sales
Mr. Jim's Pizza	35% of annual sales
Pasquale's Pizza	35%–40% of annual sales
Pizza by George	50% of annual sales
Pizza Inn	47% of annual sales

The Internal Revenue Service publishes audit guides for their agents to assist them in tracking down the revenues of what a pizza restaurant is really grossing. Their Market Segment Specialization Program (MSSP) for pizza restaurants states: "Overall, documentation of income and expenses in this industry [pizza restaurants] has been found to be lacking. In most instances, the cash register tapes are not retained and income is not deposited intact. There is generally little or no documentation to verify the gross receipts reported on the tax return. Purchases are often paid in cash and the purchase invoices are not kept. Employees are often paid in cash, sometimes in order to avoid the payroll taxes."

The MSSP goes on to state: "... Cash receipts books often consist of a sheet of paper with a summary of 12 months' sales...The restaurant usually keeps the cash register tapes long enough to determine if the employees are stealing, then the tapes are not kept.... It was found in many cases that business expenses as well as personal living expenses were paid with cash taken from the cash drawer." The following excerpt from the MSSP is especially insightful: "The examiner noticed that certain ingredients were not reflected on the purchase invoices. In addition, there were missing invoices. From the original received from the supplier, it was determined that the owner understated purchases by over $50,000. This was done to camouflage the skimming by keeping the gross profit percentage in line."

"The cost of food, paper, soda & labor should be between 47% and 51%, before rent & utilities. If it is more than 51%, the store is losing money."

Guide to a Successful Pizza Business by Paul Shakarian (See Resources below)

According to the MSSP, the number of pizza boxes used and the number of grinder rolls [if grinders, hoagies or submarine sandwiches are served] should be confirmed from the suppliers. The MSSP goes on to suggest to the agents that different size pizzas be purchased and sent to a laboratory to discover how much flour, cheese, etc. is used in making the pizzas. This is done to attempt to establish the number of pizzas that can be made from 100 pounds of flour, to compare the amount of cheese per pizza with the amount purchased, etc. This is not practical for a would-be purchaser or business appraiser to do, but there are some rough rules that can be applied. Once again, these are from the MSSP:

(1) Determine the total number of pounds of flour and cheese purchased and the number of cans of pizza sauce purchased.

(2) Multiply the total number of pounds of flour and cheese by 16 to calculate the total number of ounces of flour and cheese, respectively.

(3) Multiply the total number of cans of pizza sauce by 105 ounces (the total number of ounces in a #10 size can).

(4) Divide the total ounces of flour, sauce and cheese purchased by the respective average weight of each ingredient per laboratory results. [You might ask another pizza restaurant owner, supplier, or industry expert for these average weights.]

(5) The result is the total estimated number of pizzas sold based on flour, cheese, or sauce purchased. The three methods (flour, cheese or sauce) should closely approximate pizza sales and should be relatively close. Attempt to use the lower, more conservative, number of pizzas sold. If there is a large discrepancy between the three methods, there is a chance that not all of the suppliers have been identified, or possibly some products were purchased with cash.

(6) Multiply the units sold by the average menu price of a large and small cheese pizza to arrive at pizza sales.

Example
Assume that the purchases for flour, cheese, and sauce were 12,000 lbs., 9,000 lbs., and 800 cans (#10 size), respectively. Also, laboratory testing of one large and one small pizza found the average weight of the flour, cheese and sauce were 9.5, 7, and 4 ounces respectively. The average menu price for pizza is $6.

	Flour	Cheese	Sauce
Purchases	12,000	9,000	800
converted to ounces	x16	x16	x105
Total ounces	192,000	144,000	84,000
Divided by average weight	9.5	7	4
Total units sold	20,210	20,571	21,000

Since the discrepancy here is not substantial, continue with steps 5 and 6.

Take the lowest of the three results—in this case, the amount is 20,210 units—and multiply the total units sold by the average menu price for pizza.

Total Estimated Pizza Sales = 20,100 units x 6 = $121, 260.

The MSSP contains a similar explanation for sandwiches. Here is an example:

Assume 500 pounds of roast beef were purchased. Laboratory testing shows the average weight of the meat in a grinder [sub, etc.] is 5 ounces. The average menu price for a roast beef grinder is $4.

Meat purchased	500 lbs.

Convert to ounces	x16
Meat in ounces	8,000
Divide by average weight	5
Grinder sold in units	1,600
Average menu price	x4
Roast beef grinder sales	$6,400

The MSSP suggests that "Generally, a reasonable spoilage factor should be allowed (a 10 percent spoilage factor was allowed in one audit)."

The MSSP shows the knowledge and effort placed in the audits conducted by the IRS. The above information may be too cumbersome for many business brokers and business appraisers, but it should provide some methods of calculating some rough figures.

Pricing Information
As a multiple of annual gross sales, 30 percent seems to be the consensus, according to the 2005 Edition of *Bizcomps Special Food Service Edition.* The multiplier of Seller's Discretionary Earnings is 1.6. The average down payment is 69.1%

Food Cost	28% to 30%
Payroll/Labor	25% to 30%
Occupancy	6% to 8%

Source: Industry Experts

Labor is an ever-increasing figure. Help is hard to get and, in the case of delivery, can be especially difficult. Occupancy costs for good locations are also expensive. *The 2005 Bizcomps Restaurant Edition* shows a 9.6 percent occupancy cost for pizza restaurants. A slow economy can lower both labor and occupancy costs. For more information on the *Bizcomps Restaurant Edition* go to www.bizcomps.com.

Plastics Processing—Fabricators, Converters, Molders

Rule of Thumb:

- 4 to 5 times EBIT (adjusted for non-recurring expenses)
- 65 to 70 percent of annual sales
- 2 times book value

Pricing Tips

"Goodwill often 75 percent of price"

"Is the management in place and will it stay? Will the seller protect the buyer from short- term (12 to 18 months) loss of key accounts, i.e., 80 percent of purchase at closing with balance at the end of 24 months, or some equitable basis? Is the company growing at a substantial rate?"

Expenses as a percentage of annual sales:

Cost of Goods Sold	65%
Payroll/Labor Costs	8%–10%
Profit (EBIT estimate)	12%

Seller Financing

- "Maximum 3 years"

Resources

Society of the Plastics Industry, Inc.
www.socplas.org

www.plasticsdatasource.org—This is also a site for the Society and has a lot of data and information on the industry.

THE INSTITUTE OF BUSINESS APPRAISERS
IBA
SINCE 1978

Franchise

Play It Again Sports

450 units

Approximate Total Investment: $186,800

Rule of Thumb:

- 45% of annual sales plus paid for inventory

Resources
www.playitagainsports.com

> **Rule of Thumb**
>
> Start with the so-called wealth effect. If people tend to spend more when their net worth increases, they'll spend less when it decreases. Economists use this rule of thumb: a $1 change in household wealth leads to a roughly 5-cent change in consumer spending. By that measure, a 10 percent decline in real estate prices would knock about half a percent off the gross domestic product

Plumbing and Heating Contractors *(See also HVAC)*

Pricing Tips
"Selling price should be fixtures and equipment, tools, plus the inventory at wholesale cost. If it is well established, you can add an additional 10 percent for goodwill. After a healthy draw for the owner, the business should show a net profit averaging from 14 to 17 percent. Some of these businesses have entered into contract agreements with various businesses to service their heating and air conditioning units. If this is true, you can add 25 percent of one year's net profit to them for these existing service-contract agreements."

Franchise

PODS (Portable On Demand Storage)

(See also Moving & Storage)

66 units	
Approximate Total Investment:	$2,000,000

General Information

"PODS revolutionized the moving and storage business industry by originating the concept of transporting mobile storage containers. The convenient, cost-effective service is unique in the patented hydraulic lift system available only with PODS, and which is designed to significantly reduce shift in contents and securely transport PODS brand containers to a dry and secure warehouse, or from state to state.

"Currently, the PODS network services 8,329 cities in 45 states. The company has serviced over 303,000 customers accommodating over 24,000 inter-franchise relocations. There are approximately 63,000 PODS brand containers in service."

Resources

www.podsusa.com

Podiatrists

21,167		

Rule of Thumb:

- 35 percent of annual sales
- 3 to 4 times SDE

Pricing Tips

"Inventory varies widely. Some podiatrists sell products and some don't. Product sales can be profitable, but surgical podiatry is usually the most profitable."

Benchmarks

"Variables include whether 'midlevels' like nurse practitioners or P.A.s are employed; orthotic sales or referral; surgical components."

Expenses as a percentage of annual sales:	
Cost of Goods Sold	5%–6%
Payroll/Labor Costs	21%–23%
Occupancy Cost	6%–7%
Profit (estimated)	40%–43%

General Information

"Many states prohibit owning podiatric practices without podiatry licenses."

Advantages of this Business

- "High entry barrier threshold requiring licensure"

Disadvantages of this Business

- Malpractice litigation exposure. Income is dependent on health insurances.

Industry Trend

"Good as baby boomers age. Loss of manufacturing industries to offshore businesses reduces the number of workers' compensation foot injuries, a large source of businesses."

Resources

American Podiatric Medical Association
www.apma.org

Pool Service (Swimming)

1,600	SIC: 7389-09	NAIC: 561790

Rule of Thumb:

- 10 to 12 times the "Monthly Service Only Gross Income"—swimming pool routes throughout the country sell for this multiple.

Note: The monthly service gross income is just that. It does not include income from maintenance or repair. "This is already considered in the multiple, because most pool service technicians agree that whatever your monthly service billing is, half of that again will translate into maintenance/repair income."

Source: Industry Expert

General Information

Questions to ask a seller: "How long have the pool service accounts been established? What is the average monthly service fee? How many times a week do they service the account? Do they charge extra for filter cleaning, conditioner and other treatments?"

"There are several income sources in owning and operating a pool service route.

"The two main sources of income are monthly service billing and maintenance/repair income. An average pool service technician can earn approximately $40.00 per hour servicing pools (this will vary depending on the area of the United States your pool route is located in) and approximately $100 to $150.00 per hour doing minor maintenance/repair on the pool equipment. This business is not difficult for the average person to learn. Most pool route sellers will train the new owner for a period of two to four weeks and provide a consulting period. The accounts are guaranteed to transfer to the new owner during a transition period. A letter notifying the customer of the new owner's billing information should be sent within 30 days of taking over the route. The attrition rate during a transition period should be less than two percent.

"If you are in the Northeast or the Northwest, your hourly fee for service will vary from the Sunbelt area. Most pool service professionals in the North will have an abbreviated swimming season. However, the opening and closing of the swimming pool supplement their service income. The opening and closing of a pool in the North can run into several hundred dollars. This will average out to be the same income as pool service technicians across the country during the year for the same number of hours worked. The Sunbelt area of the southern and western United States operate their routes all year and charge an average monthly service fee of $60 to $120.

"In the North, pool service technicians, with their abbreviated swim season, average the same income as Sunbelt service technicians; they just do it in a shorter period of time. This is because pools are shut down and closed for the winter months. However, they make it up by charging the accounts an opening and closing fee usually around $200.00 to open in the spring and another $200.00 to close the pool down in the fall.

"The average pool service technician, if running his route correctly, should be netting between $75,000.00 and $80,000.00 per year. If you have a monthly gross service billing income of $4,000.00 per month, that equates to $48,000.00 per year generated from weekly 'service only.' Your expenses should be approximately 2 months of your service income, or, in this example, $8,000.00. This will cover your three major expenses: gas, insurance and chemical replacement. Therefore, your service income totaling $48,000.00 for the year, less estimated expense of $8,000.00, should produce a net profit of $40,000.00, assuming you are operating in a diligent manner. In addition to this profit, you will have a second income on the same accounts for maintenance (filter cleanings, algae, conditioner treatments and other preventive maintenance) charges that you will bill your account extra for, plus repairs (motors, pumps, heaters, etc.) This second income should be fifty percent of your service net. If your net income from service is $40,000.00, then your net from maintenance and repairs should be $20,000.00. This is assuming that you are providing full service to your accounts.

"Operating a pool service route correctly is not difficult. Your overhead should be kept to a minimum. Operate your business from your home. Use a small truck, comparing your wholesale prices with different suppliers; charge the proper service rate for your area. Let your accounts know of the different services that you provide, alert them to the preventive maintenance services, and upgrade their equipment as necessary.

"As stated, there are two main sources of income, monthly service billing and maintenance/repair income. Throughout the United States, the purchase price of a pool service route is based on a multiple times the Monthly Service Billing Only income. The multiple will vary from state to state and even within some states. However, it is an industry standard to use a multiple times the Monthly Service Billing Only income. In other words, the maintenance/repair income should not be included to arrive at a fair purchase price. Any other method of appraising the value of a pool route would be contrary to the industry standards. The maintenance and repair income is already considered in the multiple, because most pool service technicians agree that whatever your monthly service billing is, half of that again will translate into maintenance/repair income.

"We have been selling businesses for over 28 years. Pool routes are our specialty. We can tell that the most important step in purchasing a pool route is in verifying the monthly service billing. Financial statements, profit and loss statements and balance sheets are usually not available, mainly because it is not necessary to keep an expensive bookkeeping system for one person operating out of their home. Therefore, there are not usually records available to satisfy a bank or financial institution to borrow the money to buy the route. Individual tax returns usually will not help either, because if you were buying 50 accounts of a route of 100, the tax returns would not be broken down that way. Also, if he is a pool builder or does a lot of business in major pool repairs or pool remodeling, again the tax returns would reflect all this income. What if he had 100 accounts and sold 50 accounts? His tax return would show an income for 100 accounts and you would have no way of knowing this. The next couple of paragraphs will discuss what we find to be the best way to verify the income of the accounts you are purchasing. Pool routes are sold for cash, and no terms are generally available. Therefore, you should have the funds available at the time of purchase, unless you are arranging for an equity loan, line of credit or other means to enable you to purchase a pool route.

"While most pool routes have the same expenses, they do not have the same income. Income is what you will be purchasing. One of the best ways to get a handle on the monthly service income, as well as what the owner is charging for repairs, is to look at his ledger cards. A ledger card is a monthly history for each account. A ledger card should show when an account was billed and when the account was paid. The payment history of the customer is one of the most important items to review during the purchase. Who wants an account that does not pay his or her bill. The ledger card also shows what the account was billed for repairs. This part of the ledger card will show if the owner is charging for the proper extras. In addition, the ledger card will show how long the account has been on service. While this is very important to some, the length of time on service is not as important as the payment history. If the average age of the accounts is over a year and they have a good payment history, that would be more of a good account.

"Another big question on the minds of most potential purchasers is the radius of the route and the quality of the neighborhoods. The overall radius of a pool route is not as important as the daily radius. Almost everyone has to drive to work or the office. Some people drive 30 minutes, some an hour, some much more. If you purchase a pool route that is within an overall radius of twenty miles but is under a five-mile daily radius, this would be considered a good route in the industry. Try to keep your pools clustered (tight) by service day. The neighborhood of your accounts is not as important as the way they pay their bills. There are several high-priced neighborhoods where collection is a problem. Most people in just average neighborhoods have a far better collection record than some so-called upper-class neighborhoods.

"How many pools can I service in a day? A good question, but difficult to answer. The average pool service technician will service approximately 16 full-service pools a day, while some can service 25 to 30 in a day. It depends on the individual and what type of pools he or she is servicing. The average pool service technician will service two pools an hour, including driving time. If the accounts are chemical only, he can do many more. If the accounts are commercial, he or she will do less.

"A full-service account is one in which the pool service technician takes complete care of the cleaning and chemical treatment of the pool. A chemical account is one which has only their water balanced by the pool service technician. This owner will clean his own pool. A chemical account can take as little as five minutes. A commercial account is a public pool: hotel/motel, park pool, apartment pool, homeowner association, etc. A commercial account can be very demanding, but they will pay double or even triple monthly service billing compared to residential. If something goes wrong, they want it fixed immediately. Repairs are great for your pocketbook. The more you fix, the more you make.

"After you purchase your pool route what then? Can you expand? The answer is yes. There are more accounts out there than you will ever want or need (depending on where you live). Thousands of pools are built each year, but there are already millions in the ground.

"If a seller is only concerned with the sale of their route, and how much money they receive from this sale, then that seller will not be concerned with the quality of service provided by the new owner. This is the type of seller you should try to avoid. If a seller's interest lies only in the money received from the sale, more than likely, he will not care about how well you are trained or if you succeed at all in your new business. While this is a simple business, you will need to be trained properly. Try to find a seller who is concerned with who purchases his route. This will go a long way in assuring that you will receive proper training. A seller who is concerned about his customers is a good seller. He should have some compassion for the way his customers are treated after the sale. Verification of the accounts is one reason not to purchase from a for sale by owner. A buyer should have a pool broker involved in the sale and purchase, for his protection. Pool route brokers have no interest in taking the accounts away from the seller or in causing the buyer any harm. Pool brokers will be able to take the list of customers being sold, and contact a percentage of the accounts to verify their authenticity. If you do purchase a route from a for sale by owner, you should complete this process prior to giving the seller ANY funds, or at least have them held by a third party. A seller may want you to give him half of the funds now, and half after the verification, or half after training. If the seller is dishonest, you could still lose half of your money. It is always better, for your protection, to have a pool route broker involved, as a third party, in the sale and purchase of a pool route. The purchase price will remain the same. There is no discount in the purchase price when you purchase a route directly from the owner. However, there is a discount in your protection.

"When purchasing pool accounts, be sure to obtain the following:

1. The seller should train the buyer for thirty (30) days. During the thirty (30) day training period, the buyer receives all of the income derived from the accounts for both monthly service billing and maintenance/ repairs.

2. The seller should train the buyer for the first two (2) weeks on service and preventive maintenance items, and the final two (2) weeks on repairs and any other questions the buyer may have that were not covered during the first two (2) weeks. Furthermore, the seller should be willing to provide consultation to the new owner during the transition period.

3. The seller should also guarantee the transfer of accounts. The guarantee period should run for ninety (90) days from the close of escrow. During this period, the seller should replace any account that did not transfer, due to any reason except negligence of the buyer, with an account of equal monthly service billing or refund to the buyer, the amount paid for the account that discontinued service. Some funds should be held in escrow for the ninety (90) day guarantee period to assure seller compliance, and also to assure that the buyer's training is properly completed.

4. The seller should also be willing to sign a Five (5) year Covenant Not to Compete on the accounts being transferred. Sometimes the seller is

only selling part of his route; this should not negatively affect your business, or your expansion plans, if the seller continues to service other pool customers. If the seller is remaining in the pool business, he is usually more available for advice and consultation.

5. The seller should provide the buyer, for his examination, the current billing history for each customer being purchased. The buyer should review this customer billing history prior to the opening of an escrow. It is important for the buyer to review this customer history, prior to the purchase, to determine the acceptability of the accounts. Billing history should disclose the following:

   - When the account was billed; when the account was paid; the monthly service charge; repair charges; sometimes, but not always, the start date for each customer. All information pertaining to the customers will remain in the possession of the seller or deposited into escrow, until after the close of escrow. After the close of escrow, the seller should deliver copies of all customer histories to the buyer.
   - Possession of the account histories will assist the buyer when a customer has a question on a repair that was done by the seller. Since most repairs have a one (1) year warranty, the seller will remain responsible for warranty work on all repairs done, prior to the close of escrow. Pool route brokers will receive a list of the accounts being purchased, prior to the close of escrow, for the purpose of transferring them to the buyer through escrow.

"Buyer should be counseled in the following items:

- Business license
  -Fictitious business name filing
  -Notification to accounts
- Establishing account with chemical and parts wholesaler
- Obtaining proper service equipment
  -Proper account billing procedure (account software)
  -Extra services information
- Proper charges for extra services
  -Establishing account with Employment Development Department (if applicable)
- Establishing account with State Board of Equalization
  -Account expansion

- When and how to raise customer rates
- Pool associations information
- Seminar and training information
  -Employee or independent contractor information (if applicable)
- Subscription to *Service Industry News*
- Liability insurance information (best sources)

"Throughout the United States the purchase price of a pool service route is based on a multiple times the Monthly Service Billing Only income. The multiple will vary from state to state and even within some states. However, it is an industry standard to use a multiple times Monthly Service Billing Only income."

Source: Pool Route Brokers

Industry Trend

"This business has been on a steady up since I have been selling them over 30 years."

Resources

www.poolroutebrokers.com—This is an Industry Expert's Web site and it is superb. If you need any information on swimming pool routes, it's on this site. You may have to do a little searching, but this site contains a lot of information. And the site contains industry links for additional information. If we were buying a pool route, we would call these people first as an industry consultant.

Portable Toilet Companies

3,574	SIC: 7359-22	NAIC: 326191

Rule of Thumb:

- $1,000 per unit
- 100 percent of annual revenues

General Information

"The portable sanitation industry has developed into a 1.5 billion-dollar-a-year business. Worldwide, there are an estimated 1,400,000 portable restrooms in use, serviced by a fleet of 9,400 trucks.

"A portable sanitation company may own from several hundred to several thousand portable toilet units, as well as service vehicles and related equipment required to provide the sanitation service. The toilet units are rented and serviced on scheduled service routes on a weekly, or more frequent, basis. On a construction site, each weekly serviced toilet unit can accommodate 10 workers (working a single 40-hour shift).

"The basic resources of a portable sanitation company are its toilet units, its service vehicles, its personnel (vehicle drivers, service technicians and salespeople) and a centrally located headquarters facility where surplus units may be stored and vehicles can be parked and maintained. Ideally, the headquarters facility should have a connection to a sanitary sewer system for the convenient disposal of effluent. Officially approved disposal sites that are conveniently located are important to the economic success of the business.

"The basic equipment needed includes portable toilet units and service trucks. The toilet unit is a small toilet room built over a watertight waste-holding tank. The service truck has a pump and a large tank that is divided into two compartments, one for fresh charge for use in cleaning the units, and the other for receiving and transporting the effluent for proper disposal.

"Portable toilet units on work sites normally are serviced on a weekly basis. The servicing is scheduled for the service driver, and his daily route schedule is arranged to minimize mileage between units. In a metropolitan area, a service person should be able to perform service on forty to fifty units per day."

Source: Portable Sanitation Association International www.psai.org

Resources
Portable Sanitation Association International
www.psai.org

Power/Pressure Washing

		NAIC: 333319

Rule of Thumb:

- 50 percent of annual revenues

Franchise

Precision Tune Auto Care

460 units	
Approximate Total Investment:	$123,000 to $208,075

Rule of Thumb:

- 36 percent of annual sales plus inventory

Resources
www.precisiontune.com

Print Shops/Commercial Printers

(See Print Shops/Quick Print)

47,930	SIC: 2752-02	NAIC: 323114

Rule of Thumb:

- 40 percent of annual sales plus inventory
- 2.5 to 3 times recast EBITDA if sales under $2 million
- 2.5 to 3.5 times recast EBITDA if sales $2 to $5 million.
- 3.5 times recast EBITDA if sales $5 to $25 million
- 1 to 1.5 SDE plus fair market value of assets (for smaller companies)
- 2.5 to 3 times SDE plus inventory

5 times EBITDA for Commercial Flexographic Printing

Pricing Tips

"There are two primary methods of valuing printing companies. A multiple of EBITDA and fair market value of assets plus1.5 x EBITDA. If everything is equal, these two methods should come relativly close. Multiples will range from 3 to 7 depending on sales, profitability and segment of the printing industry."

"Age of equipment is big issue and customer base"

"Should use adjusted EBITDA, with normalized owner compensation included, non-recurring add backs and a 5-year weighted average for cap x deducted from the total."

"The higher the gross sales and/or SDE, the higher the multiple. If sales are over $3 million or SDE over $500,000, look for a 3 multiple of SDE."

"Multiples depend on size, profitability, trend, customer base and percentage. Flexo companies can range from 3 to 6.5 EBITDA with higher multiple applied to larger companies with great potential, which are very profitable."

"Equipment value plays a big part in total valuation."

Profit and Loss Analysis

	All Firms	Single Firms	Franchise Firms	Independent Firms
Total Gross Sales	$1,010,864	$915,100	$996,320	$1,014,246
Cost of Sales	29.18%	29.40%	27.49%	29.57%
Payroll	32.55%	31.52%	30.67%	32.99%
Total Overhead	26.83%	27.08%	33.01%	23.35%
Total Costs	88.55%	88.01%	91.17%	87.91%
Net Owner's Compensation	11.45%	11.99%	8.83%	12.09%

Note: The above does not include firms with sales less than $150,000 or more than $5 million.

Source: Printimage International 2004 Operating Ratio Study, covering fiscal year 2003

Industry Experts' Ratings:

Amount of Competition (1 = Lot of: 4 = Not much) 1.2
Amount of Risk (1 = Very: 4 = Not much) 1.4
Historical Profit Trend (1 = Down: 4 = Up) 1.8
Location & Facilities (1 = Poor: 4 = Excellent) 2.2
Marketability (1 = Low: 4 = High) 2.0
Industry Trend (1 = Declining: 4 = Growing) 1.6
Ease of Replication (1 = Easy: 4 = Difficult) 1.6

-cont'd-

Industry Experts' Ratings: *(cont'd)*

"There is currently a dramatic shift in equipment and marketing trends in this industry."

"There is lots of competition and a lot of over-capacity. Risk is high unless you have experience and are in a niche area because of competition; profits for some segments are trending down and a few are up slightly; location has little bearing unless a retail shop; marketability is declining because the general buyer believes the Internet is putting printers out of business, but size will have a bearing. Printing revenues in general are up slightly year over year."

"Difficult to find good press operators. Newer digitial equipment is a good alternative for short run color."

"Printing is slow growth industry."

Benchmarks

"Payroll less than 30% of sales"

"Sales per employee should be in the $150,000 range."

"No customer big than 10%, and direct-to-plate image making"

"Profit (estimated) 0 to 17 percent depending on segment. Digital printing will be on high side, commercial printing will be much less."

Expenses as a percentage of annual sales:	
Cost of Goods Sold	35%
Payroll/Labor Costs	25%
Occupancy Cost	7%–8%
Profit (estimated)	6%–8%

General Information

Questions to ask a seller: "Why would a customer do business with you, other than quality, price and turnaround time?"

"Find a niche to operate from for higher profit margins."

"You can't compete on price; you must be a solutions provider."

"Look at cleanliness of shop and equipment. A messy shop with dirty presses indicates a lack of maintenance."

"Study the customer base and equipment."

"The printing industry (including commercial printing, newspaper and magazine printing, and book publishing) is the largest manufacturing industry in the U.S. in terms of number of establishments. With its 52,000 firms, this industry generates $142 billion in annual sales. These organizations employ more than 1 million workers, making printing the fourth largest U.S. industry in terms of employees.

"The commercial printing segment of the U.S. printing industry represents all printers that produce commercial products on a custom basis: everything from annual reports to business cards, stock certificates, voting ballots, menus, brochures, catalogs, and much more. This sector employs 567,200 workers and generated $89.7 billion in annual sales in the year 2000. It represents an exceptionally broad range of markets that span the entire economy. Virtually every commercial activity in the U.S. depends on the printing industry. Printed materials are used by virtually every sector of the economy, from the smallest household to the largest corporation.

"Overall, commercial printing is the fourth largest manufacturing employer in the U.S., providing jobs for nearly 570,000 workers in 2000. In fact, industry employment has increased by 4.3 percent in the last 10 years (1991–2000). During the same period, total manufacturing employment increased by 0.2 percent."

Source: National Association for Printing Leadership (NAPL)

In a survey conducted by the National Association for Printing Leadership (NAPL), the annual sales breakdown for 2002 was:

Annual Sales	% of Firms
$1M or Less	13.5%
$1M+ to $3M	17.3%
$3M+ to $5M	13.9%
$5M+ to $10M	22.6%
$10M+ to $20M	13.5%
$20M+ to $40M	13.5%
Over $40M	5.8%
Minimum Sales	$120,000
Maximum Sales	$220,000,000
Average Sales	$13,058,801

"The printing industry is facing considerable challenges because of the economy, changes in how customers use print, and technology. Printers, especially commercial printers, must separate themselves from the rest. This can be a specialty, with other services, etc.; otherwise they are competing with many other printers on price."

"Consolidation. Most transactions are survival motivated, with the transaction being rapidly followed by a culling of equipment, employees, and customers; with the end result being that after an acquisition, the resulting business may be no bigger than before, but it will be more viable. Overall, the volume and complexity of business is increasing, but changes in technology and productivity are such that it can produce with far fewer people, facilities, equipment, etc. Consequently, although gross volumes are increasing, the industry trend is shrinkage. Many businesses will simply cease to exist."

Advantages of this Business

- "Great family business; can be fun and creative for the owners; we will always need printing, but you need to find the right company in the right segment."
- "A well run company can have EBITDA margins of 15%–20%."
- "Tangible product that people understand"
- "Huge number of prospects—every business needs printing. There is a fallout for the technology laggards."

- "Equipment value provides a bottom."
- "Flexo printing—growing, and much less capital expenditures than commercial printing."

Disadvantages of this Business

- "Competition, competitors competing on price"
- "Highly competetive. Customers look at printing as a commodity, not as customized manufacturing."
- "Equipment costs are hard to control."
- "Growth is difficult."
- "Competition, being in the wrong segment"
- "Heavy capital expenditures and industry fluctuations"
- "High cost of making technology purchase mistakes; it can be fatal."

Trend

"The overall U.S. market for business printing—including commercial offset printing—is projected to grow 1.5% annually until 2007."

Source: InfoTrends/Cap Ventures. From: *The Boston Sunday Globe*, June 20, 2004

"Printing establishments will continue to decline. We lost 4,500 in the past 4 years."

"The well-run shops with state-of-the-art equipment will do well."

"Facing pressure from Asia"

Seller Financing

- " 5 years"

Resources

National Association for Printing Leadership
www.napl.org

PrintImage
www.printimage.org
Site offers studies and operating ratios for a fee. Much of it used to be free; now available only to members or non-members for a very high fee.

An IRS Audit Technique Guide (Market Segment Specialization Program—MSSAP) on Commercial Printing is a good resource. They are an excellent source of information and are available at www.bookstore.gpo.gov (search under IRS—IRS Audit Technique Guides).

Parker-Nelson publishes a valuation software program especially for the printing industry called *Valuware.* www.bizbooksoftware.com

"Valuing Printing Businesses," *Handbook of Business Valuation*, West & Jones, 2nd Edition, published by John Wiley & Sons

American Printer
www.americanprinter.com

www.piworld.com—*Printing Impressions*, an online publication

Graphic Arts Information Network, www.gain.net

2003 U.S. Market Segment Breakout

Commercial Printing	# of Establishments
General Commercial Printing*	20,205
Quick Printing*	6,710
Magazine Printing	254
Newspaper Printing	5,042
Book Printing	343
Financial, Legal Printing	172
Screen Printing	1,174
Thermography	256

*The small commercial (<10 employees) and quick printing market totals:

Total	18,265

Source: 2004 Print Market Atlas. www.gain.net

Print Shops/Quick Print *(See Print Shops/Commercial Printers)*

Rule of Thumb:

- 40 percent of annual sales plus iventory
- 4 times EBIT
- 3 to 4 times EBITDA
- 2.7 times SDE plus iventory

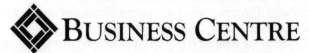

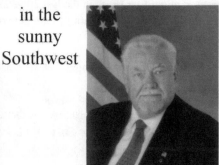

Pricing Tips

"There are two primary ways to value printing companies. One is a multiple of adjusted EBITDA, and the other is fair market value of assets plus one year's EBITDA."

"These businesses have high fixed costs and very low marginal costs of production. Incremental sales beyond breakeven have a big effect on profitability and value. Industry norms of sales per employee have increased about four times in the last 20 years, but profit percentages have trended down. Industry earnings are generally declining."

Industry Experts' Ratings:

Marketability (1 = Low: 4 = High)	1.8
Industry Trend (1 = Declining: 4 = Growing)	2.3
Ease of Replication (1 = Easy: 4 = Difficult)	2.3

Benchmarks

"The dollar amount of sales per employee, on average, is $140,000."

"Sales per employee are more a measure of automation and type of work than a meaningful value. Net profit after allowance for equipment is the main factor."

Expenses as a percentage of annual sales:

Cost of Goods Sold	20%
Payroll/Labor Costs	40%
Occupancy Cost	20%
Profit (estimated)	20%

Advantages of this Business

- "Most of these businesses provide a job for the owner and/or family members. These businesses exist everywhere, and usually promote a fair income and active community involvement."
- "If offering the right services in a good location, it can be profitable."

Disadvantages of this Business

- "Competition, changing market, changing technology."

- "High capital investment, high risk of loss due to technology change, high fixed costs."

General Information

Print Shops/Quick Print

	All Firms	Franchise Firms	Independent Firms
Total Gross Sales	$953,164	$979,929	$949,762
Total Cost of sales	$288,177	$285,100	$291,157
Payroll	$299,655	$306,332	$299,606
Total Overhead	$257,967	$301,450	$245,764
Total Costs	$845,799	$892,881	$836,527
Net Owner's Compensation	$107,366	$87,048	$113,234

Source: Printimage International 2002 Operating Ratio Study
(The latest we could locate.)

Resources

(See Print Shops above)

PrintImage
www.printimage.org

Trade Publications

(See Print Shops above)

Franchise

Print Shops — Quick Print *(See Print Shops/Quick Print above)*

Rule of Thumb;

- Pricing Rules of Thumb would be the same as the Quick Print listed above, with perhaps the franchise fee added to the price calculated. Here are a few examples:

Franchise

Allegra Printing

450 units

Approximate Total Investment: Starting under $200,000

Rule of Thumb:

- 70 percent of annual sales plus inventory

Note: Allegra Network includes Allegra Print and Imaging, but also American Speedy Printing Centers, Instant Copy, Insty Prints, Quik Print, Speedy Printing Centers (Canada) and Zippy Print (Canada).

Franchise

Franklin's Printing

50+ units

Approximate Total Investment: $305,000 to $395,000

Rule of Thumb:

- 52 percent of annual sales plus inventory

Franchise

Kwik Kopy Business Center

17 units

Approximate Total Investment: $216,735 to $320,600

Franchise

Sir Speedy Printing

500 units

Approximate Total Investment: $200,000 to $225,000

Rule of Thumb:

- 25 percent of annual sales plus inventory

Note: One Sir Speedy sale was reported at 70 percent of sales.

Franchise Company

	# of Units	Investment
AlphaGraphics Inc.	281	$350,000 to $550,000
Minuteman Press	900	$100,000 to $150,000
PIP Printing	290	$250,000 to $350,000

"The U.S. market for quick print copying and digital printing was nearly $12 billion in 2003, with more than 22,000 retail locations.

Independent copy centers .... $6.6 billion
Franchises and chains, such as Kinko's .... $3.6 billion
Office superstores, mail service chains .... $1.7 billion"

Source: Source: InfoTrends/Cap Ventures.
From: *The Boston Sunday Globe*, June 20, 2004

Quick *Profile* Print Shops/Quick Print

The quick print business provides printing and copying services for businesses, associations and other groups. These businesses specialize in smaller quantities with a fast turnaround. They can generally provide two-color work, desktop publishing, collating and bindery services for their customers. Big jobs, multi-color work and complicated binding are done by the large commercial printers. However, new technology is allowing the quick print industry to compete with the smaller commercial printers. In some cases, it is hard to distinguish between what used to be termed a quick print and a small commercial printer. Quick printers are becoming more and more sophisticated. One primary difference is that quick printers still tend to be located in retail-type space, while the commercial printer is located in a more industrialized location with cheaper rent and more space. Quick printers will be limited in the services they provide by their very locations. Several of the franchised quick printers advertise themselves as full-service printers. Generally, however, the quick print

"The traditional quick printing business is largely gone; all are now mainly copy shops or have become more capable commercial printers."

Source: Industry Expert

industry cannot compete in price for larger, more complicated jobs.

Equipment Necessary

Most quick print businesses will have several high-speed copiers, a color copier, and some will have copiers for oversized work such as engineering and architectural blueprints. The copy equipment of yesterday is now really a high-speed duplicator. They will also have at least a two-color press. Almost all quick printers have folding equipment, binders for booklets—staples, plastic or metal spirals. They will also have collators, cutters and drillers. Desktop publishing is a rapidly growing—and changing— part of the quick print industry. New technology will continue to allow the quick print business to offer more services.

The cash investment necessary to start a quick print business is approximately $100,000 to $150,000, or even more depending on the equipment and technology desired. Most major franchises quote a start-up cost of well over $150,000—with $250,000 and up not unusual. The copying and duplicating equipment is often leased, along with a maintenance agreement. This can substantially reduce the initial investment.

Note: For total investment required for several of the larger franchise quick print companies, see Quick Print/Franchises above.

Pluses of this Business

It is an ideal business for the first-time buyer who is not overwhelmed by the mechanical equipment of the business. He or she should be able to provide the sales and marketing skills necessary to build this type of business. They should also be able to stay abreast of the technical knowledge of this rapidly changing industry. A plus of this business is the fact that it is changing. For example, more and more small businesses, and other organizations, find it more economical to have the short runs necessary to incorporate changes. Long runs are cheaper, but because the printed word is constantly changing, no one wants to be stuck with outdated material.

A quick print business also allows an owner to build a company. It is not just a job, but an opportunity to own a growing firm. It is an ideal business for husband and wife. One can handle the outside work and the other can run the inside.

Minuses of this Business

Some of the pluses can also be the minuses. It is a rapidly changing business and the owner must keep apprised of these changes. The growing technology, and its cost, can also be a minus. It is a very competitive business. The owner of a quick print business must be a good manager. The business usually has a printer, a counter-person, someone who does desktop publishing, a person who can do layout, and others who may do copying, accounting, etc. The quick print business is not a one-person operation.

What to Look For?
Some of the things to look for in a quick print business are: the cost of sales, how much of the work is brokered (that is, work sent out like wedding invitations, etc.), how much business is walk-in, and what the margins are for the different kinds of work performed, for example, printing versus copying.

Produce Markets

8,830	SIC: 5431-01	NAIC: 422480

Rule of Thumb:

- 3 times monthly sales plus inventory

General Information
"Retail Fresh Produce Industry sales—Retail fresh produce industry sales surpassed $50 billion in the United States in 2003. Last updated February 2005.

"Fresh-Cut Produce Industry—With 18% sales growth in 2004, fresh-cut produce approaches $12 billion."

Resources
Produce Marketing Association
www.pma.com

Propane Companies *(See Liquefied Petroleum Gas and Heating Oil Dealers)*

Property Management Companies (Non-residential)

35,000	SIC: 6531-08	Non-residential real estate NAIC: 531312 Residential real estate NAIC: 531311

Rule of Thumb:

- 100 percent of annual revenues
- 6 to 7 months revenues for firms selling under $500K
- 10 to 12 months revenues for firms above $500K
- 2.5 to 5 times SDE based on a cash sale
- 3.5 to 6 times SDE with sales involving notes and/or contingencies

Pricing Tips

"Key item is the longevity of accounts (i.e., any property managed for more than 3 years is good). Also, the transition period should have the owner (seller) remain visible for 2 to 3 months."

Industry Experts' Ratings:

Marketability (1 = Low: 4 = High) 3.6
Industry Trend (1 = Declining: 4 = Growing) 1.2
Ease of Replication (1 = Easy: 4 = Difficult) 2.4

Benchmarks

"Most property management firms earned 10 to 30 percent of their revenue from non-management activities; e.g., lease fees, maintenance contracts."

Expenses as a percentage of annual sales:

Cost of Goods .... n/a
Payroll/Labor Costs 40%–50%
Occupancy Cost 7%–10%
Profit* (estimated) 15%–20%

*(well-run company with other services such as leasing fees)

General Information

"...Analyzing key factors...most important ones are: Property portfolio—type(s) of properties, number and size, and quantity of buildings. Ownership—type(s) of owners, duration and transferability of contracts. Property location—desirability of area, concentration of accounts, and area economic strength. Assets—tangible (furniture/equipment), intangible (goodwill)."

Advantages of this Business

- "Offers a more steady and stable revenue flow in contrast to real estate sales/brokerage/leasing"

Disadvantages of this Business

- "Fairly competitive, and can be a 'loss leader' for major full-service real estate firms that will 'buy' property management businesses in order to get the more lucrative sales/leasing."

Seller Financing

- "Seller financing is less common for property management companies larger than $500,000 gross income, but for smaller companies would be 3 to 5 years."
- "4 years. Note typically has fixed amortized payment, but may be contingent upon payments based on retention of accounts."

Resources

Institute of Real Estate Management
www.irem.org

National Property Management Association
www.npma.org—an informative site

Property Management Association
www.pma-dc.org

Publishers—Books *(See Publishers in General)*

5,534	SIC: 2731-01	NAIC: 511130

Rule of Thumb:

- 80 percent of annual sales plus inventory
- 4 to 6 times EBIT
- 4 to 6 times EBITDA

Pricing Tips

"Professional publishing is valued higher than educational publishing, and both are valued higher than consumer publishing. Proprietary and niche-specific publishing is most attractive."

Benchmarks

"Sales per employee should be $200,000 or over. Returns should be below 15 percent. Mostly valued on cash flow, the balance sheet is rarely considered unless the company is losing money. Company needs to have clear rights to their intellectual property."

General Information

"In book publishing, COGS (cost of goods sold) of under 50 percent and operating income above 10 percent are two optimal benchmarks. In trade publishing (i.e., titles sold through the book trade or consumer book stores), 'returns' (of unsold books by booksellers back to publishers) under 20 percent is considered very laudable. Lastly, strategic buyers in the professional book publishing market have reportedly paid 2–3 times revenues for new acquisitions (properties)! That said, we must add that 'revenue multiples' are very unreliable statistics and should not be used to determine real value."

Source: Association of American Publishers

Advantages of this Business

- "Low operating cost. High potential return to owner. Interesting and clean business."

Disadvantages of this Business

- "Not everybody can run a publishing company. Capital intensive. Can be volatile. Distribution relationships are key to success."

Trend

"The publishing industry continues to put out more books than the public is prepared to buy, according to a report issued Monday by the Book Industry Study Group.

"The number of books sold dropped by nearly 44 million between 2003 and 2004, even as the annual number of books published approaches 175,000.

"The Book Industry Study Group, a nonprofit research organization, reported estimated sales of 2.295 billion books in 2004, compared to an estimated 2.339 billion the previous year. Higher prices enabled net rev-

Small-time publishers add up to big business

"Boys Town Press, an 11-year-old company that publishes parenting and educational materials, generated sales of $1.7 million last year, a fraction of what Random House, Scholastic and other billion-dollar companies bring in.

"Boys Town may appear to be an industry exception, but a new study says it's more the rule. In a report issued Wednesday, the Book Industry Study Group says there are thousands of such publishers, earning between $1 million and $50 million on their own, but adding up to an estimated $11 billion market.

"For several years, we knew there was a segment of book industry activity that was not being covered by traditional research," said Jeff Abraham, executive director of the study group, a non-profit research and policy organization funded by publishers, booksellers and others in the industry."

Source: The Associated Press, April 6, 2005. From www.msnbc.com

enues to increase 2.8 percent, to $28.6 billion, but also drove many readers, especially students, to buy used books, Greco said.

"The BISG anticipates a better year in 2005, thanks to the new Harry Potter book, *Harry Potter and the Half-Blood Prince,* and to a surge in high school and elementary textbook sales, with many states due to order new editions.

"After 2005, the BISG expects a flat market for the following four years. Religious titles are an exception, with both dollar sales and the number of actual books sold expected to average more than 6 percent annual growth into 2009.

"'The key isn't so much Bibles and prayer books, it's what we call *other* religious books,' says Greco, citing such multimillion sellers as Rick Warren's *The Purpose Driven Life* and the *Left Behind* novels of Tim LaHaye and Jerry B. Jenkins.

"An especially troubled area, Greco says, is college textbooks. While no hard statistics have been compiled, many believe that students are increasingly turned off by prices for new books and instead are buying used editions. The BISG anticipates a steady drop in sales for new works, from 68 million in 2004 to 64.4 million in 2009."

Source: "Publishers Putting Out Too Many Books,"Associated Press, May 16, 2005, From *Forbes*

Resources
Publishers Marketing Association
www.pma-online.org

American Booksellers Association
www.bookweb.org

Association of American Publishers
www.publishers.org

Publishers—Internet (and Broadcasting)

Rule of Thumb:

- 100 percent of annual revenue
- 2 to 6 times SDE
- 8 times EBITDA

Pricing Tips
"Larger companies and those with high renewal rates for subscription-based services command a premium. Also companies with long-term agreements and/or verifiable recurring revenue streams should be valued on the high end of the multiple."

Industry Experts' Ratings:

Marketability (1 = Low: 4 = High) 2.6
Industry Trend (1 = Declining: 4 = Growing) 2.8
Ease of Replication (1 = Easy: 4 = Difficult) 2.0

"The ease of replication depends on the content being published. The more unique, the more valuable, the more timely—the better."

Benchmarks
"For every dollar in employee expense, a successful Internet publishing company should generate at least two dollars in sales."

Expenses as a percentage of annual sales:	
Cost of Goods Sold	25%
Payroll/Labor Costs	40%
Occupancy Cost	10%
Profit (estimated)	25%

Advantages of this Business

- "No incremental cost of distribution once you cover the cost of production. Also, the business is populated by interesting people who are making a contribution to society overall."

Disadvantages of this Business

- "Business depends on creative types. These can be expensive, high-maintenance employees. Also, many people that think information should be free … especially when it is available on the Internet."

Publishers—Magazines *(See Publishers in General)*

5,111	SIC: 2721-02	NAIC: 511120

Rule of Thumb:

- 5 times EBITDA
- 2 times annual net sales

Pricing Tips

"Magazines generally fall into two categories, trade and consumer. Both are valued by a multiple of EBITDA generally ranging from 3 to 10 depending on size, industry trend and profitability. Trade magazines are suffering because people no longer want to wait a month to get their news. In some cases, consumer magazines are suffering as well, but not nearly as much."

"84% of adults 18+ read magazines."

Source: The Magazine Handbook, www.magazine.org

"Circulation questions are key, including various details of subscriptions and newsstand. Advertisers—number, new advertisers. Share of market in the specific specialty area such as log-home magazines, fishing — # of pages and revenue dollars."

"Prices have been hurt due to low advertising and magazines not embracing an Internet strategy."

"In magazine publishing, operating profits or EBITDA (earnings before interest, taxes, depreciation and amortization) of 15 to 20 percent are desired and frequently exceeded, while paid subscription renewals above 50 percent and newsstand 'sell-through' above 35 percent will support a higher selling price."

Industry Experts' Ratings:

Marketability (1 = Low: 4 = High) 2.4
Industry Trend (1 = Declining: 4 = Growing) 2.0
Ease of Replication (1 = Easy: 4 = Difficult) 1.0

"There is competition in almost every segment and category. Risk is on the high side because it takes deep pockets to stay in until profitability. Recent trend in profitability has been down because advertising is down. There is good demand for magazines; however profitability will be a key factor. It is easy to get into the industry; you don't need much in the way of equipment, since it is generally printed by a third party."

General Information

"Gruner & Jahr, a division of the German media giant Bertelsmann, reached an agreement last night to sell its two American business magazines, *Inc.* and *Fast Company*, for about $35 million, a fraction of what it paid for the publications, according to someone close to the deal.

"Gruner & Jahr bought both magazines five years ago for $550 million—*Inc.* from Bernard Goldhirsch for $200 million and *Fast Company* from Mortimer Zuckerman for $350 million.

"The deal follows last month's sale of Gruner & Jahr's women's magazines—*Family Circle, Parents, Child and Fitness*—to the Meredith Corporation for $350 million. With the sales, the company, troubled by a two-year-old circulation scandal, is effectively rid of its American magazines."

Source: *The New York Times*, Tuesday, June 21, 2005

"When the Meredith Corporation announced its purchase of Gruner & Jahr's women's magazines last Tuesday, Meredith said that Gruner's business magazines, *Fast Company* and *Inc.* were not 'material' to the sale. What that means is that two magazines that sold for more than a half a billion dollars four years ago now have a value of zero."

Source: *The New York Times*, May 30, 2005

"Last year, according to Media Industry Newsletter, the big three in business sold just over 10,000 advertising pages, a shadow of the 18,300 they sold in 2000. That drop is almost axiomatic, but they have yet to crawl back to their 1995 level of more than 11,500 pages sold. Collectively, the three are reporting almost half a billion dollars less in revenues in 2004 than they did in 2000. Those ad revenue numbers are notoriously inexact, but still represent a breathtaking hemorrhage."

Source: *The New York Times*, May 30, 2005

Advantages of this Business

- "Can be very profitable, low barrier to entry"

Disadvantages of this Business

- "Competition, competition for advertising"

Resources

The Magazine Publishers of America
www.magazine.org

Publishers—Newsletters

		NAIC: 511120

Rule of Thumb:

- 1 to 2 times revenues

Pricing Tips

"High renewal rate (70 percent plus) increases value"

Publishers—Newspapers (Dailies)

(See Publishing in General)

Rule of Thumb:

- 1 to 2.5 times revenues (only very large will get 2.5)
- 5 times EBITDA
- 5 times EBIT
- 3 times SDE

Pricing Tips

"5x EBITDA is a current average for newspaper properties with a history of stable earnings. Number may be considerably higher if publication is positioned for sale to a strategic buyer."

"Prices for dailies have been strong, trading at 10 to 14 times EBITDA (earnings before interest, taxes, depreciation and amortization), the same range they enjoyed during the go-go years.

"The year's largest deal was the purchase by Journal Register Co. in Trenton, NJ., of 21st Century Newspapers Inc. in Pontiac, MI, for $415 million in cash—11.5 times EBITDA. This summer, Cribb & Associates in Bozeman, MT, negotiated a private daily newspaper transaction that closed at 18 times EBITDA.

"'The current level of multiples,' says John T. Cribb, principal broker at the firm, 'is as good as it gets.'"

Source: "Business Matters" by Ann Lallande, *Presstime*, February 2005

"... eight out of 10 adults in the top 50 markets, 77.3%, read the newspaper over the course of a week, compared to 78.6% in spring 2004."

Source: Newspaper Association of America, www.naa.org

"Key factors include: size of market, years in business, is the newspaper geographically desirable by contiguous publishers or buyers looking to roll-up smaller publications into larger groups and take advantage of economies of scale? How active and dominant is the publication in its market and how dominant are its online activities?

"Six to 12 times depending on size, profitability, circulation and advertising trend. Some smaller weekly papers will have lower multiples in the 3 to 5 EBITDA area. Current trends in revenue and profitability will have an impact on multiple. Recent large daily newspaper transactions have gone at 11 plus times EBITDA."

Industry Experts' Ratings:

Amount of Competition (1 = Lot of: 4 = Not much) 2.0
Amount of Risk (1 = Very: 4 = Not much) 2.8
Historical Profit Trend (1 = Down: 4 = Up) 3.2
Location & Facilities (1 = Poor: 4 = Excellent) 2.8
Marketability (1 = Low: 4 = High) 3.0
Industry Trend (1 = Declining: 4 = Growing) 1.8
Ease of Replication (1 = Easy: 4 = Difficult) 3.2

"Established newspapers with 10+ year track record tend to be extremely stable and low risk. Competition from Internet has not had a material impact on revenues or valuations...at least not yet."

"Subscriber acquisition and gaining solid market position takes many, many years for paid circulation newspapers, therefore time is the greatest barrier to entry."

"There is very little competition in newspapers. The days of cities having two newspapers is long gone, with only a handful of exceptions. Newspapers are still getting high multiples. In recent years, the trend has been for newspaper circulation to decline. For most of the last 30 years, average daily circulation was 62 million; two years ago that slipped to 60 million."

Benchmarks

"Benchmarks vary greatly by type of publication. For instance, sellers of daily paid circulation newspapers may find that valuations based on subscriber base may be most advantageous. Publishers of free distribution publications are often tied to multiple of discretionary cash flow."

"Generally multiple of EBITDA. Another is $50 to $400 per paid subscriber."

"Sales per subscriber, number of subscribers, revenue per household reached (if free distribution publication)"

"Ratios, benchmarks, etc. vary according to the type of publication and geographic area. Daily newspapers, weekly newspapers, free circulation newspapers, coupon book, local magazines, niche magazines, etc."

Expenses as a percentage of annual sales:	
Cost of Goods Sold	65%
Payroll/Labor Costs	25%
Occupancy Cost	05%
Profit (estimated)	30%

General Information

Number of Daily Newspapers

	Morning	Evening	Total
1940	380	1,498	1,878
1950	322	1,450	1,772
1960	312	1,459	1,763
1970	334	1,429	1,748
1980	387	1,388	1,745
1990	559	1,084	1,611
2000	766	727	1,480
2001	776	704	1,468
2002	777	692	1,457
2003	787	680	1,456
2004	814	653	1,457

Source: Newspaper Association of America, www.naa.org

Advantages of this Business

- "Stability, very good margins—(typically over 30% for paid circulation papers and 15% to 30% for free circulation publications). Print media properties historically sell for high multiples to strategic buyers and attract, on a cyclical basis, financial buyers and private equity group dollars."
- "Owning a small newspaper can be a lifestyle change. Editors and writers have long desired to own their own newspapers. Can be a relatively low barrier to entry."
- "Stability. Influence in communities that they serve. Predictable cash flow."

Disadvantages of this Business

- "Losing some of its 'sizzle.' Tends to be slow to develop new products and services."
- "High cost of capital equipment, highly competitive in major markets, slow but steady growth (not easy to catapult earnings)."
- "With the diversions, newspaper circulation is declining. Advertising is more fragmented where at one time newspapers were the main advertising venue for cities and towns. As advertising and circulation trend down, so will the price of the newspaper. In order to grow, they will have to adapt to the new electronic age."

Industry Trend

"Continued stability. Continued and increasing investment in online divisions. Continued consolidation and 'trading' of publications to create regional powerhouses."

"Since 2002, when new guidelines changed how newspapers could count their paid circulation, an increasing number of newspapers have bolstered their circulation by counting copies delivered for free but paid for by a third party, like an advertiser."

Source: *The New York Times*, Monday, January 10, 2005

Seller Financing

- "5 years"

Resources

National Newspaper Publishers Association
www.nnpa.org

Cribb & Associates, www.cribb.com—an excellent site full of good information. Cribb & Associates is a newspaper appraisal firm and also a newspaper brokerage firm.

Editor & Publisher
www.editorandpublisher.com

Presstime
www.naa.org/presstime

Publishers—Newspapers (Weeklies/Community papers) *(See Publishing in General)*

Rule of Thumb:

- "Average gross of past three years or 6 times cash flow EBITDA"
- "Some smaller weekly papers will have lower multiples in the 3 to 5 EBITDA area."
- "Community monthlies will sell for 3 x SDE if they produce at least $150,000 in SDE. Otherwise, multiple comes down to the 2 x SDE area."
- "6 to 10 times EBITDA"
- 1 times annual income for mid-sized weekly newspaper
- 3 to 4 times SDE

Pricing Tips

"There is a lot of buyer interest in this business. Small papers with revenues below $100,000 are difficult to sell and will go for about 2 x SDE. Once SDE gets into the $150K plus range, then the SDEs go to 3 x especially in higher end communities."

"Interest in weekly newspapers continues to grow, pushing up multiples in this market, too. In 1993, weekly newspapers sold for six times EBITDA, Cribb recalls. 'Now, they're trading at ten times EBITDA.'"

"Two recent weekly newspaper transactions commanded prices that exceeded EBITDA by a factor of 12. In growth markets, both rural and suburban properties trade at the higher multiples.

"The strength in weekly newspapers is a trend, not a fluke, Cribb insists. According to *Editor & Publisher*, between 1996 and 2003, circulation at daily newspapers declined 3.2 percent while circulation for all weeklies grew 9.4 percent. Free weeklies enjoyed even larger gains, exceeding 17 percent over the same period. The trend is forcing publishers to look for readership wherever it exists, Cribb says."

Source: "Business Matters" by Ann Lallande, *Presstime*, February 2005

"Weekly—priced at 1 to 1 ½ times annual, or 2 to 3.5 times recasted cash flow"

"Strategic buyers are key. Seek help or broker experienced in, and with contacts in, newspaper field. Consolidation of neighboring publications adds to value."

"Press not necessarily included in above rules of thumb. Competition a major factor in buyer interest."

Industry Experts' Ratings:

Amount of Competition (1 = Lot of: 4 = Not much)	1.0
Amount of Risk (1 = Very: 4 = Not much)	2.8
Historical Profit Trend (1 = Down: 4 = Up)	3.2
Location & Facilities (1 = Poor: 4 = Excellent)	1.2
Marketability (1 = Low: 4 = High)	3.6
Industry Trend (1 = Declining: 4 = Growing)	3.2
Ease of Replication (1 = Easy: 4 = Difficult)	2.0

"There is a lot of competition for local advertising dollars. Specialty and community based publications provide for a good value to local advertisers vs. the local section of the daily paper. Papers mailed into homes produce better results (i.e., more repeat advertisers) than rack-distributed publications (a lot are thrown out.)."

Benchmarks

"Look for businesses where the owner does very little selling. You have to make a negative adjustment to SDE to account for sales commissions to replace an overactive seller."

Expenses as a percentage of annual sales:

Cost of Goods Sold	10%
Payroll/Labor Costs	40%
Occupancy Cost	05%
Profit (estimated)	40%

General Information

"Bigger, good quality, weekly and twice-weekly newspapers, small dailies, and large dailies are actively sought.

"Everyone wants to buy the dailies. They are selling for high multiples of cash flow. The bigger ones are going for 12 to 15 times cash flow, and that can be over four times revenues.

"Smaller dailies, under 10,000 circulation, are only getting half that. For big weeklies— those selling for $1 million and up—there is a lot of interest. They are selling at their highest prices in history. 6 to 10 times cash flow and 1.25 to 2.5 times publishing revenues have been seen. For a couple of recent sales… three times publishing revenues.

"Intermediate weeklies, ones going for between $400,000 and $1 million, are selling well, but are not as actively sought as the ones at more than $1 million.

"Small weeklies—$400,000 and down—are in a totally different market. The buyers in this market have evaporated.

"For about three years now…we've been riding right on the crest of values. They are not going up anymore, and there's evidence that they might be easing back a bit."

Source: John Cribb, Cribb & Associates

Advantages of this Business

- "No inventory, very few hard assets, mostly commission-based payroll, scalable, could be home based.."

Disadvantages of this Business

- "It's a selling business; not everyone is comfortable asking for money. It's competitive."

Industry Trend

"Community papers are following the rise in the housing market. New communities are receptive to local papers that educate them as to local restaurants, salons, etc. This trend will continue."

Resources

National Newspaper Publishers Association (NNPA)
www.nnpa.org

Cribb & Associates, www.cribb.com—an excellent site full of good information. Cribb & Associates is a newspaper appraisal firm and also a newspaper brokerage firm.

Publishers—Newspapers (Shoppers) *(See Publishing in General)*

General Information

"What is a shopper? The broad definition of a shopper is a free circulation publication, published on a regular basis, with primarily advertising content. The typical shopper is distributed free to households by mail or carrier, is weekly, and has display advertising, classified (private party) advertising, and some non-advertising content which can be news features, TV listings or other material.

"The shopper business started as long as 60 to 75 years ago, but the shopper in most markets is just fifteen to twenty years old. The entrepreneurs who started these papers are just now thinking about bringing in younger management and/or selling out. The industry is changing, and has attracted the interest of big media groups who recognize that shoppers are a solid and profitable business. It is interesting that some of the most active buyers of existing shoppers and backers of new start-ups are daily newspaper companies."

Source: Cribb & Associates, www.cribb.com

Publishing (In General)

Rule of Thumb:

- 3.5 times SDE
- 5 to 6 times EBITD
- 5 times EBIT
- 100 percent of annual revenues

Pricing Tips

"Business are essentially goodwill, with little consideration of fixed assets. Strategic and financial buyers (PEGs) figure predominantly in valuation with considerably higher valuations, some as high as 8 to 10 times EBITDA, possble for a publisher of strategic interest. Size is also a critical factor in valuation, as most strategic buyers will not be attracted to publishing business with gross revenue less than $3 to $4 million annually."

"Respondents to an industry-wide survey conducted by Ad Media Partners Inc. reported a Median Multiple @ 7x to11x for business-to-business publications (similar to the 8x to 11x from 1999) and compared to 8x to12x for consumer magazines and 12x to14x for daily newspapers. A second report, from JEGI, is based upon ten recent (1999) publishing transactions, which also included some trade show activity in addition to business publications. Recorded as 'trailing twelve month multiples' (TTM), these deals are reported at the mean and median as follows: revenue (EV) multiples, 3.5x and 2.9x; EBITDA multiples, 12.2x and 10.3x. The sizes of these ten transactions were at the mean, $73.2 million and at the median, $48.0 million...."

Industry Experts' Ratings:

Amount of Competition (1 = Lot of: 4 = Not much) 1.0
Amount of Risk (1 = Very: 4 = Not much) 1.0
Historical Profit Trend (1 = Down: 4 = Up) 2.4
Location & Facilities (1 = Poor: 4 = Excellent) 1.2
Marketability (1 = Low: 4 = High) 2.8
Industry Trend (1 = Declining: 4 = Growing) 3.2
Ease of Replication (1 = Easy: 4 = Difficult) 3.2

"The defensibility of the publishing franchise and the ranking of the business in a specific niche are of high importance in terms of valuation."

"Competition will depend on the publishing and the industry. Risk will depend on the publishing segment and competition for advertisiers and subscribers if applicable. Profits in many sectors have trended downward because of competition for advertising dollars, particularly from the interactive segment."

Benchmarks

"Publishing cost of goods solely will be based on the type of publication, as will labor and occupancy costs. Profits will range from 10% to 30%

based on type of publication. Publishing is undergoing a change. Successful publishing companies will be in a growth industry and will have an interactive presence."

"The niches in this business are too diverse to have a common set of benchmarks. Book publishing, consumer magazines, trade magazines, trade shows, scientific and technical publishing are all separate and distinct segments with varying benchmarks."

Expenses as a percentage of annual sales:	
Cost of Goods Sold	30%
Payroll/Labor Costs	25%
Occupancy Cost	10%
Profit (estimated)	15%

General Information

"Book, journal and magazine publishers are all valued differently. A key to valuation is the company's portability. If it can be easily moved across country, it is more valuable. Regional publishers are generally less valuable than the national ones."

Advantages of this Business

- "Yes, once you are up and profitable, it can be an exceedingly profitable business. It is also a 'fun' business, such that some of the valuation is driven by money which cash-rich individuals will invest in publishing properties without reference to the underlying economics."
- "Consumer and trade magazines that embrace an interactive component will do well."

Disadvantages of this Business

- "The business has a long startup; much of its assets are the personnel who can talk out the door; and the barriers to entry for local or regional publications are not too high. Also, a buyer should have expertise in publishing, due to the significant expertise which is required."
- "Competition, fragmented advertising dollars, competition for readers' time"

Industry Trend

"High multiples due to consolidation and lessening of competition. Internet has created both opportunity and increasing competition in specific instances."

Pumps & Valves (Manufacturers)

Rule of Thumb:

- "Multiples of recast earnings plus special assets"

General Information

Questions to ask a seller: "What is the technology involved with products? What is the technology on shop floor?"

Pushcarts

General Information

"The once-humble pushcart, some now equipped with electricity and plumbing, has become a darling of mall operators and other landlords as a way of squeezing rental income from areas formerly occupied by mall rats.

"The wheeled carts, now called retail merchandising units, can add 2 percent to 3 percent to a mall rental stream. The greatest income is generated in the fourth quarter, when vendors of high-margin holiday knickknacks are packed as close as fire safety codes allow, experts say. During the two-month holiday shopping season, a vendor at a top mall can pay more than $20,000 for a 45-square-foot pushcart, and annual rents can reach $50,000.

"Much of this income comes from mom-and-pop peddlers.

"For peddlers it is a way to start a business without much capital or long-term risk. Holiday sales for a single pushcart can exceed $100,000 at a top mall."

From: An article in *The New York Times*, January 22, 2003, "Islands in the Mall: Pushcarts as Revenue Streams"

Note: We have not heard of any sales of pushcart businesses, but they sound like very viable small businesses. In addition to the normal financial questions, a major concern would be the rental or lease arrangements for the location. Until enough sales are made, we suggest that you treat it as any other retail business—approximately 40 percent of annual sales plus inventory. If the business has a solid lease or rental arrangement, we could make a case for a higher multiple.

Quick Print *(See Print Shops/Quick Print)*

Franchise

Quick Stop Oil Change

Rule of Thumb:

- 30 percent of annual sales plus inventory

Franchise

Quizno's Classic Subs

1,950 units	
Estimated Annual Sales per Unit:	$438,000
Approximate Total Investment:	$185,450 to $264,950

Rule of Thumb:

- 48 percent of annual sales plus inventory

Pricing Tips

"Two sales in the western states were reported at 99 percent of annual sales and another at 65% of annual sales. However, two sales in the lower Midwest were reported at 38% and 40% of annual sales."

Benchmarks

One franchisee, in his analysis of stores, estimated that one has to make $10,000 to $12,000 per week to break even. He reported that the average per store in some areas he checked was about $8,700 a week. Quizno's executives stated that there were no average breakeven figures and that it depended on the location of the stores.

Source: *Nation's Restaurant*, June 20, 2005

Resources

www.quiznos.com

Race Tracks/Auto

2,437	SIC: 5531-13	NAIC: 711212

General Information

"There still isn't any. Have been unsuccessful at developing a model. The income approach is the best way to develop value."

Resources

www.race-tracks.net

Racquet Sports Clubs *(Also includes Health and Fitness Centers—See Fitness Centers)*

Rule of Thumb:

- 50 percent to 55 percent of annual sales plus inventory

Resources

International Health, Racquet and Sportsclub Association (IHRSA)
www.ihrsa.org
This is an excellent site and well worth visiting if you require information on health clubs.

Fitness, Racquet Sports, and Spa Projects: A Guide to Appraisal, Market Analysis, Development, and Financing by Arthur E. Gimmy, MAI, and Brian B. Woodworth, published by the Appraisal Institute. www.appraisalinstitute.org

Radio Stations

14,547	SIC: 4832-01	NAIC: 513112

Rule of Thumb:

- 8 to 10 times EBITDA
- 10 to 12 times cash flow in medium markets
- 15 times cash flow—large markets
- 1.5 to 6 times annual sales

Pricing Tips

"Some Advice to Sellers...You are not going to get 22 times cash flow on a small market station. Yes, I know that some stations recently, and one in particular in Texas, were reported as having sold for 22 times cash flow. This is only going to happen in probably the top 50 markets. Most banks will only (if you can get them to look at the deal) do 4 to 5 times cash flow. That means the buyer will have to put in the balance in cash unless you carry the paper yourself (and be in 2nd position behind the bank). The only way you are going to get a big premium is if your FM station has the potential to upgrade into a much larger market. My associate Burt Perrault has been in discussions with the owner of a small market combo, billing in the $150,000 range, about listing the stations for sale. The market has about 6,000 population, with 40,000 or so in the country. There are 3 other radio stations in the county also. He wants close to $1,000,000 for the combo. In a market his size, to bring $1million he needs to cash flow $125K to bring 8 times cash flow (which is a realistic multiple) in a market his size. He also does not want to do the work to bring his station's cash flow, and, as a result, the value up to where he wants it. That is to be left to the hoped-for buyer to do. Yes his combo may be worth $1million one day but not on a present 'as is...where is' basis. There are lots of people wanting to get into the radio station ownership business, but pricing has got to be realistic in relation to market size. That's the way it is...deal with it."

Source: David Garland, Media Brokerage, www.radiobroker.com

"A multiple of broadcast cash flow (revenues minus operating expenses before interest, depreciation, taxes). Multiple varies by service (AM/FM/TV) & market size. All broadcasters need to own tower site. Consolidation opportunities within a market add value."

"Try 8 to 12 times cash flow depending on market size."

"With rapid consolidation taking place in the radio industry sellers and buyers are happy with the multipliers they are achieving—buyers of multiple properties can reduce expenses. Ask about buyer's investment horizon. What expenses are in the business of the owner/operator that an investor may not have?"

Benchmarks

Profit (estimated)—25 percent for well-run stations

General Information

Questions to ask a seller: "Can your signal be upgraded or moved to cover a larger market? How are you spending your revenue? How much do you do in trade? Can any barter be converted to cash? Do you really need to buy that new gadget, just because you have a few extra bucks this month? Spend the money to find out what can be done to expand or move that signal to more ears. Are you being a partner in your advertisers' business? The more you expand your advertisers' businesses, the more you expand yours and are therefore able to ask for more dollars on the selling market.

Source: www.buysellradio.com

The Contract - "The FCC's rules require that every application for assignment or transfer of a broadcast license must be accompanied by a written contract or narrative outlining the terms of the deal. The FCC needs to know whether the agreement between the parties complies with its rules.

"For example, the Commission is especially interested in knowing whether the assets conveyed include the broadcast license. This is a frequent mistake, since the license can only be transferred or assigned with the consent of the Commission. Moreover, the Commission will want to be certain that the broadcast license is not being used as collateral for a loan or whether there is any other form of 'reversionary interest' on the part of the seller; that is, whether the seller retains any rights in the license. Both of these practices are prohibited by the Communications Act. Finally, the Commission's rules prohibit the transfer or assignment of a bare license. The contract must also include assets sufficient for the station to broadcast.

"You should engage the services of an experienced communications attorney to prepare or review the contract, to be certain that your interests are fully protected and that the contract complies with all applicable FCC rules."

Source: Prepared by Pepper & Corazzini, L.L.P., Attorneys at Law, www.commlaw.com

Seller Financing

- Rarely is there seller financing except for smallest of deals.

Resources

"Broadcast investment analysts have a great deal of helpful information."

www.buysellradio.com—This is a brokerage site, but loaded with good information.

www.radiobroker.com—David Garland, Media Brokerage, also, a brokerage site, but well worth a visit.

Real Estate/Business Brokerage Offices

Real Estate: 212,977 Business Brokerage: 3,453	SIC: 6531-18 SIC: 7382-22	NAIC: 531210

Rule of Thumb:

- ➢ 20 to 25 percent of annual commissions; may require earnout
- ➢ 1 to 1.5 times SDE; may require earnout
- ➢ 30 to 50 percent of annual gross commissions; may require earnout
- ➢ $10,000 per sales person; may require earnout

Resources

National Association of Realtors
www.realtor.com

Value of a Real Estate Brokerage Firm published by the National Association of Realtors (see address above)

(See Business Brokerage Information)

Records Management

Rule of Thumb:

- ➢ 8 times SDE
- ➢ 200 percent of annual sales

Pricing Tips

"Pricing [above] specifically for Records Management businesses."

Industry Experts' Ratings:

Amount of Competition (1 = Lot of: 4 = Not much)	1.6
Amount of Risk (1 = Very: 4 = Not much)	2.8
Historical Profit Trend (1 = Down: 4 = Up)	2.4
Location & Facilities (1 = Poor: 4 = Excellent)	2.0
Marketability (1 = Low: 4 = High)	3.6
Industry Trend (1 = Declining: 4 = Growing)	2.4
Ease of Replication (1 = Easy: 4 = Difficult)	2.0

"Market has undergone significant consolidation."

Benchmarks

"Internal account growth of 5 to 7%. Sixty percent storage revenues with 40% service revenues."

Expenses as a percentage of annual sales:

Cost of Goods Sold	0%
Payroll/Labor Costs	35%
Occupancy Cost	25%
Profit (estimated)	30%

General Information

"Consolidators paying premiums for key markets."

Advantages of this Business

- "Annuity revenues with steady growth prospects"

Disadvantages of this Business

- "Increased competition from national consolidators pushing national accounts"

Industry Trend

"Continued industry growth with emphasis on document-destruction services"

Rental Equipment

	SIC: 7359-59	NAIC: 532310

Rule of Thumb:

- 100 percent of annual sales
- 5.5 times SDE
- 6 times EBITDA
- Depending on type of business (general, tool, construction, industrial, party) values will range from 3.0 to 5.5 EBITDA, $1.00 to $2.00 per annual revenues.

Pricing Tips

"A. Type of rental business: tool versus construction equipment versus party/event rental —earnings have a different set of criteria. B. Key ratios: rental equipment inventory; rental revenues; EBITDA percent of net revenues."

Who's Who

"According to a 1998 Readex study (the latest available), today independent rental dealers make up 77 percent of the rental industry. Most of these have one or two store locations. Franchise operations account for about 6 percent. And regional or national corporations now account for more than 13 percent of all rental operations. A growing number of these are publicly held."

Source: "Equipment Rental Industry Profile," American Rental Association (ARA). www.ararental.org

"Percentage of rent to sales; capitalization versus expense policy for equipment purchases; age of rental fleet (inventory for rent); rental inventory is a fixed asset, not a current asset such as inventory for sale."

"ROI—Return on Investment (annual rental revenues divided by original cost of equipment). Varies from $0.70:$1.00 to $2.00:$1.00, 1:1 depending on whether equipment is construction, general tool, or party. Values primarily based on multiple of EBITDA, net revenues, value of assets plus goodwill factor, customer base, organizational structure/employees & staff, physical plant facilities, including location and expansion area availability."

"Areas to look at: Rental equipment inventory mix, type, unit investment, ROI, revenues, net earnings, EBITDA, customer (type) base, location,

physical plant facilities, organization structure, market position, and overall thrust of the business."

"To be successful, a general equipment rental store should be doing a minimum of $800,000 gross sales per year."

Industry Experts' Ratings:

Marketability (1 = Low: 4 = High) 2.5
Industry Trend (1 = Declining: 4 = Growing) 2.8
Ease of Replication (1 = Easy: 4 = Difficult) 3.0

Benchmarks

Expenses as a percentage of annual sales:

"Revenues of $100,000 per employee"

"A well-run store will have approximately $100,000 in net revenues per full-time equivalent employee."

"The American Rental Association divides equipment into three broad categories:

1. Construction and industrial equipment, including the full range from heavy to light contractor equipment. Examples are backhoes, cranes, mini-excavators, scaffolding, air compressors...

2. General tools, including all equipment for do-it-yourself projects in lawn, garden and home improvement or repair. Examples are floor-care equipment, rototillers, thatchers, wallpaper steamers, pressure washers...

3. Party and special event equipment, including everything for special events, theme parties, weddings and receptions. Examples are tents, party props, table linens, gazebos, silverware...

Some rental businesses carry inventory from all of these broad categories, and others specialize in equipment from one or two areas."

Source: "Equipment Rental Industry Profile," American Rental Association (ARA). www.ararental.org

"Rental revenues should be $0.70 to $2.00 the value of inventory at cost and be in reasonable rental condition."

Expenses as a percentage of annual sales:	
Cost of Goods Sold*	N/A
Payroll/Labor Costs	30%–40%
Occupancy Cost**	4%–7%
Profit (estimated)	10%–20%
EBITDA	20%–35%

*in a rental store where rental is 90+% of revenue
**dependent on revenue mix and size

Advantages of this Business

- "Excellent potential cash flow—20 to 25 EBITDA is common. However, substantial portion thereof must be reinvested in new rental equipment inventory"
- "Thrives under an entrepreneurial principal"

Disadvantages of this Business

- "Does not operate well in an absentee owner situation"
- "Do not overpay; off-season sales can be 50% of high season. Be prepared to carry your key people through the period."
- "Very capital intensive"

Seller Financing

- "7 year amortization."
- "Limited to 20 percent of the sales price"

Resources

American Rental Association
www.ararental.org

Rental Management
www.rentalmanagementmag.com

Rental—Party & Event *(See also Rental—Equipment)*

Rule of Thumb:

- ➢ 5 times SDE (Party & Tent Rental)

Rent-To-Own Stores

8,300	SIC: 7359-30	

Pricing Tips

"Eight (8) times monthly gross receipts (tops), includes lock, stock (inventory) and barrel. All underlying debts would be paid off by seller at this price. I think the multiple is now less because the industry has sustained a shake-out."

Benchmarks

- The average store has an annual revenue of $588,676 and has 596 items to rent at any one time.
- The average income per unit is $70.20.
- Operating costs for rent-to-own businesses are higher than traditional retail because of the ultimate return of merchandise, merchandise repair and replacement expenses, the need to continually market the industry's services to a rotating customer base and other unique factors.

Source: 2005 RTO Industry Statistics, Association for Progressive Rental Organizations (APRO)

Profit Margins

1 to 4 stores:	4.4%
5 to 10 stores:	4.8%
11 to 40 stores:	8.4%
41 or more stores:	6.0%

Source: 2005 RTO Industry Statistics, Association for Progressive Rental Organizations (APRO)

General Information

Most states have some sort of regulations or laws governing rent-to-own. For example, Michigan law requires that 45 percent of rental payments must go towards the purchase. Other states have similar requirements. Some states just outline what the agreement must contain between the store and the customer. Here is a paragraph from California's Rental-Purchase Act, which is 24 pages long.

> "There are approximately 8,300 stores in all 50 states. RTO serves 2.7 million customers (households) a year."
>
> Source: www.apro-rto.com

"It is further the intent of the Legislature to (a) prohibit unfair or unconscionable conduct toward consumers in connection with rental-purchase transactions, (b) prohibit unfair contract terms, including unreasonable charges, (c) prevent the forfeiture of contract rights by consumers, (d) provide a right of reinstatement and a reasonable formula for the exercise of purchase option rights under a rental-purchase contract, (e) provide reasonable requirements or the servicing, repair, and replacement of improperly functioning rental property, and (f) cover rental-purchase transactions under existing laws, including laws governing debt collection, cosigners, home solicitation contracts, and warranties. This title shall be liberally construed to achieve its remedial objectives."

Product Breakdown

Furniture	38%
Appliances	22.7%
Electronics	22%
Computers	5.3%
Tires & Wheels	4.7%
Other	7.3%

Source: 2005 RTO Industry Statistics, Association for Progressive Rental Organizations (APRO)

Resources

Association for Progressive Rental Organizations (APRO)
www.aprovision.org—a very good site with lots of data and information

Rent to Own Online
www.rtoonline.com

> "2.3 percent of U.S. households had used rent-to-own transactions in the last year, and 4.9 percent had done so in the last five years. Compared to households who had not used rent-to-own transactions, rent-to-own customers were more likely to be African American, younger, less educated, have lower incomes, have children in the household, rent their residence, live in the South, and live in non-suburban areas."
>
> Source: Survey of Rent-to-Own Customers, Federal Trade Commission (FTC)

Resources

Association for Progressive Rental Organizations (APRO)
www.aprovision.org—a very good site with lots of data and information

Rent to Own Online
www.rtoonline.com

> **Publicly Held Counterparts**
>
> Many types of independent businesses, big and small, have their counterparts in the publicly held sector. For example, there are at least six companies in the rent-to-own type of business that are publicly held: Rent-A-Center, Rent-Way, Aaron Rents Inc, Easy Home Ltd., Rainbow Rentals, and BestWay Inc. Obtaining a copy of the latest annual report (usually available on the company's Web site) can provide a lot of material and information on the industry.

Repair Services

Pricing Tips

"General type—When establishing a price for a repair business which caters to the general public, the selling price should be fixtures and equipment; inventory, which is usually rather small;, plus two-thirds of one year's profit."

Resort Businesses *(See Ski Resort Businesses)*

Restaurants - An Introduction *(See also individual listings)*

900,00	SIC: 5812-08	NAIC: Full Service—722110 Fast Food/Carry Out—722211

Introduction

Restaurants are, by far, the biggest section in the *Reference Guide*. Restaurants cover many different types of eating places, from fine dining to fast food, coupled with many different ethnic varieties of both. We have had quite a few Industry Expert contributions to this section, along with data from many publications such as *Nation's Restaurant, Forbes, Business Week*, the *Boston Globe* and the *New York Times,* plus many other miscellaneous publications as well as the wonderful information available from the National Restaurant Association. This site sets a standard for what an industry trade association side should be and the information it makes available to the general public. And, if you do any work in the restaurant industry, you need to get *Nation's Restaurant News*

If you need additional information, we suggest that you refer to the listing for the particular business type you are looking for—the main section is arranged alphabetically. For example Pizza Restaurants have their own very large section. You may find some additional information, or in some cases, you may be referred right back to this section.

There are also several web sites that handle only restaurants and related businesses. They may also supply additional information. They are:

- www.restaurants.com
- www.restaurantbizops.com

And, when all else fails, we have an extensive list of Industry Experts listed under that section in the Guide. Or, you can visit our Web site at www.bbpinc.com for a current list of Industry Experts.

The Two Main Segments

The restaurant industry is divided into two main segments: full-service restaurants and quick-service restaurants. Quick service [also referred to as limited service] is the word currently used to cover fast food, limited-service establishments and fast casual.

Since the information for full service is different than limited service/quick service, we have separated the information into each category. Full service is basically restaurants, full-serve coffee shops, specialty restaurants such as steak houses, and seafood restaurants, Limited service includes fast food type businesses and the fast growing quick casual, which is a hybrid between fast food and restaurants. Many fast food type businesses are integrating their quick-serve concept with a more casual type operation. As the quote at the beginning of this section points out, approximately 60 percent of fast food goes out the drive-up window. Within each type of food service business, there are differences, in some cases big differences. We have tried to identify the type of restaurant operation throughout this section. It is becoming increasingly difficult to do this, since some fast-food operations include several different concepts.

Because of the overlap between concepts and the fact that most industry experts handle both full service and quick service, the lines are often crossed. It is important that, when pricing a food-service business, you read the whole section. Information on the specific type of food-service business you are looking for may be located in a different part of this section than what you had expected.

Basic Information on the Various Categories of Restaurants

On a very practical level, Charles Perkins of the Boston Restaurant group and one of the leading restaurant experts in the country has divided restaurant concepts into the following categories:

Segment Profile

Restaurant Theme	Menu Price Range	Facility Size	Serves Alcohol	Representative Chains
Fine Dining	\$40–\$60	1,500–7,000	Yes	Ruth's Chris, Morton's
Casual Dining	\$10–\$20	4,000–6,000	Yes	Applebee's, Chili's, Bennigan's
Dinner House	\$15–\$25	4,000–6,000	Yes	Outback Steakhouse, Olive Garden
Family Style	\$8–\$13	4,000–5,000	No	Denny's, IHOP, Friendly's
Quick Casual	\$6–\$12	1,500–3,000	No	Panera, Boston Market, Baja Fresh
Fast Food	\$4–\$7	1,500–3,000	No	McDonald's, Burger King, Wendy's

Courtesy: Charles Perkins, Boston Restaurant Group

Full-Service Restaurants

Rule of Thumb:

- 30 to 40 percent of annual sales plus inventory
- 2.5 to 3 times SDE plus inventory
- 3 times EBITDA
- 4 times EBIT
- For restaurants 200+ seats—1.5 to 2 times SDE plus inventory

Pricing Tips

"A restaurant grossing $1 million + in sales is approximately $9,000 per seat; and pre- tax profit is $250 per seat."

"The rent factor is key to the value. 6% of sales is a good guideline for 'normal' rent. If the restaurant has higher rent than 6% of revenue, the price should be lower; and, conversely, if the rent is less than 6% of revenue and no percentage rent is paid, the price should be higher."

"Prices as % of annual sales vary from 40% for a Monday through Friday breakfast-lunch to 25% of annual sales for a full-service 7-day-a-week restaurant."

"Sometimes the real estate values get co-mingled with the business values due to financing."

"Seven out of 10 eating-and-drinking places have fewer than 20 employees."

Source: The National Restaurant Association, Restaurant Industry Forecast-2004

"Competition, location, area disposable income, time established at location. COGs should be approximately 38%. Payroll/labor to include management would be approximately 30%."

"Multiple may vary based on type and brand of restaurant, e.g., franchise, days/hours of operation, buildout, etc."

"Financial records do not usually reflect the true gross or SDE."

"Every dollar in owner financing affects the predicted selling price of the restaurant by 50 percent of that dollar. This means a $200,000 all-cash sale is the same as a $250,000 sale with $100,000 financed. Typical terms are five years at 6% to 8% compounded interest, a personal guarantee, but no other security other than a first lien on the restaurant."

"3 times monthly gross value in place of the FF&E plus license and any capital value, if any, on the lease"

"1 times annual gross profit plus inventory for business only"

"Condition of equipment. Lease terms & Conditions. Owner financing. Definitely location."

Industry Experts' Ratings:

Amount of Competition (1 = Lot of: 4 = Not much) 1.0
Amount of Risk (1 = Very: 4 = Not much) 1.2
Historical Profit Trend (1 = Down: 4 = Up) 2.2
Location & Facilities (1 = Poor: 4 = Excellent) 2.9
Marketability (1 = Low: 4 = High) 2.9
Industry Trend (1 = Declining: 4 = Growing) 2.6
Ease of Replication (1 = Easy: 4 = Difficult) 2.4

"Multi units are better for profitability, assuming the concept works, and easier management by the owne,r since you can build a general-manager-run management team."

"This is a highly competitive field. Franchise or chain restaurants with name recognition generally do better than locals unless the locals manage to capture a steady clientele."

"Extremely competitive business with an average five year shelf life prior to re-inventing the concept"

"Competition increasing as the food-service industry becomes a larger part of the manufacturing sector in the economy."

"Population and tourist growth has continued to fuel this industry."

"Business model is easy to replicate and grow with multiple locations."

"Clean facility and good service"

"Trends for the type of restaurant and competition add to the viability of the operation. If too many locations are the same type, it will be more difficult to be successful. There must be an aspect that sets a certain operation apart from the others— a reason to visit the restaurant."

Food Costs

"Food costs—sub shops < 30%, fine dining 35% +, breakfast/lunch < 30%, pizza & pasta 29%–32%."

Benchmarks

(See also General Benchmarks below)

"On an SDE basis, a quality benchmark would be a profit of $56 per sq. ft. to equate to approximately a 10% net profit."

"Average check = $25 + per person; average sales per employee is $55K to 60K; sales per sq. ft. is $300; food cost is 32%; and income before taxes is 4% to 5%."

"Depending on menu mix, food cost ranges from 26% to 32%."

"Occupancy costs + debt service < 10%; food cost < 30%."

"Strong capitalization—Limited direct competition—Strong emphasis on customer service."

"Most chains realize over 60% of their business through this one window [drive-thru]. That's like saying we get 60% of our business on one product.

"The QSR (Quick Service Restaurant) industry is looking to reinvent the Drive-Thru," Source Unknown

"Tight food costs and employee costs result in a successful business. Those that are loose in these two critical areas generally fail."

"Rent at 6% of sales. Average restaurant rent of $20 per square foot divided by 6% = sales of $333 per square foot."

"Median sales per seat is approximately $7,500/seat. Average sales for a 200-seat, full- service restaurant are $1.5 to $2 million/year. Most restaurants lease land and buildings. Average sales per square foot is $300."

"A full-service restaurant needs at least $400 per square foot in annual sales to be considered successful."

"Total COGS, labor and rent expenses should be less than 65% of total revenues."

"Sales per foot is not necessarily as prevalent as occupancy cost. Anything over 10% must have a direct reduction somewhere else; e.g., labor.

Labor should be looked at by breaking down the labor for FOH (front-of-the-house), BOH (back-of-the-house), and management.

"Owner with a rent factor of around 6% should produce 15% to 20% SDE."

Expenses as a percentage of annual sales:	
Cost of Goods Sold	35%
Payroll/Labor Costs	27%
Occupancy Cost	08%
Profit (estimated)	15%–20%

Full-Service Restaurant Model

Use this as a model for a full-service restaurant as to the various categories of sales. A fine-dining restaurant might have 10 to 15 percent wine sales, while an Irish pub might have 10 to 15 percent beer sales.

Representative Sales Profile

<u>Sales</u>

Food	75.4%
Liquor	10.3%
Beer	5.5%
Wine	8.8%
Net Sales	100%

The following is based upon a typical ratio of 75 percent food and 25 percent beverage. Food costs for a steakhouse or fish restaurant may approach 35 to 37 percent. Food cost for an Italian pizzeria might be in the 25 to 30 percent range. Wine costs will vary, based upon sales by the bottle or by the glass. Bottle wine sales will have a higher cost of goods, as there is a lot of customer resistance to a markup above 100 percent.

Representative Cost of Sales Profile

<u>Sales</u>

Food	32.5%
Liquor	21.0%
Beer	21.4%
Wine	28.4%
Combined Cost	30.4%

Source: Charles Perkins, The Boston Restaurant Group

General Information

"It can be very profitable, but also so is the risk."

"Don't be afraid to price your product accordingly. People pay for quality. The industry continues to show strong growth. Not too many people have the time or want to cook at home anymore."

"A good operation can be successful if it is unique and interesting. It must be a fun place to come. Fine dining is very difficult. Never start too big. Must have a good physical plant. Ease of operation. Good kitchen. Storage and buying ability a must. Good system. Good accounting. Theft is a major problem. Most employees do not understand the damage which can be done when food and drinks are given away."

"Eating-and-drinking places are extremely labor intensive—sales per full-time-equivalent employee were $57,567 in 2003 and notably lower than other industries."

Source: *Restaurant Industry 2005 Fact Sheet*, National Restaurant Association

Advantages of this Business

- "It is the 'hospitality' industry. If you are a people person with a nurturing nature, you will find the work very satisfying."
- "Can be very profitable with the right concept. More folks are and will continue to eat out."
- "Need no education, it's a cash business, determine your own hours, work hard and make more."
- "A good location and strong management generally result in steady profits."
- "You have to love it. Many do."
- "Highly profitable after breakeven is reached. People always need to eat & drink. More eating out, especially by singles."
- "Restaurants can be very profitable. If the establishment is busy enough, the owner does not have to be married to the location, and should always strive for that outcome. There is a lot of work, but the people in the business are great people who always treat everyone like family."
- "Setting own levels of accomplishment. Working with people. Pride of ownership and seeing people enjoy the menu and amenities. Must love people and make people happy."

Disadvantages of this Business

- "Your work hours may be different from the 9 to 5 office/ business environment."

- "Long hours and employees are always a big problem, especially in the fast food end of things."
- "Growing competition, difficulty in finding a competent work force, employee benefits are too costly, governmental oversight is too costly, can't afford quality help."
- "Continuous supervision is required. Employee turnover and finding employees, especially during the day shifts, continues to be a real problem."
- "The three main reasons for failure are undercapitalization, level of experience, and concept/location. Everything must be right."
- "Risk and employee nonsense"
- "Can be long hours, can be a lot of work. You should have strong operating experience before owning an establishment."
- "Amount of competition, food costs and health issues"
- "Many hours. Sustaining power. Difficulty of under-financing. Employee apathy. Not recognizing the tax consequences."

Industry Trend

"Generally, I see a shift away from the independent operator to more multi-unit operators. I see sales trends declining in the full-service Northeast market a small amount, but the profit picture looks much weaker, with additional governmental expenses rising dramatically."

Neal Moro, the napkin business leader at Kimberly-Clark, said the standard rule of thumb at a fast-food restaurant is that a couple will have dinner for two and napkins for 12.

Source: *The Boston Globe*, March 30, 2002

"The industry will continue to grow, as the market continues to grow, but competition and growing governmental regulations will continue to put a strain on it."

"The trend in this industry is on a definite growth path. Consumers are dining out more often, yet are careful of the amount of money spent on each meal."

"Continued upward trend"

"Labor costs and finding qualified and willing workers continue to be difficult."

"Growing in the meal replacement area"

Seller Financing

- It ranged from 3 to 7 years, with most most industry experts reporting 5 years.

Quick-Service Restaurants

Rule of Thumb:

- 40 to 45 percent of annual sales for independents; 45 to 50 percent for many franchises plus inventory
- 2 to 2.5 times SDE plus inventory
- 2.5 to 3 times EBIT

Pricing Tips

"Pricing should be tempered by the type of restaurant (drive thru, sit down, franchise or nonfranchise) and the location. Pricing is adjusted up or down in relationship to the rent factor and length of lease."

"2.5 times SDE and 50 percent of annual sales are agressive for independent quick- service restaurants. Most franchises such as Subway, Quizno's etc. sell at these numbers. Nonfranchised sell closer to 2 times SDE. Biggest problem with comps: some brokers state EBITDA without a manager's salary, which is really SDE. Numbers below are from the Restaurant Industry Operations Report (median).

"35 percent of annual sales for independents and 50 percent for franchises"

"Sales are a much better indicator of value than bottom-line numbers. Different operators can have huge a impact on food and labor costs running the same business."

"Popular business, sandwich shops can create high gross profits."

"Limited menu a bonus; delivery and length of lease major considerations."

"Look for dramatically out-of-line cost of sales. Often indicates owner skimming."

"Location, lease, concept, operating manuals, recipes"

"If business is a franchise, usually priced between 45% to 50% of annual sales."

"Normal situation—I would take last year's net plus any adjustments such as cars, insurance for owner, depreciation and interest, and make it a multiple of .72 to 2 times that number depending upon location, growth or decline of sales, age of fixtures and condition of building, then add value of FF&E, liquor license and other assets for a good value number."

"Increase in upcoming rental amount; ease of menu; delivery and competition in the market"

Industry Experts' Ratings:

Amount of Competition (1 = Lot of: 4 = Not much)	1.0
Amount of Risk (1 = Very: 4 = Not much)	1.2
Historical Profit Trend (1 = Down: 4 = Up)	2.2
Location & Facilities (1 = Poor: 4 = Excellent)	2.6
Marketability (1 = Low: 4 = High)	2.4
Industry Trend (1 = Declining: 4 = Growing)	2.2
Ease of Replication (1 = Easy: 4 = Difficult)	1.8

"Easy to open, hard to master. Very difficult to run absentee, owner must be present."

"Competition is very heavy from chains, franchises as well as independants."

"Very much location driven"

"Heavy foot traffic locations like malls, airports, office buildings"

"Fast food is here to stay. People like the fast route, and fast food is it. There is a ready work force always coming up with the next generation of your people and first time workers.

"Lots of competition. Risk factor: must give consistent product, with good quality. Catering a plus for today's business environment. Many sandwich shops add catering. Some catering only locations with delivery, in low-rent areas with little highway exposure."

"Great service followed by good food are keys to success."

Benchmarks

"Combined food cost, labor and occupancy (the big 3) must not exceed 70% in total."

"Food costs need to be kept under 38%. Rents need to be kept under 10%."

"Lower quartile per seat is $5,115, median is $7,510, and $14,293 is upper. $10,000 per seat is a benchmark for a sucessful quick-service restaurant."

"Better operators keep food costs down closer to 30%, adds to bottom line."

"Food usually maximum of 35%. Sandwich shops very popular today. Catering a plus, hard to prove without good reliable records."

"I look for a 20% plus EBIT and 'Prime Costs' (Cost of Sales & Labor) combined below 50%."

"Good menu can add to sucess. Location, visability, and parking key ingredients for profitable business."

"Mall fast food should be $1,000 + per square foot."

"Ownership of real estate very desirable. Franchise stores more marketable than independents. Franchise presence in market place very important."

"Median sales per full-time employee = $55,240; sales per square foot = $291"

Expenses as a percentage of annual sales:	
Cost of Goods Sold	25%–30%
Payroll/Labor Costs	20%–25%
Occupancy Cost	8%–10%
Profit (estimated)	15%

General Information

"Watch your prices and quality, as they are directly related to income."

"Quick casual is the fastest growing segment, rather than quick service."

Advantages of this Business

- "Ease of operation, lower start-up costs (compared to full service)"
- "Run right, they can be much more lucrative than most types of businesses, and they deal in large amounts of cash which limits collection time and effort."
- "Quality of life, few employees, usually shorter work hours"
- "Ease of operation. Low food costs. Little waste. Low skilled workforce. Less total hours less than a full-service restaurant. Very nice profit margins."
- "A fast-paced lifestyle will continue to support fast-food operations. People like it quick and easy. If managed properly, this can be a very lucrative field."
- "Cash business. Low costs."

Disadvantages of this Business

- "Huge competition, higher start-up costs (general retail) due to restaurant infrastructure"
- "Long hours and unforgiving customers, along with high employee turnover"
- "Most of the major franchises now deliver and accept credit cards."
- "Hours, spoilage, theft by employees"
- "Usually fierce competition and a lot of long gruelling hours"
- "Confining, low sales"
- "Long hours, dealing with personnel who are always looking for a better position"
- "Owner must be there and maintain quality levels of business."

Industry Trend

"Quick-casual, or modified, service will continue to grow. The quick-casual segment has better quality food at lower price points. This can be achieved due to lower labor costs."

Seller Financing

- "Five years—8 percent"
- "Three years max. in California"
- "3 to 4 years"
- "7 to 10 years with a 3 to 5 year stop"
- "Average of 5 years and prime plus 2 percent"
- "Depends on size and cash flow; 8 years is an average of our last 20 restaurant transactions."
- "7 to 10 years in leased space; 15 to 20 years if real estate is included"

Additional Information on the Foodservice Business
Following are comments from prior editions of *The Guide* that we feel are still pertinent and helpful.

"Also, in the restaurant business, it is not uncommon for an owner/operator to work excessive hours and not be compensated correctly. Therefore, it is very important to normalize the owner's salary."

"Focus on top-line sales growth over past 2 to 3 years and determine why there are substantial variances or abnormalities."

"Amount of cooking, length of lease, rental amount, seating capacity"

"Is it currently profitable? What's happening in the neighborhood? What makes your restaurant unique?"

"The lease and lessor can make or break the deal."

"An undervalued lease has great value in our market [So. CA] Are the FF&E's updated and is the interior décor current and won't take a lot renovation? Is there sufficient parking to meet code? Have there been any infractions on the liquor license?"

"How long since last menu update?"

"1 year's SDE plus FF&E and inventory (when only 1 year's financials are available)"

"When pricing fast food types or locations in major mall food courts, the price may range from 5 percent to 15 percent higher."

"Current average price for all restaurant deals over the last three years is

> "Most models project labor as a percentage of total sales, but I find this method highly inaccurate. I view the majority of labor as a fixed expense. A restaurant needs the majority of its staff whether or not any customers are served. As a result, unpredictable sales generate high labor cost as a percentage of sales. Sending an hourly employee home can reduce labor only slightly. Therefore I recommend treating labor as a fixed expense."
>
> Source: "*The New Restaurant Entrepreneur* by Kep Sweeney, Dearborn Trade Publishing

approx. 35 percent of gross annual sales."

"The price is right if the cash flow after owner's salary of $40,000 can pay for the restaurant's total purchase in 5 years. Restaurants are so competitive today that there is nothing proprietary about any concept. After 5 years, major renovations are needed to upgrade and stay competitive. Can the cash flow of the business service 100 percent of the total purchase price and pay the owner/operator base pay of $40,000 year? The seller will have to discount for deferred maintenance, an out-of-date concept, and a concept change if needed."

For Sale: Closed Restaurant—Only $500,000

... The attendees could not believe that I sold a restaurant in Cambridge, MA for $500,000. The restaurant was closed, there was no cash flow, it had a very short lease, and the new buyer spent $300,000 to remodel it as a brew pub. He bought the location.

What the buyer purchased was the following:

- The use of the existing leasehold improvements
- The existing plumbing and electrical features
- The exhaust system in place
- The 'Grandfather Rights' to the use of the existing sign and the non-compliance with current building code issues, parking spaces, green space, etc.
- A location that had permits and licenses in place
- The cost savings in legal fees and the time it takes to get zoning variances, neighborhood association approvals, etc.

The above is an example of a valuation method that is getting a lot of consideration in several types of businesses, including restaurants. It is a method under the Cost or Asset-Based Approach that is referred to as the Cost to Create Method.

"Grandfathered Rights add significant value to a location. The current restaurant may not be operating profitably; however, under new management and with a different concept, the location may have a great deal of potential. If a buyer feels a location can generate $900,000 in revenue and he wants his investment to be 1/3 of projected sales, he may commit as much as $300,000 to the project, paying the seller for whatever equipment he can use.

Source: Charles Perkins, The Boston Restaurant Group

"Cost approach—First year sales should be 3 times the total investment. Spend $300,000 to do sales of $900,000. Income Approach—Cap rate today is 35 to 40 percent."

"One-third of sales for full-service restaurant. 50 percent of sales for franchise restaurants. 40 to 50 percent of sales for fast-food, donuts, pizza. Bars will sell for 50 to 60 percent of sales. The rent should be 6 percent of sales; real estate taxes, 1 percent of sales. A lease with 5 years plus options of 5 years each."

"Many restaurants can demand a good price regardless of profit if: Is there a good lease, what is the condition of the assets, will new owner have to renovate? Cash flow analysis —will it service debt? Good hours? Shopping center—'red hot' locations. Questions to ask seller: Assumable loans? Will they execute a non-compete? Health Dept. status? Will equipment & premises pass all inspections? Pending competition? How will they prove all income? Will employees stay? Why are they really selling? Can buyer obtain a reasonably long-term lease—at least 10 years?"

"Good condition, turnkey condition, and are sales dependent on the original owner?"

"Location, location, lease value, buildout adaptation to new concept & seller financing?"

"(1) #1 selling feature—location! (2) Contemporary concepts add value, dated concepts subtract (3) Equipment age and condition (4) Health rating (5) Good books with positive cash flow (6) Stable employee base that can be retained (7) Competition +/- (8) Below market leases add value. In order to market and sell by standard valuation methods, restaurant must have a favorable lease, good location and concept, be well established and have a proven stream of income. If not, we attempt to market on a concept conversion basis using approximate replacement cost of assets and leasehold improvements. Restaurants continue to be difficult to sell, but will always sell with a low down payment and good terms!"

"A long-term lease is important. Good books and records bring a higher price. A free-standing building will increase the price. Good chemistry between the buyer and seller is very important to getting a higher price. A fresh cleanup and painting helps a lot. Rent to sales ratio should be 6 to 8 percent of sales."

"Casual style restaurant .... 25%–30% of annual sales
Fine dining .... 25%–30% of annual sales
Full-service tablecloth restaurant............ 2.5–3 times annual net (SDE)*
Family restaurant .... 30% of annual sales
"Asian Formula .... 3 times monthly sales (30% if sold to Asian)"
Restaurants overall 20%–30%

**depending on the condition of the premises."*

"You cannot sell or expect to be paid for sales or profit you cannot or will not show. Debt service should not exceed 70 percent of adjusted cash flow after owner's compensation. Restaurant must be established 2.5 to 3 years minimum on independents. Look at how long it has been since a remodel or upgrade; it should be no longer than 5 years. How old and what condition are the FF&E? Is there any specialized equipment needed?"

"1. Buyers are not paying for goodwill as much as they did in the past due to many factors:
    - -increased competition in area
    - -higher rent/lease costs
    - -shorter lease costs
    - -sloppy books—no goodwill.
2. Exclusive concept rights in strong shopping centers = more dollars.
3. Security is a concern for many first time buyers
4. Restaurants that are not doing strong numbers on books are more difficult to sell. The economy is very strong in our area [North Carolina]; it doesn't make any sense for a buyer to pay $100K for a $25K-a-year job.
5. Long-term assignable leases at below market rates add to the value of the business.
6. Parking is at a premium in our area! Good parking is a +."

"Pluses are location, location, location, and can concept be expanded."

"Fast Food (Hot Dog stands, Pizza, etc.) . 40–55 percent of annual sales
Casual Restaurants .... 33 percent of annual sales
Bars .... 45–50 percent of annual sales
Franchised Restaurants .... 50–60 percent of annual sales"

"The higher the sales, the higher the percentage they will sell for. Any fast food above $700,000 in annual sales will sell for 45 percent to 50 percent. Full service above $1 million in annual sales will sell for 35 percent to 40 percent, as long as the rent is 6 percent to 8 percent of annual sales."

"35 percent of gross annual sales if in leased space; or one time gross annual sales if real estate is included (at high end)."

"Good staff in place adds to value. Absentee current owner adds value. Premium real estate would add some value but still needs to have cash flow."

"As a 'rule of thumb' most full-service restaurants in our area [San Diego] market will sell for 30 to 40 percent of most current annual gross sales, assuming there is positive cash flow (profit)."

"Cost of goods (Fast Food—Mexican, Asian, Italian, etc.) .... 30%+/-
Cost of goods (Full Service, Midscale, Fine Dining) .... 35%+/-
Payroll/Labor costs (Fast Food) ....20% to 25%
Payroll/Labor costs (Full Service) 30%
Occupancy cost .... 6%+/-

Note: Labor shortage is affecting sales. Occupancy costs may be a deal killer if higher with increasing labor costs decreasing margins."

"Sales/Investment Ratio—30 percent of sales/3 times SDE after owner's salary of $40,000"

"85 to 95 percent of annual sales/real estate; 40 to 50 percent of annual sales w/o real estate; 40 percent (needs renovation); 50 percent (renovated within last 3 years); lease is 5 to 7 percent of annual sales."

"Lease—10 percent of annual sales or above is too much for restaurants."

"Lease should be no more than 5 to 7 percent of annual sales. Restaurants with leased premises are more difficult to sell (unless heavy cash cow). Buyers prefer to buy business with less income, as long as real estate is included."

Additional Restaurant Benchmarks

Restaurants by the Numbers

$1.3 billion—Restaurant-industry sales on a typical day in 2005

Two out of three—Percentage of quick-service operators who have added low-carb items to their menu as a result of the low-carb diet trend

Nearly half—Percentage of table-service operators reporting that takeout represents a larger proportion of their total sales compared to two years ago

One out of three—Percent of consumers who have used curbside takeout at a table- service restaurant

4%—Median pre-tax income in 2003 for full-service restaurants with average per-person checks of $15 to $24.99

45%— Percentage of 25 to 34 year olds who have used the Internet to find out information about a restaurant they have not patronized before

Source: "Restaurant Industry 2005 Fact Sheet," National Restaurant Association

Sales per Square Foot

A good benchmark for many businesses is the sales per square foot. Restaurants are no exception. Following is a selection of restaurants with this information. They are all franchised operations; and while they may not match a business under review, you may find enough similarities to help you in pricing a business.

Restaurant Sales

Sales Company	Sales Per Foot	Avr. Store Size	Avr. Sales Per Store
Applebee's	454	5,000	$2,269,332
Bugaboo Steakhouse	557	6,400	$3,567,668
California Pizza Kitchen	$579	5,000	$2,897,024
Carabbas	471	6,650	$3,133,000
Checkers	$759	870	$659,990
Cheescake Factory	$1,020	10,730	$10,940,800
Denny's	$270	4,800	$1,294,765
Dominos Pizza	$527	1,150	$605,879
Frisch's Big Boy	$324	5,610	$1,819,000
Krispy Kreme	$859	4,600	$3,952,000
Lone Star Steakhouse	$328	5,800	$1,900,000
Papa John's	$575	1,300	$747,000

Restaurant Sales *(cont'd)*

Sales Company	Sales Per Foot	Avr. Store Size	Avr. Sales Per Store
McDonald's	$543	3,000	$1,628,000
Outback Steakhouse	$548	6,200	$3,399,000
Panera Bread	$418	4,400	$1,840,000
Ruby Tuesday's	$377	5,600	$2,111,000
Scholtzsky's Deli	$147	4,000	$588,000
Starbucks	$521	1,500	$781,669

Source: www.Bizstats.com

The Restaurant Industry Dollar

The following figures are from the National Restaurant Association's *Restaurant Operations Report—2005,* which is available online at www.restaurant.org. This site, as we said before, sets a very high standard for association Web sites. If you are working in the restaurant category, you need to visit this site and also order the latest *Operations Report.* The figures below are great for benchmark guidelines.

	Full Service	Limited Service*
Where It Came From		
Total Sales	100%	100%
Where It Went		
Cost of Food Sold and Beverage Sales	33%	31%
Salaries and Wages (including employee benefits)	33%	30%
Restaurant Occupancy Costs	6%	7%
Corporate Overhead	3%	4%
General & Administrative Expenses	3%	2%
Other	18%	19%
Income Before Income Taxes	4%	7%

*Includes quick-service and quick/fast casual restaurants

Note: All figures are averages, are computed individually for each cost category, and are rounded. All amounts are reflected as a percentage of total sales.

Source: National Restaurant Association, *2004 Restaurant Operations Report,* November 2, 2005

Representative Restaurant Ratios

- Owner Salary $40,000
- Cash Flow 10%–15%
- Rent—Full-Service Restaurant 5%–7%
- Rent—Fast-Food Restaurant 9%–11%
- Lease Length .... 5 + 5 + 5
- Rent + Debt Service ..... Not more than 75% of Cash Flow
- Advertising 1%–3%
- Maintenance 1%–3%
- Utilities 3%–4%
- Rent Increases .... 12%–15% every 5 years
- Refurbish .... 5 years
- Renovate .... 10 years
- Chain Requirements .... Sewer/Parking/Demographics
- Food Cost 28%–32%
- Payroll Costs 30%–34%
- Primary Costs .... Food & Payroll 60%–65%

Source: Charles Perkins, Boston Restaurant Group

Restaurants—QUICK CHECK—2005

Bagels .... 30% of annual sales
Bars .... 50% of annual sales
Bar & Grills (50% Liquor) .... 40%-50% of annual sales
Barbecues .... 30% of annual sales
Bistros .... 30% of annual sales
Brew Pubs .... 40% of annual sales
Billiard Parlors .... 45% of annual sales
Cajun .... 30% of annual sales
Catering Businesses .... 30% to 40% of annual sales
Caribbean .... 30% of annual sales
Chicken .... 30% of annual sales
Chinese .... 30% of annual sales
Coffee Houses .... 40% of annual sales
Continental .... 30% of annual sales
Delis .... 30% to 40% of annual sales
Diners .... 30% of annual sales
Fine Dining .... 30% of annual sales
French .... 30% of annual sales
Gourmet Shops .... 40% of annual sales
Hamburgers .... 35% of annual sales
Ice Cream .... 35% to 40% of annual sales
Irish .... 40% of annual sales
Italian .... 30% of annual sales
Mexican .... 30% of annual sales

Night Clubs .... 25% of annual sales
Pancake Houses .... 30% of annual sales
Pizza (if delivery) .... 30% of annual sales
Pizza (if no delivery) .... 40% of annual sales
Sandwiches .... 40% of annual sales
Seafood .... 40% of annual sales
Sports Bars .... 40% to 45% of annual sales
Steakhouses .... 40% of annual sales

Franchised Food Operations—2005—Quick Check

A&W Restaurants .... 45% to 55% of annual sales
Arctic Circle .... 50% of annual sales
Atlanta Bread Company .... 28% of annual sales
Baskin-Robbins Ice Cream .... 46% to56% of annual sales
Between Rounds .... 3 to 4 times SDE
Big Apple Bagel .... 42% of annual sales
Black Jack Pizza .... 55% to 60% of annual sales
Blimpies .... 48% of annual sales
Bresler's Ice Cream .... 35% to 40% of annual sales
Buffet Nest .... 40% of annual sales
Burger King .... 40% of annual sales
Carvel Ice Cream/Restaurants .... 60% of annual sales
Chester International .... 45% of annual sales
Chicago Pizza .... 26% of annual sales
Dairy Queen .... 50% of annual sales
Del Taco .... 90% of annual sales
Dunkin Donuts .... 60% to 80% of annual sales
Godfather's Pizza .... 52% of annual sales
Great Harvest Bread Company .... 3.3 to 3.4 times SDE
Great Steak & Potato .... 55% to 60% of annual sales
Heavenly Hams .... 48% of annual sales
Hungry Howie's Pizza & Subs .... 30% of annual sales
Iceberg Drive Inn .... 40% to 45% of annual sales
Jersey Mike's .... 50% of annual sales
KFC (Kentucky Fried Chicken) .. 30% to 35% of annual sales
Lil' Dinos Subs .... 64% of annual sales
Little Caesar's Pizza .... 55% of annual sales
Logan Farms (honey-glazed hams) .... 30% of annual sales
Maggiemoo's Ice Cream .... 32% of annual sales
Marble Slap Creamery .... 44% of annual sales
Mountain Mike's Pizza .... 27% of annual sales
Orange Julius .... 32% of annual sales
Quizno's Classic Subs .... 50-60% of annual sales
Pasquale's Pizza .... 35-40% of annuals sales
Pizza by George .... 50% of annual sales
Pizza Inn .... 47% of annual sales
Red Robin Gourmet Burgers .... 32% of annual sales
Rita's – Ices, Cones, Shakes .... 80-1.3% of annual sales

Roly Poly Sandwiches .... 34% of annual sales
Subway .... 50-60% of annual sales
Taco Johns .... 31%of annual sales
TCBY .... 50% of annual sales
Wingstop Restaurants .... 33% of annuals sales

Note: Many of the listings above have footnotes that contain additional information. Go to Franchises for them and/or the individual listings. For franchises or restaurant types not listed, or for more information, check the alphabetical listing.

More General Information

The Restaurant industry is composed of eight major markets:

Employee—Food service facilities in office complexes, manufacturing and industrial plants

Educational—Food and drink facilities at schools, colleges and universities

Recreational—Sports complexes, movie theatres and other recreational facilities make up this market

Transportation—Airlines, cruise lines and railroads are the bulk of this market

Health Care—Hospitals, nursing homes, assisted living and similar facilities are all part of this growing market

Lodging Places—Hotels and other lodging places make up this market

Military—Sales for this portion of the market was expected to be $1.3 billion in 2000

Retail—This is by far the biggest segment in the market

Source: National Restaurant Association

Restaurants – The cornerstone of our nation's economy

- Restaurant-industry sales are forecast to advance 4.9% in 2005 and equal 4% of the U.S. gross domestic product.
- The overall economic impact of the restaurant industry is expected to exceed $1.2 trillion in 2005, including sales in related industries such as agriculture, transportation and manufacturing.
- Every dollar spent by consumers in restaurants generates an additional

$1.98 spent in other industries allied with the restaurant industry.

- Every additional $1 million in restaurant sales generates an additional 42 jobs for the nation's economy.
- Average unit sales in 2002 were $730,000 at full-service restaurants and $619,000 at limited-service restaurants.
- More than seven out of 10 eating and drinking places are single-unit (independent) operations.

Source: "Restaurant Industry 2005 Fact Sheet," National Restaurant Association

Unit Breakdown of Liquor

The following items are unit breakdowns of liquor that are useful in computing liquor cost percentages or markup percentages.

Keg of Beer = 15 ½ gallons = 1984 ounces
16 ounces = 1 pound = pint = 500 milliliters
32 ounces = 1 quart = 100 liter
128 ounces = 1 gallon
25.6 ounces = 1 fifth = 750 milliliters
½ gallon = 64 oz. = 1.75 liter
1.6 oz. = miniature = 50 milliliters

	U.S.	*Number of drinks in Bottle*				
Metric Size	Fluid oz.	¾ oz.	1 oz.	1 1/8 oz.	1 ¼ oz.	1 ½ oz.
1.75 Liter	59.2	78.9	59.2	52.6	47.4	39.5
100 Liters	33.8	45.1	33.8	30.0	27.0	22.5
750 Milliliters	25.4	33.9	25.4	22.6	20.3	16.9
500 Milliliters	16.9	22.5	16.9	15.0	13.5	11.3
200 Milliliters	6.8	9.1	6.8	6.0	5.4	4.5

The above is excerpted from an IRS Audit Technique Guide (Market Segment Specialization Program—MSSAP). This is an excellent source of information and is available at www.bookstore.gpo.gov (search under IRS—IRS Audit Technique Guides).

Resources

National Restaurant Association—Their Web site is an excellent example of what an industry Web site should be.
www.restaurant.org

Food Service Study2004 published by Bizcomps. www.bizcomps.com

The Sale and Purchase of Restaurants by John Stefanelli, second edition, 1990, published by John Wiley & Sons ISBN 0-471-51209-5. This book may be difficult to locate, and slightly dated, but it is an excellent resource.

(See list of liquor associations in this Guide)

"The Dynamics of Restaurant Business Valuation," *Business Valuation Review*, March 1997, published by The Business Valuation Committee of the American Society of Appraisers, Business Office: 2777 S. Colorado Blvd., Suite 200, Denver, CO 80222. (303) 758-6148.

How to Value Your Restaurant, published by the National Restaurant Association (see address above).

"Valuing Restaurants," *Handbook of Business Valuation*, West & Jones, 2nd Edition, published by John Wiley & Sons.

The New Restaurant Entrepreneur by Kep Sweeney, Dearborn Trade Publishing—This is a very informative book. If you're selling or valuing restaurants, buy this book. It's a paperback and inexpensive.

Trade Publications
Nation's Restaurant News
www.nrn.com

Pricing Information
The following figures are from the current Bizcomps *2005 Special Food Service Edition of Recent Small Business Sales.* We strongly urge anyone who needs information on the food service industry to get a copy. Note that the percentages do change from year to year, so having a current edition is a must. Contact Bizcomps at www.bizcomps.com .

The first column of figures is the Sale Price as a Percentage of Annual Sales and the second is the SDE Multiple:

Business Type	% of Total Sales	SDE
All Food Service Businesses	39	1.9
Western States	39	2.1
Central States	40	2.2
Eastern States	40	1.8
Rest/Cocktails	34	2.2
Rest/Full Service	38	2.6
Rest/Family	35	2.0
Rest/Breakfast-Lunch	40	1.6

Business Type	% of Total Sales	SDE
Rest/Coffee Shops	35	2.0
Rest/Seafood	32	2.5
Rest/Oriental	38	2.5
Rest/Italian	32	1.7
Rest/Mexican	33	2.0
Fast Food Takeout	37	1.8
Fast Food/Hamburgers	42	2.8
Fast Food/Pizza	30	1.6
Fast Food/Chicken	35	1.6
Fast Food/Mexican	41	2.0
Fast Food/Ice Cream	53	2.3
Fast Food/Yogurt	46	1.8
Fast Food/Juice Bars	42	2.1
Deli/Retail	50	1.8
Deli/Sandwich	42	2.0
Deli/Industrial	51	1.8
Deli/Office Bldg	51	1.6
Bakery/Rest.	34	1.7
Coffee Houses	42	2.0
Catering Businesses	42	2.0
Catering-Truck Routes	49	1.2
Cocktail Lounges	45	2.1

Source: Bizcomps, *Special Food Service Edition 2005*

Retail Business (In General)

Rule of Thumb:

- 25 to 50 percent annual sales plus inventory plus inventory
- 47 percent of annual sales plus inventory
- 3 times EBIT

Pricing Tips

"Occupancy – Lease terms"

Industry Experts' Ratings:

Amount of Competition (1 = Lot of: 4 = Not much)	1.0
Amount of Risk (1 = Very: 4 = Not much)	1.2
Historical Profit Trend (1 = Down: 4 = Up)	2.8
Location & Facilities (1 = Poor: 4 = Excellent)	4.0
Marketability (1 = Low: 4 = High)	2.0
Industry Trend (1 = Declining: 4 = Growing)	2.4
Ease of Replication (1 = Easy: 4 = Difficult)	2.0

Benchmarking

No business lends itself more to benchmarking than retailing. Two important benchmarks for retail operations that may measure profitability, or just how a particular business may stack up against its peers, are Sales per square Foot and Sales per Employee.

Pat O'Rourke, the creator of BizStats, has written a very interesting—and informative —article titled "Why Sales per Foot is the critical benchmark for Retailers." Here are a few excerpts. For the complete article and lots of other benchmarking data go to www.bizstats.com.

"Think of Sales per Foot in terms of sun protection factor—SPF—a healthy SPF will help prevent you from getting burned in a retail business. SPF is one of many retail benchmarks, but I believe it's the best gauge of a

Some Definitions

"Super Regional Shopping Centers—Malls that are typically about 1 million square feet with several anchor department stores

"Regional Shopping Centers—Smaller malls typically 500,000 square feet with two or more anchor stores

"Community Shopping Centers—Strip centers ranging from 100,000 to 300,000 square feet

"Neighborhood Shopping Centers—Strip centers under 100,000 square feet, typically built around a supermarket"

Source: Bizstats, www.bizstats.com

retailer's efficiency, and, ultimately, its profitability. It's also easy to compute—just divide sales by the store's gross square feet. Some retailers calculate SPF based on selling feet (excluding in-store administrative, storage and other space), but this can be subjective and impair meaningful comparisons.

"SPF differs among industries. For example, a big box discounter with high inventory turnover (such as Costco) is going to have a much higher SPF than a clothing chain or sports equipment outlet. Another key element is location, SPF is typically much higher for merchants in a destination mall, than for similar stores in a local shopping center—of course you pay much higher rent in the big mall.

"An upward trend in SPF is almost always a positive sign of a retailer's health, whereas a downward trend in SPF is often a warning sign that business performance is suffering—even if the company's total sales are increasing.

"There can be many reasons for a low SPF. The first reason is obvious—the retailer simply has too much space. By having excessive space, a retailer will be adversely impacted by high fixed costs:

- Rent costs are excessive
- Labor costs are excessive, since additional floor space requires additional personnel
- Flooring costs are excessive, since additional space requires additional merchandise
- Insurance utilities and theft costs all increase with additional floor space

"Assuming the store size is reasonable, there are many reasons for a poor SPF relative to competitors. Here are 10 primary reasons for a low SPF—these are considerations for retailers of all sizes:

1. Poor product/merchandising mix
2. Insufficient floor inventory (e.g., empty shelves, missing sizes)
3. Un-competitive pricing
4. Poor location
5. Poor sales and customer service personnel
6. Non-optimal store hours
7. Poor store layout and design

8. Cannibalization of nearby owned stores
9. Insufficient/poor marketing
10. Fixed consumer perception"

Also from the BizStats site are some average sales per foot based on information from U.S. shopping malls. Since the data is based on shopping malls, keep in mind that rents, and related costs, are generally higher than most "main street" locations.

Type Business	Sales per Square Foot
Jewelry	$880
Restaurants— Food courts & kiosks	$648
Shoes— Men's	$514
Accessories—Women's	$478
Restaurants—Fast food	$453
Shoes—Children's	$439
Specialty food stores	$430
Personal care & health	$411
Restaurants	$369
Electronics	$355
Sporting goods	$246
Stationary & card shops	$229
Toys & hobbies	$221
Automotive parts	$210
Books	$199

Source: Newspaper Association of America, as shown at www.bizstats.com

And, for comparison purposes, BizStats also provides the following for Neighborhood Shopping Centers, defined as strip centers under 100,000 square feet, typically built around a supermarket.

Type of Business	Sales per Square Foot
General merchandise	$100
Clothing & accessories	$201
Shoes	$145
Automotive	$136
Hobby/special interest	$163
Gifts/specialty	$149
Jewelry	$280
Liquor	$217
Drugs	$241
Other Retail	$143

Following are some Sales per Square Foot figures for various retail public company outlets. Although the following companies are publicly held, they will provide some example of various types of retail operations. Many of their outlets are in malls or are box stores and most privately owned and operated retail operations will not have as high a figure as they do.

Name of Company	Sales per Square Foot
Gymboree	$511
Ann Taylor	$434
J. Crew	$365
Children's Place	$263
Foot Locker	$316
Payless ShoeSource	$181
Wal-Mart	$422
Dollar Tree Stores	$199
Williams-Sonoma	$410
Linens 'n Things	$171
Dick's Sporting Goods	$192
Sports Authority	$164
Borders Books	$237
Barnes & Noble	$243
Radio Shack (company store)	$342
AutoZone	$258
Pep Boys	$169
PetSmart	$189
PETCO	$188
Bath & Body Works	$507

Another of the important benchmarks is employee productivity. The number of employees includes both full-time and part-time employees. The following sampling of employee productivity will provide some rough rule of thumb for comparison purposes.

Type of Retailer	Payroll as % Of Sales	Sales per Employee
Automotive parts & accessories	15.6%	$129,024
Tire dealers	18.1%	$137,821
Floor covering stores	14.9%	$171,250
Camera & photographic supplies store	14.4%	$128,609
Nursery & garden centers	10.0%	$198,428
Children's & infants' clothing stores	10.2%	$99,699
Family shoe stores	11.0%	$112,517
Athletic footwear stores	10.5%	$118,111

-cont'd-

Type of Retailer	Payroll as % Of Sales	Sales per Employee
Sporting goods, hobby & musical instrument stores	11.6%	$114,100
Hobby, toy & games stores	09.5%	$128,746
Book stores—general	11.8%	$103,517
Florists	21.3%	$52,359
Gift, novelty & souvenir stores	14.2%	$69,574
Used merchandise stores	19.9%	$61,692
Pet & pet supplies stores	12.9%	$89,763
Vending machine operators	19.4%	$103,763

The data above gives you an idea of the information that is available. We have found that BizStats has lot of valuable information. *Nation's Restaurant* has a lot of data on restaurants. For subscription information, go to www.nrn.com.

Expenses as a percentage of annual sales:

Cost of Goods Sold	25%
Payroll/Labor Costs	20%
Occupancy Cost	18%
Profit (estimated)	28%

General Information

"Visual appearance and merchandising trends are in constant need of updates and modernization to enhance sales."

"Retail is the second largest industry in the United States in both the number of businesses and the number of employees.

"The term 'retail' is derived from the French word *retaillier,* which means to cut a piece off or to break bulk.

"$3.8 trillion—annual retail sales in the United States
$56 million—the amount of those annual sales which are Wal-Mart's
14.9 million—the number of people employed in retail trade in 2003."

Source: About Business Web site, a *New York Times* Company, appeared in *Franchise Times*

Advantages of this Business

- "Quality operators can have impact on sales if location has excellent salespeople and service for the customer."

Disadvantages of this Business

- "New and intense competition from Big Box retailers and Internet sites. Rising costs for wages, insurance, energy (utilities) and legal representation."

Industry Trend

"Difficult. Big box retailers and Internet sites are crimping margins."

Resources

"Valuing Retail Businesses," *Handbook of Business Valuation*, West & Jones, 2nd Edition, published by John Wiley & Sons

National Retail Federation
www.nsf.com

Quick *Profile* Retail Businesses

Pricing the Retail Business

Pricing retail businesses is unlike any other. The major difference, of course, is inventory. In pricing all small retail operations, the inventory is the key. One other issue —most statistics for retail include the restaurant industry: quick food outlets, tablecloth restaurants, bars, taverns and the like. This is not the forum to make the argument that these businesses are an industry in themselves, but we think they are and should not be included in the retail category. They, for the most part, take an unfinished product and turn it into a finished one. The final stage may be a retail operation, but they do not maintain high inventory levels. We believe that the main difference between retail and other types of business operations is the high dollar amount invested in inventory.

What is Retail?

The Dictionary of Business Terms defines retailing as "The promoting and selling of merchandise directly to customers, augmented by advertising, store promotions, and personal contacts in the community where the retailer's outlet is located. Retailing is the selling of finished goods and services to the consumer for personal or family consumption..."

Ed Telling, in his chapter on Valuing Retailing Businesses in the 2nd Edition of the *Handbook of Business Valuation,* says, "Many retail business characteristics are unlike those of manufacturing and service businesses.

- "Typically, a retail business's largest dollar investment is in inventory, followed by accounts receivable (if credit is offered).
- To stay competitive, often retail businesses stay open around the clock to serve their customers. [Non-store retailers are open 24 hours a day, every day of the year.]
- In general, retail employees are paid less than manufacturing employees.
- It can be argued that retailing has less control over value-added pricing of the product it sells."

In defining small retail operations and attempting to outline some pricing guidelines, we are looking at such businesses as hardware stores, book stores, sporting goods, building materials and supply, apparel stores, gift and card shops, and the like. Operations such as department stores, the box stores retailing electronic goods, home supply and hardware, books and music, housewares—and companies like Amazon, L.L. Bean, and Land's End, although obviously retail, are not included in this pricing discussion.

Inventory – the Key

Since we are discussing pricing small retail operations, we have to return to the subject of inventory. As we mentioned earlier, we believe the defining difference in pricing retail operations from pricing every other business is the inventory. In many cases, the inventory dollar amount can be substantial. To price small businesses, most business brokers use Seller's Discretionary Earnings. We should add that this method is also being used by many business appraisers to actually place a value on a small business.

And here is the dilemma. One school of thought is that the price arrived at by the SDE method should include the inventory—or, at least, a level sufficient to run the business. If there is more than what might be considered adequate, the surplus can be added to the price. The other school of thought is that, after performing the calculations and arriving at a figure, the inventory, regardless of the amount, is then added to this number to arrive at the asking price.

Some Background on the Inventory Issue

A bit of history from the business broker's vantage point may be helpful in understanding this quandary. Prior to 1980, most business brokers listed a business exclusive of the inventory. The commission was based on this figure, and inventory was not part of the asking price, nor was it commissionable. After the closing, the buyer and seller, usually with the broker's help, worked out the inventory figure; and this amount was then given by the buyer to the seller, outside of the escrow or closing. This method presented several problems. Although it reduced the asking price considerably—especially in retail businesses—it could, and did, create a real problem after the closing. Generally, the buyer did not have sufficient funds to pay for the inventory in cash; and since the sale was already closed, serious problems developed. The asking price was low, but the inventory still had to be paid for, and in cash. Of course, another big negative to this method was that the business broker did not get a commission on the amount of the inventory.

Finally, some business brokers saw the light and changed the way the business was done. Their thinking was based on—and correctly so, in our opinion—the fact that the buyer had to have sufficient funds to pay for the inventory—which made the task more difficult. Inventory was to be added to what the seller wanted for his or her business to arrive at an asking price. Although complicating matters in one sense, it also did the following: (1) it allowed for the commission to be based on the total price including the inventory, (2) by including the inventory, it provided better terms to be arranged with the seller, (3) the buyer knew exactly what he was paying and how much cash was required, and finally (4) it eliminated a lot of problems.

Obviously, the difference in the two applications can impact the final price considerably. This difference can also greatly impact the ultimate salability of a small retail operation, and/or substantially influence the amount the seller receives for his or her business. Who's right?

Inventory & the SDE Pricing Method

The first school feels that the price arrived at via the SDE calculations should be the price one pays for a business ready to operate—in essence, a turnkey operation. The other school, of which we are one, thinks that inventory is such a variable that it should be added to the price calculation.

The thing we have always liked about the SDE method is that it equalizes all businesses based on their cash flow. Since whatever equipment exists is necessary for the operation of the business, placing a value on it is not necessary. This makes sense because attempting to place an actual dollar value on used equipment is almost impossible. Of course, one could argue that if the equipment is included, why not inventory? Our response is that placing a dollar amount on inventory is relatively easy. Also, inventory inclusion can really skew the numbers, since the amount can vary from month to month and even year to year.

Take a gift store that has been in business for 10 or more years. Many of these businesses reinvest much of their profits in adding more inventory. We have seen gift stores bulging with inventory—every nook and cranny filled. Or, take the local toy store a month before Christmas—its inventory may be two to three times the normal levels.

Another concern we have is that trying to calculate the inventory necessary to adequately operate the business is about the same as trying to place a dollar value on the used equipment necessary to operate the business. In many small businesses, the value of the fixtures and equipment necessary to operate the business, which is currently in place in the business, is minimal. Fixtures and equipment normally do not influence the price as the inventory would. In larger, manufacturing-type businesses, the investment in fixtures and equipment can be substantial.

Where Does the Inventory Go?

Bizcomps, in its regional editions of Recent Small Business Studies, does not include inventory, but rather assumes that it is or has been added to the prices submitted for inclusion. Here is what is said in the Introduction to the Studies:

"The exclusion of inventory from the financial averages requires further discussion. In business sale transactions, inventory transfers at the date of closing are based on the wholesale cost of 'good' inventory existing at that date. Since the amount of inventory can vary so significantly from business to business, Bizcomps believes that the financial ratios of the selling price of a business should exclude this relatively volatile asset. Also, there may be external reasons to manipulate the amount of inventory at the time of closing that, if included, would distort the selling price of the business. If it could be assumed that the optimal level of inventory was included in every business sale transaction or that the aggregate statistics would produce the optimal level of inventory, then inventory could be meaningfully included. The author does not believe this is a safe assumption, and therefore inventory is excluded from the statistical averages."

When writing about this issue in *The Business Broker* newsletter, we received a lot of letters. Again, there was a division among those who responded. Those who work in the General Business Brokerage area feel that the inventory should be added to the price derived from the SDE calculations. Some of the opinions are very practical. By building in the inventory, the price can be greatly increased (in many cases inventory can be reduced, returned or sold off) creating a difficult situation in talking to potential buyers. One writer used the example that if $100,000 in liquid cash on hand was required to operate the business, would the business sell for $300,000 or $400,000 including the requisite cash. Obviously not, says the writer. "The buyer is expected to have the cash required to replace the $100,000 as a working capital injection. Why should the expectation be any different for inventory?" The writer also says that by including the inventory, the buyer begins business with, for example, 60 days of free inventory. He further states, "... The seller not only pays for every bit of inventory he's sold but pays for the inventory the buyer will be selling, giving the buyer a 100 percent profit margin on that inventory."

It should also be noted that the rules of thumb contained in the *Business Reference Guide* provide that inventory be added. For example, in the case of a gift shop, the rule of thumb is 35 percent of annual sales + inventory.

There is one caveat in all this. Ed Telling, in his article referenced earlier, says: "[Inventory] is probably the largest asset for most retail operations ... A business that has inventory probably has in inventory merchandise it would rather not own. A prudent analysis should determine how much and how troublesome the 'how much' will be to dispose of. Does disposal mean a trip to the dump, or a discount in price (how deep a discount, as compared to cost and/or normal), which will result in an immediate or rapid sale? We should determine with some reasonable accuracy that total amount of inventory that represents 'good clean saleable merchandise.' Inventory that is other than that should be discounted—even in an extreme case 'carried to the dump' (the ultimate discount for lack of marketability, as in today's world there are probably costs attached to disposal)." Adding the inventory allows the process outlined in Ed's article to take place without actually influencing the negotiated price of the business.

Pricing Tips

The following table is from Toby Tatum's book, *Transaction Patterns: A Pictorial Review of the Bizcomps Database*. It indicates that in a retail business, the value of the furniture, fixtures and equipment (FF&E) is not in the high end, the inventory is the highest, and, very interestingly, the intangibles (goodwill) are the lowest in value of all the categories. This might indicate that the marketplace builds in a decrease in goodwill to allow for the increase in inventory, in comparison to other major business types or groups.

A further review of all three editions of the Bizcomps data would seem to indicate that retail businesses, in general, have a lower sale price in both the percentage of Sales to Gross, and also in SDE, than all of the other major categories.

What all of this suggests is that the marketplace, in its own way, builds in inventory in the small retail business. Keep in mind that Bizcomps does not include inventory in its data, so the price indicated would be plus inventory, whatever the amount.

The average for the three regions in Bizcomps is a bit over 30 percent and is probably a realistic figure. Obviously, this is plus inventory. A review of the rules of thumb in Bizcomps, on average, for SDE is 1.8.

Keep in mind that an SDE multiple contains a lot of subjective analysis. When working with the small retail store, start with the 1.5 to 2.0 range and build up or scale down, whichever is easier. We have seen some excellent retail stores go for more than the 2.0 figure. In retail, the old expression "Location, Location, Location" is still a very important element. A great location with a great lease will add great value, assuming everything else is equal.

Type of Business	FF&E.	Inventory	Intangibles
Personal Service Industry	18.1%	0.6%	81.3%
Distribution Business	18.7%	28.4%	52.9%
Manufacturing	24.3%	17.6%	58%
Retail	25.5%	31.3%	43.1%
Construction	35.2%	4.6%	60.2%
Dry Cleaning	52.9%	2.0%	45.1%
Grocery/C-Stores	35.2%	21.1%	43.7%

Franchise

Rita's—Ices, Cones, Shakes & Other Cool Stuff

261 units

Approximate Total Investment:	$161,900 to $337,000

Rule of Thumb:

- 80 percent to 1.3 times annual sales plus inventory

Resources
www.ritasice.com

Routes *(See also Amusement and Vending Routes)*

Rule of Thumb:

- 50 percent of annual sales plus inventory
- 10 to 20 times weekly gross plus inventory
- 3 times SDE. Add inventory; name brands—3 times; no name brand—1 to 2 times

Pricing Tips
"Franchised Routes: Approximately 2 times SDE. Note that franchised routes, which usually exist on the more consumer-recognized products, have 'Distribution Agreements' in force between wholesales and distributor."

"Non-Franchised Routes: Approximately 1 times SDE. Non-franchised routes have no such contracts [Distribution Agreements] and they usually distribute staple items and/or non-consumer recognized products."

"What is a route?
A route is a collection of stops where a specific product is picked up and delivered to customers. These customers may include supermarkets, delis, grocery stores, diners, restaurants, schools, nursing homes and even factories and office buildings. Payment is usually made to the owner of the route for the product that has been delivered, either by C.O.D. or on a weekly basis.

"What types of routes are there?
There are many different types of routes that can be purchased. Some categories include bread, meat and provisions, beverage, cookie, cake, snacks, coffee catering, dairy, vending, newspaper, ice cream, Fed Ex and even office cleaning. Some of these are name brand routes and others are not. The ones which are not are called independent routes.

"How much does a route cost?
The price of routes varies according to how much the route is netting, the route type, the vehicle, area and days/hours per week. The general rule of 2x the yearly net (double net) still holds true for many routes, including some independent routes. Name-brand routes start at 2x and can now go for 2 ½ to 3x the net, with some even going for as high as 4x net. [Ex: Pepsi, Boar's Head, Snapple, and Pepperidge Farm Cookies]. Most route owners who are willing to hold a note want at least 50% to 70% down."

Source: www.mrrouteinc.com—Mr. Route is a route brokerage firm that has an excellent Web site that is full of information on the subject.

Industry Experts' Ratings:

Amount of Competition (1 = Lot of: 4 = Not much) 1.0
Amount of Risk (1 = Very: 4 = Not much) 1.0
Historical Profit Trend (1 = Down: 4 = Up) 2.0
Location & Facilities (1 = Poor: 4 = Excellent) 3.2
Marketability (1 = Low: 4 = High) 3.6
Industry Trend (1 = Declining: 4 = Growing) 2.4
Ease of Replication (1 = Easy: 4 = Difficult) 2.0

Benchmarks
"Cost of goods should never be more than 35 percent."

Expenses as a percentage of annual sales:	
Cost of Goods Sold	30%
Payroll/Labor Costs	25%
Occupancy Cost	12%
Profit (estimated)	20%

General Information

"Owner operated typically"

"Each business is different, based upon the answers to the following: product distributed; years owned; years established; protected territory; protected stops; unprotected; location of business; vehicles & condition/age; hours of operation; days/nights; condensed territory; distribution contract; percentage cash volume; net profit."

"Down payment will be approx. one year's net. Total price approx. two years' net. Protected stops or territory with major company will sell for more."

"Years established, age of vehicles, protected territories, years owned, brand names, hours needed to operate, number of stops, weekly gross sales, gross purchases"

"Verification of product purchases for the last 12 months, a confirmation of profit margin worked on and policy, amount of returns"

"Routes established less than 2 to 3 years definitely reduce the price of the business. Where is route distribution territory? Category of business: bread, soda, provisions, juice, snacks, cookies, etc. Protected stops or territory? Condition of vehicle included? Contracts?"

Advantages of this Business

- "The market is broader than in retail."
- "Distribution routes are not complicated to operate. Most are owner operated."

Disadvantages of this Business

- "The increases in fuel costs will impact this business tremendously."

- "If a prospective purchaser does not like working outside, this is not the right business for them."

Seller Financing

- "Enough years (at prevailing rate of interest) to insure monthly debt service of no more than one week's net income"
- "8 years"

RV Dealerships

3,823	SIC: 5561-03	

Rule of Thumb:

- 15 percent of annual sales + RV inventory & parts, etc.

General Information

Recreational vehicles come in two basic types, those that need to be towed and those that power themselves. Within those categories, here are the options:

Towables

- Travel trailers: Offered in a wide range of floor plans and sizes. They sleep up to 10 people. The price range is $8,000 to $65,000.
- Fifth-wheel travel trailers: Have two-level floor plans and are towed by pickup trucks. Sleep up to six. $13,000 to $100,000.
- Truck campers: Are mounted on a pickup bed or chassis. Sleep up to six. $4,000 to $26,000.

Motorized RVs

- Class A: The roomiest RVs, they look like buses in front and can sleep up to six. $50,000 to $400,000, though some luxury models can top $1 million.
- Class B: Known as van campers. Sleep up to four. $41,000 to $74,000.
- Class C: Have amenities similar to those in Class A, but with fronts that hang over the cab. Sleep up to eight. $48,000 to $140,000.

Source: *The New York Times,* Sunday, January 16, 2005

Industry Trend

"Despite fuel prices, the RV industry is experiencing one of its best sales years on record. Even though RV sales are down slightly, 2005 is forecasted to be the second-best year for RV sales in 27 years. The past 24 months (July 2003 to June 2005) have been the best two-year period in RV sales in 27 years."

Source: *RV Business Indicators*, September 12, 2005, Prepared by the Recreation Vehicle Industry Association

Resources

Recreational Vehicle Industry Association, (RVIA)
www.rvia.org—A very informative site

RV Parks *(See also Camp Grounds)*

Pricing Tips

"Too variable for rules of thumb. Cap rates of 9 to 15 percent. Urban parks at low end of cap rate spectrums. Destination parks are at higher end. Number of ancillary revenue sources will affect cap rates on destination parks—more revenue sources, lower cap rates. Parks with fewer than 100 sites are very inefficient, and value tends to be exclusively in the real estate, with little or no intrinsic value."

Benchmarks

Expenses as a percentage of sales:	
Marketing	10%
Utilities	14%
Payroll	25%
G&A	5%

General Information

"The Association of RV Parks and Campgrounds estimates the cost of building a new park at between $15,000 and $20,000 a space, which is very costly, considering most new parks have as few as 150 spaces.

"The cost of buying an existing park is much less, and most of the sales are structured so that a buyer can make a 10 to15 percent return on his or her investment when it changes hands.

"The problem for most owners is they want to make improvements when they buy an existing park. That can be costly, depending on the state of the park when it changes hands.

"Modern RVs are much more sophisticated than RVs that pulled into parks even five years ago. Many are outfitted with satellite technology, computers and televisions.

"Modern travelers, too, have different expectations than earlier RVers and like a lot of amenities. To keep up with the times, park owners now have retail outfits where they sell T-shirts and sweatshirts and provisions. Most have upgraded game rooms and pools and offer ancillary services such as RV repair.

"Many owners are eager to add amenities these days because such amenities are great sources of additional revenue. In some parks, they are more lucrative than renting the spaces.

"One owner stated that his good fortune cane be attributed to excellent timing and understanding his customers. An avid camper himself, this owner understands well what customers want from an RV park. Neatness counts, as does the continental breakfast he serves and the top-shelf amenities such as cable television and a brand new clubhouse."

Source: www.money.cnn.com

Resources

Guide to Appraising Recreational Vehicle Parks published by the Appraisal Institute
www.appraisalinstitute.org

RV Life—an industry publication
www.rvlife.com

National Association of RV Parks and Campgrounds
www.arvc.org

Sales Businesses (In General)

Rule of Thumb:

- 1 times SDE plus inventory

Sand and Gravel Mining

Rule of Thumb:

- 100 percent of annual sales plus inventory
- 5 times EBITDA

Benchmarks

"At least 150,000 tons/year is the minimum usually necessary for a profitable site."

General Information

"All commodity markets by definition are generally quite competitive, although this changes by the number of producers, size of market and proximity of resources to market. This is a very capital intensive industry and nothing is proprietary except the quality, quantity and location of the resource. The opportunity trends for the industry are declining, due to consolidation and availability of permitted resource."

Advantages of this Business

- "Declining resource availability equates to real price increases and growing margins."

Disadvantages of this Business

- "Cost of regulation and equipment makes this highly capital intensive compared to other industries."

Sandwich Shops

(See individual sandwich shops for more information)

7,700	SIC: 5812-19	NAIC: 722211

Rule of Thumb:

- 50 percent of annual sales plus inventory
- 2 times SDE50 percent of annual sales plus inventory
- 50 percent of annual sales plus inventory
- 3 times EBIT
- 6 times monthly sales plus inventory

Sandwich Shops	
Blimpie	48% of annual sales
Hungry Howie's Pizza & Subs	30% of annual sales
Lil' Dino's Subs	64% of annual sales
Quiznos Classic Subs	50%–60% of annual sales
Roly Poly Sandwiches	34% of annuals sales
Subway	50%–60% of annual sales

Pricing Tips

Industry Experts' Ratings:

Marketability (1 = Low: 4 = High)	2.4
Industry Trend (1 = Declining: 4 = Growing)	2.4
Ease of Replication (1 = Easy: 4 = Difficult)	2.4

Benchmarks

Expenses as a percentage of annual sales:	
Cost of Goods Sold	28%
Payroll/Labor Costs	22%
Occupancy Cost	10%
Profit (estimated)	20%

General Information

"Ownership of real estate is very desirable. Franchise stores more marketable than independents. Franchise presence in marketplace is very important."

Advantages of this Business

- "Ease of operation. Low food costs. Little waste. Low-skilled workforce. Fewer total hours than a full-service restaurant. Very nice profit margins. Franchise sub shops can usually qualify for SBA loans."

Disadvantages of this Business

- "Employees. Customers look for, and use, coupons. Hard to compete with 'big' names in the industry, which have a media presence."

Schools—(Educational—Non-Vocational)

(See also Day Care)

Rule of Thumb:

- 2.8 times SDE plus inventory

Pricing Tips

Industry Experts' Ratings:

Amount of Competition (1 = Lot of: 4 = Not much)	1.2
Amount of Risk (1 = Very: 4 = Not much)	2.0
Historical Profit Trend (1 = Down: 4 = Up)	2.0
Location & Facilities (1 = Poor: 4 = Excellent)	2.8
Marketability (1 = Low: 4 = High)	2.8
Industry Trend (1 = Declining: 4 = Growing)	2.0
Ease of Replication (1 = Easy: 4 = Difficult)	1.6

"There are no physical barriers to entry, but creating a quality school or day care takes more than a facility. It takes quality teachers and leaders. Finding these is the real barrier to entry."

Benchmarks

Some people use a crude measure to value of between $1,500 and $2,500 per student enrolled for childcare facilities in leased space."

Expenses as a percentage of annual sales:

Cost of goods sold	1%
Payroll/Labor costs	35%
Occupancy cost	30%
Profit (estimated)	5%

General Information

"Most successful operators get into it to make a decent living while doing something they want to do. Don't get into it if profit is your only motive. Also, if you have not had children of your own, it is hard to understand the business or the parents."

Advantages of this Business

- "A chance to work with children, much like the benefit of being a teacher."

Disadvantages of this Buisness

- "Maintaining state compliance, dealing with problem parents and children."

Industry Trend

"There is plenty of growth as the population increases. Franchises and corporate-owned schools are increasingly popular."

"Always students who need help, fall behind, need passing grades to pass"

Seller Financing

- "5 years"

Schools (In General)

Rule of Thumb:

- 50 percent of annual sales plus inventory
- 3 times SDE plus inventory
- 1.5 times EBIT

Pricing Tips

"Pricing is all over the board because of the size of a facility. The larger the school the more the owners profit."

"I am in the process of closing a second sale on truck-driver-training schools in Missouri and Alabama. Unfortunately the same buyers of Franklin College are my buyers for the Missouri and Alabama schools. Their criteria are straight up and simple, and I quote:

'Invested capital has to come back to buyer 100 percent + Cost of Money (Interest) in 24 months or less.'

"My sale, being a truck-driver-training school, is a somewhat different business than a typical trade school where the 'class' time or number of months to complete school would be say 1 year or 2 years. The CDL licensing school is a 'short' 3-week, high-turn business. Asset/Liability structure is much different for other 'long-term' schools, as they invest higher percentages in fixed assets and typically do not get the margin as the CDL licensing schools.

"The 'deal' on Franklin College was an equity purchase of $2,600,000+, plus cash payments to owner principals of $120,000. In the following, I will use the $2.6 million as a sale price.

Amount and % Seller financed: .... $1,000,000 or 38.46%
Term Financed: .... 5 years
x Historical Cash Flow .... 3.43 x (based on last two years' average)
x Forecasted Two Yr. Cash Flow .... 2.5x (buyer's forecast)
x Book Equity .... 98.48% (net depreciation and amortization)
x Blue Sky 0%
x Annual Gross Revenue lx
Cost of Goods % to Gross Revenue* 16.6%
Recruitment Expense** 18.00%
Administrative Expense 17.8%
All Other & Misc. 6.9%
Net Operating Income .... 40.7% (before income tax)

**(Cost of teaching supplies for training, including instructor/teacher wages and wage burden)*
***(Cost of commissioned salesmen,* advertising)

"The buyer of this particular school has never owned or operated a truck-driver-training school or been involved in the trucking industry. I had earlier sold them a structural-steel- fabrication company, and they wanted to look at ALL my sell deals and became interested because of the high margins of this particular school and the well-known truck driver shortage, nationally. Since that date, they have acquired 7 other operating schools in 5 states and are now in the process of purchasing 2 more in 2 states, as I earlier mentioned.

"Until this buyer came along, my best offer came from PGT Trucking, a Northeast, PA firm that was not considered acceptable to the sellers. It is also interesting to note that I marketed to 14 different truck-driver-training schools and only had one principal to inquire, without an offer of any kind."

"Value is driven by type of program (longer, more expensive programs are more valuable), enrollment, and enrollment growth."

Industry Experts' Ratings:

Amount of Competition (1 = Lot of: 4 = Not much)	2.8
Amount of Risk (1 = Very: 4 = Not much)	1.2
Historical Profit Trend (1 = Down: 4 = Up)	4.0
Location & Facilities (1 = Poor: 4 = Excellent)	3.2
Marketability (1 = Low: 4 = High)	4.0
Industry Trend (1 = Declining: 4 = Growing)	3.6
Ease of Replication (1 = Easy: 4 = Difficult)	1.2

"Great industry with room to grow. The childcare, private school and adult education industry is on the move."

Benchmarks

"Sales per license cap can range from $6000 to $ 14000. An example: a 100 student licensed school could sell for as much as $1.4 million. Most schools sell based on Cash Flow."

Expenses as a percentage of annual sales:

Cost of goods sold	20%
Payroll/Labor costs	40%
Occupancy cost	20%
Profit (estimated)	20%

General Information

The following is a definition of private vocational schools in New Jersey: "In accordance with the New Jersey Administration Code … a 'private vocational school' means a business enterprise operated for either profit or nonprofit which maintains a place of business within the State of New Jersey and which:

1. Solicits pupils from the general public
2. Charges tuition and/or fees
3. Offers instruction to a group or groups of four or more pupils at one time

4. Offers preparatory instruction to pupils for entry-level employment or for upgrading in a specific occupational field

"After they have been in business for at least two years, then they may apply for accreditation. That takes anywhere from six to nine months for that process to be completed and if you are successful, then you may apply for student financial aid, (student loans and grants) if your accredited programs meet the required number of credit hours to be funded.

"Then you must staff the financial aid office, submit the necessary financial aid packages, and be prepared to wait thirty to sixty days to receive your federal funds. When your client is buying an accredited school that has financial aid, you must examine their default rate for the past several years and also contact the accrediting body to determine if there are any complaints, any conditional accreditation, and the renewal date for accreditation.

"The default rate, if too high, would jeopardize the school's continuation in federal financial programs and in fact could jeopardize its accreditation. In other words, without accreditation, there is no financial aid.

"Job skill training that has a low entry-level income has a higher risk of default for lack of income to make necessary payments. The lower the default rate for a great number of years, the more valuable the school is and therefore the higher multiple rate should apply."

"Big difference between schools that are not accredited and do not qualify for federally backed student loans. Schools that can qualify for student loans can be very profitable, but do have to deal with government bureaucracy and interference. These schools need experienced owners or managers, especially someone with experience in dealing with federally backed student loans. It can take schools four or five years normally to qualify for these student loans. Owners of vocational/technical schools should be sales oriented, as they need to recruit good teachers who can relate to the students and 'teach the market' so they can get jobs upon completion of the program. Then the owners must sell students on attending. Difficult business for the novice."

Number of Schools	
Business & Secretarial	2,332
Business & Vocational	4,827
Cooking	303+
Dancing	15,556
Driving	6,589
Floral Design	48,670
General Interest	689
Industrial Technical & Trade	2,737
Language	1,680

Source: American Business Information, Inc.

Advantages of this Business

- "Good income. Good hours. Clean work. FUN."

Seller Financing

- "10 years"

Resources

RWM provides a database of private postsecondary vocational schools in all 50 states. www.rwm.org

www.schoolsforsale.com

Franchise

Sears Carpet & Upholstery Care

130 units

Approximate Total Investment: $71,510 to $362,300

Rule of Thumb:

- 30 percent of annual sales plus inventory

Secretarial Services *(See also Answering Services)*

Rule of Thumb:

- 50 percent of annual revenues plus inventory

Security is a Small-Business-Dominated Industry

"Approximately one-half of the businesses installing alarm systems have annual revenues of less than $250,000 per year and employ four or fewer employees."

Source: STAT Resources, Inc.

Security Services/Systems *(See also Guard Services)*

2,300	SIC: 7382-02	NAIC: 561621

Rule of Thumb:

- 2 to 3 times SDE plus inventory
- 24 to 28 times monthly revenue based on an average $18 mo. per account plus inventory

Benchmarks

"No one disregards the sale and installation of a typical home security system, especially with continued strength of new home construction and existing home sales in the United States. Still, the average price of a home security system was flat last year ($1,471) when compared to an average price tag of $1,425 in 2002. Previous high prices (($1,995 in 1998 and $2,000 in 1999) occurred just before the economy started to slow and overall consumer prices started to soften. For those that define themselves as serving the mass market, the price of an average home security system is $911 compared to that $1,471 across all types of dealer firms. About a third of dealers (32 percent) believe that the average price of home security systems will increase this year; most believe pricing will remain the same.

"Monthly home monitoring fees, the meat to product sales potatoes, remain static on average, with the average monthly fee pegged at $22.80, although 30 percent of dealers who monitor report billing higher than the average. About two in 10 (21 percent) expect that the price of monitoring will increase this year. That's less than the number of respondents who expect the price of an average home installation to increase.

"Last year, for instance, surveyed dealers say they lost, on average, 59 customers, with about one-fourth reporting that the number of lost customers increased as compared to 2002. Still, on average, dealers say they sold 150 monitoring contracts last year, with about one-fourth saying the number of monitoring contracts sold in 2003 increased compared to 2002.

"Emerging remote video monitoring services, which some claim may one day replace or overtake traditional alarm monitoring, have grown and bring in higher monthly monitoring revenues, thanks in large part to the increased monthly expenses inherent in the service. A healthy 26 percent of respondents say that they now sell remote video monitoring services, and the average monthly video monitoring price charged is $101."

Source: *Security Distributing and Marketing*

Expenses as a percentage of annual sales:	
Cost of Goods	10%
Payroll/Labor Costs	70%
Occupancy Cost	10%
Profit (estimated)	10%

General Information

Questions to ask a seller: "What are the contract terms? How long have you had this account? Buyers do not like government contracts."

"Another finding of the survey points out the ongoing consolidation of security companies. 'Security companies—and smaller ones in particular—should be aware that it will be increasingly difficult to successfully pursue niche marketing strategies in the business in the future. This is because the large diversified companies that are achieving dominance in the industry are in effect erecting barriers to entry in the form of economies of scale and scope that did not exist traditionally. Smaller companies that desire to stay independent may be forced to pool resources in the form of joint ventures and other strategic partnerships to achieve and sustain market share and profitability."

Source: Ed Hester, VP, The Freedonia Group, in *Research Update*, Report for First Quarter 2004, published by the Security Industry Association

"While the average price of $1,425 for a residential security system seems relatively high, it's important to note that the survey measures pricing for 'traditional systems.' The average price for a mass market type system clocked in at $416 in 2002."

Source: *Security Distributing and Marketing*

"Service Revenue Generators

Following are the types of services from which security dealers and system integrators expect to earn their revenues in 2004.

Burglar alarms	38%
Video surveillance	20%
Fire alarms	15%
Access control	11%
Home systems (other than burg./fire)	6%
Integrated security systems	6%
Other	4%"

Source: *Security Distributing and Marketing*

Industry Trend

"This is a stable industry; with 9/11, it is almost like a temp business; make sure they have low turnover which will mean satisfied clients."

"The demand for U.S. private security services will grow 7.3 percent yearly through 2006. Continued outsourcing of in-house security in both commercial offices and warehouses and the increasing privatization of some prisons will fuel the $33.5 billion U.S. private security services market. Heightened concerns about crime and the perceived inadequacy of public safety officials will also drive growth.

"U.S. sales of $7 billion; U.S. electronic security industry will grow nearly ten percent yearly through 2006. Gains will be driven by heightened security awareness as government agencies, the air travel industry, power plants, office buildings, factories and schools invest heavily in new protective measures. Bomb detectors, CCTV cameras, access controls and biometrics will lead gains."

Source: The Freedonia Group

Seller Financing

- "3 to 5 years and an average of 20 to 50 percent of transaction value financed by seller"

Resources

The American Society for Industrial Security (ASIS)
www.asisonline.org

Security Industry Association (SIA)
www.siaonline.org

National Burglar & Fire Alarm Association
www.alarm.org

Security Distribution and Marketing magazine
www.sdmmag.com—An excellent site with lots of good information and data. It's everything one needs to know about the security industry.

Self-Storage

41,000	SIC: 40,981	NAIC: 531130

Rule of Thumb:

- 1 times EBITDA

Pricing Tips

"Pricing is driven by capitalization rates and expense ratios."

"The typical buyer is looking for about a 20% cash-on-cash return plus an opportunity to eventually sell the ground for a profit when development reaches the area."

Cap Rate Adjustments

The little chart that follows is about the best thing we have seen in pricing a business. It outlines specific business issues and assigns them an adjustment to the cap rate. What is so good about this chart is the specific areas it covers and that it essentially assigns a rating to each one that impacts the valuation or pricing of each business.

Item	9.50 - 10.00	10.00 - 11.00	11.00 - 11.50
Vacancy (last 2 years)	95%–100%	90%–95%	<90%
Rates (last 2 years)	Continuous Rise	Steady	Falling
Size	>45,000	30,000–45,000	<30,000
Competition (3 mile radius)	None	One	More than One

Cap Rate Adjustments - (cont'd)

Item	9.50 - 10.00	10.00 - 11.00	11.00 - 11.50
Competition's Vacancy	95%–100%	90%–95%	<90%
Surrounding Area	Growing Metro	Large City	Rural
Density (5 mile radius)	>200,000	100,000–200,000	<100,000
Median Household Income	Above Average	Average	Below Average
Manager	Full-time	Full-time	Other
Records (last 3 years)	Computerized & Professionally Audited	Computerized	Other
Computer System	Computers & SS Accounting Software	Computers	None
Construction	Concrete or Brick	Combination Brick & Metal	Metal
Maintenance	Pristine	Little Deferred Maintenance	Modest Deferred Maintenance
Security	Full Gate & Card Access	Full Gate	Other
Access	Very Direct	Clear, but Not Direct	Difficult
Visibility	Can see Sign & Facility	Can see Sign & Entrance	Can see Sign only
Drives	Concrete	Paved	Gravel

Source: Argus Real Estate, Inc., Denver, CO

Note: This is from an excellent article by Michael L. McCune, Cap Rates and Sales Prices. For more information visit www.selfstorage.com—an excellent site.

"You can look at it a couple of different ways. It depends on your location; but here in Southern Indiana, Mini-Storage facilities are being appraised based upon the number of units. Age, condition and income are also looked at. Our appraiser just today told us that they are ranging from $3,000 to $3,500 per unit. So your 131-unit facility would appraise for around $393,000 if it were located here.

"Another way to figure out what your potential income will be: if you are totally full, then multiply that number by 60 to 75 percent, because of the reality of occupancy. Use those numbers to figure out what your income/expense ratio will be. Your income should be at least 1.25 over your debt service (if it's not, then you're paying too much for the property). That extra 25 percent will help cover vacancies, utilities, labor, etc."

Source: www.autocareforum.com

"American families own such a surfeit of consumer goods that they've turned self-storage into a $17 billion-a-year industry."

Source: "Pomp and Circumspect" by Daniel H. Pink, *The New York Times*, June 4, 2005

"We sold a 195-unit mini-storage in Idaho last year. It had annual gross receipts of $105,000 and an annual net cash flow of $80,000. It sold for $640,000 with $235,000 cash down payment and the balance at 8.3 percent over 15 years.

"We have another mini-storage in the process of being sold. It looks like it will go for $500,000 with $150,000 cash down payment, the balance over 20 years at 8.5 percent. It has annual gross income of $70,000 and cash flow debt service of $61,000.

"I believe that a cash-on-cash return of 15 percent to 20 percent is required to sell one of these mini-storage projects. A minimum of 15 percent seems to be required."

Industry Experts' Ratings:

Marketability 2.8
(1 = low marketability; 4 = high marketability)
Industry Trend 1.2
(1 = declining trend; 4 = growing trend)
Ease of Replication 3.2
(1 = easily replicated; 4 = difficult to replicate)

"Barriers of entry to prospective competitors drive rental rates."

Benchmarks

Sample facility

"Size	40,000 SF
Average Rent	$71/month
Rent/SF	$8.52/yr
Current Occupancy	88%
Market Occupancy	70%
Potential Rent	$341,000
Rents Collected @ 88%	$300,000/yr
Expenses	$100,000
Net Operating Income	$200,000/yr
Value @ 9.5	$2,100,000
Loan Amount @ 75%	$1,575,000
Debt Service @ 6.5%	$128,000/yr"

Source: "The State of Self Storage Real Estate"
by Michael L. McCune, Argus Self-Storage Sales Network

"Expenses as a percentage of annual sales:

On-site management	22.91%
Taxes	13.62%
Insurance	4.95%
Off-site management	14.55%
Repairs & Maintenance	6.81%
Utilities	6.50%
Advertising	7.12%
Administration	8.36%
Misc.	15.17%"

2004 Mini-Storage Messenger published by MiniCo., Inc.and compiled by Self Storage Data Economics.

"The most common 'state of the art' facility will be about 60,000 to 80,000 net rentable square feet, cost $25 to $50 per square foot, outside of existing land costs, to construct, and have breakeven operating expenses in the 25 to 40 percent range (not including debt service) of total stabilized income.

"A well-designed and located facility will successfully operate in the 83 to 93 percent occupancy range, with many projects having been successful at occupancies as low as 70 percent, depending upon cost, rental rates and the method of financing applied and age of project. As a general rule, the investor should open his facility in the spring of the year and allow at least 18 to 24 months to realize its potential in a competitive market, 36+ months for 'Jumbo' 1,000,000 square foot size facilities to reach stabilization."

Source: Self Storage Association. www.selfstorage.org

General Information

"Cost and Operating Expenses -

As with all types of real estate, costs and operating results vary widely with self-storage. Who, what, when, where and how determine the final results. General comments are based upon experience; results from many self-storage facilities are obtained from associates in the industry, articles from various real estate and financial publications, and from numerous offering proposals on public record. Averaged nationally, operating costs range from a low of 20 percent to 40 percent (plus or minus) of actual stabilized income.

Expenses include:

- Maintenance—Includes supplies, pest control, contract services, equipment, building, doors, gates, elevator, and landscaping
- Taxes—Property taxes
- Utilities—Includes electric, gas, water, sewer, and garbage fees
- Insurance—Includes fire, property, liability, sales and disposal, customer goods, legal liability and general business insurance
- Administrative—Includes legal and accounting fees, office supplies, printing, computer supplies, and postage
- Advertising—Includes yellow-page advertising, promotional items, marketing and collateral pieces
- Operations—Includes eviction cost, telephone, security services, auto expense, truck operations, equipment rental
- Capital improvements and owner's home, office, automobile, or personal expenses are not normally included

"The 'proper' price for land has long been debated in the self-storage industry, as it is in any real estate scenario. At $1.25 per gross square foot and assuming 40 percent coverage, net cost for land is $3.13 per rentable foot of building. This used to be the 'upper limit' rule of thumb in the self-storage industry. However, this cost has been exceeded successfully many, many times. The current general rule of thumb for land cost is 25 to 30 percent of total development cost. It should be mentioned that two-story, or higher, self-storage facilities are no longer uncommon (even in northern states), and numerous three and four-story facilities do exist.

"The most common cost/operating description of self-storage is the comparison with apartments. As a general rule, self-storage projects will generate the same per-square- foot income as medium priced apartment properties in a market area. They can achieve this performance at roughly one-half the construction cost and at one-half the operating expense."

Source: Self Storage Association. www.selfstorage.org

Note: Self-Storage businesses are generally real estate intensive—a real estate license may be necessary to handle the sale.

Advantages of this Business

- "Ease of management, low construction costs"

Disadvantages of this Business

- "Increasing competition, few sellers of existing facilities"

Seller Financing

- "10 to 15 years"

Resources

Self Storage Association
www.selfstorage.org

MiniStorageMessenger—They provide excellent resources for the self-storage business. Their publications are published by MiniCo, Inc. www.selfstoragenow.com

Argus Self Storage Sales Network—A large real estate firm that specializes in the self-storage industry. Their Web site contains lot of articles and research on the industry. For information visit www.selfstorage.com/Argus

Marcus & Millichap—This is a large commercial real estate firm that has a group specializing in the sale of mini-storage units, or, as they call it, self-storage. Their Web site www.marcusmillichap.com is excellent. It contains lots of information and should be visited by anyone researching the self-storage industry.

This industry has many excellent resources. Every once in a while, in our research, we find an industry that has wonderful resources—and the self-storage industry is one of them. All of the firms and associations above have excellent Web sites full of information, and instructions on how to purchase additional data.

Service Businesses

Rule of Thumb:

- 50 percent of annual revenues [sales] plus inventory; however it is not unusual for service businesses to sell for a much higher figure
- "Conventional wisdom dictates that service firms are valued between .5 to 1.0 times revenues...."

Source: "Selling Services Companies," *M& A Today*, April 2004

Pricing Tips

Service Businesses

Sectors	LTM Revenue	LTM EBITDA
IT Services	1.0x	9.1x
Outsource Business Services	3.8x	15.5x
Professional Employer Org.	0.4x	8.5x
Healthcare Services	1.6x	10.0x
Consulting Firms	2.2x	14.9x
Advertising/Marketing	1.4x	12.8x"

Source: "Selling Service Companies," *M&A Today*, April 2004

Note: Information above furnished by Susan Pravda, a transaction attorney with Epstein Becker & Green (spravda@ebglaw.com) and Robert Cronin of Stonebridge Technology Associates, an investment banker (rcronin@stonebrtech.com), and appeared in *M&A Today*, April 2004. LTM is Last Twelve Months.

"Goodwill does not attach to a business that depends on the owner's skill, ability, or integrity or personal characteristics, unless the business has a future claim to that owner's services."

"Separating Personal and Business Goodwill," *The Tax Advisor*, June 2003, by Darrell Arne and James Hamill

General Information

"Deal Structure/Personal goodwill indicators

- Buyer has insisted on, and bargained for, a separate personal Covenant Not-to-Compete and/or employment agreement.
- There is a separately bargained for agreement to purchase personal goodwill.
- Personal seller financing is part of the consideration, with right of offset (e.g., loss of existing customers).
- An earnout is part of the consideration; payout depends on future

company sales and/or earnings.

- A strategic buyer's acquisition premium can be traced to attributes found in personal goodwill."

"Separating Personal and Business Goodwill," *The Tax Advisor*, June 2003, by Darrell Arne and James Hamill

Quick *Profile* Service Businesses (Personal Service)

A personal service business is one in which the owner is the driving force for its success and profitability. The seller's discretionary cash may be solid; the business may have everything going for it, except for one problem—the owner is responsible for much of its success.

This owner may just be the rainmaker, meeting and greeting the customers or clients, or the "brains" behind the operation, or have the loyalty of the clientele and employees. The longer the owner has been this driving force, the more likely it is that he or she is responsible for much of the business's success. Service businesses comprise about 40 percent of all businesses, and we suspect that many of them are what we would call personal service type operations. How does one separate the owner from his or her business in attempting to price this type of business?

This issue is also one that impacts any small business, whether it is service, retail, or the food-service business. Customers will go to the local hardware store because the owner is always there and can answer any question and provides that personal service that many people want. The local drug store [unfortunately a relic of the past] delivers prescriptions to those who can't drive or are otherwise unable to pick them up. The local dry cleaner [one of the few service businesses where a working owner doesn't seem to impact the price] is always quick with the quip and makes his customers laugh. Or take the local flower shop that will make that last-minute delivery or stay open past closing to allow someone to pick up flowers because they just remembered an important event. Although retail businesses often have an owner who is integral to its success, the service business seems to be the one most people identify with the owner.

What is a personal service business?

Those that come immediately to mind are the barbershop, the tax accountant, the lawn service, the travel agent, and the employment agency. However, others that are not used in the normal course of daily living also come to mind: advertising agencies, distributors of

all kinds, manufacturers' representatives, brokers of all types, service providers such as plumbers and electricians. Then there are the professional practices: doctors, lawyers, CPAs, architects, veterinarians, etc. All of these and many others develop personal relationships with their customers, patients, and clients that may not be transferable.

It is important to keep in mind that "goodwill" does not exist if it is not transferable. Since business broker professionals are being called on to represent a diverse business community, how does one put a price on a business in which the goodwill may disappear immediately after the closing? To tell the owner of a business such as those we have described that it is only worth the price of the fixtures and equipment, and maybe a pittance for a customer list, is asking for trouble if not a physical response.

Personal service businesses tend to have all or most of the following qualities:

- repeat business, customers, clients (not a one-time occurrence)
- personal contact between business and user (customer or client)
- provides a service that is more personal than business related
- requires some form of personal contact
- exceptional service is appreciated (almost required)
- usually geographically localized
- loyalty or friendship easily developed

Who owns the goodwill—the individual or the company?
In an important legal case, Martin Ice Cream Company v Commissioner of Internal Revenue, the tax court addressed the issue of goodwill—does it belong to the company or is it personal goodwill? We don't intend to discuss the tax implications, but to point out that the tax court did, indeed, recognize personal goodwill as distinct from company goodwill.

The court summed it up this way [keep in mind that the seller was just a partner in the company—so there is a distinction between the two]: "The benefits of the personal relationships developed by [seller] with supermarket chains and [seller's assets] ... not assets of [the selling company] that were transferred to [the buyer] by the [selling company] ... [the seller] was the owner and seller of these assets."

The above is a bit confusing, but basically the court ruled that an owner of the company owned the vast majority of the goodwill [personal goodwill] and the company owned only what was left.

Despite the fact that he was an owner of the company, he was the owner of much of the firm's goodwill and so could do with it as he saw fit.

This partial owner of the selling company "formed close personal relationships with supermarket owners and managers." These "close personal relationships" led to continuing orders. How does one sell that personal goodwill or place a price on the business that included this personal goodwill?

Some key questions to get answered

When considering the impact of this personal goodwill derived from the owner/seller, you should get answers to questions such as:

- If this owner/seller left the business tomorrow, could he or she be replaced by anyone else in the business?
- How much of the revenue of the business is derived from the personal relationships or contacts of the seller/owner?
- Does the business have contracts or written agreements with these customers despite the personal relationships with the owner/seller?
- Is the owner/seller willing to continue as an employee or consultant for a reasonable length of time after the sale?
- What percentage of total revenues of the business is a direct result of the personal relationships of the owner/seller?

Personal relationships

A prospective buyer understands that nothing stays the same. His or her concern is not that they will lose all the business, but that the business dependent on these relationships will be severed when they buy the business. In many cases, a customer, client, supplier, etc., is remaining in the business relationship due to loyalty. In fact, they may be relieved that they can now extricate themselves from it. Further, anyone who has been involved in the sale of such businesses knows that, in many cases, a new owner increases the business, because the seller's relationships weren't as strong as first perceived. Let's face it; a long-term business relationship is based on the quality of the product, service and price. Personal relationships can only go so far!

So, what do personal service businesses sell for?

The latest information we had from the BizComps Studies shows the following breakdown for service businesses:

Eastern Study .... 60% of annual sales and 1.9 times SDE
Central Study .... 54% of annual sales and 2.1 times SDE

Western Study .... 62% of annual sales and 2.0 times SDE

And, in their National Industrial Edition for businesses that sell for over $1 million, the percentage of annual sales was 68% and the SDE multiple was 2.6

For the most current data, contact BizComps at www.bizcomps.com

In reviewing data on the selling prices of businesses that are perceived to be personal service type businesses, we are struck by the disparity between the multiple of seller's discretionary cash (SDE) and that of other businesses. The average for all businesses based on Bizcomps data in *Transaction Patterns: A Pictorial Review of the Bizcomps Database*, authored by Toby Tatum, was 2.42, although the median was 2.03. In our informal averaging using data from *The Business Reference Guide* and current studies of Bizcomps, personal service businesses were priced significantly less than 2.0 x SDE Our guess is that the average multiple is about 1.5.

Goodwill versus hard assets
Toby, in his book, also calculated that only a small percentage of personal service businesses sell at a price where FF&E plus inventory represent more than 25 percent. Goodwill represents about 80 percent of the selling price. Remember, we are trying to determine what, if any, do we lower the SDE multiple for a small, personal service type business. Below is a table that depicts the amount of goodwill (intangibles) for the major business types.

The following are the result of some 3,800 transactions taken from the Bizcomps database. They have been compiled by Toby for the book mentioned above.

Allocation of Goodwill from the Bizcomps database for all of the SIC codes as a percentage of the sales price:

"Furniture, Fixtures & Equipment 30.5%
Inventory 14.5%
Intangibles (Goodwill)... 54.9%

Type of Business	FF&E	Inventory	Intangibles
Personal Service Industry	18.1%	0.6%	81.3%
Distribution Business	18.7%	28.4%	52.9%
Manufacturing	24.3%	17.6%	58%
Retail	25.5%	31.3%	43.1%
Construction	35.2%	4.6%	60.2%

Type of Business	FF&E	Inventory	Intangibles
Dry Cleaning	52.9%	2.0%	45.1%
Grocery/C-Stores	35.2%	21.1%	43.7%
Restaurants	52.9%	3.7%	43.4%"

The average for all business is about 54 percent, while the personal service type business is about 80 percent. Clearly, a large part of the value of a personal service type business is its goodwill.

A discount for personal service businesses?

It appears that the marketplace has already placed a discount on the multiple of SDE for these types of businesses. The average multiple for all businesses is over 2.0 (and we assume that this includes the personal service businesses; so the multiple would be higher, we suspect, if they were not included). The range for personal service type businesses seems to be between 1.0 and 1.9. The average for personal service businesses is about 1.5—so the multiple has been discounted by about .5 percent. That's a 25 percent reduction in the selling price.

We have found that many personal service businesses really sell for closer to a 1.0 multiple of SDE. We think the problem may be that those working on pricing models are so used to a routine 2.0 multiple of SDE, that they don't take into account the value of the owner/seller. So, in working with personal service type businesses, they try to make the deal work at the end by using earnouts, non-competes, or employment agreements. In some cases, they may use lengthy time periods in which the owner/seller agrees to stay with the new owner.

"With service companies, there is almost always a contingent portion of the purchase price. It can be based on one or several factors such as the following:

- retention of key employees
- retention of key customers
- performance milestones based over 2 to 5 years measured by a certain percentage of sales, EBITDA, etc., with certain operational restrictions

"The contingent part, commonly known as the earnout, can be tricky and controversial, but is a necessary part in selling service companies. The inherent problem with earnouts is that the seller has short-term objectives ... not just in the length of years for the payout but whether new capital equipment is purchased now or later.

> "Invariably sellers want to peg the earnout to total revenue, while the buyer wants to peg the earnout to earnings, such as EBITDA. Additionally, the seller might want to insist that the buyer provide a certain level of working capital; the seller has control of issues like hiring and firing personnel; the buyer will share their synergies; the earnout is cumulative for the period; and that there is 'no cap' to the earnout amount."
>
> Source: "Selling Services Companies," *M&A Today*, April 2004.

It looks as if, in many cases, the buyer wins both ways. The price is quite a bit less than other businesses, and the buyer usually receives some concessions at the tail-end as described above. Psychologically, this may be the best tactic. The seller gets closer to what he or she anticipates, or at least in asking price; and the buyer is more comfortable with the business because the seller is staying, or at least some concessions are included.

Any business in which the owner plays a significant role in its profitability is going to have to pay the price when it comes time to sell. They probably should have replaced themselves before it was time to sell. The price they receive appears to be about a 25 percent discount of what they would have if they had replaced themselves some years back. However, the use of earnouts and/or employment agreements may lessen or soften this discount in many cases.

Our recommendation is to begin with a 1.5 multiple; and by reviewing the answers to the questions mentioned earlier, add or subtract from this multiple. The multiple should end somewhere between 1.0 and 1.9. Obviously, these are only suggestions, and each business brings its own nuances to the table. It is also important to discuss the problem with the seller and bring up such issues as: management agreements, non-competes and staying with the seller until customer relations are transferred. Working out some of the solutions prior to going to market can result in a higher price for the seller.

Franchise

Service Master

4,400 + units

Approximate Total Investment: $22,586 to $90,544

Rule of Thumb:

- 45 percent of annual sales plus inventory

Resources

www.ownafranchise.com

Service Stations *(See Gas Stations)*

Franchise

Shell Rapid Lube

Rule of Thumb:

➢ 50 percent of annual sales plus inventory

Shoe Stores *(See also Retail Businesses)*

29,587	SIC: 5661-01	NAIC: 451110

General Information

"The shoe retail industry is segmented across the following product lines:

Products/Services	Share
Children's Shoes	15.0
Men's Shoes	19.3
Women's Shoes	24.2
Athletic Shoes	41.5

Source: "Starting a Shoe Retail Store," www.powerhomebiz.com

Resources

National Shoe Retailers Association
www.nsra.org

Shopping Centers

47,718		

General Information

"New York (May 2005) – U.S. enclosed malls achieved record annual growth in 2004 as sales per square foot for non-anchor tenants totaled $366, a 4.2 percent increase over 2003 figures, according to the International Council of Shopping Centers (ICSC) U.S. Mall monthly Merchandise Index. This was the strongest sales productivity growth in the eleven-year history of this report.

"The strongest tenant group at malls in 2004 was furnishings, which includes home furniture and furnishings, home entertainment and electronics, as sales productivity increased by 5.8 percent. Productivity for apparel and accessories retailers, which accounts for nearly half of non-anchor mall space, improved by 4.8 percent. Within the apparel and accessories group, women's accessories and specialties saw sales per square foot increase by 8.1 percent. It was followed by children's shoe stores (6.0%), women's shoe stores (5.3%), and family apparel (5.2%). For the stationery/cards/gifts/novelty (-0.4%)."

Source: International Council of Shopping Centers (ICSC) News, May 2005

"In 2002, U.S. regional malls generated $302.54 per square foot in sales, on average, versus $277.72 at lifestyle centers. But the centers cost $10.25 per square foot a year to operate, versus $25.25 at a traditional mall, he noted.

"The average asking rent at shopping centers and strip malls, as opposed to enclosed shopping malls, stands at $18.89, from $18.54 in 2003."

Source: *The Boston Globe*, Saturday, November 20, 2004. Note the information is from 2002, but we felt it was still pertinent – and informative.

"The vast majority of shopping centers (95%) are open-air centers. California has the most shopping centers. There are approximately 1,130 enclosed malls in the United States. Currently, the average enclosed mall contains 859,828 square feet of non-anchor space and 505,067 square feet of anchor space."

Short Line Railroads

Pricing Tips

"These are highly regulated businesses that, as businesses, tend to be basically real estate businesses. Many buyers tend to be hobby buyers. Historically, buyers have grossly overpaid to purchase these businesses, then not exploited the potential of the real estate business. Buyers are almost always industry related in some way. Sellers are mainly large operating corporations who cannot operate these units economically."

"Buyers are quoting 1.6 to 1.85 times gross revenues and in most cases it is a seller's market."

"If it's for sale, that pretty much guarantees that someone with expertise has determined that they cannot operate it profitably and/or make the capital investments required. Sellers have usually deferred capital investment and maintenance to an extreme degree prior to sale."

General Information

What are "Short Line" and "Regional" railroads?

"Short line" and "regional railroad" are generic terms without precise definitions, generally used to refer to small and middle-sized railroads, respectively.

There is a precise revenue-based definition of categories of U.S. railroads found in the regulations of the Surface Transportation Board (STB). The STB's accounting regulations group rail carriers into three classes for purposes of accounting and reporting (49 CFR Part 1201 Subpart A):

Class I: Carriers with annual carrier operating revenues of $250 million* or more

Class II: Carriers with annual carrier operating revenues of less than $250 million* but in excess of $20 million*

"RailAmerica, Inc. (NYSE:RRA) October 3 announced the completion of its acquisition of four short line railroads from Alcoa for a purchase price of $77.5 million in cash. The cash purchase price is based on RailAmerica assuming a targeted working capital deficit. RailAmerica funded substantially all of the cash purchase price through a $75 million increase in the term loan portion of its existing senior secured credit facility.

"The four railroads acquired serve Alcoa aluminum manufacturing operations in Texas and New York and a former Alcoa-owned specialty chemicals facility in Arkansas. For the twelve months ended June 30, 2005, the four railroads handled 30,000 carloads, generated revenue of $20.8 million, resulting in operating income of $10.1 million, and had depreciation and amortization expense of $0.2 million. The four railroads, which operate a total of 25 miles, had capital expenditures of $50,000 for the twelve months ended June 30, 2005."

Source: Rail America News, www.aslrra.org

Class III: Carriers with annual carrier operating revenues of $20 million* or less, and all switching and terminal companies regardless of operating revenues

Generally, Class III carriers are referred to as short lines, and Class II carriers are referred to as regional railroads.

*These threshold figures are adjusted annually for inflation using the base year of 1991.

Source: American Short Line and Regional Railroad Association

"New federal rules on transactions, which I haven't had time to wade through in detail, will limit the ability of many traditional buyers to do a deal. The incentive for cars and car leasing income/business is history, now nobody is buying or selling for that reason anymore. Recent purchasers are very interested in selling those they have been unable to make profitable, but the buyer better be looking for a hobby. Increasingly, they are becoming real estate development deals. Real estate values drive most deals, not operating revenue or profit. Most transactions will be structured as 1033 exchanges, or stock deals, and that needs to be planned for early.

"The 'groups' have come to dominate this business, and although I'd like to remain active in this, there just aren't any deals to be had. Prices have been drifting up rapidly because of several factors: public company purchasers; ability to secure low interest rate, long- term financing; and additional revenue sources, like fiber optics. These should be viewed primarily as local real estate deals.

"Activity has picked up. Almost all properties being offered are ones where existing operators cannot turn them around or get enough government subsidy. These are basically now plays on the local real estate, and can be great transactions. Financing availability is very good. Pricing is based usually on hard asset values including full potential values of often unique real estate."

Resources

American Short Line and Regional Railroad Association
www.aslrra.org

Franchise

Sign-A-Rama *(See also Manufacturing—Sign)*

700 units

Approximate Total Investment: $130,000 to $135,000

Rule of Thumb:

- 55 to 60 percent of annual sales plus inventory

Resources
www.signarama.com

Sign Manufacturing *(See Manufacturing—Sign)*

Silk Screen Printing

		NAIC: 541430

Rule of Thumb:

- 40 to 45 percent of annual sales plus inventory

Resources
Screen Printing Technical Foundation (SPTF)
Main St.
Fairfax, VA 22031-3489
(703) 385-1417

Franchise

Sir Speedy Printing

500 units

Approximate Total Investment: $500,000 to $550,000

Rule of Thumb:

- 25 percent of annual sales plus inventory
- "One sale was reported at 70% of sales."

Resources

www.sirspeedy.com

Ski Shops

500	SIC: 7011-10	NAIC: 721110

Rule of Thumb:

- 1.8 to 2.5 times EBIT; very rare 3.0 times (plus inventory), unless store is very exclusive with no competition in area
- 40 to 45 percent of gross annual sales plus inventory
- 2.5 to 3.5 times SDE plus inventory

Pricing Tips

"Key is long-term lease, since location is so important in resort retail sales. If lease is less than 3 years, a heavy discount in percentage of gross sales is appropriate. The price goes down the higher the inventory—which is always in addition to price [calculated on rules of thumb]. Every store is different. Be careful, the trend is for ski companies to get into the retail business and compete with independent shops. Must be disclosed."

"In resort businesses, location is key. Businesses must be in the tourist foot traffic areas. A strong lease securing such a location is the key in determining the multiple of cash flow. Since most areas have limited real estate, competition plays a large factor in determining price; e.g., how many ski shops are in your immediate area?"

Benchmarks

Expenses as a percentage of annual sales:

Cost of goods	45% to 50%
Payroll/Labor	22% to 28% (Rising due to labor shortages)
Occupancy cost*	8% to 12%

*(Seeing some 18% to 20% in very hot locations—ski in/ski out.)

General Information

"The National Ski Area Association (NSAA) reports 492 ski areas opened during the 2004–2005 season, according to the 2004–2005 *Kottke National End of Season Survey.*" Interestingly, in 1984–1985, the first year records were apparently maintained, there were 727 ski areas.
Source: National Ski Area Asociations.

Seller Financing

- "3 years maximum"

Snack Bars *(See also Sandwich Shops & Restaurants)*

Benchmarks

"Turnover of stock, hours of operation, type of snack bar, products offered"

Expenses as a percentage of annual sales:

Cost of goods	55%
Payroll/Labor	17%
Occupancy cost	10%
Profit (estimated)	18%

Quite variable depending on type, location-size, hours of operation

Seller Financing

- "5 years if renting; 11 years if real estate is included"

Soft Drink Bottlers

		NAIC: 445299

Rule of Thumb:

- $10/case sold annually

Software Companies

Rule of Thumb:

- 2 to 3 times revenue (trailing 12 months) plus inventory

Pricing Tips

"There is no 'typical' rule of thumb because individual software companies can have widely different cycles and growth phases. Classic measures focus on revenue amounts, consistency, and growth, although revenue recognition policies vary and market conditions can change quickly."

"Usually no bank financing involved, companies can be unprofitable or have negative net worth and still sell. Average deal is 50 percent liquid, 2 year employment agreement—3 to 4 year non-compete. Most buyers are public and hi tech in order to leverage the purchase—35 percent international buyers."

General Information

Questions to ask a seller: "Calculations of net cash flow, consistently applied, are good for historical analysis. Discounted cash flow models vary widely, but commonly use higher rates because of risk and uncertainty. Premiums for control, discounts for illiquidity are usually magnified from more 'stable' industries. The broker/intermediary should inquire about capitalization policies of the software 'asset.' Many companies will not capitalize their product; others will be based on cost accumulation. 'Niche' software with an established client base will attract buyers because of the ongoing service revenues."

Industry Trend

Projections for Software Industry Growth

	2003	2004	2005	2006	2007
U.S.	2.5%	3.5%	4.5%	6.0%	7.0%"

Source: SIIA Software Division, www.siia.net/software

"Growth Drivers (percent answering 'important' or 'most important')

Developing New Upgraded Products & Services	87.4%
New Distribution Channels/Key Partnerships	76.4%
Acquisition of Companies	35.4%"

Source: Spencer Stuart/Software & Information Association

Sound Contractors

Rule of Thumb:

- 2 to 3 times SDE and/or 30 to 60 times monthly contract billing for music services plus inventory

Pricing Tips

"Any inventory over 24 months is dead inventory and should not be part of sale."

Seller Financing

- "5 to 8 years"

Sporting Goods Stores

21,217	SIC: 5941-13	NAIC: 451110

Rule of Thumb:

- 4 times monthly sales plus inventory
- 30 percent of annual sales plus inventory

General Information

"These should turn their inventory a minimum of 3 times per year. The markups above wholesale vary considerably. Generally most of the items carry 35 percent to 45 percent profit, others 25 percent to 30 percent. Rent should never run over 5 percent of the gross volume. Selling price, fixtures and equipment plus inventory at wholesale cost, plus some allowance if they have exclusive sales rights for some of the larger items or contracts with school districts."

Sales of Sporting Goods (in billions of dollars)—2004

Equipment	$22.9 billion
Footwear	$14.75 billion
Clothing	$11.2 billion
Total	$48.9 billion
	(versus $47.4 billion in 2003)

Source: National Sporting Goods Association

Resources
National Sporting Goods Association
www.nsga.org

Steel Fabrication

Rule of Thumb:

➢ 4 to 5 times EBIT

Franchise

Subway

21,000 units	
Estimated Annual Sales per Unit:	$365,000
Approximate Total Investment:	$86,300 to $251,000

Rule of Thumb:

➢ 60 percent of annual sales plus inventory

➢ 2.3 times SDE plus inventory

➢ "Premium for a Subway franchise—60 to 80 percent of sales"

Pricing Tips
"Dramatic increase in number of Subway stores is causing a decrease in salability and price. Factor appears to be heading to 2 times SDE if trend of new units continues."

"Lease of less than 8 years diminishes the value. This is typical valuation for Subway type store."

"On stores with gross sales of $300,000 to $500,000, multiple of 40% of annual sales. On stores with sales of $500,000 +, a multiple of 50% of annual sales. Franchisor would like 30% as a down payment on resales."

"...the chain now has more than 18,000 units in the United States, according to the company. Subway surpassed McDonalds U.S. unit count in 2002."

Source: *Nation's Restaurant News*, February 7, 2005

"I would suggest for Subway, in New England and maybe all of New England, due to the high number of pizza restaurants, Subways tend to sell for a much lower of percentage of sales than 47%—sometimes as low as 20% to 25%."

Benchmarks

Sales per square Foot - "Average sq. ft. per location—1,200/at $300/sf (malls significantly higher)"

Expenses as a percentage of annual sales:	
Cost of Goods Sold	29%
Payroll/Labor Costs	20%
Occupancy Cost	09%
Profit (estimated)	22%

General Information

"High demand for Subways. Many buyers won't look at any other type of sandwich shop."

Advantages of this Business

- "National exposure, price pointed, controllable costs, can be operated with minimal employees"

Disadvantages of this Business

- "Too many on the market. Limited market and market share."

Industry Trend

"Flooding of market…reduction in old-fashioned delis"

Seller Financing

- "5 years"

Resources

www.subway.com

Franchise

Superior Inspection (Home Inspection Services)

Rule of Thumb:

- 1.3 times annual sales plus inventory

Supermarkets *(See also Grocery Stores)*

Rule of Thumb:

- 3 times SDE plus inventory
- 10 percent of annual sales plus inventory

Pricing Tips

"3 times yearly net income"

Industry Experts' Ratings:

Amount of Competition (1 = Lot of: 4 = Not much)	1.2
Amount of Risk (1 = Very: 4 = Not much)	1.2
Historical Profit Trend (1 = Down: 4 = Up)	2.0
Location & Facilities (1 = Poor: 4 = Excellent)	2.8
Marketability (1 = Low: 4 = High)	2.8
Industry Trend (1 = Declining: 4 = Growing)	2.4
Ease of Replication (1 = Easy: 4 = Difficult)	3.2

Benchmarks

"Larger and better. Full-service grocery store in a larger strip center. Plenty of parking."

Expenses as a percentage of annual sales:

Cost of Goods Sold	75%
Payroll/Labor Costs	3%
Occupancy Cost	5%
Profit (estimated)	5%

General Information

"A clean store with good customer service"

Advantages of this Business

- "High sales. $5 million to $10 million yearly."

Disadvantages of this Business

- "Volume with lower profit and higher rest costs. Competition from larger chains."

Industry Trend

"More products"

Seller Financing

- "5 years"

Sustainable Businesses

What is a Sustainable Business?

"A sustainable business is one that operates in an environmentally responsible way. Its products and business processes are such that no negative environmental impact is felt as a result of their existence."

Source: The Evergreen Group

Pricing Tips

"These are typically values or lifestyle based purchases. The cash flow analysis is often based on future expectations for this young and rapidly growing industry."

General Information

"Organic products are a subset of sustainable business. That segment has been growing at 20 percent annually for 10 years. Green building products and renewable energy are other examples."

"Selling your business doesn't have to mean selling out. The Evergreen Group is committed to helping you find not only the best price for your business, but also a buyer who will continue to implement environmental principles and practices."

Resources

The Evergreen Group—a business brokerage firm specializing in sustainable businesses For more information visit www.theevergreengroup.com

Franchise

Swisher (Restroom Hygiene Service)

Rule of Thumb:

- 75% of annual sales plus inventory

Resources

www.swisheronline.com

Franchise

Taco Johns

400 + units	
Estimated Annual Sales per Unit:	$575,000
Approximate Total Investment:	$443,000 to $681,500

Rule of Thumb:

- 31 percent of annual sales plus inventory

Resources

www.tacojohns.com

Tanning Salons

25,000	SIC: 7299-44	NAIC: 812199

Rule of Thumb:

- 2.3 to 2.5 SDE plus inventory

Pricing Tips

"Most tanning salons sell between 2 and 3 x SDE (Seller's Discretionary

Average Tans per Day	2004 vs. 2003
In-season	2004—315 vs. 346 for 2003
Off season	2004—125 vs.132 for 2003

Source: *Looking Fit*, February 15, 2005

Earnings). Factors influencing sales price include the following: asset value, whether assets are owned or leased, age of equipment, facility lease term and amount of rent, threats of competition, long-term memberships in place."

Industry Experts' Ratings:

Amount of Competition (1 = Lot of: 4 = Not much)	1.2
Amount of Risk (1 = Very: 4 = Not much)	1.6
Historical Profit Trend (1 = Down: 4 = Up)	2.0
Location & Facilities (1 = Poor: 4 = Excellent)	2.0
Marketability (1 = Low: 4 = High)	2.0
Industry Trend (1 = Declining: 4 = Growing)	2.0
Ease of Replication (1 = Easy: 4 = Difficult)	2.0

"Competition varies greatly by location. California, Nevada, Arizona, Texas, and Florida are highly competitve in most areas. Some college towns (i.e., Ann Arbor, Michigan) also see a great deal of competition."

Benchmarks

"No industry benchmarks exist, as equipment values range from a $375 hand-held spray unit to a $45,000 high-pressure bed."

"Average monthly revenue in 2004—$26,319 (2003—$20,874)
"Adjusted Monthly Revenue in 2005—$32,475 (2004—$25,541)"

Source: *Looking Fit*, February 2005

"Average 2004 Gross Revenue—$315,828 (2003—$250,488)"

Source: *Looking Fit*, September 2004

"Adjusted Gross Revenue for 2005—$389,700 (2004—$306,492)"

Source: *Looking Fit*, February 2005

"In 2004, 50 percent of salons reported an average single session price as $7; only four percent charged $5 or less."

Source: *Looking Fit*, September 2004

Expenses as a percentage of annual sales:	
Cost of Goods Sold	4%–8%
Payroll/Labor Costs	15%–30%
Occupancy Cost	15%–30%
Profit (estimated)	30%

General Information

"The factors that influence price are amount of SDE, amount of provable skim, newness of tanning beds and whether standup spray-on beds are or are not available. If the equipment is more than 3 or 4 years old, the sale will be more difficult. If there are high- intensity bulbs where customers can tan more quickly, this will make the business more desirable to purchase. Some owners do extensive skimming which in and of itself is not a problem. If the skim cannot be proven with believable computer-generated reports, the price for the salon will be less.

"The risk of owning a tanning salon is directly related to its seasonality. If you buy at the end of January, you inherit the cream of the season, which is February, March, April, May and part of June. Business dries up until the holiday season when people want tans for November and December social functions. You need staying power to make it through the possibly negative cash flow months of January, July, August, September and October.

"I see the trend as being very positive. We live in a vain society, and the beautiful people will always want a tan. Even with warnings regarding skin cancer, people will believe that tanning in a tanning salon is safer than tanning outside.

"This business is a people business. You constantly meet new and different people. It is a very casual business where you can wear shorts, T-shirts, tennis shoes, tank tops, etc.

"The disadvantages are the seasonality of the business and the fact that it is very capital intensive. If you do not have the latest and best equipment, customers will look elsewhere. Every shopping center has a tanning salon, and you have to be very good with your customers. If you are not hands-on and do not have sophisticated equipment, your employees can give away free time.

"The most profitable salons have state-of-the-art technology to track time and usage. Free time cannot be given away without the owner finding out."

Advantages of this Business

- "High cash businesses; often up to 50% of gross revenues. Salons are fantastic investments for absentee owners."
- "Up to 50% of revenues are cash. Great absentee-owned businesses."

Disadvantages of this Business

- "Very few disadvantages. Many of the employees who attract the 'target' segment (i.e., 18 to 35 year old image-conscious females) make unreliable employees. Employee theft is a problem unless owners install timers and software systems to manage beds."

Industry Trend

"While the overall industry grows, owners in more saturated markets are experiencing diminishing returns. Saturated markets will see consolidation in the next 10 years."

"Overall growth in industry"

"While the majority of freestanding tanning salons have 10 beds or less, the industry saw a shift in business tactics as a number of savvy salon chains acquired smaller facilities, improved them, made them bigger and added them into their tanning fold. Industry experts predict this consolidation trend will continue in larger markets but not in smaller, rural markets that don't have the populace to support bigger salons."

Resources

Tanning Trends magazine
www.tanning-trends.com

Suntanning Association for Education (SAE)
www.smarttan.com

Looking Fit magazine
www.lookingfit.com—a great Web site, lots of good information. And, for a nominal sum, you can get pretty much all of the information available, including their annual survey. We like what they have done. The nominal sum buys 7 days of usage. So, if you are working on a tanning-salon project, this site will help.

Taverns *(See Bars & Restaurants)*		
53,544	SIC: 5813-01	NAIC: 722410

Taxicab Businesses		
10,755	SIC: 4121-01	NAIC: 485310

Rule of Thumb:

- 40 to 45 percent of annual sales plus inventory

Pricing Tips

"Selling price should be between 1 year's and 2 years' net profit, depending upon the number of cabs and their respective ages."

General Information

"At one time, cab companies required cab drivers to report the meter readings and the money collected to a company official at the end of their shift. The drivers were employees who received a minimum salary and a commission at the end of the pay period. In that scenario, income from tips was the big issue. Now, a company finds it easier to charge drivers a flat rate for using the vehicles and not have the problems of employment taxes and the review and manipulating of meter readings. This method of operation for the cab companies is the subject of Revenue Ruling 71-572, 1971-2CB347.

"Taxicab companies are issued franchises by a political body or organization, such as the county, city, airport, etc., to operate in their respective jurisdiction.

"In order to get the franchise, a company must guarantee that its vehicles will be in a clean condition, available at specified times to have a specified response time rate, and will have drivers who meet certain standards.

"There is also a franchise fee, costing between $25,000 and $40,000, that drivers must pay to the taxicab company. If a taxi does not meet the requirements of the franchise, it is referred to as a 'bandit' and is considered illegal and subject to fines. Taxicab companies encourage their drivers to drive 10 to12 hours per day, six days a week. To keep the license, they must have drivers available to answer the radio dispatch within minutes of the customer's request.

"Since taxi drivers are treated as independent contractors, no record of fares earned is maintained by the company. If the cab company owns the taxis, the driver must pay a rental fee for the use of the vehicle. The rental fee is computed on a weekly basis and may include charges for property damage insurance.

"Drivers who own their vehicles are allowed to operate under the company license, but they are charged a fee for the dispatch service and insurance."

The above is excerpted from an IRS Audit Technique Guide (Market Segment Specialization Program—MSSAP). This is an excellent source of information and is available at www.bookstore.gpo.gov (search under IRS—IRS Audit Technique Guides).

Resources
International Taxicab & Livery Association (ITLA)
www.taxinetwork.com

Franchise

TCBY

1,366 units	
Estimated Annual Sales per Unit:	$110,000
Approximate Total Investment:	$142,000 to $347,200

Rule of Thumb:

- 50 percent of annual sales plus inventory

Resources
www.mrsfieldsfranchise.com

Technology—Information

Rule of Thumb:

- 100 percent of annual sales plus inventory
- 3 times SDE plus inventory
- 3 times EBIT
- 3 times EBITDA

Pricing Tips

"Renewal rates are paramount, whether the business is advertiser supported or subscription supported."

Industry Experts' Ratings:

Amount of Competition (1 = Lot of: 4 = Not much) 1.0
Amount of Risk (1 = Very: 4 = Not much) 2.0
Historical Profit Trend (1 = Down: 4 = Up) 3.2
Location & Facilities (1 = Poor: 4 = Excellent) 2.0
Marketability (1 = Low: 4 = High) 3.2
Industry Trend (1 = Declining: 4 = Growing) 3.2
Ease of Replication (1 = Easy: 4 = Difficult) 1.2

"Content that is unique is always a plus for both electronic and published information. Also business content tends to have greater value than consumer content."

Benchmarks

"The sales ratio to employee expense should exceed 1.5 to 1.

Expenses as a percentage of annual sales:

Cost of Goods Sold 40%
Payroll/Labor Costs 25%
Occupancy Cost 5%
Profit (estimated) 20%

Advantages of this Business

- "The work is interesting and ever changing, and clients tend to renew if they are satisfied with the product. This creates an annuity revenue stream. The information business is not particularly capital intensive."

Disadvantages of this Business

- "The competition is always raising the bar."

Industry Trend

"I see continued consolidation as smaller providers are rolled into larger companies. It is easier for larger companies to buy than to build."

Seller Financing

- "5 years"

Technology Companies—Manufacturing

Rule of Thumb:

- Niche market—4.25 to 4.75 adjusted net plus inventory
- PCB—4.65 to 5.0 plus inventory
- Software—4.50 to 6.0 plus inventory
- Non-niche—4.35 to 5.5 plus inventory

Pricing Tips & Information

"Adjusted net times [EBIT] 4 to 5.5 (depending on prior growth curves)"

"Additions: location, 1st impression on walk-through, how competitive is marketplace, how clear P&L is. High tech or low tech? How much is straightforward in P&L & how much has to be recast?"

Technology Companies—Service

Rule of Thumb:

- Temporary Agencies—1.25 to 3.5 EBITDA
- Test Services—2.75 to 3.35 EBITDA
- Design Services—2.5 to 3.5 EBITDA

-cont'd-

Technology Companies—Service *(cont'd)*

- (Adjusted net for large companies is EBITDA, for smaller ones SDE is used as adjusted net)

Tee Shirt Shops

11,500	SIC: 5699-17	NAIC: 448190

Rule of Thumb:

- 30 percent of annual sales plus inventory

Telecommunications

Rule of Thumb:

- $700 to $1,400 per line

Pricing Tips

"Three variables—$1,000 to $2,000 per installed port; 20 to 40 percent of annual revenues, depending upon sales mix & earnings; earnings impact selling price, but on a case by case basis relating to the first two variables plus cash flow analysis. This industry is far from exact, as market share, client base revenues, product line exclusivity, market potential (saturation) & earnings all impact market value. The old adage 'beauty is in the eyes of the beholder' definitely applies to the telecom industry. Client (installed) base revenue mix & profit margin? New system sales product mix? Competition? Service reputation? Customer retention rate? Inventory obsolescence factor? Overall pretax profit?"

General Information

Questions to ask a seller: "Are there any Competitive Local Exchange Carriers (CLECs) operational in market area? Do they have their own facilities or are they reselling?"

Resources

Telephony Magazine
www.tmcnet.com

dealtrax.com

DEALTRAX™ is an office management system created by the experts at Business Brokerage Press, Inc. exclusively for business transaction professionals. DEALTRAX™ allows agents to manage buyers and sellers, communicate interactively online, share confidential files, and helps match buyers and listings—from anywhere, without limitations. This revolutionary management system tracks every detail of the transaction process, so that all work is documented and protected. In addition, with DEALTRAX™ you will be able to manage and connect your entire office, and it can be easily integrated into your existing website.

DEALTRAX™ is built on 76 years and 4 generations of business transaction experience and knowledge. The system knows the work you do and assists at every stage, tracking each deal and keeping you organized so you have more time to focus on what you do best—selling businesses.

Featured system highlights include:

- Tracks and manages all data on every listing, every buyer, and every deal.
- Allows all agents in a single office to work together and stay on the same page, but gives each agent unique permissions and ownership of their listings and buyers. Centralizes both your buyer and listing databases for easy access and searching from anywhere.
- Assists with the matching of buyers and prospective businesses for sale and creates a relationship between the two for easy prospect tracking. Also displays level of access buyers have to each listing and sends notifications of when their permissions expire.
- Permits each agent to receive all faxes directly into their online office.
- DEALTRAX™ dashboard gives the office owner an up to the minute snapshot of their entire business including:
  - ✔ Number of listings by agent with breakdown by industry
  - ✔ Listings about to expire
  - ✔ New listings and price changes on current listings as well as listings recently renewed
  - ✔ Number of active buyers by agent
  - ✔ Access to system preferences, user accounts, and management rights of all buyers and listings
- DEALTRAX™ agent dashboard gives each agent an up to the minute snapshot of their business activity and of their schedule, tasks, client messages and requests, plus:
  - ✔ Price updates on office listings
  - ✔ Postings of new office listings
  - ✔ Listings about to expire as well as listings recently renewed
  - ✔ Recent incoming faxes
  - ✔ New messages and listing requests from buyers and sellers
  - ✔ New buyers assigned from website
  - ✔ Broker messages
  - ✔ Potential sales and commissions
  - ✔ Current number of listings and buyers, both individually and for the entire office
  - ✔ Tasks and appointments
  - ✔ List of hot listings and buyers currently working with

Telephone Answering Services *(See also Answering Service)*

5,000	SIC: 7389-03	NAIC: 561421

"A well-run answering service will generate a 30 percent profit. Your labor should run you around 40 percent, with 10 percent going to phones and taxes, and 20 percent for administration. Installing a voice mail system for message delivery should reduce your labor by at least 15 percent to 20 percent."

Source: www.tasmarketing.com

Telephone Companies/Independent

Pricing Tips

"Sales price throughout the nation has been established at between $800 and $1,200 per subscriber."

Television Sales & Service

Rule of Thumb:

- 2 times monthly sales plus inventory

Television Stations

4,000	SIC: 4,158	NAIC: 513120

Rule of Thumb:

- 9 to 12 times EBITDA

Pricing Tips

"…a recent published analysis of other sports networks done by Salomon Smith Barney valued them at 10 times their annual pretax cash flows, at a minimum."

Source: *Boston Globe*, September 11, 2001

Temporary Services/Staffing *(See also Employment Agencies)*

23,000	SIC: 7363-04	NAIC: 561320

Rule of Thumb:

- 1 to 2 times annual sales plus inventory
- 2 to 5 times EBIT (smaller deals under $25 million)
- 5 to 7.5 times EBIT (larger deals over $25 million)
- 6 to 9 times EBIT (Information Technology)
- 3 to 6 times EBITDA—Depending on revenues

General Information

"Noting that the temporary staffing industry is 'a leading [economic] indicator in and a leading indicator out [of a recession],' Joerres said he believes the current hiring crunch 'is absolutely cyclical' and conditions will improve.

"In fact, the Bureau of Labor Statistics reported in December that the personnel supply services industry is one of the 10 fastest growing of this decade and, during that time, is expected to grow 49 percent—from 3.887 million to 5.8 million workers."

Source: *The Boston Sunday Globe*, February 10, 2002

"This is a consolidating industry so there are good buyers looking to add market share and services they are not already offering."

"Here are some factors that add value: Multiple offices or regional strength (have more critical mass); nice business is good, such as nursing (medical); high gross margin. Negatives are: one customer represents 10 percent or more of customers; is owner/manager leaving."

"Management in place after sale is much more attractive. Customer concentration & higher workman's comp.—higher risk categories bring multiples down."

Seller Financing

- "3-year earnouts are most typical"
- "2 to 5 years"

Resources
National Association of Temporary and Staffing Services
www.natss.org

Franchise

Texaco Express Lube

Rule of Thumb:

- 30 to 40 percent of annual sales plus inventory

Textile Rental *(See also Uniform Rental and Dust Control)*

General Information
The textile rental industry consists primarily of SIC numbers 7213 and 7218. Linen Supply, SIC #7213 and #7218, is defined as "establishments primarily engaged in supplying to commercial establishments or household users, on a rental basis, such laundered items as uniforms, gowns, and coats of the type used by doctors, nurses, barbers, beauticians, and waitresses; and table linens, bed linens, towels and toweling and similar items." Industrial Launderers, SIC #7218, are defined as "establishments primarily engaged in supplying laundered or dry-cleaned industrial work uniforms and related work clothing, such as protective apparel (flame and heat resistant) and clean- room apparel; laundered mats and rugs; dust control items, such as treated mops, rugs, mats, dust tool covers, and cloths; laundered wiping towels; and other selected items to industrial, commercial, and government users." The textile rental industry has been described as a "derived demand, business-to-business service industry.

"In 2001, [the latest available] the industry had revenues of about $10.3 billion and employed more than 150,000 people. Textile rental companies serve hygienically clean textile items to millions of customers in commerce, industry, and the professions. Major customers of most industrial laundry, linen supply, and commercial launderers include: automobile service and repair facilities; food processing companies; pharmaceutical manufacturers; hotels and restaurants; hospitals, nursing homes, doctors' and dentists' offices and clinics; retail stores and supermarkets; and a variety of other manufacturing and service companies."

Source: The Textile Rental Services Association (TRSA)

Resources

The Textile Rental Services Association (TRSA)
www.trsa.org—a very interesting and informative site

Ticket Services

1,600	SIC: 7999-73	NAIC: 561599

Rule of Thumb:

- 3 times EBITDA for small to midsize operations; 4 times EBITDA for larger companies

Pricing Tips & Information

"Length of time in business? Stability of earnings? How do they get tickets? Average markup? Repeat business?"

General Information

"With the age of computers, ticket services were replaced as primary ticket sellers by companies such as Ticketronâ*. At that time, our business industry evolved into the secondary market. No longer do ticket services get provided with tickets on consignment from venues. Today, with the greatest demand for many sporting events, concerts, and theater events, ticket services now serve the public in three ways. First, we provide tickets to events that are sold out through the primary market. Second, we provide premium upfront seats which are the most desirable. Third, we provide ticket holders a place to sell their unwanted, or unneeded or extra tickets."

*Ticketron© and Ticketmaster© are copyrighted trademarks of Ticketmaster®. The NATB and their members are not affiliated with Ticketmaster®.

Source: National Association of Ticket Brokers (NATB)

Resources

National Association of Ticket Brokers
www.natb.org

Tire Stores *(See also Auto Tire Stores)*

41,500	SIC: 5531-23	NAIC: 441320

Rule of Thumb:

➢ 25 percent of annual sales plus inventory

Title Abstract and Settlement Offices

Rule of Thumb:

➢ 60 percent of annual sales plus inventory

➢ 35 times SDE plus inventory

➢ 5 times EBIT

➢ 4.5 times EBITDA

Pricing Tips

"'Affiliated Business Arrangements' (ABAs) are in vogue. Make sure the ABA is transferable upon sale. Title agencies will command higher prices in states with higher filed premiums."

"Criteria include the sales history and trends. Title companies' revenues are affected by interest rates, but the stronger ones will maintain profits through the ups and downs by adjustments of variable expenses."

Industry Experts' Ratings:

Amount of Competition (1 = Lot of: 4 = Not much) 1.0
Amount of Risk (1 = Very: 4 = Not much) 1.2
Historical Profit Trend (1 = Down: 4 = Up) 3.8
Location & Facilities (1 = Poor: 4 = Excellent) 3.2
Marketability (1 = Low: 4 = High) 3.6
Industry Trend (1 = Declining: 4 = Growing) 3.1
Ease of Replication (1 = Easy: 4 = Difficult) 2.8

"Buyers for title agencies have increased due to legislative changes."

Benchmarks

"Labor/Gross Revenues = <35% for metropolitan markets
Labor/Gross Revenues = <30% for rural markets"

Expenses as a percentage of annual sales:	
Cost of Goods Sold	18%
Payroll/Labor Costs	35%
Occupancy Cost	4.5%
Profit (estimated)	14%

General Information

"The buyer must be financially substantial to be approved by the underwriters and should procure a title agent license regulated by the state."

Advantages of this Business

- "Highly esteemed, profitable, specialized legal knowledge, regular business hours..."
- "Professional settings, few weekend hours"

Disadvantages of this Business

- "Seasonal cash flow challenges, ruthless competitive environment, rapid technological changes..."
- "It is important to control overhead expenses to account for the normal ups and downs."

Tour Operators

6,700	SIC: 4725-01	NAIC: 561520

Rule of Thumb:

- 4 times EBITDA for larger operations; 3 times EBITDA for smaller operations

Pricing Tips

"Length of time in business? Single destination operators a bit higher; type of travel (golf, ski, scuba, etc.)—specialist vs. generalist."

Towing Companies

50,000	SIC: 7549-01	NAIC: 488410

Rule of Thumb:

- 70 percent of annual revenues plus inventory
- 2.75 times EBITDA
- Nominal value + "contracts" + real estate + equipment value

Pricing Tips

"Extreme care with adding back depreciation, and/or allowance to replace trucks. Define which segment of industry, and check to see if the insurance premium is fair market value. Small companies and those in non-consent business are hard to sell."

"The last of the consolidators has liquidated its acquisitions at a loss. The implication is that there are negative economies of scale at both ends of the scale; large and small, i.e., above some size these businesses based on revenue etc. have a declining value, and that optimal values are found within the span of control of one person. Ease of entry has been increasing, so going-concern values have been declining."

"More than 85 percent of all tows in the U.S. involve passenger cars and light trucks. The majority of these tows are provided by small, family-owned towing businesses."

Source: Towing and Recovery Association of America (TRAA)

Industry Experts' Ratings:

Marketability (1 = Low: 4 = High) 2.4
Industry Trend (1 = Declining: 4 = Growing) 2.0
Ease of Replication (1 = Easy: 4 = Difficult) 2.0

"These businesses vary widely. Hands-on management is almost always a critical element. Control of operating real estate is usually a major element in profitability."

Benchmarks

Expenses as a percentage of annual sales:	
Cost of Goods Sold	30%
Payroll/Labor Costs	30%
Occupancy Cost	08%
Profit (estimated)	20%

General Information

"Many towing operators are AAA contractors. This is, in most cases, a loss leader. It is a high volume of business at a very low revenue rate, that for all but the most efficient operators is less than the cost of doing the business. Its 'value' is in its ability to convert other business that does have a significant profit margin. For valuation, AAA costs and revenues should be looked at almost as an advertising activity rather than as a business in and of itself. Also, an AAA relationship is often unsaleable due to contractual relationships on change of ownerships, and a sale can be expected to trigger a renegotiation or a cancellation."

Advantages of this Business

- "Can be very profitable with minimal skills"

Disadvantages of this Business

- "Unattractive industry image and working conditions"

Trend

"Trend is positive, but competition is fierce. Many companies come and go."

Seller Financing

- "5 years"

Resources

Tow Times Magazine
www.towtimes.com

Toy Stores

8,500	SIC: 5945-17	NAIC: 451120

Rules of Thumb:

- ➢ 35 percent of annual sales plus inventory

Resources
Toy Industry Association
www.toy-tma.org—a very good site

Transportation (all types) *(See also Trucking Companies)*

General Information
Questions to ask a seller: "Annual revenue mileage per vehicle?"

Trash Routes *(See Garbage/Trash Collection)*

11,000	SIC: 4953-02	NAIC: 562111

Travel Agencies

40,000	SIC: 4724-02	NAIC: 561510

Rule of Thumb:

- ➢ "Small operations, $1 to $3 million—35 percent of annual commissions and fees; $4 to $8 million—40 percent; $9 to $20 million—45 percent; 3.5 times EBITDA above $20 million in revenues"
- ➢ 2 times SDE plus inventory
- ➢ "For agencies with $1 to $4 million in sales, 1.5 to 2.0 SDE is customary. If $5 to $10 million, then 2.0 to 2.5 SDE"
- ➢ 35 percent of gross profit plus inventory
- ➢ "One-quarter down, balance earned out over 24 months"
- ➢ "Earnouts are very common, with a percentage of the income generated from the selling agency's customer list paid over a 2-year period—maximum."

Pricing Tips

"Gross Income is more important than Gross Sales. Management team to stay. Higher commission structure and specialty is the key."

"30 to 40 percent of travel agents now bypassing airlines and booking through consolidators (consolidators buy air seats in bulk and resell to travel agents at a reduced rate). The agent is now able to mark up tickets to a higher price and sell to the client at a better rate of commission. In most cases, the price of the ticket is less than what the client can get through the airlines."

"GDS (Global Distribution System) or CRS (Computer Reservation Service) contract length is critical; the shorter the length, the higher the value. How long have agents been on staff, mix of business, overrides vs. base commission, full-time agents or independent contractors?"

Benchmarks

"Higher net commissions due to special contracts. Service fee income. Overall control on expenses."

"Look for preferred supplier and override agreements, written contractual agreements with corporate customers, relationships with wholesalers on airline tickets. GDS (airline computer system) contract situation is a key factor."

Expenses as a percentage of annual sales:	
Cost of Goods Sold	90%
Payroll/Labor Costs	5%
Occupancy Cost	1%
Profit (estimated)	1.5%

General Information

Questions to ask a seller: "Ask about who controls the business, is it under contract? Length of GDS contract, location, lease expiration date? Any net pricing?" "Do customers have written contracts to use the agency? Is there a database of past leisure customers? How often is this database contacted?" "The net commissions earned, service price charged, special override commission contracts from the vendors. Employees' goodwill, inside or independent contractors, all licenses, covenant not to compete."

"Agency should be fully appointed by ARC (Airlines Reporting Corp.), which is for domestic travel, as well as IATAN (International Travel Agent Network) for international travel. You must have ARC—you don't have to have IATAN."

"Profitability? Agency more than 3 years old? Agency does not depend on more than one account for more than 10 percent of gross? Agency does not rebate? Manager stays on?"

"Would need last 18 months' financials to spot any trends"

Advantages of this Business

- "No cost inventory"
- "Exciting life, full of travel and meeting the world community"

Disadvantages of this Business

- "At suppliers' mercy—suppliers dictate a lot"

Trend

"Currently there are 10,400 owners of retail agencies. Turnover is 7 percent per year, so in 2006 we expect 735 ownership changes—sales of agencies, hopefully."

"According to the National Associated of Commissioned Travel Agents, it's estimated that there are about 20,000 agents nationwide who work from their homes, mostly women who specialize in leisure travel."

Source: *The Boston Sunday Globe*, August 8, 2004

Seller Financing

- "2 to 2.5 years"
- "2 to 5 years"

Resources

American Society of Travel Agents (ASTA)
www.astanet.com

Institute of Certified Travel Agents
www.icta.com

Travel Industry Association of America
www.tia.org

Travel Weekly
www.twcrossroads.com

Travel Agent magazine
www.travelagentcentral.com

Travel Trade
www.traveltrade.com

www.travelbusinessbroker.com

Travel Wholesalers/Consolidators

Rule of Thumb:

- 3 times EBITDA for small to midsize companies; 4 times EBITDA when profits exceed $350,000

Pricing Tips

"Booking patterns have decreased the value of these operations, as public is trained to wait for last-minute distressed inventory, and suppliers e-mail customers directly."

"Length of time in business? Salary vs. commission? Who controls the business? How long are contracts valid?"

Trophy Studios

Rule of Thumb:

- 60 to 70 percent of annual sales plus inventory

General Information

Questions to ask a seller: "What is seller willing to finance, since the intangible side of the transaction could be 75% + of the transaction value."

"A large studio can have a net profit greater than 25 percent."

"In the trophy business, 70 to 80 percent of the charge is for the engraving service, a service function."

Industry Trend

"Should be about the same as it has been, but technology is changing the business."

Truck Stops *(See also Gas Stations)*

3,063	SIC: 5541-03	NAIC: 447190

Rule of Thumb:

- 4 1/4 times SDE plus inventory for units 10 to 15 years or older. May deduct cost of cosmetic update.
- 3 times SDE plus inventory
- 2.75 times EBITDA
- 7 to 10 times SDE (truck stops with property) plus inventory

Pricing Tips

"Limited buyers who buy this kind of business, due to the large number of employees and size of operation"

"Business Only 2.5 to 3.5 times the Net/EBITDA; Real Estate + Business 7 to 10 times Net/EBITDA"

"I only do cash deals. Environmental risk can turn into nightmare on contract sales."

"Net profit median is 2 to 2.5 percent of sales; high net profit truck stops make 5 to 7 percent of sales. Note: Truck stops have an overall higher gross profit because there are various departments—restaurants, trucker's store, motel, scale, C-store, laundromat, showers, movies, phones, gas, diesel, repairs, truck wash, barber shop, shoeshine shop, check cashing and much more sometimes."

Industry Experts' Ratings:

Amount of Competition (1 = Lot of: 4 = Not much) 1.6
Amount of Risk (1 = Very: 4 = Not much) 1.6
Historical Profit Trend (1 = Down: 4 = Up) 2.0
Location & Facilities (1 = Poor: 4 = Excellent)......................... 2.0
Marketability (1 = Low: 4 = High).. 1.2
Industry Trend (1 = Declining: 4 = Growing) 2.0
Ease of Replication (1 = Easy: 4 = Difficult) 2.4

"Even though the travel plazas are profitable, the size of operation and management acumen required can be daunting. Also the upfront monies required are pretty hefty as compared to most small businesses."

"The average return on investment for a truck stop is 6 to 8 percent. The high profit return on investment for a truck stop is 16 to 17 percent. In order for a buyer to determine a good deal—12 to 15 percent ROI for a truck stop should provide a good rule of thumb."

"Replication is difficult because 5 to 25 acres of prime real estate is required, and the cost can be between $5 and $10 million to build one. Truck stops/travel plazas have been steady, but also the older or small mom/pops are being eliminated due to competition."

Benchmarks

"Convenience/Retail combined is approx $500 per sq. ft"

"Per Employee Sales Annually: $135,000
Gross Profit Margins: 24%
Net Profit Margins: .... 1.8%"

"Average annual sales are nearly $7 million with the larger, high-profit centers doing in excess of $20 million annually with a net of 6% of sales."

"Typical Full-Service Travel Plaza Statistics

At a typical full-service travel plaza you will find:

- Convenience or retail stores (97%)
- Check cashing (98%)
- Private showers (89%)
- Free parking (93%)
- Buses welcome (82%)
- Public fax machines (81%)
- Restaurants or delis (77%)
- Platform scales (59%)
- Laundry facilities (58%)
- Truck repair (50%)
- Emergency road service (63%)
- ATM machines (91%)
- Security/local police patrol (54%)
- Load boards (75%)
- Postal service (53%)
- Truck washes (28%)
- Hotels or motels (28%)
- Driver lounges (48%)
- Recreational vehicle facilities (23%)
- On-site fast food (51%)
- Church services (38%)
- Food court (15%)
- Internet services (39%)

"Employment: The typical travel plaza or truck stop employs 75 to 95 individuals. The largest percentage work in restaurants, followed by retail/convenience stores, administrative offices and maintenance shops.

"Sales: The average travel plaza or truck stop has annual sales of about $7.8 million (median $6.6 million).

"Fuel: NATSO member travel plazas and truck stops average 6.5 diesel islands and 3.0 gasoline islands. A typical fuel stop sells an average of 250,000 gallons of diesel fuel per month, while a typical full-service truck stop sells an average of 1 million gallons per month. Sales of gasoline at fuel stops average 150,000 gallons per month, while sales at full-service truck stops average 100,000 gallons.

"Restaurants: Almost all NATSO travel plazas and truck stops operate a restaurant as part of their facility—90 percent operated by the facility itself, with 10 percent either leased or franchised. The average travel plaza or truck stop restaurant has a seating capacity of 132, with 60 percent of the restaurants designating separate sections for professional drivers. Truckers account for the greatest share of truck stop restaurant business (57 percent), followed by local patrons (26 percent) and tourists (17 percent). The average meal ticket is $4.97.

"Retail Operations: The typical travel plaza or truck stop convenience store or retail store measures 2,100 square feet. The most common retail offering is a combined convenience and retail store (70 percent), followed by in-store fast food, separate retail stores, and separate convenience stores."

Source: National Association of Truck Stop Operators(NATSO). (The figures in the data above are from an industry survey of 1999, but the information is still of interest).

Expenses as a percentage of annual sales:	
Cost of Goods Sold	63%
Payroll/Labor Costs	8%
Occupancy Cost	2.5%
Profit (estimated)	4%

General Information

"There is constant consolidation in the industry, and the bigger chains are buying out and/or partnering with the smaller mom-and-pop operations."

Advantages of this Business

- "Very stable, since there are several profit centers. The good ones can produce a very high ROI."
- "Extremely stable because of multiple profit centers, high rate of return"

Disadvantages of this Business

- "Large number of employess, especially in the restaurant area. Again, open 24 hours x 365 days a year."
- "Large number of employees, high turnover, cash business, fuel on credit"

Industry Trend

"Very slow growth due to the nature of the business. Large lots of 10+ acres required, and investments upwards of $10+ million per site make the field of players very limited."

Seller Financing

- "Property and land included: 10 to 15 years (8% to 11%)"
- "Business only: 3 to 8 years (8% to 10%)"

Resources

National Association of Truck Stop Operators
www.natso.com—an excellent site, full of interesting information and data

Trucking Companies *(See Motor Carriers & Transportation)*

Rule of Thumb:

- 5 times EBIT
- 2 to 3 times EBITDA
- 1 to 1.5 times SDE + market value of assets
- $4,000 to $6,000 per driver

Pricing Tips

Operating Ratio (EBIT divided by gross sales)	
Excellent	85% or less
Good	86% to 92%
Fair	93% to 96%
Poor	97% or greater

Revenues per Mile	
Excellent	1.40 or more
Good	1.35 to 1.39
Fair	1.30 to 1.34
Poor	1.29 or less

"Special Equipment +15 percent; special services +5 to 25 percent; routes & relationships +10 to 25 percent."

Industry Trend

"The ranks of long-haul truck drivers expanded 1.6 percent last year, according to federal data, while industry expansion is projected at 2.2 percent a year over the next decade. If those trends hold, a current 20,000-driver shortfall will balloon to 110,000 by 2014, a figure that doesn't include the approximately 219,000 truckers expected to retire during that period, according to a study commissioned by American Trucking Associations."

Source: *The Boston Globe*, Tuesday, July 12, 2005

Resources
American Trucking Association
www.ata.com

Franchise

Two Men and a Truck

120 units	
Approximate Total Investment:	$112,400 to $245,100

Rule of Thumb:

- 43 percent of annual sales plus inventory

Uniform Rental and Dust Control

Rule of Thumb:

- 40 to 45 times weekly sales plus inventory

Pricing Tips
An industry expert says that if there are contracts with the accounts serviced, the rule of thumb will be 70 percent of gross annual sales.

Uniform Sales

5,500	SIC: 5699-22	NAIC: 448190

Rule of Thumb:

- 35 percent of annual sales plus inventory

Franchise

UPS Store (Formerly Mail Boxes, Etc.)

(See also Mail & Parcel Centers)

4500 + units

Approximate Total Investment: $141,079 to $239,687

Rule of Thumb:

- "The average MBE store transferred for 65 percent of STR from a period of nine years ending in 1998. STR is gross sales less sales tax, the cost of metered mail, stamps, money orders and select other items that are not very profitable. The valid range was 50 percent of STR for a store earning under $250,000 STR to perhaps as high as 75 percent of STR for a store earning $1,000,000 STR. But the old rule of 1.5 to 2.5 times SDE is very much applicable. I have personally not seen a store transfer in So. Cal. for more than 2.25 times SDE + inventory where inventory is less than $5,000."
- 39 percent of annual sales plus inventory
- 2 to 3 times SDE plus inventory

Resources

www.mbe.com

Franchise

U Save (Auto Rental)

300 units

Rule of Thumb:

- "10 percent of annual sales (price does not include cost of vehicles, and revenues do not include auto sales)"

Resources

www.usave.net

Variety Stores

12,400	SIC: 5331-01	NAIC: 452990

Pricing Tips

"These should turn their inventory 4 times per year. Sales price is based upon market value of fixtures and equipment, plus inventory at wholesale cost. The rent shouldn't be more than 5 percent of the gross sales. These stores usually do two-thirds of their volume through October, November, and December."

Vending Industry (Routes) *(See also Routes)*

Rule of Thumb:

- 75 to 75 percent of annual sales plus inventory
- 1.5 to 2 times SDE plus inventory
- "Smaller, one-man operations sell for less than one year's gross sales. Larger vending businesses are based on cash flow and asset value. A common rule of thumb would be 1 to 2 times SDE plus assets. Again, companies with new assets would be closer to 2 times SDE plus hard assets."
- "Listing price should be less than 1 year's gross. Some vending businesses are heavy in assets, so assets plus 1 to 1½ times cash flow. Highly profitable may sell for 2 to 3 times cash flow."

Pricing Tips

"Price could be 70 to 80 percent of last year's sales if business is well established."

"How much does a route cost? The net profit of the route is the main factor in determining its value. Other significant factors include the type of route, the gross, the area, days and hours, and the vehicle. A general rule to keep in mind for the purchase of a route is 'double net.' The amount that you net in one year will be the approximate down payment amount, and double that figure will be the total purchase price. (Example: route netting $1,000/wk would cost approximately $100,000 with $50,000 down.) As a rule of thumb, the bigger the name a brand route is, the more the route will cost. Independent routes and service routes, on the other hand, cost usually 1 to 1 ½ year's net as opposed to 2 years' net (double net)."

Source: Mr. Route, www.mrrouteinc.com—a very informative Web site

"These factors will also influence price determination: ownership status of the machines coming with the sale; are they leased, owned, financed; the type of machines that the route consists of and the service schedule that they would need to have the machines produce income (sandwiches need daily servicing ... soda/snacks many need weekly servicing); the locale of the machines ... inside, outside, 24-hour access, limited access; is the commission paid to accounts above the normal 10% to 15%?"

"As in all businesses, the size of the business, the value of the equipment and the provable cash flow by the business must be considered. It is difficult to value this type of business on cash flow basis alone."

"Ratios of investment dollars (borrowed or asset) and estimated length of return"

"Caution should always be prime in price of equipment, location risk, and percentage of payouts."

Industry Experts' Ratings:

Marketability (1 = Low: 4 = High) 3.4
Industry Trend (1 = Declining: 4 = Growing) 2.4
Ease of Replication (1 = Easy: 4 = Difficult) 2.4

"The vending industry (at least in the metro New York area) is dominated by several large companies. However, the market usually views this business as being a 'good part-time,' making it generally a highly desirable business opportunity."

Benchmarks

"Bulk machines should sell at least $100 per month/per location to be considered viable; soda machines should vend at least four cases per week to be considered viable, and snack machines should produce a minimum of $50 per week/per location to be viable."

"Gross sales in vending businesses are directly related to the number of employees per location. A few locations with 100 or more employees normally make for a good business."

"Profit depends on volume and percentage paid to customer providing space & power."

Industry Profitability

Item	<$1M	$1–$3M	$3–$5M	$5–$10M	>$10M
Sales	100%	100%	100%	100%	100%
Product Cost	50%	49.9%	47.4%	47.5%	44.5%
Gross Margin	50%	50.1%	52.6%	52.5%	55.5%
Labor Costs	22.6%	22.6%	21.8%	23.8%	21.7%
Commissions	5.2%	6.4%	8.0%	7.6%	10.1%
Other Costs	24.7%	19.9%	19.2%	18.1%	18.4%
Op. Profit	(2.5%)	1.2%	3.6%	3.0%	5.3%

M = Million

Source: National Automatic Merchandise Association (NAMA)

Expenses as a percentage of annual sales:

Cost of Goods Sold	45%–50%
Payroll/Labor Costs	15%–20%
Occupancy Cost	15%–20%
Profit (estimated)	25%–35%

General Information

Questions to ask a seller: "Will seller finance the deal? Lenders do not want to own a lot of vending machines in case the loan would go bad."

"Buying an established vending business with established, well-documented locations has value. Someone selling you vending equipment that they will place for you is not the way to go into vending."

"A well-established vending business with contracts on locations and newer equipment tends to sell for more. As in most businesses, good books and records are very helpful."

Advantages of this Business

- "This is a cash business. Few employees are needed to run this type of business as compared to most other businesses. Hours can be flexible. There is no need for a retail location or showroom."

- "In many cases, this business can generate a good income, yet be operated part-time."

Disadvantages of this Business

- "The high investment in hard assets (machines) is disproportionate to the amount of immediate return."
- "This is an equipment intensive business. Often when a new location is contracted, there will be a need to purchase additional equipment. It is not easy for smaller venders to take a long vacation."

Seller Financing

- "3 to 5 years. A seller will need to carry for a longer period if the cash flow is low and assets high. Could carry for 5 to 7 years—10 percent interest."

Resources

National Automatic Merchandising Association (NAMA)
www.vending.org—a very good site with lots of educational information on the industry

Automatic Merchandiser
www.amonline.com—This is an excellent site full of good information.

Amusement & Music Operators Association (AMOA)
www.amoa.com

Quick *Profile* — Vending Industry

Vending Operator Definition

NAMA, the industry association, informally defines the term Vending Operators as "people who are in the business of buying, placing on location, filling with product, removing the cash and maintaining vending equipment." There are seven major categories under Vending Routes. They are as follows, with a brief definition of each furnished by NAMA.

"1. 4C's: an abbreviation standing for what were the basics of vending as it evolved; i.e., Coffee—Cup Soda—Candy—Cigarettes.

"2. Full Line: as equipment evolved and the customers demanded more alternatives, operators who began to offer such things as hot canned food, canned soda, refrigerated food, frozen food, dairy, etc. were said to be 'full line,' meaning that they were still concentrated in food and refreshments but offered a broader service than the basic 4C's.

"3. Specialty: as the technology and sophistication of vending grew, many operators either got into the business or chose to concentrate their efforts in one particular line of equipment or product. Having its roots in routes that focused in just this way on items such as dairy, cigarettes, soda, etc., today's specialty operator is more often offering service in equipment such as French fries, pizza, popcorn and other tightly focused items.

"75% of all vending companies do less than $1 million in annual revenues."

Source: *Automatic Merchandiser, 2004 State of the Vending Industry Report,* August 2005

"4. OCS: the commonly used abbreviation for the Office Coffee Service marketplace, wherein operators provide equipment and "kits" containing coffee and related items such as sweeteners, creamers, stir sticks, etc. It is very common for full-line vending operators to migrate into OCS, and for OCS operators to migrate into vending, serving the demand of their customers.

"5. Bulk: a broad category used to define vending of candy, gum, novelties, etc. This segment has evolved from the small, commonly sited machines into a broader approach using oversize equipment. Once again, it is not uncommon for there to be crossover between full-line and bulk operators in both directions, but not as frequently as the OCS-vending connection.

"6. Music/Game: another broad-based term used to describe what began as the juke box/pool side of the business, but today has evolved into music machines, video games of all sorts, coin-operated amusement devices, etc. This is another area that often sees diversification to/from full line, but most often in the form of a separate operation within a company due to the specific needs of this market.

"7. Street: in many quarters, street vending is viewed as a subset or a combination of specialty, full-line and music/games vending. Most often it is used to describe the type of location being served, that of "public" such as restaurants, taverns, etc. The service can encompass cigarettes, snacks, jukeboxes, video games, pool tables or any combination of these.

"Vending is very much an entrepreneur's business. It started that way and for the most part, it still is that way."

Operator Sales

Size	Revenue Range	% of 2003 Operators	Projected 2004 sales	% of of 2004 sales
Small	under $1 million	75%	$485 million	2.4%
Medium	$1 M to $4.9 M	18%	$1.33 billion	6.6%
Large	$5 M to $9.9 M	4%	$1.07 billion	5.3%
Extra large	$10 M +	3%	$17.3 billion	85.7

M = Million

Note: Does not include 5% of total industry revenue for machines owned and operated by locations.

Source: *Automatic Merchandiser, 2004 State of the Vending Industry Report,* August 2005 www.AMonline.com

"In 204, these extra-large operators increased their total market share [by 13 percent] at the expense of other operators."

Source: *Automatic Merchandiser, 2004 State of the Vending Industry Report,* August 2005 www.AMonline.com

Machines Installed by Location Type

Manufacturing, fabrication, warehouse facilities	28.4%
Offices	26.8%
Other retail locations	21%
Schools, colleges, universities	11%
Hospitals, nursing homes	3.8%
Hotels/motels	2.1%
Restaurants, bars, clubs	1.7%
Correctional facilities	1.6%
Other	2.4%
Military bases	1.2%

Source: *Automatic Merchandiser, 2004 State of the Vending Industry Report,* August 2005 www.AMonline.com

The Industry Mix of Products Sold

Cold Beverages	28.8%
Candy/Snacks/Confections	19%
Manual Food service	30%
Vend Food	6.2%
Hot Beverages	4.9%
OCS	4.1%
Milk	1.5%
Ice Cream	1.1%
Cigarettes	.06%
Other	3.8%

Source: *Automatic Merchandiser, 2004 State of the Vending Industry Report,* August 2005
www.Amonline.com

Another important component of the vending business is coin-activated equipment on location. These would include games, jukeboxes, pool tables, dart boards, and other amusement equipment.

What Equipment Is on Location

Jukeboxes	15%
Video Games	14%
Pinball Games	13%
Pool/Billiards	11%
Electronic Darts	10%
Foosball/Air Hockey	10%
Cigarettes/Pay Phones	8%
Redemption	6%
Kiddie Rides	4%
Bulk Vending	2%
Food Vending/Confections	2%
Legalized Gaming	2%
Virtual Reality	1%
Other	2%

Where Is this Equipment Placed?

Amusement Arcades	11%
Street Locations	23%
Amusement Parks	2%
Family Entertainment Centers	7%
Bars/Restaurants	29%
Food Vending/Confections	7%
Miniature Golf Courses	3%
Bowling Centers	12%
Other	3%
Unspecified	2%

Source: Amusement & Music Operators Association (AMOA)

Veterinary Practices

Rule of Thumb:

- 70 percent of annual sales plus inventory
- 2.0 times SDE for small animal practices plus inventory
- "Usually 70 to 80 percent of past 12 months' gross revenues [sales] (includes tangible and intangible assets)"

Pricing Tips

"Profitable small animal practices are the easiest to sell. Mixed and large animal practices are harder to sell (fewer buyers) and often sell for less. Wide variance +/- 35% of selling price; rule of thumb (72%) above based on a wide variety of factors."

"Rules of thumb can be very unreliable for some practices due to great differences in profitability and demand for different types of veterinary practices. There is moderate demand for small animal type practices and low demand for large animal practices in many parts of the country."

"Range 50% to 90% of gross revenues; 1.5 to 3.0 SDE. Multi-doctor, small animal practices in urban areas bring higher prices than most others. Mixed practice (large and small animal) are very difficult to sell as there are few buyers and they are generally less profitable. The above rules of thumb are probably inappropriate for mixed or large animal practices."

> "For new veterinarians, pets are far more lucrative patients than farm animals."
>
> Source: *The New York Sunday Times*, July 31, 2005

"Small animal practices are much easier to sell than larger animal practices. Most small animal practices grossing less than $500K will be sold for 50 to 70 percent of gross revenue. Small animal practices grossing more than $500K will sell for 70 to 90 percent of gross revenue. Large, or predominately large, animal practices with significant retail/resale/dispensing activity will be discounted significantly from what small animal practices sell for, due to limited market and low profitability."

"Size of customer base, frequency of visits, special services offered, related service and products offered"

"Prices generally run from 60 percent to 95 percent of gross with smaller hospitals on the lower end, larger on the upper."

"Small animal clinics in good locations can command premium prices. Generally, these practices can sell for 75 to 125 percent of the last year's revenues for the goodwill, equipment, and supplies."

Industry Experts' Ratings:

Amount of Competition (1 = Lot of: 4 = Not much) 1.2
Amount of Risk (1 = Very: 4 = Not much) 3.6
Historical Profit Trend (1 = Down: 4 = Up) 2.4
Location & Facilities (1 = Poor: 4 = Excellent)......................... 2.0
Marketability (1 = Low: 4 = High).. 2.8
Industry Trend (1 = Declining: 4 = Growing) 3.2
Ease of Replication (1 = Easy: 4 = Difficult) 2.8

"Risk is low. Loan default rates very low. Can get up to 100% financing. Cost of entry for vet practice is higher than for human medical practice."

"Market for veterinary practices appears to be declining. Fewer young doctors want to own. Also greater number of sellers is coming into the market place (baby-boomers coming of retirement age). The larger practices with good profit histories, better facilities, and multiple doctors are in greatest demand."

"Some states now allow non-vets to own vet practices, providing that the licensed vet runs the medical practice."

Benchmarks

"3.4 employees per FTE veterinarian"

"Vet wages should be approximately 23% of gross vet professional fees generated."

"Revenues of $250,000 to $500,000/doctor typical. Compensation of doctors should be 20% to 25% of revenue production. High end of this range if managing practice; lower end if just being a doctor."

Expenses as a percentage of annual sales:	
Cost of Goods Sold	20%–25%
Payroll/Labor Costs	20%–23%
Occupancy Cost	8%–10%
Profit (estimated)	10%–20%

General Information

Questions to ask a seller: "Standard recasting info for sellers. Types of surgery performed? 1 or 3 vaccination schedule? Relationship with local shelters/humane societies? How are emergencies handled?"

"Small animal practices have a limited market. Other types of practices are much more difficult to sell. Rural locations add to the difficulty."

Advantages of this Business

- "Less liability/malpractice costs than other medical professionals"
- "Business owners control their own business path, have control of their destiny and directly benefit from their efforts. Compensation for owners can be many times that for what an employed associate can earn."
- "Helpful service to pet lovers and community. Many vets caring and compassionate people, and highly regarded."

Disadvantages of this Business

- "Longer hours than many other medical professionals"
- "Long education time frame, with pay considerably less than dentists, MDs, and other medical professionals."
- "Management responsibilities and operating a business can be a distraction from the practice of veterinary medicine."

Trend

"More female veterinarian buyers. Fewer DVMs treating large animals."

"Currently, there are many consolidators looking for profitable practices. Also, financing is more easily obtained in this business than others."

Seller Financing

- "10 years"

Resources

American Veterinary Medical Association (AVMA)
www.avma.org—The site offers publications that would be of interest to anyone involved in the sale of veterinary practices.

Video Stores

	SIC: 7841-02	NAIC: 451220

Rule of Thumb:

- Most buyers want to recover their investment within 24 months, so 2 times SDE is a safe bet.
- "It used to be one year's SDE plus the fair market value of the tapes and games, but inventory drops in value too dramatically after the 'new release' prime period (90 days) has passed."
- "1 to 2 times SDE plus fair market value of videos, furniture & equipment"
- "1 to 2 times SDE to a working owner plus fair market value for videos, games & DVDs"
- .65 to 1.0 annual revenues plus inventory

Pricing Tips

"I have sold more mom-and-pop video stores in the state of Georgia than anyone else. But these stores are not coming on the market very frequently, and when they do, they typically are making very little money if any. This, of course makes them unsaleable. The video industry is primarily composed of the chains like Blockbuster, Hollywood Video, etc."

"The inventory price of the videos and games drops drastically from its original retail. Unit prices can be as low as $5.00 or less."

"If the current owner can computer-generate a video rental report that shows you how many times each video in inventory has been rented and the income associated with it, you will see how much 'dead inventory' could be replaced to increase revenues. Special- interest videos and games like Nintendo and PlayStation 2, etc. would be good profit generators."

Industry Experts' Ratings:

Marketability (1 = Low: 4 = High)	1.2
Industry Trend (1 = Declining: 4 = Growing)	2.0
Ease of Replication (1 = Easy: 4 = Difficult)	1.0

"The industry has changed with the switch to games."

Benchmarks

"Stores should have well-stocked concession areas including popcorn, candy, soft drinks. They should be close to cash registers."

Expenses as a percentage of annual sales:

Cost of Goods	33%
Payroll/Labor Costs	27%
Occupancy Cost	15%
Profit (estimated)	approx. 25%

General Information

Questions to ask a seller: "You want to know how large a percentage late-fee income is as a percentage of total revenue. It should be approximately 20% to 25%. In some instances, late-fee income has dropped due to 5-day rentals and other promotions offered by Blockbuster Video and Hollywood Video." "Distance from the nearest Blockbuster or Hollywood Video and likelihood of one opening that is closer."

"If someone wants to stay in business, they need to carve out a niche for games and keep them leading edge to keep customers coming back for more. You can develop monthly memberships where for a flat fee a person can rent one item per day for a month."

Advantages of this Business

- "It is a people business and you get to interact with all types every day. It is a heavy cash business for those who want this. If you develop niches like foreign films, historic documentaries, sports, wars, heavy children's categories, etc. you can carve out your own business."

Disadvantages of this Business

- "The larger chains and pay-per-view are hurting the independents. If you are prevented from carrying adult titles, you will lose a great deal of potential business."

Industry Trend

"Video store operators already have dealt with declining rental revenue for the past three years, according to data from research firm Adams Media Research and accounting firm PricewaterhouseCoopers.

"The size of the U.S. video rental market peaked at $10.26 billion in 2001 before falling 3.3% in 2002, 4.4% in 2003, and about 7.4% last year, according to PwC.

"For this year, the company forecasts a 7.1% decline, which will be reduced to a 1.1% decrease next year, PwC said. Although PwC sees continued reductions in market size through at least 2008, the worst should be behind chains like Blockbuster, according to its estimates."

Source: *Reuters Know Now*, www.reuters.com, Sunday, January 9, 2005

Seller Financing

- "12 to 24 months"
- "3 years"

Resources

Video Software Dealers Association
www.vsda.org

Visa/Passport Companies

Rule of Thumb:

- "3 times EBITDA for small to midsized operations, 4 times EBITDA for larger ones"

Pricing Tips

"How do they execute quick turnaround? How long does it take them to fulfill applications?"

Water Companies

Pricing Tips
"The market price varies greatly, between $75 and $150 per metered customer. The normal meter hookup charge is approximately $100. These are saleable unless they have a minimum of 250 customers with growth potential."

Franchise

We the People (Legal Document Preparation)

138 units	
Approximate Total Investment:	$109,500 to $119,500

Rule of Thumb:

- 86 percent of annual sales plus inventory

General Information
"40 percent of all franchisees own more than one unit."

Resources
www.wethepeople.com

Web-Based Companies *(See also Internet Services)*

Rule of Thumb:

- "Right now it's 2 times SDE maximum or asset liquidation value. ISP's are being sold for 3 – 6 times monthly gross sales."

Pricing Tips
"It depends on if there is any profit. If there is, about 2 times SDE."

Seller Financing
- "Very short—2 to 4 years"

Wedding Stores *(See Bridal Shops)*

Wholesale/Distributors—Durable Goods

Rule of Thumb:

- 5 times EBITDA
- 2 to 2.5 times SDE plus inventory

Pricing Tips

"Worth approximately one-half of sales volume; watch out for large, stale inventory."

"% of annual gross sales is a poor guide to follow. EBITDA drives ROI and ability to service debt."

"Add cost of replacing current ownership with professional management to SDE, and then multiply this number by 4 to 6 to get price. Variance is for security of earnings, competition, assets, etc."

Industry Experts' Ratings:

Amount of Competition (1 = Lot of: 4 = Not much)	2.2
Amount of Risk (1 = Very: 4 = Not much)	2.4
Historical Profit Trend (1 = Down: 4 = Up)	2.8
Location & Facilities (1 = Poor: 4 = Excellent)	2.0
Marketability (1 = Low: 4 = High)	2.6
Industry Trend (1 = Declining: 4 = Growing)	2.6
Ease of Replication (1 = Easy: 4 = Difficult)	2.8

"There are significant competitive cost barriers to entry into this industry, where size does matter along with quantity and quality of product lines, adequate logistical distribution channels, good supplier pricing and terms, adequate facilities sizing and location. Solid, well-diversified customer base mitigates risk and wards off competitive challenges."

Benchmarks

"Cost of goods should be less than 74%, with 70% as ideal; operating expenses of less than 20%; sales/assets ratio of 3.0; W/C ratio of 13% to 15% of revenues; current ratio of 3.0 or greater; A/R turnover ratio of 12.0;

inventory turns of 6.0 or greater; sales per employee greater than $250,000; sales per sq. ft. in excess of $300,000."

Expenses as a percentage of annual sales:	
Cost of Goods Sold	70%–72%
Payroll/Labor Costs	15%–20%
Occupancy Cost	3%–8%
Profit (estimated)	8%–15%

Advantages of this Business

- "Barriers to entry—size, product lines"
- "Most are growing because of Internet sales"

Disadvantages of this Business

- "Most are growing because of Internet sales."
- "Large players trying to squeeze out smaller players"

Industry Trend

"Self-service options will change the way you do business with customers and transform your sales force. Customers will roam online, searching for information and taking over more of the pre-sales and transactional activities typically handled by their wholesaler-distributors. Distributors will not have a lock on information needed by customers to make purchasing and sourcing decisions, since manufacturers and online sources will make such information readily available.

"In response, wholesaler-distributors of all sizes will complement their traditional selling methods with online technologies. Wholesaler-distributors will catch up to larger companies by 2008, as the costs and complexity of today's technologies drop.

"Customer self-service will also significantly erode the perceived value of the wholesale distribution sales force in educating customers about new products. The majority of wholesale distribution executives believe the Internet could actually replace their sales force as a source of product information. Manufacturers will seriously question the effectiveness of the distributor's sales force going forward. As a result, sales positions in wholesale distribution are forecast to grow at half the rate of overall U.S. job growth over the next five years."

Source: *The Road to Opportunity in Wholesale Distributation* by Adam J. Fein, Ph.D., Pembroker Consulting, Inc., www.pembrokeconsulting.com

Wholesale/Distributors—Fuel Dealers

(See Fuel Dealers)

Wholesale/Distributors—Green Groceries

Rule of Thumb:

- 1 times SDE plus inventory

Pricing Tips

"Actual gross sales achieved is not an important analysis tool … since there is usually an inverse relationship between sales volume & amount of profit that may be achieved (for instance, the more a box of tomatoes costs, the less profit may be added on). Better to determine how many packages/boxes of product are handled weekly & what 'profit per unit' is achieved."

Benchmarks

Expenses as a percentage of annual sales:	
Cost of Goods Sold	25%
Payroll/Labor Costs	45%
Occupancy Cost	15%
Profit (estimated)	15%

Disadvantages of this Business

- "A retail customer may go to a local market on his own and pick up produce; most large food wholesalers carry (at least) a limited line of produce items."

Wild Bird Shops

Sells bird houses, feeders, feed and other wild-bird and nature products

Rule of Thumb:

- 30 percent of annual sales plus inventory

General Information

"How big is the market for Wild Birds Unlimited?

Imagine a backyard that can fit 52 million people and still have room to grow! Across North America, that's the number of people who participate in bird feeding and wildlife watching in their own backyards, according to the most recent U.S. Fish and Wildlife Service Survey of Fishing, Hunting and Wildlife Associated Recreation.

"And they spend money to support their hobby. The most recent statistics for consumer spending show people spend nearly $4.7 billion annually on bird feeding and watching wildlife. Of that, they spend $3.2 billion on birdseed and wildlife food; $832 million on birdfeeders, birdbaths and nesting boxes; and $636 million on binoculars and spotting scopes."

Source: Wild Birds Unlimited, www.wbu.com

Window Treatment

Rule of Thumb:

- 35 percent of annual sales plus inventory

Resources

Draperies & Window Coverings magazine
www.dwcdesignet.com

Wireless Communications (Carriers, dealers & resellers of cellular, PCs, & paging)

Rule of Thumb:

- 2 to 5 times EBITDA
- $50 to $130 per pop for operational market—less if naked license

General Information

Questions to ask a seller: "Ask if market is built out (to what percentage of population and geography) and if it is operational (how long)."

Industry Trend
"There will be large consolidations of operators, and wireless penetration in U.S. will continue to increase. More use of data."

Resources
www.10meters.com—a Web site that provides current news

www.rcrnews.com—a magazine that has a Web site for the industry

Yardage Shops

Pricing Tips
"You must take into consideration that, even though the markup is high, the gross profit is often reduced to a low figure of 35 percent because of the amount of sales which have to be spent to merchandise the products. Prices of this type of store usually include a very minimal amount for the fixtures and equipment, plus inventory, and at wholesale. Rent should not exceed 4 percent to 4.5 percent of the gross sales."

Franchise

Your Office USA

Rule of Thumb:

- 60 percent of annual sales plus inventory

Yum! Brands

General Information
"In the eight years that have passed since KFC, Pizza Hut, and Taco Bell were spun off by PepsiCo Inc. into a stand-alone company singularly focused on restaurants, parent Yum! Brands Inc. has wasted no time demonstrating its dominance among fast feeders.

"Today Yum's chains have nearly 34,000 restaurants in almost 100 countries with a diverse portfolio of mega-brands that now includes A&W All American Foods and Long John Silver's, making Yum overseer of the world's largest restaurant system.

"The five concepts generated nearly $28 billion in sales last year—up by a whopping $5.6 billion system-wide from their 2001 year-end tally—and currently employ some 850,000 workers."

Source: *Nation's Restaurant News*, August 15, 2005

Yum! Brands

Brand	# of units	2004 average sales per unit
KFC	5,145	$896,000
Pizza Hut	6,284	$794,000
Taco Bell	5,017	$1.07 million
Long John Silver's	1,197	n/a
A&W All American Food	461	n/a

Source: *Nation's Restaurant News*, August 15, 2005

Franchise

Ziebart International (auto services)

450 units

Approximate Total Investment: $105,000 to $210,000

Rule of Thumb:

- 42 percent of annual sales plus inventory

Resources

www.ziebart.com

industry experts

Accounting Firms

Roy Braatz
Accounting Practice Sales
888-783-7822
roy@accountingpracticesales.com

John Ezell, CPA
ProHorizons
800-729-3242
john@prohorizons.com

Leon W. Faris, CPA
Professional Accounting Sales
800-729-9031
leon@cpasales.com

William Pipes
Breckenridge Pipes & Co
904-264-4888
bpipes@breckbroker.com

David Snyder
Strategic Success Business Brokers
803-644-4000
david@dmsnyder.com

Arts and Crafts Stores

Randall (Randy) Ferrian
Ferrian, Tifft & Spannaus, LLC
952-912-0333
randy@ftsbrokers.com

Auto Body Shop

David Sweeten
Sweeten Business Brokerage
210-697-8760
busforsale@prodigy.net

Auto Dealerships – New

Patrick Anderson
Anderson Economic Group LLC
517-333-6984
panderson@andersoneconomicgroup.com

Pat McNulty
McNulty & Associates, LLC
800-800-4728
pmcnulty@prodigy.net

John Sliman
USA Business Brokers, Inc.
866-343-1266
info@usabbi.com

Auto Lube/Tune-up
Hal Janke
Hal Janke & Associates, Inc.
760-431-6767
haljanke@aol.com

Auto Rental
Patrick Anderson
Anderson Economic Group LLC
517-333-6984
panderson@andersoneconomicgroup.com

Auto Repair
Richard Haugland
West USA
602-862-0749
AFC1@cox.net

Hal Janke
Hal Janke & Associates, Inc.
760-431-6767
haljanke@aol.com

Bob McDowell
McDowell Business Associates
972-991-9588
mcdowellbb@sbcglobal.net

Aaron Muller
KR Business Brokers
425-766-3940
aaron@krbrokers.com

Kavi Pannu
American Business Advisors, Inc.
856-235-6700
Kavi_Pannu@yahoo.com

Auto Tire Centers
Hal Janke
Hal Janke & Associates, Inc.
760-431-6767
haljanke@aol.com

Auto Transmission Centers
Hal Janke
Hal Janke & Associates, Inc.
760-431-6767
haljanke@aol.com

Bob McDowell
McDowell Business Associates
972-991-9588
mcdowellbb@sbcglobal.net

Aviation/Aerospace
Leonard Nock
Aviation Capital Advisors, Inc.
305-931-6820
ddmincfl@yahoo.com

Bakeries
Ken Leif
Route World Brokers, Inc.
516-825-6050
Rwbkr@aol.com

Bakeries – Commercial and Wholesale
Bob Lucido
Lucido & Company
508-878-2900
BobBusBkr@comcast.net

Bars
Larry Battershell
Indiana Business Resource
317-848-1200
inbizsales@aol.com

Steve Chiaet
Dickman Business Brokers
973-627-1490
icediver007@aol.com

Scott Dickman
Dickman Business Brokers
973-627-1490
nacdman@aol.com

Dan Jones
Aaction Business Sales
530-620-4947
danjones@directcon.net

Edward Resha
#1 Business Brokers
714-777-1727
a1bizbroker@aol.com

Terri Sokoloff
Specialty Tavern & Restaurant Brokers
412-369-1555
terri@specialtygroup.com

David Sweeten
Sweeten Business Brokerage
210-697-8760
busforsale@prodigy.net

Bars – Adult

H. Winston Hines
HWH Properties
864-580-3826
updaze@aol.com

Bars – Nightclubs

Michael Wildeveld
The Veld Group
310-652-8353
contact@theveldgroup.com

Beauty Salons

Franco Ferrari
Ferrari Sunbelt Business Brokers
407-339-3101
ferrarisunbelt@cfl.rr.com

Sharon Matle
Empire Business Brokers Southeast Office
313-382-6277
smatle1@comcast.net

Bed and Breakfasts

Bob Fuehr
The Inn Broker, Inc.
800-926-4667
fuehr@innbroker.com

Beer and Ale Merchant Wholesalers

Patrick Anderson
Anderson Economic Group LLC
517-333-6984
panderson@andersoneconomicgroup.com

Bowling Centers

Sandy Hansell
Sandy Hansell & Associates
800-222-9131
sandyh@sandyhansell.com

Ken Mischel
Mischel & Company
619-423-2001
mischelco@msn.com

Building Supplies

Bud Howe
Howe & Ely Co.
314-302-9248
budhowe@aol.com

Jeffrey Wolpin
Accredited Business Appraisals & Brokerage
661-263-0911
bizvalu@earthlink.net

Car Washes
Hal Janke
Hal Janke & Associates, Inc.
760-431-6767
haljanke@aol.com

Kavi Pannu
American Business Advisors, Inc.
856-235-6700
Kavi_Pannu@yahoo.com

Carvel Ice Cream
Anthony Citrolo
NY Business Brokerage, Inc.
866-449-6922
anthony@nybbinc.com

Cemeteries and Crematories
Paul Kuper
Kuper Consulting, LLC
877-624-5107
paul@kuperconsulting.com

Check Cashing
Steven Seidner
siegel financial group
609-468-6315
sseidner@siegelfg.com

Chiropractic Practices
Keith Borglum
Professional Management and Marketing
707-546-4433
kborglum@practicemgmt.com

Coin Laundries
Andrew John Cunningham
ACE, LLC
310-951-4556
ace@socal.rr.com

Tom Paspalas
Dickman Business Brokers
973-627-1490
icediver007@aol.com

Rob Ruby
Realty Associates
415-455-1700
robruby@sbcglobal.net

Collection Agencies
Thomas M. Edens
Marion Financial Corp.
713-988-8000
edens@marionfinancial.com

Michael Ginsberg
Kaulkin Ginsberg Company
301-907-0840, x111
mike@kaulkin.com

Construction
Andy Anderson
719-540-2200
andy@bizsale.com

Joel Bowie
JBowie@Tworld.com

Convenience Stores with or without Gas
Mike Baskin
PetroConsulting, Inc.
703-242-2042
mbaskin@petroconsulting.com

Robert Bunn
Robert E. Bunn & Associates
573-651-6014
rover@showme.net

A. DeMarco
Sunbelt Business Brokers
205-807-5909
apd@sunbeltnetwork.com

Hal Janke
Hal Janke & Associates, Inc.
760-431-6767
haljanke@aol.com

William Lops
K&W Business Brokers
386-257-1905
kwbusinessbroker@aol.com

Jim Martinez
Sunbelt Business Brokers
919-787-0566
jmartinez@sunbelt-raleigh.com

Terry Monroe
American Business Brokers
217-347-5758
tmonroe@abbunitedstates.com

Stanley Myszkowski
BR Business & Loan Brokers, Inc.
630-434-7519
myszkowski_stanley@hotmail.com

Kavi Pannu
American Business Advisors, Inc.
856-235-6700
Kavi_Pannu@yahoo.com

Gary Papay
CK Business Consultants, Inc.
570-584-6488
gpapay@ckbc.net

Coupon Books
Bob Sweeney
Innovative Travel Acquisitions, Inc.
800-619-0185
bob@travelbusinessbroker.com

CPA Practices
Roy Braatz
Accounting Practice Sales
888-783-7822
roy@accountingpracticesales.com

John Ezell, CPA
ProHorizons
800-729-3242
john@prohorizons.com

Leon W. Faris, CPA
Professional Accounting Sales
800-729-9031
leon@cpasales.com

William Pipes
Breckenridge Pipes & Co
904-264-4888
bpipes@breckbroker.com

David Snyder
Strategic Success Business Brokers
803-644-4000
david@dmsnyder.com

Curves
Kevin Nery
508-990-9800
nerycorp@verizon.net

Dairy Queen
Bill Dougherty
Bill Dougherty Business Brokerage, Inc.
763-477-4022
billdbb@aol.com

Day Care Services — Child
Curt A. Cyliax
E Edge, Inc.
215-489-8881
ccyliax@eedge.com

Randall (Randy) Ferrian
Ferrian, Tifft & Spannaus, LLC
952-912-0333
randy@ftsbrokers.com

Karen Stieve
Dickman Business Brokers
973-627-1490
dickmanbrokers@aol.com

Deli's
Scott Dickman
Dickman Business Brokers
973-627-1490
nacdman@aol.com

Dental Practices
Keith Borglum
Professional Management and Marketing
707-546-4433
kborglum@practicemgmt.com

Cindy Eddins Collier
Valuation Solutions
614-433-7545
cindycollier@cindycollier.com

Mark Epstein
Epstein Practice Brokersage, Inc.
201-291-3888
me40@verizon.net

Direct Mail
Steve Ferber
The Wheatley Group
602-312-6808
steve@ideatron.com

Direct Selling — Advertising
Michael Hoesly
Hoesly and Company, Incorporated
608-288-9700
mhoesly@hoesly.com

Display Advertising
Paul Wright
SignValue, Inc.
480-657-8400
paul@signvalue.com

Distribution Businesses
Kenneth S. Sussman
Route Brokers, Inc.
516-482-8250
theroute@aol.com

Dollar Stores
Kavi Pannu
American Business Advisors, Inc.
856-235-6700
Kavi_Pannu@yahoo.com

Donuts
Bernie Siegel
Siegel Business Services
bsiegel@siegelbusinessservices.com

Drycleaners
Terry Doyle
Metro Business Brokers, Inc.
651-641-1606
mbbi@qwest.net

Richard Ehrenreich
Ehrenreich & Associates Cleaner Broker Network
301-570-3000
ehrenassoc@aol.com

Ovanes Mikaelian
Venture Business Brokers, Ltd.
847-437-4070
venturebus@hotmail.com

Tom Paspalas
Dickman Business Brokers
973-627-1490
icediver007@aol.com

Dunkin Donuts
Bernie Siegel
Siegel Business Services
bsiegel@siegelbusinessservices.com

Educational Services
Charles Barnett
The Barnett Capital Group, LLC.
713-291-1203
cbarnett@barnettcapitalgroup.com

Electrical Contractors
Bob McDowell
McDowell Business Associates
972-991-9588
mcdowellbb@sbcglobal.net

Electronic Shopping
Ross Whittaker
eBizBrokers, Inc.
888-882-4324 x202
rossw@ebizbrokers.com

Event Companies
Bob Sweeney
Innovative Travel Acquisitions, Inc.
800-619-0185
bob@travelbusinessbroker.com

Fitness Centers
Stewart Hamel
Empire Mergers and Acquisitions
318-865-6363
stewart@empirebc.com

Flower Shops
Gregory Kovsky
425-454-3052
gregory@ibainc.com

Julie Gordon White
FlowerShop Brokers
510-812-2233
julie@flowershopbrokers.com

Funeral Homes/Services
Jeff Boutwell
The New Bridge Group
404-249-9582
jeff@newbridgegroup.com

Paul Kuper
Kuper Consulting, LLC
877-624-5107
paul@kuperconsulting.com

Gas Stations
Joel Bowie
JBowie@Tworld.com

Steve Chiaet
Dickman Business Brokers
973-627-1490
icediver007@aol.com

Hal Janke
Hal Janke & Associates, Inc.
760-431-6767
haljanke@aol.com

Scott Manker
Oakwood Associates
561-658-1404
smanker@flabrk.com

Thomas Messler
Transworld Business Brokers
954-772-1122
tmessler@tworld.com

Gasoline – Wholesale
Thomas Messler
Transworld Business Brokers
954-772-1122
tmessler@tworld.com

Gift Shops
Kevin Nery
508-990-9800
nerycorp@verizon.net

Golf Courses
Harry Kushner
518-458-7740
hhkush@aattglobal.net

Grocery Stores
Scott Dickman
Dickman Business Brokers
973-627-1490
nacdman@aol.com

Ground Transportation Companies
Bob Sweeney
Innovative Travel Acquisitions, Inc.
800-619-0185
bob@travelbusinessbroker.com

Hardware Stores
Fred Hall
209-296-5236
fredh@volcano.net

Heating Oil Dealers
Gary Papay
CK Business Consultants, Inc.
570-584-6488
gpapay@ckbc.net

Home Centers
Fred Hall
209-296-5236
fredh@volcano.net

Home Nursing Agencies
Don Cummins
Stoneridge Partners
239-561-0826
don@stoneridgeonline.com

Hotels and Motels
Jim Harley
Sunbelt Business Advisors
859-806-3352
Harley@sunbeltnetwork.com

Henry Votel
Motels by Gudim
651-426-1610
gudim1@isd.net

Incentive Travel Companies
Bob Sweeney
Innovative Travel Acquisitions, Inc.
800-619-0185
bob@travelbusinessbroker.com

Inns
Bob Fuehr
The Inn Broker, Inc.
800-926-4667
fuehr@innbroker.com

Insurance Agencies
Bob Lucido
Lucido & Company
508-878-2900
BobBusBkr@comcast.net

Raymond Messier
The Nery Corporation
508-990-9800
nery.corp@verizon.net

John Erb
All Southern Business Brokers
407-894-8237
johnbizbroker@aol.com

Janitorial Services – Distribution and Wholesale
Dr. Gary Solondz
Sunbelt Business Advisors of Hawaii
808-879-4981
drgary@sunbelthawaii.com

Jewelry Stores
Bobby Wilkerson
Wilkerson and Associates
800-631-1999
bwsi@biz.com

Liquefied Petroleum Gas (Bottled Gas) Dealers
Gary Papay
CK Business Consultants, Inc.
570-584-6488
gpapay@ckbc.net

Liquor Licenses
Michael Brewer
Alcoholic Beverage Consulting
mbrewer@abcconsulting.com

James Stariha
231-670-0878
jimstariha@hotmail.com

Liquor Stores
Stephen Atkins
Atkins Realty Group, Inc.
410-757-4965
steve.atkinrealtygroup@comcast.net

C. R. Blohm
Allied Business Group, Inc.
901-767-2354
cblohm@alliedbroker.com

Scott Dickman
Dickman Business Brokers
973-627-1490
nacdman@aol.com

Christopher R. George
George & Company
508-753-1400
cgeorge@georgeandco.com

David Humphrey
Liquor Store Brokers
781-551-9911
david@lsbrokers.com

Robert Rodriguez
The Veld Group
619-368-7468
robertr@theveldgroup.com

Lumberyards

Fred Hall
209-296-5236
fredh@volcano.net

Bud Howe
Howe & Ely Co.
314-302-9248
budhowe@aol.com

Machine Shops

Christopher R. George
George & Company
508-753-1400
cgeorge@georgeandco.com

Mailing Services

Keith Lehmann
American Business & Commercial Brokerage, Inc.
407-260-ABC (1222)
keicor@earthlink.net

Manufacturing

Ralph A. Bellizzi
Aaron, Bell International, Inc.
720-200-0470
rab@aaron-bell.com

Jan Fowler
Acquisitions Unlimited, Inc.
813-920-7880
acqunltd@tampabay.rr.com

Ray Gorcyca
Ray M&A
501-823-4ray
mergerray@aristotle.net

Kris Karlson
Bowman/Hanson
415-292-5227
karlson@bowmanhanson.com

Timothy McDonald
909-337-9570
timothy@leland-group.net

Rosalind Newton
401-463-6950
hwittnewtonre@aol.com

Manufacturing – Chemical

Charles Lorelli
Lorelli & Co., Inc.
919-967-1120
lorelli@chemicaldeals.com

Manufacturing – Electrical

Dennis L Watford
ICI Associates
423-676-6829
larry@larrywatford.com

Manufacturing – Machinery

Andre Teissier-duCros
404-284-1828
atc@geanoverseas.com

Manufacturing – Metal Fabricator

Layne Kasper
817-738-4220
kasper@kasperassociates.com

Richard Mowrey
Management Services & Development, Ltd.
814-938-8170
mgtserv@go-des.net

Manufacturing – Pharmaceutical

Carol R Berry
International Business Brokerage & Realty Inc
305-663-3494
cberry@internationalbrokerage.net

Yali Friedman
ThinkBiotech
716-308-7668
info@thinkbiotech.com

Manufacturing – Plastics

James Zipursky
Corporate Finance Associates
402-330-2160
jaz@cfaomaha.com

Manufacturing – Valves

Joe F. Cannon
Louisiana/Gulf Coast Business Brokers
225-928-3473
jfcannon@eatel.net

Marinas

J. Michael Wood
Johnson & Glazebrook, Inc.
540-372-4343
Jmpwood@aol.com

Medical – Health Care Sales

Camille Todd
321-217-3625
camille@tworld.com

Medical Labs

Dennis Forgione
Transworld Business Brokers, LLC
954-772-1122
dforgione@tworld.com

Medical Practices

Keith Borglum
Professional Management and Marketing
707-546-4433
kborglum@practicemgmt.com

Ben Bulot
800-546-4160
tapservices@yahoo.com

Cindy Eddins Collier
Valuation Solutions
614-433-7545
cindycollier@cindycollier.com

Thomas Jones
Transworld
800-205-7605
info@healthcarebizsales.com

Motorcycle Dealers

Bill O'Shields
Vercor
615-844-6199
bill@vercoradvisor.com

Non-medical Health Practices

Keith Borglum
Professional Management and Marketing
707-546-4433
kborglum@practicemgmt.com

Nursing Homes

Karen Stieve
Dickman Business Brokers
973-627-1490
dickmanbrokers@aol.com

Optometrist Practices
Andrew Cagnetta
Transworld Business Brokers, Inc.
954-772-1122
ac@tworld.com

Scott Daniels
Practice Concepts
877-778-2020
scottd@practiceconcepts.com

Gary Ware
Practice Consultants
800-576-6935
gary@practice-consultants.com

Pharmacies
Andrew John Preston
Preston Business Consultants, Inc.
973-838-5804
andypreston@pharmacybusinessbrokers.com

Physical Therapy
William Deaton
253-573-9500
carydeaton@qwest.net

Plumbing and Heating
Marty McHugh
973-635-5625
ridge@webspan.net

Podiatrist Practices
Keith Borglum
Professional Management and Marketing
707-546-4433
kborglum@practicemgmt.com

Printing
Ralph A. Bellizzi
Aaron, Bell International, Inc.
720-200-0470
rab@aaron-bell.com

Theodore Burbank
Lighthouse Financial, LLC
508-794-1200
tburbank@buysellbiz.com

Rick Hammond
VR Inland Empire
951-587-2475
rick@vrinlandempire.com

Kris Karlson
Bowman/Hanson
415-292-5227
karlson@bowmanhanson.com

Professional Practices
Paul Goldman
Goldman Group – Professional Practice Brokers
248-569-0508
goldmangroup2000@aol.com

Publishers – Newspapers
(Weeklies, Community Newspapers)
Peter Berg
Transworld Business Brokers, LLC
954-772-1122
pberg@tworld.com

Publishing
Ronald Hoxter
Sunbelt of Philadelphia
215-487-3900
RHoxter@sunbeltpa.com

Publishing – Newspapers

Charles Oppenheimer
Amvest Financial Group, Inc.
816-461-3312
coppenheimer@amvest.com

Radio Stations

Robert Schlegel
Houlihan Valuaton Advisors
317-264-1005
rschlegel@houlihan.com

Real Estate Offices

William Loftis
Legacy Assurance
888-694-9520
bill@legacy-assurance.com

Record Managaement

Bill O'Shields
Vercor
615-844-6199
bill@vercoradvisor.com

Rental Equipment

Edward Latek
Latek Capital Corporation
866-370-4960
elatek@latekcapital.com

Restaurants

Steve Bragg
Calhoun Companies
218-663-7682
sbragg@boreal.org

Steve Chiaet
Dickman Business Brokers
973-627-1490
icediver007@aol.com

A. DeMarco
Sunbelt Business Brokers
205-807-5909
apd@sunbeltnetwork.com

Bill Dougherty
Bill Dougherty Business Brokerage, Inc.
763-477-4022
billdbb@aol.com

Bob Dowdy
National Restaurant Associates
704-365-9774
restaurantstore@bellsouth.net

Franco Ferrari
Ferrari Sunbelt Business Brokers
407-339-3101
ferrarisunbelt@cfl.rr.com

Dennis Forgione
Transworld Business Brokers, LLC
954-772-1122
dforgione@tworld.com

Paul Hyde
Hyde Valuations, Inc.
208-722-7272
prh@hydevaluations.com

David Judkins
Business Brokers LLC
drj@aug.com

Jack Kimball
Kimball & Company
919-782-1110
jack@kimballandcompany.com

Keith Lehmann
American Business & Commercial Brokerage, Inc.
407-260-ABC (1222)
keicor@earthlink.net

Ron Nies
Restaurant Realty Associates
732-968-0001
rnies76408@aol.com

Charles M. Perkins
The Boston Restaurant Group
978-887-9895
weperk@ix.netcom.com

Edward Resha
#1 Business Brokers
714-777-1727
a1bizbroker@aol.com

Shawn Sanborn
Sanborn Company
303-220-7919
shawn@sanbornandcompany.com

Terri Sokoloff
Specialty Tavern & Restaurant Brokers
412-369-1555
terri@specialtygroup.com

Tom Sundeen
T.R. Sundeen, Inc./Page Olson
858-314-1300
tsundeen@san.rr.com

David Sweeten
Sweeten Business Brokerage
210-697-8760
busforsale@prodigy.net

Retail
Carl Pallini
908-887-4959
carlrball@aol.com

Retirement Continuing Care
Tony Green
Business Solutions 2020, LLC
662-842-2618
greenfrog@dixie-net.com

Routes
Ken Leif
Route World Brokers, Inc.
516-825-6050
Rwbkr@aol.com

Kenneth S. Sussman
Route Brokers, Inc.
516-482-8250
theroute@aol.com

Schools
Dennis Mope
407-909-6277
SchoolsForSale@aol.com

Self Storage
Paul Hyde
Hyde Valuations, Inc.
208-722-7272
prh@hydevaluations.com

Software
Robert Schlegel
Houlihan Valuaton Advisors
317-264-1005
rschlegel@houlihan.com

Subway
Anthony Citrolo
NY Business Brokerage, Inc.
866-449-6922
anthony@nybbinc.com

Supermarkets
Stanley Myszkowski
BR Business & Loan Brokers, Inc.
630-434-7519
myszkowski_stanley@hotmail.com

Sustainable Businesses
Chris Bartle
The Evergreen Group LLC
415-750-1220
chris@theevergreengroup.com

Tanning Salons
Ryan Clark
The Veld Group
310-652-8353
ryanc@theveldgroup.com

Loren Marc Schmerler
Bottom Line Management, Inc.
770-587-4847
lms@botline.com

Michael Wildeveld
The Veld Group
310-652-8353
contact@theveldgroup.com

Tax Practices
John Ezell, CPA
ProHorizons
800-729-3242
john@prohorizons.com

Leon W. Faris, CPA
Professional Accounting Sales
800-729-9031
leon@cpasales.com

Technology
Craig Allsopp
Harbourton Group
609-466-3100
coallsopp@harbourtongroup.com

Ticket Services
Bob Sweeney
Innovative Travel Acquisitions, Inc.
800-619-0185
bob@travelbusinessbroker.com

Title Companies
William Loftis
Legacy Assurance
888-694-9520
bill@legacy-assurance.com

Tour Operators
Bob Sweeney
Innovative Travel Acquisitions, Inc.
800-619-0185
bob@travelbusinessbroker.com

Travel Agencies
Bob Sweeney
Innovative Travel Acquisitions, Inc.
800-619-0185
bob@travelbusinessbroker.com

R. Stephen Thomson
Sunbelt Business Brokers of Orange Coast
949-727-2412
steve@sunbeltorange.com

Travel Plazas
Kavi Pannu
American Business Advisors, Inc.
856-235-6700
Kavi_Pannu@yahoo.com

Travel Wholesalers/Consolidators
Bob Sweeney
Innovative Travel Acquisitions, Inc.
800-619-0185
bob@travelbusinessbroker.com

Truck Stops
Terry Monroe
American Business Brokers
217-347-5758
tmonroe@abbunitedstates.com

Kavi Pannu
American Business Advisors, Inc.
856-235-6700
Kavi_Pannu@yahoo.com

Trucking
Bill Smalley
Sunbelt Business Brokers
813-831-5990
wjsmalley@earthlink.net

Vending Routes
Ken Leif
Route World Brokers, Inc.
516-825-6050
Rwbkr@aol.com

Kenneth S. Sussman
Route Brokers, Inc.
516-482-8250
theroute@aol.com

Veterinary Practices
David Greene
Medical Practice Brokers, Inc.
719-487-9973
dave@practicebrokers.com

Michael Terry
Plains States Professional Practice
785-566-8353
mike@vetbrokerage.com

Video Stores
Loren Marc Schmerler
Bottom Line Management, Inc.
770-587-4847
lms@botline.com

Visa/Passport Companies
Bob Sweeney
Innovative Travel Acquisitions, Inc.
800-619-0185
bob@travelbusinessbroker.com

Wholesale Trade
C. R. Blohm
Allied Business Group, Inc.
901-767-2354
cblohm@alliedbroker.com

Karen Stieve
Dickman Business Brokers
973-627-1490
dickmanbrokers@aol.com